TH   _~~~

Annual reports in this edition mostly cover the period 1 May 2006 to 30 April 2007. The staff lists and details of centres of work are generally accurate to 30 September 2007.

Statistics are those for the year ending 31 December 2006.

Officers and lay staff serving in countries other than their own are counted in the statistics of the territory/command in which they are serving.

The 'Biographical Information' section is as accurate as possible at the time of going to press.

THE
SALVATION ARMY
YEAR BOOK

2008

INTERNATIONAL
MISSION STATEMENT

The Salvation Army, an international movement, is an
evangelical part of the universal Christian Church.
Its message is based on the Bible. Its ministry is motivated by
love for God. Its mission is to preach the gospel of Jesus Christ
and meet human needs in his name without discrimination.

THE SALVATION ARMY
INTERNATIONAL HEADQUARTERS
101 QUEEN VICTORIA STREET, LONDON EC4V 4EH, UNITED KINGDOM

First published 2007

Copyright © 2007 The General of The Salvation Army

ISBN 978 0 85412 775 7

Editor: Major Trevor Howes

Cover design: Berni Georges

Full-colour inserts: Nathan Sigauke

Published by Salvation Books
The Salvation Army International Headquarters
101 Queen Victoria Street, London EC4V 4EH, United Kingdom

Printed in the United Kingdom by Polestar Wheatons Ltd
Exeter, Devon, England

Contents

(Continued on the next page)

Contents (continued)

FOREWORD
by General Shaw Clifton
International leader of The Salvation Army

GOD continues to pour his love into the hearts of Salvationists all over the world and thus the global work and witness of the Army go on. All that can be found in these pages – all the programmes, reports, events, people, places – should point the reader to the love of God shown to the world in the person of Jesus Christ. No Salvationist works in his or her own strength. No programme, no project, no fresh initiative, no success among us can be attributed to human achievement. It all belongs to God.

Our primary purpose is, and always has been, to introduce men and women and girls and boys to Jesus Christ, the Saviour of us all. In every land where the Army flag flies, daily we seek to share the good news of Jesus Christ.

General Shaw Clifton and Commissioner Helen Clifton

We have a message and it is a message of hope – hope for today and for the future; hope for this life and for the life to come. It is a message that burns in our hearts. It cannot be held back for it is about life and death. The love of God within us compels us to offer Jesus Christ to the whosoever. It is the most loving thing anyone can do for another.

That same divine love, indwelling every Christian believer, drives us forward into compassionate service for others. Again, we cannot hold back. Faith without good works is a dead thing. Christ's people become his hands and feet, available, ready to be spent, putting the needs of others first.

The result is a life of self-sacrifice and self-denial, a life lived for those in need. It can also mean a life of risk-taking. Sometimes the risk

1

is physical, sometimes reputational as we become a voice for the voiceless. Social service and social action are two sides of the same coin.

Dear reader and user of this book: if you are not a Salvationist I thank you deeply for your interest in The Salvation Army's work and for your encouragement which we need so much; if you are a Salvationist I thank you from my heart for your service in the ranks of God's Salvation Army.

We bring all that is recorded in these pages as an offering to the Lord, seeking his blessing upon it all and asking humbly that he will continue to use the Army according to his holy will for the world.

International Headquarters, London
September 2007

The General talks with a family in Parliament Square, Bern, Switzerland. As he writes in his foreword: 'Our primary purpose is, and always has been, to introduce men and women and girls and boys to Jesus Christ.'

DOCTRINE IS THE DRAMA OF OUR MISSION

Commissioner William Francis writes about the International Doctrine Council

RENOWNED British author and lay Anglican theologian Dorothy Sayers (1893-1957) produced a popular series of 12 radio dramas depicting Jesus' life. *The Man Born to be King* was broadcast in war-torn Britain on Sunday evenings, the monthly episodes beginning in December 1941.

Prior to the debut performance, a reporter asked Dorothy Sayers, 'What do you hope to teach through these plays?' Without hesitation she replied, 'Doctrine!' After an awkward pause, the reporter probed, 'Doctrine? Won't that be boring?' 'Indeed not,' Dr Sayers rejoined – 'Doctrine is the drama!'

The Salvation Army's doctrine – its theological underpinnings – provides the firm foundation for the drama of its mission. What we believe to be true about the Scriptures, the Triune God, sin, salvation and sanctification supports and empowers that mission.

In 1931 General Edward Higgins created a doctrine council at International Headquarters. Its duties were 'to examine and report to the General as to the correctness and harmony with Salvation Army principles and doctrines, as defined in our Deed Poll of 1878, of the teaching contained in all Salvation Army publications such as song books, company orders, directories, advanced training, and similar lesson courses and text books, and other publications in which doctrinal teaching appears in any form'.

Over the years the most arduous and challenging task of the council has been to recommend to the General the content of successive editions of *The Handbook of Doctrine*, including the 1942 and 1969 handbooks and their successor volume titled *Salvation Story*, published in 1998.

In 1982 the doctrine council published *The Doctrine We Adorn*, a condensed study of Salvation Army doctrines deliberately targeting those for whom English is not their first language.

Membership

The General appoints members of the International Doctrine Council (IDC) for normally a five-year period. To enhance the gender and cultural balance, in January 2007 General Shaw Clifton increased the number of members by 60 per cent (from 10 to 16), of which 70 per cent are new members. The General also introduced a new category of 'corresponding members' who participate via email and conference calls.

Academic qualifications of the

newly constituted membership include 14 bachelor degrees, 13 masters degrees, and four doctorates, with a sprinkling of other diplomas and qualifications. Intentionally placed on the council are members who have no formal theological qualifications but who have demonstrated a capacity to think theologically.

Role of the Council

In his address to the IDC at the start of its meeting at IHQ in April 2007, General Clifton outlined the council's principal duties and responsibilities. The council is:

□ entrusted to be 'faithful custodians of Army doctrinal positions' including the articles of faith and other positions set down in approved Salvation Army publications or statements;

□ asked to recommend ways in which Salvation Army beliefs might be taught more effectively;

□ empowered to undertake interchurch dialogue at the General's direction;

□ expected to keep in touch with theological trends internationally, maintaining contacts with relevant institutions and academics both inside and outside The Salvation Army.

Inter-church dialogues

In recent years the council has participated in formal dialogues with other Christian denominations. Presently, the IDC is in dialogue with representatives of the General Conference of the Seventh Day Adventist Church. Formal dialogue

was commenced in Washington DC, USA, in January 2004 at the initiative of the Adventists. This was followed by the most recent meeting in Toronto, Canada, in March 2005. Bilateral dialogue with the Seventh Day Adventists will conclude with a third and final meeting in February 2008.

The goal of these meetings is to enhance mutual understanding between The Salvation Army and the Adventists, who from time to time have partnered with the Army in emergency responses and other community endeavours.

Similar dialogue has occurred with representatives of the World Methodist Council (WMC), an umbrella group that includes the United Methodists, the Church of the Nazarene, the Free Methodists, and other Wesleyan churches.

Mutual understanding

The WMC represents 77 separate denominations in 130 countries with a combined membership of 37 million. Despite its Wesleyan theology and origins, the Army is not a member of the WMC because that council recognises the Army as a Christian world communion in its own right.

The goal is one of increased mutual understanding through dialogue. Both bodies stand firmly in the historic Wesleyan tradition of free and full salvation through faith in Christ.

The first meeting with the WMC was held in June 2003 and a second in January 2005. Future plans anticipate further meetings until 2011. Bilateral

Congo (Brazzaville) Territory: Cadets in a class at the training college receive a lecture on the doctrines of The Salvation Army

dialogues will not take place if the other denomination sees these meetings as leading to ecclesiological merger, absorption or organic union of any kind. The goal must always be that of strengthening friendship, learning from each other and affirming fellow believers.

The IDC members ask Salvationists around the world to pray earnestly for them as they strive to fulfill their sacred mandate – that of articulating, promoting, resourcing, teaching, proclaiming and participating in the Army's doctrinally based, mission-driven divine drama.

Commissioner Francis (Territorial Commander, Canada and Bermuda) is Chairperson of the International Doctrine Council

---

International Doctrine Council Members

Commissioner William Francis (Chairman), Canada and Bermuda Territory; **Commissioner Robert Street** (Vice-chairman), IHQ; **Colonel Brian Tuck** (Secretary), Southern Africa Territory; **Commissioner Linda Bond**, IHQ (residing in Canada); **Colonel Vibeke Krommenhoek**, IHQ (residing in The Netherlands); **Colonel Oscar Sanchez**, Latin America North Territory; **Major Rosemarie Brown**, IHQ; **Major Kapela Ntoya**, Congo (Kinshasa) and Angola Territory; **Major Edwin Okorougo**, Nigeria Territory; **Major Karen Shakespeare**, United Kingdom Territory; **Major P. John William**, India Central Territory; **Captain Juliana Musilia**, Kenya Territory; **Captain Gordon Sparks**, USA Eastern Territory; **Mr Lars Lydholm**, Denmark Territory; **Mrs Irma Made Patera**, Indonesia Territory; **Dr Jonathan Raymond**, Canada and Bermuda Territory

Corresponding Members

Major Philip Cairns, Australia Eastern Territory; **Major Florante Parayno**, The Philippines Territory; **Major JoAnn Shade**, USA Eastern Territory; **Captain Philip Layton**, United Kingdom Territory; **Captain Masataka Tateishi**, Japan Territory

ONE HUNDRED YEARS ON THE KOREAN PENINSULA

Lieut-Colonel Kim, Joon-chul records significant moments in the Korea Territory's history

ONE hundred years ago Colonel and Mrs Robert Hoggard sowed seeds of good news, talking about Jesus to people in Korea. The Salvation Army 'opened fire' in a poor country prevalent with strong superstitious beliefs, struggling against foreign aggression; and yet, at the same time, experiencing a great revival in the churches.

When the Army commenced on the peninsula there was a complexity of religions such as Buddhism, Confucianism and Taoism. These had lost their positive influence on social and political life. People were extremely poor so they still relied on Shamanism, a kind of superstitious belief in spirits.

The political situation was difficult too. There was a resistance movement against the foreign aggression and annexation of Korea. As a result, Koreans were indignant and discontented with an external invasion of their homeland. They could find strong inspiration and new strength in Christianity.

It was in the Christian Church that they found independence and self-esteem; in the Church they learned to trust, believe and love each other. This led to a great revival in Korea, with centres in Wonsan and Pyongyang, where missionaries gathered to study the Bible and to pray.

When William Booth visited Japan in 1907 he met a group of Koreans who were studying there. They asked him to commence the Army's mission in Korea so he despatched Commissioner George Scott Railton to survey prospects on the Korean peninsula. The next year, Colonel and Mrs Hoggard were commissioned to start the mission there and on 1 October 1908, with a group of five other officers, arrived in Seoul to begin Salvation Army work.

Revival tradition

In the great revival tradition, they were encouraged to go out in uniform, blowing trumpets, beating the drum, playing tambourines and gathering people around them so they could share the gospel.

They put more emphasis on a community concept, encouraging people to do social service by managing institutions, schools and hospitals. In order to achieve peace in the community, they combatted social evils by preaching the gospel.

There have been three distinct crises in the history of The Salvation Army in Korea. The first was the 1926 protest which happened in November when General Bramwell Booth was visiting. The 'big tower' of the Army's inaugural years was collapsing. Cultural difficulties between missionaries and Koreans, and problems with meagre allowances were combining with the sentiment of national and racial antagonism throughout the country.

The Army's dynamic growth slowed after the resignation of a number of Korean officers. Eighteen months later, Korea's Territorial Commander, Colonel James Toft, was promoted to Glory.

Contact ceased

The second crisis was the period of *Koo Sei Dahn* (The Salvation 'Brigade' or 'Group'). If up until 1940 had been the domination by Western missionaries, then next came domination of The Salvation Army by Japan.

Use of the name *Koo Sei Goon* (The Salvation Army) was not allowed since as far as the Japanese occupation was concerned there was only one army – the Imperial Army. When a Japanese officer became the head of *Koo Sei Dahn* many Korean officers resigned, moving to other denominations. All contact with International Headquarters ceased.

The third crisis was the Korean War. The year 1945 saw the end of the Second World War, thus the end of Japanese occupation; so once again The Salvation Army was able to operate normally.

However, war broke out on the Korean peninsula on 25 June 1950, ending with the signing of a peace agreement in July 1953. There was much devastation during those three years; many lives were lost, properties totally destroyed.

During the war, six comrades died for their faith: Senior-Major Noh, Young-soo; Senior-Captain Kim, Sam-suk; Lieutenant Kim, Jin-ha; Lieutenant Park, Jong-sup; Lieutenant Kang, Ki-mo; and Corps Sergeant-Major Yoo, Young-bok. They died as martyrs for the Christian faith and the Korean Church.

From its commencement through to the year 1973, The Salvation Army in the Korea Territory, led by territorial commanders from overseas, developed into a vibrant expression of this international movement.

The overseas comrades had persevered through the difficulties of pioneering the ministry, then the sufferings of the Japanese invasion, followed by the Korean war. They used every ounce of their energies toward the Army's growth and development. Hence, their sacrifice was the foundation for The Salvation Army in Korea.

Spiritual growth

In 1973 the first Korean territorial commander was appointed and he aimed to bring greater localisation of the Army's work through the Korean culture. There was great success in spiritual growth and evangelism in small groups.

Making the most use of the sterling characteristics of the Army – spreading the gospel and serving with love – corps grew into well-developed, strong churches. They expanded God's Kingdom by practising holistic mission and serving people: with people and for people.

The territory realises that for growth

in the next 100 years, youth can become a key; so investment in youth work is essential. In an age of information technology, young people will be a bridge to the 'new homeless' in 'cyber ghettos' in order for Jesus Christ to save them from spiritual destruction. Leadership-training of officers is also important, and many women and lay-leaders also need to be trained.

To fulfill its prophetic ministry and important mission role in the territorial and worldwide scenes, The Salvation Army in Korea is moving forward to the lost and abandoned, wanting them to be saved, seeking to be life in a dying world.

Lieut-Colonel Kim, a retired officer, is the Territorial Archivist, Korea

SPORT HAS MISSION PURPOSE

Major Stephen Yoder outlines possibilities for evangelism through sports ministry

FEW things excite people as much as sport. Nothing opens the door to lively conversation like a discussion on sport, the players and their teams! Whether participating, watching or somehow supporting an event, anyone can enjoy sports and games: men, women, boys, girls, young, old – there's something for everyone!

Sport is a universal language that transcends culture, economic status, religious backgrounds and human diversity.

The possibilities for outreach, evangelism, character-building programmes and fellowship through sports ministry are limited only by the creative approach of Salvationists. And such a mission initiative can be brought to life at every level of Salvation Army life: one-to-one; at corps and centres; in divisions and regions; within a territory or command.

But what is sports ministry? Here

are examples I have seen in people and situations.

Junior soldier David knows his school friends may not be comfortable going to the youth Bible study with him, but they're certainly happy to join him at the youth club and turn up when World Cup football matches are screened at the corps.

Playing golf

While four friends are playing golf together most Saturdays they share each other's concerns about home and work, and regularly pray for each other. (What if they invite an unsaved friend and talk in much the same way around the course?)

My friend John is specialising in sports therapy at his university. As he lives in close proximity to athletes he witnesses for Jesus Christ.

Mission teams from around the world converge on Gelshenkirchen,

USA Southern Territory: Commissioner Israel L. Gaither (USA National Commander) greets Tuskegee University and Morehouse College players at the Annual Tuskegee-Morehouse Football Classic in Columbus, Georgia

Singapore, Malaysia and Myanmar Territory: Captain Hary Haran joins in a game of football at Gracehaven Children's Home, Singapore, knowing that taking part in their games helps him share the gospel with the young people
(see inside front cover)

Cologne and numerous other venues during the FIFA World Cup tournament in Germany. A territorial football competition is included in the All-Africa Congress. A corps officer arranges a fathers-and-sons outing to their local football club.

Mini-marathon

A men's fellowship golf event raises thousands of dollars for Salvation Army World Services and gives the guys a great opportunity for fellowship and outreach among their unsaved friends. Home league members walk the course during a mini-marathon to raise money for a worthy cause.

In Brazil, I get to join a bunch of street kids in a game of football. Children play cricket in a field in India – bricks for a wicket and using some kind of makeshift bat and ball. Smiles and laughter are the hallmarks of these games.

Kroc centres are springing up across America – providing facilities for swimming, ice-skating, basketball, hockey and much more.

If you want to know what's already being done around the world – not just in the Army – do a quick Google search using 'sports ministry' as your search reference. The results on my computer totalled more than 30 million possibilities! Here's an example of the kind of stimulating material you'll find – and it sits very comfortably in the Army ethos:

'Sports is culturally relevant and, therefore, a strategic way to introduce people to the Church and to the person of Jesus Christ. It doesn't matter if I am interested in sports; the key is to recognise that lost people are interested and that is where they congregate. Where would Jesus be?' (former NFL football player and US representative Steve Largent, www.sportzplay.org/sportzplay.htm).

Olympics

Of course none of this is new to The Salvation Army. Salvationists have been enjoying sports for their own personal interest for years. Many territories/commands are well-advanced in their use of sports and games as a means of outreach, evangelism and fellowship.

And we have been actively involved in major international sports events for many years, in particular through mission teams at Olympic Games and World Cup events. Future possibilities await us at the 2008 Summer Olympics (China), 2010 Winter Olympics (Canada) and 2010 Soccer World Cup (South Africa).

The Chief of the Staff's approval (in August 2006) of a Sports Ministry Desk being established within the Programme Resources Department at International Headquarteras formalised sports ministry within The Salvation Army's structure. The Sports Ministry Desk/Network exists to facilitate the development of sports as a mission opportunity within the Army, and this mission will be enlivened on a wider scale by sharing resources via a Lotus Notes database and discussion forum.

Objectives

The objectives of the Sports Ministry Desk/Network are: (1) to cast vision to the Salvation Army world; (2) identify, equip, mobilise and encourage Salvation Army sports ministry leaders; (3) connect The Salvation Army with the global sports ministry community.

The key is getting the stories told so that we can all learn from each other's successes. Salvationists need to share the wealth of resources they are creating and using.

Our challenge is to acknowledge the sports activities which create the most excitement – and which people enjoy – and then dare to believe that God can and will use that passion and energy for Kingdom-building. Put in the simplest terms: sports and games have mission purpose.

At the time of writing Major Yoder was the Under-Secretary for Programme Resources, IHQ, with additional responsibility for the Sports Ministry Desk/Network. He is now CO, Norridge Citadel Corps, USA Central Territory.

WHAT IS THE SALVATION ARMY?

RAISED up by God, The Salvation Army is a worldwide evangelical Christian church with its own distinctive governance and practice. The Army's doctrine follows the mainstream of Christian belief and its articles of faith emphasise God's saving purposes.

Its religious and charitable objects are 'the advancement of the Christian religion ... and, pursuant thereto, the advancement of education, the relief of poverty, and other charitable objects beneficial to society or the community of mankind as a whole'.*

The Army (then known as The Christian Mission) was founded in London, England, in 1865 by William and Catherine Booth and has spread to many parts of the world.

The rapid deployment of the first Salvationists was aided by the adoption of a quasi-military command structure in 1878 when the title 'The Salvation Army' was brought into use. A similarly practical organisation today enables resources to be equally flexible.

Responding to a recurrent theme in Christianity which sees the Church engaged in spiritual warfare, The Salvation Army has used to advantage certain soldierly features such as uniforms, flags and ranks to identify, inspire and regulate its endeavours.

Evangelistic and social enterprises are maintained, under the authority of the General, by full-time officers and employees, as well as soldiers who give service in their free time. The Army also benefits from the support of many adherents and friends, including those who serve on advisory boards.

Leadership in The Salvation Army is provided by commissioned and ordained officers who are recognised as fully accredited ministers of religion.

Salvationists commit to a disciplined life of Christian moral standards, compassion toward others, and witnessing for Christ.

From its earliest days The Salvation Army has accorded women equal opportunities, every rank and service being open to them, and from childhood the young are encouraged to love and serve God.

Raised to evangelise, The Salvation Army spontaneously embarked on schemes for the social betterment of the poor. Such concerns develop, wherever the Army operates, in practical, skilled and cost-effective ways. Evolving social services meet endemic needs and specific crises worldwide. Highly trained staff are employed in up-to-date facilities.

The need for modernisation and longer-term development is under continual review. Increasingly The Salvation Army's policy and its indigenous membership allow it to cooperate with international relief agencies and governments alike.

The Army's partnership with both private and public philanthropy will continue to bring comfort to the needy, while the proclamation of God's redemptive love revealed in Jesus Christ offers individuals and communities the opportunity to know spiritual fulfilment here on earth and a place in Christ's eternal Kingdom.

*Section 3 of the Salvation Army Act 1980

THE DOCTRINES OF THE SALVATION ARMY

We believe that the Scriptures of the Old and New Testaments were given by inspiration of God, and that they only constitute the Divine rule of Christian faith and practice.

We believe that there is only one God, who is infinitely perfect, the Creator, Preserver and Governor of all things, and who is the only proper object of religious worship.

We believe that there are three persons in the Godhead – the Father, the Son and the Holy Ghost, undivided in essence and co-equal in power and glory.

We believe that in the person of Jesus Christ the Divine and human natures are united, so that he is truly and properly God and truly and properly man.

We believe that our first parents were created in a state of innocency, but by their disobedience they lost their purity and happiness, and that in consequence of their fall all men have become sinners, totally depraved, and as such are justly exposed to the wrath of God.

We believe that the Lord Jesus Christ has by his suffering and death made an atonement for the whole world so that whosoever will may be saved.

We believe that repentance towards God, faith in our Lord Jesus Christ, and regeneration by the Holy Spirit, are necessary to salvation.

We believe that we are justified by grace through faith in our Lord Jesus Christ and that he that believeth hath the witness in himself.

We believe that continuance in a state of salvation depends upon continued obedient faith in Christ.

We believe that it is the privilege of all believers to be wholly sanctified, and that their whole spirit and soul and body may be preserved blameless unto the coming of our Lord Jesus Christ.

We believe in the immortality of the soul; in the resurrection of the body; in the general judgment at the end of the world; in the eternal happiness of the righteous; and in the endless punishment of the wicked.

FOUNDERS OF THE SALVATION ARMY

William Booth

The Founder of The Salvation Army and its first General was born in Nottingham on 10 April 1829 and promoted to Glory from Hadley Wood on 20 August 1912. He lived to establish Salvation Army work in 58 countries and colonies and travelled extensively, holding salvation meetings. In his later years he was received in audience by emperors, kings and presidents. Among his many books, *In Darkest England and the Way Out* was the most notable; it became the blueprint of all The Salvation Army's social schemes. It was reprinted in 1970.

Catherine Booth

The Army Mother was born in Ashbourne, Derbyshire, on 17 January 1829 and promoted to Glory from Clacton-on-Sea on 4 October 1890. As Catherine Mumford, she married William in 1855. A great teacher and preacher, she addressed large public meetings in Britain with far-reaching results, despite ill health. Her writings include *Female Ministry* and *Aggressive Christianity*.

William Bramwell Booth

The eldest son of the Founder, and his Chief of the Staff from 1880 to 1912, Bramwell (as he was known) was born on 8 March 1856. He was largely responsible for the development of The Salvation Army. His teaching of the doctrine of holiness and his councils with officers and young people were of incalculable value. In 1882 he married Captain Florence Soper (organiser of the Women's Social Work and inaugurator of the Home League), who was promoted to Glory on 10 June 1957. During his time as General (1912-1929), impetus was given to missionary work. Published books include *Echoes and Memories* and *These Fifty Years*. He was appointed a Companion of Honour shortly before his promotion to Glory from Hadley Wood on 16 June 1929.

GLOSSARY OF SALVATION ARMY TERMS

Adherent: A member of The Salvation Army who has not made a commitment to soldiership.

Advisory Board: A group of influential citizens who, believing in the Army's programme of spiritual, moral and physical rehabilitation and amelioration, assist in promoting and supporting Army projects.

'Blood and Fire': The Army's motto; refers to the blood of Jesus Christ and the fire of the Holy Spirit.

Cadet: A Salvationist who is in training for officership.

Candidate: A soldier who has been accepted for officer training.

Chief of the Staff: The officer second in command of the Army throughout the world.

Chief Secretary: The officer second in command of the Army in a territory.

Citadel: A hall used for worship.

Colours: The tricolour flag of the Army. Its colours symbolise the blood of Jesus Christ (red), the fire of the Holy Spirit (yellow) and the purity of God (blue).

Command: A smaller type of territory, directed by an officer commanding.

Command leaders: An officer commanding and spouse in their joint role of sharing spiritual leadership and ministry, providing pastoral care and exemplifying the working partnership of officer couples.

Commission: A document conferring authority upon an officer, or upon an unpaid local officer, eg, secretary, treasurer, bandmaster, etc.

Congress: Central gatherings often held annually and attended by most officers and many soldiers of a territory, command, region or division.

Corps: A Salvation Army unit established for the preaching of the gospel and to provide Christian-motivated service in the community.

Corps Cadet: A young Salvationist who undertakes a course of study and practical training in a corps, with a view to becoming efficient in Salvation Army service.

Corps Sergeant-Major: The chief local officer for public work who assists the corps officer with meetings and usually takes command in his/her absence.

Dedication Service: The public presentation of infants to the Lord. This differs from christening or infant baptism in that the main emphasis is upon specific vows made by the parents concerning the child's upbringing.

Division: A number of corps grouped together under the direction of a divisional commander (may also include social service centres and programmes), operating within a territory or command.

Divisional Commander: The officer in charge of the Army in a division.

Envoy: A local officer whose duty it is to visit corps, societies and outposts, for the purpose of conducting meetings. An envoy may be appointed in charge of any such unit.

General: The officer elected to the supreme command of the Army throughout the world. All appointments are made, and all regulations issued, under the General's authority (see under High Council – p 22).

General Secretary: The officer second in charge of the Army in a command (or, in some territories, a large division).

Halfway House: A centre for the rehabilitation of alcoholics or parolees (USA).

Harbour Light Centre: A reclamation centre, usually located in inner city areas.

High Council: See p 22

Home League: See p 34

International Headquarters (IHQ): The offices in which the business connected with the command of the worldwide Army is transacted.

International Secretary: A position at IHQ with responsibility for the oversight and coordination of the work in a specific geographical zone or functional category, and for advising the General on zonal and worldwide issues and policies.

Junior Soldier: A boy or girl who, having accepted Jesus as their saviour, has signed the junior soldier's promise and become a Salvationist.

League of Mercy: Salvationists who visit prisons, hospitals and needy homes, in their own time, bringing the gospel and rendering practical aid (see p 35).

Lieutenant: A Salvationist giving service to the Army for an agreed period of time without becoming a commissioned officer.

Local Officer: A soldier appointed to a position of responsibility and authority in the corps; carries out the duties of the appointment without being separated from regular employment or receiving remuneration from the Army.

Medical Fellowship: See p 35

Mercy Seat or Penitent Form: A bench provided as a place where people can kneel to pray, seeking salvation or sanctification, or making a special consecration to God's will and service. The mercy seat is usually situated between the platform and main area of Army halls as a focal point to remind all of God's reconciling and redeeming presence.

Officer: A Salvationist who has left secular concerns at God's call and has been trained, commissioned and ordained to service and leadership. An officer is a recognised minister of religion.

Officer Commanding: The officer in charge of the Army in a command.

Order of Distinguished Auxiliary Service: See p 37

Order of the Founder: See p 36

Outpost: A locality in which Army work is carried out and where it is hoped a society or corps will develop.

Pastoral Care Council: Established in each corps for the care of soldiers, etc, and maintenance of the membership rolls. Previously called the census board.

Promotion to Glory: The Army's description of the death of Salvationists.

Ranks of Officers: Captain, major, lieut-colonel, colonel, commissioner, General.

Red Shield: A symbol identifying a wide range of Army social and emergency services.

Red Shield Appeal: A financial appeal to the general public; also known as the Annual Appeal in some countries.

Red Shield Centre: A club for military personnel.

Salvation: The work of grace which God accomplishes in a repentant person whose trust is in Christ as Saviour, forgiving sin, giving meaning and new direction to life, and strength to live as God desires. The deeper experience of this grace, known as holiness or sanctification, is the outcome of wholehearted commitment to God and enables the living of a Christlike life.

Self-Denial Appeal: An annual effort by Salvationists and friends to raise funds for the Army's worldwide operations.

Sergeant: A local officer appointed for specific duty, usually in a corps.

Society: A company of soldiers who work together regularly in a district, without an officer, but with the approval of the divisional commander.

Soldier: A converted person at least 14 years of age who has, with the approval of the pastoral care council, been enrolled as a member of The Salvation Army after signing the Soldier's Covenant.

Soldier's Covenant: The statement of beliefs and promises which every intending soldier is required to sign before enrolment. Previously called 'Articles of War'.

Territorial Commander: The officer in command of the Army in a territory.

Territorial leaders: A territorial commander and spouse in their joint role of sharing spiritual leadership and ministry, providing pastoral care and exemplifying the working partnership of officer couples. The chief secretary is the second-in-command of the territory.

Territory: A country, part of a country or several countries combined, in which Salvation Army work is organised under a territorial commander.

Young People's Sergeant-Major: A local officer responsible for young people's work in a corps, under the commanding officer.

Chronological Table of Important Events in Salvation Army History

1829 Catherine Mumford (later Mrs Booth, 'the Army Mother') born at Ashbourne, Derbyshire (17 Jan); William Booth born at Nottingham (10 Apr).

1844 William Booth converted.

1846 Catherine Mumford converted.

1855 Marriage of William Booth and Catherine Mumford at Stockwell New Chapel, London (16 Jun).

1856 William Bramwell Booth (the Founder's eldest son and second General of the Army) born in Halifax (8 Mar).

1858 William Booth ordained as Methodist minister (27 May). (Accepted on probation 1854.)

1859 *Female Teaching*, Mrs Booth's first pamphlet, published (Dec).

1860 Mrs Booth's first public address (27 May, Whit Sunday).

1865 **Rev William Booth began work in East London** (2 Jul); The Christian Mission, founded; Eveline (Evangeline) Cory Booth (fourth General) born in London (25 Dec).

1867 First Headquarters (Eastern Star) opened in Whitechapel Road, London.

1868 *The East London Evangelist* – later (1870) *The Christian Mission Magazine* and (1879) *The Salvationist* – published (Oct).

1874 Christian Mission work commenced in **Wales** (15 Nov).

1875 *Rules and Doctrines of The Christian Mission* published.

1876 *Revival Music* published (Jan).

1878 First use of the term 'Salvation Army' – in small appeal folder (May); 'The Christian Mission' became **'The Salvation Army'**, and the Rev William Booth became known as the General; deed poll executed, thus establishing the doctrines and principles of The Salvation Army (Aug); first corps flag presented by Mrs Booth at Coventry (28-30 Sep); *Orders and Regulations for The Salvation Army* issued (Oct); brass instruments first used.

1879 First corps in **Scotland** opened (24 Mar) and **Channel Islands** (14 Aug); cadets first trained; introduction of uniform; first corps band formed in Consett; issue No 1 of *The War Cry* published (27 Dec).

1880 First training home opened, at Hackney, London; first contingent of SA officers landed in the **United States of America** (10 Mar); SA work commenced in **Ireland** (7 May); children's meetings commenced at Blyth (30 Jul); SA work extended to **Australia** (5 Sep).

1881 Work begun in **France** (13 Mar); *The Little Soldier* (subsequently *The Young Soldier*) issued (27 Aug); *The Doctrines and Disciplines of The Salvation Army* prepared for use at training homes for Salvation Army officers; Headquarters removed to Queen Victoria Street, London (8 Sep).

1882 The Founder's first visit to France (Mar); former London Orphan Asylum opened as Clapton Congress Hall and National Training Barracks (13 May); work begun in **Canada** (21 May), **India** (19 Sep), **Switzerland** (22 Dec) and **Sweden** (28 Dec).

1883 Work begun in **Sri Lanka** (26 Jan), **South Africa** (4 Mar), **New Zealand** (1 Apr), **Isle of Man** (17 Jun) and **Pakistan** (then a part of India); first prison-gate home opened in Melbourne, Australia (8 Dec); *The Doctrines and Disciplines of The Salvation Army* published in a public edition.

1884 Women's Social Work inaugurated; *The Soldier's Guide* published (Apr); work begun in **St Helena** (5 May); *The Salvation Army Band Journal* issued (Aug); *All the World* issued (Nov).

1885 *Orders and Regulations for Divisional Officers* published (10 Jun); *The Doctrines of The Salvation Army* published; Purity Agitation launched; Criminal Law Amendment Act became law on 14 Aug; trial (began 23 Oct) and acquittal of Bramwell Booth – charged, with W. T. Stead, in connection with the 'Maiden Tribute' campaign.

1886 Work begun in **Newfoundland** (1 Feb); first International Congress in London (28 May-4 Jun); *The Musical Salvationist* issued (Jul); first Self-Denial Week (4-11 Sep); first slum corps opened at Walworth, London, by 'Mother' Webb (20 Sep); work begun in **Germany** (14 Nov); *Orders and Regulations for Field Officers* published; the Founder first visited the United States and Canada.

1887 Work began in **Italy** (20 Feb), **Denmark** (8 May), **Netherlands** (8 May) and **Jamaica** (16 Dec); the Founder's first visit to Denmark, Sweden and Norway.

1888 Young people's work organised throughout Great Britain; first food depot opened, in Limehouse, London (Jan); work begun in **Norway** (22 Jan); first junior soldiers' brass band (Clapton); the Army Mother's last public address at City Temple, London (21 Jun).

1889 Work begun in **Belgium** (5 May) and **Finland** (8 Nov); *The Deliverer* published (Jul).

1890 Work begun in **Argentina** (1 Jan); *Orders and Regulations for Soldiers of The Salvation Army* issued (Aug); the Army Mother promoted to Glory (4 Oct); *In Darkest England and the Way Out*, by the Founder, published (Oct); work begun in **Uruguay** (16 Nov); banking department opened (registered as The Salvation Army Bank, 1891; Reliance Bank Ltd, 28 Dec 1900).

1891 The Founder publicly signed 'Darkest England' (now The Salvation Army Social Work) Trust Deed (30 Jan); £108,000 subscribed for 'Darkest England' scheme (Feb); Land and Industrial Colony, Hadleigh, Essex, established (2 May); International Staff Band inaugurated (Oct); work begun in **Zimbabwe** (21 Nov) and **Zululand** (22 Nov); the Founder's first visit to South Africa, Australia, New Zealand and India; the charter of The Methodist and General Assurance Society acquired.

1892 Eastbourne (UK) verdict against Salvationists quashed in the High Court of Justice (27 Jan); Band of Love inaugurated; League of Mercy begun in Canada (Dec).

1893 Grace-Before-Meat scheme instituted; *The Officer* issued (Jan).

1894 Second International Congress (Jul); work begun in **Hawaiian Islands** (13 Sep) and **Java** (now part of **Indonesia**) (24 Nov); naval and military league (later

red shield services) established (Nov); Swiss Supreme Court granted religious rights to SA (Dec).

1895 Work begun in **British Guiana** (now **Guyana**) (24 Apr), **Iceland** (12 May), **Japan** (4 Sep) and **Gibraltar** (until 1968).

1896 Young people's legion (Jan) and corps cadet brigades (Feb) inaugurated; work begun in **Bermuda** (12 Jan) and **Malta** (25 Jul until 1972); first SA exhibition, Agricultural Hall, London (Aug).

1897 First united young people's meetings (later termed 'councils') (14 Mar); first International Social Council in London (Sep); first SA hospital founded at Nagercoil, India (Dec).

1898 *Orders and Regulations for Social Officers* published; work begun in **Barbados** (30 Apr) and **Alaska**; first united corps cadet camp at Hadleigh (Whitsun).

1899 First bandsmen's councils, Clapton (10 Dec).

1901 Work begun in **Trinidad** (7 Aug).

1902 Work begun in **St Lucia** (Sep) and **Grenada**.

1903 Migration Department inaugurated (became Reliance World Travel Ltd, 1981; closed 31 May 2001); work begun in **Antigua**.

1904 Third International Congress (Jun-Jul); Founder received by King Edward VII at Buckingham Palace (24 Jun); Founder's first motor campaign (Aug); work begun in **Panama** (Dec).

1905 The Founder campaigned in the Holy Land, Australia and New Zealand (Mar-Jun); first emigrant ship chartered by SA sailed for Canada (26 Apr); opening of International Staff Lodge (later College, now International College for Officers) (11 May); work begun in **St Vincent** (Aug). Freedom of London conferred on the Founder (26 Oct); Freedom of Nottingham conferred on the Founder (6 Nov).

1906 *The YP* (later *The Warrior*, then *Vanguard*) and *The Salvation Army Year Book* issued; Freedom of Kirkcaldy conferred on the Founder (16 Apr).

1907 Anti-Suicide Bureau established (Jan); Home League inaugurated (28 Jan); *The Bandsman and Songster* (later *The Musician*) issued (6 Apr); honorary degree of DCL, Oxford, conferred on the

Founder (26 Jun); work begun in **Costa Rica** (5 Jul).

1908 Work begun in **Korea** (Oct).

1909 Leprosy work commenced in **Java** (now part of **Indonesia**) (15 Jan); SA work begun in **Chile** (Oct).

1910 Work begun in **Peru**, **Paraguay** and **Sumatra** (now part of **Indonesia**).

1912 Founder's last public appearance, in Royal Albert Hall, London (9 May); **General William Booth promoted to Glory** (20 Aug); **William Bramwell Booth appointed General** (21 Aug).

1913 Inauguration of life-saving scouts (21 Jul); work begun in **Celebes** (now part of **Indonesia**) (15 Sep) and **Russia** (until 1923).

1914 Fourth International Congress (Jun).

1915 Work begun in **British Honduras** (now **Belize**) (Jun) and **Burma** (now **Myanmar**); life-saving guards inaugurated (17 Nov).

1916 Work begun in **China** (Jan until 1951), in **St Kitts** and in **Portuguese East Africa** (now **Mozambique**) (officially recognised 1923).

1917 Work begun in **Virgin Islands** (USA) (Apr); chums inaugurated (23 Jun); Order of the Founder instituted (20 Aug).

1918 Work commenced in **Cuba** (Jul).

1919 Work begun in **Czechoslovakia** (19 Sep until 1950).

1920 Work begun in **Nigeria** (15 Nov) and **Bolivia** (Dec).

1921 Work begun in **Kenya** (Apr); sunbeams inaugurated (3 Nov).

1922 Work begun in **Zambia** (1 Feb), **Brazil** (1 Aug) and **Ghana** (Aug); publication of a second *Handbook of Salvation Army Doctrine*.

1923 Work begun in **Latvia** (until 1939).

1924 Work begun in **Hungary** (24 Apr until 1950), in **Surinam** (10 Oct) and **The Færoes** (23 Oct).

1927 Work begun in **Austria** (27 May), **Estonia** (31 Dec until 1940) and **Curacao** (until 1980); first International Young People's Staff Councils (May-Jun).

1928 General Bramwell Booth's last public appearance – the stonelaying of the International (William Booth Memorial) Training College (now William Booth College), Denmark Hill, London (10 May).

1929 First High Council (8 Jan-13 Feb); **Comr Edward J. Higgins elected General**;

General Bramwell Booth promoted to Glory (16 Jun); Army work begun in **Colombia** (until 1965).

1930 Inception of goodwill league; Order of the Silver Star (now Fellowship of the Silver Star) inaugurated (in USA, extended to other lands in 1936); work begun in **Hong Kong**; Commissioners' Conference held in London (Nov).

1931 Work begun in **Uganda** and the **Bahamas** (May); The Salvation Army Act 1931 received royal assent (Jul).

1932 Work begun in **Namibia** (until 1939).

1933 Work begun in **Yugoslavia** (15 Feb until 1948), Devil's Island, **French Guiana** (1 Aug until closing of the penal settlement in 1952) and **Tanzania** (29 Oct).

1934 Work begun in **Algeria** (10 Jun until 1970); second High Council elected Commander Evangeline Booth General (3 Sep); work begun in **Congo (Kinshasa)** (14 Oct); **General Evangeline Booth took command of The Salvation Army** (11 Nov).

1935 Work begun in **Singapore** (28 May).

1936 Work begun in **Egypt** (until 1949).

1937 Work begun in **Congo (Brazzaville)** (Mar), **The Philippines** (6 Jun) and **Mexico** (Oct).

1938 Torchbearer group movement inaugurated (Jan); *All the World* re-issued (Jan); work spread from Singapore to **Malaysia**.

1939 Third High Council elected Comr George Lyndon Carpenter General (24 Aug); **General George Lyndon Carpenter took command of The Salvation Army** (1 Nov).

1941 Order of Distinguished Auxiliary Service instituted (24 Feb); International Headquarters destroyed in London Blitz (10 May).

1943 Inauguration of The Salvation Army Medical Fellowship (16 Feb) (SA Nurses' Fellowship until 1987).

1944 Service of thanksgiving to mark centenary of conversion of William Booth (in 1844) held in St Paul's Cathedral, London (2 Jun).

1946 Fourth High Council elected Comr Albert Orsborn General (9 May); **General Albert Orsborn took command of The Salvation Army** (21 Jun).

1948 First Army worldwide broadcast (28 Apr).

1950 Work begun in **Haiti** (5 Feb); first TV

broadcast by a General of The Salvation Army; official constitution of students' fellowship; first International Youth Congress held in London (10-23 Aug); reopening of Staff College (later International College for Officers) (10 Oct).

1954 Fifth High Council elected Comr Wilfred Kitching General (11 May); **General Wilfred Kitching took command of The Salvation Army** (1 Jul).

1956 Work begun in Port Moresby, **Papua New Guinea** (31 Aug); first International Corps Cadet Congress (19-31 Jul).

1959 Over-60 clubs inaugurated (Oct).

1962 Work begun in **Puerto Rico** (Feb).

1963 Sixth High Council elected Comr Frederick Coutts General (1 Oct); Queen Elizabeth the Queen Mother declared International Headquarters open (13 Nov); **General Frederick Coutts took command of The Salvation Army** (23 Nov).

1965 Queen Elizabeth II attended the International Centenary commencement (24 Jun); Founders' Day Service held in Westminster Abbey, London (2 Jul); work re-established in **Taiwan** (pioneered 1928) (Oct).

1967 Work begun in **Malawi** (13 Nov).

1969 Seventh High Council elected Comr Erik Wickberg General (23 Jul); *The Salvation Army Handbook of Doctrine* new edition published (Aug); **General Erik Wickberg took command of The Salvation Army** (21 Sep); work begun in **Lesotho.**

1970 Cyclone relief operations in East Pakistan (later **Bangladesh**) (25 Nov) lead to start of work in 1971.

1971 Work begun in **Spain** (23 Jul) and **Portugal** (25 Jul).

1972 Work begun in **Venezuela** (30 Jun).

1973 Work begun in **Fiji** (14 Nov).

1974 Eighth High Council elected Comr Clarence Wiseman General (13 May); **General Clarence Wiseman took command of The Salvation Army** (6 Jul).

1976 Work begun in **Guatemala** (Jun); **Mexico and Central America Territory** (now **Latin America North Territory** and **Mexico Territory**) formed (1 Oct).

1977 Ninth High Council elected Comr Arnold Brown General (5 May); **General Arnold Brown took command of The Salvation Army** (5 Jul).

1978 Fifth International Congress (Jun-Jul), with opening ceremony attended by HRH the Prince of Wales.

1979 The Salvation Army Boys' Adventure Corps (SABAC) launched (21 Jan).

1980 Inauguration of International Staff Songsters (8 Mar); The Salvation Army Act 1980 received royal assent (1 Aug); work begun in **French Guiana** (1 Oct).

1981 Tenth High Council elected Comr Jarl Wahlström General (23 Oct); **General Jarl Wahlström took command of The Salvation Army** (14 Dec).

1984 International Conference of Leaders held in Berlin, West Germany (May).

1985 Work begun in **Colombia** (21 Apr) and **Marshall Islands** (1 Jun); second International Youth Congress (Jul) held in Macomb, Illinois, USA; work begun in **Angola** (4 Oct) and **Ecuador** (30 Oct).

1986 Work begun in **Tonga** (9 Jan); *Salvationist* first issued (15 Mar); 11th High Council elected Comr Eva Burrows General (2 May); **General Eva Burrows took command of The Salvation Army** (9 Jul); International Development Conference held at Sunbury Court, London (Sep).

1988 Work begun in **Liberia** (1 May); International Conference of Leaders held in Lake Arrowhead, California, USA (Sep).

1989 Work begun in **El Salvador** (1 Apr).

1990 Work begun in **East Germany** (Mar), **Czechoslovakia** (May), **Hungary** (Jun) and re-established in **Latvia** (Nov); sixth International Congress held in London (Jun-Jul); **United Kingdom Territory** established (1 Nov).

1991 Restructuring of **International Headquarters** as an entity separate from UK Territory (1 Feb); work reopened in **Russia** (6 Jul); International Conference of Leaders held in London (Jul-Aug).

1992 Opening of new **USA National Headquarters** building in Alexandria, Virginia (3 May).

1993 The 12th High Council elected Comr Bramwell H. Tillsley General (28 Apr); **General Bramwell H. Tillsley took command of The Salvation Army** (9 Jul); work begun in **Micronesia**.

1994 First International Literary and Publications Conference held at Alexandria, Virginia, USA (Apr); General Bramwell H. Tillsley retired due to ill health (18 May); 13th High Council elected Comr

Paul A. Rader General (23 Jul); **General Paul A. Rader took command of The Salvation Army immediately**; work begun in **Guam**.

1995 International Conference of Leaders held in Hong Kong (Apr); all married women officers granted rank in their own right (1 May); work begun in **Dominican Republic** (1 Jul); work reopened in **Estonia** (14 Aug); following relief and development programmes, work begun in **Rwanda** (5 Nov).

1996 Work begun in **Sabah (East Malaysia)** (Mar); first meeting of International Spiritual Life Commission (Jul).

1997 International Youth Forum held in Cape Town, South Africa (Jan); first-ever congress held in Russia/CIS; Salvation Army leaders in Southern Africa signed commitment to reconciliation for past stand on apartheid; work begun in **Botswana** (20 Nov).

1998 International Conference of Leaders held in Melbourne, Australia (Mar), receives report of International Spiritual Life Commission; publication of a fourth Handbook of Doctrine entitled *Salvation Story* (Mar); International Commission on Officership opened in London (Oct).

1999 International Education Symposium held in London (Mar); work begun in **Romania** (May); 14th High Council elected Comr John Gowans General (15 May); **General John Gowans took command of The Salvation Army** (23 Jul).

2000 International Commission on Officership closed and subsequent Officership Survey carried out (Mar-May); work begun in **Macau** (25 Mar); The Salvation Army registered as a denomination in **Sweden** (10 Mar); International Conference of Leaders held in Atlanta, Georgia, USA (Jun); seventh International Congress held in Atlanta, Georgia, USA (28 Jun-2 Jul) (first held outside UK); work begun in **Honduras** (23 Nov).

2001 International Conference for Training Principals held in London (Mar); International Theology and Ethics Symposium held in Winnipeg, Canada (Jun); International Music Ministries Forum held in London (Jul); International Poverty Summit held on the Internet and Lotus Notes Intranet (Nov 2001-Feb 2002).

2002 The 15th High Council elected Comr John Larsson General (6 Sep); **General John Larsson took command of The Salvation Army** (13 Nov).

2004 International Conference of Leaders held in New Jersey, USA (29 Apr-7 May); International Music and Other Creative Ministries Forum (MOSAIC) held in Toronto, Canada (Jun); New International Headquarters building at 101 Queen Victoria Street, London, opened by Her Royal Highness, The Princess Royal (9 Nov); IHQ Emergency Services coordinates disaster relief work after Indian Ocean tsunami struck (26 Dec).

2005 Indian Ocean Tsunami Summit held in London (Jan); Eastern Europe Command redesignated Eastern Europe Territory; Singapore, Malaysia and Myanmar Command redesignated Singapore, Malaysia and Myanmar Territory (both 1 Mar); International Literary and Publications Conference held at Alexandria, Virginia, USA (Apr); European Youth Congress held in Prague, Czech Republic (4-8 Aug); All-Africa Congress held in Harare, Zimbabwe (24-28 Aug); work in **Lithuania** officially recognised by IHQ, and Germany Territory redesignated Germany and Lithuania Territory (Sep); 'Project Warsaw' launched to begin Army's work in **Poland** (23-25 Sep); East Africa Territory redesignated Kenya Territory, with Uganda Region given command status (1 Nov)

2006 The 16th High Council elected Comr Shaw Clifton General (28 Jan); **General Shaw Clifton took command of The Salvation Army** (2 Apr); Salvation Army Scouts and Guides World Jamboree held in Almere, Netherlands (Aug); 2nd International Theology and Ethics Symposium held in Johannesburg, South Africa (Aug)

2007 Web site for Office of the General launched (Feb); first of General's pastoral letters to soldiers dispatched electronically (15 Mar); first-ever International Conference of Personnel Secretaries held in London (27 May-3 Jun); International Social Justice Commission established (1 Jul), headed by an International Director for Social Justice; work begun in **Burundi** (5 Aug) and **Greece** (1 Oct)

SIGNIFICANT EVENTS 2006-2007

2006
October
Eastern Europe: European Court of Human Rights ruled in favour of The Salvation Army regarding its registration in Moscow (6 Oct)

New Zealand, Fiji and Tonga: Twenty months of unbroken 24-7 prayer throughout the territory ended with 'New Zeal' Convention (13-15 Oct)

USA: Pan American Conference held at Camp Hoblitzelle, Texas (18-20 Oct)

November
Papua New Guinea: 50th anniversary of Salvation Army work celebrated during congress meetings led by the General in Port Moresby (22-26 Nov)

Korea: Commissioner Chun, Kwang-pyo (TC) elected President of the National Council of Churches in Korea (20 Nov)

Italy: The Salvation Army became an official member of *Federazione delle Donne Evangeliche* (Federation of Evangelical Women's Groups)

2007
January
IHQ: Home League Centenary Year launched with 'While Women Weep' slogan and logo

February
IHQ: New web site dedicated to the Office of the General launched at www.salvationarmy.org/thegeneral (1 Feb)

India: Chief of the Staff presides over All-India Training Seminar at Surrenden Conference Centre in Tamil Nadu (24-27 Feb)

IHQ: An international delegation of 10 women led by Commissioner Janet Street (WSWM) attended United Nations 51st session of the Commission on the Status of Women at UN Headquarters, New York (26 Feb-9 Mar)

March
IHQ: First of General's pastoral letters to soldiers dispatched electronically (15 Mar)

April
Italy: Lieut-Colonel Massimo Paone (OC) appointed General's Personal Representative to the Vatican (16 Apr)

United Kingdom Territory: Commissioner Betty Matear (TPWM) became first Salvationist to be inducted as Moderator of the Free Churches in England and Wales (25 Apr)

May
Switzerland, Austria and Hungary: 125 years of Salvation Army work in Switzerland celebrated at congress in Bern, led by the General (17-20 May)

IHQ: First-ever International Conference of

One of 125 doves is released in Bern during 125th anniversary celebrations of The Salvation Army in Switzerland Photo: Cédric Fague

Personnel Secretaries held at Sunbury Court (27 May-3 June)

July
IHQ: International Social Justice Commission established (1 July), headed by an International Director for Social Justice

August
Africa: New opening in Burundi commenced (5 Aug), linked to Rwanda Region

IHQ: Centenary of Salvation Army suicide prevention work recognised at biennial congress of International Association for Suicide Prevention held in Killarney, Ireland (28 Aug-1 Sep)

October
Europe: New opening in Greece commenced (1 Oct), linked to Italy Command

21

THE HIGH COUNCIL

THE High Council was originally established by William Booth in 1904 as a safeguard to allow the removal from office of an incumbent General who had become, for whatever reason, unfit to continue to exercise oversight, direction and control of The Salvation Army. Should such an allegation be made and receive significant support from officers of the rank of commissioner, a High Council would be called to decide upon the matter and to appoint a successor should the General be found unfit.

The Founder intended, however, that the normal method of appointment would be for the General in office to select his or her successor, but only one General – Bramwell Booth in 1912 – was ever selected in this way.

By November 1928, Bramwell Booth had been absent from International Headquarters for seven months on account of illness, and a High Council was called. The 63 members, being all the commissioners on active service and certain territorial commanders, gathered at Sunbury Court near London on 8 January 1929 and eventually voted that the General, then aged 73, was 'unfit on the ground of ill-health' to continue in office. On 13 February 1929 the High Council elected Commissioner Edward Higgins as the Army's third General.

Subsequently, a commissioners' conference agreed to three major constitutional reforms later passed into law by the British Parliament as the Salvation Army Act 1931, namely:

i. the abolition of the General's right to nominate his or her successor, and the substitution of the election of every General by a High Council;

ii. the fixing of an age limit for the retirement of the General;

iii. the creation of a trustee company to hold the properties and other capital assets of the Army, in place of the sole trusteeship of the General.

The High Council is currently constituted under provisions of the Salvation Army Act 1980 as amended by deeds of variation executed in 1995 and 2005.

Since 1929, High Councils have been held in 1934 (electing General Evangeline Booth), 1939 (General Carpenter), 1946 (General Orsborn), 1954 (General Kitching), 1963 (General Coutts), 1969 (General Wickberg), 1974 (General Wiseman), 1977 (General Brown), 1981 (General Wahlström), 1986 (General Burrows), 1993 (General Tillsley), 1994 (General Rader), 1999 (General Gowans), 2002 (General Larsson) and 2006 (General Clifton). The next is currently scheduled to convene in January 2011.

High Councils are normally called by the Chief of the Staff and have usually met at Sunbury Court but can meet anywhere in the United Kingdom. Since 1995 the High Council has been composed of all active commissioners except the spouse of the General, and all territorial commanders.

GENERALS ELECTED BY A HIGH COUNCIL

The place and date at the beginning of an entry denote the corps from which the General entered Salvation Army service and the year

Edward J. Higgins

Reading, UK, 1882. General (1929-34). b 26 Nov 1864; pG 14 Dec 1947. Served in corps and divisional work, British Territory; at the International Training Garrison, as CS, USA; as Asst Foreign Secretary, IHQ; Brit Comr (1911-19); Chief of the Staff (1919-29). CBE. Author of *Stewards of God*, *Personal Holiness*, etc. m Capt Catherine Price, 1888; pG 1952.

Evangeline Booth

General (1934-39). b 25 Dec 1865; pG 17 Jul 1950. Fourth daughter of the Founder, at 21 years of age she commanded Marylebone Corps, its Great Western Hall being the centre of spectacular evangelistic work. As Field Commissioner this experience was used to advantage throughout Great Britain (1888-91). The Founder appointed her to train cadets in London (1891-96); then as TC, Canada (1896-1904); Commander of The Salvation Army in the United States of America (1904-34). Author of *Toward a Better World*; *Songs of the Evangel*, etc.

George L. Carpenter

Raymond Terrace, Australia, 1892. General (1939-46). b 20 Jun 1872; pG 9 Apr 1948. Appointments included 18 years in Australia in property, training and literary work; at IHQ (1911-27) for most part with General Bramwell Booth as Literary Secretary; further service in Australia (1927-33), including CS, Australia Eastern; as TC, South America East (1933-37); TC, Canada (1937-39). Author of *Keep the Trumpets Sounding*; *Banners and Adventures*, etc. m Ens Minnie Rowell, 1899; pG 1960. Author of *Notable Officers of The Salvation Army*; *Women of the Flag*, etc.

Albert Orsborn

Clapton, UK, 1905. General (1946-54). b 4 Sep 1886; pG 4 Feb 1967. Served as corps officer and in divisional work in British Territory; as Chief Side Officer at ITC (1925-33); CS, New Zealand (1933-36); TC, Scotland & Ireland (1936-40); Brit Comr (1940-46). CBE, 1943. Writer of many well-known Army songs. Author of *The House of My Pilgrimage*, etc. m Capt Evalina Barker, 1909; pG 1942. m Maj Evelyn Berry, 1944; pG 1945. m Comr Mrs Phillis Taylor (née Higgins), 1947; pG 1986.

Wilfred Kitching

New Barnet, UK, 1914. General (1954-63). b 22 Aug 1893; pG 15 Dec 1977. Served in British Territory corps, divisional and NHQ appointments, then as CS, Australia Southern (1946-48); TC, Sweden (1948-51); Brit Comr (1951-54). Composer of many distinctively Salvationist musical works. Hon LLD (Yonsei, Seoul, Rep of Korea), 1961; CBE, 1964. Author of *Soldier of Salvation* (1963) and *A Goodly Heritage* (autobiography, 1967). m Adjt Kathleen Bristow (Penge, 1916), 1929; pG 1982.

Generals of The Salvation Army

Frederick Coutts

Batley, UK, 1920. General (1963-69). b 21 Sep 1899; pG 6 Feb 1986. Served in British Territory in divisional work (1921-25) and as corps officer (1925-35); for 18 years in Literary Dept, IHQ; writer of *International Company Orders* (1935-46); Editor of *The Officers' Review* (1947-53); Asst to Literary Secretary (1947-52); Literary Secretary (1952-53); Training Principal, ITC (1953-57); TC, Australia Eastern (1957-63). Author of *The Call to Holiness* (1957); *Essentials of Christian Experience* (1969); *The Better Fight* (1973); *No Discharge in this War* (1975), *Bread for My Neighbour* (1978); *The Splendour of Holiness* (1983), etc. Order of Cultural Merit (Rep of Korea), 1966; Hon Litt D (Chung Ang, Rep of Korea), 1966; CBE, 1967; Hon DD (Aberdeen), 1981. m Lt Bessie Lee, BSc, 1925; pG 1967. m Comr Olive Gatrall (Thornton Heath, 1925), 1970, pG 1997.

Erik Wickberg

Bern 2, Switzerland, 1925. General (1969-74). b 6 Jul 1904; pG 26 Apr 1996. Served as corps officer in Scotland; in Germany as Training (Education) Officer, and Private Secretary to CS and TC (1926-34); at IHQ as Private Secretary to IS and Asst to Under Secretary for Europe (1934-39); in Sweden as IHQ Liaison Officer (1939-46) and DC, Uppsala (1946-48); as CS, Switzerland, (1948-53); CS, Sweden (1953-57); TC, Germany (1957-61); Chief of the Staff (1961-69). Commander, Order of Vasa, 1970; Order of Moo Koong Wha (Rep of Korea), 1970; Hon LLD (Rep of Korea), 1970; Grand Cross of Merit, Fed Rep of Germany, 1971; King's Gold Medal (Grand Cross) (Sweden), 1980. Author of *Inkallad (God's Conscript)* (autobiography, Sweden, 1978) and *Uppdraget (The Charge – My Way to Preaching)* (1990). m Ens Frieda de Groot (Berne 1, Switz, 1922), 1929; pG 1930. m Capt Margarete Dietrich (Hamburg 3, Ger, 1928), 1932; pG 1976. m Major Eivor Lindberg (Norrköping 1, Swdn, 1946), 1977.

Clarence Wiseman

Guelph, Ont, Canada, 1927. General (1974-77). b 19 Jun 1907; pG 4 May 1985. Served in Canada as corps officer and in editorial work; chaplain with Canadian forces overseas (1940-43); Senior Representative, Canadian Red Shield Services Overseas (1943-45); back in Canada as divisional commander (1945-54), Field Secretary (1954-57) and CS (1957-60); as TC, East Africa (1960-62); Training Principal, ITC (1962-67); TC, Canada & Bermuda (1967-74). Order of Canada, 1976, Hon LLD, Hon DD (Yonsei, Seoul, Rep of Korea). Author of *A Burning in My Bones* (1980) and *The Desert Road to Glory* (1980). m Capt Jane Kelly (Danforth, Ont, Can, 1927), 1932; pG 1993. Author of *Earth's Common Clay*; *Bridging the Year*; *Watching Daily*.

Arnold Brown

Belleville, Canada, 1935. General (1977-81). b 13 Dec 1913; pG 26 Jun 2002. Served in Canada in corps, editorial, public relations and youth work (1935-64); as Secretary for Public Relations at IHQ (1964-69); Chief of the Staff (1969-74); TC, Canada & Bermuda (1974-77). MIPR, Hon LDH (Asbury, USA); Freeman, City of London; Hon DD (Olivet, USA), 1981; Officer, Order of Canada, 1981. Author of *What Hath God Wrought?*; *The Gate and the Light* (1984); *Yin – The Mountain the Wind Blew Here* (1988); *With Christ at the Table* (1991); *Occupied Manger – Unoccupied Tomb* (1994). m Lt Jean Barclay (Montreal Cit, Can, 1938), 1939. Author of *Excursions in Thought* (1981).

Generals of The Salvation Army

Jarl Wahlström

Helsinki 1, Finland, 1938. General (1981-86). b 9 Jul 1918. pG 3 Dec 1999. Served in corps, youth and divisional work in Finland; as Second World War chaplain to Finnish armed forces; in Finland as a divisional commander (1960-63), Training Principal, Secretary of Music Dept (1963-68) and CS (1968-72); as CS, Canada & Bermuda (1972-76); TC, Finland (1976-81); TC, Sweden (1981); Knight, Order of the Lion of Finland, 1964; Order of Civil Merit, Mugunghwa Medal (Rep of Korea), 1983; Hon DHL (W Illinois), 1985; Paul Harris Fellow of Rotary International, 1987; Commander, Order of the White Rose of Finland, 1989. Author of *A Traveller's Song* and *A Pilgrim's Song* (autobiography, Finnish/ Swedish, 1989). m Lt Maire Nyberg (Helsinki 1, 1944).

Eva Burrows

Fortitude Valley, Qld, Australia Eastern, 1951. General (1986-93). b 15 Sep 1929. Appointed to corps in British Territory, before post-graduate studies; served at Howard Institute, Zimbabwe (1952-67), Head of Teacher Training (1965), Vice-Principal (1965-67); as Principal, Usher Institute (1967-70); Asst Principal, ICO (1970-74), Principal (1974-75); Leader, WSS (GBI) (1975-77); TC, Sri Lanka (1977-79); TC, Scotland (1979-82); TC, Australia Southern (1982-86). BA (Qld); M Ed (Sydney); Hon Dr of Liberal Arts (Ehwa Univ, Seoul, Rep of Korea), 1988; Hon LLD (Asbury, USA), 1988; Paul Harris Fellow of Rotary International, 1990; Hon DST (Houghton), 1992; Hon DD (Olivet Nazarene Univ), 1993; Hon Dr Philosophy (Qld), 1993; Hon Dr of University (Griffith Univ), 1994; Companion of Order of Australia, 1994; Living Legacy Award from Women's International Center, USA, 1996.

Bramwell Tillsley

Kitchener, Ont, Canada, with wife née Maude Pitcher, 1956. General (1993-94). b 18 Aug 1931. Served in Canada in corps, youth, training college and divisional appointments, including Training Principal (1974-77), Provincial Commander in Newfoundland (1977-79) and DC, Metro Toronto (1979-81); as Training Principal, ITC (1981-85); CS, USA Southern (1985-89); TC, Australia Southern (1989-91); Chief of the Staff (1991-93). Retired in 1994 due to ill health. BA University of Western Ontario. Has written extensively for SA periodicals. Author of *Life in the Spirit*; *This Mind in You*; *Life More Abundant*; *Manpower for the Master*.

Paul Rader

Cincinnati Cit, USA Eastern, w wife née Frances Kay Fuller, BA (Asbury), Hon DD (Asbury Theol Seminary) 1995, Hon LHD (Greenville) 1997, 1961. General (1994-99). b 14 Mar 1934. Served in corps prior to transfer to Korea in 1962; in Korea in training work (1962-73), as Training Principal (1973), Education Secretary (1974-76), Asst Chief Secretary (1976-77) and CS (1977-84); in USA Eastern as Training Principal (1984-87), DC, Eastern Pennsylvania (1987-89) and CS (1989); as TC, USA Western (1989-94). BA, BD (Asbury); MTh (Southern Baptist Seminary); D Miss (Fuller Theological Seminary); Hon LLD (Asbury); 1984 elected to board of trustees of Asbury College; 1989 elected Paul Harris Fellow of Rotary International; Hon DD (Asbury Theol Seminary), 1995; Hon LHD (Greenville), 1997; Hon DD (Roberts Wesleyan), 1998.

John Gowans

Grangetown, UK, 1955. General (1999-2002). b 13 Nov 1934. Served in British Territory as corps officer, divisional youth secretary, National Stewardship Secretary and divisional commander; as Chief Secretary, France (1977-81); in USA Western as Programme Secretary (1981-85) and DC, Southern California (1985-86); TC, France (1986-93); TC, Australia Eastern & Papua New Guinea (1993-97); TC, UK (1997-99). Paul Harris Fellow of Rotary International; Hon DLitt (Yonsei, Seoul, Rep of Korea); Freedom of the City of London (2000). Songwriter. Author of *O Lord!* series of poetry books and *There's a Boy Here* (autobiography, 2002). Co-author with John Larsson of 10 musicals. m Lt Gisèle Bonhotal (Paris Central, France, 1955) 1957.

John Larsson

Upper Norwood, UK, 1957. General (2002-06). b 2 Apr 38. Served in corps; at ITC; as TYS (Scotland Territory); NYS (British Territory); CS, South America West (1980-84); Principal, ITC (1984-88); Assistant to Chief of the Staff for UK Administrative Planning, IHQ (1988-1990); TC, UK (1990-93); TC, New Zealand & Fiji (1993-96); TC, Sweden & Latvia (1996-99); Chief of the Staff (1999-2002). BD (London). Author of *Doctrine without Tears* (1964); *Spiritual Breakthrough* (1983); *The Man Perfectly Filled with the Spirit* (1986); *How Your Corps Can Grow* (1989), and *Saying Yes to Life* (autobiography, 2007). Composer of music and co-author with John Gowans of 10 musicals. m Capt Freda Turner (Kingston-upon-Thames, UK, 1964) 1969.

Shaw Clifton

Edmonton, UK, with wife née Helen Ashman, 1973. General (2006-present). b 21 Sep 45. Served as corps officer in British Territory; in Literary Department, IHQ (1974); in Zimbabwe as Vice Principal, Mazoe Secondary School (1975-77) and CO, Bulawayo Citadel (1977-79); in further BT corps appointments (1979-82, 1989-92); at IHQ as Legal & Parliamentary Secretary (1982-89); in UK as divisional commander (1992-95); in USA Eastern as DC, Massachusetts (1995-97); as TC, Pakistan (1997-2002); TC, New Zealand, Fiji & Tonga (2002-04); TC, UK (2004-06). LLB (Hons), AKC (Theol), BD (Theol) (Hons), PhD. Author of *What Does the Salvationist Say?* (1977); *Growing Together* (1984); *Strong Doctrine, Strong Mercy* (1985); *Never the Same Again* (1997); *Who are these Salvationists?* (1999); *New Love – Thinking Aloud About Practical Holiness* (2004), etc.

> ❛ Our Lord is the Prince of Peace who gives peace to our hearts such as the world cannot give. Therefore I call the Army to prayer for peace in the world. We can begin by shunning strife in our own personal lives and praying that God will grant us grace for this day by day. ❜

General Shaw Clifton

COUNTRIES WHERE THE SALVATION ARMY IS AT WORK

THE Salvation Army is at work in 113 countries. A country in which the Army serves is defined in two ways:

(i) Politically

(ii) Where the General has given approval to the work, thus officially recognising it, ensuring it has legal identity and a Deed Poll is published to acknowledge this.

As far as political status is concerned, for the Army's purposes, three categories are recognised:

(a) Independent countries, eg USA and New Zealand;

(b) Internally independent political entities which are under the protection of another country in matters of defence and foreign affairs, eg The Færoes, Isle of Man, Puerto Rico;

(c) Colonies and other dependent political units, eg Bermuda, French Guiana, Guernsey, Jersey.

Administrative subdivisions of a country such as Wales and Scotland in the UK are not recognised as separate countries for this purpose. The countries fulfilling the quoted criteria, with the date in brackets on which the work was officially recognised, are as follows:

Angola ....(1985)
Antigua ....(1903)
Argentina ....(1890)
Australia.............(1881)
Austria ....(1927)

Bahamas.............(1931)
Bangladesh..........(1971)
Barbados ....(1898)
Belgium ....(1889)
Belize ....(1915)
Bermuda.............(1896)
Bolivia ....(1920)
Botswana ....(1997)
Brazil ....(1922)
Burundi ....(2007)

Canada ....(1882)

Chile...................(1909)
China ....(1916)
Colombia ....(1985)
Congo (Brazzaville)
.............................(1937)
Congo (Kinshasa)
.............................(1934)
Costa Rica ....(1907)
Cuba...................(1918)
Czech Republic ..(1919)
.............................(1990)

Denmark ....(1887)
Dominican Republic
.............................(1995)

Ecuador ....(1985)
El Salvador ....(1989)

Estonia ....(1927)
.............................(1995)

Færoes, The ....(1924)
Fiji ....(1973)
Finland ....(1889)
France ....(1881)
French Guiana ....(1980)

Georgia ....(1993)
Germany ....(1886)
Ghana.................(1922)
Greece ....(2007)
Grenada ....(1902)
Guam ....(1994)
Guatemala ....(1976)
Guernsey ....(1879)

Countries where The Salvation Army is at work

Guyana...............(1895)
Haiti ....(1950)
Honduras ....(2000)
Hong Kong ....(1930)
Hungary ....(1924)
 ....(1990)

Iceland ....(1895)
India ....(1882)
Indonesia ....(1894)
Ireland, Republic of
 (Eire) ....(1880)
Isle of Man..........(1883)
Italy ....(1887)

Jamaica ....(1887)
Japan ....(1895)
Jersey ....(1879)

Kenya..................(1921)
Korea ....(1908)

Latvia..................(1923)
 ....(1990)
Lesotho ....(1969)

Liberia ....(1988)
Lithuania ....(2005)

Macau ....(2000)
Malawi................(1967)
Malaysia..............(1938)
Marshall Islands..(1985)
Mexico ....(1937)
Micronesia ....(1993)
Moldova..............(1994)
Mozambique ......(1916)
Myanmar ....(1915)

Netherlands, The
 ....(1887)
New Zealand ......(1883)
Nigeria ....(1920)
Norway ....(1888)
Pakistan ....(1883)
Panama................(1904)
Papua New Guinea
 ....(1956)
Paraguay ....(1910)
Peru ....(1910)
Philippines, The ..(1937)

Poland ....(2005)
Portugal ....(1971)
Puerto Rico ....(1962)

Romania..............(1999)
Russia..................(1913)
 ....(1991)
Rwanda ....(1995)

St Christopher Nevis
 (St Kitts) ....(1916)
St Helena ....(1884)
St Lucia ....(1902)
St Maarten ....(1999)
St Vincent ....(1905)
Singapore ....(1935)
South Africa........(1883)
Spain ....(1971)
Sri Lanka ....(1883)
Suriname ....(1924)
Swaziland............(1960)
Sweden................(1882)
Switzerland ....(1882)

Taiwan ....(1965)
Tanzania..............(1933)
Tonga ....(1986)
Trinidad and Tobago
 ....(1901)

Uganda................(1931)
Ukraine ....(1993)
United Kingdom (1865)
United States of
 America ....(1880)
Uruguay ....(1890)

Venezuela ....(1972)
Virgin Islands ....(1917)

Zambia ....(1922)
Zimbabwe ....(1891)

Italy Command: Children help celebrate The Salvation Army's 120 years in Italy as the Chief of the Staff cuts a 'birthday' cake during the National Congress in Rome

INTERNATIONAL STATISTICS
(as at 1 January 2007)

Countries and other territories where
SA serves (see pp 27-28)..............113
Languages used in SA work, including
some tribal languages....................175
Corps, outposts, societies, new
plants and recovery churches....15,175
Goodwill centres 1,155
Officers 25,974
Active..16,945
Retired...9,029
Auxiliary-captains..............................143
Lieutenants 604
Envoys/sergeants, full-time 793
Cadets...998
Employees...................................107,902
Senior soldiers 1,082,166
Adherents....................................190,215
Junior soldiers 360,222
Corps cadets..................................36,374
Senior band musicians..................25,653
Senior songsters............................94,921
Other senior musical group
members....................................45,753
Senior and young people's
local officers 128,854
Women's Ministries (all groups) –
members 564,566
League of Mercy – members......110,924
SAMF – members..........................8,257
Over-60 clubs – members..........359,230
Men's fellowships – members......74,072
Young people's bands –
members 10,652
Young people's singing
companies – members..............79,665
Other young people's music
groups – members....................55,776
Sunday schools – members........612,533
Junior youth groups
(scouts, guides, etc, and clubs) –
members...................................236,067
Senior youth groups – members......79,912

Corps-based community development
programmes..............................23,035
Beneficiaries/clients 2,845,288
Thrift stores/charity shops
(corps/territorial) 1,603
Recycling centres 26

Social Programme
Residential
Hostels for homeless and transient....647
Capacity 34,945
Emergency lodges.............................373
Capacity 21,047
Children's homes 209
Capacity 8,500
Homes for the elderly.......................121
Capacity 6,744
Homes for the disabled 54
Capacity 2,583
Homes for the blind 10
Capacity 986
Remand and probation homes.............36
Capacity 988
Homes for street children...................31
Capacity 669
Mother and baby homes.....................40
Capacity 1,016
Training centres for families 27
Capacity 590
Care homes for vulnerable people 60
Capacity 808
Women's and men's refuge
centres 68
Capacity 1,691
Other residential care
homes/hostels 113
Capacity 5,555

Day Care
Community centres............................492
Early childhood education centres....186
Capacity 26,195

Day centres for the elderly..................78
   Capacity 22,744
Play groups..102
   Capacity 1,422
Day centres for the hearing
   impaired 2
   Capacity 60
Day centres for street children 10
   Capacity 924
Day nurseries 174
   Capacity 15,127
Drop-in centres for youth..................183
Other day care centres 368
   Capacity 48,137

Addiction Dependency

Non-residential programmes 57
   Capacity 26,260
Residential programmes....................191
   Capacity 15,245
Harbour Light programmes 38
   Capacity 70,361
Other services for those with
   addictions 1,695
   Capacity 17,252

Service to the Armed Forces

Clubs and canteens...............................27
Mobile units for service personnel......18
Chaplains 18

Emergency Disaster Response

Disaster rehabilitation schemes 268
   Participants 1,109,469
Refugee programmes –
   host country 3
   Participants.....................................138
Refugee rehabilitation programmes....58
   Participants 13,886
Other response programmes 1,962
   Participants 111,768

Services to the Community

Prisoners visited 409,014
Prisoners helped on discharge....151,405
Police courts – people helped 272,920
Missing persons – applications....10,143
   Number traced..............................5,660
Night patrol/anti-suicide –

number helped........................345,948
Community youth programmes 2,780
   Beneficiaries 189,837
Employment bureaux –
   applications 96,331
   initial referrals........................185,630
Counselling – people helped......435,789
General relief – people
   helped...................................13,534,571
Emergency relief (fire, flood,
   etc) – people helped 1,632,409
Emergency mobile units 2,562
Feeding centres 1,066
Restaurants and cafes........................121
Thrift stores/charity shops
   (social)......................................1,409
Apartments for elderly 437
   Capacity 6,700
Hostels for students, workers, etc......86
   Capacity 2,640
Land settlements (SA villages,
   farms etc) 21
   Capacity 1,656
Social Services summer camps 205
   Participants 17,991
Other services to the community
   (unspecified)....................................79
   Beneficiaries........................1,625,094

Health Programme

General hospitals 22
   Capacity 2,580
Maternity hospitals..............................24
   Capacity 319
Other specialist hospitals 25
Capacity 1,956
Specialist clinics..................................68
   Capacity 1,784
General clinics/health centres 133
   Capacity 887
Mobile clinics/community health
   posts 63
Inpatients......................................281,110
Outpatients 981,568
Doctors/medics 3,459
Invalid/convalescent homes................29
   Capacity 1,083

Health education programmes
    (HIV/Aids, etc) 365
    Beneficiaries.............................355,786
Day care programmes...........................26

Education Programme
Kindergarten/sub primary..................732
Primary schools 934
Upper primary and middle
schools 176
Secondary and high schools..............185
Colleges and universities 6
Vocational training schools/centres ...253

Pupils...494,491
Teachers 15,831
Schools for the blind (included in
    above totals)......................................8
Schools for the disabled (included in
    above totals)....................................16
Boarding schools (included in
    above totals)....................................27
Evening schools 2
Colleges, universities, staff training
    and development study and distance
    learning centres...............................27

SALVATION ARMY PERIODICALS
BY TERRITORY/COMMAND

Australia National: *Kidzone, Warcry*

Australia Eastern Territory: *Creative Ministry, Pipeline, Venue, Women in Touch*

Australia Southern Territory: *Kidzone, On Fire, Warcry*

Belgium Command: *Espoir* (French), *Strijdkreet* (Flemish)

Brazil Territory: *Notas e Notícias, O Oficial, Rumo Magazine*

Canada and Bermuda Territory: *Edge for Kids, En Avant, Faith & Friends, Foi & Vie, Salvationist*

Caribbean Territory: *The War Cry*

Congo (Brazzaville) Territory: *Le Salutiste*

Congo (Kinshasa) and Angola Territory: *Echo d'Espoir*

Denmark Territory: *Mennesker & Tro, Kids Alive, Vision-Mission, Young Connection*

Eastern Europe Territory: *Vestnik Spaseniya* (*The War Cry*), *The Officer* (both Russian)

Finland and Estonia Territory: *Krigsropet* (Swedish), *Nappis, Sotahuuto* (both Finnish)

France Territory: *Avec Vous, Le Bulletin*

de la Ligue du Foyer, Le Fil, Le Magazine, L'Officier, Quand Même

Germany and Lithuania Territory: *Danke, Der Kriegsruf, Heilsarmee-Forum*

Ghana Territory: *Salvationist Newsletter*

Hong Kong and Macau Command: *Army Scene, The War Cry*

India Central Territory: *Home League Magazine, Udyogasthudu, Yovana Veerudu, Yudha Dwani*

India Eastern Territory: *Sipai Tlangau* (Mizo *War Cry*), *The Officer, Young Salvationist, Chunnunpar* (all Mizo)

India Northern Territory: *Home League Quarterly* (Hindi), *Mukti Samachar* (Hindi and Punjabi), *The Officer* (Hindi); *Yuva Sipai* (Hindi)

India South Eastern Territory: *Chiruveeran* (Tamil), *Home League Quarterly, Poresathan* (Tamil), *The Officer* (Tamil)

India South Western Territory: *Home League Quarterly* (Malayalam/English), *The Officer, Youdha Shabdan, Yuva Veeran* (all Malayalam)

India Western Territory: *Home League Quarterly, The Officer, The War Cry,*

The Young Soldier (all Gujarati and Marathi)

International Headquarters: *All the World, Global Exchange, The Officer, Words of Life*

Italy Command: *Il Bollettino dell' Unione Femminile, Il Grido di Guerra*

Japan Territory: *Home League Quarterly, The Officer, The Sunday School Guide, Toki-no-Koe*

Kenya Territory: *Sauti ya Vita* (English and Kiswahili)

Korea Territory: *Home League Quarterly, The Officer, The Sunday School Guide, Toki-no-Koe, Toki-no-Koe Junior*

Latin America North Territory: *Voz de Salvación (Salvation Voice), Arco Iris de Ideas (Rainbow of Ideas)*

The Netherlands and Czech Republic Territory: *Dag in Dag Uit, Heils-en Strijdzangen, InterCom, Strijdkreet, Voor Werk* (all Dutch), *Prapor Spásy* (Czech)

New Zealand, Fiji and Tonga Territory: *War Cry*

Nigeria Territory: *Salvationist, The Shepherd, The War Cry*

Norway, Iceland and The Færoes Territory: *Herópid* (Icelandic), *FAbU nytt, Krigsropet, Frelsesoffiseren* (all Norwegian)

Pakistan Territory: *Home League Quarterly, The War Cry* (Urdu)

Papua New Guinea Territory: *Tokaut*

The Philippines Territory: *Home League Programme Aids, The War Cry*

Singapore, Malaysia and Myanmar Territory: *The War Cry*

South America East Territory: *El Cruzado, El Oficial, El Salvacionista, El Mensajero*

South America West Territory: *El Grito de Guerra, El Trebol*

Southern Africa Territory: *Echoes of Mercy, Home League Highlights, Home League Resource Manual, Outer Circle Newsletter, SAMF Newsletter, The Reporter, The War Cry*

Sri Lanka Territory: *Yudha Handa*

Sweden and Latvia Territory: *FA-musikant, Stridsropet, William*

Switzerland, Austria and Hungary Territory: *Espoir* (French), *Dialog* (German), *Dialogue* (French), *IN* (French and German), *Just 4 U* (French), *Trialog* (German), *Klecks* (German)

Taiwan Region: *Taiwan Regional News*

United Kingdom Territory with the Republic of Ireland: *Kids Alive!, Salvationist, The War Cry*

USA National: *The War Cry, Word & Deed – A Journal of Theology and Ministry, Women's Ministries Resources, Young Salvationist*

USA Central Territory: *Central Connection*

USA Eastern Territory: *¡Buenas Noticias!, Cristianos en Marcha* (both Spanish), *Good News!, Good News!* (Korean), *Priority!, Ven a Cristo Hoy* (Spanish)

USA Southern Territory: *Southern Spirit*

USA Western Territory: *Caring, New Frontier, Nuevos Fronteras* (Spanish)

Zimbabwe Territory: *Zimbabwe Salvationist, ZEST*

Books Published during 2006-07

International Headquarters: *For Such a Time* by Jenty Fairbank; *Purity of Heart* by William Booth ('Classic Texts' reprint); *Saints Alive: A Brief History of the Christian Church* by John Coutts; *Saying Yes to Life* by John Larsson (autobiography); *Seasons: A Woman's Calling to Ministry* by JoAnn Shade; *The Salvation Army Year Book 2007*; *Unsung Heroes* by Derek Elvin (International Literature Programme); *Adventurers* Junior Soldiers Training Course (International Literature Programme); *Discovery* Discipling Programme for Young People (International Literature Programme)

Books Published 2006-07

Australia Eastern Territory: *God-incidences How Beautiful* by William Cairns

Canada and Bermuda Territory: *Celebration Morning* by Ian Howes; *New Day Dawning* by Fred Ash

Caribbean Territory: *Salvation Story –* Salvationist Handbook of Doctrine (French)*

Congo (Kinshasa) and Angola Territory: *Bible Studies for Home Leagues**

Eastern Europe Territory: *Holiness Unto the Lord –* a compilation of works (Russian)*; *Salvation Army Ceremonies Book* (Russian)*; *Servants Together* (Russian)*

Finland and Estonia Territory: *Holiness Unwrapped* by Robert Street (Finnish); *History of Salvation Army Scouting in Finland 1917-2007* (Finnish)

Ghana Territory: *God's Kingdom Culture**

India National: *The General Next to God* by Richard Collier*; *The Song Book of The Salvation Army* (Urdu)*

India Central Territory: *Discovery* Discipling Programme for Young People*; *Heroes of the Faith* by Derek Elvin*; *Nothing Without Love* by Ken Lawson*

India Eastern Territory: *Discovery* Discipling Programme for Young People (Mizo)*; *Never the Same Again* by Shaw Clifton (Mizo)*; *Senior Sunday School Bible Lessons* (Mizo)*; *The Song Book of The Salvation Army* (Bru) (Mizo tonic sol-fa)*; *Warriors for Christ* (Mizo)*; *Young People's Bible Lessons* (Beginners, Primary, Junior, Intermediate, Senior) (Mizo)*

India Northern Territory: *Adventurers* Junior Soldiers Training Course*; *Discovery* Discipling Programme for Young People*; *Heroes of the Faith* by Derek Elvin*; *We Need Saints!* by Chick Yuill*

India South Western Territory: *Nothing Without Love* by Ken Lawson*

India Western Territory: *Finding New Hope in Christ*; *Gospel Hymns* (for women's ministry)

Italy Command: *The Salvation Army: An Introduction* by Antonio Lesignoli

Kenya Territory: *Cadets' Bible Lessons**; *Never the Same Again* by Shaw Clifton*

Korea Territory: *Corps Cadet Lessons* (Courses A and B); *Corps Cell Group Study Manual 2007*; *Daily Devotions for Salvationist Families 2007*; *Orders and Regulations for Officers* (Korean, revised); *Summer Bible School 2007* (handbook and workbooks); *The Salvation Army Ceremonies Book* (Korean, revised); *Women's Ministry* by Catherine Booth (Korean); *Young People's Company Lessons 2007* (manual and workbooks)

New Zealand, Fiji and Tonga Territory: *Leadership in The Salvation Army: A Case Study in Clericalisation* by Harold Hill; *Like a Tree: A Collection of Meditations* by Colleen Marshall; *On the Road to Recovery: 12 Step Meditations for Aotearoa* by Sue Hay

Papua New Guinea Territory: *God's Plan for Man* (English and Pidgin)*; *Life After Birth* (English and Pidgin)*; *Salvation Assault* The History of The Salvation Army in Papua New Guinea by Alan Satterlee*

Singapore, Malaysia and Myanmar Territory: *The Song Book of The Salvation Army* (Burmese, Mizo)*; *International Bible Lessons (*1, 2, 3) (Burmese)*; *Orders and Regulations for Officers* (Burmese)*; *Servant Leadership* by Robert Street (Burmese)*

South America West Territory: *A Great Christmas Adventure* by Allen Satterlee*; *A Great Easter Adventure* by Grace Bringans*; *Beside Still Waters* by Marlene Chase*; *Cradle Roll Ministries Manual**; *Called to be God's People* by Robert Street*; *Hallelujah Choruses**; *Holiness Unwrapped* by Robert Street*; *Training Manual for Sunday School Leadership* (all Spanish)*

Sri Lanka Territory: *Resource Manual for Women's Ministries**

Tanzania Command: *Preparing for Junior Soldiership**; *The Salvationist and the Sacraments* by William Metcalf (Kiswahili)*

United Kingdom Territory: *Hey God ... Wot U Up2?* compiled by Children's Ministries Unit; *Kids Alive 125*

   Available on UKT web site: *Booth's Boots* by Jenty Fairbank; *Female Ministry* by Catherine Booth

USA National: *I Knew William Booth* edited by R. G. Moyles; *Man with a Mission* by Henry Gariepy; *Saying Yes to Life* by John Larsson (published jointly with IHQ)

* Published with the assistance of a grant from the International Literature Programme, IHQ

MINISTRIES AND FELLOWSHIPS

WOMEN'S MINISTRIES

THE ideal basic unit of society is the home and family, where women play a vital and definitive role. Furthermore, as natural providers of hope, women play an important part in shaping society. Therefore, any fellowship of women in which Christian influence is exerted and practical help given benefits not only the individual and the family, but also the nation.

Women's Ministries provide a programme of meetings and other activities based on the fourfold aim of the Army's international women's organisation, the Home League, which was inaugurated in 1907. Those aims are worship, education, fellowship, service. The motto of the Home League is: 'I will live a pure life in my house' (Psalm 101:2 *Good News Bible*).

The mission of Women's Ministries is to bring women into a knowledge of Jesus Christ; encourage their full potential in influencing family, friends and community; equip them for growth in personal understanding and life skills; address issues which affect women and their families in the world.

Japan Territory: Commissioner Helen Clifton (World President of Women's Ministries) meets two young women Salvationists from The Philippines who live and work in Japan

THE LEAGUE OF MERCY AND COMMUNITY CARE MINISTRIES

THE League of Mercy began in 1892 in Canada and is made up of people of all ages whose mission is to engage in a caring ministry. The main objective of the League of Mercy is to respond to the spiritual and social needs of the community. The ministry is adapted according to the local situation, the size of its membership and the skill of its members, and endeavours to follow Christ's injunction, 'Inasmuch as ye have done it unto one of the least of these my brethren, ye have done it unto me' (Matthew 25:40 *Authorised Version*).

THE FELLOWSHIP OF THE SILVER STAR

THE Fellowship of the Silver Star, inaugurated in the USA in 1930 and extended worldwide in 1936, expresses gratitude to parents or other significant life mentors of Salvation Army officers.

THE SALVATION ARMY MEDICAL FELLOWSHIP

THE Salvation Army Medical Fellowship, instituted in 1943 by Mrs General Minnie Carpenter, is an international fellowship of dedicated medical personnel. Physical suffering in our world today challenges both the medical and the physical and emotional resources of medical personnel. The fellowship encourages a Christian witness and application of Christian principles in professional life while at the same time being involved with practical application in hospitals, clinics and various other places of medical care. The motto of the Fellowship is: 'If we walk in the light, as he is in the light, we have fellowship one with another' (1 John 1:7 *Authorised Version*).

THE SALVATION ARMY STUDENTS' FELLOWSHIP

THIS fellowship started in Norway in 1942 and later spread to other countries, receiving an official constitution in 1950. It comes under the world presidency of the General. The aim of the fellowship is to unite Salvationist students and graduates of universities, colleges and other centres of higher education in Christian fellowship and such Salvation Army service as may be appropriate.

THE SALVATION ARMY BLUE SHIELD FELLOWSHIP

IN 1974 the Blue Shield Fellowship was formed by two British Salvationist policemen to provide friendship and support to Christian policemen as they face present-day challenges. Membership is open to both active and retired police officers, and there are members in many countries.

SALVATION ARMY HONOURS

ORDER OF THE FOUNDER

**Instituted on 20 August 1917 by General Bramwell
Booth, the Order of the Founder is the highest
Salvation Army honour for distinguished service**

HISTORY OF THE ORDER

IN 1917, five years after the death of William Booth, his son, General Bramwell
Booth, inaugurated the Order of the Founder 'to mark outstanding service
rendered by officers and soldiers such as would in spirit or achievement have been
specially commended by the Founder'.

The first awards were made in 1920 to 15 officers and one soldier. Three years
later, seven officers and one local officer were honoured, but since then the
awards have been made much more sparingly and, to date, 154 officers and 90 lay
Salvationists have been recognised with the Army's highest honour – a mere 244
in total over 90 years.

The first presentation was to a soldier, Private Herbert Bourne, for outstanding
Christian witness and service during military service in the First World War.
A few senior leaders such as Commissioner Henry Howard, General Evangeline
Booth and Commissioner Catherine Bramwell-Booth have been recipients but,
much more commonly, faithful and devoted service by less well-known
personalities has been acknowledged.

The honour is rarely given because every nomination is carefully scrutinised by
a panel of senior leaders at International Headquarters. Salvationists have every
reason to be proud of those who have been awarded this outstanding recognition
for meritorious Christian example, witness and service.

Recipients of the Order of the Founder 2006-07

Major Catherine Pacquette
(Caribbean Territory). Having given
56 years of sacrificial and pioneering
service to the people of Haiti, Major
Catherine Pacquette continues to serve
in her local corps and community,
exemplifying a strong Christian commitment to prayer and service for
others. Admitted to the Order of the
Founder on 5 November 2006.

Colonel Sawichhunga (India Eastern
Territory). Over many years Colonel
Sawichhunga has exemplified the
spirit of Salvationism, shown in his
zeal for Christ, his heart for lost souls,
his compassion for the needy and his
steadfastness in the face of persecution.
He remains, even in retirement, a true
Christian example and inspiration to
others, both within the ranks of The

Salvation Army and beyond. Admitted to the Order of the Founder on 4 February 2007.

Colonel Henry Gariepy (USA Eastern Territory). Having devoted himself to his sacred calling as an officer, through a notable, tireless ministry of writing Colonel Henry Gariepy has inspired and blessed countless others around the world. With more book titles to his name than any other writer in the Army's history, he has humbly continued through the years of both active and retired service to teach, mentor and influence others for Christ. His vast output of writings, often translated, includes works of devotion, history, biography, Bible teaching, compilations and educational matter. He has regularly made telling contributions to other Salvationist and Christian publications. He has always helped and encouraged others to write for Christ. In 2000 he wrote the eighth volume of

The Salvation Army's official history. He remains a faithful and active soldier of his corps in Lancaster, Pennsylvania. This selfless, creative and unique contribution to the life of the Army would commend itself to the Founder. Admitted to the Order of the Founder on 10 June 2007.

Major Catherine Pacquette receives her Order of the Founder medal and certificate from the Caribbean territorial leaders, Commissioners Raymond and Judith Houghton

ORDER OF DISTINGUISHED AUXILIARY SERVICE

On 24 February 1941 General George Carpenter instituted this order to mark the Army's appreciation of distinguished service rendered by non-Salvationists who have helped to further its work in a variety of ways

Recipients of the Order of Distinguished Auxiliary Service 2006-07

Sir Brian Bell (Papua New Guinea Territory) received the order on the occasion of the 50th anniversary of The Salvation Army in Papua New Guinea in recognition of unstinting dedicated service to The Salvation Army and to the people of Papua New Guinea through the Red Shield Advisory Board. Admitted to the Order of Distinguished Auxiliary Service on 24 November 2006.

Dr William Norrie (Canada and Bermuda Territory) received the order for outstanding service and distinguished active support of the mission of The Salvation Army and the William and Catherine Booth College in Winnipeg. Admitted to the Order of Distinguished Auxiliary Service on 27 April 2007.

'Serving suffering humanity' is more than a slogan

by Major Cedric Hills (International Emergency Services Coordinator, IHQ)

THE mission of The Salvation Army has been described using a number of phrases or slogans. 'Soup, soap and salvation' was a well-known motto that described the holistic approach to ministry that has marked the Movement's service from earliest days.

'Where there's need, there's The Salvation Army' was a phrase coined during the last century and described the desire of Salvationists to be the practical presence of Christ whenever times of difficulty arose.

In more recent years the Army's mission has been summarised within the three-part slogan: 'To save souls, grow saints and serve suffering humanity'.

Around the world the compassionate ministry of Salvationists allows us to demonstrate and introduce our faith in Christ through practical and caring ministry. This practical translation of the compassion of Jesus is shown through the provision of shelter for the homeless, food for the hungry and protection for the oppressed and stateless.

For more than a century, through emergency relief, hundreds of thousands of suffering people have been recipients of the incarnational ministry of Jesus through acts of service; touching them at a time when they were in greatest need and at their most vulnerable.

During 2006-07, many parts of the world were impacted by disaster. The effects of terrorism were felt again when bombs exploded on trains in Mumbai, India. Salvationists were quickly at the scene to provide basic relief supplies of blankets and refreshments. Follow-up visits were made to care for the wounded and hospitalised.

As a reminder that the effects of disaster outlive the interests of the media, a winterisation programme in Pakistan provided roofing sheets and blankets for thousands of families still without shelter some 15 months after the earthquake of 2005.

In March 2007, Mozambique was hit by the worst cyclone ever known in Africa. The areas worst affected were in the north of the country – many hours' drive from Salvation Army centres. A grant of US$25,000 from International Headquarters allowed relief teams to provide materials for the rebuilding of homes (such as the one pictured on the facing page) and a community centre.

As a result of Salvation Army territories around the world generously responding to appeals from the International Emergency Services (IES) at International Headquarters, grants were given to India, Pakistan, Argentina, The Philippines, Mozambique, Rwanda, Peru, Indonesia, Bolivia and Brazil.

Training plays an important part in IES work. Increasingly, training courses are planned to bring together representatives from within neighbouring countries. Zonal training courses held in Hong Kong drew personnel from around the South Pacific and East Asia Zone, while an eight-day course convened at Sunbury Court, London, brought together delegates from across Europe.

A highlight of 2006 was an opportunity for IES personnel to lead sessions for Salvation Army delegates at the International Conference of Social Welfare, in Brazil.

The IES mandate is clearly defined in teaching of Jesus found in Matthew 25:40 (*New International Version*): 'I tell you the truth, whatever you did for one of the least of these brothers of mine, you did for me.'

Believing this to be gospel truth, serving suffering humanity becomes an essential aspect of Christian life.

Pakistan Territory: When the mountainous northern region of Pakistan, earlier hit by a massive earthquake, was hit by heavy monsoon rains, Salvation Army Emergency Services workers – in the area to supervise the ongoing response to the earthquake – took much-needed supplies to families whose stocks of food had became dangerously low

Providing new skills and knowledge

Update from the International Projects and Development Services, IHQ

ACROSS the developing world The Salvation Army's International Projects and Development Services (IPDS) is working through its network of community development programmes to meet human need. With a current portfolio of around 600 projects, The Salvation Army is making a significant difference worldwide – changing individual lives and communities.

Projects range in value from US$2,000 to US$8.3 million and include ongoing support to established Salvation Army community services such as children's homes, schools, hospitals and clinics. The Army is also pioneering developmental initiatives in anti-human trafficking, micro-credit and psycho-social counselling.

These projects represent the ongoing collaboration and partnership between The Salvation Army's grant aided territories and financially independent territories. IPDS gives important support and oversight to this process.

During 2006-07, IPDS commenced a programme of capacity-building workshops for Salvation Army personnel in grant aided territories. These workshops focus on providing new skills and knowledge for Salvation Army community workers, and encouraging the exchange of community experiences.

'We need to get in more with the community,' said a workshop participant in Sri Lanka, 'and get all the information from them – the problems and difficulties they face.' Another reflected on the valuable role The Salvation

India Central Territory: Community members from a village in Andhra Pradesh map their community resources and discuss their future plans with Salvation Army project personnel

Army plays in communities: 'In one appointment in a remote area, I walked around on house-to-house visits every day, to find out people's needs and to help them. If a baby was sick I would pray for him; if someone had died, the family could cry on my shoulder because I was there.'

Through community projects The Salvation Army is achieving its mission daily. IPDS is committed to continue playing its part – offering support and developing expertise in some of the world's most needy places.

FUNDING THE MINISTRY

The Salvation Army thanks those listed below who, during 2006, assisted in its ministry to some of the world's most vulnerable people through community development projects. These involved:

Combating the HIV/Aids pandemic; developing savings and loans groups; promoting healthy communities; supporting formal and non-formal educational services; improving access to safe water and sanitation; supporting social service programmes to the aged, the marginalised and the young; responding to disaster-hit areas

Country	Donor	US $
Australia	Eastern & Southern Territories (through SAADO)	
	AusAID	841,982
	D. Knowles	54,278
Canada	CIDA (Canada)	500,000
Germany	Brot fur die Welf	27,589
	Christoffel Blindenmission	183,497
	Dr Walter Herter	107,599
	Kindernothilfe	733,331
Netherlands	Kerk in Actie (tsunami support)	1,072,000
	Ministry of Foreign Affairs	844,359
Norway	NORAD	1,760,160
Sweden	Dispurse Foundation	313,000
	Radio Help	24,050
	Swedish Ecumenical Council for Women	7,000

Latin America North Territory: An educational project in Bogotá, Colombia, funded by new donors, The Netherlands Ministry of Foreign Affairs

Switzerland	
Accentus Foundation	14,334
Bread for All	121,262
Fontes Foundation	10,576
Solidarity Third World	30,670
Stanley Thomas Johnson Foundation	20,286
Swiss Government	1,084,346
Swiss Solidarity	521,973

United Kingdom	
Count Zoltan Trust	4,179
Hope HIV	125,379
Lord Michelham of Hellingly Foundation	29,692
Oxfam UK	30,000
Roger Carllson Foundation	59,700
Saga Shipping	18,980
Spring Harvest	59,700
Tear Fund International	351,629
Tear Fund UK	99,500
Vidi Trust	5,970

USA	
SAWSO	8,297,075
USAID	2,952,395
TOTAL	**US$ 20,306,491**

INTERNATIONAL HEADQUARTERS

**Postal address: The Salvation Army,
101 Queen Victoria Street, London EC4V 4EH,
United Kingdom**

Tel: (020) 7332 0101 (national)
[44] (20) 7332 0101 (international)
Fax: (020) 7192 3413; email: websa@salvationarmy.org
Web site: www.salvationarmy.org

General
SHAW CLIFTON
(2 April 2006)

Chief of the Staff
COMMISSIONER ROBIN DUNSTER
(2 April 2006)

INTERNATIONAL Headquarters exists to support the General as he leads The Salvation Army to accomplish its God-given worldwide mission to preach the gospel of Jesus Christ and meet human need in his name without discrimination. In so doing, it assists the General:

☐ To give spiritual leadership, promote the development of spiritual life within the Army, and emphasise the Army's reliance on God for the achievement of its mission.
☐ To provide overall strategic leadership and set international policies.
☐ To direct and administer the Army's operations and protect its interests – by means of appointments and delegation of authority and responsibility with accountability.
☐ To empower and support the territories and commands, encourage and pastorally care for their leaders, and inspire local vision and initiatives.
☐ To strengthen the internationalism of the Army, preserve its unity, purposes, beliefs and spirit, and maintain its standards.
☐ To promote the development, appropriate deployment and international sharing of personnel.
☐ To promote the development and sharing of financial resources worldwide, and manage the Army's international funds.
☐ To promote the development and international sharing of knowledge, expertise and experience.
☐ To develop the Army's ecumenical and other relationships.

The General directs Salvation Army operations throughout the world through the administrative departments of International Headquarters, which are headed by international secretaries. The Chief of the Staff, a commissioner appointed by the General to be second-in-command, is the Army's chief executive whose function is to implement the General's policy decisions and effect liaison between departments.

The Christian Mission Headquarters, Whitechapel Road, became the Army's first International Headquarters in 1880. However, the Founder soon decided that a move into the City of London would be beneficial and in 1881 IHQ was moved to 101 Queen Victoria Street. Sixty years after this move the IHQ building was destroyed by fire during the Second World War. The rebuilt International Headquarters was opened by Queen Elizabeth, the Queen Mother, in November 1963.

When it was decided to redevelop the Queen Victoria Street site, IHQ took up temporary residence at William Booth College, Denmark Hill, in 2001. Three years later IHQ returned to 101 Queen Victoria Street and the new building was opened by Her Royal Highness The Princess Royal in November 2004.

Web site of the Office of the General:
www.salvationarmy.org/thegeneral

INTERNATIONAL MANAGEMENT COUNCIL

The International Management Council (IMC), established in February 1991, sees to the efficiency and effectiveness of the Army's international administration in general. It considers in detail the formation of international policy and mission. It is composed of all London-based IHQ commissioners, and meets monthly with the General taking the chair.

Sec: Lt-Col Miriam Frederiksen
Asst Sec: Maj Richard Gaudion

GENERAL'S CONSULTATIVE COUNCIL

The General's Consultative Council (GCC), established in July 2001, advises the General on broad matters relating to the Army's mission strategy and policy. The GCC is composed of all officers who qualify to attend a High Council, and operates through a Lotus Notes database. Selected members also meet three times a year in London with the General taking the chair.

Sec: Lt-Col Miriam Frederiksen
Asst Sec: Maj Richard Gaudion

ADMINISTRATION DEPARTMENT

The Administration Department is responsible for all matters with which the Chief of the Staff deals; for the effective administration of IHQ; for IHQ personnel; for international external relations; for providing legal advice; and for ensuring that the strategic planning and monitoring process is implemented and used effectively.

International Secretary to the Chief of the Staff

COMR ROBERT STREET (1 Jul 2006)

Sec for Administration: Lt-Col Michael Williams
Executive Sec to the General/Research and Planning Sec: Lt-Col Miriam Frederiksen
P/S to the General: Maj Richard Gaudion
P/S to the Chief of the Staff: Maj Rob Garrad
Sec for Spiritual Life Development and International Ecumenical Relations: Comr Linda Bond
International Director for Social Justice: Comr M. Christine MacMillan
General's Representative for Global Evangelisation: Col Dick Krommenhoek
International Youth Ministries Coordinator/ Leader, Project Warsaw (Poland): Col Vibeke Krommenhoek
International Doctrine Council: Chair: Comr William Francis
Sec for IHQ Staff Development: Comr Nancy Roberts
Legal and Parliamentary Sec: Maj Peter J. M. Smith (Solicitor of the Supreme Court)

WOMEN'S MINISTRIES

World President of Women's Ministries

COMR HELEN CLIFTON (2 Apr 2006)

World Secretary for Women's Ministries and World President, SA Scouts, Guides and Guards

COMR JANET STREET (1 Jul 2006)

Women's Ministries Administrative Asst: Capt Teresa Everett

INTERNATIONAL PERSONNEL DEPARTMENT

The International Personnel Department works in the interests of international personnel in support of the Chief of the Staff and the zonal international secretaries. Responsibilities include facilitating the personal and vocational development of all personnel, their pastoral care and physical well-being. The department exists to encourage and facilitate the sharing and appropriate deployment of personnel resources on a global basis; to assist in the identification of officers with potential for future leadership; to monitor training and development; to register and coordinate all offers for international service.

International Secretary for Personnel

COMR LYN PEARCE (1 Dec 2004)

Under Sec: Maj Wendy Caffull
Sec for International Training and Leader Development: Lt-Col Wayne Pritchett
Medical Consultant: Dr John Thomlinson

BUSINESS ADMINISTRATION DEPARTMENT

The Business Administration Department is responsible for international accounting, auditing, banking, property and related matters. The International Secretary for Business Administration has the oversight of the finance functions in territories and commands.

International Secretary for Business Administration

COMR WILLIAM ROBERTS (1 Feb 2005)

Finance Sec: Lt-Col Ann Woodall
Chief Accountant: Maj Jeffrey Wills
Chief International Auditor: Lt-Col Graeme Reddish
  Auditors: Lt-Col Gustave Allemand, Col Gordon Becker, Maj Francis Nyakusamwa, Maj João Paulo Ramos, Lt-Col Wynne Reddish, Lt-Col John Rowlanes; Maj Randall Sjogren; Maj John Warner
Facilities Manager: Mr Graham Twist
Information Technology Manager: Mr Mark Calleran
Property Manager: Mr Graham Reynolds
Travel Manager: Mr Mark Edwards

PROGRAMME RESOURCES DEPARTMENT

The mission of the Programme Resources Department is to participate with others in envisioning, coordinating, facilitating and raising awareness of programmes that advance the global mission of The Salvation Army.

International Secretary for Programme Resources

COMR B. DONALD ØDEGAARD (11 Jul 2005)

Under Sec: Lt-Col Gillian Downer
'Sally Ann' – Fair Trade:
  International Coordinator: Comr Berit Ødegaard
  Business Manager: Mr Paul Pirie
International Emergency Services:
  IES Coordinator: Maj Cedric Hills
  Field Operations and Training Officer: Capt Elizabeth Haywood
  Field Operations Officer: Maj Mike Caffull
International Health Services:
  IHS Coordinators: Majs Dean and (Dr) Eirwen Pallant
International Projects and Development Services:
  IPDS Sec: Maj Ted Horwood
  Mission Support Projects and Feeding Programmes: Maj Deborah Horwood
Communications:
  Communications Sec/Editor-in-Chief/ Literary Sec: Maj Charles King
  Editor *All the World*: Mr Kevin Sims
  Editor *Global Exchange*: Capt Kathy See
  Editor *The Officer*: Maj Charles King
  Editor *The Year Book*: Maj Trevor Howes
  Writer *Words of Life*: Maj Evelyn Merriam
  International Literature Programme Officer: Maj Helen Bryden
  Editorial fax: (020) 7332 8079

ZONAL DEPARTMENTS

The zonal departments are the main administrative link with territories and commands. The international secretaries give oversight to and coordinate the Army's work in their respective geographical areas.

AFRICA

International Secretary

COMR AMOS MAKINA (1 Jul 2004)

Under Sec: Lt-Col David Burrows
  fax: (020) 7332 8231
Sec WM: Comr Rosemary Makina
Regional Consultant HIV/Aids: Mr Ricardo Walters

AMERICAS AND CARIBBEAN
International Secretary
COMR BARRY C. SWANSON (1 Jul 2007)

Under Sec: Maj Joan Canning
 fax: (020) 7332 8199
Sec WM: Comr E. Sue Swanson

EUROPE
International Secretary
COMR HASSE KJELLGREN (1 Nov 2006)

Under Sec: Maj David Shakespeare
 fax: (020) 7332 8209
Sec WM: Comr Christina Kjellgren
Officer for European Affairs: Maj Göran
 Larsson

SOUTH ASIA
International Secretary
COMR LALKIAMLOVA (1 Jan 2004)

Under Sec: Lt-Col John Dyall
 fax: (020) 7332 8219
Sec WM: Comr Lalhlimpuii

SOUTH PACIFIC AND EAST ASIA
International Secretary
COMR BARRY POBJIE (1 Jul 2007)

Under Sec: Maj Alison Cowling
 fax: (020) 7332 8229
Sec WM: Comr Raemor Pobjie

STATISTICS **Officers** 78 **Employees** 76

During the first-ever International Conference of Personnel Secretaries, held at Sunbury Court, delegates from South America West, Japan, India Eastern, Tanzania, Finland and Estonia, and USA Southern enjoy conversation with the General and Commissioner Helen Clifton. Fifty-five delegates responsible to their territorial or command leaders for the care and deployment of officers gathered for a week of significant and beneficial discussions under the theme 'Creating a Climate of Care'.

International Administrative Structure

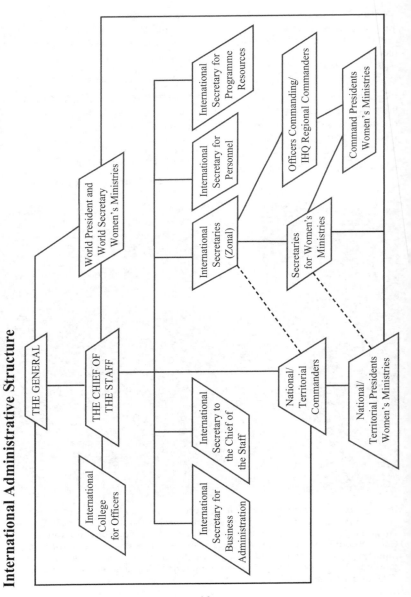

The Salvation Army International Trustee Company

Registered Office: 101 Queen Victoria Street, London EC4V 4EH

Registration No 2538134. Tel: (020) 7332 0101

Company Secretary: Lieut-Colonel Ann Woodall

DIRECTORS: Comr Robin Dunster (Chair), Comr William Roberts (Managing Director and Vice Chair), Mr Andrew Axcell, Mr David Kidd, Comr Hasse Kjellgren, Comr Lalkiamlova, Comr Amos Makina, Comr Donald Ødegaard, Comr Lyn Pearce, Comr Barry Pobjie, Maj Peter Smith, Mr Trevor Smith, Comr Robert Street, Comr Barry C. Swanson, Lt-Col Ann Woodall.

The company is registered under the Companies Acts 1985 and 1989 as a company limited by guarantee, not having a share capital. It has no assets or liabilities, but as a trustee of The Salvation Army International Trusts it is the registered holder of Salvation Army property both real and personal including shares in some of the Army's commercial undertakings. The company is a trust corporation.

Reliance Bank Limited

Faith House, 23-24 Lovat Lane, London EC3R 8EB

Tel: (020) 7398 5400; fax: (020) 7398 5401; email: info@reliancebankltd.com
web site: www.reliancebankltd.com

Chairman: Commissioner William Roberts
Managing Director: Trevor J. Smith, ACIB

Banking Manager and Company Secretary: Michael R. Meads, ACIB
Finance Manager: Kevin Dare, CIMA; Operations Manager: Paul Underwood, ACIB;
Business Development Manager: Nichola Keating

DIRECTORS: Comr William Roberts (Chairman), Comr Robert Street, Lt-Col Ann Woodall, Lt-Col William Cochrane, Maj Jeffrey Wills, Maj John Wainwright, Maj David Hinton, Mr Trevor Smith, Mr Michael Meads, Mr Philip Deer, Mr Edward Ashton, Mr Gerald Birkett, ACIB.

Reliance Bank Limited is an authorised institution under the Banking Act 1987, is regulated by the Financial Services Authority and registered under the Companies and Consumer Credit Acts.

OWNED by The Salvation Army through its controlling shareholders – The Salvation Army International Trustee Company and The Salvation Army Trustee Company – Reliance Bank accepts sterling and foreign currency deposits, carries on general banking business, and provides finance for Salvation Army corporate customers and private and business customers.

The bank can grant mortgages, personal loans and overdrafts, and also provides travel currency, cheques and safe custody facilities. It offers current accounts, together with a Reliance Bank Visa Debit Card, fixed deposits and savings accounts, and is involved in money transmission transactions both within the UK and abroad. Internet banking and telephone banking services are also offered.

The bank pays at least 75 per cent of its taxable profits by means of Gift Aid donation to its controlling shareholders.

Brochures are available on request, or visit: www.reliancebankltd.com

STATISTICS Employees 21

International College for Officers

The Cedars, 34 Sydenham Hill, London SE26 6LS, UK

Tel: [44] (020) 8299 8450; fax: [44] (020) 7192 3056

Principal: Commissioner Margaret Sutherland (1 Jul 2004)

During the International Congress held at the Crystal Palace, Sydenham, London, in 1904, Commissioner Henry T. Howard voiced what he saw as the young Salvation Army's need for leaders inspired with the aggressive spirit of Salvationism. William Booth took up the idea and the International Staff Training Lodge was opened at Clapton on 11 May 1905.

The present building was brought into service in 1950, when General Albert Orsborn declared it to be 'an investment in the great intangibles without which our cogs and wheels would soon be rusty and dead'. In 1954, a broadening of scope promoted a change of name to the International College for Officers.

ICO MISSION STATEMENT

The Salvation Army's International College for Officers exists to further develop officers by:

- **nurturing personal holiness and spiritual leadership**
- **providing opportunity to experience the internationalism of the Army**
- **encouraging a renewed sense of mission and purpose as an officer**

TIME and again delegates who come to 'The Cedars' remark what a wonderful setting it is for a spiritual retreat. While close to central London, the house has large grounds not visible from the road which are very conducive to spiritual and physical refreshment.

The interiors of the main house and the delegates' rooms are maintained to a good standard and very comfortable, thus also contributing to a relaxed atmosphere. A varied menu ensures that all delegates can eat healthily and enjoy what they eat. A wonderful team of employees and volunteers, fully committed to the mission of the ICO, enables all this to happen.

At the same time the ICO is a place of learning and there is the constant challenge to bring the facilities to the standard expected of an educational establishment in the 21st century. Each of the delegates' room now has a computer point and a project is underway to install a phone in each room – for many years there has only been one telephone for delegate use.

Session 190 had the distinction of being featured in one of the United Kingdom Territory's *LINK* DVDs. It is hoped that as people watch this, it will increase understanding of what the ICO is and what happens there. In addition, the ICO now has its own website at www.salvationarmy.org/ico

Praise God for his faithfulness which enables the ICO to go on fulfilling its mission in the lives of 100 officer delegates each year!

STATISTICS
Officers 4 **Employees** 5

STAFF
Programme Sec: Maj Rosemarie Brown
Business Sec: Maj Steven Howard
Personnel Sec: Maj Janice Howard

The Salvation Army Leaders' Training College of Africa

16 Private Rd, off General Booth Rd, Braeside, Harare, Zimbabwe

Postal Address: PO Box GT 650, Graniteside, Harare, Zimbabwe

Tel: [263] (4) 743 039; fax: [263] (4) 743 010; email: leadcoll_africa@sal.salvationarmy.org

Principal: Major David Sterling (12 Feb 2002)

Prompted by the request of territorial leaders of Africa, The Salvation Army Leaders' Training College of Africa (SALT College) was established in 1986. Its purpose is to coordinate officer and local officer in-service training across the continent through SALT College distance-learning courses and seminars, implemented by an extension training officer in each territory.

THE Salvation Army Leaders' Training College of Africa (SALT College) facilitates distance-learning in 15 countries across the Africa Zone. Reporting to territorial leaders through the International Secretary for Africa, it aims to develop informed, theologically aware Christian leaders for Salvation Army ministry.

The diverse college roll includes officers, local officers and soldiers. Guided by extension training officers (ETOs), students work in either English, French, Portuguese or Kiswahili. Their assignments are assessed by a team of skilled and dedicated tutors from three continents.

The goal is one of continuous development to enable students to achieve their full potential. To succeed in this the college has plans to widen its academic network by drawing upon the experience of educators and theologians from other colleges to critique and develop its curriculum.

The college student base continues to expand, recording 375 new student registrations in 2006. There were 353 subject passes at certificate level, with 37 students achieving their final Certificate in Salvation Army Ministry award.

Congratulations are due to Captain Alfred Banda (Malawi Command) who completed with merit the Australian College of Theology Associate in Theology award (ThA) in 2006 and to Captain Musa Barasa (Kenya Territory) who completed with a pass.

Evaluating his ThA studies, Major Obed Mgbebuihe (Nigeria Territory) writes: 'My ThA studies broadened my knowledge and understanding and helped me to handle issues and situations more maturely. The tutoring is challenging and encouraging.'

STATISTICS
Officers 4 Employees 5

STAFF
Senior Tutor: Maj Brenda Sterling
Associate Principal: Maj Kapela Ntoya
Assistant: Maj Nicole Ntoya

OVERSEAS SERVICE FUNDS 2006-2007 INCOME

	International Self-Denial Contributions £	International Self-Denial Special £	Special Projects £	Donations via IHQ £	Total £
Australia Eastern	562,590	-	412,530	85,836	1,060,956
Australia Southern	437,666	-	416,470	422	854,557
Bangladesh	697	-	-	-	697
Belgium	2,091	-	-	-	2,091
Brazil	8,872	-	-	258	9,130
Canada	955,277	-	1,097,278	314,425	2,366,980
Caribbean	14,944	-	-	-	14,944
Congo (Brazzaville)	21,334	-	-	-	21,334
Congo (Kinshasa) & Angola	21,007	-	-	-	21,007
Czech Republic	1,074	-	-	-	1,074
Denmark	47,500	-	51,953	11,860	111,313
Eastern Europe	6,064	-	-	4,268	10,332
Finland	38,055	-	39,073	46,261	123,389
France	12,441	-	9,411	798	22,651
Germany	44,487	-	41,918	48,991	135,396
Ghana	5,513	-	-	-	5,513
Hong Kong	52,814	-	878,899	3,511	935,224
India Central	14,829	-	-	-	14,829
India Eastern	17,055	-	-	140	17,195
India Northern	13,979	-	-	543	14,522
India South Eastern	21,805	-	-	1,261	23,066
India South Western	15,825	-	-	-	15,825
India Western	13,919	-	-	-	13,919
Indonesia	18,696	-	-	-	18,696
Italy	5,687	-	-	716	6,403
Japan	60,681	-	-	11,296	71,977
Kenya	20,648	-	-	-	20,648
Korea	56,933	-	-	17,809	74,742
Latin America North	6,073	-	-	127	6,200
Malawi	1,039	-	-	-	1,039
Mexico	14,865	-	-	2,572	17,437
Myanmar	815	-	-	-	815
Netherlands	128,350	-	1,217,901	3,122	1,349,373
New Zealand	185,823	-	509,873	15,794	711,490
Nigeria	6,894	-	-	-	6,894
Norway	266,578	-	818,654	542,710	1,627,942
Pakistan	1,655	-	-	-	1,655
Papua New Guinea	2,964	-	-	-	2,964
Philippines	2,952	-	-	-	2,952
Portugal	1,185	-	-	100	1,285
Rwanda	561	-	-	-	561
Singapore & Malaysia	52,973	-	17,845	2,925	73,743
South America East	7,946	-	-	-	7,946
South America West	4,956	-	-	1,077	6,033
Southern Africa	14,055	-	-	-	14,055
Spain	2,706	-	1,651	13,189	17,546
Sri Lanka	806	-	-	-	806
Sweden	89,829	-	140,731	117,869	348,429
Switzerland	359,785	-	1,436,838	367,538	2,164,161
Taiwan	4,615	-	-	-	4,615
Tanzania	2,557	-	-	-	2,557
Uganda	247	-	-	-	247
United Kingdom	1,450,970	-	799,650	89,948	2,340,568
USA Central	2,056,175	151,607	1,000,594	592,508	3,800,884
USA Eastern	2,052,688	181,589	1,011,486	657,349	3,903,112
USA Southern	2,222,273	185,267	1,593,833	253,514	4,254,887
USA Western	1,484,748	42,826	657,213	16,236	2,201,023
USA SAWSO	-	-	395,233	761,304	1,156,537
Zambia	19,429	-	-	-	19,429
Zimbabwe	51,075	-	-	-	51,075
TOTAL	**£12,990,068**	**£561,289**	**£12,549,034**	**£3,986,277**	**£30,086,668**

OVERSEAS SERVICE FUNDS 2006-2007 EXPENDITURE

	Support of Overseas Work	Special Projects	Donations via IHQ	Total
	£	£	£	£
Africa, General	27,785	-	93,233	121,018
Americas, General	3,251	-	13,952	17,203
Austria	28,707	-	-	28,707
Bangladesh	122,110	67,028	154	189,292
Brazil	656,843	352,048	21,788	1,030,679
Caribbean	564,613	945,903	19,236	1,529,752
Congo (Brazzaville)	363,080	128,533	17,127	508,740
Congo (Kinshasa) & Angola	398,899	338,861	10,806	748,566
Czech Republic	311,583	388,082	519	700,184
Eastern Europe	1,581,581	524,653	89,483	2,195,717
Estonia	9,338	56,178	9,519	75,035
Europe, General	2,045	-	7,906	9,951
Fiji & Tonga	-	450,361	2,491	452,852
France	-	1,600	-	1,600
Germany (East)	102,733	88,242	35,576	226,551
Ghana	169,092	120,485	23,172	312,749
Hong Kong	15,031	139,178	7,409	161,618
Hungary	51,105	3,922	8,510	63,537
India National Secretariat	83,409	5,452	10,678	99,539
India Central	178,690	428,760	8,964	616,414
India Eastern	71,399	214,233	34,071	319,703
India Northern	198,777	515,346	37,503	751,626
India South Eastern	173,411	268,310	43,960	485,681
India South Western	258,443	438,984	25,793	723,220
India Western	172,550	93,526	62,830	328,906
Indonesia	42,207	1,137,909	227,651	1,407,767
Italy	130,970	49,714	347	181,031
Kenya	546,486	997,651	135,175	1,679,312
Korea	10,699	190,940	675	202,314
Latin America North	506,874	253,388	5,816	766,078
Latvia (Sweden)	90,187	60,744	13,174	164,105
Liberia	120,338	40,743	546	161,627
Malawi	76,137	149,937	3,784	229,858
Mexico	285,608	172,879	6,844	465,331
Mozambique	113,642	226,792	3,286	343,720
Myanmar	67,099	107,052	500	174,651
Nigeria	135,968	139,311	39,462	314,741
Pakistan	349,131	240,132	24,246	613,509
Papua New Guinea	333,184	165,138	94,334	592,656
Philippines	297,271	533,556	14,236	845,063
Poland	-	141	21,997	22,138
Portugal	194,747	57,527	100	252,374
Rwanda	85,263	83,970	21,478	190,711
SALT College	33,219	-	22,693	55,912
Singapore & Malaysia	51,940	106,575	2,691	161,206
South America East	418,484	112,643	29,552	560,679
South America West	363,689	467,883	38,542	870,114
South Asia, General	24,513	-	16,435	40,948
Southern Africa	140,466	147,020	20,483	307,969
SPEA, General	5,978	990	3,551	10,519
Spain	241,223	270,766	302	512,291
Sri Lanka	128,438	391,757	14,105	534,300
Taiwan	35,436	10,734	310	46,480
Tanzania	140,018	200,650	11,798	352,466
Uganda	64,051	161,854	6,814	232,719
Zambia	312,132	190,780	7,505	510,417
Zimbabwe	320,280	310,173	47,561	678,014
TOTAL	**£11,210,153**	**£12,549,034**	**£1,420,674**	**£25,179,861**

AUSTRALIA

National Secretariat: 2 Brisbane Ave, Barton, Canberra, ACT 2600
Postal address: PO Box 4256, Manuka, ACT 2603, Australia

Tel: [61] (02) 6273 3055; fax: [61] (02) 6273 1383; email: Peter.Holley@aue.salvationarmy.org

Two Christian Mission converts, John Gore and Edward Saunders, pioneered Salvation Army operations on 5 September 1880 in Adelaide. These were officially established on 11 February 1881 by the appointment of Captain and Mrs Thomas Sutherland. In 1921 the work in Australia was organised into Eastern and Southern Territories with headquarters in Sydney and Melbourne.

A National Secretariat serving the whole of Australia and funded jointly by both territories was established in 1987.

Periodicals: *Kidzone, Warcry*

THE National Secretariat represents the views of both Australian territories to the Australian Government as required or requested by both territorial commanders.

It addresses issues of spiritual, moral, ethical and social welfare by means of submissions, personal dialogue with members of parliament and attendance at open forums. It maintains a watching brief over legislation which is related to Salvation Army programmes.

With a view to accomplishing The Salvation Army's mission, the Secretariat is responsible for the operations of the Salvation Army Australia Overseas Development Office (SAADO) and the Red Shield Defence Services (RSDS), and chairs the National Moral and Social Issues Council (MASIC) and the National Public Relations Committee. It is responsible for negotiating funding from the Australian Government.

Through SAADO, the Secretariat monitors overseas aid community development projects jointly funded with the Australian Agency for International Development (AusAID).

To date SAADO has managed more than 300 projects in 25 developing countries.

Successful non-Salvation Army partners have included the YMCA in Lebanon and the Propeller Club of Manila in The Philippines, World Concern in Vietnam and the Eugene Bell Foundation in South Korea.

Innovative projects established by SAADO include income-generating windmills in India and 400 self-help groups in three Indian territories. The Australian office was the first Salvation Army donor to fund a programme to deal with the trafficking of children in India.

National Sec: Maj Peter Holley

Overseas Development Consultant:
Mr Gordon Knowles
Overseas Development Officer: Leigh O'Donoghue
Editorial Department: Level 1, 19-23 Prospect St, Box Hill, Vic 3128 (PO Box 451); tel: (03) 9818 1438; fax: (03) 9819 4864
National Editor-in-Chief: Maj Laurie Robertson
Red Shield Defence Services: PO Box 3246, Manuka, ACT 2603; tel: (02) 6273 2280; fax: (02) 6273 1383
Chief Commissioner: Capt Mel Stephens

AUSTRALIA EASTERN TERRITORY

Territorial leaders:
Commissioners Leslie and Coral Strong

Territorial Commander:
Commissioner Leslie Strong (1 Mar 2003)

Chief Secretary:
Lieut-Colonel Geanette Seymour
(1 Aug 2006)

Territorial Headquarters: 140 Elizabeth Street, Sydney, NSW 2000

Postal address: PO Box A435, Sydney South, NSW 1235, Australia

Tel: [61] (02) 9264 1711 (10 lines); fax: [61] (02) 9266 9638; web site: www.salvos.org.au

Zone: South Pacific and East Asia
States included in the territory: New South Wales, Queensland, The Australian Capital Territory (ACT)
Languages in which the gospel is preached: Cantonese, English, Korean, Mandarin
Periodicals: *Creative Ministry, Pipeline, Venue, Women in Touch*

WITH its acceptance of the three-fold mission statement – 'Save Souls, Grow Saints and Serve Suffering Humanity' – the Australia Eastern Territory places great emphasis on the outworking of The Salvation Army's mission. Salvationists are showing their belief in transformation, integrity and compassion in many ways.

There is an increasing number of first-time spiritual decisions being made by people at corps throughout the territory; these are supplemented by the conversions recorded at social services centres – especially in the Recovery Services programme.

The territorial emphasis on prayer has been particularly targeted at the 'growing of saints', with corps continuing to hold 24/7 prayer events and

developing steady growth in the number of weekly home groups for Bible study and prayer.

The outflow of the prayer emphasis is a call to evangelism: corps members are being challenged to step out of their comfort zones, reach out to unchurched people in their communities, and bring them into the corps fellowship and to a knowledge of Jesus Christ as Saviour.

Homelessness, family crisis, substance abuse and unemployment force many people to seek help at Salvation Army refuges and community centres.

Rural chaplains work round the clock to give relief, counsel and assistance, particularly to farmers who have been the most affected by the worst drought on record. They are also involved with many communities whose livelihood is affected by farmers being unable to purchase goods they normally would.

The territory's Aged Care programme is seeing a major overhaul of its buildings after stringent government requirements were placed upon such facilities. There are many rebuilding schemes under way, with the first new complex – Gill Waminda, at Goulburn – having opened on 12 May 2007.

As part of a territorial drive on candidate recruitment, the first *Salvationist Story – a Life Worth Living* DVD was issued free with the May 2007 edition of *Pipeline* – the territory's internal magazine for Salvationists and friends.

The DVD features the life story of a young captain in his first appointment, having come into The Salvation Army through the Recovery Services programme. Although designed for candidate promotion, it is also meeting a great need in the families of people with addictions.

A great deal of emphasis is being placed on volunteerism, an officer having been appointed to the recruitment and development of volunteers. One such volunteer, Mrs Ruth Alley, was presented with the Law and Justice Society Volunteer Award, the highest recommendation award possible, for her services to the courts.

Mrs Alley received her trophy in front of an audience of 500 people, among whom was a former Prime Minister of Australia, the Hon Malcolm Frazer.

STATISTICS

Officers 953 (active 544 retired 409) **Cadets** (1st Yr) 19 (2nd Yr) 9 **Employees** 3,951 **Corps** 174 **Outposts/Corps plants** 39 **Institutions** 73 **Community Care Services** 156 **Thrift stores/Charity shops** 210

Senior Soldiers 9,730 **Adherents** 3,104 **Junior Soldiers** 695

Personnel serving outside territory Officers 32 Layworkers 10

STAFF

Business: Lt-Col John Hodge
Personnel: Maj Peter Farthing
Programme: Lt-Col Lynette Green
Women's Ministries: Comr Coral Strong (TPWM) Maj Glenys Holley (TSWM)

Asst Chief Sec: Maj Brian Holley
Asst Sec for Business: Maj Mervyn Holland
Audit: Mr Tim Green
Booth College: Maj Philip Cairns
Candidates: Capts Craig & Donna Todd
Communications & Public Relations: Maj Mark Campbell
Counselling Service: Major (Dr) Christine Unicomb
Emergency Services: Maj Kevin Hentzschel
Finance: Mr Ian Minnett
Information Technology: Mr Wayne Bajema
Legal: Maj Mervyn Holland
Mission & Resource Team:
　Territorial Mission Directors: Majs Neil & Sharon Clanfield
　Music & Creative Arts: Mr Graeme Press
Moral & Social Issues Council: Lt-Col Lynette Green
Property: Capt Edwin Cox
Red Shield Defence Services: Capt Mel Stephens
Rep to Nat Council of Churches: Maj Graham Harris
Salvationist Supplies: Mr Graham Lang
Salvos Stores: Mr Neville Barrett
Social Programme Dept: Maj Cec Woodward
Sydney Staff Songsters: S/L Graeme Press

DIVISIONS

Australian Capital Territory and South NSW: 2-4 Brisbane Ave, Barton 2600, PO Box 4224, Kingston 2604; tel: (02) 6273 2211; fax: (02) 6273 2973; Maj Rodney Ainsworth

Central and North Queensland: 54 Charles St, North Rockhampton, QLD 4701, PO Box 5343, CQMC, Rockhampton, QLD 4702; tel: (07) 4999 1999; fax: (07) 4999 1915; Maj Gary Baker

Newcastle and Central NSW: 94 Parry St,
PO Box 684, The Junction 2291;
tel: (02) 4926 3466; fax: (02) 4926 2228;
Maj Peter Laws

North NSW: 4 Salmon Ave, PO Box 1180,
Armidale 2350; tel: (02) 6771 1632;
fax: (02) 6772 3444; Maj John Rees

South Queensland: 342 Upper Roma St,
Brisbane 4000, GPO Box 2210, Brisbane,
Qld 4001; tel: (07) 3222 6699;
fax: (07) 3229 3884; Maj Wayne Maxwell

Sydney East and Illawarra: 61-65 Kingsway,
Kingsgrove 2208, PO Box 740, Kingsgrove
1480; tel: (02) 9336 3320;
fax: (02) 9336 3359; Lt-Col Ian Hamilton

The Greater West: 93 Phillip St, Parramatta,
2150, PO Box 66, Parramatta, NSW 2124;
tel: (02) 9635 7400; fax: (02) 9689 1692;
Maj Kelvin Alley

BOOTH COLLEGE

Bexley North, NSW 2207: 32a Barnsbury
Grove, PO Box 226; tel: (02) 9502 0460;
fax: (02) 9502 4177

SCHOOL FOR OFFICER TRAINING

Bexley North, NSW 2207: 120 Kingsland Rd,
PO Box 63; tel: (02) 9502 1777;
fax: (02) 9554 3298

SCHOOL FOR CHRISTIAN STUDIES

Bexley North, NSW 2207: 32a Barnsbury Grove,
PO Box 237; tel: (02) 9502 0432;
fax: (02) 9502 0476

SCHOOL FOR LEADERSHIP TRAINING

Stanmore, NSW 2048: 97 Cambridge St;
tel: (02) 9557 1105; fax: (02) 9550 2005

SCHOOL FOR YOUTH LEADERSHIP

Lake Munmorah, NSW 2259: 42 Greenacre Ave;
tel: (02) 4358 8886; fax: (02) 4358 8882

HERITAGE CENTRE

Bexley North, NSW 2207: 120 Kingsland
Rd, PO Box 226; tel: (02) 9502 0424;
fax: (02) 9554 9204;
email: AUEHeritage@aue.salvationarmy.org;
Envoy George Hazell, OF

RECOVERY SERVICES COMMAND

Sydney: 85 Campbell St, Surry Hills 2010;
tel: (02) 9212 4000; fax: (02) 9212 4032;
Maj Jennifer Allen

BRIDGE ADDICTION RECOVERY PROGRAMME
(Drugs, alcohol and other substances)

Brisbane: 'Moonyah', 58 Glenrosa Rd, PO Box 81,
Red Hill 4059; tel: (07) 33690922;
fax: (07) 3369 9294 (acc men 76 Detox Unit
13 Halfway House 3)

Canberra: Canberra Recovery Services Centre, 5-
13 Mildura St, Fyshwick 2609, PO Box 4181,
Kingston 2604; tel: (02) 6295 1256/1644; fax:
(02) 6295 3766 (acc men 37 Halfway House
3)

Fountaindale: 'Selah', 60 Berkeley Rd, Berkeley
Vale, PO Box 5019, Chittaway 2261;
tel: (02) 4388 4588; fax: (02) 4389 1490
(acc women 36)

Gold Coast: 'Fairhaven', 497 Parklands Drive,
Southport 4215; PO Box 482, Ashmore
City 4214; tel: (07) 5594 7288;
fax: (07) 5594 7218 (acc men 54 Detox Unit
11 Halfway House men 3 Halfway House
women 3)

Hunter Region Recovery Services –
Morisset: 'Endeavour Community', 8 Russell
Rd, PO Box 346, Morisset 2264;
tel: (02) 4973 4146/4156;
fax: (02) 4973 4173 (acc men 26)
Morisset: 'Miracle Haven', Russell Rd,
PO Box 93, Morisset 2264;
tel: (02) 4973 1495/1644;
fax: (02) 4970 5807 (acc men 84)
Newcastle: 100-102 Hannell St, PO Box 125,
Wickham 2293; tel: (02) 4961 1257;
fax: (02) 4965 3295 (acc men 19)

Leura: 'Blue Mountains Recovery Services
Centre', 6 Eastview Ave, Leura; PO Box 284,
Wentworth Falls 2782; tel: (02) 4782 7392;
fax: (02) 4782 7392 (acc men 22)

Shoalhaven: Bridge Programme, 4 Smith Lane,
Nowra 2541; tel: (02) 4422 4604;
fax: (02) 4422 4672

Sydney: 'William Booth House Recovery
Services Centre', 56-60 Albion St, Surry Hills
2010, PO Box A127, Sydney South 1232;
tel: (02) 9212 2322; fax: (02) 9281 9771
(acc men 105 women 18)

Townsville: 'Rehabilitation Services Centre',
312-340 Walker St; PO Box 803,
Townsville 4810; tel: (07) 4772 3607;
fax: (07) 4772 3174 (acc men 26 Detox Unit 6
Halfway House 4)

Salvos Stores

General Manager: Mr Neville Barrett
ACT and Monaro Area: 5-15 Mildura St,
Fyshwick 2609, PO Box 4181, Kingston;

tel: (02) 6295 1644; fax: (02) 6295 3766 (retail stores 8)

Brisbane: 80 Glenrosa Rd, PO Box 81, Red Hill, 4059; tel: (07) 3369 0922; fax: (07) 3368 6344 (retail stores 18)

Central Coast Area Administration Office: 342 Mann St, Gosford 2250; tel: (02) 4325 3101; fax: (02) 4325 4879 (retail stores 4)

Gold Coast: 497 Parklands Drive, Southport 4215; tel: (07) 5571 5777; fax: (07) 5574 4893 (retail stores 12)

Illawarra Area: 29 Ellen St, Wollongong 2500; tel: (02) 4228 5644; fax: (02) 4228 1040 (retail stores 7)

Newcastle: 900 Hunter St, Newcastle 2300; tel: (02) 4961 3889; fax: (02) 4961 2623 (retail stores 9)

Sydney: 5 Bellevue St, St Peters 2044; tel: (02) 9519 1477; fax: (02) 9516 2924 (retail stores 12)

Sydney West: 4 Archbold Rd, Minchinbury 2770; tel: (02) 9625 8883; fax: (02) 9625 2253 (retail stores 10)

Townsville: 314-340 Walker St, PO Box 803, Townsville 4810; tel: (07) 4772 3844; fax: (07) 4772 3084 (retail stores 5)

RURAL CHAPLAINS

ACT & South NSW Div: c/o DHQ Canberra; tel: (02) 6273 2211; fax: (02) 6273 2973

Longreach, Qld 4730: 149 Eagle St, PO Box 127; tel: (07) 4658 3590

North NSW Div: c/o DHQ Armidale; tel: (02) 6771 1632; fax: (02) 6772 3444

AERIAL SERVICE

Flying Service Base: 107 Transmission St, Mt Isa

CONFERENCE AND HOLIDAY HOMES

Budgewoi, NSW 2262: Holiday Cottage, 129 Sunrise Ave; bookings through THQ; tel: (02) 9266 9502 (acc 6)

Cairns, Qld 4870: 281-289 Sheridan St; bookings through DHQ Rockhampton; tel: (07) 4999 1902 (5 motel units)

Caloundra, QLD 4551: 4 Michael St, Golden Beach; bookings through DHQ Brisbane; tel: (07) 3222 6666

Collaroy, NSW 2097: The Collaroy Centre, Homestead Ave, Collaroy Beach, PO Box 11; tel: (02) 9982 9800 (office); (02) 9982 6570 AH; fax: (02) 9971 1895

Margate, QLD 4019: 2 Duffield Rd; bookings through DHQ Brisbane; tel: (07) 3222 6666

Monterey NSW 2217: 3/34 Burlington Ave; bookings through THQ; tel: (02) 9266 9502

Tugun, QLD 4224: Holiday Unit, 3/15 Elizabeth St; bookings through DHQ Brisbane; tel: (07) 3222 6666

RED SHIELD DEFENCE SERVICES

RSDS Administration, Canberra ACT; tel: (02) 6273 2280; fax: (02) 6273 1383

Gallipoli Barracks, Brisbane, QLD: RSDS representative; tel: (07) 3332 7943

Holsworthy Military Camp, Sydney, NSW: RSDS representative; mobile: 0428 680 556

Kokoda Barracks, QLD: RSDS representative; tel: (07) 5541 6569

Lavarack Barracks, Townsville, QLD: RSDS representative; tel: (07) 4771 8571

Royal Military College, Duntroon, ACT: RSDS representative; mobile: 0417 236 183

Singleton Infantry Centre, NSW: RSDS representative; tel: (02) 6570 3279

SOCIAL SERVICES
Aged Care

Arncliffe, NSW 2205: Macquarie Lodge, 171 Wollongong Rd; tel: (02) 9556 6900; fax: (02) 9567 5043 (acc nursing home 65 hostel 49 units 99)

Balmain, NSW 2041: Montrose, 13 Thames St, PO Box 2; tel: (02) 9818 2355; fax: (02) 9818 5062 (acc hostel men 44)

Bass Hill, NSW 2197: Weeroona Village, 14 Trebartha St; tel: (02) 9645 3220; fax: (02) 9645 1390 (acc hostel 44 units 44 respite care 1)

Burwood, NSW 2134: Shaftesbury Court, 75a Shaftesbury Rd; tel: (02) 9560 4457 (acc units 35)

Canowindra, NSW 2804: Moyne, Eugowra Rd, PO Box 156; tel: (02) 6344 1475; fax: (02) 6344 1902 (acc nursing home 29 hostel 44)

Chelmer, QLD 4068: Warrina Village, 35 Victoria Ave, PO Box 239, Indooroopilly 4068; tel: (07) 3379 9800; fax: (07) 3278 1127 (acc nursing home 40 hostel 42 units 13)

Dee Why, NSW 2099: Pacific Lodge, 15 Fisher Rd, PO Box 109; tel: (02) 9982 8090; fax: (02) 9982 9174 (acc hostel 59)

Dulwich Hill, NSW 2203: Maybanke, 80 Wardell Rd, PO Box 286; tel: (02) 9560 4457; fax: (02) 9569 1301 (acc nursing home 39 hostel 38)

Goulburn, NSW 2580: Gill Waminda,

2 Combemere St, PO Box 233;
tel: (02) 4821 6533; fax: (02) 4821 7405
(acc hostel 67)

Marrickville, NSW 2204: Bethesda, 80 Victoria
Rd, PO Box 286 Dulwich Hill 2203;
tel: (02) 9519 7079; fax: (02) 9565 1327
(acc nursing home 46)

Merewether, NSW 2291: Carpenter Court,
46 John Pde, PO Box 246; tel: (02) 4963 4300;
fax: (02) 4963 6489 (acc 42)

Narrabundah, ACT 2604: Mountain View,
Goyder St, PO Box 61; tel: (02) 6295 1044
(acc 65)

Narrabundah, ACT 2604: Karingal Court,
11 Boolimba Cresc; tel: (02) 6295 1044;
fax: (02) 6295 1473 (acc 36)

Parkes, NSW 2870: Rosedurnate, 46 Orange St,
PO Box 100; tel: (02) 6862 2300;
fax: (02) 6862 3756 (acc nursing home 29
hostel 45 units 17)

Port Macquarie, NSW 2444: Bethany, 2-6 Gray
St, PO Box 2016; tel: (02) 6584 1127;
fax: (02) 6584 1045 (acc nursing home 50
hostel 40)

Riverview, QLD 4303: Moggill Ferry Rd,
PO Box 6042; tel: (07) 3282 1000;
fax: (07) 3282 6929 (acc nursing home 50
hostel 143 units 44)

Rockhampton, QLD 4700: Bethesda Hostel,
58 Talford St, PO Box 375; tel: (07) 4922 3229;
fax: (07) 4922 3455 (acc hostel 50 respite
care 1)

Resident Funded Accommodation

Collaroy, NSW 2097: Warringah Place,
1039 Pittwater Rd, PO Box 395;
tel: (02) 9971 1933; fax: (02) 9971 4155
(acc self care units 64 serviced apartments 44)

Erina, NSW 2250: Woodport Village, 120-140
The Entrance Rd; tel: (02) 4365 2660;
fax: (02) 4365 1812 (acc hostel 79 nursing
home 96 units 67)

Crisis Accommodation and Day Care (Aged)

'Burrangiri', 1-7 Rivett Place, PO Box 65,
Rivett, ACT 2611; tel: (02) 6288 1488;
fax: (02) 6288 0321 (acc 15 day care 20)

Children's Services (Child care centres and family day care and after-school programmes)

Carina, QLD 4152: 202 Gallipoli Rd;
tel: (07) 3395 0744

Gladstone, QLD 4680: 198 Goondoon St;

tel: (07) 4972 2985: fax: (07) 4972 7835

Macquarie Fields, NSW 2564: Eucalyptus Drive,
PO Box 1; tel: (02) 9605 4717;
fax: (02) 9618 1492

Counselling Service

Head Office: Rhodes, NSW 2138, PO Box 3096;
tel: (02) 9743 4535

Brisbane, QLD 4122: 5/46 Mount Gravatt-
Capalaba Rd, Upper Mount Gravatt, PO Box
6266, Upper Mount Gravatt; tel: (07) 3349 5046

Campbelltown: refer to Penrith Office

Gosford, NSW 2250: 59 Mann St, Gosford;
tel: (02) 9743 2831

North Lyneham, ACT 2602: Ste 3, Southwell Park
Offices, Montford Cresc; tel: (02) 6248 5504

Penrith, NSW: Ste 15, Lethbridge Ct,
20-24 Castlereagh St, PO Box 588;
tel: (02) 4731 1554

Pine Rivers, QLD 4501: 27-29 Lawnton Pocket
Rd, Lawnton; tel: (07) 3285 2401

Stafford, QLD 4054: refer to Brisbane Office

Sydney, NSW 2138: 15 Blaxland Rd, PO Box
3096, Rhodes 2138; tel: (02) 9743 2831

Tuggeranong, ACT 2900: Ste 3, Southwell Park
Offices, Montford Cresc, PO Box 2324, North
Lyneham 2902; tel: (02) 6248 5504

Moneycare Financial Counselling Service

Brisbane, 4001: 342 Upper Roma St, PO Box
2210; tel: (07) 3222 6621; fax: (07) 3229 3884

Campbelltown, NSW 2560: 27-31 Rudd Rd,
PO Box 204 Leumeah; tel: (02) 4620 7482

Campsie, 2194: 30 Anglo Rd, PO Box 399;
tel: 9787 5375; fax: 9718 6775

Central Qld 4701: 54 Charles St, North
Rockhampton, PO Box 5343 CQMC 4702;
tel: (07) 4999 1999; fax: (07) 4999 1915

Dickson, ACT 2602: 4 Hawdon Pl, PO Box
1038; tel: 6247 1340 (Direct Line),
6247 3635; fax: 6257 2791

Hurstville, NSW 2220: 23 Delcassia St;
appointments through DHQ; tel (02) 9336 3320;
fax (02) 9336 3359

Kingsgrove, 1480: 61-65 Kingsway, PO Box 740;
tel: 9336 3320; fax: 9336 3359

Lethbridge Park, 2150: 2-6 Bougainville Rd;
tel/fax: (02) 9835 2756

Newcastle West, NSW 2302: DHQ, Union and
Parry Sts; tel: (02) 4926 0231;
fax: (02) 4926 2228

Parramatta, 2150: Ste 1, 2nd Fl, 95 Phillip St,
PO Box 3681; tel: 9633 5011; fax: 9633 5214

Taree, NSW 2430: 140a Victoria St;
tel: (02) 6592 4404; fax: (02) 6892 4405

Tuncurry, NSW 2428: 7 South St;
tel: (02) 6554 6101; fax: (02) 6555 3347

Crisis and Supported Accommodation (Homeless persons programmes)
Adults

Broken Hill, NSW 2880: Catherine Haven,
633 Lane St, PO Box 477;
tel: (08) 8087 1999

Broken Hill, NSW 2880: Algate House Carer's
Respite Centre, 633 Lane St, PO Box 477;
tel: 08 8087 0011

Cairns North, QLD 4870: Centennial Lodge,
281 Sheridan St, PO Box 140N;
tel/fax: (07) 4031 4432 (acc men 24, women 20,
women with children 6, patient transfer
scheme 5)

Campbelltown, NSW 2560: Shekinah, 127b
Lindesay St; tel:02 4625 9022 (acc women
and children 5 units)

Carrington, NSW 2294: The Anchor, PO Box 134,
cnr Young and Cowper St; tel: (02) 4961 6129;
fax: (02) 4961 4038 (acc men 18)

Chermside, QLD 4032: Glen Haven, 1000
Gympie Rd, PO Box 82, Aspley, QLD 4034;
tel: (07) 3350 3455; fax: (07) 3256 3601
(acc women/children units 10)

Griffith, NSW 2680: Anzac St;
tel: (02) 6964 3388 (acc men)

Kemblawarra, NSW 2505: 'Carinya Cottage',
1/3 Kemblawarra Rd, PO Box 269,
Warrawong 2502; tel: (02) 4276 2968;
fax: 4276 1412 (acc women and children 38)

Leeton, NSW 2705: 9 Mulga St;
tel: (02) 6953 4941 (client units)

Mackay, QLD 4740: Samaritan House,
Shakespeare St, PO Box 6642;
tel: (07) 4957 7644 Silent (acc mothers and
children, families 4)

Merewether, NSW 2291: Clulow Court,
49 Frederick St, PO Box 414, The Junction
2291; tel: (02) 4963 6616 (acc women 8)

Mount Isa, QLD 4825: Serenity House,
4 Helen St, PO Box 2900; tel: (07) 4743 3198
(acc women and children 11)

Southport, QLD 4215: Still Waters, 173 Wardoo
St, PO Box 888, Ashmore City 4214;
tel: (07) 5591 1776 (acc women 36, women
and children 7 units)

Spring Hill, QLD 4004: Pindari, 28 Quarry St,
PO Box 159; tel: (07) 3832 1491 (acc hostel
120, flats 9, medical centre 3)

Spring Hill, QLD 4004: Pindari Women's
Programme, 28 Quarry St; tel: (07) 3832 6073
(acc 18)

Surry Hills, NSW 2010: Foster House (including
Alf Dawkins Detox Unit), 5-19 Mary St;
tel: (02) 9212 1065; fax: (02) 9218 1248
(acc men 117, community houses 85)

Surry Hills, NSW 2010: Samaritan House,
348 Elizabeth St, PO Box 583, Surry Hills;
tel: (02) 9211 5794; fax: (02) 9212 5430
(acc women 38)

Tewantin, QLD 4565: 26 Donella St, PO Box
671; tel: (07) 5447 1184; fax: (07) 5447 1854
(acc families)

The Junction (Newcastle), NSW 2291: Faith
Cottage, 28 Farquhar St, PO Box 366;
tel: (02) 4969 4275 (acc mothers and
children 16)

Toowoomba, QLD 4350: 5 Russell St, PO Box
2527; tel: (07) 4632 5239; fax: (07) 4639 1821
(acc men)

Toowoomba, QLD 4350: 5 Russell St, PO Box
2527; tel: (07) 4639 1998 (acc Family Crisis)

Youth

Bundaberg QLD 4670: The Salvation Army Youth
Refuge, 71 Woongarra St, Bundaberg 4670;
tel: (07) 4151 3400; fax: (07) 4152 6044

Canberra, ACT 2601: Oasis Support Network,
PO Box 435; tel: (02) 6248 7191;
fax: (02) 6249 8116

Fortitude Valley, QLD 4006: 20 Baxter St,
PO Box 701; tel: (07) 3854 1245;
fax: (07) 3854 1552

Newcastle, NSW 2293: The Ark, 116-120
Hannell St, PO Box 94 Wickham;
tel: (020) 4969 8066; fax: (02) 4969 8073
(acc 24)

Surry Hills, NSW 2010: Oasis Youth Support
Network, 365 Crown St, PO Box 600
Darlingshurst 1300; tel: (02) 9331 2266

Wyong, NSW 2259: Oasis Youth Support,
5 Hely St, PO Box 57, Wyong;
tel: (02) 4353 9799; fax: (02) 4353 9550

Handicapped Persons: accommodation

Bardon, QLD 4065: SAILSS (Salvation Army
Individual Lifestyle Support Service),
3/63 Macgregor Tce; tel: (07) 3368 0700
(home support services 31 adults)

Toowoomba, QLD 4350: Horton Village,
2 Curtis St, PO Box 289; tel: (07) 4639 4026
(acc 28)

Family Tracing Service

Brisbane, QLD 4000: 342 Upper Roma St, GPO
Box 2210, Brisbane 4001; tel: (07) 3236 5544;
fax: (07) 3221 6228

Sydney, NSW 2000: PO Box A435, Sydney South,
1232; tel: (02) 9211 0277; fax: (02) 9211 2044

Special Search Service

Sydney, NSW 2000: 85 Campbell St, Surry Hills 2010, PO Box A435, Sydney South, 1232; tel: (02) 9211 6491, 1300 667 366 Australia Wide; fax: (02) 9211 2044

Court and Prison Ministry

Brisbane, QLD 4000: 342 Upper Roma St, GPO Box 2210, Brisbane 4001; tel: (07) 3222 6670

Sydney South, NSW 1232: PO Box Corrective Services Ministry NSW/ACT

Parramatta, NSW 2105: 30-32 Smith St; tel: (02) 9687 9005; fax: (02) 9687 9544

Community Service

Brisbane, QLD 4003: 97 Turbot St, PO Box 13688, George St 4003; tel: (07) 3211 9230; fax: (07) 3211 9234

Broken Hill, NSW 2880: Algate House Community Centre, 633 Lane St, PO Box 477; tel: (08) 8088 2044

Campsie, NSW 2194: 30 Anglo Rd, PO Box 399; tel: (02) 9787 2333; fax: (02) 9718 6775

Canberra, ACT 2602: 4 Hawdon Pl, Dickson, PO Box 1038 Dickson; tel: (02) 6247 3635

Dulwich Hill: 54 Dulwich St; tel: (02) 9569 4511; fax: (02) 9569 4677

Eastern Beaches, NSW 2035: 100 Boyce Rd, PO Box 321; tel: (02) 9314 2166; fax: (02) 9344 3160

Greenslopes, QLD 4120: 627 Logan Rd; PO Box 221 Stones Corner; tel: (07) 3394 4184

Illawarra, NSW 2500: Northcliffe Dr, Kemblawarra 2505, PO Box 6102 Wollongong; tel: (02) 4275 1188; fax: (02) 4275 2944

Inala, QLD 4077: 83 Inala Ave, PO Box 1050; tel: (07) 3372 1889

Inner City (Sydney), NSW 2000: 339 Crown St, Surry Hills 2010; tel: (02) 9360 1000

Ipswich, QLD 4305: 14 Ellenborough St; PO Box 227; tel: (07) 3812 2462

Logan City, QLD 4114: Shop 5, 41 Station Rd, Woodridge, PO Box 816; tel: (07) 3808 2564

Macquarie Fields, NSW 2564: Eucalyptus Drive, PO Box 1; tel: (02) 9605 4771

Nerang, QLD 4211: Shop 5, Dalmar Centre, 43-45 Price St, PO Box 599; tel: (07) 5596 0764

Newcastle West, NSW 2302: 12-16 Union St; tel: (02) 4929 2300

Northern Beaches, NSW 2099: 1 Fisher Rd, PO Box 210, Dee Why; tel: (02) 9981 4472

St George, NSW 2208: 23 Dalcassia St, Hurstville 2220; tel: (02) 9579 3897, fax: (07) 9579 6094

Southport, QLD 4215: 48 Nind St, PO Box 1680; tel: (07) 5591 2729

Townsville, QLD 4810: 165 Ross River Rd, Mundingburra, PO Box 1152 Aitkenville MC QLD 4814; tel: (07) 4755 0722

Wynnum/Capalaba, QLD 4178: 107 Akonna St, PO Box 701; tel: (07) 3393 4713

Zillmere, QLD 4034: 8/35 Handford Rd, PO Box 182, Zillmere; tel: (07) 3865 1416; fax: (07) 3865 1705

Hostels for Students

Marrickville, NSW 2204: Stead House, 12 Leicester St, PO Box 3015; tel: (02) 9557 1276 (acc women 25)

Toowong, QLD 4066: 15 Jephson St, PO Box 1124; tel: (07) 3371 1966 (acc 66)

Telephone Counselling Service

Salvo Care Line, NSW 2046: tel: (02) 8736 3297 (office); (02) 9331 6000 (24-hr counselling); (02) 9331 2000 (suicide prevention); (02) 9360 3000 (youth line)

Salvo Care Line, QLD 4000: 342 Upper Roma St, GPO Box 2210, Brisbane 4001; tel: (07) 3222 6678 (24-hr counselling)

Work Skill Training

Bundaberg QLD 4670: The Salvation Army Tom Quinn Community Centre, 8 Killer St, Bundaberg 4670; tel (07) 41533557; fax: (07) 41511746

Job Link, Blacktown, NSW 2148: 15-21 Boiler Close, PO Box 20; tel: (02) 9831 4247

Newcastle Youth Crisis and Training Service: The Ark, 116-120 Hannell St, PO Box 94 Wickham NSW 2293; tel: (02) 4969 8066; fax: (02) 4969 8073

This Way Up Furniture Co: 46 Maitland Rd, Islington 2296; tel: (02) 4969 5695; fax: (02) 4969 5665

JPET (Job Placement & Employment Training)

Caboolture, QLD 4510: Unit 1, 75 King St; tel: (07) 5428 2811

Lawnton, QLD 4501: 27-29 Lawnton Pocket Rd; tel: (07) 3285 8522

Redcliffe, QLD 4020: Shop 4, 3 Violet St; tel: (07) 3283 5977

Employment Plus

National Office: Level 3, 10 Wesley Court, East Burwood, VIC 3151; tel: 136 123 Australia Wide

AUSTRALIA SOUTHERN TERRITORY

Territorial leaders:
Commissioners James and Carolyn Knaggs

Territorial Commander:
Commissioner James Knaggs (1 Aug 2006)

Chief Secretary:
Lieut-Colonel Raymond Finger (1 Dec 2007)

Territorial Headquarters: 3-7 Hamilton St, Mont Albert 3127, Vic

Postal address: Locked Bag 1, Mont Albert 3127, Victoria, Australia

Tel: [61] (03) 9896 6000; fax: [61] (03) 9899 2337; email: Salvosaus@aus.salvationarmy.org;
web site: www.salvationarmy.org.au

Zone: South Pacific and East Asia
States included in the territory: Northern Territory, South Australia, Tasmania, Victoria,
 Western Australia
Languages in which the gospel is preached: Cantonese, English, Korean, Mandarin, local aboriginal
 languages
Publications: *Kidzone, On Fire, Warcry*

DROUGHT has affected much of Australia for the past decade. Water supplies for most cities have been at an all-time low; many farmers and rural property owners have had to leave the land; suicide in rural communities has risen dramatically.

On 12 January 2007 the territory launched its 'Living Water' Drought Relief Appeal at the Melbourne Showgrounds. The territorial leadership pledged two million Australian dollars to provide the infrastructure for a long-term distribution of funds and goods through the ongoing 'Living Water' operation.

By end-April more than $1 million had come in from the public and corporate Australia. This amount doubled to $2.2 million during May .

Despite the drought, Australians gave generously to the annual Red Shield Appeal in 2006. The amount raised – $26.6 milion – was an increase of $1.7 million on the 2005 result. These finances help fund the territory's social welfare programmes. The territorial leadership praise God for his provision through these appeals.

Further priority was given to youth ministry: an increased number of people were placed in youth leadership positions and the territory launched the 2Love youth brand that encompasses all youth programmes and processes.

The 2Love model is based on the United Kingdom's ALOVE programme and intentionally connects youth work with the Australia Southern Territory's four mission intentions – caring for people, transforming lives, making disciples and reforming society.

On 25 March 2007 the 2Love team organised a 'Stop the Traffick' event at Melbourne's Southbank, involving 500 Salvationists and thousands of onlookers. People listened to a number of bands and speakers included Territorial Commander Commissioner James Knaggs. Everyone was invited to sign a 'freedom wall'.

Women also came to the fore early in 2007 through the 'While Women Weep' campaign. The Women's Ministries Department combined with the territory's *On Fire* magazine to communicate the impact women and their ministry are making within the Army's mission.

There is still a need for more soldiers to commit to officership as innovative models of corps planting and outreach-focused social programmes are explored. A continued interest has been shown in lieutenancy, with 70 people serving in that capacity during the period of this report.

The development of resources and assistance to corps for evangelism and growth took a large step forward in November 2006 with the establishment of the Growing Healthy Corps Network coordinated from THQ.

Other significant occasions included the re-branding of Family Stores to Salvos Stores (June 2006); the inaugural conference for Chinese-speaking officers (June 2006); the rolling-out of new risk management procedures; the training college joining with the Melbourne College of Divinity on 5 February 2007, and the Melbourne Staff Songsters celebrating their 20th anniversary on 11 April 2007.

A commemoration on 22 October 2006 marked the cessation of 111 years' continuous use of 69 Bourke Street, Melbourne, as a Salvation Army headquarters. At various times the building has housed the Australasian, Australia Southern Territorial and Melbourne Central Divisional Headquarters.

STATISTICS

Officers 859 (active 466 retired 393) **Lieutenants** 60 **Cadets** (1st Yr) 10 (2nd Yr) 29 **Employees** 4,924

Corps 161 **Outposts** 18 **Social Centres/ Programmes** 218 **Salvos Stores** 183 **Family Support Centres** 72 **Outback Flying Service** 1

Senior Soldiers 9,010 **Adherents** 2,937 **Junior Soldiers** 981

Personnel serving outside territory Officers 28 Layworkers 2

STAFF

Asst Chief Sec: Lt-Col Elaine Hood
Asst to Chief Sec/Overseas Personnel Officer: Lt-Col Lyndon Spiller
Training Principal: Capt Stephen Court
National Editor-in-Chief: Maj Laurie Robertson
Business Administration: Lt-Col Brian Hood
  Asst Business Sec: Capt Malcolm Roberts
  Audit: Mr Cameron Duck
  Salvo Stores: Mr Allen Dewhirst
  Finance: Mr Gregory Stowe
  Information Technology: Mr Larry Reed
  Legal: Capt Malcolm Roberts
  Property: Mr David Perry
  Public Relations: Maj Wayne Pittaway
Personnel: Maj Frank Daniels
  Asst Personnel Sec – Officer Resource Unit: Maj Karyn Rigley
  Asst Sec for Personnel – Leader Dev: Maj Colin Corkery
  Candidates and Lieutenants Sec: Maj Len Turner

Human Resources: Mr John Cullinan
Pastoral Care: Maj Graeme Faragher
Spiritual Development: Maj Robert A. Paterson
Programme: Maj John Vale
   Corps Programme: Maj Winsome Merrett
   Family Tracing: Maj Sophia Gibb
   Melbourne Staff Band: B/M Ken Waterworth
   Melbourne Staff Songsters: S/L Brian Hogg
   Social Programme: Maj Graeme Rigley
   Youth: Lt David Collinson
Women's Ministries: Comr Carolyn Knaggs (TPWM) Lt-Col Aylene Finger (TSWM) Maj Adele Vale (Director) Mrs Wendy Smith (Child Sponsorship:

DIVISIONS

Eastern Victoria: 347-349 Mitcham Rd, Mitcham, Vic 3132; tel: (03) 8872 6400; Maj Ronald Clinch
Melbourne Central: 1/828 Sydney Rd, North Coburn 3058; tel: (03) 9353 5200; Maj Rodney Barnard
Northern Victoria: Bramble St, Bendigo, Vic 3550; tel: (03) 5443 4288; Lt-Col Jocelyn Knapp
South Australia: 39 Florence St, Fullarton, SA 5063; tel: (08) 8379 9388; Maj Dennis Rowe
Tasmania: 'Maylands', 27 Pirie St, Newtown, Tas 7008; tel: (03) 6278 7184; Maj Allan Daddow
Western Australia: 333 William St, Northbridge, WA 6003; tel: (08) 9227 7010; Maj Iain Trainor
Western Victoria: 102 Eureka St, Ballarat, Vic 3350; tel: (03) 5337 1300; Maj Peter Walker

REGION

Northern Territory: Level 2 Suite C, Paspalis Centre, 48-50 Smith St, Darwin, NT 0800; tel: (08) 8944 6000; Maj Ritchie Watson

OFFICER TRAINING COLLEGE

Parkville, Vic 3052: 303 Royal Parade; tel: (03) 9347 0299

ARCHIVES AND HERITAGE CENTRES

Melbourne, Vic 3000: Territorial Archives and Museum, 69 Bourke St, PO Box 18137, Collins St E, Melbourne, Vic 8003; tel: (03) 9653 3201
Nailsworth, SA 5083: Heritage Centre, 2a Burwood Ave; tel: (08) 8342 2545
Northbridge, WA 6003: Historical Society

Display Centre, 3rd Floor, 333 William St; tel: (08) 9227 7010

CONFERENCE AND HOLIDAY CENTRES

Bicheno, Tas 7215: Holiday Home, 11 Banksia St
Busselton, WA 6280: Holiday Unit 2, 12 Gale St; tel: (08) 9227 7010/7134
Daylesford, Vic 3460: Holiday Flat, Unit 5/28, Camp St
Geelong, Vic 3219: Conference Centre, Adams Court, Eastern Park; tel: (03) 5226 2121
Mount Dandenong, Vic 3767: Holiday Home, 6 Oakley St
Ocean Grove, Vic 3226: Holiday Home, 4 Northcote Rd
Victor Harbor, SA 5211: Encounters Conference Centre, 22 Bartel Blvd; tel: (08) 8552 2707 (acc 148)
Weymouth, Tas 7252: Holiday Camp, Walden St; tel: (03) 6382 6359 (acc 32)

EMPLOYMENT PLUS

National Office: Level 3, 10 Wesley Crt, Burwood, Vic 3151; tel: (03) 9847 8700; Maj John Simmonds
Service Delivery Centres: New South Wales 23; Queensland 16; South Australia 8; Tasmania; Victoria 25; Western Australia 7
Enquiries: tel: 136 123

FLYING PADRE AND OUTBACK SERVICES

PO Box 43289, Casuarina, NT 0811; Tel: (08) 8945 0176; Capt David Shrimpton

RED SHIELD DEFENCE SERVICES

Puckapunyal Representative; tel: (03) 5793 1294
Robertson Barracks Representative; tel: (08) 8935 2526/8981 7663

SOCIAL SERVICES

Pathways Accommodation and Support (including Personal Support Programme, Community Connections Programme, and Homeless Services)
43b Wyndham St, Shepparton, Vic 3630; tel: (03) 5821 2131

Pathways Shepparton
43a & 43b Wyndham St, Shepparton, Vic 3630; Postal address: PO Box 7352, Shepparton, Vic 3632;
email: pathways@aus.salvationarmy.org

Homelessness Support Service

Outreach Connections: tel: (03) 5821 2131; fax: (03) 5822 4424

Family Support Services

Tel: (03) 5822 4420; fax: (03) 5821 7627

Adult Services

Abbotsford, Vic 3067: The Anchorage, 81 Victoria St; tel: (03) 9417 5820

Geelong, Vic 3216: Community Access, Community Support, Adult Outreach, 1 Riverview Tce; tel: (03) 5243 3364

Kensington, Vic 3031: Community Outreach, 133 Rankins Rd; tel: (03) 9372 2488

New Town, Tas 7008: Accommodation and Housing for the Aged, 115 New Town Rd; tel: (03) 6278 3256

North Melbourne, Vic 3051: Community Aged Care, Food Services, Cleaning Maintenance, 9 Roden St; tel: (03) 9329 5777

Aboriginal Ministry

Alice Springs, NT 0870: Aboriginal Programme, 88 Hartley St; tel: (08) 8951 0207

Swan Hill, Vic 3585: 190 Beveridge St; tel: (03) 5033 1718

Chaplaincy – Police, Fire and Emergency Services

Darwin, NT 0800 (PFES): tel: 0407 797 197

Kununurra, WA (FES)

Child Care and Family Services

Balga, WA 6061: Family Day Care and Long Day Care, 10-18 Lavant Way; tel: (08) 9349 7488

Ballarat, Vic 3550: 6 Crompton St; tel: (03) 5329 1100

Bendigo, Vic 3552: Fairground Family Access Programme, 65-71 Mundy St; tel: (03) 5441 5405

Melton, Vic 3337: Melton Foster Care, 38 Station Rd; tel: (03) 9747 8310

North Coburg, Vic 3031: 2/828 Sydney Rd; tel: (03) 9353 1011

Sunshine, Vic 3020: Child and Adolescent Services, Home-Based One-to-One Care, Intensive Case Management Services, 34 Devonshire Rd; tel: (03) 9312 3544

Intensive Living and Learning Environments – ILLE Programmes

St Albans; Taylor's Lakes; Sunshine; North Altona; Kealba; Melton: contact through Westcare, 34 Devonshire Rd, Sunshine; tel: (03) 9312 3544

Children's Homes and Cottages

Sunshine, Vic 3020: Westcare, 34 Devonshire Rd, Sunshine; tel: (03) 9312 3544

Community Programmes

Bendigo, Vic 3552: Community Programmes including Youth Ministries, Personal Support Programme, Creative Arts and Technology, Gravel Hill Community Gardens, HillSkills Workshop, Hilltop Café, Fairground Children's Contact Service, 65-71 Mundy St; tel: (03) 5442 7699

Berri, SA 5343: Riverland Community Services, 20 Wilson St; tel: (08) 8582 3182

Brunswick, Vic 3056: 256 Albert St; tel: (03) 9387 6746

Hawthorn, Vic 3122: Hawthorn Project, Homeless Outreach Project, Community Connection Project, Equity and Access Project, 16 Church St; tel: (03) 9851 7800

Kununurra, WA 6743: Community Outreach Centre, 106 Coolibah Drive; tel: 0429 802 885

Mornington, Vic 3931: PYFS, Reconnect Programme, Shop 9, 234 Main St; tel: (03) 5976 2231

Port Augusta, SA 5700: Community Services, 35 Flinders Tce; tel: (08) 8641 1021

Rosebud, Vic 3939: Peninsula Community Support Programme, 17-19 Ninth Ave; tel: (03) 5986 7268

Crisis Services

Balga, WA 6061: Family Accommodation Programme, 10-18 Lavant Way; tel: (08) 9349 7488

Croydon, Vic 3136: Gateways Crisis Services, PO Box 1072; tel: (03) 9725 8455

Frankston, Vic 3199: Peninsula Counselling Service, Peninsula Crisis Centre, 37 Rossmith Ave East; tel: (03) 9784 5050

Geraldton, WA 6530: Family Crisis Accommodation, 42 Ainsworth St; tel: (08) 9964 3627

Leongatha, Vic 3953: GippsCare Domestic Violence Outreach Service, 51 McCartin St; tel: (03) 5662 4502

St Kilda, Vic 3128:
Inner South Domestic Violence Service, 27 Grey St; tel: (03) 9536 7730, toll free: 1800 627 727
Verve Programme, 31 Grey St; tel: (03) 9536 7780
Crisis Accommodation, 31 Grey St; tel: (03) 9536 7730, toll free 1800 627 727
Health and Information, 29 Grey St; tel: (03) 9536 7703, toll free 1800 627 727

Access Health Service, 31 Grey St;
tel: (03) 9536 7780
Inner South Domestic Violence Services,
29 Grey St; tel: (03) 9536 7720

Emergency Accommodation

Albany, WA 6330: 152-160 North Rd;
tel: (08) 9841 1068 (acc family units 2)
Alice Springs, NT 0870: 11 Goyder St;
tel: (08) 8952 1434 (acc service, single men,
dual diagnosis)
Ballarat, Vic 3350: Karinya, 6 Crompton St;
tel: (03) 5329 1100 (acc mothers 8)
Berri, SA 5343: Riverland Community Services,
20 Wilson St; tel: (08) 8582 3182 (acc 30)
Bunbury, WA 6230: Cnr Bussell H'way and
Timperly Rd; tel: (08) 9721 4519 (acc family
units 2)
Burnie, Tas 7320: 24 View Rd;
tel: (03) 6431 5791 (acc 61)
Darwin, NT 0800: 49 Mitchell St;
tel: (08) 8981 5994 (acc 64, family units 5)
Geraldton, WA 6530: Ainsworth St;
tel: (08) 9964 3667 (acc family units 3)
Hobart West, Tas 7000: 15 Lansdowne Cresc;
tel: (03) 6234 5777 (acc 16, exit houses 2)
Horsham, Vic 3400: 12 Kalkee Rd;
tel: (03) 5382 1770 (acc family units 3,
single 3)
Jacana, Vic 3047: 23 Sunset Blvd;
tel: (03) 9309 6289 (acc family units 4,
community houses 6)
Kalgoorlie Boulder, WA 6430: Oberthur St;
tel: (08) 9021 2255 (acc family units 2)
Sale, Vic 3850: Cnr Cunningham and Marley Sts;
tel: (03) 5144 4564 (acc 6)
Shepparton, Vic 3630: 23 Middleton St;
tel: (03) 5821 2131 (acc extended care house 1,
family units 3, single women unit 1, single
men units 2)
Stawell, Vic 3380: 26-30 Ligar St;
tel: (03) 5358 4072 (youth and singles)
Sunbury, Vic 3429: 27-37 Anderson St;
tel: (03) 9740 8844
Sunshine, Vic 3020: 1 St Andrew St;
tel: (03) 9364 9744

Emergency Family Accommodation

Burnie, Tas 7320: Oakleigh House, 24 View Rd;
tel: (03) 6431 5791 (acc 61)
Darwin, NT 0800: 49 Mitchell St;
tel: (08) 8981 5994 (family units 5)
Horsham, Vic 3400: 12 Kalkee Rd;
tel: (03) 5382 1770 (acc family units 3, single 3)
Port Augusta, SA 5700: 35 Flinders Tce;
tel: (08) 8641 1021 (acc 65)

St Kilda, Vic 3182: 27 Grey St;
tel: (03) 9536 7730 (acc 20)

Family Outreach (Community Programme)

Brunswick, Vic 3056: 256 Albert St;
tel: (03) 9387 6746
Geelong, Belmont, Vic 3216: Kardinia,
1 Riverview Tce; tel: (03) 5243 3364
Jacana, Vic 3047: 23 Sunset Blvd;
tel: (03) 9309 6289
Moonah, Tas 7008: 73 Hopkins St;
tel: (03) 6228 0910
Port Augusta, SA 5700: 35 Flinders Tce;
tel: (08) 8641 1024
Seymour, Vic 3660: Pathways, 6 Tallarook St;
tel: (03) 5799 1581

Salvos Stores

Administration: 233-235 Blackburn Rd,
Mt Waverley 3149; tel: (03) 9845 4000
Stores: Northern Territory 6; South Australia 39;
Tasmania 10; Victoria 92; Western
Australia 45

Family Support Services

Aberfoyle Park, SA 5159: The Hub Worship and
Community Complex, tel: (08) 8370 5003
Adelaide, SA 5000: 277 Pirie St;
tel: (08) 8227 0199
Albany, WA 6330: 152-160 North Rd;
tel: (08) 9841 1068
Alice Springs, NT 0870: 88 Hartley St;
tel: (08) 8951 0206
Armadale, WA 6112: 57 Braemore St;
tel: (08) 9497 1803
Arndale, Kilkenny, SA 5009: 1-7 Gray St;
tel: (08) 8445 2044
Bairnsdale, Vic 3875: 63 McLeod St;
tel: (03) 5152 4201
Balga, WA 6061: 10-18 Lavant Way;
tel: (08) 9349 7488
Ballarat, Vic 3350: 102 Eureka St;
tel: (03) 5337 0600
Beechworth, Vic 3747: 35 Ford St;
tel: (03) 5728 3245
Benalla, Vic 3672: 72 Fawkner Dr;
tel: (03) 5762 6396
Bendigo, Vic 3550: 65-71 Mundy St;
tel: (03) 5442 7699
Bentleigh, Vic 3204: 87 Robert St;
tel: (03) 9557 2644
Bentley, WA 6102: Dumond St;
tel: (08) 9458 1855
Berwick, Vic 3806: Cnr Parkhill Dr and Ernst
Wanke Rd; tel: (03) 9704 1940

Box Hill, Vic 3128: 17-23 Nelson Rd;
  tel: (03) 9890 2993
Broadford, Vic 3658: 25-27 Powlett St;
  tel: (03) 7584 1635
Brunswick, Vic 3056: 256 Albert St;
  tel: (03) 9387 6746
Burnie, Tas 7320: 99 Wilson St;
  tel: (03) 6431 8722
Busselton, WA 6280: Kent St;
  tel: (08) 9754 2733
Camberwell, Vic 3124: 7 Bowen St;
  tel: (03) 9889 2468
Campbelltown, SA 5074: Cnr Roma Grv and
  Florentine Ave; tel: (08) 8365 2301
Carrum Downs, Vic 3201: 1265 Frankston-
  Dandenong Rd; tel: (03) 9782 0383
Castlemaine, Vic 3450: 47 Kennedy St;
  tel: (03) 5470 5389
Chelsea, Vic 3196: 4 Swan Walk;
  tel: (03) 9773 1027
Colac, Vic 3250: 35 Corangamite St;
  tel: (03) 5231 1178
Cranbourne, Vic 3977: 1 New Holland Dr;
  tel: (03) 5991 1777
Darwin, Anula, NT 0812: Cnr Lee Point Rd and
  Yanyula Dr; tel: (08) 8927 9566
Doncaster, Vic 3109: 37 Taunton Street;
  tel: (03) 9842 4744
Doveton, Vic 3177: 1A Frawley Rd;
  tel: (03) 9793 3933
Echuca, Vic 3564: 50-52 Sturt St;
  tel: (03) 5482 6722
Ellenbrook, WA 6069: Cnr Highpoint and
  Woodlake Blvds; tel: (08) 9296 7172
Ferntree Gully, Vic 3156: 37 Wattletree Rd;
  tel: (03) 9752 3604
Frankston, Vic 3200: 15 Forest Dr;
  tel: (03) 9776 9155
Geelong, Vic 3220: 26-28 Bellerine St;
  tel: (03) 5223 2434
Geraldton, WA 6530: 42 Ainsworth St;
  tel: (08) 9965 2467
Glenroy, Vic 3046: 2 Finchley Ave;
  tel: (03) 9300 4099
Greensborough, Vic 3088: 2 Flodden Way;
  tel: (03) 9434 6990
Healesville, Vic 3777: 114 Maroondah Hwy;
  tel: (03) 5962 2486
Heathridge, WA 6027: 36 Christmas Ave;
  tel: (08) 9401 3408
Hobart, Tas 7000: 250 Liverpool St;
  tel: (03) 6231 1345
Horsham, Vic 3400: Cnr Kalkee Rd and
  Lynott St; tel: (03) 5382 1770
Ingle Farm, SA 5098: Cnr Bridge and Maxwell
  Rds; tel: (08) 8264 4166

Kalgoorlie/Boulder, WA 6430: Oberthur St;
  tel: (08) 9021 2255
Karratha, WA 6714: 2 Bond Pl;
  tel: (08) 9185 2148
Keilor, Vic 3037: 2a Roseleigh Boulevard;
  tel: (03) 9390 6111
Kwinana, WA 6167: Cnr Medina Ave and Hoyle
  Rd; tel: (08) 9439 1585
Kyabram, Vic 3620: 24 Unitt St;
  tel: (03) 5853 2684
Launceston, Tas 7250: 7 Cameron St;
  tel: (03) 6334 2950
Leongatha, Vic 3953: 52 Anderson St;
  tel: (03) 5662 4670
Marion, SA 5047: Cnr Sturt and Morpett Rd,
  Seacombe Gdns; tel: (08) 8377 0001
Mandurah, WA 6210: Lot 5 Lakes Rd;
  tel: (08) 9535 4951
Maryborough, Vic 3465: 58 High St;
  tel: (03) 5461 2789
Melbourne, Vic 3000: 69 Bourke St;
  tel: (03) 9653 3259
Merriwa, WA 6030: 26 Jenolan Way;
  tel: (08) 9305 2131
Mildura, Vic 3500: 1401-1415 Etiwanda Ave;
  tel: (03) 5021 2229
Moonee Ponds, Vic 3040: Cnr Mount
  Alexander Rd & Buckley St;
  tel: (03) 9375 3249
Mooroolbark, Vic 3138: 55 Manchester Rd;
  tel: (03) 9727 4777
Morley, WA 6062: 565 Walter Rd;
  tel: (08) 9279 4500
Mountain View, Vic 3154: 1 The Basin - Olinda
  Rd; tel: (03) 9762 3490
Mt Gambier, SA 5290: Cnr Gray and Wyatt Sts;
  tel: (08) 8725 9900
Narrogin, WA 6312: Doney St;
  tel: (08) 9881 4004
Noarlunga, Morphett Vale, SA 5162:
  186 Elizabeth St; tel: (08) 5382 1600
Northam, WA 6401: Wellington St;
  tel: (08) 9622 1228
Northbridge, WA 6003: Perth - 333 William St;
  tel: (08) 9328 1690
Norwood, SA 5067: 55 George St;
  tel: (08) 8332 0283
Oakleigh, Vic 3166: 50 Atherton Rd;
  tel: (03) 9563 0786
Pakenham, Vic 3810: 51 Bald Hill Rd;
  tel: (030 5941 4906
Palmerston, NT 0830: Cnr Temple Tce and
  Woodroffe Ave; tel: (08) 8932 2103
Playford, Elizabeth East, SA 5112: Cnr Kinkaid
  Rd and Aylwin St; tel: (08) 8255 8811
Plenty Valley, Vic 3075: Cnr Morang Dr and

Fred Hollows Way, Mill Park;
tel: (03) 9436 9200

Port Lincoln, SA 5606: 41 Marine Ave;
tel: (08) 8682 4296

Preston, Vic 3072: 263 Gower St;
tel: (03) 9471 9111

Ringwood, Vic 3134: 47 Wantirna Rd;
tel: (03) 9879 2894

Rivervale, WA 6103: Cnr Norwood Rd and
Francisco St; tel: (08) 9355 2799

Rochester, Vic 3561: Cnr Elizabeth and Ramsay
Sts; tel: (03) 5484 1364

Rockingham, Cooloongup, WA 6168: Cnr Read
St and Willmot Dr; tel: (08) 9527 3460

Rosebud, Vic 3940: 2 Melaleuca Ave;
tel: (03) 5986 4206

Rowville, Vic 3178: Police Rd;
tel: (03) 9701 0491

Seymour, Vic 3660: Victoria St;
tel: (03) 5799 2583

Shepparton, Vic 3630: 43a Wyndham St;
tel (03) 5831 1551

St Arnaud, Vic 3478: 14 Queens Ave:
tel: (03) 5495 1385

Sunshine, Vic 3020: 34 Devonshire Rd;
tel: (03) 9312 4624

Swan Hill, Vic 3585: 190 Beveridge St;
tel: (03) 5033 1718

Swan View, WA 6056: 371-379 Morrison Rd;
tel: (08) 9294 2811

Tea Tree Gully, Modbury, SA 5092:
138 Reservoir Rd; tel: (08) 8264 8729

Traralgon, Vic 3844:
Latrobe Valley Community Services Network,
Admin Office, 51-57 Post Office Pl;
tel: (03) 5174 1955
Moe, Vic 3825: 18-22 George St;
tel: (03) 5126 1683
Morwell, Vic 3840: 160 Commercial Rd;
tel: (03) 5133 9366
Traralgon, Vic 3844: 51-57 Post Office Pl;
tel: (03) 5174 7153

Wangaratta, Vic 3677: 13-17 Garnet Ave;
tel: (03) 5722 1129

Warragul, Vic 3820: 120 Burke St;
tel: (03) 5623 1090

Warrnambool, Vic 3280: Cnr Lava and
Henna Sts; tel: (03) 5561 6844

Waverley, Glen Waverley, Vic 3150: 958 High
Street Rd; tel: (03) 9803 2587

Werribee, Vic 3030: 1-3 Thames Blvd;
tel: (03) 9731 1344

Whyalla, Whyalla Norrie, SA 5608: 5-7 Viscount
Slim Ave; tel: (08) 8645 7101

Wodonga, Vic 3690: 210 Lawrence St;
tel: (03) 6024 2886

Wonthaggi, Vic 3995: McKenzie St;
tel: (03) 5672 1228

Family Tracing Service

Adelaide, Fullarton, SA 5063: 39 Florence St;
tel: (08) 8379 9388

Darwin, Anula, NT 0812: Cnr Lee Point Rd and
Yanyula Dr; tel: (08) 8927 6499

Hobart, New Town, Tas 7008: 27 Pirie St;
tel: (03) 6278 7184

Perth, Northbridge, WA 6003: 333 William St;
tel: (08) 9227 7010

Victoria and Inter-Territorial enquiries only:
Mont Albert, Vic 3127: 3-7 Hamilton St;
tel: (03) 9896 6000

Home and School Support Service

Broadford, Vic 3658: 25-27 Powlett St;
tel: (03) 5784 1635

Hostels for Homeless Men

Abbotsford, Vic 3067: Anchorage Hostel,
81 Victoria Cres; tel: (03) 9417 8520

Adelaide, SA 5000: Towards Independence,
277 Pirie St; tel: (08) 8223 4911 (acc 75)

Alice Springs, NT 0870: 11 Goyder St;
tel: (08) 8952 1434 (acc 27)

Darwin, NT 0820: Sunrise Centre, Lot 5344
Salonika St; tel: (08) 8981 4199 (acc 26)

Melbourne North, Vic 3051: The Open Door,
166 Boundary Rd; tel: (03) 9329 6988
(acc 45)

Melbourne West, Vic 3003: Flagstaff Crisis
Accommodation, 9 Roden St;
tel: (03) 9329 4800 (acc 64)

Perth, Mount Lawley, WA 6050: Tanderra
Hostel, 68 Guildford Rd;
tel: (08) 9271 1209 (acc 27)

Perth, WA 6000: Lentara, Cnr Short and Nash
Sts; tel: (08) 9328 3102 (acc 55)

St Kilda, Vic 3182: St Kilda Crisis
Accommodation Centre, 31 Grey St;
tel: (03) 9525 4473 (acc 20)

Hostels for Homeless Youth

Fitzroy, Vic 3065: 12 Tranmere St;
tel: (03) 9489 1122

Frankston, Vic 3199: 37 Rossmith Ave East;
tel: (03) 9784 5050 (4 houses)

Kalgoorlie/Boulder, WA 6430: 10 Park St;
tel: (08) 9091 1016 (acc 12)

Lansdale, WA 6065: Lansdale House,
460 Kingsway; tel: (08) 9302 1433 (acc 8)

Leongatha, Vic 3953: GippsCare Cross-target
Transitional Support, 51 McCartin St;
tel: (03) 5662 4502

Mirrabooka, WA 6061: Oasis House,
68-70 Honeywell Blvd; tel: (08) 9342 6785
(acc adolescents 8)

Pooraka, SA 5095: Muggy's, 88 Henderson Ave;
tel: (08) 8260 6617 (acc 10)

Salisbury, SA 5108: Burlendi, 22 Spains Rd;
tel: (08) 8281 6641 (acc 8)

Shepparton, Vic 3630: Brayton, 360 River Rd;
tel: (03) 5823 2277

St Kilda, Vic 3182: 27 Grey St;
tel: (03) 9536 7730

Hostels for Intellectually Disabled Persons

Manningham, SA 5086: Red Shield Housing
Network Services, 109 Hampstead Rd;
tel: (08) 8368 6800 (properties 310)

Social Housing – SASHS

Adelaide, Manningham, SA 5086: Red Shield
Housing Network Services, 109 Hampstead
Rd; tel: (08) 8368 6800

Box Hill, Vic 3128: 31-33 Ellingworth Pde;
tel: (03) 9890 7144

Geelong, Grovedale, Vic 3216: Barwon South
West Region, 142 Torquay Rd;
tel: (03) 5244 2500

Hawthorn, Vic 3122: EastCare Housing
Services, 16 Church St; tel: (03) 9851 7800

Hobart, Tas 7000: Red Shield Housing,
223 Macquarie St; tel: (03) 6223 8050

Kew, Vic 3101: EastCare Housing Services,
85 High St; tel: (03) 9851 7800

Leongatha, Vic 3953: Gippsland Region,
51a McCartin St; tel: (03) 5662 4538

Melbourne, Vic 3000: SACHS, 69 Bourke St;
tel: (03) 9653 3288

Newtown, Tas 7008: 117 Main Rd;
tel: (03) 6278 2817

Sunshine, Vic 3020: Western Metropolitan
Region, 27 Sun Cres; tel: (03) 9312 5424

Warragul, Vic 3820: 64 Queen St;
tel: (03) 5622 0351

Warrnambool, Vic 3280: 70 Henna St;
tel: (03) 5561 6844

Mobile Ministry

Karratha, WA 6714: 1 Nelson Court;
tel: (08) 9144 2895

Darwin, Jingili, NT 0810: 5 Murphy St (Flying
Padre); tel: (08) 8945 0176

Independent Units for Intellectually Handicapped Persons

Ottoway, SA 5013: Centennial Ct, 30-32 Edward
St; tel: (08) 8341 0413 (acc 18)

Men's Support Service

Medina, WA 6167: Cnr Hoyle Rd and Median
Ave; tel: (08) 9439 1585

Migrant and Refugee Services

Brunswick, Vic 3056: 12-14 Tinning St;
tel: (03) 9384 8334

Non-Residential Domestic Violence Programme

Adelaide, SA 5000: Central Violence Intervention
Project, 440 Morphett St; tel: (03) 8231 0655

Prison Chaplaincy, Police Court, Probation Work

Adelaide, Manningham, SA 5086:
109 Hampstead Rd; tel: (08) 8368 6800

Alice Springs, NT 0870: 88 Hartley St;
tel: (08) 8951 0200

Ballarat, Vic 3350: tel: (03) 0409 963 673

Bendigo, Vic 3552: Bramble St;
tel: (03) 5443 4288

Darwin, Anula, NT 0812: Cnr Lee Point Rd and
Yanula Dr; tel: (08) 8927 5189

Darwin, Stuart Park, NT 0820: Lot 5043
Salonika St; tel: (08) 8981 4199

Geelong, Vic 3220: Gordon St;
tel: (03) 5225 3353

Hobart, Tas 7000: Prison Support Service,
250 Liverpool St; tel: (03) 6234 1870

Horsham, Vic 3400: 12 Kalkee Rd;
tel: (03) 5382 1770

Manningham, SA 5086: 109 Hampstead Rd;
tel: (08) 8368 6800

Perth, Northbridge, WA 6003: 333 William St;
tel: (08) 9227 7010

Sale, Vic 3869: PO Box 45, Yinnar, Vic;
tel: (03) 5169 1503

Swan Hill, Vic 3583: 190 Beveridge St;
tel: (03) 5033 1718

Wangaratta, Vic 3677: 13-17 Garnet Ave;
tel: (03) 5722 1129

West Melbourne, Vic 3033: Senior Courts and
Prisons Chaplain, 9 Roden St;
tel: (03) 9329 6022

Wodonga, Vic 3690: PO Box 130, Beechworth,
Vic 3747; tel: (03) 5728 3245

Red Shield Hostels

Alice Springs, NT 0870: 11 Goyder St;
tel: (08) 8952 1434 (acc 27)

Darwin, NT 0800: 49 Mitchell St;
tel: (08) 8981 5994 (acc 64, 5 family units)

Rehabilitation Services

Abbotsford, Vic 3067: Detox Unit, 81 Victoria

Cres; tel: (03) 9495 6811

Adelaide, SA 5000: Central Violence Intervention Programme, 118 Wright St; tel: (08) 8231 0655

Adelaide, SA 5000:
Sobering Up Unit, 62A Whitmore Sq; tel: (08) 8212 2855 (acc 25)
Warrondi Stabilisation Unit, 146 Gilbert St; tel: (08) 8212 1215 (acc 22)

Bendigo, Vic 3550:
Northern Victoria Drug & Alcohol Coordinator, 65-67 Mundy St; tel (03) 5442 7931
Bendigo Bridge Community Outreach, 65-71 Mundy St; tel: (03) 5442 8558

Box Hill, Vic 3128: Aurora Women's Accommodation Service, 310 Elgar Rd; tel: (03) 9890 4549

Brunswick, Vic 3056: Outreach Service, 256 Albert St; tel: (03) 9387 6746

Corio, Vic 3214: Geelong Adult Withdrawal Unit; tel: (03) 5243 3364

Darwin, Stuart Park, NT 0820: Drug and Alcohol Services – Top End, Lot 5344, Salonika St; tel: (08) 8981 4199 (acc 26)

Geelong, Vic 3220: Geelong Bridge, Goldsworthy St; tel: (03) 5275 3500

Gosnells, WA 6110: Harry Hunter Adult Rehabilitation, 2498 Albany H'way; tel: (08) 9398 2077

Hawthorn, Vic 3122: Aurora Women's Accommodation Service, Drug and Alcohol Counselling Programme, 16 Church St; tel: (03) 9851 7800

Highgate, WA 6003: Bridge House, 15 Wright St; tel: (08) 9227 8086 (acc 27)

Hobart, Tas 7008: The Bridge Programme, Creek Rd; tel: (03) 6278 8140

Kew, Vic 3101: Drug and Alcohol Counselling Programme, 85 High St; tel: (03) 9851 7800

Kilmore, Vic 3664: Overdale Rural Residential Programme, 455 O'Grady's Rd; tel: (03) 5782 2744 (acc 10)

Preston, Vic 3072: Bridgehaven, 1a Jackman St; tel: (03) 9480 6488 (acc 15)

St Kilda, Vic 3182: The Bridge Centre, 12 Chapel St; tel: (03) 9521 2770

Swan Hill, Vic 3585: 190 Beveridge St; tel: (03) 5033 1718

The Basin, Vic 3154: New Hope Rehabilitation Centre, Basin-Olinda Rd; tel: (03) 9762 1166

Warrnambool, Vic 3280: 52-54 Fairy St; tel: (03) 5561 4453

Rural Outreach Worker

Eaglehawk, Vic 3556: 51 Church St; tel: (03) 5446 8135, mobile: 0429 337 408

Senior Citizens' Residences

Adelaide, SA 5000: Linsell Lodge, 430 Morphett St; tel: (08) 8231 4687 (acc hostel 53)

Clarence Park, SA 5034: Jean McBean Ct, 35 Mills St; tel: (08) 8231 4687 (acc units single 10, double 4)

Footscray, Vic 3011: James Barker House, 78 Ryan St; tel: (03) 9689 7211 (acc 45)

Fremantle North, WA 6159: Hillcrest, 23 Harvest Rd; tel: (08) 9335 9955 (acc hostel 49, nursing home 30, day care 30)

Geelong, Belmont, Vic 3216: Kardinia, 1 Riverview Tce; tel: (03) 5243 3364 (acc hostel 27, day care 12 with extended care)

Gosnells, WA 6110: Seaforth Gardens, 2542 Albany H'way; tel: (08) 9398 5228 (acc hostel 53, units 50)

Lenah Valley, Tas 7008: Macfarlane Ct, 16-22 Ratho St (acc units single 22, double 8)

New Town, Tas 7008: Barrington Lodge, 21 Tower Rd; tel: (03) 6228 2164 (acc res beds 10)

Soup Runs

Adelaide, SA 5000: 277 Pirie St (care of Adelaide Congress Hall; tel: (08) 8223 7776

Melbourne, Vic 3001: 69 Bourke St; tel: (03) 9653 3222

Perth, Northbridge, WA 6003: 333 William St; tel: (08) 9328 1690

Telephone Counselling Service

Perth, WA 6000: Salvo Care Line, Cnr Short and Nash Sts; tel: (08) 9227 8655

Women's Refuge Centres

Ballarat, Vic 3350: Karinya; tel: (03) 5329 1100 (mothers 8)

Darwin, NT 0801: Catherine Booth House, PO Box 189; tel: (08) 8981 5928 (acc 8)

Fullarton, SA 5063: Bramwell House, PO Box 305; tel: (08) 8379 7223 (acc 5 adults with children)

Geelong, Belmont, Vic 3216: Kardinia Women's Services; tel: (03) 5241 9149

Highgate, WA 6003: Byanda/Nunyara; tel: (08) 9328 8529 (acc 43)

Hobart, Tas 7000: McCombe House; tel: (03) 6243 5777 (acc 16)

Karratha, WA 6714: tel: (08) 9185 2807 (acc 16)

Richmond, Vic 3121: Mary Anderson Lodge, Refer Crossroads; tel: (03) 9353 1011

Youth and Family Services

Alice Springs, NT 0870: Towards Independence, 88 Hartley St; tel: (08) 8951 0203

NICOLE KIDMAN SUPPORTS THE 'SALVOS'

Stars Nicole Kidman and Hugh Jackman pause during the filming of Baz Luhrmann's new film *Australia* for a photo shoot to promote Australia's nationwide Red Shield Appeal. They are pictured with Captain Mervyn Dovey of Bowen Corps (North Queensland, Australia Eastern Territory).

Box Hill, Vic 3128:
Intensive Case Management Service, Specialist Consulting and Assessment Service, Children in Residential Care Education Support, Work and Recreation Programme with Education, Residential Youth Services, Leaving Care, 31-33 Ellingworth Pde; tel (03) 9890 7144
Box Hill, Vic 3128:
JJHIP (Juvenile Justice Housing Initiative Pathways); tel: (03) 9890 7144
Brunswick, Vic 3056: Creative Opportunities, 10-18 Tinning St; tel: (03) 9386 7611
Darwin, Anula, NT 0812: Towards Independence, Cnr Lee Point Rd and Yanula Dr; tel: (08) 8927 5189
Kew, Vic 3101: The Hawthorn Project, 85 High St; tel: (03) 9851 7800
Leongatha, Vic 3953: GippsCare Adolescent Community Placement, 51 McCartin St; tel: (03) 5662 4502
Melbourne, Vic 3000: Melbourne Counselling, 69 Bourke St; tel: (03) 9653 3250
Moonee Ponds, Vic 3039: Crosslink Employment Services, 33a Taylor St; tel: (03) 9372 0675
Mornington, Vic 3931:
Peninsula Home and Community-Based Care Services, Shop 9, 234 Main St; tel: (03) 5976 2231
Peninsula Adolescent Community Placement, Peninsula High Risk Adolescent Programme, Peninsula Special Support Unit, Peninsula Supported Independence, Reconnect

Programme, Shop 9, 234 Main St; tel: (03) 5976 2747
Northbridge, WA 6003: Crossroads West – Perth, 333 William St; tel: (08) 9328 1600
North Coburg, Vic 3058: Transitional Support, Independent Living Programmes (including Youth Services, Transitional Support Accommodation for Youth (TSAY), Anger Management, Reconnect), 2/828 Sydney Rd; tel: (03) 9353 1011
Salisbury, SA 5108: CHIPS Internet Cafe, 20B John St, Salisbury; tel: (08) 8285 9406
Shepparton, Vic 3630:
Brayton Young Activities Service, Brayton Young Offenders Pilot Programme, Strengthening Families and Sexual Abuse Prevention, 360 River Rd; tel: (03) 5823 2277
JPET, 360 River Rd; tel: (03) 5821 8144
Swan Hill, Vic 3585: Y-Space, 5 Campbell St; tel: (03) 5033 1411

Youth Centres for Homeless Unemployed

Mornington, Vic 3931:
Peninsula JPET, Shop 8, 234 Main St; tel: (03) 5976 5500
Burnt Toast Cyber Cafe, Shop 7, 234 Main St; tel: (03) 5976 5500
North Coburg, Vic 3058: 2/828 Sydney Rd; tel: (03) 9353 1011
St Kilda, Vic 3182: Crisis Centre, 29 Grey St; tel: (03) 9536 7777
Wonthaggi, Vic 3995: GippsCare Cyber Café Net, 59 McBride Ave; tel: (03) 5672 5506

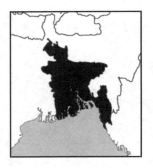

BANGLADESH COMMAND

Officer Commanding:
Lieut-Colonel Ethne Flintoff (1 Jul 2002)

General Secretary:
Major Joginder Masih (1 Sep 2005)

Command Headquarters: House 96, Road 23, Banani, Dhaka

Postal address: GPO Box 985, Dhaka 1000, Bangladesh

Tel: [880] (2) 9882836/7; fax: [880] (2) 8823568

Work in Bangladesh began immediately after the Liberation War with Pakistan in 1971. Thousands of people moved from refugee camps in Calcutta, where Salvationists had served them, and a team of Salvationists accompanied them. A year earlier, relief operations had been carried out by The Salvation Army in East Pakistan (later Bangladesh) following a severe cyclone. On 21 April 1980, The Salvation Army was incorporated under the Companies Act of 1913. Bangladesh was upgraded to command status on 1 January 1997.

Zone: South Asia
Country included in the command: Bangladesh
'The Salvation Army' in Bengali: Tran Sena
Languages in which the gospel is preached: Bengali, English

IN The Salvation Army's 35th year of operations in Bangladesh, the command continued its focus on Youth Capacity Development (YCD). Following a YCD seminar a corps officer was appointed as part-time YCD Coordinator, later becoming the first national officer as Command Youth and Candidates Officer.

A planned 35-year celebration was cancelled due to political unrest; however, the commissioning of 14 new officers took place and was a joyous occasion.

The command conducted its first organisational review to focus on mission. Questionnaires completed by officers, employees, volunteers and soldiers, along with interviews, gave insights for the consultants to consider and formed the basis of the 'Review and Strategic Planning' process. The command is now working on a five-year strategic action plan to achieve its purposes. These are:

Vision – All peoples united in Christ, acting justly, loving mercy and walking humbly with God.

Mission – To live and share the gospel, to disciple believers, and to address human need without discrimination.

Strategy – Engage with the whole person in community towards fullness of life.

Another first was a Mission Team visit by women officers from Canada. Their women's leadership seminars were a source of much encouragement.

A team visited Kolkata, India, to inspect programmes among trafficked women and children. Networking contacts were made, and discussions with like-minded Christian organisations back in Bangladesh resulted in a networking group being formed.

STATISTICS

Officers active 78 **Cadets** (1st Yr) 8
Employees 290
Corps 30 **Outposts** 17 **Institution** 1 **Schools** 14
Clinics 9 **HIV/Aids Counselling Centres** 2
Senior Soldiers 1,534 **Adherents** 642 **Junior Soldiers** 178

STAFF

Director of Finance: Mrs Sarah Biswas
Information Technology Development:
Mr Palash (Paul) Baidya
Projects: Capt Elizabeth Nelson
Training :
Women's Ministries: Lt-Col Ethne Flintoff
(CPWM) Maj Shanti Masih (CSWM)
Youth and Candidates: Capt Stephen Baroi

DISTRICTS

South Western: PO Box 3, By-Pass Rd,
Karbala, Jessore 7400; tel: (0421) 68759;
Capt Ganendro Baroi
Dhaka: Hse 96, Rd 23, Banani, Dhaka 1213;
tel: (0171) 1546012; Capt Alfred Mir

TRAINING COLLEGE

Genda, Savar, Dhaka; tel: (02) 7712614

COMMUNITY WORK

HIV/Aids Counselling Centres: Jessore, Old
Dhaka
Micro-Credit Projects: Dhaka Mirpur, Jessore,
Khulna
Income-generating Cooperatives: Jessore, Khulna

EDUCATIONAL WORK

Adult Education: Jessore, Khulna
Schools for the Hearing Impaired: Dhaka
(acc 30); Jessore (acc 30)
Primary Schools: (pupils 2,053)
Jessore: Arenda, Bagdanga, Fatepur, Ghurulia,
Kholadanga, Konejpur, Ramnagar,
Sitarampur, Suro
Khulna: Andulia, Komrail, Krisnanagar
Gopalgonj: Rajapur
**Integrated Education for Sighted and Visually
Impaired:** Savar (pupils 154)
Vocational Training: Dhaka, Jessore,
Khulna

MEDICAL AND DEVELOPMENT WORK

**Urban Health and Development Project
(UHDP):**
Mirpur Clinic, Dhaka, with Leprosy and
TB Control Programmes
**Community Health and Development Projects
(CHDP):**
Jessore: New Town and Kholadanga Clinics,
with Leprosy and TB Control Programmes
Village Clinics: Fatepur, Ghurulia, Konejpur,
Ramnagar, Sitarampur and mobile clinic to
five villages
Khulna: Andulia Clinic

SOCIAL WORK

Integrated Children's Centre (Sishu Niloy),
Savar (acc 48)

FAIR TRADE PROGRAMME

Sally Ann Bangladesh Ltd
email: sallyann@ban.salvationarmy.com
web site: www.sallyann.com
Manager: Greg Warkentin
Chair of Board: Maj Joginder Masih
Shop: House 96, Road 23, Banani, Dhaka;
Satu Barua (shop manager)
Employees 25
Production units: 13
Knitting Factory: Genda, Savar, Dhaka
(staff 6, trainees 20)

❛ Vision – All peoples united in Christ . . . Mission – To live and share the gospel, to disciple believers, and to address human need without discrimination **❜**

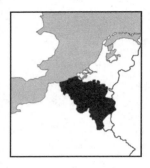

BELGIUM COMMAND

Command leaders:
Majors Christian and Joëlle Exbrayat

Officer Commanding:
Major Christian Exbrayat (1 Aug 2003)

General Secretary:
Major Noélie Lecocq (1 Aug 1999)

Command Headquarters: Place du Nouveau Marché aux Grains, 34, 1000 Brussels, Belgium

Tel: [32] (02) 513 39 04; fax: [32] (02) 513 81 49

web sites: www.armeedusalut.be; www.legerdesheils.be

Salvation Army operations, which were pioneered on 5 May 1889 by Adjutant and Mrs Charles Rankin and Captains Velleema and Hass, are now carried out among both French and Flemish-speaking people. Legal recognition was granted by Act 1007 on 8 December 1930.

Zone: Europe
Country included in the command: Belgium
'The Salvation Army' in French: Armée du Salut; in Flemish: Leger des Heils
Languages in which the gospel is preached: Flemish, French
Periodicals: *Espoir* (French), *Strijdkreet* (Flemish)

DURING a wonderful National Congress weekend in Brussels, 25 people made spiritual decisions at the mercy seat. United musicians headed Sunday's march before all the congress participants, some 200 in total, held an open-air meeting.

The congress leader was Colonel Robert Redhead, from Canada, and a highlight of the event was a mini-musical that had been prepared during a youth camp.

Earlier in the year Commissioners Alex and Ingeborg Hughes (United Kingdom Territory) conducted officers' councils; they were a source of blessing and encouragement.

There is a lack of officers in the command, but for many years two retired officers (now in their 70s) have continued to give active oversight of two corps; and a former officer who resigned his commission some years ago has returned to The Salvation Army and is now in charge of a corps.

Three young people have followed a training course to be registered as youth workers.

As an initiative at Easter, the officers in two corps took children from door to door distributing small plants – a symbol of life – together with Bible texts. Home leagues are progressing well in corps, particularly Brussels Central where more than 40 women meet each week.

Belgium Command

The social services establishments continue to provide satisfaction, especially in the mother and baby home where its Salvationist director brings human warmth and Christian care to the residents. The 'Foyer Selah' centre is a welcoming home for more than 90 refugees from several countries.

In the face of adversity the command's Salvationists are maintaining an optimistic spirit: 'With God, the mission continues!'

STATISTICS
Officers 28 (active 16 retired 12) **Auxiliary-Captain** 1 **Lieutenants** 2 **Employees** 74
Corps 10 **Institutions** 7 **Stores** 3 **Youth Centre** 1
Senior Soldiers 242 **Adherents** 113 **Junior Soldiers** 55

STAFF
Editor: Maj Christian Exbrayat
Family Tracing: Esther Tesc
Finance: Maj Patrick Naud, Capt Marc Dawans
Personnel: Maj Noélie Lecocq
Property: Maj Noélie Lecocq
Public Relations: Maj Patrick Naud
Social: Maj Noélie Lecocq
Women's Ministries: Maj Joëlle Exbrayat (CPWM)
Youth and Candidates: Maj Anne Dore Naud

SOCIAL SERVICES
Hostels for Men
Home Georges Motte, Bd d'Ypres 24, 1000 Brussels; tel: (02) 217 61 36 (acc 75)
'Le Foyer', Centre d'accueil, rue Bodeghem 27-29, 1000 Brussels; tel: (02) 512 17 92 (acc 70)

Family Aid (food, counselling)
Bd d'Ypres 26, 1000 Brussels; tel: (02) 223 10 44

Guidance Centre (Housing help and Recovery Dept)
102 rue de l'église ste Anne, 1180 Brussels; tel: (02) 414 19 16

Refugee Centre
'Foyer Selah', Bld d'Ypres 28, 1000 Brussels; tel: (02) 219 01 77 (acc 90)

Mothers' and Children's Home
Chaussée de Drogenbos 225, 1180 Brussels; tel: (02) 376 17 01 (acc mothers 14, children 25)

Children's Home
'Clair Matin', rue des Trois Rois 88, 1180 Uccle-Brussels; tel: (02) 376 17 40 (acc 41)

SHOPS
Antwerp: Ballaerstraat 94, 2018 Antwerpen
Brussels: bld d'Ypres 24, 1000 Brussels
Courcelles: rue Général de Gaulle 145, 6180 Courcelles
Liège: 6 Quai Bonaparte, 4000 Liège

YOUTH AND CONFERENCE CENTRE
Villa Meyerbeer, route de Barisart 256, 4900 Spa; tel: (087) 77 49 00

During a women's camp at Spa Conference Centre, Major Joëlle Exbray (CPWM) greets the arrival of two huge '100th birthday' cakes baked to celebrate the centenary of the Home League

BRAZIL TERRITORY

Territorial leaders:
Commissioners Peder and Janet Refstie

Territorial Commander:
Commissioner Peder Refstie (1 Dec 2006)

Chief Secretary:
Lieut-Colonel Torben Eliasen (1 Jul 2001)

**Territorial Headquarters: Rua Juá 264 - Bosque da Saúde,
04138-020 São Paulo-SP**

**Postal address: Exército de Salvação; Caixa Postal 46036, Agência Saúde
04045-970 São Paulo-SP, Brazil**

Tel: [55] (011) 5591 7070; fax: [55] (011) 5591 7075; email: exercitodesalvacao@salvos.org.br;

web site: www.exercitodesalvacao.org.br

Pioneer officers Lieut-Colonel and Mrs David Miche unfurled the Army flag in Rio de Janeiro on 1 August 1922. The Salvation Army operates as a national religious entity, Exército de Salvação, having been so registered by Presidential Decree 90.568 of 27 November 1984. All its social activities have been incorporated in APROSES (Assistência e Promoção Social Exército de Salvação) since 1974 and have had Federal Public Utility since 18 February 1991.

Zone: Americas and Caribbean
Country included in the territory: Brazil
'The Salvation Army' in Portuguese: Exército de Salvação
Language in which the gospel is preached: Portuguese
Periodicals: *O Oficial (The Officer)*, *Rumo*, *Women's Ministries Annual Magazine*

'GROWING in Relationships' – the theme set for 2007 in the territory's strategic plan – was highlighted in many different contexts. The basic message has been the need for God's people to develop good relationships within families, corps and communities.

For many Salvationists the building of relationships with neighbours and in local communities became an important vehicle for conveying the gospel.

Building good relationships was also an important theme during the conference for leaders of Salvation Army social centres, held at Suzano Conference Centre. New legislation and ever more stringent regulations imposed by the civil authorities are providing the Army's social services with many challenges.

At the same time the excellent and dedicated work done by officers and employees in many places is being recognised by the authorities and local communities.

An accentuated fall in the value of the US dollar coinciding with a steady rise in the value of the Brazilian real caused serious financial difficulties in the territory. The value of grants and sponsorship monies has more than halved, forcing the territory to economise on all fronts and maximise fully the use of all available funds.

The positive side is that this situation is forcing the territory to double its efforts to achieve a higher degree of financial independence.

'Salvashopping' – a recycling business launched six years ago – has experienced continuous growth and is now an important source of income. It sustains much of the Army's social work in addition to being a service much appreciated by many clients.

The most important part of building God's Kingdom in Brazil is the work done week by week in corps, outposts and social centres across the territory.

The young people's enthusiastic testifying and singing, the sharing of God's Word and the consistent teaching given to children and young people from the streets and the many *favelas* (shanty towns) bear fruit in lives being changed. Hope and faith are replacing the hopelessness of poverty and difficult circumstances.

After many years of highly influential leadership on numerous levels in the territory, Commissioners Paulo and Yoshika Rangel handed over the reins of leadership to new leaders, Commissioner Peder and Janet Refstie. The Rangels' retirement ceremony was conducted by Commissioner William Francis (then International Secretary for the Americas and Caribbean).

STATISTICS

Officers 170 (active 138 retired 32) **Cadets** (2nd Yr) 7 **Employees** 231
Corps 47 **Outposts** 7 **Social Institutions** 32
Senior Soldiers 1,755 **Adherents** 123 **Junior Soldiers** 567
Personnel serving outside territory Officers 2

STAFF

Personnel: Lt-Col Deise Eliasen
Candidates: Maj Nara Strasse
Editor-in-Chief/Communications: Maj Paulo Soares
Education: Lt-Col Deise Eliasen
Finance: Maj Joan Burton
Legal/Property: Maj Giani Azevedo
Music: Maj Paulo Soares
National Band: B/M João Carlos Cavalheiro
National Songsters: S/L Vera Sales
Social: Mrs Marilene Oliveira
Training: Maj Wilson Strasse
Women's Ministries: Comr Janet Refstie (TPWM) Maj Iolanda Camargo (TSWM, ORRO/FT)
Youth: Lt-Col Deise Eliasen (responsible)

DIVISIONS

North East: Rua Rua Carlos Gomes, 1016, 50710-310 Recife, PE; tel/fax: (81) 3227-7513; email: regional.ne@salvos.org.br; Maj Maruilson Souza
Paraná and Santa Catarina: Rua Mamoré 1191, 80810-080 Curitiba, PR; tel/fax: (041) 3336-8624; email: regional.pr@salvos.org.br; Maj Verônica Jung
Rio de Janeiro and Minas Gerais and Centre West: Rua Visconde de Santa Isabel no 20, salas 712/713, 20560-120, Rio de Janeiro, RJ; tel/fax: (21) 3879-5594; email: regional.rj@salvos.org.br; Maj Edgar Chagas
Rio Grande do Sul: Rua Machado de Assis 255, 97050-450, Santa Maria, RS; tel/fax: (55) 3026-1935; email: regional.rs@salvos.org.br; Lt-Col Tomas de Sá
São Paulo: Rua Taguá 209, Liberdade 01508-010, São Paulo-SP; tel/fax: (11) 3207-3402; email: regional.sp@salvos.org.br; Maj Márcio Mendes

TRAINING COLLEGE

Rua Juá 264, Bosque da Saúde, 04138-020, São Paulo-SP; tel: (11) 5071-5041

Young Salvationists in Brazil are enthusiastic in testifying, singing and the sharing of God's Word. Here, prayer is offered for a family during a street meeting.

SOCIAL WORK
Children's Homes and Day Centres

Arco Verde: 'Maria Felisbina de Souza' Home, Av Antonio Pires 1790, 35715-000, Prudente de Moraes-MG; tel: (31) 3711-1370 (acc 50)

Joinville: 'João de Paula', Rua 15 de Novembro 3165, 89216-201, Joinville-SC; tel: (47) 453-0588 (acc 50)

Paranaguá: 'Honorina Valente', Rua Manoel Jordão Cavalheiro s/no, 83200-000, Paranaguá-PR; tel: (41) 423-6115 (acc 36)

Pelotas: Av Fernando Osório, 6745, 96065-000, Pelotas-RS; tel: (53) 273-6909 (acc 30)

Rio de Janeiro: Méier, Rua Garcia Redondo 103, 20775-170, Rio de Janeiro-RJ; tel: (21) 2595-5694 (acc 50)

Suzano: 'Lar das Flores', Rua Gal. Francisco Glicério 3048, 08665-000, Suzano-SP; tel: (11) 4747-1098 (acc 30)

Uruguaiana: Rua Gal. Câmara 1403, 97500-281, Uruguaiana-RS; tel: (55) 3412-4930 (acc 50)

Clinics (medical and dental)

Porto Alegre: 'Dr Leopoldo Rössler', Av São Pedro 1116, 90230-123, Porto Alegre-RS; tel: (51) 3342-4170

Suzano: 'Lar das Flores', Rua Gal. Francisco Glicério 3048, 08665-000, Suzano-SP; tel: (11) 4747-1098

Community Centres

*Cubatão: 'Vila dos Pescadores', Rua Amaral Neto 211, 11531-070, Cubatão-SP; tel: (13) 3363-2111

*Curitiba: Rua Manoel de Abreu 247, 80215-060, Curitiba-PR; tel: (41) 363-1537

Guarulhos: Rua NS Aparecida 10, 07111-190, Guarulhos-SP; tel: (11) 6409-1500

*Itaquaquecetuba: Rua Antônio Fugas 190, 08572-730, Itaquaquecetuba-SP; tel: (11) 4640-4304

*Recife: 'Centro Comunitário Integração', Rua Conde de Irajá, 108/135, 50710-310, Recife-PE; tel: (81) 3228-4740

*Rio de Janeiro: 'Nova Divinéia', Rua Bambuí 36, 20561-210, Rio de Janeiro-RJ; tel: (21) 2298-2574

* *These centres have programmes for children at risk*

Crèches and Kindergartens

Carmo do Rio Claro: 'Recanto da Alegria', Rua Luiz Amélio Freire 260, 37150-000, Carmo do Rio Claro-MG; tel: (35) 3561-2175 (acc 100)

Cubatão: 'Recanto dos Sirizinhos', Rua Amaral Neto 211, 11531-070, Cubatão-SP; tel: (13) 3363-2111 (acc 300)

Guarulhos: Rua NS Aparecida 10, 07111-190, Guarulhos-SP; tel: (11) 6409-1500 (acc 50)

Recife: 'Centro Comunitário Integração', Rua Conde de Irajá 108, 50710-310, Recife-PE; tel: (81) 3228-4740 (acc 420)

São Gonçalo: 'Arca de Noé', Rua Rodrigues da Fonseca 315, 24.610-000, São Gonçalo-RJ; tel: (21) 2604-9821 (acc 150)

São Paulo: 'Ranchinho do Senhor', Rua Bertioga 470/480, 04141-100, São Paulo-SP; tel: (11) 5589-4609 (acc 60)

Suzano: 'NUDI - Lar das Flores', Rua Gal. Francisco Glicério, 3048, 08665-000, Suzano-SP; tel: (11) 4747-1098 (acc 160)

Centres for Street Children

Curitiba: Rua Bartolomeu Lourenço de Gusmão 5167, 81730-040, Curitiba-PR; tel: (41) 286-3662 (acc 11)

São Paulo: Rua Taguá 209, Liberdade, 01508-010, São Paulo-SP; tel: (11) 3275-0644 (acc 50)

Brazil Territory

São Paulo: Rua Diogo Vaz 248, Cambuci,
01527-020, São Paulo-SP; tel: (11) 3271-8511
(acc 10)

Mother and Baby Home
São Paulo: Rancho do Senhor, Rua Caramurú 931,
04138-020, São Paulo-SP; tel: (11) 275-4487
(acc mothers 25, babies 18)

Old People's Home
Campos do Jordão: Lar do Outono, Rua João
Rodrigues Pinheiro 335, 12460-000, Campos
do Jordão-SP; tel: (12) 262-2154 (acc 24)

Prison Work
Piraí do Sul and Carmo do Rio Claro

Social Services Centres
Santa Maria: Rua Jerônimo Gomes 74, 97001-
970, Santa Maria-RS; tel: (55) 3221-8922

São Paulo: Rua Taguá 209, 01508-010, São
Paulo-SP; tel: (11) 3209-5830

Students' Residences
Brasília: Av L2 Sul, 610B Mod 69, 70259-970,
Brasília-DF; tel: (61) 443-3332 (acc 20)
Santa Maria: Rua Jerônimo Gomes, 74,
97050-350, Santa Maria-RS;
tel: (55) 3222-1935 (acc 26)

Territorial Camp
Suzano: Rua Manuel Casanova 1061, 08664-
000, Suzano-SP; tel: (11) 4476-3843

Thrift Stores
São Paulo:
Salvashopping I, Av Santa Catarina 1781,
04146-020, São Paulo-SP; tel: (11) 5563-1442
Salvashopping II: Av Cupecê 3254,
04366-000, São Paulo-SP;
tel: (11) 5563-9937

AN ENTHUSIASTIC AND GROWING ARMY

Kenya Territory: Enthusiastic Salvationists in Lokitaung, Turkana, welcome the Territorial Leader of Women's Ministries, Lieut-Colonel Jolene Hodder, to their corps. In a single year the territory has established a new division, five new districts, 26 corps and 78 outposts.

CANADA AND BERMUDA TERRITORY

Territorial leaders:
Commissioners William W. and Marilyn D. Francis

Territorial Commander:
Commissioner William W. Francis (1 Jul 2007)

Chief Secretary:
Colonel Glen Shepherd (22 Jun 2003)

Territorial Headquarters: 2 Overlea Blvd, Toronto, Ontario M4H 1P4, Canada

Tel: [1] (416) 425-2111; fax: [1] (416) 422-6201;

web sites: www.salvationarmy.ca; www.salvationist.ca; www.SendTheFire.ca

There are newspaper reports of organised Salvation Army activity in Toronto, Ontario, in January 1882, and five months later the Army was reported holding meetings in London, Ontario. On 15 July the same year, Major Thomas Moore, sent from USA headquarters, established official operations. In 1884 Canada became a separate command. The League of Mercy originated in Canada in 1892. An Act to incorporate the Governing Council of The Salvation Army in Canada received Royal Assent on 19 May 1909.

The work in Newfoundland was begun on 1 February 1886 by Divisional Officer Arthur Young. On 12 January 1896 Adjutant (later Colonel) Lutie Desbrisay and two assistant officers unfurled the flag in Bermuda.

Zone: Americas and Caribbean
Countries included in the territory: Bermuda, Canada
Languages in which the gospel is preached: Creole, English, French, Indian languages (Gitxsan, Nisga'a, Tsimshian), Korean, Lao, Portuguese, Spanish, Thai
Periodicals: *Edge for Kids*, *En Avant*, *Faith & Friends*, *Foi & Vie*, *Salvationist*

THE territory marked a significant milestone in its history on 1 May 2006 with the opening of a new college for officer training in Winnipeg. The ceremony was the culmination of years of planning that saw the closure of colleges in Toronto and St John's, Newfoundland. The new facility is in the same building as the new John Fairbank Memorial Library, shared with students of nearby William and Catherine Booth College.

The opening was held in conjunction with Booth College's annual graduation weekend, with special guest Commissioner Hasse Kjellgren (then Territorial Commander, Sweden and Latvia). A total of 60 students made it the largest graduating class in the college's history.

Salvationists from the Pacific Northwest Region met in Prince

Rupert, British Columbia, for the Great Pacific Congress (19-21 May) under the theme 'Where the Nations Gather'. Events centred on community, God's calling and covenant. Nine First Nations auxiliary-captains were promoted to substative rank when ordained and commissioned as captains.

Thousands found their way to St John's for the 120th Newfoundland and Labrador provincial congress (23-25 June). Excitement filled the air from the opening event through to the closing salvation meeting. Participants were not disappointed as God's presence brought fresh renewal, deep commitment and, for some, the start of a new life in Christ.

Events included the official closing of the St John's College for Officer Training and the ordination and commissioning of new officers from the Visionaries Session, the last cadets to be trained on the island.

It was an emotional weekend for many, yet filled with hope for the new direction God is taking The Salvation Army in this part of the territory.

During the weekend of 30 June-2 July, simultaneous events brought together Salvationists from across the territory. At Jackson's Point, Ontario, delegates to SAROOTS considered the theme 'Metamorphoses – From Glory to Glory' and were challenged to consider how Christ's resurrection can radically transform lives.

Salvationists also met in Red Deer, Alberta, for Forward '06, with guest leaders Retired General John Gowans and Commissioner Gisèle Gowans.

In September, former Staff Bandmaster Brian Burditt returned to lead the Canadian Staff Band, embarking on a year of ministry that included the band's second visit to southern California in January 2007.

A new initiative at Yorkminster Citadel, Toronto, came with the launch of a community choir to reach people beyond its doors. Members were thrilled to participate as part of the massed chorus for the annual 'Christmas With The Salvation Army' concert.

Straddling the Army of yesterday, today and tomorrow, the 2006 Bermuda Congress (27-29 October) was definitely 'outside the box'. Meetings were marked by inspirational and joyous singing, unique dance and drama presentations and meaningful testimonies. Many people responded to the stirring Bible messages by kneeling at the mercy seat.

An announcement was made in January 2007 that the historic Montreal Citadel had been sold to Alcan Inc, who will redevelop the site to expand its headquarters. It marked the end of an era, with the corps being relocated as part of a strategic plan to redevelop Salvation Army ministries in Quebec.

In March, delegates came together for a conference on rural ministries titled 'Strengthening the Fields for Harvest'. It was the initial step in deploying new strategies to enhance small-town ministry throughout the territory.

April saw the first official visit to

the territory of General Shaw Clifton and Commissioner Helen Clifton. Inspiring Salvationists in Toronto and Winnipeg, the international leaders also took part in events celebrating the 25th anniversary of William and Catherine Booth College and The Salvation Army's 125th anniversary in Canada.

STATISTICS

Officers 1,863 (active 948 retired 915) **Cadets** (1st Yr) 23 (2nd Yr) 9 **Employees** 8,345

Corps 321 **Outposts** 10 **Institutions** 113 **Bible College** 1

Senior Soldiers 20,935 **Adherents** 51,546 **Junior Soldiers** 3,988

Personnel serving outside territory Officers 38 Layworkers 4

STAFF

Personnel: Maj Jean Moulton

Programme: Lt-Col David Hiscock

Business: Maj Neil Watt

Asst Chief Sec: Maj James Champ

Corps Ministries: Maj Floyd Tidd

Editor-in-Chief and Literary Sec: Lt-Col Raymond Moulton

Finance: Mr Paul Goodyear

Information Technology: Mr Robert Plummer

National Recycling Operations: Mr John Kershaw

Property: Maj Pearce Samson

Public Relations and Development: Mr Graham Moore

Social: Mrs Mary Ellen Eberlin

Training: Maj Sandra Rice (Winnipeg)

WCBC Bible College: Dr Donald Burke

Women's Ministries: Comr Marilyn Francis (TPWM) Col Eleanor Shepherd (TSWM)

DIVISIONS

Bermuda: PO Box HM 2259, 10 North St, Hamilton, HM JX Bermuda; tel: (441) 292-0601; fax: (441) 295-3765; Maj Douglas Lewis

British Columbia: 103-3833 Henning Dr, Burnaby, BC V5C 6N5; tel: (604) 299-3908; fax: (604) 299-7463; Maj William Blackman

Manitoba and Northwest Ontario: 203-290 Vaughan St, Winnipeg, MB R3B 2N8; tel: (204) 946-9101; fax: (204) 975-1010; Maj Susan van Duinen

Maritime: Metropolitan Pl, 99 Wyse Rd, Suite 1420, PO Box 54, Dartmouth, NS B3A 4S5; tel: (902) 455-1201; fax: (902) 453-2192; Maj Larry Martin

Newfoundland and Labrador East: 21 Adams Ave, St John's, NF A1C 4Z1; tel: (709) 579-2022/3; fax: (709) 576-7034; Maj Raymond Rowe

Newfoundland and Labrador West: 157 Airport Blvd, Gander, NF A1V 1K6; tel: (709) 256-6088/7135; fax: (709) 256-7955; Maj Junior Hynes

Ontario Central-East: 1645 Warden Ave, Scarborough, ON M1R 5B3; tel: (416) 321-2654; fax: (416) 321-8136; Lt-Col Donald Copple

Ontario Great Lakes: 371 King St, London, ON N6B 1S4; tel: (519) 433-6106; fax: (519) 433-0250; Maj Alfred Richardson

Ontario North: 76 Coldwater St E, Orillia, ON L3V 1W5; tel: (705) 325-4416; fax: (705) 325-4667; Maj Brenda Holnbeck

Prairie: 9618 101A Ave NW, Edmonton, AB T5H OC7; tel: (780) 423-2111; fax: (780) 425-9081; Maj Eric Bond

Quebec: 1655 Richardson St, Montreal, QC H3K 3J7; tel: (514) 288-2848; fax: (514) 288-4657; Maj Kester Trim

COLLEGE FOR OFFICER TRAINING

Winnipeg Campus: 100-290 Vaughan St, Winnipeg, MB R3B 2N8; tel: (204) 924-5606

EDUCATION

The William and Catherine Booth College, 447 Webb Pl, Winnipeg, MB R3B 2P2; tel: (204) 947-6701/6950; fax: (204) 942-3856; President: Dr Donald Burke (acc 104)

ETHICS CENTRE

203-290 Vaughan St, Winnipeg, MB R3B 2N8; tel: (204) 924-5627; fax: (204) 957-2418; email: ethics.centre@can.salvationarmy.org; Dr James Read

SALVATION ARMY ARCHIVES

Archives: 26 Howden Rd, Scarborough, ON M4H 1P4

Museum: 2 Overlea Blvd, Toronto, ON M4H 1P4; tel: (416) 285-4344; fax: (416) 285-7763; Col John Carew

NATIONAL RECYCLING OPERATIONS

2 Overlea Blvd, Toronto, ON M4H 1P4; tel: (416) 425-2111; fax: (416) 422-6167

Atlantic Region: 2 Overlea Blvd, Toronto, ON
M4H 1P4; tel: (416) 425-2111;
fax: (416) 422-6167

Montreal Region: 1620 Notre Dame W,
Montreal, QC H3J 1M1; tel: (516) 935-7128;
fax:514-935-6093

Ontario Central and Southwestern Region:
2360 South Service Rd W, Oakville, ON
L6L 5M9; tel: (905) 825-9208;
fax: (905) 825-9182

Prairies Region: 1-111 Inksbrook Dr,
Winnipeg, MB R2R 2V7; tel: (204)-954-1504;
fax: (204)-953-1505

Western Canada Region: 2520 Davies Ave,
Port Coquitlam, BC V3C 4T7;
tel: (604) 944-8747; fax: (604) 944-3158

SOCIAL SERVICES (UNDER THQ)
Hospitals (public)
Rehabilitation
Montreal, QC H4B 2J5, Catherine Booth
Hospital, 4375 Montclair Ave

General (B Class)
Scarborough, ON M1W 3W3, Scarborough
Hospital, 3030 Birchmount Rd;
tel: (416) 495-2400

Windsor, ON N9A 1E1, Hotel-Dieu Grace
Hospital, 1030 Ouellette Ave;
tel: (519) 973-4444

Winnipeg, MB R3J 3M7, Grace General
Hospital, 300 Booth Dr; tel: (204) 837-8311

Complex Continuing Care
Toronto, ON M4Y 2G5, Toronto Grace Health
Centre, 650 Church St; tel: (416) 925-2251

Family Tracing Services
2 Overlea Blvd, Toronto, ON M4H 1P4;
tel: (416) 422-6291; fax: (416) 422-6221

SOCIAL SERVICES (UNDER DIVISIONS)
Hospice
Calgary, AB T2N 1B8, Agape Hospice, 1302
8 Ave NW; tel: (403) 282-6588 (acc 20)

Regina, SK S4R 8P6, Wascana Grace Hospice,
50 Angus Rd; tel: (306) 543-0655 (acc 10)

Richmond, BC V6X 2P3, Rotary Hospice,
3111 Shell Rd; tel: (604) 244-8022 (acc 10)

Winnipeg, MB R3J 3M7, Grace Hospice, 300
Booth Dr; tel: (203) 837-8311 (acc 20)

Adult Services to Developmentally Handicapped
Fort McMurray, AB T9H 1S7, 9919 MacDonald
Ave; tel: (780) 743-4135

Hamilton, ON L8S 1G1, Lawson Ministries,
1600 Main St W; tel: (905) 527-6212
(acc 21)

Toronto, ON M4K 2S5, Broadview Village,
1132 Broadview Ave (Residential Living for
Developmentally Handicapped Adults);
tel: (416) 425-1052; fax: (416) 425-6579
(acc 160)

Winnipeg, MB R3A 0L5, 324 Logan Ave;
tel: (204) 946-9418

Adult Services Mental Health
Toronto, ON M6K 1Z3, Liberty Housing,
248 Dufferin St; tel: (416) 531-3523
(acc 23)

Sheltered Workshops
Etobicoke, ON M8Z 4P8, Booth Industries, 994
Islington Ave; tel: (905) 255-7070 (acc 160)

Toronto, ON M3A 1A3, 150 Railside Rd;
tel: (416) 693-2116 (acc 44)

Addictions and Rehabilitation Centres (Alcohol/Drug Treatment)
Men
Calgary, AB T2G 0R9, 420 9th Ave SE;
tel: (403) 410-1150 (acc 34)

Edmonton, AB T5H 0E5, 9611 102 Ave NW;
tel: (780) 429-4274 (acc 158)

Glencairn, ON L0M 1K0, PO Box 100;
tel: (705) 466-3435/6 (acc 35)

Hamilton, Bermuda HM JX, PO Box HM 2238;
tel: (441) 292-2586 (acc 10)

Kingston, ON K7L 1C7, 562 Princess St;
tel: (613) 546-2333 (acc 24)

Mission, BC V2V 4J5, PO Box 3400;
tel: (604) 826-6681 (acc 171)

Montreal, QC H3J 1T4, 800 rue Guy;
tel: (514) 932-2214

Sudbury, ON P3E 1C2, 146 Larch St;
tel: (705) 673-1175/6 (acc 32)

Toronto, ON M4K 3P7, 450 Pape Ave;
tel: (416) 363-5496 (acc 80)

Vancouver, BC V6A 1K8, 119 East Cordova St;
tel: (604) 646-6800 (acc 70)

Victoria, BC V8W 1M2, 525 Johnson St;
tel: (250) 384-3396 (acc 109)

Winnipeg, MB R3B 0A1, 72 Martha St;
tel: (204) 946-9401 (acc 32)

Women
Toronto, ON M5R 2L6, The Homestead, 78
Admiral Rd; tel: (416) 921-0953 (acc 18)

Vancouver, BC V6P 1S4, The Homestead, 975
57th Ave W; tel: (604) 266-9696 (acc 32)

Residential Services (Hostels, Emergency Shelters)

Men

Barrie, ON L4M 3A5, Bayside Mission Centre, 16 Bayfield St; tel: (705) 728-3737 (acc 32)

Brampton, ON L6T 4M6, Wilkinson Road Shelter, 15 Wilkinson Rd; tel: (905) 452-6335 (acc 85)

Brantford, ON N3T 2J6, Booth Centre, 187 Dalhousie St; tel: (519) 753-4193/4 (acc 32)

Calgary, AB T2G 0J8, Booth Centre, 631 7 Ave SE; tel: (403) 262-6188 (acc 276)

Calgary, AB T2G 0R9, Centre of Hope, 420 9th Ave; tel: (403)410-1111 (acc 235)

Halifax, NS B3K 3A9, 2044 Gottingen St; tel: (902) 422-2363 (acc 49)

Hamilton, ON L8R 1R6, Booth Centre, 94 York Blvd; tel: (905) 527-1444 (acc 75)

Iqaluit, NU X0A 0H0, Box 547; tel: (867) 975-2605 (acc 20)

London, ON N6C 4L8, Centre of Hope, 281 Wellington St; tel: (519) 661-0343 (acc 253)

Mississauga, ON L5C 1T9, Mavis Shelter, 3190 Mavis Rd; tel: (905) 848-8922 (acc 24)

Montreal, QC H3J 1T4, Booth Centre, 880 Guy St; tel: (514) 932-2214 (acc 195)

New Westminster, BC V3L 2K1, 32 Elliot St; tel: (604) 526-4783 (acc 10)

Oakville, ON L6L 6X7, Lighthouse Shelter, 750 Redwood Sq; tel: (905) 339-2918 (acc 25)

Ottawa, ON K1N 5W5, Booth Centre, 171 George St; tel: (613) 241-1573 (acc 142)

Pembroke, Bermuda HM JX, 5 Marsh Lane; tel: (441) 295-5310 (acc 83)

Quebec City, QC G1R 4H8, Hotellerie, 14 Côte du Palais; tel: (418) 692-3956 (acc 60)

Regina, SK S4P 1W1, 1845 Osler St; tel: (306) 569-6088 (acc 75)

Regina, SK S4P 1W1, Waterston Centre, 1865 Osler St; tel: (306) 566-6088 (acc 40)

Richmond, BC V6X 2P3, Richmond House Emergency Shelter, 3111 Shell Rd; tel: (604) 276-2490 (acc 10)

Saint John, NB E2L 1V3, 36 St James St; tel: (506) 634-7021 (acc 75)

St Catharine's, ON L2R 3E7, Booth Centre, 184 Church St; tel: (905) 684-7813 (acc 21)

St John's, NL A1E 1C1, Wiseman Centre, 714 Water St; tel: (709) 739-8355/8 (acc 30)

Saskatoon, SK S7M 1N5, 339 Avenue C S; tel: (306) 244-6280 (acc 50)

Thunder Bay, ON P7A 4S2, CARS, 545 Cumberland St N; tel: (807) 345-7319 (acc 46)

Toronto, ON M5T 1P7, Hope Shelter, 167 College St; tel: (416) 979-7058 (acc 108)

Toronto, ON M4M 2G9, 312 Broadview Ave; tel: (416) 465-6970 (acc 60)

Toronto, ON M5C 2H4, The Gateway, 107 Jarvis St; tel: (416) 368-0324 (acc 100)

Toronto, ON M5A 2R5, Maxwell Meighen Centre, 135 Sherbourne St; tel: (416) 366-2733 (acc 427)

Vancouver, BC V6B 1K8, Belkin House, 555 Homer St; tel: (604) 681-3405 (acc 198)

Vancouver, BC V6A 1K7, James McCready Residence, 129 East Cordova St; tel: (604) 646-6800 (acc 44)

Vancouver, BC V6A 1K7, The Haven, 128 East Cordova St; tel: (604) 646-6800 (acc 40)

Windsor, ON N9A 7G9, 355 Church St; tel: (519) 253-7473 (acc 133)

Winnipeg, MB R3B 0J8, Booth Centre, 180 Henry Ave; tel: (204) 946-9460 (acc 208)

Women

Brampton, ON L6X 3C9, The Honeychurch Family Life Resource Center, 535 Main St N; tel: (905) 451-4115 (acc 73)

Brampton, ON L6T 4M6, Wilkinson Road Shelter, 15 Wilkinson Rd; tel: (905) 452-6335 (acc 24)

Mississauga, ON L5C 1T9, Mavis Shelter, 3190 Mavis Rd; tel: (905) 848-8922 (acc 24)

Montreal, QC H3J 1M8, L'Abri d'Espoir, 2000 Notre Dame W; tel: (514) 934-5615 (acc 36)

Quebec City, QC G1R 4H8, Maison Charlotte, 14 Cote du Palais; tel: (418) 692-3956 (acc 25)

Toronto, ON M6P 1Y5, Evangeline Residence, 2808 Dundas St W; tel: (416) 762-9636 (acc 71)

Toronto, ON M6J 1E6, Florence Booth House, 723 Queen St W; tel: (416) 603-9800 (acc 60)

Vancouver, BC V5Z 4L9, Kate Booth House, PO Box 38048 King Edward Mall; tel: (604) 872-0772 (acc 12)

Vancouver, BC V6B 1G8, The Crosswalk, 138-140 W Hastings St; tel: (604) 669-4349

Family

Mississauga, ON L5R 4J9, Angela's Place, 45 Glen Hawthorne Rd; tel: (905) 791-3887

Mississauga, ON L5A 2X3, SA Peel Family Shelter, 2500 Cawthra Rd; tel: (905) 272-7061 (acc 148)

Montreal, QC H3J 1M8, L'abri e'espoir, 2000 rue Notre-Dame oust; tel: (514) 934-5616 (acc 25)

Youth

Sutton, ON L0E 1R0, 20898 Dalton Rd, PO Box 1087; tel: (905) 722-9076

Community and Family Services

Abbotsford, BC V2S 2E8, 34081 Gladys Ave; tel: (604) 852-9305

Ajax, ON L1S 2L8, 35 King Cresc;
  tel: (905) 683-0454
Bathurst, NB E2A 1A4, 112 Main St;
  tel: (506) 548-5270
Belleville, ON K8N 3B3, 295 Pinnacle St;
  tel: (613) 968-6834
Bowmanville, ON L1C 2N8, 75 Liberty St S;
  tel: (905) 623-2185
Brampton, ON L6T 3T2, 8054 Torbram Rd;
  tel: (905) 451-8840
Brandon, MB R7A 1R8, 9 Princess St E;
  tel: (204) 727-4334
Brantford, ON N3T 3E5, 23 West St;
  tel: (519) 752-7814
Bridgewater, NS B4V 2K7, 199 Dominion St;
  tel: (902) 543-5471
Brockville, ON K6V 3B6, 175 First Ave;
  tel: (613) 342-5211
Burlington, ON L7L 6A1, 14-1800 Applyby
  Line; tel: (905) 637-3893
Calgary, AB T2B 0X6, 3301-17 St SE;
  tel: (403) 220-0432
Cambridge, ON N1R 4J5, 12 Shade St;
  tel: (519) 623-1221
Campbell River, BC V9W 2M4, 291 McLean St;
  tel: (250) 287-3720
Campbelltown, NB E3N 2G8, 110B Roseberry
  St; tel: (506) 753-6592
Charlottetown, PEI C1A 1S1, 158 Fitzroy St;
  tel: (902) 892-8870
Chatham, ON N7L 5H1, 46 Orangewood Blvd;
  tel: (519) 354-1430
Chilliwack, BC V2P 2N4, 45746 Yale Rd;
  tel: (604) 792-0001
Cobourg, ON K9A 1K5, 66 Swayne St;
  tel: (905) 373-9440
Collingwood, ON L9Y 3K2, 162 St Marie St;
  tel: (705) 445-9222
Corner Brook, NL A2H 4C7, 61 Broadway;
  tel: (709) 639-1719
Cornwall, ON K6J 3Z8, 500 York St;
  tel: (613) 932-8311
Courtenay, BC V9N 8P1, 10-2966 Kilpatrick
  Ave; tel: (250) 383-5133
Cranbrook, BC V1C 4Y5, 533 Slater Rd NW;
  tel: (250) 426-3612
Dauphin, MB R7N 0Z4, 38 2nd Ave NE;
  tel: (204) 638-3764
Dawson Creek, BC V1G 2J8, 1436-104 Rd Ave;
  tel: (250) 782-8669
Drumheller, AB T0J 0Y4, 242 First St W;
  tel: (403) 823-2722
Duncan, BC V9L 3P9, 280 Trans Canada Hwy;
  tel: (250) 746-8669
Edmonton, AB T5H 0C7, 9620 101A Ave NW;
  tel: (780) 424-9222

Essex, ON N8M 1A7, 26 Talbot St S;
  tel: (519) 776-4750
Etobicoke, ON M8W 3B7, 5 Thirtieth St;
  tel: (416) 252-1289
Etobicoke, ON M9W 4K9, 2152 Kipling Ave N;
  tel: (416) 743-1282
Fenelon Falls, ON K0M 1N0, 42 Bond St W;
  tel: (705) 887-1408
Fernie, BC V0B 1M0, 741 2nd St;
  tel: (250) 423-4661
Flin Flon, MB R8A 1S6, 3 Hemlock Dr;
  tel: (204) 687-7812
Fort Frances, ON P9A 2C2, 316 Victoria Ave;
  tel: (807) 274-3871
Fort McMurray, AB T9H 1S7, 9919 MacDonald
  Ave; tel: (780) 791-9903
Fort St John, BC V1J 1Y6, 10116 100 Ave;
  tel: (250) 785-0500
Fredericton, NB E3A 8H4, 531 St Mary's St;
  tel: (506) 453-1706
Gananoque, ON K7G 1H9, 120 Garden St;
  tel: (613) 382-3105
Gander, NL A1V 1A9, 111 Memorial Dr;
  tel: (709) 256-4480
Georgetown, ON L7G 5K8, 271 Mountainview
  Rd; tel: (905) 877-9470
Gibsons, BC V0N 1V0, PO Box 1625;
  tel: (604) 886-3665
Glace Bay, NS B1A 5V1, 40 Union St;
  tel: (902) 849-7886
Goderich, ON N7A 3H8, 303 Suncoast Dr;
  tel: (519) 524-4188
Grand Falls Windsor, NL A2B 1C7, 27 Park St;
  tel: (709) 489-7751
Grande Prairie, AB T8V 3Y1, 9525 83 Ave;
  tel: (780) 532-3720
Gravenhurst, ON P1P 1E7, 620 Muskoka Rd N;
  tel: (705) 687-7271
Guelph, ON N1E 1E9, 210 Victoria Rd S;
  tel: (519) 836-9360
Halifax, NS B3K 3A9, 2038 Gottingen St;
  tel: (902) 422-1598
Hamilton, Bermuda, 92 Reid St;
  tel: (441) 292-5159
Hamilton, ON L8R 3N3, 80 Bay St N;
  tel: (905) 540-1888
High River, AB T1V 1G3, 22 4th Ave SE;
  tel: (403) 653-7530
Huntsville, ON P1H 1W4, 4 Mary St E;
  tel: (705) 789-3398
Ingersoll, ON N5C 2T5, 192 Thames St S;
  tel: (519) 485-4961
Jacksons Point, ON L0E 1L0, 1816 Metro Rd;
  tel: (905) 722-4613
Kamloops, BC V2B 3L7, 175 Leigh Rd;
  tel: (250) 376-1754

Kelowna, BC V1Y 4B8, 344 Poplar St;
tel: (250) 860-3442

Kemptville, ON K0G 1J0, 2 Oxford St W St;
tel: (613) 258-3583

Kenora, ON P9N 1T8, 104 Matheson St S;
tel: (807) 468-8918

Kentville, NS B4N 1K7, 401 Main St;
tel: (902) 678-4534

Kingston, ON K7L 3S5, 326 Alfred St;
tel: (613) 548-4411

Kirkland Lake, ON P2N 2C7, 6 Sylvanite Ave;
tel: (705) 567-6151

Kitchener, ON N3M 2C8, 300 Gage Ave Unit 1;
tel: (519) 745-4215

Labrador City/Wabush, NL A2V 1G3, PO Box
369; tel: (709) 944-3200

Leamington, ON N8H 1T6, 88 Setterinton St;
tel: (519) 326-0319

Lethbridge, AB T1J 0E3, 1212 2 Ave S;
tel: (403) 328-2860

Lindsay, ON K9V 2Y2, 46 Kent St W;
tel: (705) 878-5331

Listowel, ON N4W 2C8, 611 Main St E;
tel: (519) 291-2900

Lloydminster, AB T9V 2P9, 2302 53rd Ave;
tel: (306) 825-4840

London, ON N6C 4L8, 281 Wellington St;
tel: (519) 434-1651

Maple Ridge, BC V2X 2S8, 22188 Lougheed
Hwy; tel: (604) 463-8296

Medicine Hat, AB T1A 1M6, 737 8th Ave;
tel: (403) 526-9699

Midland, ON L4R 1R1, 555 Dominion Ave;
tel: (705) 526-2751

Milton, ON L9T 5B2, 100 Nipissing Rd;
tel: (905) 875-1022

Miramichi, NB E1V 1Y8, 231 Pleasant St:
tel: (506) 622-7826

Mississauga, ON L5A 2X4, 3173 Cawthra Rd;
tel: (905) 279-3941

Mississauga, ON L5N 4W8, 3020 Vanderbilt Rd;
tel: (905) 824-0452

Mississauga, ON L5L 1V3, 2460 The Collegeway;
tel: (905) 607-2151

Moncton, NB E1E 4E4, 20 Centennial Dr;
tel: (506) 389-9901

Montreal, QC H4E 1C8, 1545 Cabot St;
tel: (514) 766-2155

Moose Jaw, SK S6H 0Y9, 175 1st Ave NE;
tel: (306) 692-5899

Naniamo, BC V9R 4S6, 19 Nicol St;
tel: (250) 754-2621

Napanee, ON K7R 1H2, 135 Mill St W;
tel: (613) 354-7633

Nelson, BC V1L 4E9, 601 Vernon St;
tel: (250) 352-3488

New Glasgow, NS B0K 2A0, 134 James St;
tel: (902) 752-3299

New Liskeard, ON P0J 1P0, 260 Whitewood
Ave; tel: (705) 647-1588

New Westminster, BC V3L 3A9, 325 6th St;
tel: (604) 521-2421

Newmarket, ON L3Y 8G8, 415 Pickering Cres;
tel: (905) 895-0577

Niagara Falls, ON L2G 5S3, 5720 Dorchester
Rd; tel: (905) 354-2834

North Bay, ON P1B 1C4, 134 McIntyre St E;
tel: (705) 474-7859

North Vancouver, BC V7M 1N2, 105 12th St W;
tel: (604) 988-7225

North York, ON M3A 1A3, 150 Railside Rd;
tel: (416) 285-0080

North York, ON M2M 2L4, 25 Centre Ave;
tel: (416) 225-6683

Oakville, ON L6L 1Z1, 1225 Rebecca St;
tel: (905) 827-6523

Orillia, ON L3V 3L7, 157 Coldwater Rd W;
tel: (705) 326-3472

Oshawa, ON L1H 1B2, 45 King St E;
tel: (905) 723-7422

Ottawa, ON K1N 5W5, 165 George St;
tel: (613) 241-5188

Owen Sound, ON N4K 5P7, 365 14th St W;
tel: (519) 371-0957

Parksville, BC9P 2H6, 866 Webley Rd;
tel: (250) 248-8793

Pasadena, NL A0L 1K0, 12 Third Ave;
tel: (709) 686-5209

Peace River, AB T8S 1G8,9613-90 Ave;
tel: (780) 624-5980

Pembroke, ON K8A 5N9, 484 Pembroke St W;
tel: (613) 735-5601

Penticton, BC V2A 5J1 2399 South Main St;
tel: (250) 492-4788

Perth, ON K7H 1R9, 40 North St;
tel: (613) 267-4652

Peterborough, ON K9H 2H6, 219 Simcoe St;
tel: (705) 742-4391

Port Alberni, BC V9Y 1V9, 4815 Argyle St;
tel: (250) 723-6913

Portage La Prairie, MB R1N 0S6, 220 Duke
Ave; tel: (204) 857-4672

Powel River, BC V8A 3A6, 4500 Joyce Ave;
tel: (604) 485-6067

Prince Albert, SK S6V 4V3, 900 Central Ave;
tel: (306) 763-6078

Prince George, BC V2M 3R5, 777 Ospika Blvd;
tel: (250) 564-4000

Prince Rupert, BC V8J 1R3, 25 Grenville Crt;
tel: (250) 624-6180

Quebec City, QC G1J 2C3, 1125 De La
Canardiere; tel: (418) 641-0050

Canada and Bermuda Territory

Quesnel, BC V2J 2N9, 374 McLean St;
 tel: (250) 635-1829

Red Deer, AB T4N 5E9, 4837 54 St;
 tel: (403) 346-6145

Regina, SK S4P 3M7, 2240 13th Ave;
 tel: (306) 757-4600

Renfrew, ON K7V 4A3, 8 Argyle St S;
 tel: (613) 432-7721

Richmond, BC V7C 3W7, 8280 Gilbert Rd;
 tel: (640) 277-2424

Ridgetown, ON N0P 2C0, 7 Eric St N;
 tel: (519) 674-2472

Saint John, NB E2L 3S1, 27A Prince Edward St;
 tel: (506) 634-1633

Salmon Arm, BC V1E 1H6, 191 2nd Ave NE;
 tel: (250) 832-9194

Sarnia, ON N7A 1A1, 970 Confederation St.;
 tel: (519) 334-1142

Sault Ste Marie, ON P6C 3K9, 670 John St;
 tel: (705) 759-4143

Scarborough, ON M1H 2W6, 2085 Ellesmere
 Rd; tel: (416) 438-2573

Sherbrooke, QC J1H 5C7, 112 Rue Wellington
 Sud Suite 101; tel: (819) 566-6298

Simcoe, ON N3Y 3V3, 184 Colborne St N;
 tel: (519) 426-3640

Smiths Falls, ON K7A 3Z5, 243 Brockville St;
 tel: (613) 3563

Springdale, NL A0J 1T0, PO Box 127;
 tel: (709) 673-3576

St-Hubert, QC J4T 2S5, 3228 Grande Allée;
 tel: (450) 676-8060

St Albans, AB T8N 6A7, 165 Liberton Dr;
 tel: (780) 458-1937

St Anthony, NL A0K 4S0, PO Box 699;
 tel: (709) 454-3172

St Catharines, ON L2M 7N5, 400 Niagara St;
 tel: (905) 935-4311

St John's, NL A1C 4Z1, 21 Adams Ave;
 tel: (709) 726-0393

St Mary's, ON N4X 1A9, 220 Queens St E;
 tel: (519) 284-4822

St Thomas, ON N5P 1E2, 852 Talbot St:
 tel: (519) 633-4509

Stephenville, NL A2N 3A3, PO Box 464;
 tel: (709) 643-3482

Stratford, ON N4Z 1C8, 230 Lightbourne Ave;
 tel: (519) 271-2762

Strathroy, ON N7G 1C2, 71 Maitland Terrance;
 tel: (519) 245-5398

Sudbury, ON P3E 4S1, 107 Lome St;
 tel: (705) 566-8915

Summerside, PEI C1N 1B2, 163 Water St;
 tel: (902) 888-3870

Surrey, BC V3W 8V3, 4-13570 78th Ave;
 tel: (604) 507-4860

Sussex, NB E4E 1S8, 95 Main St;
 tel: (506) 433-5461

Sydney, NS B1P 1W6, 55 Inglis St;
 tel: (902) 562-5442

Terrace, BC V8G 2N5, 3236 Kalum St;
 tel: (250) 635-1829

Thompson, MB R8N 1W2, 305 Thompson Dr;
 tel: (204) 677-3658

Thunder Bay, ON P7A 4S2, 545 Cumberland St
 N; tel: (807) 344-7300

Tillsonburg, ON N4G 1R7, 110 Concession St
 W; tel: (519) 842-9491

Toronto, ON M3N 1J3, 20 Yorkwoods Gate;
 tel: (416) 398-1566

Toronto, ON M6H 2X4, 789 Dovercourt Rd;
 tel: (416) 532-4511

Toronto, ON M5A 3P1, 77 River St;
 tel: (416) 304-1982

Trail, BC V1R 1N3, 2030 Second Ave;
 tel: (250) 386-3814

Trenton, ON K8V 1L9, 244 Dundas St E;
 tel: (613) 392-9905

Trois-Rivieres, QC G8V 1G7, 501 A boul
 Ste-Maurice; tel: (819) 373-0831

Truro, NS B2N 7B8, 14 Outram St;
 tel: (902) 893-1862

Vancouver, BC V5V 4B8, 3213 Fraser St;
 tel: (604) 872-7676

Vernon, BC V1T 3N5, 2801 45 Ave;
 tel: (250) 549-4111

Victoria, BC V8T 4E3, 2695 Quadra St;
 tel: (250) 386-8521

Wallaceburg, ON N8A 1M8, 17 Gillard St;
 tel: (519) 627-1163

Welland, ON L3B 3W3, 30 East Main St;
 tel: (905) 735-5700

Westville, NS B2H 5E3, 134 James St;
 tel: (905) 752-3299

Whitby, ON L1N 6S5, 607 Palace St;
 tel: (905) 430-3454

White Rock, BC V4B 2G4, 15417 Roper Ave;
 tel: (604) 531-7314

Whitehorse, YT Y1A 1J5, 4169 4th Ave;
 tel: (867) 668-2327

Williams Lake, BC V2G 1R3, 272 Borland St;
 tel: (250) 392-2429

Windsor, ON N9A 7G9, 355 Church St;
 tel: (519) 253-7473

Winnipeg, MB R3B 0J8, 180 Henry Ave;
 tel: (204) 945-9485

Winnipeg, MB R3A 0L5, 324 Logan Ave;
 tel: (204) 946-9136

Woodstock, ON N4V 1E9, 769 Juliana Dr;
 tel: (519) 539-6166

Yarmouth, NS B5A 2G9, 103 Brunswick St;
 tel: (902) 742-7749

Correctional and Justice Services
Community Programme Centres

Barrie, ON L4M 5A1, 400 Bayfield St, Ste 255;
tel: (705) 737-4140

Burnaby, BC V5C 6N5, 3833 Henning Dr;
tel: (604) 299-3908

Calgary, AB T2G 0R9, 420 9th Ave SE;
tel: (403) 410-4119

Chilliwack, BC V2P 2N4, 45742B Yale Rd;
tel: (604) 792-8581

Guelph, ON N1L 1H3, 1320 Gordon St;
tel: (519) 836-9360

Halifax, NS B3J 1Y9, 1329 Barrington St,
Halifax; tel: (902) 429-6120

Kingston, ON K7K 4B1, 472 Division St;
tel: (613) 549-2676

Kitchener, ON N2H 2M2, 151 Frederick St,
Ste 502; tel: (519) 742-8521

London, ON N6B 2L4, 281 Wellington St;
tel: (519) 432-9553

Medicine Hat, AB T1A 0E7, 874 2 St E;
tel: (403) 529-2111

Moncton, NB E1C 1M2, 68 Gordon St;
tel: (506) 853-8887

Ottawa, ON K1Y K1N, 171 George St;
tel: (613) 725-1733

Peterborough, ON K9H 2H6, 219 Simcoe St;
tel: (705) 742-4391

Prince Albert, SK S6V 4V3, 900 Central Ave;
tel: (306) 763-6078

Regina, SK S4P 3M7, 2240 13th Ave;
tel: (306) 757-4711/2

Saint John, NB E2L 1V3, 36 St James St;
tel: (506) 634-7021

St Catharines, ON L2R 3E7, 184 Church St;
tel: (905) 684-7813

St John's, NL A1C 4Z1, 21 Adams Ave;
tel: (709) 726-0393

Saskatoon, SK S7M 1N5, 339 Avenue C S;
tel: (306) 244-6280

Stoney Creek, ON L8J 3Y1, 300 Winterberry Dr;
tel: (905) 573-0635

Thunder Bay, ON P7A 4S2, 545 Cumberland
St N; tel: (807) 345-5785

Toronto, ON M5A 3P1, 77 River St;
tel: (416) 304-1974

Winnipeg, MB R3A 0L5, 324 Logan Ave,
2nd Floor; tel: (204) 949-2100

Adult/Youth Residential Centres

Brampton, ON L6X 1C1, 44 Nelson St W;
tel: (905) 453-0988

Dartmouth, NS B3A 1H5, 318 Windmill Rd;
tel: (902) 465-2690

Dundas, ON L9H 2E8, 34 Hatt St;
tel: (905) 627-1632

Ilderton, ON N0M 2A0, PO Box 220;
tel: (519) 666-0600

Kitchener, ON N2G 2M4, 657 King St E;
tel: (519) 744-4666

Moncton, NB E1C 8P6, 64 Gordon St,
PO Box 1121; tel: (506) 858-9486

Sydney, NS B1P 1B4, 571 Esplanade;
tel: (902) 564-0032

Toronto, ON M4X 1K2, 422 Sherbourne St;
tel: (416) 964-6316/967-6618

Whitehorse, YT Y1A 6E3, 91678 Alaska
Highway; tel: (867) 667-2741

Yellowknife, NWT X1A 1P4, 4927 45th St;
tel: (867) 920-4673

Health Services
Long-Term Care/Seniors' Residences

Brandon, MB R7A 3N9, Dinsdale Personal Care
Home, 510 6th St; tel: (204) 727-3636
(acc 60)

Calgary, AB T3C 3W7, Jackson/Willan Seniors'
Residence, 3015 15 Ave SW;
tel: (403) 249-9116 (acc 18)

Edmonton, AB T5X 6C4, Grace Manor, 12510
140 Ave; tel: (780) 454-5484 (acc 100)

Kitchener, ON N2H 2P1, A. R. Goudie Eventide
Home, 369 Frederick St; tel: (519) 744-5182
(acc 80)

Montreal, QC H4B 2J4, Montclair Residence,
4413 Montclair Ave; tel: (514) 481-5638
(acc 50)

New Westminster, BC V3L 4A4, Buchanan
Lodge, 409 Blair Ave; tel: (604) 522-7033
(acc 112)

Niagara Falls, ON L2E 1K5, The Honourable
Ray and Helen Lawson Eventide Home,
5050 Jepson St; tel: (905) 356-1221
(acc 100)

Ottawa, ON K1Y 2Z3, Ottawa Grace Manor,
1156 Wellington St; tel: (613) 722-8025
(acc 128)

Regina, SK S4R 8P6, William Booth
Special Care Home, 50 Angus Rd;
tel: (306) 543-0655 (acc 81)

Riverview, NB E1B 4K6, Lakeview Manor, 50
Suffolk St; tel: (506) 387-2012/3/4 (acc 50)

St John's, NL A1A 2G9, Glenbrook Lodge, 105
Torbay Rd; tel: (709) 726-1575 (acc 114)

St John's, NL A1A 2G9, Glenbrook Villa, 107
Torbay Rd; tel: (709) 726-1575 (acc 20)

Toronto, ON M4S 1G1, Meighen Retirement
Residence, 84 Davisville Ave;
tel: (416) 481-5557 (acc 84)

Toronto, ON M4S 1J6, Meighen Manor, 155
Millwood Rd; tel: (416) 481-9449 (acc 168)

Vancouver, BC V5S 3T1, Southview Terrace,

While conducting The Salvation Army's 125th anniversary in Canada, the General and Commissioner Helen Clifton took part in events celebrating the 25th anniversary of William and Catherine Booth College in Winnipeg. They are picured with staff and graduates. Since it was opened as Catherine Booth Bible College in 1982 students from 40 countries, including representatives from every continent, have studied at the institution. In addition to graduates from Canada, the class of 2007 included students from the USA, Haiti, India, Ukraine and Zimbabwe.

3131 58th Ave E; tel: (604) 438-3367/8 (acc 57)
Vancouver BC V5S 3V2, Southview Heights
 7252 Kerr St; tel: (604) 438-3367/8 (acc 47)
Victoria, BC V9A 7J6, Matson Sequoia
 Residence, 554 Garrett Pl Ste 211;
 tel: (250) 383-5821 (acc 30)
Victoria, BC V9A 4G7, Sunset Lodge, 952 Arm
 St; tel: (250) 385-3422 (acc 108)
Winnipeg, MB R2Y 0S8, Golden West
 Centennial Lodge, 811 School Rd;
 tel: (204) 888-3311 (acc 116)

Immigrant and Refugee Services
Toronto, ON M5A 1Z1, 7 Labatt Ave Suite
 B116; tel: (416) 360-6036

Women's Multi-Service Programmes
(and unmarried mothers)
Hamilton, ON L8P 2H1, Grace Haven,
 138 Herkimer St; tel: (905) 522-7336 (acc 12)

London, ON N6J 1A2, Bethesda Centre,
 54 Riverview Ave; tel: (519) 438-8371
 (acc 14)
Ottawa, ON K1Y 2Z3, Bethany Hope Centre,
 1140 Wellington St; tel: (613) 725-1733
Regina, SK S4S 7A7, Grace Haven, 2929 26th
 Ave; tel: (306) 352-1421 (acc 7)
Saskatoon, SK S7K 0N1, Bethany Home,
 802 Queen St; tel: (306) 244-6758 (acc 15)
Thunder Bay, ON P7B 1E3, 219 Pearl St;
 tel: (807) 345-3772

Children's Treatment Facilities
Calgary, AB T3C 1M6, Children's Village,
 1731 29 St SW; tel: (403) 246-1124
 (acc 40)
Regina, SK S4S 0X5, Gemma House, 3820 Hill
 Ave; tel: (306) 586-5388 (acc 8)

CARIBBEAN TERRITORY

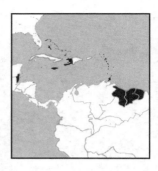

Territorial leaders:
Commissioners Raymond and Judith Houghton

Territorial Commander:
Commissioner Raymond Houghton
(1 Jul 2006)

Chief Secretary:
Lieut-Colonel Raphael Mason (1 Jun 2005)

Territorial Headquarters: 3 Waterloo Rd, Kingston 10, Jamaica

Postal address: PO Box 378, Kingston 10, Jamaica, WI

Tel: [1876] 929 6190/91/92; fax: [1876] 929 7560; web site: www.salvationarmycarib.org

In 1887 The Salvation Army 'opened fire' in Kingston, and thence spread throughout the island of Jamaica and to Guyana (1895), Barbados (1898), Trinidad (1901), Grenada (1902), St Lucia (1902), Antigua (1903), St Vincent (1905), Belize (1915), St Kitts (1916), Suriname (1924), the Bahamas (1931), Haiti (1950), French Guiana (1980) and St Maarten (1999). The General of The Salvation Army is a Corporation Sole in Jamaica (1914), Trinidad and Tobago (1915), Barbados (1917), Belize (1928), Guyana (1930), the Bahamas (1936) and Antigua (1981).

Zone: Americas and Caribbean
Countries included in the territory: Antigua, Bahamas, Barbados, Belize, French Guiana, Grenada, Guyana, Haiti, Jamaica, St Kitts, St Lucia, St Maarten, St Vincent, Suriname, Trinidad and Tobago
'The Salvation Army' in Dutch: Leger des Heils; in French: Armée du Salut
Languages in which the gospel is preached: Creole, Dutch, English, French, Surinamese
Periodical: *The War Cry*

THIS diverse territory of 15 nations continues to experience growth as Salvationists seek the Holy Spirit's inspiration and guidance in the advancement of The Salvation Army's mission. Souls are being won for Christ; increases in membership rolls were recorded in the year under review.

Chief of the Staff Commissioner Robin Dunster visited the territory in June 2006 and commissioned eight cadets of the Visionaries Session.

The next month Commissioner William Francis (then International Secretary for Americas and the Caribbean) installed Commissioners Raymond and Judith Houghton as territorial leaders. The new leaders immediately reinforced the mission direction of the territory: 'Together – Building Tomorrow, Today'.

In the midst of Antigua's 25th independence celebrations His Royal Highness Prince Edward, along with His Excellency Governor-General Sir James and Lady Emma Carlisle and the British High Commissioner

Duncan Taylor, were welcomed to the Sunshine Home for Girls. Prince Edward toured the centre and was introduced to the girls, who interpreted the song 'I Know My Redeemer Lives' in dance.

Congress meetings in Port-au-Prince, Haiti, conducted by the new territorial leaders, were attended by more than 1,200 enthusiastic Salvationists from that part of the Haiti Division. A highlight was the presentation of the Order of the Founder medal and certificate to Major Catherine Pacquette in recognition of her pioneering work and continuing selfless service in Haiti.

Medical work continues to expand in Haiti as more groups seek to partner with The Salvation Army. The Army's HIV/Aids work in Haiti is known for its comprehensive nature and effectiveness.

During the floods in Suriname in 2006 local Salvationists responded effectively to the disaster-ravaged communities. Their efforts did not go unnoticed and, because of this, one of the communities that had been assisted has requested The Salvation Army's permanent presence in the village.

A major social services project has been completed in Bridgetown, Barbados. The new centre provides accommodation for the homeless and a daily feeding programme.

In the Bahamas celebrations were held throughout 2006 to mark the 75th anniversary of Salvation Army witness. An extensive mission study has been completed to take the Army's work forward in these islands.

The Hanbury Home for Children in Jamaica celebrated its 50th anniversary. Many former residents returned to give thanks for the care and instruction received there in their formative childhood years.

The territory continues to have strong partnerships with other territories. In addition to receiving financial support, the territory provides opportunities for mission and work teams to become involved with people of the developing Caribbean nations. Members of such teams invariably return home the richer for their experience.

Advisory boards make a significant contribution to Salvation Army work in the territory. A territorial delegation attended the National Advisory Organisations Conference in Dallas, Texas, in April 2007.

STATISTICS

Officers 293 (active 222 retired 71) **Cadets** (1st Yr) 11 (2nd Yr) 8 **Employees** 1,035 **Lieutenants** 4
Corps 126 **Outposts** 59 **Institutions** 59 **Schools** 76
Senior Soldiers 9,306 **Adherents** 1,196 **Junior Soldiers** 3,650
Personnel serving outside territory Officers 9

STAFF

Business: Maj Ward Matthews
Coordinator for Disasters/Services: Capt Michele Matthews
Editor: Capt Prescilla Kellman
Field/Property: Lt-Col Sydney McKenzie
Projects/Sponsorship: Capt Michele Matthews
Training: Lt-Col Joan Dunwoodie (pro tem)
Women's Ministries: Comr Judith Houghton (TPWM) Lt-Col Winsome Mason (TSWM & TWMS, inc HL) Lt-Col Trypheme McKenzie (TLOMS & TWAS)
Youth and Candidates: Capt Jonathan Kellman

Caribbean Territory

DIVISIONS

Antigua: PO Box 2, 36 Long St, St John's; tel: [1 268] 562-5473; fax: [1 268] 462-9134; Maj Stanley Griffin

Bahamas: PO Box N 205, Nassau, NP; tel: [1242] 393-2340; fax: [1242] 393-2189; Maj Lester Ferguson

Barbados: PO Box 57, Reed St, Bridgetown; tel: [1246] 426-2467; fax: [1246] 426-9369; Maj Dewhurst Jonas

Guyana: PO Box 10411, 237 Alexander St, Lacytown, Georgetown; tel: [592] 22 72619/ 54910; fax: [592] (22) 50893; Maj Sinous Theodore

Haiti: PO Box 301, Port-au-Prince; tel: [509] 510-3671; Maj Lucien Lamartiniere

Jamaica Eastern: Box 153, Kingston; 153B Orange St, Kingston; tel: [1876] 922-6764/ 0287; fax: [1876] 967-1553; Maj Devon Haughton

Jamaica Western: PO Box 44, Lot #949 Westgreen, Montego Bay, St James; tel: [876] 952-3778; Maj Keith Graham

Trinidad and Tobago: (temporary DHQ) 131-133 Henry St, Port-of-Spain, Trinidad, PO Box 248, 27 Edward St, Port-of-Spain; tel: [1868] 625-4120; fax: [1868] 625-4206; Maj Vilo Exantus

REGIONS

Belize: PO Box 64, 41 Regent St, Belize City; tel: [501] 2273 365; fax: (501) 2278 240; email: salvationarmyrhqbelize@yahoo.com; Maj Errol Robateau

Suriname: PO Box 317, Henck Arron Straat 172, Paramaribo; tel: [597] 47-3310; fax: [597] 41-0555; email:salvationarmy@inbox.com; Maj Kervin Harry

COUNTRIES NOT IN DIVISIONAL OR REGIONAL LISTS

French Guiana: Route de la Madeleine, Cite Mortin, Boite Postale 329, 97327 Cayenne Cedex, Guyane Francaise; tel: [594] 594-315832

Grenada: Grenville St, St George's, Grenada; tel: [1473] 440-3299

St Kitts: PO Box 56, Cayon Rd, Basseterre, St Kitts; tel: [1869] 465-2106; fax: [1869] 465-4429

St Lucia: PO Box 6, High St, Castries, St Lucia; tel: [1758] 452-3108; fax: [1758] 451-8569

St Maarten: 59 Union Rd, Cole Bay, PO Box 5184, St Maarten, Netherlands Antilles; tel: [599] 580-8588

St Vincent: Melville St, PO Box 498, Kingstown, St Vincent; tel: (809) 456-1574; fax: [1784] 456-1082

TRAINING COLLEGE

GPO Box 437, 174 Orange St, Kingston, Jamaica; tel: [1876] 922-2027; fax: [1876] 967-7541

CITY WELFARE OFFICES

Bahamas: 31 Mackey St, Nassau NP
Jamaica: 57 Peter's Lane, Kingston

COMMUNITY CENTRES

Bahamas: Freeport, Grantstown
Barbados: Checker Hall, St Lucy, Wellington St, Bridgetown, Wotton, Christchurch
Jamaica:
Rae Town Goodwill Centre, 24 Tower St, Kingston; tel: [1876] 928-5770/930-0028
Allman Town, 18-20 Prince of Wales St, Kingston 4; tel: [1876] 92-27279

FEEDING CENTRES

Antigua: Meals on wheels (60)
Bahamas: Mackey St and Grantstown, Nassau
Barbados: Reed St, Bridgetown
Belize: 9 Glynn St, Belize City (acc 50)
Guyana: 6-7 Water St, Kingston, Georgetown (Soup Kitchen); Third Avenue, Bartica
Haiti: Port-au-Prince (Nutrition Centre)
Jamaica: Peter's Lane, Kingston; Jones Town, Kingston; Spanish Town, St Catherine; May Pen, Clarendon; St Ann's Bay, St Ann; Port Antonio, Portland; Montego Bay, St James
Suriname: Gravenstraat 126, Paramaribo

For Children
Bahamas: Nassau, Mackey St
Grenada: St Georges
Guyana: Georgetown, Bartica, Linden
St Vincent: Kingstown

MEDICAL WORK

Haiti: Bethel Maternity Home and Dispensary, Fond-des-Negres
Bethesda TB Centre, Fond-des-Negres
Primary Health Care Centre and Nutrition Centre, Port-au-Prince
Jamaica: Rae Town Clinic, 24 Tower St, Kingston; tel: (876) 928-1489/930-0028

PRISON, PROBATION AND AFTERCARE WORK

Antigua, Grenada, Guyana (Georgetown, Bartica, New Amsterdam), Jamaica, St Kitts, Suriname, Tobago, Trinidad

The General leads Salvationists in a flag-waving celebration at the Russia 15th Anniversary Congress in St Petersburg

The flag is yours, the flag is mine,
That flies o'er lands and seas;
From north to south, from east to west,
Unfurled by every breeze.
The blood-stained flag, the fiery flag,
The flag of purity,
That brings new life, new hope, new joy,
And tells of victory.

Song Book of The Salvation Army, 779

Above: Flags are paraded during the Newfoundland and Labrador Provincial Congress in St John

Left: Kneeling at a flag-draped altar, n captains in USA Western Territory a ordained and commissioned

BLOOD & FIRE

e General and Commissioner Helen Clifton share a joyful moment at
e territorial congress in Sweden

'flag of all sessions' is created at the Philippines commissioning

A cross on a Salvation Army flag creates a powerful focal point in a corps prayer room set up during the 24/7 prayer event in Switzerland, Austria and Hungary Territory

Prison Visitation Services
Belize: directed by Regional Commander

RETIRED OFFICERS' RESIDENCES
Jamaica: Francis Ham Residence, 57 Mannings
Hill Rd, Kingston 8; tel: (876) 924-1308 (acc 7)
Barbados: Long Bay, St Phillip
Guyana: East La Penitence

SOCIAL SERVICES
Blind and Handicapped
Adults
Bahamas: Visually Handicapped Workshop,
Ivanhoe Lane, PO Box N 1980, Nassau NP;
tel: (242) 394-1107 (acc 19)
Jamaica: Francis Ham Residence (home for
blind women), 57 Mannings Hill Rd,
Kingston 8; tel: (876) 924-1308 (acc 30)

Children (schools)
Bahamas: School for the Blind, 33 Mackay St,
PO Box N 205, Nassau NP;
tel: (242) 394-3197 (acc 15)
Jamaica:
School for the Blind and Visually Impaired,
57 Mannings Hill Rd, PO Box 562,
Kingston 8; tel: (876) 925-1362 (residential
acc 120)
Deaf/Blind Unit, 57 Mannings Hill Rd,
Kingston 8 (residential acc 20)

Women (vocational training)
Jamaica: Evangeline Residence, Kingston; Port
Antonio, Portland
St Vincent: Melville St, Kingstown

SOCIAL SERVICES
Children
Day Care Centres (nurseries)
Barbados: Wellington St, Bridgetown (acc 50)
Wotton, Christchurch (acc 50)
Grenada: St Georges (acc 25)
Jamaica: Allman Town, Kingston (acc 40)
Havendale, Kingston (acc 16) Lucea,
Hanover (acc 30) Montego Bay, St James
(acc 40) Rae Town, Kingston (acc 50)
St Lucia: Castries (acc 50)
St Vincent: Kingstown (acc 20)
Trinidad: San Juan (acc 20)

Homes
Antigua: St John's Sunshine Home (acc 12)
Haiti: Bethany, Fond-des-Negres (acc 22)
La Maison du Bonheur, Port-au-Prince (acc 52)
Jamaica:
Hanbury Home, PO Box 2, Shooter's Hill PO,

Manchester; tel: [1876] 603-3507 (acc 90)
The Nest, 57 Mannings Hill Rd, Kingston 8;
tel: [1876] 925-7711 (acc 45)
Windsor Lodge, PO Box 74, Williamsfield PO,
Manchester; tel: [1876] 963-4031 (acc 80)
Suriname: Ramoth, Henck Arron Straat 172,
PO Box 317, Paramaribo; tel: [597] 47-3310
(acc 62)

Playgrounds
Jamaica: Rae Town, Kingston; Lucea, Hanover;
Montego Bay, St James
Suriname: Henck Arron Straat 126, Paramaribo

Schools
Basic (kindergartens)
Antigua: St John (acc 150)
Barbados: Checker Hall (acc 50) Wellington St
(acc 10) Wotton (acc 20)
Guyana: Bartica (acc 90)
Haiti: Aquin (acc 72) Carrefour (acc 23)
Duverger (acc 50) Fond-des-Negres (acc 114)
La Colline (acc 35) Laferonnay (acc 40)
LeBlanc (acc 40) Vieux Bourg (acc 70)
Jamaica: Bath (acc 25) Bluefields (acc 49) Cave
Mountain (acc 30) Cave Valley (acc 75)
Falmouth (acc 86) Great Bay (acc 40)
Kingston Allman Town (acc 150) Kingston
Havendale (acc 90) Kingston Rae Town
(acc 100) Lime Hall (acc 83) Linstead (acc 65)
Lucea (acc 200) May Pen (acc 60) Montego
Bay (acc 240) Port Antonio (acc 50) St Ann's
Bay (acc 36) Savanna-la-mar (acc 110) Top
Hill (acc 93)
St Kitts: Basseterre (acc 80)
St Lucia: Castries (acc 100)
Trinidad and Tobago: San Fernando (acc 80)
Scarborough, Tobago (acc 70) Tragarette Rd,
Port-of-Spain (acc 20)

Home Science
Barbados: Project Lighthouse (acc 12)
Haiti: Aquin, Carrefour, Desruisseaux, Duverger,
Fond-des-Negres, Gros Morne, Vieux Bourg

Primary Schools
Belize: 12 Cemetery Road, Belize City;
tel: (501) 227-2156 (acc 250)
Haiti: Abraham (acc 171) Arcahaie (acc 210)
Aquin – William Booth (acc 400) Bainet
(acc 150) Balan (acc 156) Baptiste (acc 60)
Bas Fort National (acc 198) Bellamie (acc 130)
Bellegarde (acc 245) Belle Riviere (acc 140)
Boco Lomond (acc 250) Bodoun (acc 80)
Brodequin (acc 140) Campeche (acc 100)

Carrefour/Desruisseaux (acc 235)
Cayot (acc 175) Couyot (acc 140) Dessources (acc 125) Duverger (acc 190) Fond-des-Negres (acc 630) Gardon (acc 250) Gros Morne (acc 200) Guirand (acc 130) Jacmel (acc 40) Kamass (acc 100) L'Azile (acc 190) Laferonnay (acc 100) L'Homond (acc 250) La Jovange (acc 171) La Zandier (acc 170) La Colline (acc 275) Le Blanc (acc 105) La Fosse (acc 500) Lilette (acc 110) Limbe (acc 35) Luly (acc 210) Mapou (acc 80) Montrouis (acc 250) Moulin (acc 150) Peirigny (acc 165) Petit Goave (acc 200) Plaisance (acc 216) Port-au-Prince – College Verena (acc 1,410) Port-de-Paix (acc 100) Puits Laurent (acc 200) Rossignol (acc 230) St Louis du Sud (acc 75) St Marc (acc 235) Vieux Bourg (acc 440) Violette (acc 120)

Evening Schools
Guyana: Happy Heart Youth Centre, New Amsterdam (acc 20)
Haiti: Port-au-Prince (acc 83)

Secondary Schools
Haiti: Port-au-Prince (acc 450) Gros-Morne (acc 85)

SOCIAL SERVICES
Men and Women
Centre for Homeless
Belize: Raymond A. Parkes Home, 18 Cemetery Rd, Belize City; tel: [501] 207-4309 (acc 24)

Eventide Homes
Trinidad: Senior Citizens' Centre, 34 Duncan St, Port-of-Spain; tel: [868] 624-5883 (acc 57)

SOCIAL SERVICES
Men
Guyana: MacKenzie Guest House, Rainbow City, PO Box 67, Linden Co-op MacKenzie, Guyana; tel: [592] 444-6406 (acc 30)

Hostels and Shelters
Guyana:
Men's Hostel, 6-7 Water St, Kingston, Georgetown; tel: [592] 226-1235 (acc 40)
Drug Rehabilitation Centre, 6-7 Water St, Kingston, Georgetown; tel: [592] 226-1235 (acc 20)
Jamaica:
Men's Hostel, 57 Peter's Lane, Kingston; tel: [1876] 922-4030 (acc 25)
William Chamberlain Rehabilitation Centre, 57 Peter's Lane, Kingston (acc 25)

Suriname: Night Shelter, Ladesmastraat 2-6, PO Box 317, Paramaribo; tel: [597] 4-75108 (acc 31)
Trinidad: Working Lads' Hostel, 154a Henry St, Port-of-Spain; tel: 36514 (acc 28)

SOCIAL SERVICES
Women
Eventide Homes
Belize: Ganns Rest Home, 60 East Canal St, Belize City; tel: [501] 227 2973 (acc 12)
Guyana: 69 Bent and Haley Sts, Wortmanville, Georgetown; tel: [592] 226-8846 (acc 22)
Suriname:
Elim Guest House, Gravenstraat 126, PO Box 317, Paramaribo; tel: [597] 47-2735 (acc 15)
Emma House, Dr Nassylaan 76, PO Box 2402, Paramaribo; tel: [597] 4-73890 (acc 22)

Hostels and Shelters
Bahamas: Women and Children's Emergency Residence, Grantstown, PO Box GT 2216, Nassau NP; tel: [242] 323-5608 (acc 14)
Jamaica: Evangeline Residence, 153 Orange St, Kingston; tel: 922-6398 (acc 48)
Trinidad:
Geddes Grant House, 22-24 Duncan St, Port-of-Spain; tel: 623-5700 (acc 36)
Josephine Shaw House, 131-133 Henry St, Port-of-Spain; tel: 623-2547 (acc 106)
Night Shelter, 34 Duncan St, Port-of-Spain; tel: 624-5883 (acc 10)

❝ This diverse territory of 15 nations continues to experience growth . . . souls are being won for Christ; increases in membership rolls recorded ❞

CONGO (BRAZZAVILLE) TERRITORY

Territorial leaders:
Commissioners Mfon J. and Ime Akpan

Territorial Commander:
Commissioner Mfon J. Akpan (1 Apr 2004)

Chief Secretary:
Lieut-Colonel Ambroise Zola (1 Apr 2004)

**Territorial Headquarters: Rue de Reims, Brazzaville,
République du Congo**

Postal address: c/o Africa Department, International Headquarters, 101 Queen Victoria St,
London EC4V 4EH, United Kingdom

Tel: [242] 881144; email: ads_congo_brazzaville@yahoo.com

In 1937 The Salvation Army spread from Léopoldville to Brazzaville, and in 1953 French Equatorial Africa (now Congo) became a separate command. Commissioner and Mrs Henri Becquet were the pioneers. The command was upgraded to a territory in December 1960.

Zone: Africa
Country included in the territory: The Republic of Congo
'The Salvation Army' in French: Armée du Salut; in Kikongo: Nkangu a Luvulusu; in Lingala: Basolda na Kobikisama; in Vili: Livita li Mavutsula
Languages in which the gospel is preached: French, Kikongo, Kituba, Lingala, Vili
Periodical: *Le Salutiste*

GOD has been good to the territory throughout the year under review, and Salvationists praise the Almighty for everything. Work is expanding. A new corps was planted in the town of Dongou in the far north of the country.

Six plots of land were purchased to erect a worship hall, corps officers' quarters and other buildings. Four new halls for worship were opened at Missama, Mbaya, Tanaf and Owando. A quarters for the training principal was opened in the training college compound.

The first visit to Cameroon in anticipation of beginning Salvation Army work there took place (17-24 July 2006). People gave the delegation a positive response to establishing a ministry in Cameroon.

The cabinet system of administration came into operation (1 April 2006). The territory was restructured by carving out Tchitondi District from the then Kouilou Division, which was renamed Point-Noire Division. The inauguration meeting of Tchitondi District was conducted by the territorial commander (6 January 2006).

The first ever Divisional Youth

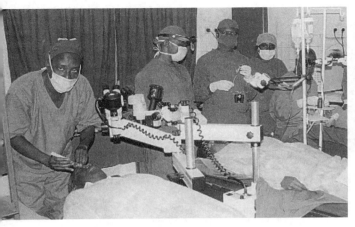

Medical staff carry out surgery at the Salvation Army clinic and eye treatment centre in Moukoundji-Ngouaka. The territory also operates five other clinics and two maternity units.

Officers Conference was conducted in Brazzaville. Various aspects of young people's work was discussed, practical areas of youth and children's ministries were demonstrated, and the DYOs are now more keenly aware of their responsibilities in work among young people.

The Women's Ministries Department conducted an empowerment training seminar for all the DDWMs and officers in Brazzaville 1 and 2 Divisions, led by Commissioner Ime Akpan (Territorial President of Women's Ministries) with Commissioner Véronique Ludiazo (then TPWM, Congo Kinshasa and Angola) as guest speaker.

A coordinator of the newly opened corps schools has been appointed. He is working hard to see that all these schools' curricula are the same as those of the country's public schools.

The territory's bi-monthly publication *Le Salutiste* (*The Salvationist*) has opened doors of contact not only with the Congolese public but also among Government institutions such as the Senate, National Assembly and Ministry of Communication.

STATISTICS

Officers 301 (active 248 retired 53) **Cadets** (2nd Yr) 30 **Employees** 231
Corps 99 **Outposts** 51 **Maternity Unit** 2 **Clinics** 6 **Centres** 2 **Schools** 15
Senior Soldiers 21,843 **Adherents** 2,025 **Junior Soldiers** 6,055
Personnel serving outside territory Officers 4

STAFF

Sec for Personnel: Maj Prosper Bakemba
Sec for Programme: Maj Alexis Sakamesso
Sec for Busness Administration: Maj Jean Pierre Sonda
Extension Training: Maj Anatole Massengo
Financial Administrator: Sgt Jean Mayandu
Health Services Coordinator: Capt Grégoire Mamete
Information Technology: Passi Loukeba Richard
Music: Wilfrid Milandou
Projects: Sgt Edy Seraphin Kanda
Property: Capt Aristide Samba
Public Relations: Capt Pascal Matsiona
Social: Maj Cécile Loukoula
Territorial Bandmaster: Sgt Sensa Malanda

Congo (Brazzaville) Territory

Territorial Songster Leader: Wilfrid Milandou
Training: Maj Frédéric Diandaga
Women's Ministries: Comr Ime Akpan (TPWM) Lt-Col Alphonsine Zola (TSWM) Maj Monique Bakemba (THLS)
Youth and Candidates: Capt Pierre Mounsambote

DIVISIONS

Brazzaville 1: BP 20, Brazzaville; tel: 21 13 15; Maj Eugène Bamanabio (mobile: 5 58 63 92)
Brazzaville 2: tel: 68 95 14; Maj Antoine Massiélé (mobile: 5 35 53 21)
Pointe Noire: BP 686, Pointe Noire; tel: 94 00 16; Maj François Mavouna (mobile: 5 58 68 08)
Lekoumou: BP 20, Brazzaville; tel: 58 63 92; Maj Alexandre Mabanza
Louingui: BP 20, Brazzaville; Maj Jérôme Nzita (mobile: 5 47 09 75)
Mbanza-Ndounga: BP 20, Brazzaville; Maj Daniel Taty (mobile: 5 38 76 31)
Niari: BP 85, Dolisie; tel 5364319; Capt Urbain Loubacky
Yangui: BP 10, Kinkala; Maj Patrick Tadi (mobile: 5 56 38 72)

DISTRICTS

Bouenza: BP 20, Brazzaville; Maj Jean-Pierre Douniama (mobile: 5 39 50 87)

North: BP 20, Brazzaville; Maj Gabin Mbizi (mobile: 5 31 35 09)
Tchitondi: c/o THQ; Maj Alphonse Mayamba-Debi

TRAINING COLLEGE

Nzoko, BP 20, Brazzaville; tel: 56 95 72

SOCIAL AND EDUCATIONAL CENTRES

Day Care Centre: Ouenze Corps, Brazzaville
Guest House: Pointe-Noire
Home for the Needy: Yenge, Nzoko
Institute for the Blind: BP 20, Brazzaville
Nursery School: Commissioner V. Makoumbou Nursery School, Nzoko
Primary School: John Swinfen Primary School, Loua

HEALTH SERVICES

Clinic and Eye Treatment Centre
Moukoundji-Ngouaka: BP 20, Brazzaville

Clinics with Maternity Units
Dolisie: BP 235, Dolisie
Loua: BP 20, Brazzaville
Moungali: BP 20, Brazzaville
Nkayi: BP 229, Nkayi

GETTING TO KNOW EACH OTHER

In an international exchange programme for young Salvationists, these two young people from Norway and three from Peru worked and lived together for a year (six months in each country) to deepen understanding of their different cultures

CONGO (KINSHASA) AND ANGOLA TERRITORY

Territorial leaders:
Commissioners Stuart and Hope Mungate

Territorial Commander:
Commissioner Stuart Mungate (1 Feb 2007)

Chief Secretary:
Lieut-Colonel Onal Castor (1 Nov 2003)

Territorial Headquarters: Ave Ebea 23, Kinshasa-Gombe, Democratic Republic of Congo

Postal address: Armée du Salut 8636, Kinshasa 1, Democratic Republic of Congo

Tel: [243] 997-526050

The first Salvation Army corps was established in Kinshasa in 1934 by Adjutant (later Commissioner) and Mrs Henri Becquet. By decree of Léopold III, Armée du Salut was given legal status, with powers set out in a Deed of Constitution, on 21 February 1936. Work spread to Congo (Brazzaville) in 1937 and 16 years later it became a separate command. Work in Angola was officially established in 1985.

Zone: Africa
Countries included in the territory: Democratic Republic of Congo, Angola
'The Salvation Army' in French: Armée du Salut; in Kikongo: Nkangu a Luvulusu; in Lingala: Basolda na Kobikisa; in Portuguese: Exército de Salvação; in Swahili: Jeshi la Wokovu; in Tshiluba: Tshiluila Tsha Luhandu
Languages in which the gospel is preached: Chokwe, French, Kikongo, Lingala, Portuguese, Swahili, Tshiluba, Umbundu
Periodical: *Echo d'Espoir*

THE year 2007 began with the launching of a five-year strategic plan, the main objective being the doubling of Salvation Army membership in the territory. The year's slogan was 'Sharing Your Faith' and it was anticipated that 3,500 senior soldiers would be enrolled by 31 December 2007.

Some 800 local officers attended the first-ever Territorial Local Officers Congress (17-20 August 2006) and welcomed Commissioner Linda Bond (Secretary for Spiritual Life Development, IHQ) as the guest speaker. Her

Bible messages were inspiring and Spirit-filled.

On the closing day all other Salvationists and friends were invited to join the local officers for a great day of worship and celebration. Hundreds rededicated themselves to God and a large number of people sought Jesus Christ for the first time.

A 'Servant Leadership' training seminar, held during the first week of September 2006, was conducted by Lieut-Colonel Ian Southwell (then Secretary for International Training and Leadership Development, IHQ). Twenty-two delegates attended from all parts of the territory.

The Women's Ministries Department organised a women's retreat at Kavwaya (19-24 May 2006). Under the leadership of Commissioner Christina Kjellgren (then Territorial President of Women's Ministries, Sweden and Latvia), women from seven divisions were well fed spiritually by powerful and inspired Bible studies.

A new health centre was opened and dedicated to the glory of God (10 June 2006). Sanglo Plus Health Centre was built in partnership with the University of North Carolina. This new centre will serve as the family unit for HIV-positive patients. The American Ambassador to the Democratic Republic of Congo attended the opening ceremony and cut the ribbon.

The territory greatly values and thanks God for the invaluable support of its Partners in Mission territories. The Southwest Division (USA Western Territory) donated a tractor for the Cassava Project, a programme to feed 10,000 people in Congo Kinshasa who suffer from food insecurity. Eastern Victoria Division (Australia Southern Territory) provided funding to purchase new equipment and furnishings for Mbanza-Nsundi Youth Camp.

Funding also came from Switzerland to purchase a tractor to help widowers carry out small farming schemes, while Norway continued to finance a programme for victims of sex trafficking.

The first primary school in Angola Region was opened in Petrangol. Although the school building is not fully completed, more than 50 pupils attended during school year 2006/2007.

On 14 January 2007 the territory's Salvationists bade farewell to Commissioners Jean and Véronique Ludiazo. Their successors as territorial leaders, Commissioners Stuart and Hope Mungate, were installed on 5 February 2007. Warmly welcoming them back to the territory, Salvationists promised them their loyalty, love and wholehearted support.

STATISTICS

Officers 436 (active 353 retired 83) **Cadets** 12 **Employees** 4,274 **Pupils** 77,381
Corps 171 **Outposts** 111 **Health Centres** 27 **Maternity Hospitals/Clinics** 5 **Other specialist hospitals** 1 **Other specialist clinics** (inc HIV/Aid, dental, etc) 4 **Institutions** 5
Schools: Secondary 110 **Primary** 165 **Boarding** 2 **Maternal** 7 **University** 1
Senior Soldiers 20,048 **Adherents** 2,872 **Junior Soldiers** 8,235
Personnel serving outside territory Officers 8

STAFF

Sec for Personnel: Maj Eugene Dikalembolovanga
Sec for Programme: Maj Emmanuel Nsumbu
Candidates and Youth: Maj Norbert Makala
Development and Emergency Services: Maj Graçia Matondo
Editorial/Literature: Capt Denis Mafuta
Extension Training: Maj Jabhron Kibenga
Information Technology: Sgt Mbumu Muba Jean-Marc
Medical: Dr David Nku Imbie
Music: Maj L. M. Ntoya Kapel
  Sgt Jean-Marc Mbumu (Bandmaster)
  Sgt Joseph Nsilulu (Songster Leader)
  Sgt Pauline Matanu (Timbrel Leader)
Property: Mr Claude Huguenin
Public Relations: Maj Esaie Ntembi
  Schools Coordinator: Mr Raymond Luamba Ntolani

Social: Maj Odile Dikalembolovanga (Sec)
Miss Pauline Mavitu (HIV/Aids Section)
Training: Maj Norbert Nkanu
Women's Ministries: Comr Hope Mungate
(TPWM) Lt-Col Edmane Castor (TSWM) Maj
Lydia Isabel Matondo (Women's Development
Programmes) Maj Marie-José Ntembi (LOMS,
World Day of Prayer, Bible Studies) Maj
Clémentine Nsumbu (Vocational Training/
Literacy and Cafeteria) Maj Nicole Ntoya (JHLS
and Officers' Children) Maj Augustine Mpaka
(Widowed and Retired Officers)

DIVISIONS

Bas-Fleuve/Océan: BP 123, Matadi; Maj Simon
Nzeza Biyenga (mobile: 0819065803)
Inkisi: Armée du Salut, Kavwaya, BP 45,
Inkisi; Maj Célestin Pepe Pululu (mobile:
0999938248)
Kasaï-Occidental: BP 1404, Kananga;
Maj Sébastien Lubaki Mbala
(mobile: 0998449971)
Kasangulu: BP 14, Kasangulu; Maj Jean-
Baptiste Mayisilwa Mata (mobile:
0998519443)
Kinshasa 1: BP 8636, Kinshasa; Maj Nsoki
Joseph Bueya (mobile: 0815184323)
Kinshasa 2: BP 8636, Kinshasa;
Lt-Col Ferdinand Nzolameso Nlabu
(mobile: 0816891161)
Kisangani: BP 412, Kisangani; Capt Dieudonné
Nzuzi Tsilulu (mobile: 0997015174)
Luozi: Armée du Salut, Luozi; Maj Isidore
Mayunga Matondo (mobile: 0990023962)
Mbanza-Ngungu: BP 160; Maj Henri Masamba
Nangi (mobile: 0815201681)
Sud-Katanga: BP 2525, Lubumbashi;
Maj Sébastien Makani Diantezulua
(mobile: 0816057064)

REGION

Angola: Exército de Salvação, Caixa Postal
1656-C, Luanda; Maj Emmanuel Manu
Mpanzu (mobile: [244] 92315211)

DISTRICTS

Bandundu: Armée du Salut, Bandundu;
Maj Abraham Dongya Naniwambote
(mobile: 0998235058)
Isiro: BP 135

SECTIONS

Bukavu: Capt Godefroid Dumbu (mobile:
0816069947)
Masamuna: Maj Pierre Masunda (mobile:
0997114730)

TRAINING COLLEGE
BP 8636, Kinshasa

UNIVERSITY
William Booth University: BP 8636, Kinshasa;
Rector: Dr Mpiutu ne Mbodi Gaston

ATTACHED TO THQ
Conference Centre: Mbanza-Nzundu

MEDICAL WORK
Health Centres
Bas-Congo: Kasangulu, Boko-Mbuba, Kifuma,
Kingantoko, Kingudi, Kinzambi, Kintete,
Nkalama, Shefu, Kavwaya, Kimayala,
Mbanza-Nsundi, Mbanza-Nzundu
Kananga: Moyo
Kinshasa: Amba (Kisenso), Bakidi (Selembao),
Bomoi, Bopeto (Ndjili), Boyambi (Barumbu),
Elonga, Esengo (Masina), Kimia (Kintambo),
Molende (Kingasani)
Kisangani: Libota, Mokela, Dengue

Clinic
Maj Leka (Maluku/Kinshasa)

Dental Clinics
Boyambi (Barumbu), Elonga (Masuna),
Kasangulu (Bas-Congo)

Diabetic Clinic
Kananga

Foot Clinic
Boyambi

Maternity Units
Bomoi Kinshasa (acc 60); Kasangulu, Bas-
Congo (acc 13); Kavwaya, Bas-Congo
maternity and centre (acc 14) Maluku
Kinshasa (acc 12)

SECONDARY SCHOOLS
Bandundu: Institut Elonga; Institut Kwango;
Institut Mabwidi; Institut Ngampo Maku;
Institut Ngobila; Institut Makaya; Institut
Wembe; Institut Luvua Kabeya; 9 primary
schools
Bas-Congo: Institut Boyokani (Matadi); Institut
Diakanwa; Institut Kavwaya (Inkisi); Institut
Beti 1; Institut Beti 2; Institut Kimbumba-
Nord; Institut Bongo-Bongo; Institut Kingudi;
Institut Pédagogique Kasi; Institut Dikal
(Lufuku); ITP Kintete; Institut Kimayasi;
Institut Kinzadi 1; Institut Kinzadi 2; CS

Sewing machines donated by the Southwest Division, USA Western, are put to good use at one of the territory's vocational training centres

Kimbongo; Institut Kinzambi 1 (Kasangulu); Institut Kinzambi 2 (Luozi); Institut Lemba Diyanika; Institut Ludiazo; Institut Mampemba; Institut Mikalukidi; Institut Kitundulu; Institut Kivunda; Institut Kumba Ndilu; ITS Kumbi; ITC Lovo; Institut Maduma; Institut Manionzi; Institut Matanda; Institut Mateso; Institut Nkundi (Mbanza-Ngungu); CS Nsanga-Mamba; ITC Mbanza-Nsanda; ITA Mbanza-Nsundi; Institut Mbanza-Nzundu; Institut Mwala-Kinsende; ITA Nsongi-Kialelua; Institut Ndandanga; ITC Ngongolo; Institut Shefu; Institut Sombala; Institut Sundi-Mamba; Collège William Booth (Kasangulu); Institut Viaza; 63 primary schools, 1 kindergarden

Equateur: ITM Bukaka; Institut Bayamwaney; Institut Elonga; ITCA Lihau; Institut Mambune; Institut Masobe; Institut Mokuta; Institut Yambo; ITA Yamwenga; Institut Yangola; 8 primary schools; 2 kindergardens

Kasaï-Occidental (Kananga): Institut Bena-Leka; Institut Bena-Mbiye; Institut Bobumwe; Institut Muzemba; Institut Mwanza-Ngoma; Institut Tshitakanioka; 10 primary schools

Kinshasa: Institut Bakidi; Collège Gabriel Becquet (Selembao); Collège Bimwala;

ITC Bimwala; Institut Dianzenza; Institut Ilona; ITC Kwamouth; Institut Lukubama; Collège John Mabwidi; Institut Mabwidi; Lycée Matonge; Lycée Technique de Matonge; ITS Mbala; ITA Menkao; Institut Mpiutu; ITC Ndjili-Kilambu; Institut Ngizulu; Institut Nsemi; ITC Ntolani; ITI Ntolani; Institut Rwakadingi; Institut Wabaluku; Institut Yanda Mayemba; Institut Yimbukulu; 38 primary schools

Province Orientale (Kisangani): Institut Bonsomi; Institut Elikya; Institut Ilota; Institut Ketele; Institut Wagenia; 10 primary schools, 3 kindergartens

Sud-Katanga (Lubumbashi): ITC Wokovu (Katuba); Institut Tujenge; 5 primary schools

SOCIAL SERVICES

Children's Home and Community Child Care: Kinshasa (acc 11 and 20)

Development and Emergencies: Kavwaya, Mbanza-Nzundu, Impini, Mato, Kasungulu

Old People's Home: Kinshasa-Kintambo (acc 24)

Vocational Training Centres: Barumbu, Kinshasa (acc 114); Lubumbashi, Sud-Katanga (acc 37); Ndjili (acc 70)

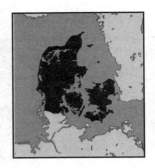

DENMARK TERRITORY

Territorial leaders:
Colonels Erling and Signe Helene Mæland

Territorial Commander:
Colonel Erling Mæland (1 Jul 2007)

Chief Secretary:
Major Graham Owen (1 Nov 2005)

Territorial Headquarters: Frederiksberg Allé 9, 1621 Copenhagen V, Denmark

Tel: [45] 33 31 41 92; fax: [45] 33 25 30 80; email: Frelsens@den.salvationarmy.org;

web site: www.frelsens-haer.dk

The work of The Salvation Army in Denmark commenced in Copenhagen in May 1887, pioneer officers being Major (later Lieut-Colonel) and Mrs Robert Perry.

Zone: Europe
Country included in the territory: Denmark
'The Salvation Army' in Danish: Frelsens Hær
Language in which the gospel is preached: Danish
Periodicals: *Mennesker & Tro*, *Kids Alive*, *Vision-Mission*, *Young Connection*

INTEGRATED Mission is a main theme of the Denmark Territory. Integrating and combining The Salvation Army's work and mission in corps, social institutions, recycling and second-hand shops is high on the agenda.

An integrated mission team was established and a series of brunch meetings were held regionally throughout the territory. These meetings enabled officers, Salvationists and employees from the different areas of Salvation Army work to come together and discuss how they might better integrate and coordinate their work at local level.

Another exciting development is the 'Kalejdoskop' project. This centre is situated in Nørrebro – an area of Copenhagen with a growing number of immigrants.

In a mentoring-project partly funded by the European Union, immigrants and Danes have partnered in small teams and attended classes in Danish culture and language, undertaken cultural visits, visited each others' homes and shared meals together. This exchange of knowledge and culture has especially helped women immigrants integrate more easily into Danish society.

The focus on family work within the social services has continued. An increasing number of camps and events, such as a trip to Legoland, provided better contact with families. The Salvation Army now has a waiting list of more than 3,000 families who want contact with the Army not just at Christmas but all year round.

A first-class conference hotel opened its doors for 130 people from poor families to enjoy a Salvation Army summer camp in 'luxurious' style. For most of the families it was the first time they had stayed in a hotel.

Christmas aid in Copenhagen also included a special surprise for every family – a 70-centimetre Lego ship. A container from the Maersk Seland company held the 50 cubic metres of Lego toys.

A new youth work initiative was the summer outreach and mission week. A mission team of youth workers was sent to Frederikshavn and helped the local corps contact young people through street mission, hockey matches and concerts.

In September 2006 the biennial congress was led by General Shaw Clifton and Commissioner Helen Clifton. The event attracted a large number of people and a new item on the congress programme was a brunch meeting for women.

In January 2007 Hendon Band (United Kingdom Territory) visited the territory and presented a festival to a full hall at Copenhagen Temple Corps.

STATISTICS

Officers 76 (active 30 retired 46) **Employees** 273
Corps 32 **Outpost** 1 **Social Institutions** 16 **Welfare Centres** 6
Senior Soldiers 994 **Adherents** 254 **Junior Soldiers** 32

STAFF

Sec for Programme: Maj Kirsten Owen
  Programme, Corps: Maj Kirsten Owen
  Asst Sec for Programme: Maj John Wahl
  Programme, Social: Maj Hannelise Tvedt
Editors: Mr Bent Dahl-Jensen (*Mennesker & Tro*) Capt Levi Giversen (*Vision-Mission*)
Finance: Mrs Annie Kristensen
Home League and Over-60s: Maj Pia Mogensen
Missing Persons: Col Jørn Lauridsen
Missionary and Child Sponsorship: Maj Ruth Christensen
Music: Mr Erik Silfverberg
Property: Maj Terje Tvedt
Public Relations and Information Technology: Mr Lars Lydholm
Women's Ministries: Col Signe Helene Mæland (TPWM)
Youth and Candidates: Capt Lone Hertz

SOCIAL SERVICES

Head Office: Frederiksberg Allé 9, 1621 Copenhagen V; tel: 33 31 41 92; fax: 36 30 70 34

Clothing Industry (Recycling Centres)
6705 Esbjerg Ø, Ravnevej 2; tel: 75 14 24 22; fax: 75 14 00 47
5000 Odense C, Roersvej 33; tel: 66 11 25 21; fax: 66 19 05 21
9560 Hadsund, Mariagervej 3; tel: 98 57 42 48; fax: 98 57 38 72
4900 Nakskov, Narviksvej 15; tel: 54 95 12 05; fax: 54 95 12 04

Community Centres
9000 Aalborg, Skipper Clementsgade 11; tel: 98 11 50 62
1408 Copenhagen K, Wildersgade 66; tel: 32 54 44 10 (acc 80)
4900 Nakskov, Niels Nielsengade 6; tel: 54 95 30 06 (acc 60)

Day Nurseries
9900 Frederikshavn Humlebien, Knudensvej 1B; tel: 98 42 33 27 (acc 40)
2000 Frederiksberg, Melita, Mariendalsvej 4; tel: 38 87 01 48 (acc 58)
2500 Valby, Solsikken, Annexstræde 29; tel: 36 16 23 11 (acc 22)
2650 Hvidovre, Kastanjehuset, Idrætsvej 65A; tel: 36 78 40 23 (acc 33)
2650 Hvidovre, Solgården, Catherine Booths vej 22; tel: 36 78 07 71 (acc 100)
7500 Holstebro Solhøj, Skolegade 51; tel: 97 42 61 21 (acc 30)

Emergency Shelters for Families

2650 Hvidovre, Svendebjerggård, Catherine
  Booths vej 20; tel: 36 49 65 77 (acc 25)
1754 Copenhagen V, Den Åbne Dør,
  Hedebygade 30; tel: 33 24 91 03 (acc 15)
4700 Næstved, Østergade 13; tel: 55 77 22 70
  (acc 6)

Eventide Nursing Centre

2200 Copenhagen N Aftensol, Lundtoftegade 5;
  tel: 35 30 55 00 (acc 43)

Social Advice Bureau and
Goodwill Centre

Grundtvigsvej 17 st, 1864 Frederiksberg C;
  tel: 33 24 56 67

Project for Long-term Unemployed

Nørholmlejren, Oldenborrevej 2, 9000 Aalborg;
  tel: 98 34 18 10 (acc 10)

Rehabilitation Centre

Hørhuset, 2300 Copenhagen S, Hørhusvej 5;
  tel: 32 55 56 22 (acc 64)

Students Residence

2100 Copenhagen Ø, Helgesengade 25;
  tel: 35 37 74 32 (acc 41)

SOCIAL SERVICES (field administered)
Community Centres

2200 Copenhagen N, Kalejdoskop,
  Thorsgade 48 A; tel: 35 85 00 87
3000 Helsingør, Regnbuen Community Centre,
  Strandgade 60; tel: 49 21 10 06
4800 Nykøbing Falster, Jernbanegade 42,

Community Centre and Corps activities;
  tel: 54 85 71 89
9560 Hadsund, Nørregade 10, Den Åbne Dør
  Community Centre; tel: 23 26 19 15
2500 Valby, Valby Langgade 83;
  tel: 36 45 67 67
7100 Vejle, Midtpunktet, Staldgårdsgade 4;
  tel: 75 82 78 38

Summer Camps

9000 Aalborg, Nørholmlejren, Oldenborrevej 2;
  tel: 98 34 18 10 (acc 50)
8700 Horsens, Hjarnø; tel: 75 68 32 24 (acc 25)
5450 Otterup, Rømhildsminde, Ferievej 11-13,
  Jørgensø; tel: 64 87 13 36

UNDER THQ
Holiday Home and Conference Centre

Lillebælt, Nørre Allé 47, Strib, 5500 Middelfart;
  tel: 64 40 10 57; fax: 63 40 02 82 (acc 30)

Investigation Bureau

Frederiksberg Allé 9, 1621 Copenhagen V;
  tel: 33 31 41 92

Radio Station (Copenhagen area)

Frederiksberg Allé 9, 1621 Copenhagen V;
  tel: 33 31 41 25 (studio)

Youth and Conference Centre

Baggersminde, Fælledvej 132, 2791 Dragør;
  tel: 32 53 70 18; fax: 32 53 70 98 (acc 80)

New Project

Community Centre: 2700 Brønshøj, Ruten 14;
  tel: 36 17 70 06

PRAISE FROM THE PRESIDENT

Finland and Estonia Territory: The President of Finland, Tarja Halonen, is welcomed to The Salvation Army's Christmas Kettle Concert in Helsinki by territorial leaders Colonels André and Silvia Cox. The president spoke warmly of The Salvation Army and its contribution to the betterment of Finnish society.

EASTERN EUROPE TERRITORY

Territorial leaders:
**Commissioners Willem and
Netty van der Harst**

Territorial Commander:
Commissioner Willem van der Harst
(1 Jul 2007)

Chief Secretary:
Lieut-Colonel Alistair Herring (16 Sep 2006)

Territorial Headquarters: Krestiansky Tupik 16/1, Moscow

Postal address: Russian Federation, 109044 Moscow, Krestiansky Tupik 16/1

Tel: [7] (495) 911 2600/2956; fax: [7] (495) 911 2753; email: Russia@eet.salvationarmy.org;
web site: www.thesalvationarmy.ru

Work was initiated in Russia in 1910 by Colonel Jens Povlsen of Denmark but circumstances necessitated his withdrawal after 18 months. Army operations then recommenced in St Petersburg in 1913 as an extension to the work in Finland. After the February 1917 revolution the work flourished, Russia became a distinct command and reinforcements arrived from Sweden. As a result of the October revolution they had, however, to be withdrawn at the end of 1918, leaving 40 Russian and Finnish officers to continue the work under extreme hardship until the Army was finally proscribed in 1923.

Salvation Army activities were officially recommenced in July 1991, overseen by the Norway, Iceland and The Færoes Territory with the arrival of Lieut-Colonels John and Bjorg Bjartveit. It became a distinct command in November 1992. Work was extended to Ukraine (1993), Georgia (1993), Moldova (1994) and Romania (1999). On 1 June 2001 the command was redesignated the Eastern Europe Command. It was elevated to territory status on 1 March 2005.

Zone: Europe
Countries included in territory: Georgia, Moldova, Romania, Russian Federation, Ukraine
'The Salvation Army' in Georgian: Khsnis Armia; in Moldovan/Romanian: Armata Salvarii; in Russian: Armiya Spaseniya; in Ukrainian: Armiya Spasinnya
Languages in which the gospel is preached: Georgian, Moldovan, Romanian, Russian, Ukrainian
Periodicals: *Vestnik Spaseniya* (*The War Cry*), *The Officer* (both Russian)

'HOPE Starts Here' – at the cross – was the theme for the Russia 15th Anniversary Congress in St Petersburg, led by General Shaw Clifton and Commissioner Helen Clifton (2-3 September 2006).

The event celebrated 15 years of ministry since the work was reopened in Russia in 1991 and also looked forward to what God would do, in years to come, in this and the other four nations of the territory.

Some of the way ahead became clearer when the then Territorial Commander, Commissioner Barry Pobjie, presented his 'New Horizon' vision – a plan to see The Salvation Army go gradually to other major cities of this vast territory.

The commitment to this expansion was evident when the corps flags of targeted cities entered the auditorium to much enthusiastic applause. Since that time five new cities have received corps planting officers.

On 6 October 2006, in Strasbourg, France, the European Court of Human Rights unanimously ruled for The Salvation Army saying that the Russian Federation's refusal to register the Moscow branch of The Salvation Army in 1999 violated the religious organisation's rights to 'freedom of religion and association' under Europe's human rights convention. It is hoped that registration in Moscow will soon be completed.

A project which offers services to Moscow's street children and youth was transferred from another international agency to The Salvation Army on 13 December 2006. The centre is open five days a week for six hours.

Young people come in off the street to receive a meal provided by a local church, medical attention from a doctor, social help and educational assistance, and have access to a shower and laundry.

A corps officer has been appointed to the centre so that Sunday worship can be offered to the youths and other homeless people from the area.

The development of officers and their role in leadership has continued to be a priority for the territory, with a marriage enrichment and training seminar and a further Brengle Institute being held in the past 12 months.

The first national Romanian Regional Officers, Captains Valery and Victoria Lalac, were appointed in April 2007.

STATISTICS
Officers 131 (active) **Aux-Capts** 2 **Cadets** (1st Yr) 19 **Employees** 319
Corps 60 **Corps Plants** 5 **Rehabilitation Centres** 2 **Seniors Centres** 2
Senior Soldiers 2,001 **Adherents** 1,027 **Junior Soldiers** 370

STAFF
Candidates: Capt Vitaly Chiriac
Editorial: Capt Anna Kotrakadze
Education: Capt Brad Caldwell
Emergency Response: Capt David Kotrikadze
Finance: Maj Richard Herivel
  Audit and Asst Finance Officers: Capt Natalia Pismeniuk and Capt Olga Kootsnesova
Leadership Development: Mr Cliff Worthing
League of Mercy: Maj Maria Kharkova
Mission Development: Lt-Col Astrid Herring
Mission Training: Capt Anita Caldwell
Pastoral Care: Capt Elena Shulyanski
Prayer Ambassador: Capt Vadim Kolesnik
Property: Capt David Kotrikadze
Public Relations: Mr and Mrs Cliff and Simone Worthing
Territorial Sergeant-Major: Yuri Gulanitsky
Training Principal: Capt Svetlana Sharov
Women's Ministries: Comr Netty van der Harst (TPWM) Capt Galina Drozdovsky (TWMO)
Projects Cordinators: Mr Neale Rudd

DIVISIONS
Russia: 105120 Russia, Moscow, Khlebnikov Pereulok, 7 bld, 2; tel: 495 678 03 51; fax: 495 678 91 60; Maj Alexander Kharkov
Moldova: Moldova, Chisinau, 2012, Armata Salvarii, PO Box 137, Str P. Movila #19; tel: (37322) 235076; telefax: (37322) 237972; Maj Jostein Nielsen
Ukraine: 01023, Ukraine, Kiev, Shota Rustavely St 38, Suite 3 3; tel/fax:(380 44) 287 4598, 287 3705; 246 6689; Maj Marie Willermark

REGIONS
Georgia: Tbilisi, 2-nd Microregion Nutsubidze, Area 1, Build 2, Apart 3, Georgia;

tel: 995 (32) 39 9654, 39 9764;
fax: 995 (32) 31 7383; Capt Giorgi Salarishvili
Romania: 722212 Bucharest, Sector 2, Str Maica
Domnului Nr 2, Bl T58, Scara 1, Et 5, Ap 14;
tel: [10] (4021) 211 11 99; Capt Valery Lalac

MISSION TRAINING AND EDUCATION CENTRE INSTITUTE FOR OFFICER TRAINING

Russia, Moscow, 105120 Karl Larson Centre,
Khlebnikov Per 7/2;
tel: (495) 678 55 14, 678 03 51

SOCIAL SERVICE CENTRES
(Community outreach, HIV/Aids, alcohol, drugs, programmes for homeless)

Georgia
Children's Centre: Didi Digomi, 35 Giorgi
Brtzinsvale St
Youth Centre: Rustavi, Baratashvili St 26

Moldova
Medical Clinic: Chisinau, Mesterul Manole 1;
tel: (373 22) 47-2382
Mobile Clinic; Project Shoes; Roma Project

Romania
Laundry

Russia
Moscow: Karl Larsson Centre, Khlebnikov
pereulok 7, bld 2
Rostov-on-Don: The Bridge Programme,
Lermontovskaya St 229;
tel/fax: (8632) 48-2410;
email: rostov_doncorps@mail.ru
St Petersburg:
Liteini Prospect # 44 B, 191104;
tel: (812) 273-9297
Chaplaincy Centre: Usst Izhora Village
Mobile Canteen: Novoribinskaya St 19
Medical Clinic, Feeding Programme, Food
and Clothing Distribution, Rehabilitation
Programme, Shoe Repair Workshop, Home
Care Programme

CORPS-BASED SERVICES
Feeding Programmes (33); After-school
Programmes; Homeless Children Outreach;
Orphan Outreach; Medical Programmes;
Haircutting Programmes; Prison Ministry
Programmes

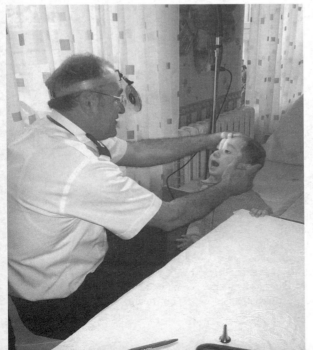

Dr Nicolai Caraman, a Salvationist from Moldova Division, is seen working at the Army's medical clinic in Chisinau. The Salvation Army also operates a mobile clinic in Moldova.

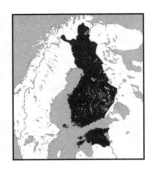

FINLAND AND ESTONIA TERRITORY

Territorial leaders:
Colonels André and Silvia Cox

Territorial Commander:
Colonel André Cox (11 Jul 2005)

Chief Secretary:
Lieut-Colonel Arja Laukkanen (1 Jun 2004)

Territorial Headquarters: Uudenmaankatu 40, 00120 Helsinki

Postal address: Post Box 161, 00121 Helsinki, Finland

Tel: [358] (09) 6812300; fax: [358] (09) 601131; email: finland@pelastusarmeija.fi

Web site: www.pelastusarmeija.fi

Work in Finland was commenced on 8 November 1889 in Broholm's Riding School, Helsinki, by four aristocratic Finns – Captain and Mrs Constantin Boije with Lieutenants Hedvig von Haartman and Alva Forsius. Within six months Hedvig von Haartman was appointed leader of the work in the country.

Work in Estonia first commenced in 1927 and continued until 1940 when it was closed due to the Second World War. It recommenced in the autumn of 1995 when three Finnish officers were assigned to start the work in Tallinn.

Zone: Europe
Countries included in the territory: Estonia, Finland
'The Salvation Army' in Estonian: Päästearmee; in Finnish: Pelastusarmeija; in Swedish: Frälsningsarmén
Languages in which the gospel is preached: English, Estonian, Finnish, Russian, Swedish
Periodicals: *Krigsropet* (Swedish), *Nappis* (Finnish), *Sotahuuto* (Finnish)

SALVATIONISTS see the confirmation that God is doing 'a new thing' within The Salvation Army in Finland and Estonia as they continue to witness the spiritual results of the Territorial Roots Congress (22-25 June 2006). The venue was packed for the event, which offered a rich mix of plenary sessions and various workshops.

Cadets from Finland and Switzerland joined forces in an evangelical campaign in Estonia, held shortly after Easter. People were greatly challenged and there have been positive responses from contacts made in each of the centres visited.

In November, 36 officers underwent the disaster management training course, 'PREPARE' (Prepare to Respond to Emergencies: Planning and Readiness Education). Many of the tools taught in this course are relevant to work undertaken every day by Salvation Army officers in the communities in which they serve.

Significant publicity and media

interest was generated by the 100th celebration of the Christmas Kettle collection in Finland.

On Sunday 17 December 2006 the territory organised its second Christmas charity concert. The main TV channel YLE1 recorded concert highlights which were broadcast two days before Christmas during prime-time viewing.

The highlight of the event, widely covered in the national and local press, was the presence of Finland's President Tarja Halonen and members of the diplomatic corps. President Halonen spoke very warmly about The Salvation Army and its contribution to the betterment of Finnish society.

The territory's five-year strategic plan for spiritual renewal focuses on the implementation of integrated mission concepts. The first meeting of the Central House integrated mission team took place on 24-25 January 2007.

Central House is the largest of The Salvation Army's facilities in Finland with numerous social and spiritual programmes. The aim is to see how these programmes can better serve the surrounding community.

An integrated mission training workshop was held for more than 50 active officers (6-9 March 2007). Delegates were energised, equipped and encouraged to rediscover the importance of being available to engage meaningfully with people.

STATISTICS
Officers 159 (active 54 retired 105) **Cadets** 7 **Employees** 400
Corps 29 **Outposts** 10 **Goodwill Centres** 4 **Institutions** 28

Senior Soldiers 858 **Adherents** 80 **Junior Soldiers** 26

STAFF
Candidates: Maj Eija Kornilow
Editor: Maj Antero Puotiniemi
Education: Maj Eija Kornilow
Field: Majs Johnny and Eva Kleman
Finance: Liisa Kaakinen
Home and Family: Col Silvia Cox, Maj Anneli Franke
Missing Persons: Maj Osmi Laaksonen
Public Relations and Information: Maj Sirkka Paukku, Jan Jungner
Personnel: Maj Marja Meras
Social: Maj Tella Puotiniemi, Gun-Viv Glad-Jungner
Training: Maj Petter Kornilow
Women's Ministries: Col Silvia Cox (TPWM)
Youth: Capt Saga Lippo-Karvonen

SOCIAL SERVICES
Clothing Industry (Recycling Centres)
90580 Oulu, Ratamotie 22; tel: (08) 346713
33540 Tampere, Tursonkatu 3; tel: (03) 3640801
20300 Turku, Virusmäentie 65; tel: (02) 2315447
01260 Vantaa, Itäinen Valkoisenlähteentie 15; tel: (09) 8769572

Homes for Alcoholics
68600 Pietarsaari, Permontie 34; tel: (06) 7236766 (acc 15)
33100 Tampere, Tampereen Valtatie 4; tel: (03) 2235415 (acc 54)
20500 Turku, Hämeenkatu 18; tel: (02) 2329735 (acc 37)

Shelters for Men
15140 Lahti, Hämeenkatu 28; tel: (03) 7827539 (acc 29)
00530 Helsinki, Alppikatu 25; tel: (09) 7743130 (acc 234)
00550 Helsinki, Inarintie 8; tel: (09) 717377 (acc 34)
28120 Pori, Veturitallinkatu 3; tel: (02) 6333519 (acc 25)

Shelters for Women
00530 Helsinki, Papinkuja 1; tel: (09) 7533164 (acc 18)
00530 Helsinki, Castréninkatu 24-26 F 46 (acc 12)
15140 Lahti, Hämeenkatu 28 (acc 10)

Poor Relief Distribution Centres
Alppikatu 25, 00530 Helsinki; tel: (09) 7532 597

Finland and Estonia Territory

Hämeenkatu 28 B, 15140 Lahti;
  tel: (03) 7823 671
Ratamotie 22, 90580 Oulu; tel: (08) 5564 472
Tursonkatu 3, 33540 Tampere;
  tel: (03) 2124 259
Vanha Hämeentie 29, 20540 Turku;
  tel: (02) 2360 537

Service Centres
Alppikatu 25, 00530 Helsinki;
  tel: (09) 714 013
Permontie 34, 68600 Pietarsaari;
  tel: (06) 7236 766
Vanha Hämeentie 29, 20540 Turku;
  tel: (02) 2360 537

Children's Day Care Centres
48100 Kotka, Korkeavuorenkatu 24;
  tel: (05) 2108600 (acc 36)
15140 Lahti, Hämeenkatu 28 A 5;
  tel: (03) 878680 (acc 94)
90140 Oulu, Artturintie 27; tel: (08) 330706
  (acc 30)
06100 Porvoo, Joonaksentie 1;
  tel: (019) 580448 (acc 54)
28100 Pori, Mikonkatu 19; tel: (02) 6332474
  (acc 83)
95420 Tornio, Putaankatu 2; tel: (016) 445156
  (acc 47)

Children's Home
06100 Porvoo, Aleksanterinkatu 24;
  tel: (019) 580443 (acc 10)

Eventide Homes
02710 Espoo, Viherlaaksonranta 19;
  tel: (09) 8493810 (acc 60)
20740 Turku, Sigridinpolku; tel: (02) 2421238
  (acc 25)

Senior Citizens' Unit
00760 Helsinki, Puistolantie 6 (acc 75)

Goodwill Centre
00530 Helsinki, Alppikatu 25; tel: (09) 7532597

Summer Camp Centres
34300 Kuru Vanha Pappila, Tampere
  (acc 30)
03100 Nummela, Helsinki (acc 60)

Students' Hostel
40100 Jyväskylä, Ilmarisenkatu 2 E 86;
  tel: (014) 612 024 (acc 13)

Care of Domestic Violence Victims (Hedvig House)
00530 Helsinki, Castréninkatu 24-26 F;
  tel: (09) 760 328

Youth and Conference Centre
Särkijärvi, Särkilammentie 45, 01120
  Västerskog; tel: (09) 8779972;
  fax: (09) 8779069;
  email: sarkijku@saunalahti.fi; web site:
  ww.pelastusarmeija.fi/sarkijarvi/english/html

Youth Centre
Sovelontie 91, 33480 Ylöjärvi;
  tel: (03) 3491010

ESTONIA REGION
Regional Headquarters: Kopli 8-14, 10412
  Tallinn; tel: [372] 641 3330;
  fax: [372] 641 3331;
Regional Commander: Maj Aino Muikku

Corps 2 **Corps Projects** 2

Hope House (Lootusemaja): Laevastiku 1a,
  10313 Tallinn; tel: [372] 656 1047 (acc 42)
Lasnamäe Youth and Children's Centre: Pae 19,
  11414 Tallinn; tel: [372] 600 7753
Camp: Ranna 24, Loksa; tel: [372] 603 1012

❛ Significant publicity and media interest was generated by the 100th celebration of the Christmas Kettle collection in Finland . . . The territory organised its second Christmas charity concert. The main TV channel recorded concert highlights which were broadcast two days before Christmas during prime-time viewing. ❜

FRANCE TERRITORY

Territorial Commander:
Colonel Alain Duchêne (1 Nov 2006)

Chief Secretary:
Lieut-Colonel Joseph Lukau (1 Nov 2006)

Territorial Headquarters: 60 rue des Frères Flavien
75976 Paris Cedex 20, France

Tel: [33] (1) 43 62 25 00; fax: [33] (1) 43 62 25 56; web site: www.armeedusalut.fr

Since 'La Maréchale' (eldest daughter of William and Catherine Booth) conducted the Army's first meeting in Paris on Sunday 13 March 1881, Salvationist influence has grown and remarkable social and spiritual results have been achieved. French officers commenced work in Algeria in 1934 and this work was maintained until 1970.

Zone: Europe
Country included in the territory: France
'The Salvation Army' in French: Armée du Salut
Languages in which the gospel is preached: French
Periodicals: *Avec Vous, Le Bulletin de la Ligue du Foyer, Le Fil, Le Magazine, L'Officier, Quand Même*

USED as the theme of special campaigns in the territory, 'Plug 'n' Move' expressed the goal of Salvationists in France – to be 'plugged in' to Jesus and move forward in their faith.

It was also the theme of the National Youth Congress (27-30 October 2006). Bible studies, workshops, forums and question-and-answer sessions with the territorial commander provided opportunities for the 240 teenage delegates to take stock, structure their faith and consider choosing to serve God and their fellow man.

A musical presentation further challenged the young people about the realities of life, and many of them expressed a desire to be led by God. Some spent time in prayer and counselling with one of the congress chaplains.

Prayers were offered that young Salvationists would be challenged to respond to God's call to full-time service as officers.

An afternoon was devoted to open-air evangelism, such as one-to-one contacts and distributing tracts, before the young people gathered in front of a cathedral to witness by their singing.

In the 46 professionally-run social institutions of The Salvation Army Foundation, high-quality work continues to develop in a variety of social areas, from homelessness to care of the elderly, which includes an innovative programme among sufferers of Alzheimers disease. The Salvation

Army also has a centre for mentally handicapped people.

One of the country's major social problems is the large percentage of people who are unemployed. The Salvation Army Foundation leads a European project, called PRAETIC, which fights against discrimination in the search for employment.

The project aims to help people housed in Salvation Army centres find work and to give value to their integration back into employment. It is run in partnership with several businesses and associations.

The Salvation Army in France is actively involved in various national committees concerned with social justice (having taken the initiative in instigating these committees back in 1929.) Salvation Army representatives have now been requested by the Minister for Social Affairs to be part of a committee dealing with housing, a major issue in the country.

STATISTICS
Officers 179 (active 78 retired 101) **Employees** 1,660
Corps 29 **Outposts** 2 **Institutions** 43
Senior Soldiers 894 **Adherents** 185 **Junior Soldiers** 78
Personnel serving outside territory Officers 10

THE SALVATION ARMY CONGREGATION

BOARD OF DIRECTORS
Col Alaine Duchêne, Lt-Col Joseph Lukau, Lt-Col Angélique Lukau, Maj Patrick Booth, Capt Philippe Schmitter

STAFF
Asst CS: Maj Patrick Booth
Education and Prisons: Maj Jean-Paul Thoni
Field: Maj Daniel Naud
  Associate Field Sec: Maj Eliane Naud

Finance: Mr Alain Raoul
Territorial Band: B/M Mrs Arielle Mangeard
Women's Ministries: Lt-Col Angelique Lukau (TPWM) Maj Margaret Booth (TSWM)

THE SALVATION ARMY FOUNDATION

BOARD OF DIRECTORS
President: Col Alain Duchêne
Secretary: Maj Daniel Naud
Treasurer: Mr Armand Laferrere
Members: Mr Jean Benet, Mrs Irène Debu-Carbonnier, Mr Bernard Westercamp

STAFF
Director General: Mr Alain Raoul
Asst Director General – Zone A: Mrs Michelle Samson
Asst Director General – Zone B: Mr Boris Antonoff
Asst Director General – Zone C: Mr Bernard Guilhou
Asst Director General – Zone D: Mrs Christine Le Roy Fiche
Asst Director General – Zone E: Mr Denis Lebaillif
Director of Communications: Mr Christophe Rousselot
Director of Finance: Mrs Martine Dumont
Missing Persons: Maj Anne-Marie Cabanes
Publications: Maj Robert Muller
Volunteers: Maj Dominique Glories

GOODWILL CENTRES
59140 Dunkerque: 1 rue de St Pol; tel: (03) 28 29 09 37
75003 Paris: Centre St Martin, 31 blvd St Martin; tel: (01) 40 27 80 07
75019 Paris: Maison du Partage, 32 rue Bouret; tel: (01) 53 38 41 30

RESIDENCES FOR RETIRED PERSONS
74560 Monnetier-Mornex: Résidence Leirens, Chemin St Georges; tel: (04) 50 31 23 12 (acc disabled 40)
75014 Paris: 9 bis, Villa Coeur-de-Vey; tel: (01) 45 43 38 75
93230 Romainville: 2 rue Vassou; tel: (01) 48 45 12 82

SUMMER COLONY FOR CHILDREN AND YOUTH CENTRE
30530 Chamborigaud: Chausse; tel/fax: (04) 66 61 47 08

New soldiers are enrolled at Paris Coeur de Vey Corps. The goal of Salvationists in France is to be 'plugged in' to Jesus and to move forward in their faith.

SOCIAL SERVICES
* These centres include workshop facilities for the unemployed

Centres for Men
27380 Radepont: Château de Radepont; tel: (02) 32 49 03 82 (acc 73)

*76600 Le Havre: Le Phare, 191 rue de la Vallée; tel: (02) 35 24 22 11 (acc 280)
Annexe: (Atelier de récupération) 32 rue Gustave Nicolle (acc 100)

*59018 Lille Cedex: Les Moulins de l'Espoir, 48 rue de Valenciennes, BP 184; tel: (03) 20 52 69 09 (acc 124)

*69006 Lyon: La Cité de L'Armée du Salut, 131 ave Thiers; tel: (04) 78 52 60 80 (acc men 185, women 60)

*13003 Marseille: 190 rue Félix Pyat; tel: (04) 91 02 49 37 (acc 170)

57100 Thionville: 8 place de la République; tel: (03) 82 83 09 60

*68100 Mulhouse: Le Bon Foyer, 24 rue de L'Ile Napoléon; tel: (03) 89 44 43 56 (acc 60)

*75013 Paris: La Cité de Refuge, 12 rue Cantagrel; tel: (01) 53 61 82 00; including Visitation Dept, Labour Bureau and Clothing Distribution Centre (acc men 51, women 85)
Annexes: 75013 Paris: Centre Espoir, 39-43 rue du Chevaleret (Industrial Branch 'Help through Work' programme) (acc 203)

*76005 Rouen: 26 rue de Crosne; tel: (02) 35 70 38 00 (acc 50)

Annexe: 76150 Maromme, 36 rue Raymond Duflo; tel: (02) 35 76 02 27 (acc 15)

Centre for Women
30900 Nîmes: Les Glycines (home for battered wives), 33 rue de la Bienfaisance; tel: (04) 66 62 21 90 / 66 04 99 49 (acc 25)

75011 Paris: Le Palais de la Femme, 94 rue de Charonne; tel: (01) 46 59 30 00 (acc 644)

Centres for Men and Women
90000 Belfort: 3 rue de l'As de Carreau (acc 50)

74560 Monnetier-Mornex: Holiday Home, Les Hutins; tel: (04) 50 36 59 52 (acc 17)

75020 Paris: Résidence Albin Peyron, 60 rue des Frères Flavien, tel: (01) 48 97 54 50 (acc 400)

78100 St Germain en Laye: La Maison Verte, 14 rue de la Maison Verte; tel: (01) 39 73 29 39 (acc 40)

Centre for Families
94320 Thiais: Résidence Sociale, 7 bd de Stalingrad; tel: (01) 48 53 57 15

Children's Homes
35404 Saint-Malo Cedex:
La Maison des Garçons, 35 ave Eugene Herpin, BP 8; tel: (02) 99 40 21 97 (acc boys 18)

35404 Saint-Malo Cedex : Le Nid, 23 ave Paul Turpin, BP 21; tel: (02) 99 40 21 94 (acc 24)

Convalescent Centre
07800 La Voulte-sur-Rhône: Le Château de St

Georges-les-Bains; tel: (04) 75 60 81 72
(acc 50)

Emergency Accommodation
75013 Centre d'accueil d'urgence, 12 rue
Cantagrel; tel: (01) 53 61 82 00 (acc 42)
75013 Paris: Palais du Peuple, 29 rue des
Cordelières; tel: (01) 43 37 93 61 (acc 220)
75011 Paris: Résidence Catherine Booth,
15 rue Crespin du Gast;
tel: (01) 43 14 70 90 (acc 110)

Eventide Homes
60500 Chantilly: L'Arc-en-Ciel, 5 bd de la
Libération; tel: (03) 44 57 00 33 (acc 35)
42028 Saint-Etienne Cedex 01 : La Sarrazinière,
Allée Amilcare Cipriani, tel 04 77 62 17 92
47400 Tonneins: Le Soleil d'Automne, ave
Blanche Peyron, Escoutet; tel: (05) 53 88 32 00
(acc 48)

Mother and Baby Home
75019 Paris: Centre Maternel des Lilas, 9 ave de
la Porte des Lilas; tel: (01) 48 03 81 90
(acc mothers 36, babies 45)

Municipal Shelters
(managed by The Salvation Army)
90000 Belfort: Plate-forme d'urgence sociale,
7 rue Colbert; tel (03) 84 21 05 53
*51100 Reims: Le Nouvel Horizon, 10 rue Goïot;
tel: (03) 26 85 23 09 (acc 25)
Annex: 42 rue de Taissy; tel: (03) 26 05 12 08
('Help through Work' programme) (acc 75)

Rehabilitation Centre for Handicapped
45410 Artenay: Château d'Auvilliers;
tel: (02) 38 80 00 14 (acc 42)
93370 Montfermeil: MAS Le Grand Saule,
2 avenue des Tilleuls; tel: (01) 41 70 30 40

Training Centres for Children
67100 Strasbourg-Neudorf: Le Foyer du Jeune
Homme, 42 ave Jean Jaurès;
tel: (03) 88 84 16 50 (acc 42 boys)
Annex: Sora, Sce d'Adaptation en milieu
naturel
77270 Villeparisis: Domaine de Morfondé;
tel: (01) 60 26 61 61 (acc 95)
34091 Montpellier Cedex: Institut Nazareth,
13 rue de Nazareth, BP 24105;
tel: (0) 4 99 58 21 21; fax: (0) 4 99 58 21 12

Children's Day Care Centres
30000 Nîmes: Aire du Lycéen, 4/6 bd Victor
Hugo; tel: (04) 66 21 02 88
81200 Mazamet: Centre En Avant, 7 rue du Curé
Pous; tel/fax: (05) 63 61 12 30
43400 Le Chambon sur Lignon: Le Bivouac,
7 rue Neuve: tel: (04) 71 59 70 87
69007 Lyon: L'Arche de Noé, 5 rue Félissent;
tel (04) 78 58 29 66

Training Centres
68200 Mulhouse: Marie-Pascale Péan, 35 ave de
Colmar; tel: (03) 89 42 14 77 (acc 26)
30000 Nîmes: La Villa Blanche Peyron, 122
Impasse Calmette; tel: (04) 66 04 99 40 (acc 18)

JUNIOR SOLDIERS SAY 'WELCOME!'

India Northern Territory: Junior soldiers in Kolkata form a guard of honour to welcome the General and Commissioner Helen Clifton. In his Bible message to a congregation of more than 1,000 people General Clifton emphasised the importance of the family.

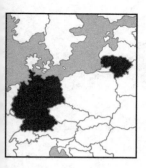

GERMANY AND LITHUANIA TERRITORY

Territorial leaders:
Colonels Horst and Helga Charlet

Territorial Commander:
Colonel Horst Charlet (12 Jun 2005)

Chief Secretary:
Lieut-Colonel Odd Berg (12 Jun 2005)

Territorial Headquarters: 50677 Köln, Salierring 23-27, Germany

Tel: [49] (221) 20 8190; fax: [49] (221) 208 1957; email: NHQ@GER.salvationarmy.org;
web site: www.heilsarmee.de

Salvation Army work in Germany began in Stuttgart on 14 November 1886 through the persistent sale of the Swiss *Kriegsruf* by Staff-Captain Fritz Schaaf who, after being converted in New York, was stationed in Switzerland and could not resist the call to bring the message over the border into his fatherland.

The Salvation Army was first registered as a limited company in Berlin in 1897 and was recognised throughout Germany as a church and public corporation on 10 October 1967 by law in Nordrhein-Westfalen. It is recognised as a religious association with public rights in the states of Berlin, Hessen, Schleswig-Holstein and Baden-Württemberg.

Salvation Army work in Lithuania having begun in 1998, the Germany Territory was redesignated the Germany and Lithuania Territory in September 2005.

Zone: Europe
Countries included in the territory: Germany, Lithuania
'The Salvation Army' in German: Die Heilsarmee; in Lithuanian: Isganymo Armija
Language in which the gospel is preached: German, Lithuanian
Periodicals: *Danke, Der Kriegsruf, Heilsarmee-Forum*

WITH the closure of the European School for Officer Training in Basle, Switzerland, cadets began being trained again within the territory after a gap of 20 years. A comprehensive training programme for officership was launched.

While following Bible study course at IGW College in Essen (whose students come from various evangelical churches), the cadets also receive teaching about Salvation Army distinctives and participate in practical Army service in preparation for future ministry.

During the 2006 FIFA World Cup, staged in Germany, The Salvation Army worked with Kick Off 2006, an ecumenical group from the Free Evangelical Churches, to undertake the largest single sustained evangelistic campaign of the territory's 120-year history.

More than 70 delegates from 12 territories (representing four of the five participating continents) shared the gospel in different ways. Throughout the campaign 75,000 copies of a special edition of *Der Kriegsruf* (*The War Cry*) were distributed.

At the same time, the territory hosted the Army's first-ever International Sports Ministries Conference. Several families and children linked up with the Army as a result of the World Cup campaign, so the Youth Department and new Sports Ministries Unit are placing a strong emphasis on sport as a way of attracting people to the gospel.

The joyful message of Christmas was presented to millions of TV viewers when the German Staff Band and the territorial commander took part in a nationwide broadcast on the first Sunday in Advent. The annual music camp in Plön attracted around 100 music-loving people, young and old. Special 'Gospel Arts' weekends were held in several places.

The territory has decided that a person does not need to be a Salvationist to participate in corps music groups. These have now been opened to adherents and other people who enjoy singing and playing instruments, and want to take part in worship and praise meetings. In this way more people will be attracted to the Army and the gos-pel, and in time find Christ as Saviour.

In Lithuania, The Salvation Army participated in a special programme for socially deprived people and over several months the hall was packed by needy people who received different forms of help.

The country holds many challenges and potential opportunities for service. In particular, in Klaipeda Corps there is a growing demand for dedicated people to undertake spiritual ministry.

STATISTICS

Officers 159 (active 89 retired 70) **Cadets** 3 **Lieutenants** 9 **Employees** 730
Corps 44 **Outposts** 5 **Institutions** 40
Senior Soldiers 1,077 **Adherents** 421 **Junior Soldiers** 72

STAFF

Evangelisation and Field Programme: Maj Marsha Bowles
Editor: Capt Alfred Preuß
Finance and Fund-raising: Mr Hans Joachim Bode
Property: Mr Wilfried Otterbach
Public Relations: Maj Fernanda van Houdt
Social: Maj Frank Honsberg
Staff Band: B/M Heinrich Schmidt
Trade: Capt Elinor Lauer
Training and Candidates: Maj Marsha Bowles
Women's Ministries: Col Helga Charlet (TPWM) Lt-Col Grethe Berg (TSWM)
Youth: Maj David Bowles

DIVISIONS

East: 12159 Berlin, Fregestr 13/14;
tel: (0)30-859 8890; fax: (0)30-859 889 99;
email: DHQ_Ost@GER.salvationarmy.org;
Maj Beat Rieder
North: 20359 Hamburg, Talstr 15;
tel: (0)40-31 3405; fax: (0)40-317 2452;
email: DHQ_Nord@GER.salvationarmy.org;
Maj Rudolf Schollmeier
South: 70178 Stuttgart, Rotebühlstr 117;
tel: (0)711-61 66 27; fax: (0)711-62 84 59;
email: DHQ_Sued@GER.salvationarmy.org;
Capt Jörg Friedl
West: 50858 Köln, Aachenerstr 1017-1019;
tel: (0)221-48 63 04; fax: (0)221-48 82 88;
email: DHQ_West@GER.salvationarmy.org;
Maj Patrick Naud

INVESTIGATION

Heckerstr 85, 34121 Kassel;
tel: (0) 561 2889945; fax: (0) 561 2889946;
email: Suchdienst@GER.salvationarmy.org;
Lt-Col Erika Siebel

SENIOR CITIZENS' RESIDENCES

12159 Berlin, Dickhardtstr 52-53;
tel: (0)30-8 51 57 90 (acc apts 42)
45127 Essen, Hoffnungsstr 23;
tel: (0)201-22 47 71 (acc apts 25)
44623 Herne, Koppenbergshof 2;
tel: (0)2323-2 22 47 (acc apts 5 flats 9)
50858 Köln, Rosenweg 1-5;
tel: (0)221-280 8979 (acc apts 42)

68159 Mannheim, G3, 1 + 20;
   tel: (0)621-2 5361 (acc apts 31)
68165 Mannheim, Augartenstr 43, Haus Marie
   Engelhardt; tel: (0)621-44 27 28 (acc apts 19)
75175 Pforzheim, Pflügerstr 37-43;
   tel: (0)7231-6 56 14 (acc apts 30)

SOCIAL SERVICES
Counselling
79106 Freiburg, Lehenerstr 115;
   tel: (0)761-89 44 92; fax (0)761-500 99 98
20359 Hamburg, Counselling Centre, Talstr 11;
   tel: (0)40-31 65 43
22117 Hamburg, Counselling for Alcoholics and
   Rehabilitation Work, Oststeinbeckerweg 2-4;
   tel: (0)40-713 65 64; fax: (0)40-713 44 37
21073 Hamburg, Counselling for Homeless, Zur
   Seehafenbrücke 20; tel: (0)40-309 53 60

Children's Day Nursery
12159 Berlin, Fregestr 13-14; tel: (0)30-850 72920;
   fax: (0)30-850 729231 (acc 30)

Drop-in Cafés
79098 Freiburg, Löwenstr 1;
   tel: (0)761-38 54616; fax: (0)761-38 546 22
22453 Hamburg, Borsteler Chaussee 23;
   tel: (0)40-514 314 0; fax: (0)40-514 314 14
90443 Nürnberg, Leonhardtstr 28;
   tel: (0)911-28 73 156

Hostels
60314 Frankfurt, Windeckstr 58-60;
   tel: (0)69-43 22 52 (acc 80)
73033 Göppingen, Markstr 58; tel: (0)7161-7 42 17;
   fax: (0)7161-7 28 10 (acc 35)
37073 Göttingen, Untere Maschstr 13b;
   tel: (0)551-4 24 84; fax: (0)551-5 31 14 22
   (acc 30)
23552 Lübeck, Engelsgrube 62-64;
   tel: (0)451-7 33 94; fax: (0)451-7 23 86
   (acc 37)
80469 München, Pestalozzistr 36;
   tel: (0)89-26 71 49; fax: (0)89-26 35 26
   (acc 56+26)
70176 Stuttgart, Silberburgstr 139;
   tel: (0)711-61 09 67/68; fax: (0)711-61 33 00
   (acc 55)
65189 Wiesbaden, Schwarzenbergstr 7;
   tel: (0)611-70 12 68; fax: (0)0611-71 40 21
   (acc 191)

Nursing Homes
14163 Berlin, Goethestr 17-21;
   tel: (0)30-3289000; fax: (0)30-32890022
   (acc 51)

47805 Krefeld, Voltastr 50; tel: (0)2151-93 72 60;
   fax: (0)2151-93 72626 (acc 65)

Therapeutic Rehabilitation Institutions
14197 Berlin, Hanauerstr 63; tel: (0)30-8 20 08 40;
   fax: (0)30-8 20 08 430 (acc 60)
22453 Hamburg, Borsteler Chaussee 23;
   tel: (0)40-514 314 0; fax: (0)40-514 314 0;
   email: HamburgJJH@GER.salvationarmy.org
   (acc 71)
34123 Kassel, Eisenacherstr 18;
   tel: (0)561-570 35 90; fax: (0)561-570 359 22
   (acc 80)
34123 Kassel-Lüderitzstr 13; tel: (0)561-40 46 78
   (acc 8)
50825 Köln, Marienstr 116/118;
   tel: (0)221-955 6090; fax: (0)221-5595 482
   (acc 80)
90443 Nürnberg, Gostenhofer Hauptstr 47-49;
   tel: (0)911-28 730; fax: (0)911-28 73 1103;
   email:
   NuernbergSozWerk@GER.salvationarmy.org
   (acc 239, including therapeutic workshops
   and facilities for alcoholics and elderly men)

Therapeutic Workshops
22453 Hamburg, Borsteler Chaussee 23;
   tel: (0)40-514 314 35; fax: (0) 40-514 314 14
90443 Nürnberg, Leonhardstr 17-21;
   tel: (0)911 28730

Women's Hostels
34134 Kassel-Niederzwehren, Am
   Donarbrunnen 32; tel: (0)561-43113 (acc 7)
90443 Nürnberg, Gostenhofer Hauptstr 65;
   tel: (0)911-272 3600 (acc 12)
65197 Wiesbaden, Königsteinerstr 24;
   tel: (0)611-80 67 58; fax: (0)611-981 23 03
   (acc 45)

CONFERENCE AND HOLIDAY CENTRE
24306 Plön, Seehof, Steinberg 3-4;
   tel: (0)4522-5088200; fax: (0)4522-5088202;
   email: seehof@GER.salvationarmy.org
   Conference and Holiday Home (acc 72 + 25)
   Youth Camp (acc 50) Camping Ground and
   5 Holiday Chalets and Homes

LITHUANIA
Isganymo Armija, Lieturvoje, Tiltu 18, LT 91246
   Klaipeda; tel/fax: [00370] 46-310634;
   email: klaipeda@isganymo-armija.org;
   Capt Susanne Kettler-Riutkenen

GHANA TERRITORY

Territorial leaders:
Colonels Dennis and Sharon Strissel

Territorial Commander:
Colonel Dennis L. Strissel (1 Feb 2007)

Chief Secretary:
Lieut-Colonel William Gyimah (1 Feb 2007)

Territorial Headquarters: PO Box CT 452 Cantonments, Accra, Ghana

Tel: [233] (21) 776 971/763 403; fax: [233] (21) 772 695; email: saghana@gha.salvationarmy.org

Salvation Army operations began in Ghana in 1922 when Lieutenant King Hudson was commissioned to 'open fire' in his home town of Duakwa. Ensign and Mrs Charles Roberts were also appointed to pioneer work in Accra.

Zone: Africa
Country included in the territory: Ghana
'The Salvation Army' in Ga: Yiwalaheremo Asrafoi Le; in Fanti and Twi: Nkwagye Dom Asraafo; in Ewe: Agbexoxo Srafa Ha La
Languages in which the gospel is preached: Bassa, Builsa, Dangme, English, Ewe, Fante, Frafra, Ga, Gola, Grushia, Twi
Periodical: *Salvationist Newsletter*

THE Lord has been gracious to Ghana Territory in diverse ways, blessing many people through The Salvation Army's ministry. Souls are being saved.

The enrolment of soldiers, recruits and junior soldiers, and the dedication of children, have taken place in many corps and societies. The officer force was strengthened by the commissioning of five new captains.

It was a great joy when the territory witnessed the Women Ministries Congress in May 2006. Commissioner Hope Mungate (then Territorial President of Women's Ministries, Nigeria) and four other women officers from that territory were the special guests.

Their presence, testimonies and teaching brought great inspiration.

A Salvation Army teachers' conference gave teachers in the territory an opportunity to meet with then Territorial Commander Colonel Graeme Harding, to discuss issues affecting The Salvation Army Education Unit.

A positive result of this conference was the teachers' affirmation to form an association to promote the welfare of Salvation Army schools and to ensure that the schools adhered to sound moral education and Army principles and disciplines.

The World Services Appeal is gaining excited support in the territory, reflected in the Salvationists' spirit of personal giving. It is worth noting that every year the territory receives an appreciable sum of income from the divisions, districts, and social and educational institutions, the amount being an increase on that raised the previous year.

The territory saw changes in leadership. The Chief Secretary and Territorial Secretary for Women's Ministries, Lieut-Colonels Peter and Jessica Dali, were appointed to Zimbabwe and the retirement and farewell meeting for territorial leaders Colonels Graeme and Anne Harding was conducted by Commissioners Amos and Rosemary Makina (International Secretary for Africa and Zonal Secretary for Women's Ministries).

The commissioners also conducted the welcome to the new CS and TSWM, Lieut-Colonels William and Mary Gyimah, and during that meeting the cabinet secretaries of Business Administration, Personnel and Programme, with their wives, were dedicated to the Lord's service.

Commissioners Jean B. and Véronique Ludiazo, the territorial leaders in Congo (Kinshasa) and Angola, were the General's representatives to conduct the installation of the new TC and TPWM, Colonels Dennis and Sharon Strissel.

Salvationists continue to pray for a mighty revival in the army of God in Ghana.

STATISTICS

Officers 228 (active 179 retired 49) **Cadets** 9
Employees 1,415

Corps 100 **Societies** 144 **Schools** 206 **Pupils** 19,482 **Clinics** 9 **Social Centres** 8 **Day Care Centres** 90
Senior Soldiers 16,671 **Junior Soldiers** 3,347
Personnel serving outside territory Officers 4

STAFF

Business Administration: Maj Samuel Amponsah
Personnel: Maj Mike Adu-Manu
Programme: Maj Samuel Baah
Women's Ministries: Col Sharon K. Strissel (TPWM) Lt-Col Mary Gyimah (TSWM) Maj Theresa Baah (Women's Development & Training) Capt Mary Adu-Gyan (TJHLS)
Communications and External Relations: Mr Kofi Sakyiamah
Editor: Capt Stephen Borbor
Extension Training: Maj Joseph Owusu-Mensah
Medical, Social and Community Services: Maj Wendy Leavey
Projects and Child Sponsorship: Maj Magda Iversen
Property: Mr Vandyke Amoako Bempah
Schools: Mr James B. Maison
Territorial Band: B/M Emmanuel Hackman
Training: Maj Margaret Wickings
Youth and Candidates: Maj John Arthur

DIVISIONS

Accra: PO Box 166 Tema; tel: (022) 215 530; Maj Seth Appeateng
Akim Central: PO Box AS 283, Asamankese; tel: (081) 23 585; Maj Peter Oduro-Amoah
Ashanti Central: PO Box 15, Kumasi; tel/fax: (051) 240 16; Maj Jonas Ampofo
Ashanti North: c/o PO Box 14, Wiamoase, Ashanti; Maj Richmond Obeng-Appau
Central: PO Box 62, Agona Swedru; tel: (041) 20 285; Maj Godfried Oduro
Nkawkaw: PO Box 3, Nkawkaw; tel: (0842) 22 208; Maj Edward Addison
West Akim: PO Box 188, Akim Oda; tel: (0882) 2 305; Maj Isaac Danso

DISTRICTS

Brong Ahafo: PO Box 1454, Sunyani; tel: (061) 23 513; Maj Edward Kyei
East Akim: PO Box KF 1218, Koforidua E/R; tel: (081) 22 580; Maj Stephen Boadu
Northern: PO Box 233, Bolgatanga; tel: (072) 22 030; Maj Ebenezer Danquah
Volta: PO Box 604, Ho, Volta Region; Capt Rockson Oduro
Western: PO Box 178, Sekondi, C/R; tel: (031) 23 763; Maj Seth Larbi

TRAINING COLLEGE
PO Box CE 11991, Tema; tel: (022) 306 252/
306 253

EXTENSION TRAINING CENTRE
PO Box CT 452, Cantonments, Accra;
tel: (021) 776 971; fax: (021) 772 695

CLINICS
Accra Urban Aid: PO Box CT 452, Cantonments,
Accra; tel: (021) 230 918 (acc 11, including
maternity)
Accra Urban Aid Outreach: PO Box CT 452,
Cantonments, Accra; tel: (021) 246 764
(mobile outreach for street children)
Adaklu-Sofa: PO Box 604, Ho, V/R (acc 4,
including maternity)
Anum: PO Box 17, Senchi, E/R (acc 11,
including maternity)
Ba: PO Box 8, Ba, C/R (acc 4, including
maternity)
Begoro: PO Box 10, Begoro, E/R (acc 10,
including maternity)
Duakwa: PO Box 2, Agona Duakwa, C/R (acc 30,
including maternity)
Wenchi: PO Box 5, Wenchi, Akim Oda (acc 8,
including maternity)

Wiamoase: PO Box 14, Wiamoase, Ashanti;
tel: (051) 32 613

EDUCATION
Sub-primary Schools: 80
Primary Schools: 89
Junior Secondary Schools: 35
Senior Secondary Schools: 2

SOCIAL WORK
Adaklu-Sofa Vocational Training Centre:
PO Box 604, Ho, V/R
Anidasofie Street Girls' Training Centre:
PO Box CT 452, Cantonments, Accra;
tel: (021) 246 764
Begoro Rehabilitation Centre: PO Box 10,
Begoro, E/R
Child Care Training Centre: PO Box 8, Ba, C/R
Community Rehabilitation Project:
PO Box 2, Agona Duakwa
Malnutrition Centre: PO Box 2, Agona
Duakwa, C/R
Rehabilitation Centre: PO Box 14, Wiamoase,
Ashanti
Voluntary Counselling and Testing Centre: PO
Box CT 452, Cantonments, Accra;
tel: (021) 776 971

Worship is held under a tree during a welcome to Ghana's new territorial leaders, Colonels Dennis and Sharon Strissel, at Doninga Corps (Builsa) in Tamale, capital of the country's northern region

HONG KONG AND MACAU COMMAND

Command leaders:
Lieut-Colonels Mervyn and Elaine Rowland

Officer Commanding:
Lieut-Colonel Mervyn Rowland
(1 Dec 2007)

General Secretary:
Major Priscilla Nanlabi (1 Dec 2007)

**Command Headquarters: 11 Wing Sing Lane, Yaumatei,
Kowloon, Hong Kong**

Postal address: PO Box 70129, Kowloon Central Post Office, Kowloon, Hong Kong

Tel: [852] 2332 4531; fax: [852] 2771 6439; email: Hongkong@hkt.salvationarmy.org;
web site: www.salvation.org.hk

In March 1930, at a meeting held at Government House, Hong Kong, The Salvation Army was requested to undertake women's work in the crown colony, a work pioneered by Majors Dorothy Brazier and Doris Lemon. This work was directed from Peking until, in 1935, the South China Command was established in Canton to promote wide evangelistic and welfare operations. In 1939 Hong Kong became the Army's administrative centre. Later, the inclusion of the New Territories determined that the Command Headquarters move to Kowloon. Since 1951 the General of The Salvation Army has been recognised as a Corporation Sole. From 1993, disaster relief and community development projects have been carried out in mainland China. In 1999, a pioneer officer was appointed to the Special Administrative Region of Macau and Salvation Army work began there officially on 25 March 2000. In 2001, an officer was appointed to the North/North Eastern Project Office in Beijing.

Zone: South Pacific and East Asia
Regions included in the command: Hong Kong and Macau (Special Administrative Regions of the People's Republic of China) and Mainland China
'The Salvation Army' in Cantonese: Kau Sai Kwan; in Putonghua: Jiu Shi Jun
Languages in which the gospel is preached: Cantonese, English, Filipino, Putonghua
Periodicals: *Army Scene, The War Cry*

THE slogan for the year under review – 'Keep in Step with the Spirit' – became the basis of teaching and preaching in the command, and a yardstick in the setting of departmental strategic goals.

Songs from *Spirit* brought challenge when the cast came together after three years to present the musical at the command's united meeting in June.

The Women's Ministries Department organised a training weekend in Macau. The event's twofold purpose was to train women in Macau in the area of ministry among women and to provide opportunity for the Hong Kong partici-pants to apply their skills in leadership.

An evangelism seminar themed

'With Christ in the City' was conducted by Commissioner Paul du Plessis (then Commissioner for World Evangelisation, IHQ) and Commissioner Margaret du Plessis. This important event drew an attendance of 121 soldiers and officers.

Chinese church leaders from around the world gathered in Macau for the Chinese Congress for World Evangelisation (CCOWE). There were 24 Salvation Army representatives. The post-congress conference brought together the officer-delegates to discuss a broadening of Chinese Salvation Army ministry worldwide.

Kowloon Central Corps Band and Timbrelists visited USA Western Territory as guests at the 120th anniversary celebration of San Francisco Chinatown Corps.

The command continues its project work in Mainland China. An example of this can be found in the extremely remote area of Qinghai, where the command – thanks to the generous support of a donor – is constructing schools and currently assessing the district's wider needs.

STATISTICS

Officers 52 (active 44 retired 8) **Cadets** 2 **Employees** 2,326

Corps 19 **Outposts** 1 **Institutions** 20 **Schools** 7 **Kindergartens** 6 **Nursery Schools** 17 **Social Centres** 50 **Hotel** 1

Senior Soldiers 2,133 **Adherents** 43 **Junior Soldiers** 435

Personnel serving outside command Officers 4

STAFF

Asst to General Secretary: Maj Simon Tso Kam-shing

China Development: Ms Puisi Chan

Community Relations: Envoy Simon Wong

Corporate Administrator: Ms Hilda Lam

Editor/Literary: Maj David Ip Kam-yuen

Educational Services: Maj Jim Weymouth

Emergency Services Coordinator: Ms Karen Ng Wai-sze

Finance: Ms Idy Lam Mei-lan

Human Resources: Ms Eva Lau

Property: Envoy Daniel Hui Wah-lun

Social: Mrs Victoria Kwok Yuen Wai-yee

Trade: Ms Karen Ng Wai-sze

Training:

Women's Ministries: Lt-Col Elaine Rowland (CPWM)

Youth and Candidates: Maj Tommy Chan Hi-wai

DIVISION

1/F, 6-8 Salvation Army St, Wanchai, HK; tel: 2591 4488; fax: 2332 3545; Maj Tony Ma Yeung-mo

TRAINING COLLEGE

6/F, 11 Wing Sing Lane, Yaumatei, Kln, PO Box 70129, Kowloon Central PO, Kln, HK; tel: 2783 2305; fax: 2332 9221; email: otc@tc.salvationarmy.org.hk

CHINA DEVELOPMENT

Hong Kong Head Office: tel: (852) 2783 2288; fax: (852) 2385 7823; China Development Director: Puisi Chan; tel: (852) 2783 2288 email: cdd@hkt.salvationarmy.org

North/Northeast Regional Project Office – China: D-102 Jin Mao Apartment, 2 Guang Hua Lane, Chao Yang District, Beijing 100020, China; tel: [86] (10) 6586 9331/2; fax: [86] (10) 6586 8382; email: nnerpo@hkt.salvationarmy.org

Southwest Regional Project Office – China: 6D, Unit 1, Block 8, Yin Hai Hot Spring Garden, Northern District, 173 Guan Xing Rd, Guan Shang, Kunming 650200, Yunnan, China; tel: [86] (871) 7166 111/222; fax: [86] (871) 7155 222; email: swrpo@hkt.salvationarmy.org

Xinghe Project Office – China: Rm 520, Xinghe Municipal Government Bldg, Xinghe County, 013650 Inner Mongolia, China; tel/fax: (86) 474 7212 010; email: xho@hkt.salvationarmy.org

EDUCATIONAL SERVICES
Kindergartens

Chan Kwan Tung: G/F and 1/F, 11 Wing Sing Lane, Yaumatei, Kln; tel: 2384 7831; fax: 2388 5310 (acc 316; 2 sessions)

u Keung: Units 121-140, G/F, Fu Keung
  House, (Block 6), Tai Wo Hau Estate, NT;
  tel: 2614 4481; fax: 2439 0666
  (acc 360; 2 sessions)

ing Yan: G/F, Commercial Centre, Area 41,
  Hau Tak Estate, Tseung Kwan O, Kln;
  tel: 2706 6222; fax: 2704 9262
  (acc 432; 2 sessions)

g Kwok Wai Memorial: G/F, 22-30 Hoi Shing
  Rd, Clague Garden Estate, Tsuen Wan, NT;
  tel: 2499 7639; fax: 2414 9214
  (acc 360; 2 sessions)

ing Tin: G/F, Ping Shing House, Ping Tin
  Estate, Lam Tin, Kln; tel: 2775 5332;
  fax: 2775 5412 (acc 270; 2 sessions) plus
  Nursery (acc 28; 2 sessions)

in Ka Ping: 15 Jat Min Chuen St, Shatin, NT;
  tel: 2647 4227; fax: 2645 1869 (acc 674;
  2 sessions)

Crèches 1 Month-2 Years

North Point: Podium Level 2, Healthy Village,
  6 Healthy St Central North Point, HK;
  tel: 2856 0892 (acc 28 full-day)

Pak Tin: G/F, Wing C, Fu Tin House, Pak Tin
  Estate, Pak Wan St, Shamshuipo, Kln;
  tel: 2778 3588 (acc 16 full-day)

Nursery Schools 2-6 Years

Catherine Booth: 2/F, 11 Wing Sing Lane,
  Yaumatei, Kln: tel: 2332 7963 (acc 110 full-day)

Hoi Fu: G/F, Wing B & C, Hoi Ning House,
  Hoi Fu Court, Mongkok, Kln; tel: 2148 2477
  (acc 112 full-day)

Jat Min: 1/F, 15 Jat Min Chuen St, Jat Min Chuen,
  Shatin, NT; tel: 2647 4897 (acc 168 full-day)

Kam Tin: G/F 103 Kam Tin Rd, Yuen Long,
  NT; tel: 2442 3606 (acc 100 full-day)

Lai Chi Kok: 1/F, Prosperity Court, 168 Lai Chi
  Kok Rd, Mongkok, Kln; tel: 2787 5788 (acc
  100 full-day)

Lei Muk Shue: G/F, Wing B & C, Yeung Shue
  House, Lei Muk Shue Estate, Kwai Chung,
  NT; tel: 2420 2491 (acc 112 full-day)

Lok Man: 1/F, Block H, Lok Man Sun Chuen,
  Tokwawan, Kln; tel: 2365 1994 (acc 145
  full-day)

Ming Tak: G/F, Wing B & C, Hin Ming Court,
  Hang Hau, Tseung Kwan O, Kln;
  tel: 2623 7555 (acc 126 full-day)

North Point: Podium Level 2, Healthy Village,
  6 Healthy St Central North Point, HK;
  tel: 2856 0892 (acc 28 full-day)

Pak Tin: G/F, Wing C, Fu Tin House, Pak Tin
  Estate, Pak Wan St, Shamshuipo, Kln;
  tel: 2778 3588 (acc 90 full-day)

Sam Shing: G/F, Moon Yu House Annex, Sam
  Shing Estate, Tuen Mun, NT; tel: 2452 0032
  (acc 100 full-day)

Tai Wo Hau: Units 215, 217, 219 & 221-232,
  2/F, Fu Keung House, Tai Wo Hau Estate,
  Tsuen Wan, NT; tel: 2614 7662 (acc 126
  full-day)

Tai Yuen: G/F, Tai Ling House, Tai Yuen
  Estate, Tai Po, NT; tel: 2664 9725
  (acc 100 full-day)

Tin Ping: G/F, Units 106-110, Wing B, Tin Hor
  House, Tin Ping Estate, Sheung Shui, NT;
  tel: 2671 9972 (acc 112 full-day)

Tsuen Wan: 1/F, Clague Garden Estate, 22 Hoi
  Shing Rd, Tsuen Wan, NT;
  tel: 2417 1400 (acc 182 full-day)

Wah Fu: 1/F-2/F, Wah Sang House, Wah Fu
  Estate, HK; tel: 2551 6341 (acc 126 full-day)

Wo Che: Bays 101-114, G/F, Tak Wo House,
  Wo Che Estate, Shatin, NT; tel: 2604 0428
  (acc 168 full-day)

Primary Schools

Ann Wyllie Memorial: 100 Shing Tai Rd, Heng
  Fa Chuen, HK; tel: 2558 2111; fax: 2898 4377
  (acc 1,536; 2 sessions)

Lam Butt Chung Memorial: Yat Tung Estate,
  Tung Chung, Lantau, NT;
  tel: 2109 0328; fax: 2109 0223 (acc 960)

Sam Shing Chuen Lau Ng Ying: Sam Shing
  Estate, Tuen Mun, NT; tel: 2458 8035;
  fax: 2618 3171 (acc 792)

Tin Ka Ping: Pok Hong Estate, Shatin, NT;
  tel: 2648 9283; fax: 2649 4305 (acc 768)

Secondary School

William Booth Secondary School, 100 Yuk Wah
  St, Tsz Wan Shan, Kln; tel: 2326 9068;
  fax: 2328 0052 (acc 1,120)

Special School

Shek Wu School, Area 8 Jockey Club Rd, Shek
  Wu, Sheung Shui, NT; tel: 2670 0800;
  fax: 2668 5353 (acc 200)

GUEST ACCOMMODATION

Booth Lodge, 7/F, 11 Wing Sing Lane,
  Yaumatei, Kln; tel: (852) 2771 9266;
  fax: (852) 2385 1140;
  email: boothlodge@salvationarmy.org.hk

RECYCLING PROGRAMME

Logistic Centre: 7/F Tat Ming Industrial Bldg,
  44-52 Ta Chuen Ping St, Kwai Chung, NT;
  tel: 2332 4433; fax: 2332 4411;
  email: Recycling@hkt.salvationarmy.org

Family Stores

Warehouse: 7/F Tat Ming Industrial Bldg, 44-52 Ta Chuen Ping St, Kwai Chung, NT; tel: 2489 8833; fax: 2332 4411

Chuk Yuen Store: Shop S202, 3/F, Chuk Yuen Shopping Centre, Chuk Yuen (South) Estate, Wong Tai Sin, Kln; tel: 2320 0050

Kwun Tong Store: No 237, G/F, Hay Cheuk Lau, Garden Estate, Kwun Tong, Kln; tel: 2331 2577

Mongkok Store: Shop 1, G/F Xing Hua Ctr, 433 Shanghai St, Mongkok, Kln; tel: 3422 3205

Nam Cheong Store: Shop7-8, Nam Cheong West Rail Stn, Kln; tel: 2387 4933

Shek Wai Kok Store: Shop 331, Shek Wai Kok Shopping Centre, Shek Wai Kok Estate, Tsuen Wan, NT; tel: 2499 8981

Stanley Store: G/F, 98 Stanley Main St, HK; tel: 3197 0070

Tai Hang Tung Store: G/F, 1 Lung Chu St, Tai Hang Tung, Kln; tel: 2784 0689

Tin Hau Store: G/F, 29 Wing Hing St, Tin Hau, HK; tel: 2887 5577

Wanchai Store: G/F, 31 Wood Rd, Wanchai, HK; tel: 2572 2879

Yaumatei Store: G/F, 1A Cliff Rd, Yaumatei, Kln; tel: 2332 4448

Yue Wan Store: Shop 29-30, Yue On House, Yue Wan Estate, Chaiwan, HK; tel: 2558 8655

SOCIAL WORK

Camps

Bradbury: 6 Ming Fai Rd, Cheung Chau Island, HK; tel: 2981 0358 (acc 108)

Ma Wan: Ma Wan Island, HK: tel: 2986 5244 (acc 40)

Children and Youth Centres

Chuk Yuen: 2-4F, Chuk Yuen Estate Community Centre, Chuk Yuen (South) Estate, Kln; tel: 2351 5321

Lung Hang: G/F, Sin Sum House, Lung Hang Estate, Shatin, NT; tel: 2605 5569

Tai Wo Hau: 2-4/F, Tai Wo Hau Estate Community Centre, Tsuen Wan, NT; tel: 2428 4581

Integrated Service for Young People

Chaiwan: Podium Level Market Bldg, Wan Tsui Est, Chaiwan, HK; tel: 2898 9750

Tuen Mun: G/F, 13-24 Hing Ping House, Tai Hing Est, Tuen Mun, NT; tel: 2461 4741

Tuen Mun East: 5/F Ancillary Facilities Block, Fu Tai Estate, No 9 Tuen Kwai Rd, Tuen Mun, NT; tel: 2467 7200

Tai Po: 2/F, Tai Man House, Tai Yuen Estate, Tai Po, NT; tel: 2667 2913

Yaumatei: 1/F, Block 4, Prosperous Garden, 3 Public Square St, Kln; tel: 2770 8933

Community Development Projects

Ngau Tam Mei: Library, Yau Tam Mei School, Yau Tam Mei Village, Yuen Long, NT; tel: 2482 7175

Sam Mun Tsai: 31 Chim Uk Village, Shuen Wan, Tai Po, NT; tel: 2660 9890

Urban Renewal Social Service Team

Hong Kong Island: Flat E, 20/F Tak Lee Commercial Bldg, 113-117 Wan Chai Rd, HK; tel: 2893 4711

Tai Kok Tsui: G/F, Bedford Tower, 68-72 Bedford Rd, Tai Kok Tsui, Kln; tel: 2391 6733

Shamshuipo: G/F, 140 Yee Kuk St, Shamshuipo, Kln; tel: 3586 3094

Education and Development Centre

6 Salvation Army St, Wanchai, HK; tel: 2572 6718

Child Development Project

Flying High: 6 Salvation Army St, Wanchai, HK; tel: 2892 1302

Community Service Team

G/F, 145-146 Azalea Hse, So Uk Estate, Shamshuipo, Kln; tel: 2728 3350

Tuen Mun Services for Young Night Drifters

5/F Ancillary Facilities Block, Fu Tai Estate, No 9 Tuen Kwai Rd, Tuen Mun, NT; tel: 2467 7200

Integrated Services for Street Sleepers

1/F, GIC Bldg, 345A Shanghai St, Kln; tel: 2710 8911

Hostels

Sunrise House: 323 Shun Ning Rd, Cheung Sha Wan, Kln; tel: 2307 8001 (acc 310)

Yee On Hostel: Unit 111-116, 1/F, Hoi Yu House, Hoi Fu Court, Mongkok, Kln; tel: 2708 9553 (acc 40)

Day Care Centres for Senior Citizens

Bradbury: G/F, Wan Loi House, Wan Tau Tong Estate, Tai Po, NT; tel: 2638 8880 (acc 44)

Chuk Yuen: 141-150 Podium Level, Chui Yuen House, Chuk Yuen (South) Estate, Kln; tel: 2326 6683 (acc 44)

Hoi Yu: G/F, Hoi Lam House, Hoi Fu Court,
2 Hoi Ting Rd, Mongkok, Kln; tel: 2148 1480
(acc 44)

Community Day Rehabilitation Service

Tak Tin: G/F, Tak Yan House, Tak Tin Estate,
Lam Tin; tel: 2177 7122

Shaukeiwan: 456 Shaukeiwan Rd, Shaukeiwan,
HK; tel: 2560 8123 (acc 40)

Community Day Rehabilitation and Residential Service

Cheung Hong: 2/F & 3/F Hong Cheung Hse,
Cheung Hong Est, Tsing Yi, NT;
tel: 2432 1588

Integrated Home Care Service Teams

Kwun Tong: Unit 1-2, Wing B, G/F, Tak Lung
House, Tak Tin Estate, Lam Tin, Kln;
tel: 2340 0100

Sai Kung: 4/F, Po Kan House, Po Lam Estate,
Tseung Kwan O, Kln; tel: 2701 5828

Tai Po: 2/F, Tai Po Community Centre, Heung
Sze Wui St, Tai Po Market, NT; tel: 2653 3941

Yau Tsim (Kowloon Central Office): G/F & 1/F,
Chee Sun Building, 161-165 Reclamation St,
Yaumatei; tel: 2300 1399

Yau Tsim (Yaumatei Office): 3/F, 11 Wing Sing
Lane, Yaumatei, Kln; tel: 2770 5266

Multi-service Centres for Senior Citizens

Tai Po: 2/F-3/F, Tai Po Community Centre,
Heung Sze Wui St, Tai Po Market, NT;
tel: 2653 6811

Yaumatei: 3/F, 11 Wing Sing Lane, Yaumatei,
Kln; tel: 2332 0005

Centres for Senior Citizens

Chuk Yuen: 1/F, Chuk Yuen Estate Community
Centre, Chuk Yuen (South) Estate, Kln;
tel: 2320 8032

Hoi Lam: 1/F, Hoi Yu House, Hoi Fu Court,
2 Hoi Ting Rd, Mongkok, Kln; tel: 2148 1481

Nam Tai: G/F, Nam Tai House, Nam Shan
Estate, Kln; tel: 2779 5983

Tai Wo Hau: 1/F, Tai Wo Hau Estate
Community Centre, Tai Wo Hau Estate,
Tsuen Wan, NT; tel: 2428 8563

Wah Fu: G/F, Wah Kin House, Wah Fu Estate,
Aberdeen, HK; tel: 2550 9971

Senior Citizens Talent Advancement Project

Tung Tau Centre: Unit 1-3, G/F, Yat Tung
House, Tung Tau Estate, Kln; tel: 2340 0266

Kwun Tong Centre: 1/F, Flat A, Yee On Centre,
31 Yee On St, Kwun Tong, Kln;
tel: 2389 5568

Carer Service

3/F, 11 Wing Sing Lane, Yaumatei, Kln;
tel: 2782 2229

Family Support Networking Team

Shamshuipo: Rm 69, 2/F Fuk Sing House,
63-69 Fuk Wing St, Shamshuipo, Kln;
tel: 2390 9361

Residential Services for Boys

Wan Tsui Home for Boys: 115-128 G/F, Chak
Tsui House, Wan Tsui Estate, Chai Wan, HK;
tel: 2557 3290 (acc 46)

Yue Wan Boys' Hostel: 3-8 Yue Tai House, Yue
Wan Estate, Chaiwan, HK; tel: 2558 4048
(acc 15)

Children (Small Group Homes)

Tai Wo Hau: Fu Yin House, Wing K, Tai Wo
Hau Estate, Phase 4, Tsuen Wan, NT;
Home of Joy: Flat 214; tel: 2615 1709 (acc 8);
Home of Love: Flat 314; tel: 2615 1784 (acc 8);
Home of Peace: Flat 112; tel: 2615 1710
(acc 8)

Ping Tin: Ping Wong House, Ping Tin Estates,
Lam Tin, Kln;
Home of Faithfulness: Flat 103; tel: 2952 3691
(acc 8);
Home of Goodness: Flat 203; tel: 2952 3692
(acc 8)
Home of Kindness: Flat 303; tel: 2775 3542
(acc 8)

Residences for Senior Citizens

Bradbury Home of Loving Kindness: 16 Tung
Lo Wan Hill Rd, Tai Wai, Shatin, NT; tel:
2601 5000 (acc 136)

Hoi Tai: 2/F, Hoi Tai House, Hoi Fu Court,
2 Hoi Ting Rd, Mongkok, Kln; tel: 2148 2000
(acc 131)

Lung Hang: 3&4/F, Wing Sam House, Lung Hang
Estate, Shatin, NT; tel: 2602 3696 (acc 155)

Nam Ming Haven for Women: G/F, Nam Ming
House, Nam Shan Estate, Shek Kip Mei, Kln;
tel: 2777 5484 (acc 38)

Nam Shan: 1&2/F, Nam Ming House, Nam Shan
Estate, Shek Kip Mei, Kln; tel: 2777 5102
(acc 150)

Po Lam: 4/F, Po Kan House, Po Lam Estate,
Tseung Kwan O, Kln; tel: 2701 5828 (acc 141)

Tak Tin: 2/F, Tak King House, Tak Tin Estate,
Lam Tin, Kln; tel: 2347 8183 (acc 81)

Kam Tin: 103 Kam Tin Rd, Yuen Long, NT;
tel: 2944 1369 (acc 150)

Warden Service in Sheltered Housing

Grace Apartments: Flat 3-95, Lotus Tower 4, 297 Ngau Tau Kok Rd, Kln; tel: 2763 6367

Kei Lok Apartments: Rm 225, Block 5, Prosperous Garden, Public Square St, Yaumatei, Kln; tel: 2782 6655

Integrated Service for Rehabilitation

Heng On Integrated Vocational Rehabilitation Service: G/F, Heng Kong House, Heng On Estate, Ma On Shan, NT; tel: 2640 0656 (acc 289)

On the Job Training Programme for People with Disabilities: G/F, Heng Kong Hse, Heng On Est, Ma On Shan, NT; tel: 2640 0656 (acc 48)

Sunnyway – On the Job Training Programme for Young People with Disabilities: G/F, Heng Kong Hse, Heng On Est, Ma On Shan, NT; tel: 2640 0656 (acc 30)

Training and Residential

Heng On Hostel: G/F, Heng Shan House, Heng On Estate, Ma On Shan, NT; tel: 2640 0581 (acc 62)

Lai King Home (Training and Residential): 200-210 Lai King Hill Rd, Kwai Chung, NT; tel: 2744 1511 (acc 100)

Agency-based Occupational Therapy

Talent Shop: G/F, Heng Sing House, Heng On Estate, Ma On Shan, Shatin, NT; tel: 2633 7116

Share-Care (Family and Community Support Service for Persons with Mental Handicaps) (cum Walk Through the Challenge): 200 Lai King Hill Rd, Kwai Chung, NT; tel: 2744 1511

Family Support Service for Persons with Autism (cum Family Support Project for Persons with Autism): 6 Salvation Army St, Wanchai, HK; tel: 2893 2537

Social Enterprise

Digital Workshop: Unit D, 5/F Kwun Tong Industrial Ctr, Phase 1, 472-484 Kwun Tong Rd, Kln; tel: 3595 2320

Shatin Family Store: Shop no 70-72, G/F Ming Yiu Lau, Jat Min Chuen, Shatin, NT; tel: 2636 6113

Shatin Park Food Kiosk: Kiosk no 4, Shatin Park, 2 Yuen Wo Rd, Shatink, NT;

The WARM Project (Wheelchair & Assistive Device Re-engagement Movement): 1/F, Flat A, Yee On Centre, 31 Yee On St, Kwun Tong, Kln; tel: 2389 5568

Tuen Mun Family Store: Shop no 41-42, Chik Lok Garden, Tuen Mun, NT; tel: 2618 2241

Kowloon Central Band and Timbrelists visit San Francisco Chinatown Corps (USA Western Territory) as guests at the 120th anniversary celebrations

INDIA NATIONAL

India is The Salvation Army's oldest mission field. Frederick St George de Latour Tucker, of the Indian Civil Service, read a copy of *The War Cry*, became a Salvationist and, as Major Tucker (later Commissioner Booth-Tucker), took the Indian name of Fakir Singh and commenced Army work in Bombay on 19 September 1882. The adoption of Indian food, dress, names and customs gave the pioneers ready access to the people, especially in the villages. In addition to evangelistic work, various social programmes were inaugurated for the relief of distress from famine, flood and epidemic. Educational facilities such as elementary, secondary and industrial schools, cottage industries and settlements, were provided for the depressed classes. Medical work originated in Nagercoil in 1893 when Harry Andrews set up a dispensary at the headquarters there. The medical work has grown from this. Work among the then Criminal Tribes began in 1908 at government invitation.

The Salvation Army is registered as a Guarantee Company under the Indian Companies Act 1913.

Several offices had been established in earlier years, including the Editorial and Literary Office and the Audit Office. Since the establishment of the Health Services Advisory Council in 1986 a regionally based national secretariat has evolved to provide support to many aspects of Salvation Army work in India.

The Conference of Indian Leaders (COIL) established in 1989, meets annually to coordinate national Salvation Army affairs and give direction to the national secretariat.

Web site: www.salvationarmy.org/ind

THE SALVATION ARMY ASSOCIATION

Chairman: Comr Chimanbhai Waghela

BUSINESS AND ADMINISTRATION OFFICE

SAIBA, TC 20/1408 Kowdiar PO,
Thiruvananthapuram 695 003, Kerala;
tel: (91) (471) 231 6112/6115;
fax: (91) (471) 231 6112
email: indiabusinessadministration
@salvationarmy.org
Executive Sec: Maj K. C. David

COMMUNICATIONS OFFICE
(including Editorial and Literary)

PO Box 8994, Dharamtala PO, Kolkata 700 013,
West Bengal; tel: (91) (33) 2249 7210/ 4140;
fax: (91) (33) 2249 7210;
email: indiacommunications@salvationarmy.org
Executive Sec and Editor: Maj J. Daniel
Jebasingh-Raj

HUMAN RESOURCES DEVELOPMENT OFFICE

Post Bag 1, Nanjundapuram PO, Coimbatore
641 036, Tamil Nadu;
tel: (91) (422) 231 9566/5593;
fax: (91) (422) 231 6153;
email: indiahumanresourcesdevelopment
@salvationarmy.org
Conference Centre: Surrenden, 15-18 Orange
Grove Rd, Coonoor 643 101, Nilgiris District,

Tamil Nadu; tel: (91) (423) 223 0242
Executive Sec: Maj Wilfred Varughese

EDUCATION

Flat No A-404, Oberoi Gardens, Thakur Village,
Kandivili (East), Mumbai 400 101;
mobile: (91) (22) 9821 652 530;
fax: (91) (22) 2884 4340;
email: indianationaleducationalconsultant
@salvationarmy.org
National Consultant: Lt-Col N. J.
Karunakara Rao

EMERGENCY SERVICES

Flat No A-404, Oberoi Gardens, Thakur Village,
Kandivili (East), Mumbai 400 101;
mobile: (91) (22) 9820 897 669;
fax: (91) (22) 2884 4340;
email:
indianationalemergencyservicesconsultant
@salvationarmy.org
National Consultant: Lt-Col N. J.
Vijayalakshmi

SOCIAL SERVICES

37 Lenin Sarani, Kolkata – 700013;
tel/fax: (91) (0) 33 2227 5780;
email: indiasocialdevelopment
@salvationarmy.org
Executive Sec: Lt-Col Thumati Vijayakumar

SALVATION ARMY HEALTH SERVICES ADVISORY COUNCIL

Post Bag 6 Ahmednagar-414 001, Maharashtra;
tel: (91) (241) 2321593;

fax: (91) (241) 2327756;
email: sahsac@salvationarmy.org
Executive Sec: Maj John Purshottam Macwan

WOMEN'S ADVISORY COUNCIL
Post Bag 1, Nanjundapuram PO, Coimbatore

641 036, Tamil Nadu;
tel: (91) (422) 231 9566/5593;
fax: (91) (422) 231 6153;
email: indiawomensadvisorycouncil
@salvationarmy.org
Executive Sec: Maj Prema Wilfred Varughese

S A YOUTH WITNESS AND WORSHIP

India Eastern Territory: SAY (Salvation Army Youth) member Jenny Lalremliani became the new world number one in the 4th Women's World Boxing Championship in the 63 kgs category. As her victory was announced she made her Christian witness by kneeling inside the ring and praying.

India South Eastern Territory: Worship was enhanced by dancing *(above)* and singing at Youth Camp 2007. Of the 650 delegates from various parts of the territory, more than 140 accepted Jesus Christ as Saviour and 45 dedicated their lives to full-time service in officership.

INDIA CENTRAL TERRITORY

Territorial leaders:
Colonels M. Y. Emmanuel and T. Regina Chandra Bai

Territorial Commander:
Colonel M. Y. Emmanuel (1 Dec 2006)

Chief Secretary:
Lieut-Colonel P. T. Abraham (1 Mar 2007)

Territorial Headquarters: 31 (15) Ritherdon Road, Vepery, Chennai 600 007

Postal address: PO Box 453, Vepery, Chennai 600 007, India

Tel: [91] (044) 2532 3148; fax: [91] (044) 2532 5987; email: ICT_mail@ICT.salvationarmy.org; web site: www.salvationarmy.org/ind

The India Central Territory comprises three regions – North Tamil Nadu (Madras-Chennai), Karnataka and Andhra Pradesh. Salvation Army work commenced at Vijayawada in Andhra Pradesh in 1895 by Staff Captain Abdul Aziz, a person of Muslim background, with his friend Mahanada. Captain Abdul attended a revival meeting led by Captain Henry Bullard in 1884 at Bangalore and subsequently dedicated himself to be a Salvation Army officer. The territory was named the India Central Territory in 1992, with its headquarters at Madras (Chennai).

Zone: South Asia
States included in the territory: Andhra Pradesh, Karnataka, Tamil Nadu
'The Salvation Army' in Tamil: Ratchania Senai; in Telugu: Rakshana Sinyamu
Languages in which the gospel is preached: English, Tamil, Telugu
Periodicals: *Home League Magazine, Udyogasthudu, Yovana Veerudu, Yudha Dwani*

MUCH progress has been made in the field of women's ministries and God is praised for his abundant grace which enabled Salvationists throughout the territory to celebrate the centenary of the Home League during 2007.

Under the leadership of Colonel Regina Chandra Bai (TPWM), celebrations were held in 14 centres. In the metropolitan city of Chennai the rejoicing began with a march of witness escorted by policewomen. Women waving Salvation Army flags,

carrying banners and singing songs as they paraded through the streets made a marvellous sight. An open jeep carried women's ministries leaders at the head of the procession.

At every centre home league members hoisted an Army flag just before their celebratory meetings and lit lamps on the platform. In commemoration of the centenary, the TPWM cut a cake and launched a souvenir brochure. Retired officers and home league local officers were honoured at the celebrations.

The following are some of the fruitful results of ministry in the territory's home leagues during the year under review: total attendances 15,321; women attending from other churches and other faiths 1,484; seekers at the mercy seat 3,296; presentations to Bible quiz winners 490; money raised for the helping-hand scheme 314,591 rupees (US$ 7,684) – an increase of 41,424 rupees (US$ 1,012) on the previous year.

The year 2006, with its theme 'Witnessing For Christ', saw a notable growth in the areas of soul-saving and corps growth. Three new corps were opened, eight societies and outposts were established, and a self-support strategy was emphasised in divisions and districts.

Refresher courses for officers were held at the training college in Nellore (19-22, 26-29 June 2006) under the supervision of the training principal. Attended by 40 officer-couples who have served 10 years, this new initiative in the territory aims to develop officers in their spiritual leadership.

The State Government approved the upgrading of the Salvation Army school of nursing at Evangeline Booth Hospital, Nidubrolu, into a BSc Nursing Degree college.

STATISTICS

Officers 696 (active 512 retired 184) **Cadets** 29 **Employees** 492
Corps 263 **Outposts** 146 **Societies** 132
  Institutions 14 **Elementary Schools** 63
  Upper Primary Schools 2 **English Medium Schools** 4 High Schools 2 **Junior College** 1
  Day Care Centres 3 **Residential School** 1
  Clinic 1 **Homes and Hostels** 13

Senior Soldiers 68,073 **Adherents** 7,242 **Junior Soldiers** 10,137

STAFF

Education: Maj Samuel Rathan Petta
Field: Maj S. P. Abbulu
Finance: Maj John Kumar Dasari
Human Resources Development: Maj Abraham Lincoln
Music and Creative Arts: Capt Prabathkumar
Outreach and Self-Support: Maj John Bhushanam
Property and Projects: Maj K. Yesudas
Social: Maj M. Daniel Raju
Sponsorship: Maj Mani Kumari
Trade: Capt I. D. Ebenezer
Training: Maj John Williams
Women's Ministries: Col T. Regina Chandra Bai (TPWM) Lt-Col C. Mariamma Abraham (TSWM) Maj S. Vimalakumari (THLS) Maj Rachel (TLOMS) Maj Ananda Kumari (S&GSS)
Youth: Maj B. Joseph

DIVISIONS

Bapatla: Bapatla, Guntur District, 522 101; tel: (086432) 23931; Maj Cheeli Samuel
Chennai: 109 Gangadeeswara Koil St, Chennai 600 084; tel: (044) 2641 5021; Maj K. Samuel Raju
Eluru: Adivarapupet, Eluru, West Godavari District, 534 005; tel: (08812) 237484; Maj P. C. Prasad
Gudivada: Krishna District, 521 301; tel: (08764) 243524; Maj Devadasi Joshi
Hyderabad: 6D Walker Town, Padmarao Nagar, Secunderabad, 500 025; tel: (040) 27502610; Maj S. Jayananda Rao
Nellore: Dargamitta, Nellore, 524 003; tel: (0861) 2322 589; Maj Alladi Nathaniel
Tanuku: West Godavari District, 534 211; tel: (08819) 225366; Maj K. Y. Dhana Kumar
Tenali: Ithanagar, Tenali, Guntur District, 522 201; tel: (08644) 225949; Maj Elisha Rao Mocharla
Vijayawada: Near Gymkhana Club East side H. No 26-191/2, Ghandi Nagar, Vijayawada, 521 003; tel: (0866) 2575 168; Maj G.V. Ratnam

DISTRICTS

Divi: PO Nagayalanka, Krishna District, 521 120; tel: (08671) 274991; Maj M. Yesuratnam
Mandavalli: Station Rd, Mandavalli, Krishna Dt., 521 345; tel: (08677) 280503; Maj K. Sunder Rao

Prakasam: Stuartpuram, Guntur District, 522 317; tel: (086432) 271131; Maj N. Jeevaratnam

Rajahmundry: Mallayapet, East Godavari District, 533 105; tel: (0883) 5579200; Maj K. Suvarna Raju

TRAINING COLLEGE
Dargamitta, Nellore, 524 003; tel: (0861) 2322687

CONFERENCE AND TRAINING CENTRE
Vadarevu: Nr Chirala, Prakasam District

HUMAN RESOURCES DEVELOPMENT
PB9, Nidubrolu, Guntur District 522 123; tel: (08643) 243447
Women's Development Officer, Nidubrolu: Maj Mani Kumari

EDUCATION
College (with hostel for boys and girls)
William Booth Junior College, Bapatla, Guntur District, 522 101; tel: (086432) 24259

High Schools (with hostels for boys and girls)
Bapatla: Guntur District, 522 101; tel: (086432) 24282 (acc 300)
Stuartpuram: Prakasham District, 522 317; tel: (086432) 271131 (acc 150)

Upper Primary School
Dargamitta, Nellore, Nellore District

Elementary Schools (Telugu Medium)
Bapatla Division: Bethapudi, Chintayapalem, Gudipudi, Kattivaripalem, Mallolapalem, MR Nagar, Murukondapadu, Valluvaripalem, Perlipadu, Pasumarthivaripalem, Pedapalli, Parli Vadapalem, Yaramvaripalem, Yazali
Eluru Division: Bhogapuram, Dendulur, Gopavaram, Gandivarigudem, Kovvali, Musunur, Pathamupparru, Surappagudem, Velpucharla
Gudivada Division: Chinaparupudi, Edulamadalli, Guraza, Gajulapadu, Gudivada, Kodur, Kancharlapalem, Kornipadu, Mandavalli, Narasannapalem, Pedaparupudi, Ramapuram
Nellore Division: Alluru, Buchireddipalem, Chowkacherla, Iskapalli, Kakupalli, Kanapartipadu, Mudivarthi, Modegunta, North Mopur, Pallaprolu, Rebala
Tenali Division: Annavaram, Burripalem,

Chukkapallivaripalem, Duggirala, Danthuluru, Emani, Ithanagar, Kollipara, Kattivaram, Nambur, Nelapadu
Prakasam District: Cherukuru, Stuartpuram

Primary Schools (English Medium)
The Haven, 21 Thiru Narayanaguru Rd, Choolai, Chennai 600 112; tel: (044) 2661 2784
Teachers' Colony, Vijayawada 500 008, Krishna District; tel: (0866) 2479854
Hyderabad, 6D Walker Town, Padmarao Nagar PO, Secunderabad 500 025 (with day care centre)
Nidubrolu; Villivakkam and Chennai; Hosur-Karnataka

English Medium High School
Teachers' Colony, Vijayawada 500 008; tel: (0866) 2479854

English Medium Matriculation School
The Haven, 21 Tiru Narayanaguru Rd, Choolai, Chennai 600 112; tel: (044) 2661 2784

Residential School
Tissot Sunrise School, PB9 Bapatla, 522 101; tel: (086432) 23336 (acc 125)

Vocational Training Centre
Adivarpet, Eluru, West Godivari District, 534 005 (with boys' hostel); tel: (08812) 550070

MEDICAL WORK
Evangeline Booth Hospital: Nidubrolu, Guntur District, 522 123; tel: (08643) 2522124 (acc 100)
Evangeline Booth Hospital (with home for the aged), Bapatla, Guntur District, 522 101; tel: (086432) 24134 (acc 75)
Clinic: Dindi, Nagayalanka PO, Nagayalanka Mandal, Krishna District, 521 120

HIV/Aids Programme
Nidubrolu, Guntur District

SOCIAL WORK
Children's Homes and Hostels
Boys' Hostel, Mallayyapet, Rajahmundry; tel: (0883) 2427926 (acc 40)
Boys' and Girls' Hostel: Stuartpuram, Bapatla Mandal; tel: (08643) 71307 (acc 80, 8 girls)
Boys' Hostel: Virugambakkam, Chennai; tel: (044) 23772723 (acc 80)
Boys' and Girls' Hostel: Nellore; tel: (0861) 2340202 (acc 120)
Girls' Home and Old Age Home: Virugambakkam,

Chennai; tel: (044) 23770400 (acc 70)
Girls' Hostel: Adivarpet, Eluru;
  tel: (08812) 226048 (acc 60)
Girls' Hostel: Nagayalanka; tel: (08671) 274512
  (acc 24)
Girls' Hostel: Gudivada, Krishna District;
  tel: (08674) 240739 (acc 25)
Girls' Hostel: 'Home of Peace', Tanuku;
  tel: (08819) 229163 (acc 30)

Emergency Disaster Relief
Nidubrolu 522 124; tel: (08643) 244408

Working Women's Hostel
The Haven, 21 Thiru Narayanaguru Rd, Choolai,

Chennai 600 112; tel: (044) 2532 1789

Day Care Centre
21 Thiru Narayanaguru Rd, Choolai, Chennai
  600 112; tel: (044) 2532 1789

Red Shield Guest House
15/31 Ritherdon Rd, Vepery, Chennai 600 007;
  tel: (044) 2532 1821 (acc 60)

**Waste Paper and Free Feeding
  Programmes**
6D Walker Town, Secunderabad 500 025, AP
8 Perianna Maistry St, Periamet, Chennai-3;
  tel: (044) 25610740

BOOKS FOR NATIONAL LIBRARY OF INDIA

India Northern Territory: Following his campaign in the territory and a visit to Kolkata (formerly Calcutta), General Shaw Clifton requested that samples of Salvation Army literature should be presented to the National Library of India. The gift was prompted by the discovery that the National Library had no Salvation Army books in its collection.

Books presented to the Director of the National Library, Professor Sudhendu Mandal, included volumes of the official history of The Salvation Army; *By Love Compelled*, a history of the Army's first 100 years in the India sub-continent; and General Clifton's *New Love – Thinking Aloud About Practical Holiness*.

Major Daniel Raj is pictured making the presentation on behalf of the General and Colonel Kashinath Lahase (TC, India Northern).

INDIA EASTERN TERRITORY

Territorial leaders:
Colonels Jayapaul and Yesudayamma Devarapalli

Territorial Commander:
Colonel Jayapaul Devarapalli (1 Dec 2006)

Chief Secretary:
Lieut-Colonel Lalngaihawmi (1 Mar 2007)

Territorial Headquarters: PO Box 5, Aizawl 796001, Mizoram, India

Tel: [91] 389 2322290 (EPABX)/321864; fax: [91] 389 2326123;

email: IET_mail@IET.salvationarmy.org; web site: www.salvationarmy.org/ind

Work in the region commenced on 26 April 1917 when Lieutenant Kawlkhuma, the first Mizo officer commissioned in India, returned to start the Army work. He was then joined by a group of earnest believers who shared his vision of an 'Army like a church, very much in line with The Salvation Army'. India Eastern became a separate command on 1 June 1991 and became a territory in 1993.

Zone: South Asia
States included in the territory: Arunachal Pradesh, Assam, Manipur, Meghalaya, Mizoram, Nagaland, Sikkim, Tripura and West Bengal (part)
'The Salvation Army' in Mizo: Chhandamna Sipai Pawl
Languages in which the gospel is preached: Adhibasi, Bengali, Bru, English, Hindi, Hmar, Manipuri (Meitei), Mizo, Nagamese, Nepali, Paite, Pali, Simte, Thadou, Vaiphai
Periodicals: *Sipai Tlangau* (Mizo *War Cry*), *The Officer* (Mizo), *Young Salvationist* (Mizo), *Chunnunpar* (Mizo Women's Ministries magazine)

WITH 'Fight the Good Fight' as the territorial theme for 2007, a number of new believers joined the good fight in outreach mission fields such as Arunachal Pradesh, Karbi Anglong, Manipur, Tripura and Fatapukur.

Commissioner Helen Clifton (World President of Women's Ministries) and Commissioner Lalhlimpuii (Zonal Secretary for Women's Ministries) joined women's ministries members in celebrating the Home League centenary.

Also to mark the centenary, the

Women's Ministries Department opened a new charity shop through which the Army will reach out to women who are oppressed, offended and shunned by their families. Women donated household goods and clothes for resale, and money received through the shop is also being donated to various Salvation Army-run homes and others run by non-governmental organisations.

During the year under review 13 officers were commissioned, and for the first time both parents of newly commissioned captains were presented with Fellowship of the Silver Star acknowledgements. Thirteen cadets entered the training college.

Young Salvationists remain a driving force in the territory and are actively participating in various ministries. They remain the biggest number of blood donors in the religious group.

SAY Member Jenny Lalremliani became the new world number one in the 4th Women's World Boxing Championship in the 63 kgs category. She knelt inside the ring and prayed as her victory was announced.

The Territorial Staff Band visited India Western Territory, giving programmes in Mumbai and Anand and playing in the Gateway of India – the spot where, on their arrival in Bombay (now Mumbai), Salvationist pioneers held a meeting to begin Army work in India in 1882.

The Territorial Songsters took part in the India South Western Territory's Youth Congress. A new Salvation Army songbook with tonic sol-fa was published in Mizo.

New initiatives for the development of self-help groups, under the Territorial Micro-credit and Health Development Projects, are being undertaken with support from the Australia Eastern and United Kingdom Territories. These will address not only economic issues, but also health and sanitation, HIV/Aids and human trafficking concerns.

The centralisation of funds has been implemented in the territory, with 60 per cent of cartridges and rice collections from every corps now submitted to headquarters. This immensely significant change of territorial policy is seen as a major move forward towards the territory becoming self-supporting.

STATISTICS

Officers 288 (active 226 retired 62) **Cadets** 13 **Employees** 253
Corps 231 **Societies/Outposts** 89 **Social Institutions** 12 **Schools** 15
Senior Soldiers 33,218 **Adherents** 704 **Junior Soldiers** 9,327

STAFF

Editor: Maj Vanlalfela
Property and Legal: Maj Jonathan Thanruma
Personnel: Maj Thanhlira
Community Health Action Network (CHAN): Maj Lalsangpuii
Finance: Capt Lalhmingliana
Human Resources and Development: Maj Khaizadinga
Projects and Sponsorship: Capt Vanlalsawmthanga
Public Relations and Communications: Maj Khaizadinga
Social: Maj Lianhlira
Trade: Maj K. Lalrinawma
Training: Maj Vanlalthanga
Women's Ministries: Col Yesudayamma Devarapalli (TPWM) Lt-Col Lalngaihawmi (TSWM) Maj Thantluangi (THLS) Maj Hmunropuii (SOSS) Maj Thanzuali (LOMS) Maj K. C. Ropari (SAMF) Capt Lalhlimpuii (WDO)
Youth and Candidates: Maj Laithanmawia

DIVISIONS

Cachar: Hospital Rd, Rangirkhari, PO Silchar, 788 005, Assam; tel: (03842) 220581; Maj Lalhriatpuia
Central: PO Aizawl, 796 001, Mizoram; tel: (0389) 2322393; Maj Sangchhunga
Eastern: Keifang, PO Saitual, 796 262; tel: (389) 256227; Maj Chawnghluna
Manipur: Salvation Rd, PO Churachanpur, 795 128, Manipur; tel: (3874) 233188; Maj Lianthanga
Midland: Chhiahtlang, PO Serchhip, 796 181, Mizoram; tel: (3838) 225058; Maj Hrangngura

Northern: PO Darlawn, 796 111, Mizoram;
  tel: (389) 269228; Maj C. Dawngliana
Southern: PO Lunglei, 796 701, Mizoram;
  tel: (95372) 2324027; Maj S. T. Dula
Western: PO Kolasib, 796 081, Mizoram;
  tel: (3837) 220037; Maj S. Biakliana

DISTRICT

Tripura: Behliangchhip Zampui Hill, 799 269, Via
  Dharmanagar, N Tripura; Maj K. Lalrinawma

TRAINING COLLEGE

Kolasib Vengthar, PO Kolasib, 796 081,
  Mizoram; tel: (3837) 220466

UNDER THQ

Shillong: Eldorado, Nongrim Hills, Shillong,
  Meghalaya; tel: (364) 2521527
Kohima: PO Box 292, Kohima, 797 001,
  Nagaland; tel: (370) 222785
Namchi: Jorethang Rd, Namchi, 737 126, South
  Sikkim; tel: (3595) 263208
Arunachal Pradesh: Dr Onik Moyong Complex,
  Mimir Tinali, Pasighat, 791 102, East Siang
  District, Arunachal Pradesh; tel: (368) 2225628
Kolkata: Liaison Office, SN Banerjee Rd,
  Kolkata; tel: (033) 22444713;
  email: liaison_saiet@yahoo.co.in

EDUCATION

Special Residential Schools for the Physically Challenged

Mary Scott Home for the Blind: Kalimpong,
  West Bengal; tel: (3552) 255252;
  email: john_pachuau@yahoo.com (acc 80)
School for Deaf and Dumb Children: Darjeeling,
  West Bengal; tel: (354) 2252332/2257645
  email: sadeaf@sify.com (acc 50)

Higher Secondary Schools

Children's Training Higher Secondary School:
  Churachandpur, Manipur; tel: (3874) 235097
Modern English Higher Secondary School:
  Aizawl, Mizoram; tel: (389) 2323248

High Schools

Blue Mount: Behliangchhip, Zampui, Tripura
Booth Tucker Memorial School: Gahrodpunjee,
  Cachar
Hermon Junior: Moreh, Manipur

Middle Schools

Children's Education School: Zezaw, Manipur
Children's Training School: Singngat, Manipur
Booth Tucker: Thingkangphai, Manipur
Hermon Junior: Moreh, Manipur

SA Middle School: Saikawt, Manipur
Willow Mount: Durtlang, Mizoram

Primary School

Integrated Primary School: Kolasib

Outreach Schools: 27

SOCIAL WORK

Home for Boys and Girls

Mary Scott Home for the Blind: Kalimpong,
  W Bengal

Homes for Boys

Hostel for the Deaf and Dumb: Darjeeling,
  W Bengal
Hostel for the Blind: Kolasib, Mizoram;
  tel: (3837) 220236 (acc 25)
Enna In: Kolasib; tel: (3837) 221419 (acc 30)
Kawlkhuma Home: Lunglei; tel: (372) 224420
  (acc 25)
Muanna In: Mualpui, Aizawl; tel: (389) 2320426
  (acc 30)
Manipur Boys' Home: Mualvaiphei,
  Churachandpur; tel: (3874) 235469 (acc 25)
Orphanage, Saiha: tel: (3835) 226140 (acc 15)
Silchar Home (acc 20)

Home for Girls

Hlimna In: Keifang, Mizoram; tel: (389) 2862278
  (acc 65)

Motherless Babies' Homes

Aizawl: Tuikal 'A', Aizawl, Mizoram;
  tel: (389) 2329868 (acc 35)
Manipur : Mualvaiphei, Churachandpur,
  Manipur; tel: (3874) 235469 (acc 10)

HIV/AIDS PROGRAMME

Community Health Action Network (CHAN)

Kawlkhuma Bldg, Tuikal 'A', PO Box 5,
  Aizawl 796001; tel: (389) 2320202/2327609;
  fax: (389) 2326106;
  email: chanaizawl@sancharnet.in

Community Caring Programme

Churachandpur, Manipur; tel: (3874) 235469;
  email: muanpuia_ccp@yahoo.co.in

CENTENARY PRESS

PO Box 5, Tuikal 'A', Aizawl, Mizoram;
  tel: (389) 2329626

INDIA NORTHERN TERRITORY

Territorial leaders:
Colonels Kashinath and Kusum Lahase

Territorial Commander:
Colonel Kashinath Lahase (1 Jan 2006)

Chief Secretary:
Lieut-Colonel Paul Peter Christian
(1 Dec 2006)

**Territorial Headquarters: Flat No 103, Aashirwad Complex,
D-1, Green Park, New Delhi 110 016, India**

Tel: [91] (11) 2651 2394; fax: [91] (11) 2619 6296/2651 6912;

email: INT_mail@INT.salvationarmy.org; web site: www.salvationarmy.org/ind

Shortly after arriving in India in 1882, Booth-Tucker visited major cities in northern India, including Allahabad, Delhi, Lucknow, Benares and Kolkata (Calcutta). Rural work was established later and operations were extended to Bihar and Orissa. The boundaries of the India Northern Territory have changed over the years; there have been headquarters in Gurdaspur, Bareilly, Lucknow, Benares and Kolkata and more recently Delhi. In 1947, part of the territory became Pakistan. The present territory was established on 1 June 1991.

Zone: South Asia

The territory is comprised of: the States of Bihar, Chattisgarh, Harayana, Himachal Pradesh, Jammu and Kashmir, Orissa, Punjab, Uttar Pradesh, Uttar Anchal, West Bengal, the Union Territories of Delhi, Chandigarh, and the Andaman and Nicobar Islands

'The Salvation Army' in Hindi, Punjabi and Urdu: Mukti Fauj

Languages in which the gospel is preached: Bengali, English, Hindi, Kui, Nepali, Oriya, Punjabi, Santhali, Tamil, Urdu

Periodicals: *Home League Quarterly* (Hindi and English), *Mukti Samachar* (Hindi and Punjabi), *The Officer* (Hindi), *Yuva Sipai* (Hindi)

AN enthusiastic welcome was given to General Shaw Clifton and Commissioner Helen Clifton when they visited the territory in January 2007. The territorial commander expressed delight that India Northern was the first Indian territory to be visited by the General after he took office.

A parade formed part of the welcome to the Army's world leaders as they arrived in Gurdaspur for Sunday's holiness meeting attended by some 4,000 Salvationists. At the close of the General's Bible message many people knelt at the mercy seat.

A Home League centenary rally was attended by more than 1,500 women and addressed by Commissioner Clifton (World President of Women's Ministries). Cadets from the training college were among 3,000 delegates at the youth rally.

International Headquarters having approved the upgrading of Angul District to a division, Delhi District to be Chandigarh Division and Mukerian Extension to be Mukerian District, Major Sabita Dass was appointed Divisional Commander of Angul Division – becoming the first woman DC in the territory's history.

People who had migrated from Bareilly and Moradabad (Uttar Pradesh) to Haldwani/Kathgodham (Uttaranchal) requested that a corps be opened. This resulted in the new Kathgodham/Haldwani Corps being opened by the territorial commander. Another new corps was opened at Bagnan (Kolkata Division)

A free feeding programme was started at New Delhi in August 2006 and 100 men and women are receiving their lunch through this project.

STATISTICS

Officers 413 (active 327 retired 84) **Cadets** 35 **Employees** 265
Corps 139 **Outposts** 381 **Societies** 1,261 **Institutions** 22 **Schools** 4 **College** 1
Senior Soldiers 55,289 **Adherents** 2,551 **Junior Soldiers** 9,176

STAFF

Church Growth: Maj Robin Kumar Sahu
Editor: Maj Manga Masih
Education: Maj Gurnam Masih
Field: Maj Edwin Masih
Finance: Maj Thomas Gera
Human Resources: Maj Samir Patra
Music Ministry: Maj Salamat Masih
Property, Projects and Legal: Maj Tarsem Masih
Public Relations and Fund-raising: Capt Anil Massey
Social: Maj Dilip Singh
Training: Maj Rounki Lal
Women's Ministries: Col Kusum K. Lahase (TPWM) Lt-Col Anandiben Christian (TSWM)
Youth/Candidates: Maj Philip Nayak

DIVISIONS

Amritsar: 25 Krishna Nagar, Lawrence Rd, Amritsar 143 001, Punjab; Maj Peter Masih
Angul: Angul 759 122, Orissa; tel: 06764-232829; Maj Sabita Das
Bareilly: 220 Civil Lines, Bareilly 243 001, UP; tel: 0581-2427081; Maj Yaqoob Masih
Batala: Dera Baba Nanak Rd, Batala 143 505, Dist Gurdaspur, Punjab; tel: 01871-243038; Maj Prakash Masih
Beas: Ajeet Nagar, Beas, Amritsar 143 201, Punjab; tel: 01853-273834; Maj Gian Masih
Chandigarh: Surajpur Rd, Firojpur, PO Dhamala Via Pinjore, Dist Panchkula, Haryana 134 102; tel: 01733-654946; Maj Makhan Masih
Dera Baba Nanak: Dist Gurdaspur, PO Dera Baba Nanak 143 604, Punjab; tel: 01871-247262; Maj Sulakhan Masih
Gurdaspur: Jail Rd, Dist Gurdaspur 143 521, Punjab; tel: 01874-220622; Maj Kashmir Masih
Kolkata: 37 Lenin Saranee, Kolkata 700 013; tel: 033-55101 591; fax: 033-22443910; Capt Manuel Masih
Moradabad: Kanth Rd, near Gandhi Ashram PAC, Moradabad 244 001; Maj Lazar Masih

DISTRICTS

Mukerian: Rikhipura Mohalla, Dist Hoshiyarpur, Mukerian – 144 211, Punjab; tel: 01883-248733; Maj Piara Masih
Simultala: Simultala 811 316, Dist Jamui, Bihar; Maj Chotka Hembrom

EXTENSION WORK

Mukerian: Rikhipura Mohalla, Dist Hoshiyarpur, Mukerian – 144 211, Punjab; tel: 01883-248733; Maj Sadiq Masih
Pathankot: Daulatpur Rd Prem Nagar, near FCI Godwan, Pathankot, Punjab; tel: 09815-358238; Maj Daniel Gill
Port Blair: Near Income Tax Office, Shadi Pur, Port Blair – 744106, Andaman Nicobar Islands; Capt Tarsem Masih
Taran Taran: Sandhu Ave, near Shota Kazi Kot Rd, Ward No 11, Taran Taran, Dist Amritsar, Punjab; Maj Tarsem Masih

TRAINING COLLEGE

Bareilly: 220 Civil Lines, Bareilly 243 001, UP; tel: 0581-2423304

MEDICAL WORK
Hospital

MacRobert Hospital: Dhariwal, Dist Gurdaspur 143 519, Punjab; tel: 01874-275152/275274 (acc 50)

Clinics

Social Service Centre: 172 Acharya Jagdish Chandra Bose Rd, Kolkata 700 014; tel: 033-22840441

Community Health Centre: 192-A, Arjun Nager, New Delhi 110 029; tel: 011-26168895

EDUCATION
Senior Secondary School

Aliwal Rd, Batala 143 505, Dist Gurdaspur, Punjab; tel: 01871-242593 (acc 900)

Extension Branch

Gurdaspur School: The Salvation Army DHQ Compound, Jail Rd, Dist Gurdaspur, Punjab; tel: 01874-20622

English Medium Schools

Behala School: 671 D. H. Rd, Hindustan Park, Behala, Kolkata 700034; tel: 033-23972692

Moradabad School: Kanth Rd, opp Gandhi Ashram PAC, Moradabad 244 001, UP; tel: 0591-2417351/2429184; (acc 400)

William Booth Memorial School: 220 Civil Lines, Bareilly 243001, UP; tel: 0581-2420007; (acc 200)

College

Catherine Booth College for Girls: Aliwal Rd, Batala 143 505, Dist Gurdaspur, Punjab; tel: 01871-242593 (acc 300)

Non-residential Tailoring Units

Dera Baba Nanak: Dist Gurdaspur, Punjab

Kancharapada, West Bengal

SOCIAL WORK
Free Feeding Programme

Kolkata: 172 Acharya Jagdish Chandra Rd, Kolkata 700 014; (beneficiaries 250)

New Delhi: 6 Malik Bldg, Chunamundi, Paharganj, New Delhi 110 055; tel: 011-23588433; (beneficiaries 100)

Homes for the Aged

Bareilly: 220 Civil Lines, Bareilly 243 001, UP; tel: 0581-2421432 (acc 20)

Dhariwal: MacRobert Hospital, Dhariwal, Dist Gurdaspur 143 519, Punjab; tel: 01874-275152/275274 (acc 20)

Kolkata: 172 Acharya Jagadish Chandra Rd, Kolkata 700 014 (acc 15)

Homes for Boys

Angul: Angul 759 122, Orissa; tel: 06764-232829 (acc 10)

Batala: Aliwal Rd, Batala 143 505, Dist Gurdaspur (acc 60)

Kolkata: 37 Lenin Saranee, Kolkata 700 013; tel: 033-55124567 (acc 30)

Moradabad: Kanth Rd, Moradabad 244 001, UP; tel: 0591-2417351 (acc 40)

Paburia: At/PO-Paburia, Dist Kandhamal, 762 112 (Orissa); tel: 06847-264063 (acc 30)

Simultala: Simultala 811 316, Dist Jamui, Bihar (acc 43)

Homes for Girls

Angul: Angul 759 122, Orissa; tel: 06764-232829 (acc 40)

Bareilly: 220 Civil Lines, Bareilly 243 001, UP; tel: 0581-2421432 (acc 40)

Batala: Aliwal Rd, Batala 143505, Dist Gurdaspur (acc 60)

Behala: 671 D. H. Rd, Hindustan Park, Behala, Kolkata 700034; tel: 033-23972692 (acc 120)

Gurdaspur: Jail Rd, Dist Gurdaspur 143 521, Punjab (acc 100)

HOSTELS
Blind (Men)

172 Acharya Jagdish Chandra Rd, Kolkata 700 014 (acc 30)

Working Men and Students

172 Acharya Jagdish Chandra Rd, Kolkata 700 014; tel: 033-22840441 (acc 200)

Young Women

Bareilly: 220 Civil Lines, Bareilly 243 001, UP; tel: 0581-2421432

Kolkata: 38 Lenin Saranee, Kolkata 700 013; tel: 033-22274281 (acc 50)

Ludhiana: 2230, ISA Nagari, Ludhiana – 141 008, Punjab

New Delhi: 192-A, Arjun Nager, New Delhi 110 029; tel: 011-26168895

RED SHIELD GUEST HOUSES

Kolkata: 2 Saddar St, Kolkata 700 016; tel: 033-22861659 (acc 80)

New Delhi: P-2 S Extension, Part II, New Delhi 110 049; tel: 011-2625 7310

WASTE PAPER DEPARTMENT

6 Malik Bldg, Chunamundi, Paharganj, New Delhi 110 055; tel: 011-2355 8433

INDIA SOUTH EASTERN TERRITORY

Territorial leaders:
Commissioners M. C. and Susamma James

Territorial Commander:
Commissioner M. C. James (1 Dec 2006)

Chief Secretary:
Lieut-Colonel Bashir Masih (1 May 2005)

**Territorial Headquarters: High Ground Road, Maharajanagar PO,
Tirunelveli – 627 011, Tamil Nadu, India**

Tel: [91] (462) 2574331/2574313; fax: [91] (462) 2577152;
email: ISE_mail@ISE.salvationarmy.org; web site: www.salvationarmy.org/ind

The Salvation Army commenced operations in south-east India on 27 May 1892 as a result of the vision received by Major Deva Sundaram at Medicine Hill, while praying and fasting with three officers when the persecution in Southern Tamil Nadu was at its height. On 1 October 1970 the Tamil-speaking part of the Southern India Territory became a separate entity as the Army experienced rapid growth.

Zone: South Asia
States included in the territory: Tamil Nadu, Pondicherry
'The Salvation Army' in Tamil: Ratchaniya Senai; in Malayalam: Raksha Sainyam
Languages in which the gospel is preached: English, Malayalam, Tamil
Periodicals: *Chiruveeran* (Tamil), *Home League Quarterly*, *Poresatham* (Tamil), *The Officer* (Tamil)

IN the year for 'Renewing the Spirit' almost all divisions and centres kept the theme in mind as they conducted many activities. This helped to win new converts. New territorial leaders Commissioners M. C. and Susamma James challenged Salvationists to renew their lives in Christ.

Youth programmes, local officers' seminars, Home League workshops, teachers' get-togethers and officers' retreats took place throughout the year.

Many children in need of education have been traced and admitted to schools; nearly 2,500 have been educated free of charge through the generous support of Caruna Bal Vikas, part of the Compassion International organisation which cooperates with regional churches to provide food, clothes, education and medicine.

The children's spiritual wellbeing is being also maintained. Some children have been awarded 'All India' prizes for special performance.

Youth Camp 2007 was a remarkable soul-winning activity which 650 delegates from various parts of the territory attended. More than 140 of the young people accepted Jesus Christ as Saviour and 45 dedicated their lives to officership.

Commissioner Susamma James (Territorial President of Women's Ministries) and her women's ministries team worked tirelessly to ensure the success of the Home League centenary. The contribution of home leaguers to corps and divisional events was greatly valued. Congregations were inspired by the testimony of Mrs Shanthi of Vadamalapuram Corps (Tenkasi Division) about her husband's road accident and the home leaguers' support and prayers.

In the Pondicherry outreach area, where Mettupalayam was a point of focus, God blessed the officers' endeavours. Seven new families were won to the Lord. However, the people living in this area are very poor and without adequate shelter, clothing and food.

The Salvationists' financial support has been very much appreciated. They participated in many activities to contribute to the Self-Denial Fund. Their fund-raising and personal giving resulted in 4,540,392 rupees (US$ 111,984).

In Radhapuram Division, which is located in a remote and very dry area, a family purchased two young calves and dedicated them to the appeal, so when an altar service took place the animals were sold for 2,900 rupees (US$ 72) and the money offered to the Self-Denial Fund. This set a good example to the other Salvationists and friends present.

STATISTICS

Officers 600 (active 445 retired 155)
Employees 486
Corps 267 **Outposts** 122 **Societies** 74 **Schools** 21
Institutions 53

Senior Soldiers 46,659 **Adherents** 17,501
Junior Soldiers 4,777
Personnel serving outside territory Officers 22

STAFF

Community Health Development:
Mr Benjamin Dhaya
Education: Maj Tharmar Alfred
Field: Maj Arulappan Paramadhas
Finance: Maj Jebamony Jayaseelan
Human Resources: Lt-Col Masilamony Ponniah
Projects: Maj Yacob Selvam
Property: Lt-Col Appavoo William
Public Relations: Maj Abraham Jeyasekhar
Social: Maj Perinbanayagam Suthanantha Dhas
Supplies: Maj Annal Peter
Training: Maj Jeyaraj Samraj
Women's Ministries: Comr L. Susamma James (TPWM) Lt-Col Bachni Masih (TSWM) Lt-Col Thavamoni William (THLS) Maj Retnam (TLOMS)
Youth and Candidates: Maj Yesudian Ponnappan

DIVISIONS

Cape North: Azhagiapandipuram PO, 629 852 tel: (04652) 281952; Maj Abel Bailis
Cape South: Vetturnimadam PO, Nagercoil 629 003; tel: (04652) 272787; Maj Chelliah Moni
Kulasekharam: Kulasekharam PO, 629 161; tel: (04651) 279446; Maj Solomon Muthuraj
Marthandam: Marthandam PO, 629 165; tel: (04651) 272492; Maj Sundaram Motchakan
Palayamcottai: 28 Bell Amorses Colony, Palayamcottai 627 002; tel: (0462) 2573676
Radhapuram: Radhapuram PO, 627 111; tel: (04637) 254318; Maj Chelliah Swamidhas
Tenkasi: Tenkasi PO, 627 811; tel: (04633) 280774; Maj Devasundaram Samuel Raj
Thuckalay: Thuckalay PO, 629 175; tel: (04651) 252443; Maj Sam Devaraj
Valliyoor: Valliyoor PO, 627 117; tel: (04637) 221454; Maj N. Edwin Sathyadhas

DISTRICTS

Coimbatore: Daniel Ngr, K. Vadamaduai PO, 641 017; tel: (0422) 2461277; Maj Yovan Dhason
Erode: 155 Amman Nager, Erode 638 002; tel: (0424) 2283909; Maj S. Yesuretinam
Madurai: TPK Rd, Palanganatham PO, 625 003; tel: (0452) 2604169; Maj J. William
Trichy: New Town, Malakovil, Thiruvarumbur 620 013; tel: (0431) 2556164; Maj Daniel Dhason
Tuticorin: 5/254 G, Caldwell Colony, Tuticorin

...or timbrelists join in Congo (Brazzaville) Territory's 70th anniversary celebrations

Make the world with music ring,
While with heart and voice we sing
Praises to our God and King,
Hallelujah!
Tell with no uncertain sound,
To the nations all around,
Of the Saviour we have found,
Hallelujah!

Song Book of The Salvation Army, 809

Young Salvationist musicians prepare for a march of witness in Fiji

Toddlers enjoy the 'Mainly Music' session at a Salvation Army pre-school group in New Zealand

Above: The world-famous Kings Singers perform Salvation Army choral music during a 'Hendon Highlights' festival in London, UK

Left: The Mizoram Songsters (India Eastern Territory) visit India South Western

Bottom: Delegates at a music camp in Sri Lanka are given guitar tuition

Above: Salvationists in Brazzaville offer their songs of praise and worship to Jesus Christ

Left: A bandsman makes sure he gets his bass – and baby! – to the Finland and Estonia Territorial Roots Congress

628 008; tel: (0461) 2376841;
Maj Sebagnanam James

Pondicherry Extension Area: opp Mahatma
Dental College, Kamaraj Ngr, Goremedu
Check Post, Pondicherry 605 006;
tel: (0413) 2271933; Maj Masilamony
Yesudhason

TRAINING COLLEGE
WCC Rd, Nagercoil 629 001;
tel: (04652) 231471

HUMAN RESOURCES DEVELOPMENT AND CONFERENCE CENTRE
Muttom, via Nagercoil 629 202;
tel: (04651) 238321

MEDICAL WORK
Catherine Booth Hospital: Nagercoil 629 001;
tel: (04652) 275516/7; fax: (04652) 275489

COMMUNITY HEALTH AND DEVELOPMENT PROGRAMMES
Catherine Booth Hospital, Nagercoil 629 001;
tel: (04652) 272068
Women's Micro-credit and Health Programme
Community-based HIV/Aids Care and
Support Programmes
Reproductive and Child Health Programme
Community Health Centre
Voluntary Counselling and Testing Centre cum
STD Clinic Programme
Community Eye Health Programme

EDUCATION
Higher Secondary School (mixed)
Nagercoil 629003; tel: (04652) 272647;
Headmaster: Mr M. Kingsley

Matriculation Higher Secondary School (mixed)
Nagercoil; tel: (04652) 272534; Principal: Mr
Monickadhas

Middle School (mixed)
Nambithoppu Middle School; Headmaster: Mr
Vethamuthu

Noble Memorial High School
Valliyoor; tel: (04637) 220380; Headmaster:
Mr A. Benjamin

Village Primary Schools: 9

Nursery and English Medium Primary Schools: 6

SOCIAL SERVICES
Hostels
Boys' Hostel: Nagercoil; tel: (04652) 272953
(acc 72)
Noble Memorial Boys' Hostel: Valliyoor;
tel: (04637) 221289 (acc 70)
Tucker Girls' Hostel: Nagercoil;
tel: (04652) 231293 (acc 135)
Girls' Hostel: Thuckalay;
tel: (04651) 252764 (acc 100)

Motherless Babies' Home
Palayamcottai 627 002; tel (04622) 584441s

Child Development Centres
Chemparuthivilai, Chemponvilai, Kadaigramam,
Madurai, Nagercoil, Pondicherry,
Radhapuram, Thuckalay, Valliyoor

Vocational Training Centres for the Physically Handicapped
Men and Boys
Aramboly 629 003; tel: (04652) 263133

Women and Girls
Nagercoil 629 003; tel: (04652) 232348

Rural Development and Vocational Training Centre
Chemparuthivilai 629 166; tel: (04651) 253292

Vocational Training Institute
Kilkothagiri Junction, 643 216 Nilgris

Industrial Training Institute
Aramboly; tel: (04652) 262198

Tailoring Institutes
Chemparuthivilai, Chemponvilai, Erode,
Kadaigramam, Katpady, Kiliancode,
Kulasekharam, Melecheval; Moolakarupatty,
Oppanayalpuramm, Osravilai, Radhapuram,
Palliyadi, Sambavarvadakarai, Thuckalay,
Trichy, Tuticorin, Vadasery, Valliyoor,
Vellachivilai

RETIRED OFFICERS' HOME
Catherine Booth Hospital, Nagercoil 629 001

More than 140 of the
young people accepted
Jesus Christ as Saviour

INDIA SOUTH WESTERN TERRITORY

Territorial leaders:
Commissioners Chimanbhai and Rahelbai Waghela

Territorial Commander:
Commissioner Chimanbhai Waghela
(3 May 2003)

Chief Secretary:
Lieut-Colonel Samuel Charan (1 May 2005)

Territorial Headquarters: The Salvation Army, Kowdiar, Thiruvananthapuram, Kerala

Postal address: PO Box 802, Kowdiar, Thiruvananthapuram 695 003, Kerala State, India

Tel: [91] (471) 2314626/2723238; fax: [91] (471) 2318790;

email: ISW_mail@ISW.salvationarmy.org; web site: www.salvationarmy.org/ind

Salvation Army work commenced in the old Travancore State on 18 March 1894 by Captain Yesudasen Sanjivi, who was a high-caste Brahmin before his conversion. His son, Colonel Donald A. Sanjivi, became the first territorial commander from Kerala. The work spread to other parts of the state through the dedication of pioneer officers, including Commissioner P. E. George. The India South Western Territory came into being on 1 October 1970 when the Southern India Territory divided into two. The territory has its headquarters at Thiruvananthapuram and comprises the entire Malayalam-speaking area known as Kerala State.

Zone: South Asia
State included in the territory: Kerala
'The Salvation Army' in Malayalam: Raksha Sainyam; in Tamil: Ratchania Senai
Languages in which the gospel is preached: English, Malayalam, Tamil
Periodicals: *Home League Quarterly* (Malayalam/English), *The Officer* (Malayalam), *Youdha Shabdam* (Malayalam), *Yuva Veeran* (Malayalam)

FOUNDERS' Day is traditionally celebrated across the territory every year with much enthusiasm. At Evangeline Booth Leprosy Hospital, Puthencruz, 2 July 2006 was marked by the opening of a diabetes club which aims to provide up-to-date information about this disorder.

Later in the month a 'Women Empowerment' seminar was held for women officers. Divisional reports and future plans were submitted by all the divisional directors of women's ministries. 'Dowry', a great challenge for girls in a community, was taken up for discussion.

As part of the annual Onam Week evangelistic campaign during August, open-air meetings and outreach activities were organised at every Salvation

Army centre in the territory.

A workshop on disaster management (2-3 August) was led by the national consultant for emergency services, supported by the national educational consultant. This training programme equipped delegates for emergency services during times of natural calamities, epidemics and the like.

The Women's Ministries Department arranged for the distribution of parcels of fruit to patients at the Government Tuberculosis Hospital, Pulayanarkotta, and a tuberculosis rehabilitation centre run by the Catholic Church in Chakkai, Trivandrum. This had been funded by Christmas caroling in Trivandrum city centre organised by THQ staff.

January 2007 saw the launch of Home League centenary celebrations. Seminars and various programmes were organised for this special year, all aimed at helping the development of women throughout the territory.

After a gap of 10 years officers met in territorial councils (9-11 April). The venue was Marthoma Youth Centre, Adoor, situated on a mountain, and the councils became a 'Mount of Transfiguration' experience for the 450 officers present.

Taking as their theme 'Jesus Glorified In You' (2 Thessalonians 1:12), guest leaders Commissioners Lalkiamlova and Lalhlimpuii (International Secretary, South Asia, and Zonal Secretary for Women's Ministries) inspired their listeners.

Marthoma Youth Centre was also the venue for the impressive Territorial Youth Congress (18-22 April). Majors Kenneth and Cheryl Maynor, divisional leaders in USA Eastern Territory, were the guest speakers on the theme 'Know Jesus Walks With You'. Bible studies, lectures, discussions and cultural programmes enriched the lives of the 747 delegates drawn from across the territory.

The territory is grateful to Swiss Solidarity and Australia for help with the tsunami rehabilitation project at Karunagappally, and United Kingdom Territory in supporting community development projects like water-supply schemes and goat distribution.

STATISTICS

Officers 701 (active 460 retired 241) **Cadets** 22 **Employees** 174
Corps 333 **Societies and Outposts** 460 **Schools** 16 **Institutions** 20
Senior Soldiers 40,227 **Adherents** 15,259 **Junior Soldiers** 3,763
Personnel serving outside territory Officers 20

STAFF

Business Administration: Maj K. C. Peter
Editor: Maj Davidson Daniel
Field: Maj K. P. Chacko
Human Resources Development and Education: Maj Simson Samuelkutty
Social and Legal: Maj John Suseelkumar
Training: Maj John Samuel
Women's Ministries: Comr Rahelbai Waghela (TPWM) Lt-Col Bimla Charan (TSWM) Maj Suseela Chacko (THLS) Maj Lillybai Samuelkutty (TLOMS) Maj M. V. Esther Davidson (SSFS)
Youth and Candidates: Maj D. Gnanadasan

DIVISIONS

Adoor: Adoor 691 523; tel: 04734-229648; Maj P. V. Stanly Babu
Cochin: Erumathala PO, Alwaye 683 105; tel: 0484-2638429; Maj C. S. Yohannan
Kangazha: Edayirikapuzha PO, Kangazha 686 541; tel: 0481-2494773; Maj P. J. Yohannan
Kattakada: Kattakada 695 572; tel: 0471-2290484; Maj Sam Immanuel

Kottarakara: Kottarakara 691 506;
tel: 452650; Maj Rajan K. John

Malabar: Veliyamthode, Chandakunnu PO
Nilambur 679 342; tel: 2222824; Maj N. S.
George

Mavelikara: Thazhakara, Mavelikara 690 102;
tel: 2303284; Maj N. J. George

Nedumangadu: Nedumangadu 695 541;
tel: 2800352; Maj Rajamani Christuraj

Neyyattinkara: Neyyattinkara 695 121;
tel: 2222916; Maj P. K. Philip

Peermade: Kuttikanam PO, Peermade 685 501;
tel: 232816; Maj T. J. Simon

Tiruvella: Tiruvella 689 101; tel: 2602657;
Maj K. M. Solomon

Thiruvananthapuram: Parambuconam,
Kowdiar PO, Thiruvananthapuram 695 003;
tel: 2433215; Maj M. Samuel

DISTRICTS

Kottayam: Pariyaram PO, Kottayam 686 018;
tel: 0481 2465652; Maj V. D. Samuel

Punalur: The Salvation Army, PPM PO, Punalur;
tel: 0475 2229218; Maj Sathiyaseelan

TRAINING COLLEGE

Kowdiar, Thiruvananthapuram 695 003;
tel: 2315313

MEDICAL WORK

Evangeline Booth Community Hospital:
Puthencruz 682 308; tel: Ernakulam 2731056

Evangeline Booth Leprosarium: Puthencruz
682 308; tel: Ernakulam 2730054 (acc 200)

General Hospital: Kulathummel, Kattakada
695 572 Thiruvananthapuram Dist;
tel: Kattakada 2290485 (acc 60)

Medical Centres:
Kanghaza 686 541, Edayappara;
tel: Kangazha 2494273 (acc 12)
Kowdiar, Thiruvananthapuram 695 003;
tel: 2723237

Community Health Centres:
Bharathannoor, Panacode, Panniyodu, Valiyodu

SCHOOLS
Higher Secondary School (mixed)
Thiruvananthapuram 695 003; tel: 2315488
(acc 1,371)

Primary Schools: 15 (acc 2,640)

SOCIAL WORK
Boys' Homes
Kangazha 686 541 (acc 30)
Kottarakara 691 506 (acc 30)

Kowdiar, Thiruvananthapuram 695 003 (acc 20)
Mavelikara 690 102 (acc 25)

Community Development Centres
North: Trikkakara – Cochin 682 021
South: Konchira, Thiruvananthapuram 695 607;
tel: 0472-2831540

Girls' Homes
Adoor 691 523 (acc 25)
Kowdiar, Thiruvananthapuram 695 003
(acc 24)
Nedumangad 695 541 (acc 30)
Peermade, Kuttikanam 685 501 (acc 30)
Trikkakara, Cochin 682 021 (acc 30)
Thiruvalla 689 101; tel: 0469-2831540 (acc 25)

Vocational Training Centre for Physically Handicapped Women
Nedumangad 695 541 (acc 25)

Vocational Training Centre for Women
Nedumangad 695 541 (acc 25)

Young Men's Training Centres
Thazhakara, Mavelikara 690 102
Thiruvananthapuram 695 003

Printing Press
Kowdiar, Thiruvananthapuram 695 003;
tel: 0471 2725358

Computer Training Centre
Kowdiar, Thiruvananthapuram; tel: 2318524

Tailoring Centres
Adoor, Cochin, Kangazha, Kattakada,
Kottarakara, Malabar, Neyyattinkara,
Peermade

Young Women's Hostel (Goodwill Hostel)
Thiruvananthapuram 695 003; tel: 2319917
(acc 20)

Youth Centre
Kowdiar, Thiruvananthapuram 695 003

RED SHIELD GUEST HOUSES
Kowdiar, Thiruvananthapuram 695 003;
tel: 0471-2319926
Kovalam, Thiruvananthapuram; tel: 0471 2485895

RETIREMENT COTTAGES FOR OFFICERS
Thiruvananthapuram (cottages 4)

INDIA WESTERN TERRITORY

Territorial Commander:
Commissioner P. Mary Rajakumari
(1 Aug 2007)

Chief Secretary:
Lieut-Colonel Lalramhluna (1 May 2007)

Territorial Headquarters: Sheikh Hafizuddin Marg, Byculla, Mumbai 400 008

Postal address: PO Box 4510, Mumbai 400 008, India

Tel: [91] (022) 2308 4705/2307 1140; fax: [91] (022) 2309 9245;

email: IWT_mail@iwt.salvationarmy.org; web site: www.salvationarmy.org/ind

The Salvation Army began its work in Bombay (later Mumbai) in 1882 as a pioneer party led by Major Frederick Tucker and including Veerasoriya, a Sri Lankan convert, invaded India with the love and compassion of Jesus. Bombay (Mumbai) was the capital of Bombay Province, which included Gujarat and Maharashtra, and the first headquarters in India was in a rented building at Khatwadi. From these beginnings the work of God grew in Bombay Province. Various models of administration were tried for the work in Gujarat and Maharashtra until the India Western Territory was established in 1921.

Zone: South Asia
States included in the territory: Gujarat, Maharashtra, Madhya Pradesh, Rajasthan
'The Salvation Army' in Gujarati and Marathi: Muktifauj
Languages in which the gospel is preached: English, Gujarati, Hindi, Marathi, Tamil
Periodicals: *Home League Quarterly* (Gujarati and Marathi), *The Officer* (Gujarati and Marathi), *The War Cry* (Gujarati and Marathi), *The Young Soldier* (Gujarati and Marathi)

MUMBAI came face to face with terror as seven bomb blasts ripped through packed compartments of rush-hour trains on the evening of 11 July 2006, killing more than 175 commuters and injuring at least 500 others.

Arriving at the scene, Salvation Army officers found the authorities already tending to the needs of the injured but noticed a great number of people were stranded due to the suburban train services having been suspended indefinitely. City bus routes were also severely hampered.

Officers and volunteers worked long into the night finding transport for people who would otherwise have had no way to get home.

As victims of the bombings were rushed to hospitals, a Salvation Army team was sent to see what was required to respond to the needs of the injured. This contact led to the Army providing much-needed emergency supplies to over-burdened hospitals. There was also invaluable work to be done in spiritual counselling for the families affected by the atrocity.

About 10 days later members of the Trauma Counselling Team visited the

143

suburbs of Nalla Sopara and Nirmal village, despite heavy rainfalls. The adverse weather conditions made it difficult to locate people, but the team managed to visit six families. Four had suffered the death of a family member, causing female relatives especially to be depressed. People in the other two families had been seriously injured in the bombings.

Severe localised flooding caused by heavy rains left more than 400 families in need of immediate assistance. Salvation Army teams distributed food baskets to many of the affected families.

As the challenge of HIV/Aids increases daily, The Salvation Army's response is growing through its hospitals situated in Gujarat and Maharashtra as well as the corps-based HIV/Aids Community Development Programme in Mumbai.

With HIV/Aids affecting the lives of many poorer women within communities, the territory has enrolled 25 women in its tailoring class. The Salvation Army provided them with sewing machines, and the income subsequently generated by these women will help buy much-needed provisions.

The local business community being very supportive of this project in partnership with the Army, it is hoped the programme will be expanded.

One of the most encouraging aspects of spiritual progress in the territory is seen in prayer cell members fervently testifying and praising God as they spread the gospel among the people.

After helpful planning and spiritual preparation, corps sought to upgrade their financial status. Thirteen have become self-supporting and by 2007 the total should increase to 21. Other corps are stepping out towards this goal.

The appointment of Commissioner P. Mary Rajakumari as territorial commander was announced following the promotion to Glory of her husband, Commissioner P. D. Krupa Das.

STATISTICS
Officers 611 (active 385 retired 226) **Cadets** 24 **Employees** 259
Corps 229 **Outposts** 290 **Institutions** 20 **Day Schools** 11
Senior Soldiers 32,504 **Adherents** 3,482 **Junior Soldiers** 9,074

STAFF
Editor: Maj B. P. Jadhav (Marathi)
Maj Ruth Macwan (Gujarati)
Education: Maj Punjalal U. Macwan (Gujarati)
Field: Maj K. K. Parmar (Gujarat) Maj B. R. Borde (Maharashtra)
Finance: Maj Jashwant D. Mahida
Human Resources: Maj Phulen Macwan (Gujarat) Maj Benjamin Gaikwad (Maharashtra)
Property and Development: Maj Vijay Dalvi (Maharashtra)
Property: Maj Jashwant Mahida (Gujarat)
Public Relations: Maj B. P. Jadhav
Social: Maj Punjalal U. Macwan (Gujarat) Maj Benjamin Randive (Maharashtra)
Training: Maj Nicolas Damor (Gujarat); Maj Ratnakar D. Kale (Maharashtra)
Women's Ministries: Comr P. Mary Rajakumari (TPWM) Lt-Col Kawlramthangi (TSWM) Maj Eunice K. Parmar (THLS-G), Maj Kanchanmala Borde (THLS-M); Maj Ruth J. Mahida (LOMS-G) Maj Rajani V. Dalvi (LOMS-M) Maj S. Retnabai (SAMF-G) Maj Asha Kamble (SAMF-M) Maj Sheila Mandgule (SSM-M) Maj Margaret Macwan (SSM-G)
Youth: Maj Yakub G. Macwan (Gujarat) Maj Ashok Mandgule (Maharashtra)

DIVISIONS
Gujarat
Ahmedabad: Behrampura, Ahmedabad 380 022; tel: (079) 539 4258; Maj Jashwant T. Macwan

Anand: Amul Dairy Rd, Anand 388 001;
tel: (02692) 240638; Maj David K. Sevak

Matar: Behind Civil Court, Matar District
Kheda 387 530; tel: (02694) 285482;
Maj Paul Maganlal

Nadiad: Nadiad, District Kheda, 387 002;
tel: (0268) 2558856; Maj Jashwant Soma
Chauhan

Panchmahal: Dohad, Panchmahal, 389 151;
tel: (02673) 221771; Maj Rasik P. Christian

Petlad: Sunav Rd, Post Petlad, District Kheda,
388 450; tel: (02679) 221527; Maj Prabhudas
J. Christian

South Gujarat: Khambla Zampa, PO Vansda,
396 580District Navsari; Maj Gabriel I.
Christian

Maharashtra

Ahmednagar: Fariabagh, Sholapur Rd, 414 001;
tel: (022) 95241 358194; Capt Sanjay Wanjare

Mumbai: Sankli St, Byculla, Mumbai 400 008;
tel: (022) 2301 3692; Maj Suresh Pawar

Pathardi: Pathardi, District Ahmednagar, 414
102; tel: (02428) 223116; Maj D. L. Kasbe

Pune: 19 Napier Rd, 411 040;
tel: (022) 95206 363198; Maj Surendra
Chopde

Satara: Satara, District Satara 415 001;
tel: (952162) 234006; Maj Philip Jadhav

Shevgaon: Shevgaon, District Ahmednagar,
414 502; tel: (952429) 223191; Maj Bhausaheb
Magar

Shrirampur: District Ahmednagar, 413 709,
Tal Shrirampur; tel: (95242) 226382

TRAINING COLLEGES

Gujarat: Anand 388 001, District Kheda, Amul
Dairy Rd; tel: (02692) 254801

Maharashtra: Fariabagh, Ahmednagar 414 001;
tel: (022) 95241 2355950

SCHOOLS
Boarding Schools (Boys and Girls)

William Booth Memorial Children's Home and
Hostel: Anand 388 001, District Kheda,
Gujarat; tel: (2692) 255580 (acc 226)

William Booth Memorial Primary and High
Schools, Farlabagh, District Ahmednagar,
414 001, Maharashtra; tel: (022) 95241 324267
(acc 513)

Day Schools

Anand: William Booth Memorial High School,
Amul Dairy Rd; tel: (2692) 254901 (acc 276)
English Medium Primary School (acc 260)
William Booth Primary School (acc 476)

Ashakiran: Primary School, Satara; under DHQ
(acc 13)

Dynanjot: English Medium School,
Vishrantwadi, 411 015; tel: 95206 692761
(acc 25)

Muktipur: PO Bareja 382 425, District
Ahmednabad; tel: 02718 233318 (acc 93)

Mumbai: Tucker English Medium School,
Sankli St, Byculla, Mumbai 400 008;
tel: (022) 307 7062 (acc 652)

Vadodara: English Medium School

MEDICAL WORK

Emery Hospital: Anand, District Kaira, Gujarat;
address: Amul Dairy Rd, 388 001;
tel: (2692) 253737 (acc 160)

Evangeline Booth Hospital: Ahmednagar 414 001,
Maharashtra; tel: (022) 95241 2345059;
tel: (022) 95241 2325976 (acc 172)

Community-Based Aids Programme and
Confidential Aids Counselling Clinic: Byculla,
Mumbai; tel: (022) 309 3566 (incl Aruna
Children's Programme and Asha Deep
Tailoring Programme)

HUMAN RESOURCES
DEVELOPMENT CENTRES

Anand (Gujarat): Faujabad Comp,
Ananda 388 001

Ahmednagar (Maharashtra):
tel: (022) 95241 2358489

SOCIAL WORK
CARE Programme Centre

Byculla, Mumbai; tel: (022) 309 3566; Community
Based Aids Programme, Confidential Aids
Counselling Clinic, Aruna Children's
Programme, Asha Deep Tailoring Programme

Farm Colony

Muktipur 382 425, Post Bareja, District
Ahmedabad; tel: (02718) 33318

Feeding Programme

Mumbai (under King Edward Home)

Homes
Children

Mumbai: Sion Rd, IOB Bldg, Sion (E) 400 022;
tel: (022) 2409 4405 (acc 170)

Hope House, Pune: Gidney Park, Salisbury Park
Plot 41 No 554/2 Pune 411 037;
tel: 9529 24271728 (acc 50)

Elderly Men

Mumbai 400 008: 122 Maulana Azad Rd,
Byculla; tel: (022) 23071346; (acc 50)

Severe flooding caused by heavy rains in parts of the territory left more than 400 families in need of immediate assistance. Salvation Army teams distributed food baskets to many of the affected families.

Industrial

King Edward Home: 122 Maulana Azad Rd, Byculla, Mumbai 400 008; tel: (022) 2307 1346

Physically Handicapped Children

Joyland, Anand 388 001, District Kheda, Gujarat; tel: (02692) 51891 (acc 60)

Ray of Hope Home

Vansda (under DHQ) (acc 60)

Hostels
Blind Working Men

Ahmedabad: Locoshed, Rajpur-Hirpur, Ahmedabad, Gujarat; tel: (079) 216 1217; (acc 40)

Mumbai 400 008: Sankli St, Byculla; tel: (022) 2305 1573 (acc 70)

Young Men

Satara: c/o DHQ Satara; tel: (952162) 234006 (acc 30)

Young Women

Anand: District Kheda, Gujarat; tel: (02692) 254499 (acc 50)

Baroda: Nava Yard, Chhani Rd, Vadodara; tel: (0265) 2775361

Mumbai 400 008: Concord House, Morland Rd, Byculla; tel: (022) 2301 4219 (acc 63)

Pune: c/o DHQ, 19 Napier Rd, Pune 411 040 (acc 16)

RED SHIELD HOTEL

30 Mereweather Rd, Fort, Mumbai 400 039; tel: (022) 2284 1824; fax: (022) 2282 4613 (acc 450)

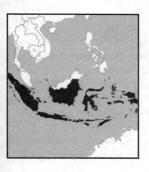

INDONESIA TERRITORY

Territorial leaders:
**Colonels Ribut Basuki and
Marie Kartodarsono**

Territorial Commander:
Colonel Ribut Basuki Kartodarsono
(1 Oct 2006)

Chief Secretary:
Lieut-Colonel Harold J. Ambitan
(1 Sep 2005)

Territorial Headquarters: Jalan Jawa 20, Bandung 40117

Postal address: Post Box 1640, Bandung 40016, Indonesia

Tel: [62] (22) 4207029/4205056; fax: [62] (22) 423 6754;

web site: www.salvationarmy.or.id

The Salvation Army commenced in Indonesia (Java) in 1894. Operations were extended to Ambon, Bali, East Kalimantan, Sulawesi (Central, North and South), Sumatra (North and South) and East Nusa Tenggara, Aceh and Papua. A network of educational, medical and social services began.

Zone: South Pacific and East Asia
Country included in the territory: Indonesia
'The Salvation Army' in all Indonesian languages: Bala Keselamatan
Languages in which the gospel is preached: Indonesian with various dialects such as Batak, Daa, Dayak, Javanese, Ledo, Makassarese, Moma, Niasnese, Tado and Uma

THE highlight of 2006 was the visit of Chief of the Staff Commissioner Robin Dunster, who led the farewell salute to territorial leaders Commissioners Johannes and Augustina Watilete and the welcome to their successors, Colonels Ribut Basuki and Marie Kartodarsono.

The Chief brought special blessings as she delivered God's words. Many of her listeners were encouraged to be strong as they dealt with problems in their ministry as Salvationists in a complex country which faces difficulties such as sickness, natural disaster and drought. They were reminded to hold on to God's promise that he is almighty and will help and take care of his people.

In Pare-pare, the territorial leaders dedicated a new building – the Catherine Booth Maternity Clinic. This is part of a new ministry located north of Makassar, South Sulawesi, in a community that is 95 per cent Muslim. Medical services have been introduced with local government support. There are also new opportunities for evangelism in this area.

A devastating earthquake in

Yogyakarta capsized five boats and all churches in Indonesia held prayer meetings for the victims. Porong, East Java, is still subject to mudslides.

Heavy rainfall was also experienced from February 2007 onwards, particularly in Jakarta and the suburbs of Polonia, Kelapa Gading and Jelambar where thousands of houses were deeply submerged. The Salvation Army Compassion in Action team in Jakarta, with the team from Bandung, assisted the whole community regardless of religion, performing medical treatment and distributing hot meals.

'While Women Weep' was the theme of workshops for women officers in leadership roles, held at THQ during January 2007. Colonel Marie Kartodarsono (Territorial President of Women's Ministries) sought to develop and encourage the delegates with a simple vision: 'Preparing trustworthy, competent and qualified women leaders who are humble and visionary in Salvation Army ministries'.

The territory was delighted to be visited by the International Legal Secretary, Major Peter Smith, to discuss Salvation Army legal matters. In both Bandung and Palu a one-day workshop was attended by 40 officers. The major also met Salvationists with professional legal skills and they examined the territory's constitution and bylaws.

The visit of Lieut-Colonels Ian and Sonja Southwell (IHQ) was also successful, their guidance on training and development matters proving very valuable and providing a starting point for the future development of the training college programme.

The territory held a projects training programme for the first time. Members of the International Projects and Development Section, IHQ, gave excellent instruction in assessing a community's needs so that the territory is better informed when developing community-based projects.

STATISTICS

Officers 664 (active 535 retired 129) **Cadets** (1st Yr) 20 (2nd Yr) 28 **Employees** 1,605
Corps 270 **Outposts** 211 **Kindergartens** 7 **Primary Schools** 60 **Secondary Schools** 13 **High Schools** 5 **Technical High School** 1 **Hospitals** 6 **Theological University** 1 **Clinics** 22 **Academies for Nurses** 2 **Social Institutions** 20
Senior Soldiers 26,417 **Adherents** 16,131 **Junior Soldiers** 7,889
Officers serving outside Territory 3

STAFF

Sec for Business Administration: Lt-Col Pieter Siagian
Asst Business Sec: Maj Yusak Tampai
Finance Sec: Maj Yusak Tampai
Auditor: Maj Yohanes Sayuti
Property: Capt Fachren Tumanduk
Information Technology: Kadek White

Sec for Programme: Maj Henoch Nore
Social Services: Maj Elisabeth Sisman
Corps Growth and Education: Maj Made Petrus
Legal and Parliament: Maj Sasmoko Hertjahjo
Youth and Children's Ministries: Maj Stanley Baginda

Sec for Personnel: Maj Selly Poa
Officers Training and Development: Maj Widiawati Tampai
Candidates: Capt Marisa Mangela

Literature and Editorial: Maj Habel Laua
Public Relations: Maj Winfrid Dalentang Jl. Kramat Raya 55, Jakarta Pusat; tel: (021) 391 4518; fax: (021) 392 8636
Training: Maj Pilemon Ngkale
Projects: Capt Nyoman Timonuli

Women's Ministries: Col Marie Kartodarsono (TPWM), Lt-Col Deetje Ambitan (TSWM) Maj Anastasia Poa (HL)

DIVISIONS

Jawa and Bali: Jalan Dr Cipto 64b, Kelurahan Bugangan, Semarang 50126, Jateng; tel: (024) 355 1361; Maj Mulyati Mitra Sumarta

Kulawi: Bala Keselamatan Post Office, Kulawi 94363, Sulteng; tel/fax: (0451) 811 017; Maj Sakius Salogi

Palu Timur: Jalan Miangas 1, Kantor Pos Palu 94112; tel: (0451) 426 821; fax: (0451) 425 846; Lt-Col Mesak Losso

Palu Barat: Jalan Miangas 1-3, Palu 94112, Sulteng; mobile: 0816 4304498; Maj Gidion Rangi

Sulawesi Utara: Jalan A. Yani 15, Manado 95114; tel/fax: (0431) 864 052; Maj Jones Kasaedja

Sumatera Utara: Jl. Sei Kera 186 Medan 20232, Sumatera Utara; tel: (061) 4510284; Maj Lidia Simatupang

DISTRICTS

East Kalimantan: Capt Benjamin Goni

Under East Palu Division
Palu: Maj Aman Mantaely
Kalawara: Capt Imanuel Subandi
Berdikari: Maj Yosren Soekaryo
Banpres Tongoa: Capt Pemri Kwantung
Lembah Elim: Capt Yunani Dongke

Under West Palu Division
Rowiga: Capt Yonas Parese
Porame: Capt Alberth Silinawa
Dombu: Maj Gidion Rikko
Gimpubia: Maj Gunawan Mantaely
Wawugaga: Capt Yusdimer Momi
Bunggu I: Capt Aser Yupa
Bunggu II: Maj Sadrakh Lanto
Malino: Capt Adreas Rantju

Under Kulawi Division
Lindu: Maj Benyamin Dama
Tobaku: Capt Henry Simanjuntak
Kulawi: under DHQ
Kantewu: Maj Albert Manik
Gimpu: Maj Tasera Ngopoh
Karangana: Capt Guntur Haku

Under North Sumatera Division
Nias: Maj Januri

TRAINING COLLEGE

Jalan Kramat Raya 55, Jakarta 10450, PO Box 3203, Jakarta 10002; tel: (021) 310 8148; fax: (021) 391 0410

EDUCATION

Jawa: 8 schools (acc 777)
Kalawara: 1 institute
Kalimantan Timur: 1 school (acc 42)
Sulawesi Selatan: 3 schools (acc 257)
Sulawesi Tengah: 79 schools (acc 6,539), 1 theological university (acc 60)
Sumatra Utara: 2 schools (acc 303)

MEDICAL WORK
General Hospitals (Jawa)

Bandung: Bungsu Hospital, Jalan Veteran 6; tel: (022) 423 1550/1695; fax: (022) 423 1582 (acc 49, poli-clinic attached)

Semarang: William Booth Hospital, Jalan Let Jen S. Parman 5 Semarang, 50232; tel: (024) 841 1800/844 8773; fax: (024) 844 8773; (acc 100, eye and general clinic attached)

Surabaya: William Booth Hospital, Jalan Diponegoro 34; tel: (031) 561 4615/4616/ 5349; fax: (031) 567 1380 (acc 200, maternity hospital and 3 poli-clinics attached)

Turen: Bokor Hospital, Jalan Jen A. Yani 89, Turen near Malang; tel: (0341) 824 453/002; fax: (0341) 823 878 (acc 150, poli- clinic and outpost clinic attached)

General Hospitals and Clinics (Sulawesi)

Palu: Woodward Hospital, Jalan L. H. Woodward 1, Kantor Pos Palu, Sulawesi Tengah; tel: (0451) 421 769/482 914/426 361; fax: (0451) 423 744 (acc 110)

Branch Hospitals

Ampera: under Woodward Hospital
Kulawi: Bethesda Hou Popakauria

Clinics

Ambon, East Kalimantan, Gimpu, Kamarora, Kantewu, Lembah Tongoa, Towulu
Sulawesi Utara: Kantor Pos Amurang, Kumelembuai, Makasili, Sulut

Maternity Hospital

Makassar, Sulawesi Selatan: Catherine Booth Mother and Child Hospital, Jalan Arif, Rate 15 or Post Box 33; tel: (0411) 873 803/852 344; fax: (0411) 873 803 (acc 53, poli-clinic attached)

Academies for Nurses' Training

Surabaya: under William Booth Hospital (acc 200)
Palu: under Woodward Hospital (acc 200)

Chief of the Staff Commissioner Robin Dunster visited Indonesia to conduct the retirement of territorial leaders Commissioners Johannes and Augustina Watilete and to install their successors, Colonels Ribut Basuki and Marie Kartodarsono, in a meeting at Bandung 3 Corps. The Chief is pictured praying with the new leaders.

Manado: Jalan Arnold Manonutu 501, Post Box 118; tel: (0431) 863 394 (acc 60)
Medan: Jalan Samanhudi 27; tel: (061) 414 2148 (acc 80)
Palu: Jalan Maluku 18, Palu 94112; tel: (0451) 424 586 (acc 80)

Centre for Homeless People
Semarang: Jalan Dr Cipto 64a, Kelurahan Bugangan, Semarang 50126, Jateng; tel: (024) 771 0501/354 2536 (acc 100, dairy farm attached)

Eventide Homes
Bandung: Jalan Jeruk 7; tel: (022) 727 1369 (acc 100)
Semarang: Jalan Musi Raya 4-6; tel: (024) 354 4855 (acc 60)
Turen: Jalan Achmad Yani 180; tel: (0341) 825 290 (acc 50)

Propeka (Social Services for School and Family Welfare)
Pulau Sicang: Kotak Pos 9, Belawan 20416, Sumatra Utara; tel: (061) 694 4003 (acc 500)
Sulawesi Tengah: Jalan Maluku 36, Palu 94112, Sul Teng; tel: (0451) 422 173 (acc 1,500)

Students' Hostels
Bandung: Jalan Dr Cipto 7; tel: (022) 423 0480 (acc 32)
Bandung: Jalan Jawa 18; tel: (022) 420 5549 (acc 32)
Medan: Jalan Samanhudi 27; tel: (061) 414 2148 (acc 30)
Surabaya: Jalan Gatotan 36; tel: (031) 352 2932 (acc 24)
Yogyakarta: Jalan Kenari 7, Miliran; tel: (0274) 563 598 (acc 8)

Transient House
Jalan Kramat Raya 55; tel: (021) 391 4518 (acc 18)

THQ GUEST HOUSES
Jalan Jawa 20; tel: (022) 420 7029 (acc 10)

SOCIAL WORK
Babies' and Toddlers' Home
Surabaya: Jalan Kombes Pol Durjat 10-12, Surabaya 60262; tel: (031) 534 1132; fax: (031) 532 2118 (acc 60)

Boys' Homes
Bandung: Jalan Dr Cipto 7; tel: (022) 423 0480 (acc 80)
Denpasar, Bali: Jalan Kebo Iwa No 29, Banjar Liligundi, Ubung Kaja, Denpasar, Bali (acc 200)
Kalawara: Kantor Pos Palu, Sul Teng (acc 60)
Medan: Jalan K. L. Yos Sudarso 10, Lorong 1A; tel: (061) 661 3840 (acc 90)
Semarang: Jalan Musi Raya 2, Kel. Rejosari, Semarang 50125; tel: (024) 355 3287 (acc 80)
Surabaya: Jalan Gatotan 36; tel: (031) 352 2932 (acc 60)
Tompaso: Post Box 1100, Manado/Desa Liba, Kecamatan Tompaso 95693, Kab Minahasa; tel: (0431) 371 524 (acc 80)
Yogyakarta: Jalan Kenari 7, Miliran Post Box 1095; tel: (0274) 563598 (acc 32)

Children's Homes
Bandung: Jalan Jawa 18; tel: (022) 420 5549 (acc 90)
Denpasar: Jalan Hos Cokroaminoto 34; tel/fax: (0361) 426 484 (acc 60)
Jakarta: Catherine Booth Children's Home, Pondok Cabe (acc 100)
Malang: Jalan Panglima Sudirman 97; tel: (0341) 362 905 (acc 80)

ITALY COMMAND

Command leaders:
Lieut-Colonels Massimo and E. Jane Paone

Officer Commanding:
Lieut-Colonel Massimo Paone (1 Aug 2002)

General Secretary:
Major Massimo Tursi (1 Aug 2007)

Command Headquarters: Via degli Apuli 39, 00185 Rome, Italy

Tel: [39] 06 4462614/06 4941089; fax: [39] 06 490078;

email: Italy_Command@ity.salvationarmy.org; web site: www.esercitodellasalvezza.org

The Salvation Army flag was unfurled in Italy on 20 February 1887 by Major and Mrs James Vint and Lieutenant Fanny Hack, though subsequent difficulties necessitated withdrawal. In 1890 Fritz Malan (later lieut-colonel) began meetings in his native village in the Waldensian Valleys. In 1893 Army work was re-established.

In a decree of the President on 1 April 1965, The Salvation Army was recognised as a philanthropic organisation competent to acquire and hold properties and to receive donations and legacies.

On 8 October 2007 The Salvation Army began operations in Greece, the work being linked to the Italy Command with the command leadership giving guidance and support to future development. Thessaloniki was identified as the centre of the new undertaking and Captains Polis Pantelidis and Maria Konti-Galinou, UK officers of Greek nationality, were entrusted with the task of launching the Army's mission in their own home country.

Zone: Europe
Countries included in the command: Greece, Italy
'The Salvation Army' in Italian: Esercito della Salvezza
Languages in which the gospel is preached: Greek, Italian
Periodicals: *Il Bollettino dell' Unione Femminile, Il Grido di Guerra*

ITALY Command continues to play an important strategic role in the international ministry and witness of The Salvation Army. Four young Salvationists from Italy, Germany and the USA received significant discipleship training during a 10-month residential course on developing spiritual leadership. It was an enriching cross-cultural occasion as well as a deeply spiritual experience for them.

Bands from USA Eastern Territory, Switzerland, the UK and Germany visited the command to take part in outreach endeavours in Brienza, Turin and Naples, and the National Congress in Rome.

Every centre throughout the command held a special week of prayer for spiritual renewal, the congress and the National Assembly. Churches Together in Rome arranged united worship during the Week For Christian Unity. This service, with the participation of Rome Corps Band and Singing Group, was transmitted by BBC

Radio to some two million people. Later in the year this interdenominational group worked together to raise funds for an irrigation project in Zimbabwe, the command's 'partner in mission'.

The officer commanding was invited to attend the installation ceremony of the newly elected President of the Republic, Giorgio Napolitano. The President later sent greetings to the 2007 National Congress, celebrating 120 years of The Salvation Army in Italy. He noted that, strengthened by its religious beliefs, the Army 'continues to write, throughout the world, noble chapters of unselfishness and dedication'.

'Strengthened by past experiences, we are certain of the future with Christ!' was the theme for 2007 and the congress weekend in Rome, led by Chief of the Staff Commissioner Robin Dunster and ably supported by the Western Divisional Band from Germany.

A DVD presenting the Army's Italian roots as well as showing its continuing mission, and a book titled *The Salvation Army: An Introduction* were launched during the congress.

STATISTICS

Officers 53 (active 28 retired 25) **Lieutenants** 6 **Employees** 10
Corps 17 **Outposts** 15 **Institutions** 7
Senior Soldiers 257 **Adherents** 90 **Junior Soldiers** 34

STAFF

General's Personal Representative to the Vatican: Lt-Col Massimo Paone
Women's Ministries (and Resources): Lt-Col E. Jane Paone (CPWM) Maj Anne-Florence Tursi (CSWM)
Finance: Capt Patricia Pavoni
Family Tracing: Maj Angela Dentico
Youth and Candidates and Training: Capt Frederick Wong
Editor: Capt Debora Wong

SOCIAL WORK

Centre for the Homeless

Centro Virgilio Paglieri, Via degli Apuli 41, 00185 Roma; tel: 06 4451351; fax: 06 4456306 (acc 225)

Workers' Lodge

Villa Speranza, Contrada Serra 57a, 85100 Potenza; tel/fax: (0971) 51245 (acc 15)

Holiday Centres

Le Casermette, Via Pellice 4, 10060 Bobbio Pellice (To); tel/fax: (0121) 957728; email: direzione@centrovacanzebobbio.it (acc 120)

Concordia, Via Casa di Majo 32-36, 80075 Forio d'Ischia (Na); tel: (081) 997324; fax: (081) 997576; email: concordia@esercitodellasalvezza.org (acc 65)

L'Uliveto, Via Stretta della Croce 20, 84030 Atena Lucana (Sa); tel/fax: (0975) 76321 (acc 70)

Guest Houses

Villa delle Rose, Via Aretina 91, 50136 Firenze; tel/fax: (055) 660445 (acc 13)

Foresteria, Via degli Apuli 41, 00185 Roma; tel/fax: 06 44 51 351; email: foresteriaroma@ esercitodella salvezza.org (acc 70)

GREECE

Polytexneiou 198 & Notara, Pylaia, GR 555 35, Thessaloniki, Greece; Capts Polis Pantelidis and Maria Konti-Galinou; mobile: 00 3069 75728790

❝ Strengthened by its religious beliefs, the Army continues to write noble chapters of unselfishness and dedication ❞

JAPAN TERRITORY

Territorial leaders:
Commissioners Makoto and Kaoru Yoshida

Territorial Commander:
Commissioner Makoto Yoshida (1 Jun 2006)

Chief Secretary:
Lieut-Colonel Naoshi Hiramoto (1 Mar 2004)

Territorial Headquarters: 17, 2-chome, Kanda Jimbocho, Chiyoda-ku, Tokyo 101-0051, Japan

Tel: [81] (03) 3237 0881; fax: [81] (03) 3237 7676; web site: www.salvationarmy.or.jp

In 1895 a small group of pioneer officers from Britain arrived in Japan at Yokohama to start operations. In spite of great difficulties, work was soon established.

Of several outstanding Japanese who were attracted to The Salvation Army, the most distinguished was Commissioner Gunpei Yamamuro OF, prominent evangelist and author, whose book *The Common People's Gospel* is now in its 527th printing.

Zone: South Pacific and East Asia
Country included in the territory: Japan
Language in which the gospel is preached: Japanese
Periodicals: *Home League Quarterly*, *The Officer*, *The Sunday School Guide*, *Toki-no-Koe*, *Toki-no-Koe Junior*

ALTHOUGH the territory saw a change in leadership at the beginning of June 2006, the spirit expressed in the year's theme, 'Making One Step Forward – Plus One Movement', continued without change. It encouraged various centres to make new attempts, however small, to reach out to the community and its people.

These initiatives included simply setting up a bench in front of a Salvation Army building to provide community space for passers-by, and an officer getting involved in a book-reading programme in a public school. This has proved to be quite an effective way to share the gospel in a society like Japan's.

In June 2006 the territory began a rural community development support project in Papua New Guinea. This three-year project is sponsored by JICA (Japan International Cooperation Agency) with the cooperation of Papua New Guinea Territory. Personnel are sent from Japan Territory, the endeavour bringing the internationalism of The Salvation Army closer to the hearts of many of Japan's Salvationists.

A focus on youth continues. Since 2004 delegates have been sent to various youth capacity development consultations and in September 2006 the Asia Pacific Regional Team made a visit to Tokyo. Due to this exposure the notion of capacity development is gradually taking shape in the form of a youth mission project, with its first workshop held in March 2007.

The project envisions equipping the Army's young people to minister to their own generation in practical and effective ways. Serious crimes, bullying, social withdrawal and suicide are some of the issues that exist among young people and their intensity is becoming a shared social concern.

The Salvation Army is hoping to serve these broken people with the unchanging love of Christ.

Major amendments are being made to government legislation in Japan, with social welfare and medical care systems being subject to change. This has required social and medical institutions to adjust their management structures to survive the changes without changing The Salvation Army's mission.

A changing society presents challenges, but the territory is experiencing divine provision and wisdom as it strives to build God's Kingdom. With vision and hope in God, the territory continues to 'make one step forward' into the future.

STATISTICS
Officers 189 (active 98 retired 91) **Cadets** (1st Yr) 2 **Employees** 973
Corps 49 **Outposts** 10 **Institutions** 20 **Hospitals** 2
Senior Soldiers 3,015 **Adherents** 26 **Junior Soldiers** 81

STAFF
Business Administration: Maj Jiro Katsuchi
Candidates: Maj Kyoko Yoshida
Editor: Sis Keiko Saito

Literary: Maj Kazumitsu Higuchi
Medical: Maj Naoko Harita
Music: B/M Hajime Suzuki
Personnel: Maj Haruhisa Ota
Programme: Maj Kazumitsu Higuchi
Social: Maj Naoko Harita
Staff Band: B/M Hajime Suzuki
Staff Songsters: S/L Mikako Ebara
Training: Maj Tsukasa Yoshida
Women's Ministries: Comr Kaoru Yoshida (TPWM) Lt-Col Seiko Hiramoto (TSWM)
Youth: Maj Hiromi Ota

DIVISIONS
Hokkaido: Nishi 1-13-1, Minami-4-jo, Chuo-ku, Sapporo-shi 064-0804; tel: (011) 231 2805; fax: (011) 231 2825; Maj Kiyoshi Namai
Kanto-Tohoku: 5 Yoriai-cho, Takasaki-shi, Gunma Ken 370-0822; tel: (027) 323 1337; fax: (027) 323 1334; Maj Masaru Yamanaka
Nishi Nihon: 3-6-20 Tenjinbashi, Kita-ku, Osaka-shi 530-0041; tel: (06) 6351 0084; fax: (06) 6351 0093; Maj Nobuhiro Hiramoto
Tokyo-Tokaido: 4-11-3 Taihei, Sumida-ku, Tokyo 130-0012; tel: (03) 5819 1460; fax: (03) 5819 1461; Maj Chieko Tanaka

TRAINING COLLEGE
1-39-5 Wada Suginami-ku, Tokyo 166-0012; tel: (03) 3381 9837

MEDICAL WORK
Booth Memorial Hospital: 1-40-5 Wada, Suginami-ku, Tokyo 166-0012; tel: (03) 3381 7236; fax: (03) 5385 0734 (acc hospital 179 hospice 20)
Kiyose Hospital: 1-17-9 Takeoka, Kiyose-shi, Tokyo, 204-0023; tel: (0424) 91 1411/3; fax: (0424) 91 3900 (acc hospital 117 hospice 25)

SOCIAL WORK
Alcoholic Rehabilitation Centre (Men)
Jiseikan, 1-17-60 Takeoka, Kiyose-shi, Tokyo 204-0023; tel: (0424) 93 5374 (acc 50)

Rehabilitation Centre (Men)
2-21-2 Wada Suginami-ku, Tokyo 166-0012 tel: (03) 3384-9114 (acc 15)

Social Service Centre (Bazaar) (Men)
2-21-2 Wada Suginami-ku, Tokyo 166-0012; tel: (03) 3384 3769

Working Men's Homes
Jijokan, 2-17-10 Tsukishima, Chuo-ku,

Tokyo 104-0052; tel: (03) 3531 3516 (acc 35)
Shinkokan, 87 Akagishita-machi, Shinjuku-ku,
Tokyo 162-0803; tel: (03) 3269 4901 (acc 40)

Women's Homes

Fujinryo: 1-43-11 Wada Suginami-ku, Tokyo
166-0012; tel: (03) 3381 0992 (acc 40)
Shinseiryo: 4-11-14 Shibazaki-cho, Tachikawa-
shi, Tokyo 190-0023; tel: (042) 522 2306
(acc 70)

Children's Homes

Aikoen: 1-3 Aoyama-cho, Kure-shi, Hiroshima
737-0023; tel: (0823) 21 6374 (acc 30)
Kibokan: 2-16-11, Nakahodzumi, Ibaraki-shi,
Osaka 567-0034; tel: (0726) 23 3758 (acc 65)
Kiekoryo: 4-12-10 Kami Ikedai, Ota-ku,
Tokyo 145-0064; tel: (03) 3729 0357
(acc 35)
Sekoryo: 2-21-1 Wada, Suginami-ku, Tokyo
166-0012; tel: (03) 3381 0545 (acc 50)
Toyohama-Gakuryo: 3082-5 Toyoshima,
Toyohama-cho, Kure-shi, Hiroshima
734-0101; tel: (08466) 8 2029 (acc 60)

Day Nurseries

Kikusui Kamimachi Hoikuen: 2-52 Kikusui
Kamimachi 3-jo, Shiroishi-ku, Sapporo-shi
003-0813; tel: (011) 821 2879 (acc 90)
Kure Hoikusho: 1-4 Aoyama-cho, Kure-shi
737-0023; tel: (0823) 21 4711 (acc 60)
Sano Hoikuen: 182 Asanuma-cho, Sano-shi
327-0831; tel: (0283) 22 4081 (acc 126)

Shiseikan Hoikuen: Nishi 7, Minami 3-jo,
Chuo-ku, Sapporo-shi 060-0063;
tel: (011) 204 9560 (acc 120)
Soen Hoikusho: Nishi 14-1, Kita 5-jo, Chuo-ku,
Sapporo-shi 060-0005; tel: (011) 221 6630
(acc 60)

Home for the Aged

Keisen Home: 1-17-61 Takeoka, Kiyose-shi,
Tokyo 204-0023; tel: (0424) 93 5161/2
(acc 50)

Hostel

Kyoto Hostel: 37 Tokushoji-cho, Tominokoji-
dori 4-jo Sagaru, Shimogyo-ku, Kyoto
600-8051; tel: (075) 361 4690 (acc 16)

Senior Citizens' Housing and Care Centre

Grace: 1-40-15 Wada, Suginami-ku, Tokyo
166-0012; tel: (03) 3380 1248;
fax: (03) 3380 1206 (acc 100)

Care House

Izumi: 1-17-24 Takeoka, Kiyose-shi, Tokyo
204-0023; tel: (0424) 96 7575 (acc 32)

RETIRED OFFICERS' APARTMENTS

Olive House: 1-39-12 Wada, Suginami-ku,
Tokyo 166-0012
Osaka Central Hall 5F: 3-6-20 Tenjinbashi,
Kita-ku, Osaka 530-0041
Tokiwa House: 1-17-12 Takeoka, Kiyose-shi,
Tokyo 204-0023

A band concert is given during the Salvation Army Fair staged in Yokohama, Japan

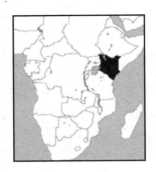

KENYA TERRITORY

Territorial Commander:
Commissioner Hezekiel Anzeze
(1 Feb 2002)

Chief Secretary:
Lieut-Colonel Kenneth G. Hodder
(1 Mar 2006)

Territorial Headquarters: Moi Avenue, Nairobi

Postal address: Box 40575, Nairobi, Kenya 00100 GPO

Tel: [254] (020) 222 7541/2/9; fax: [254] (020) 342014

In 1896 three Salvationists went to Kenya to work on the building of a new railway and made their witness while based at the Taru Camp. The first official meetings were held in Nairobi in April 1921, led by Lieut-Colonel and Mrs James Allister Smith. The first cadets were trained in 1923.

Zone: Africa
Country included in the territory: Kenya
'The Salvation Army' in Kiswahili: Jeshi La Wokovu
Languages in which the gospel is preached: English, Kiswahili and a number of tribal languages
Periodicals: *Sauti ya Vita* (English and Kiswahili)

THE Kenya Territory continues to grow, the year under review seeing the establishment of a new division, five new districts, 26 new corps and 78 new outposts.

The Salvation Army assumed sponsorship responsibilities for more educational institutions, thereby expanding the number of students it reaches with the gospel every year to more than a quarter of a million. In addition, the territory increased its contribution to the World Services/ Self-Denial Fund by raising 4.5 million Kenya shillings (US$ 70,000), an increase of more than 50 per cent over the previous year.

Evangelistic outreach increased, not only through campaigns at local, district and divisional levels but also

through cooperation with government ministries and private business.

An airport chaplaincy programme was formally established with the government of Kenya, under which The Salvation Army is authorised to appoint an officer chaplain at all airports and ports. Such chaplains have now been posted at six airports, and public meetings are held in those locations on a regular basis.

Also, in an outstanding example of cooperation with the business sector, a major sugar producer invited The Salvation Army to appoint a chaplain for the spiritual needs of its employees. A corps has since been founded on the premises.

During the commissioning weekend the territorial commander commissioned 41 captains and appointed 58 envoys. The number of candidates for officer training is growing at a steady rate, and thanks to an endowment gift of US $1 million from USA Western Territory the number of cadets that Kenya's training college is able to train will soon increase by 20 per year.

At THQ, new computers and software were installed in the Finance Department, allowing the territory for the first time to receive regular monthly reports on its financial status. Thanks to USA Southern Territory, significant strides were made in an effort to establish electronic communication between THQ and all divisional and district headquarters.

In the autumn of 2006 the territory was privileged to host the Conference of African Leaders, at which recommendations were made for implementation throughout the Africa Zone.

The development of musicianship was promoted through the Territorial Music School and Territorial Music Leaders' Conference, led by Envoy Ken Clark (United Kingdom Territory) and funded by the Kenya Trust.

In early 2007 The Salvation Army in Kenya secured formal government permission for its women officers to conduct weddings. This long-awaited development was accompanied by the appointment of the first single woman district officer in the territory's history.

STATISTICS

Officers 1,075 (active 799 retired 276) **Cadets** 71 **Envoys in training** 13 **Lieutenants** 23 **Employees** 75
Corps 567 **Outposts** 1,286 **Pre-primary**

Schools 347 **Primary Schools** 402 **Secondary Schools** 55 **Institutions** 20
Senior Soldiers 175,254 **Junior Soldiers** 173,905

STAFF

Asst CS: Maj Trustmore Muzorori
Business Administration: Maj Gabriel Kathuri
Personnel: Maj Tiras Mbaja
Programme: Maj Samuel Oklah
Women's Ministries: Lt-Col Jolene Hodder (TLWM)
Audit: Maj Jacob Olubwayo
Finance: Maj Lalbulliana
Projects: Marshall Currie
Property: Capt Ibrahim Lorot
Public Relations: Capt Julius Omukonyi
Social: Capt Armida LaMarr
Territorial Band: B/M Samuel Odiara
Territorial Songsters: S/L Joshua Rwolekya
Trade: Mr Joshua Mugera
Training: Maj Henry Nyaga
Youth: Capt Luke Khayumbi

DIVISIONS

Bungoma: PO Box 1106, Bungoma; tel: 055-30589; Maj Enock Lufumbu
Eldoret: PO Box 125, Eldoret; tel: 053-22266; Maj James Mukubwa
Embu: PO Box 74, Embu; tel: 068-20107; Maj Francis Nganda
Kakamega: PO Box 660, Kakamega; tel: 056-20344; Maj Edward Shavanga
Kangundo: PO Box 324, Kangundo; tel: 044-21049; Maj Jackson Muasa
Kibwezi: PO Box 428, Sultan Hamud; tel: 044-52200; Maj John Olewa
Machakos: PO Box 160, Machakos; tel: 044-21660; Lt-Col Julius Mukonga
Mbale: PO Box 80, Maragoli; tel: 056-51076; Maj Naphas M'memi
Musudzuu: PO Box 278, Seremi; tel: 056-45055; Maj Martin Mboto
Nairobi: PO Box 31205, Nairobi; tel: 020-767208; Maj Nahashon Njiru
Shigomere: PO Box 125, Khwisero; tel: 056-20260; Maj Moses Shavanga
Tongaren: PO Box 127, Tongaren; Maj Johnstone Kathendu

DISTRICTS

Bunyore: PO Box 81, Bunyore; Maj Isaac Kivindyo
Coast: PO Box 98277, Mombasa; tel: 041-490629; Capt Benjamin Musilia
Elgon: PO Box 274, Malakisi; tel: 055-20443; Maj Boniface Munyekhe

Kathiani: PO Box 2, Kathiani; Maj Nathan Musieni

Kimilili: PO Box 220, Kimilili; Capt Frederick Omuzee

Kisumu: PO Box 288, Kisumu; tel: 057-2025632; Capt Daniel Imbiakha

Kitale: PO Box 548, Kitale; tel: 054-30259; Capt Johnstone Wolayo

Kasikeu/Makueni: PO Box 428, Sultan Hamud; tel: 044-52200

Kathiani: PO Box 2, Kathiani

Meru: PO Box 465, Nkubu, Meru; tel: 064-51207; Capt Thomas Musyoki

Migori: PO Box 59, Suna, Migori, Kenya; Maj William Mutungi

Mwala: PO Box 19, Mwala, Kenya; Maj Frederick Khamalishi

Nakuru: PO Box 672, Nakuru; tel: 051-212455; Capt Harun Chepsiri

Thika: PO Box 809, Thika; tel: 067-22056; Capt Jonathan Barasa

Turkana: PO Box 118-30500, Lodwar; tel: 054-21010; Capt Kennedy Ombajo

Webuye: PO Box 484, Webuye; Maj Sarah Wanyama

Yatta: PO Box 29 Kithimani; Maj Peter Mutuku

TRAINING COLLEGE
PO Box 4467, Thika; tel: 067-24149

CONFERENCE CENTRE
Park Rd, PO Box 40575, Nairobi; tel: 020-6762292

FARM
Avontour Estate, PO Box 274, Thika

EDUCATIONAL WORK
SA Sponsored Primary Schools: 402

SA Sponsored and Managed Secondary Schools: 55

Special Schools
Visually Handicapped
High School
Thika: PO Box 704, Thika; tel: 067-22092 (acc 163)
Primary Schools
Kibos: PO Box 77, Kisumu; tel: 057-43135 (acc 230)

Likoni: PO Box 96089, Mombasa; tel: 041-451101 (acc 120)
Thika: PO Box 80, Thika; tel: 067-21691 (acc 297)

Physically Disabled
Primary Schools
Joyland: PO Box 1790, Kisumu; tel: 057-41864/50574 (acc 230)
Joytown: PO Box 326, Thika; tel: 067-21291 (acc 215)
Secondary School
Joytown: PO Box 1370, Thika; tel: 067-22008 (acc 110)

Multi-Handicapped Special Units
Joytown: PO Box 326, Thika; tel: 067-21291 (acc 22)
Thika Primary School: PO Box 80, Thika; tel: 067-21691
Njoro Special School: PO Box 359, Njoro

SOCIAL SERVICES
Children's Homes
Kabete: PO Box 210-00606 Sarit Centre, Nairobi; tel: 020-442766 (acc 114)
Mombasa: PO Box 90531, Mombasa; tel: 041-224387 (acc 40)

Community Centre
Kibera: PO Box 21608, Nairobi; tel: 020-567064

Feeding Programme for Destitutes
Kisumu: PO Box 288, Kisumu; tel: 057-4151

Girls' Hostel
Nairobi: PO Box 31354, Nairobi

Health Centre
Kolanya: PO Box 88, Malakisi, via Bungoma

Vocational Training Centres
Variety Village: PO Box 1472, Thika; tel: 067-21822
Nairobi Girls' Centre: PO Box 31304, Nairobi; tel: 020-766375 (acc 60)

Workshop
Kibos: PO Box 477, Kisumu (acc 12)

With effect from 1 March 2008, two territories will operate in Kenya – the Kenya East Territory with THQ in Nairobi, and the Kenya West Territory with THQ in Kakamega. Full information regarding these territories will appear on the International Headquarters web site as replacement *Year Book* pages.

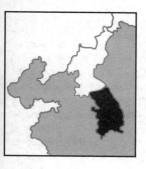

KOREA TERRITORY

Territorial leaders:
**Commissioner Chun, Kwang-pyo and
Commissioner Yoo, Sung-ja**

Territorial Commander:
Commissioner Chun, Kwang-pyo
(1 Jan 2005)

Chief Secretary:
Lieut-Colonel Park, Man-hee (1 Jan 2005)

**Territorial Headquarters: The Salvation Army Central Hall,
1-23 Chung dong, Choong Ku, Seoul 100-120**

Postal address: The Salvation Army, Central PO Box 1192, Seoul 100-611, Republic of Korea

Tel: [82] (2) 720 9494 (Korean); [82] (2) 720 9403 (English);

email: korea@kor.salvationarmy.org; web site: www.salvationarmy.or.kr

When the Founder visited Japan in 1907, he dispatched Commissioner George Scott Railton to survey prospects on the Korean peninsula. In October 1908 Colonel and Mrs Robert Hoggard (née Annie Johns) arrived with a group of officers to 'open fire' in Seoul. During the Korean conflict, which took place from 1950 to 1953, one Korean officer was martyred, one killed and two have been listed as missing.

Zone: South Pacific and East Asia
Country included in the territory: Republic of Korea
'The Salvation Army' in Korean: (sounds like) 'Koo Sei Goon'
Language in which the gospel is preached: Korean
Periodicals: *Home League Programme Helps, Loving Hands Sponsorship Magazine, The Officer, The War Cry*

AT the invitation of the Christian Forum of the National Assembly, the territorial commander visited the Democratic People's Republic of Korea (North Korea) with other dignitaries to deliver medical supplies to North Korean residents (8-10 August 2006).

Seven months later the TC again visited North Korea (28-31 March 2007), this time accompanied by Major Hwang, Sun-yup (North Korea Ministry Development Officer) and representatives of two other non-governmental organisations.

During this historic visit, made by The Salvation Army in its own right, various projects were inspected, including the Ku-bin Ri Collective Farm and yoghurt factory where the Army's yoghurt packaging is located; the Wah-woo-doh Hospital and adjacent Nampo Nursery in the second largest city, Nampo; and the very poor village of Changkyo Li located on the outskirts of the capital, Pyongyang.

Following talks with North Korean officials, an official agreement-signing ceremony was held, signifying the commencement of negotiations between The Salvation Army and North Korean officials for development projects to be undertaken.

During the 15th Territorial Strategy for Growth Rally (3 October 2006) D-730 was officially declared, being the commencement of a countdown to the centenary of the Korea Territory on 1 October 2008.

The first Policy Development Seminar for the centenary was held at Yung Deung Po Corps (5 March 2007), with 35 officers and soldiers drawing up a long-term development plan for territorial policies in preparation for the centenary celebrations in October 2008.

At the 55th Annual General Meeting of the National Council of Churches in Korea (KNCC), Territorial Commander Commissioner Chun, Kwang-pyo was elected as the council's President. This privilege is granted to heads of various churches for a 12-month period on a rotational basis. The council, inaugurated in 1924, currently has eight denominations as participating members.

About 20,000 Christians gathered at 5am on Easter Sunday (8 April) for the annual dawn service held at the Seoul Plaza in front of City Hall. The service began with Commissioner Chun, Kwang-pyo – as KNCC President – outlining the meeting's slogan: 'A flower blossom may not present the Spring but it comes in full bloom', meaning that reconciliation of society and unification of churches throughout the nation will come, in due time.

The following day saw the start of a three-day spritual retreat for 290 women officers. They considered the topic 'Launching into the Future with the Word of God'.

The appointment and dedication of staff bandsmen having taken place in May 2006, the inaugural festival of the Korea Staff Band was held on 26 November in conjunction with the dedication service for all Christmas Kettle Appeal volunteers. Captain Kim, Hai-du (Territorial Music Director) is the staff bandmaster, leading 34 bandsmen drawn from corps throughout the territory.

In July 2006, following localised major flooding during Korea's annual 'jangma' wet season, Salvation Army emergency services teams were mobilised to the worst-hit, poor village areas. Assistance was given with repairs and in providing meals and basic living necessities.

STATISTICS

Officers 708 (active 572 retired 136) **Cadets** (1st Yr) 19 (2nd Yr) 22 **Employees** 567
Corps 241 **Outposts and Societies** 15 **Institutions** 35 **School** 1 **Child Day Care Centres** 6 **Corps Child Day Care Centres** 21 **Day Care Centres for the Elderly** 6 **Community Centres** 17 **Counselling Centres** 6 **Students' Study Centres** 25 **Special Service Vehicle Units** 3 **HIV/Aids Care and Prevention Team Units** 2 **Bridge Centre for the Homeless** 1 **Sarangbang Centres** 3 **Self-Support Training Centres** 5
Senior Soldiers 40,699 **Adherents** 12,577 **Junior Soldiers** 6,290
Personnel serving outside territory Officers 15

STAFF

Sec for Personnel: Maj Lim, Hun-taek
Editor and Education Sec: Maj Lee, Choong-ho
Literary Sec: Maj Kim, Dong-jin
Overseas Service Bureau Director: Maj Kim, Dong-jin

Sec for Programme: Maj Lim, Young-sik
Church Growth: Capt Choi, Yung-mi
Social: Maj Yang, Shin-kyong
Territorial Youth Officer: Capt Kim, Kyu-han
Territorial Music Director: Capt Kim, Hai-du

Sec for Business: Maj Kim, Oon-ho
Finance and Audit: Maj Kim, Young-tae
Information Technology: Capt Lee, Hyun-hee
Property: Maj Lee, Ki-yong
Public Relations: Maj Ahn, Guhn-shik
Child Sponsorship: Maj Yang, Shin-kyung
Trade: Capt Kim, Sook-yung

Territorial Archivist: Lt-Col Kim, Joon-chul
Training: Maj Shin, Moon-ho
Women's Ministries: Comr Yoo, Sung-ja
(TPWM) Lt-Col Kim, Keum-nyeo (TSWM)
Maj Yeo, Keum-soo (THLS) Maj Chun, Soon-
ja (TLMS) Maj Pyo, Choon-yun (TSSS)
Maj Lee, Ok-kyung (TSAMFS)

DIVISIONS

Choong Buk: 704 Doosan Hansol 1 cha
Apartments 101 dong, 447-15 Kaeshin
Dong, Heungduk Ku, Chung Ju, Choong
Book 361-746; tel: (043) 276 1634;
fax: (043) 263 6387; Maj Chun, Joon-hong
Choong Chung: 603 Oosung Apartments
126 dong, 640 Chunglim dong, Suh ku,
Taejon, Choong Nam Do 302-795;
tel: (042) 584 2891; fax: (042) 584 2892;
Maj Park, Nai-hoon
Choong Saw: 401 Hyundai Apartments
3-cha 302 dong, 388-2 Ssangyong dong,
Chonan, Choong Nam Do 330-091;
tel: (041) 572 0855; fax: (041) 578 0855;
Maj Pang, Kie-chang
Chulla: 375-21 Song San Dong, Chung Eup,
Chun Buk 580-200; tel: (063) 536 1190;
fax: (063) 536 1191; Maj Kim, Nam-sun
Kyung Buk: 1302 Kongjak Hanyang
Apartments 104 dong, Eupnae dong 1366-1,
Buk ku, Taegu 702-850; tel: (053) 322 3695;
fax: (053) 322 3694; Maj Choo, Seung-chan
Kyung Nam: 1306 Green Core Apartments
301 dong, 216 7 Manduk 3 dong, Buk ku,
Pusan, Kyung Sang Nam Do 616-782;
tel: (051) 337 0789; fax: (051) 337 2292;
Maj Kang, Jik-koo
Seoul: The Salvation Army Office Building,
#705, Shinmoonro 1-ga, 58-1, Chongno gu,
Seoul 100-161; tel: (02) 720 9543;
fax: (02) 720 9546; Maj Park, Chong-duk
Seoul South: 602, Soojung Hanyang Apartments
235-dong, 1086 Sunboo 3-dong, Danwon Ku,

Ansan, Kyunggi-do 425-765;
tel: (031) 413 7811; fax: (031) 413 7812;
Maj Yang, Tae-soo
Suh Hae: 301 Dongshin Apartments 204 dong,
Eupnae Dong 624-1, Sosan, Choong Nam
356-758; tel: (041) 667 2580;
fax: (041) 667 2576; Maj Kwon, Sung-dal

TRAINING COLLEGE

83-2 Chungang-dong, Kwachun, Kyunggi-do
427-010; tel: (02) 502 9505/2927;
fax: (02) 502 7160

CONFERENCE CENTRES

Ah Hyun Corps, Kangwondo (acc 300)
Taejon Central Corps, Taejon (acc 400)
Territorial Retreat and Conference Centre,
Paekhwa-san [Paekhwa Mountain] (acc 1,000)

RETIRED OFFICERS' RESIDENCE

'Victory Lodge' Silver Nursing Home (acc 50)

TERRITORIAL HERITAGE CENTRE

1st floor, The Salvation Army Central Hall,
1-23 Chung dong, Choong Ku, Seoul 100-120

THE SALVATION ARMY OFFICE BUILDING (THE SAOB)

Shinmoon ro 1-ga 58-1, Chong Ro Ku, Seoul
110-061

SOCIAL WORK
Adult Rehabilitation Centre (ARC)
Iljook

Bridge Centre (drop-in centre)
Seoul (acc 50)

Centres for the Handicapped
Kunsan: Catherine Centre for the Handicapped
(acc 60)
Kunsan: Day Care Centre for the Handicapped
Suwon: Support Centre for the Handicapped
(acc 8)

Children's Homes
Kunsan (acc 114), Seoul Broadview (acc 160),
Taegu (acc 61), Taejon No 1 (acc 50), Taejon
No 2 (acc 75)

Community Centres
Asan, Ansung, Booyuh, Boryung, Cheju, Chilgok
Centre for the Elderly, Hapduk, Hapjung
(Pyongtaek), Hong Eun, Kang Buk, Kongdo,
Masan, Mosan, Myung Chun, Najoo, Nonsan,
Sakson, Seogwipo, Sosan, Suh San Suklim

Welfare Centre for the Elderly, Tai An, Taegu, Yongwol, Yoju,

Corps Day Care Centres

Bahnyawol (acc 52), Boo Nam (acc 32), Chin Chang (acc 32), Chin Ju [Cham Sarang] (acc 38), Chun Kok (acc 39), Hap Duk (acc 49), Kang Buk (acc 92), Kim Chon (acc 38), Kwachun (acc 91), Masan [Moonwha] (acc 44), Mil Yang [Catherine] (acc 40), Mindalae (acc 57), Mosan (acc 51), Myung Chun (acc 48), Nam Choong Ju (acc 27), Suh Taegu (acc 80) Osan [Star] (acc 43), Sae Yung Chun [Saetbyul], San Kok (acc 100), Shinchang (acc 25), Sok Cho (acc 76), Song Tan (acc 40), Suhdaemun (acc 52), Suh Taegu (acc 80), Suk Lim (acc 52), Taegu (acc 81), Tong San (acc 30), Wonju (acc 63), Yul Mok (acc 39), Yung Deung Po (acc 47)

Counselling and Friendship Centres

Chonan Counselling Centre for Women, Tong Taegu, Taegu, Suh Taejon, Taejon, Tong Taejon Tongbu

Day Care Centres

Kang Buk (acc 92), Myung Chun (acc 48), Seobu Sudaemun (acc 77), Suh San Suklim Community Welfare (acc 52), Taegu (acc 81)

HIV/Aids Care and Prevention Programme Units

Pusan Shelter; Red Ribbon Centre, Seoul

Naval Servicemen's Centre

Chin Hai

Oori Jip (transitional housing for those leaving children's homes)

Choongdong (Seoul Broadview Children's Home) (acc 3), Chun Yun (acc 4), Kunsan (acc 4), Taejon (acc 20)

Rest Centres

Ansung, Buyeo, Cheju, Hap Duk, Masan, Mosan, Muloori, Najoo,Pang Nai, SeogwipoSong Tan, Tai Kok, Wonju, Yeoju

Sarangbang Centres (hostels for the homeless)

Buk Ah Hyun Dong (acc 30), Choong Chung Ro (acc 130), Sudaemun (acc 50)

School

Inpyung Technical High School (acc 1,340)

Self-Support Training Centres

Boryung, Nonsan, Taian

Senior Citizens' Services

Ansung Peace Village Nursing Home (acc 55), Hapjung Day Centre for the Elderly (acc 15), Hongjae Dong Day Care Centre for the Elderly (acc 20), Kwachun Home for the Elderly (acc 50), Kwachun Nursing Home (acc 30), Mooan 'Silver Centre' (acc 13), Namdong Day Centre for the Elderly (acc 37), Namdong House of Love (acc 60), Pusan Home for the Elderly (acc 60), Suhsansung Day Centre for the Elderly (acc 20), 'Victory Lodge' Silver Nursing Home (acc 50), Wolsung Day Care Centre for the Elderly (acc 9)

Special Service and Relief Services

9 programmes, 3 vehicles

Students' Study Centres (and after-school programmes)

Ah Hyun, An Dong, An San, Baesan, Bang Hak, Boo Jun, Boo Kok, Boo Nam, Buk Choon Chun, Chang Yong, Chew Kok, Chin Chook, Chin Hae, Chin Ju, Cheju, Chisan, Choong Taegu, Choong Moo, Chuan, Chun An # 1, Daiyun, Dan Chun, Dong du Chun, Doriwon, Eonyak, Haeundae, Inchon, Kang Nam, Kasuwon, Kie Sung, Kong Ju, Kunsan, Kwang Chun, Mil Yang, Mooan, Nonsan, Oh Ka, On Yang, Yusung, Pochun, Pyongtaek, Sae Sungnam, Sam Sung, Sangloksoo, Seogwipo, Shim Chon, Son Chi, Soyang, Sudaejon, Suh Suwon, Suh Taegu Pisan 3-dong, Suh Chung Ju, Sunglim, Sung Nam, Syn Heung, Syn Pyung, Taechon, Taegu First, Taejon Central, Tang Jin, Togo, Tomadong, Tonam, Tonghae, Tong Kunsan, Tong Taechon, Uijungbu, Uisung, Un Po, Wadong, Wolsung, Yang Kang, Yea San, Yi Chon, Yi Won, Yong Chon, Yong Dong, Yong Ho, Yongwol, Yul Mok, Yun Hie

Student Accommodation

Taejon (university students) (acc 25)

Thrift Stores

Choong Chung Ro, Seoul; Iljook; Sally's Coffee (Namdaemun Market), Seoul

Vocational Training and Support Centres

Chung Daoon House, Taejon (acc 30); Sally Home, Pusan (acc 30)

Women's Homes

Chonan House of Hope (acc 10), Seoul (acc 35), Taejon Women's Refuge Shelter (acc 55)

LATIN AMERICA NORTH TERRITORY

Territorial leaders:
Colonels Oscar and Ana Rosa Sánchez

Territorial Commander:
Colonel Oscar Sánchez (1 Feb 2007)

Chief Secretary:
Major Zoilo Pardo (1 Jul 2006)

Territorial Headquarters: Avenida 11, Calle 20, San José, Costa Rica

Postal address: Apartado Postal 125-1005, Barrio México, San José, Costa Rica

Tel: [506] 257-7535; fax: [506] 257-5291; email: sallan@sol.racsa.co.cr;

web site: www.geocities.com/latin_america_north_territory/

The Salvation Army's work commenced in the Isthmus of Panama (1904), Costa Rica (1907), Cuba (1918), Venezuela (1972), Guatemala (1976), Colombia (1985), El Salvador (1989) and Honduras (2000).

Legal recognition was given to El Ejército de Salvación by the Republic of Panama (1946), Costa Rica (1975), Guatemala (1978), Colombia (1988), The Dominican Republic (1995), El Salvador (1996) and Honduras (2001). The territory was formed on 1 October 1976, then reformed on September 1998, when Mexico became a command.

Zone: Americas and Caribbean
Countries included in the territory: Colombia, Costa Rica, Cuba, Dominican Republic, El Salvador, Guatemala, Honduras, Panama, Venezuela
The Salvation Army' in Spanish: Ejército de Salvación
Languages in which the gospel is preached: English, Kacchikel, Spanish
Publications: *Voz de Salvación (Salvation Voice), Arco Iris de Ideas (Rainbow of Ideas)*

THE territory's Salvationists are determined that they should be 'God's Army' – an army of salvation and holiness – that uses with passion any expression of evangelism, that has a strong biblical and doctrinal foundation, that encourages the participation of lay people, that values women's ministries, and that reforms society.

A challenging opportunity for Salvationists to witness within their communities came with a call to prayer and action for victims of sex-trade trafficking – a matter of grave concern, since one of the reasons why children are victims of such abuse is because of the migration of their parents (to look for better jobs): children are often left at home with their older siblings or relatives, and become vulnerable to all kinds of danger.

Salvationists have sought to address the issue by raising awareness, organising prayer meetings and holding a protest march. The territory produced a workbook to use with parents and children at schools, day care centres and corps.

In Guatemala, talks on sex-trade trafficking were given in the Army's schools, and informative talks and workshops were arranged for parents. Corps held a series of prayer meetings.

In Cuba, every corps and outpost joined in the cry: 'God, make it stop!' The Salvationists' passion was such that they committed themselves to continue their prayers throughout the year.

In the Dominican Republic, six corps held a day of fasting and praying for sex-trade victims; they also offered counselling for young people and organised workshops for women, mothers and teenagers.

In El Salvador, members of the Integrated Development Centre (Building For Tomorrow) programme at Central Corps held a walk on the streets. Carrying signs made by the children, they expressed their security of knowing God's love and their protest against sexual trafficking.

December 2006 saw the commissioning of three cadets of the Visionaries Session in Costa Rica, while a month later an exciting 'first' was a Brengle Institute hosted by the territory at the training college. Eleven territories and commands were represented by the 34 officers who attended, coming from Brazil, Mexico, Portugal, South America East and West, Spain, the four USA territories and Latin America North.

During 2007 the territory celebrated a double centenary celebration – 100 years of both the Home League and the Costa Rica Division. The Women's Ministries Department planned rallies, camps, seminars and productions of the musical *La Rosa Blanca* (*The White Rose*) across the territory.

STATISTICS

Officers 147 (active 134 retired 13) **Cadets** (1st Yr) 7 (2nd Yr) 11 **Employees** 296
Corps 57 **Outposts** 19 **Institutions** 8 **Schools** 22
Day Care Centres 15 **Children's Development Centres** 6 **Vocational Training Centres** 20 **Feeding Centres** 16 **Camps** 2
Senior Soldiers 2,532 **Adherents** 827 **Junior Soldiers** 1,225

STAFF

Business Administration: Maj Esteban Calvo
Personnel: Maj Ileana Calvo
Programme: Maj María Eugenia Obando
Women's Ministries: Col Ana Rosa Sánchez (TPWM) Maj Magali Pardo (TSWM)
Editorial: Maj Javier Obando
Education and Candidates: Maj Javier Obando
Finance: Capt Joan Cole
Projects and Sponsorship: Grettel Mejia
Training: Maj Eduardo Almendras

DIVISIONS

Colombia: Apartado Aéreo 17756 Santa Fe de Bogotá, Colombia; tel: (571) 263 2633; fax: (571) 295 2921; email: coldiv_leadership@lan.salvatonarmy.org; web site: http/www.ejercitodesalvacion.com; Capt Odilio Fernández
Costa Rica: Apartado Postal 6227-1000, San José, Costa Rica; tel: (506) 221 8266; fax: (506) 223 0250; email: crdiv_leadership@lan.salvationarmy.org; Maj Miguel Aguilera
Cuba: Calle 96 Nª 5513 entre 55 Y 57, Marianao CP 11400, Ciudad de la Habana, Cuba; tel: (53) 7260-2171; fax: (53) 7267-2537; email: ejdivcuba@enet.cu; Capt Orestes Linares
Guatemala: Apartado Postal 1881, Guatemala CA; 2a Avenida 3-10, Sector A4 San Cristóbal 1, Zona 8 de Mixco, Guatemala; tel/fax: (502) 2478-4112/2443-2484; email: guadiv_leadership@lan.salvationarmy.org Maj Manuel Muñoz;
Panama: Apartado Postal 0843-01134 Balboa, Ancón Vía Transísmica, Pueblo Nuevo, Halo

Pintado-Casa Nº 3, República de Panamá;
tel: (507) 261-8091;
email: Jorge_Mendez@lan.salvationarmy.org;
Maj Jorge Méndez

REGIONS

Dominican Republic: Ejército de Salvación, Apartado Postal M402, Oficina Postal Los Mameyes, Calle 4ta, Esquina 26 De Enero, Santo Domingo Este, Dominican Republic; tel: (1809) 699-3818; fax: (1809) 699-3830; Capt Gerardo Góchez

El Salvador: Apartado Postal No 7, Centro de Gobierno, Calle 15 de Septiembre Nº 199 y Nº 121 Barrio Candelaria, San Salvador; tel: (503) 2280-1805; fax: (503) 2280-3293; email: ejercito-salvacion@salnet.net; Maj Max Mayorga

Project Honduras: Colonia El Hogar Bloque B Casa Nº11 Tegucigalpa Apartado Postal 6590, Honduras; tel/fax: (504) 232-4927/235-9855; email: ejercitosalvacionhn@gmail.com; Capt Eddy Obando

Venezuela: Calle San Juan de Dios Melián, Entre calle san Rafael y la Segunda de Cabudare Riviera Departamento 1, Cabudare-Barquisimento, Venezuela; tel: (058) 251 261-6318; email: Pedro_Jose_Lopez@yahoo.com; Capt Pedro López

TRAINING COLLEGE

Calle Puente de Piedra, 1 km norte del Puente de Piedra, Barrio Los Angeles, San Rafael de Heredia, Costa Rica.
Postal address: Apartado 173-3015 San Rafael de Heredia, Costa Rica; tel: (506) 262 0061; fax: (506) 262 0733

SOCIAL SERVICES
Institutions
Centres for Homeless
Costa Rica:
Centro Modelo: Calle Naranjo, Concepción de Tres Ríos, Provincia de Cartago; tel: (506) 273-6307 (acc 80)
Refugio de Esperanza: Avenida 9 Zona Roja, San José; tel: (506) 233-2059 (acc 30)

Disabled Centre
Costa Rica: Hogar Sustituto 'Tierra Prometida', Carretera Interamericana 100 metros sur de Autos Mundiales, Pérez Zeledón; tel: (506)771-2517 (acc13)

Residential Homes for the Elderly
Cuba: William Booth Home, Calle 84 No 5525 e/55 y Lindero, Mariano, CP 11400, Ciudad de la Habana; tel: (537) 260-1118
Panama: Hogar Jackson Home, Avenida Amador Guerrero y Calle 3 No 2014, Colón; tel: (507) 441-3371 (acc 30)

Residential Homes for Children
El Salvador: El Alba, Km 50, Carretera a la Herradura, Caserio los Novios, Hacienda del Cauca; tel: (503) 354-4430 (acc 20)
Panama: Hogar Dr Eno (Girls), Transísmica, Sabanitas, Colón; tel: (507) 442-0371 (acc 20)
Venezuela: Hogar Nido Alegre, Calle 71 # 14 A63, Juana de Avila, Apdo Postal 1464 Maracaibo 4001; Estado de Zulia, Venezuela; tel: (58-261) 798-3761 (acc 50)

Schools
Kindergartens
El Salvador:
Central Corps: Calle 15 Septiembre # 199 y # 121, Barrio Candelaria, San Salvador; tel: (503) 2280-1805 (acc 20)
Merliot Corps: Jardines del Volcán, Calle El Jabali # 36, Ciudad Merliot, La Libertad; tel: (503) 2278-4982 (acc 60)
Usulután Corps: 6a Avenida y 7a, Calle Oriente # 31, Barrio El Calvario, Departamento de Usulután; tel: (503) 2662-4428 (acc 80)
Guatemala:
Escuintla Outpost: 3a Avenida 2-56, Zona 3, Colonia Sebastopol; tel: (502) 7888-1559 (acc 100)
Satelite: Lote 5, Manzana 27, Proyecto 2, Ciudad Satelite, Mixto; tel: (502) 484-3052 (acc 30)
Panama:
Panamá Templo: Calle 25 y Avenida Cuba-Este; tel: (507) 262-2545 (acc 30)
Colón: Calle 14, Avenida Amador Guerrero 14201 Apartado 1163 Colón; tel: (507) 441-4570 (acc 50)

Kindergarten and School
Panama: Calle 11y1/2, La Pulida, Río Abajo; tel: (507) 224-7480 (acc 40)

Primary Schools
Dominican Republic:
Cotui: 16 de Agosto Nº 98, Cotui, Sánchez Ramírez; tel: (809) 585-3393 (acc 40)

Moca: Moca Republica Dominicana;
tel: (1809) 578-4792 (acc 20)
Tres Brazos: Calle Matadero N° 70 (acc 20)
Guatemala:
Central Corps: 15 Calle 8-29, Zona 1,
Guatemala City; tel: (502) 2232-2964 (acc 75)
Chimaltenango: 7a Avenida y 1a Calle, Zona 1,
Villas del Pilar; tel: (502) 7839-6585 (acc 150)
Mezquital: 4a Calle 3-99, Zona 12, Colonia
Mezquital; tel: (502) 2479-8443 (acc 150)
Tecpán: Calle Tte Coronel Jack Waters,
Barrio Poromá, Colonia Iximché;
tel: (502) 7840-3020 (acc 300)
Tierra Nueva: Sector B-1, Manzana D, Lote 3,
Colonia Tierra Nueva 11, Chinautla;
tel: (502) 2484-1255 (acc 150)

Primary and Secondary Schools
Honduras:
Limón: Colegio William Booth, Centro
Communal 'El Limón' Costado Derecho,
Zona 18; tel: (502) 2260-0723 (acc 395)
Maya: Colegio Nido Alegre Manzana 2,
Lote 262, Zona 18, Colonia Maya;
tel: (502) 2260-1519 (acc 150)

School for the Blind
Panama: Contact Panama DHQ

Schools
Honduras:
Avanzada de Tegucigalpa: Hospital Materno
Infantil (Classroom 4); tel: (504) 232-4927
Avanzada San Pedro Sula: Hospital Mario
Catarino Rivas (Classroom 2);
tel: (504) 556-7238

Day Care Centres
Colombia:
Armenia Outpost: Carrera 11 # 14-19 Barrio
Guayaquil; tel: (576) 746-8591
San Cristóbal Sur, Bogotá: Calle 12 Sur # 11-71
Este, Barrio San Cristóbal Sur, Santa Fe de
Bogotá; tel: (571) 333-0606/289-2672
Costa Rica:
Central Corps: Avenida 16, Entre Calle 5 y
7 San José; tel: (506) 233-6850 (acc 35)
León XIII: Ciudadela León XIII, Detrás de la
Escuela de León XIII, San José;
tel: (506) 231-1786 (acc 80)
Limón Central: Av 4 entre Calles 7 y 9;
tel: (506) 758-0657 (acc 75)
Pavas: Villa Esperanza de Pravas, Contiguo
Al Instituto Nacional de Aprendizaje, San
José; tel: (506) 231-1786 (acc 80)

El Salvador:
Central Corps: Calle 15 Septiembre # 199 y
121, Barrio Candelaria, San Salvador;
tel: (503) 2280-1805 (acc 20)
Merliot Corps: Jardines del Volcán, Calle El
Jabali # 36, Ciudad Merliot, La Libertad;
tel: (503) 2278-8249 (acc 60)
Usulután Corps: 6a Avenida y 7a, Calle Oriente
31, Barrio El Calvario Departamento de
Usulután; tel: (503) 2662-4428
Guatemala:
Central Corps: 15 Calle 8-39, Zona 1,
Guatemala City; tel: (502) 232-2964 (acc 100)
Satelite: Lote 5, Manzana 27, Proyecto 2,
Ciudad Satelite, Mixco; tel: (502) 484-3052
(acc 30)
Panama:
Panamá Templo: Calle 25 Avenida Cuba-Este;
tel: (507) 262-2545 (acc 20)
Colón: Avenida Amador Guerrero 14201,
Apartado 1163; tel: (507) 441-4570 (acc 50)
Río Abajo: Calle 11y1/2 La Pulida;
tel: (507) 224-7480 (acc 25)
Venezuela:
Cuerpo San Luis: Barrio San Luis, San
Francisco, Avenida 2 # 22-135, Estado
Zulia, Venezuela.

Children's Development Centres
Colombia:
Ibague, Tolima: Carrera 4ta Sur # 20A-34,
Barrio Yuldaima, Apartado Aéreo 792;
tel: (578) 260-8032
Itagui, Antioquía: Calle 55 # 58FF-12, Barrio
Fátima, Apartado Aéreo 90267;
tel: (094) 372-4118
Robledo, Medellín: Carrera 84B # 63-73,
Barrio Robledo, Medellín, Antioquía;
tel: (094) 234-8250
San Cristóbal Sur, Bogotá: Calle 12 Sur # 11-71
Este, Barrio San Cristóbal Sur, Santa Fe de
Bogotá; tel: (571) 333-0606/289-2672
El Salvador:
Calle 15 de Septiembre # 199 y # 121,
Barrio Candelaria, San Salvador;
tel: (503) 270-5273 (acc 246)
Usulután: 6a Avenida y 7a, Calle Oriente
31, Barrio El Calvario, Departamento de
Usulután; tel: (503) 662-4428 (acc120)

Vocational Training Centres
Costa Rica:
Centro Modelo: Carpentry and Pig Farming,
Calle Naranjo, Concepción de Tres Ríos,
Provincia de Cartago; tel: (506) 273-6307
(acc 80)

Young people from the Central Corps, El Salvador, take part in a walk on the streets to protest against sex-trade trafficking. The territory's Salvationists also organised school visits, workshops and prayer meetings to raise awareness of this social evil.

Computer Centres: 25 Julio Catalina Booth (acc 30)

Cuba:
Cuerpo Central: Computer Centre, Calle 96 Nª 5513 entre 55 y 57, Marianao 11400, La Habana; tel: (53) 260-2171
Diezmero: Dressmaking, Calle 3ra Nª 25304 entre 2da y Martí Diezmero San Miguel del Padrón, CP 130000 Guevara, La Habana

El Salvador:
Computer Centres: Central; Merliot; Usulután
Dressmaking: Central
Vocational Centre: Avanzada de Gualache

Guatemala:
Carpentry: Limón, Tecpan
Computer Classes: Chilaltenango, Limón, Mezquital, Satelite, Tecpan, Tierra Nueva, Satelite
Typing Classes: Central, Satelite, Tecpan

Venezuela:
Computer, Carpentry and Dressmaking Classes: Calle 71 # 14 A63, Juana de Avila, Apdo Postal 1464, Maracaibo 4001; Estado de Zulia, Venezuela; tel: (0261) 798-3761 (acc 50)

Feeding Centres
Colombia:
Ibague, Tolima: Carrera 4ta Sur # 20A-34, Barrio Yuldaima, Apartado Aéreo 792; tel: (578) 260-8032
Itagui, Antioquía: Calle 55 # 58FF-12, Barrio Fátima, Apartado Aéreo 90267; tel: (574) 372-4118
Robledo, Medellín: Carrera 84B # 63-73, Barrio Robledo, Medellín, Antioquía; tel: (574) 234-8250
San Cristóbal Sur, Bogotá: Calle 12 Sur # 11-71 Este, Barrio San Cristóbal Sur, Santa Fe de Bogotá; tel: (571) 333-0606/298-2672

Costa Rica:
Liberia: 500 mts Norte Estación de Bomberos

100 Este y 50 Norte, Barrio San Roque; tel: (506) 666-3603 (acc 100)
Limón 2000: Barrio Limón 2000 frente al Predio El Aragón, Alameda # 4; tel: (506) 797-1602 (acc 30)
Nicoya: Escuela de San Martín 900 al Oeste, Barrio San Martín; tel: (506) 685-5531 (acc 100)
Sagrada Familia: Costado Este Escuela Carolina Dent, Barrio Sagrada Familia; tel (506) 227-5298 (acc 100)
Salitrillos: Salitrillos de Aserri, de las Prestaciones, 300 metros al sur; tel: (506) 230-4668 (acc 80)
San Isidro del General: Barrio Los Angeles, Apartado Postal 7-8000; tel: (506) 770-6756 (acc 150)
Santa Cruz: Barrio Tulita Sandino, 300 este del IDA Guanacaste; tel: (506) 680-0724 (acc 100)
25 de Julio: Hatillo Centro, detrás de las, Bodegas de Constenla, Colonia 25 de Julio; tel: (506) 227-8380 (acc 100)

Cuba: Calle 96 Nª 5513 entre 19 y 21 Bejucal CP 32600, Habana

Panama:
Colon: Avenida Amador Guerrero 14201, Apartado 1163; tel: (507) 441-4570 (acc 75)
Chilibre: Transistmica, Lote No 175 Chilibre; tel: (507) 216-2501 (acc 100)
Paraíso: 101 X Guyana St Paraíso; tel: (507) 232-4713

Camps
El Salvador:
Km 50, Carretera a la Herradura, Caserio los Novios, Hacienda del Cauca; tel: (503) 2354-4530 (acc 150)
Tecpán: Calle Tte Coronel Jack Waters, Barrio Poromá, Colonia Iximché; tel: (502) 7840-3998 (acc 100)

LIBERIA COMMAND

Command leaders:
Majors Robert and Hester Dixon

Officer Commanding:
Major Robert Dixon (4 Nov 2004)

General Secretary:
Major Romeo Alip (1 Oct 2006)

Command Headquarters: 17th Street, Sinkor, Monrovia

Postal address: PO Box 20/5792, Monrovia, Liberia

The Salvation Army opened fire in Liberia in May 1988 as part of the Ghana and Liberia Territory, with Major and Mrs Leonard Millar as pioneer officers. Progress was monitored by Ghana during the civil war, from May 1990. Liberia became a separate command on 1 January 1997.

Zone: Africa
Country included in the command: Liberia
Languages in which the gospel is preached: Bassa, English, Gola, Krahn, Pele

AS the country received an over-abundance of rain during the rainy season, so the command was saturated with God's blessings from Heaven. The showers of blessings began with the arrival of reinforcement officer personnel: General Secretary, Command Secretary for Women's Ministries, Finance Officer and Training Principal.

The spiritual showers persisted as officers, cadets and soldiers totally immersed themselves in praying and fasting. Women attended two successful Command Prayer Fasting Retreats as well as numerous corps and regional events of a similar nature. Men celebrated their unity in Christ by planning and participating in a day of prayer and a weekend camp.

The Spirit's showers saturated lives

at two youth-focused events. During a youth leaders' training weekend the Holy Spirit set his seal on 45 young men and women who testified to a calling to youth ministry.

More than 60 men and women then met for a candidates weekend, at which many testified to being led by God to full-time service as Salvation Army officers.

Later, the 'rains' fell in torrents when 500 delegates at Command Youth Councils focused on 'Winning the Nation for God'. Taking the words of Jesus: 'If I be lifted up I will draw all men unto me' (John 12:32), they stepped out in faith to parade through the streets of Monrovia and, in small groups, undertook door-to-door visitation to share the gospel.

A chorus sung during times of praise

and worship in Liberia epitomises what God is doing in the command: 'I see my blessing coming; I see it coming'.

STATISTICS

Officers 38 **Lieutenants** 2 **Auxiliary-Captains** 6 **Envoys** 2 **Corps Leaders** 9 **Cadets** 5 **Employees** 320

Corps 21 **Outposts** 18 **District** 1 **Schools** 24 (pupils 5,642) **Commercial Institutes** 2 **Hostels/Homes** 2 **Child Day Care Centres** 18 **Clinics** 2 **Mobile Clinic** 1

Senior Soldiers 2,056 **Adherents** 45 **Junior Soldiers** 476

STAFF

Women's Ministries: Maj Hester Dixon (CPWM) Maj Elizabeth Oduro (CSWM) Maj Etta Gaymo (LOMS)
Field: Maj Ben Gaymo
Finance Officer: Maj Evelyn Alip
Property: Mr David Cooper-Bainda
Schools: Mr Ernest Suah
Trade: Mr Prince B. Siakeh
Training: Maj James Oduro
Youth: Capt Jonathan Walker
Candidates: Capt Willamena Walker

DISTRICT

Grand Bassa: contact Command HQ; Capt Anthony Sio

FLOOD VICTIMS SEE COMPASSION IN ACTION

Indonesia Territory: When heavy rainfall hit the country, particularly in Jakarta and several suburbs where thousands of houses were deeply submerged, The Salvation Army's Compassion in Action team assisted the whole community regardless of religion. Medical treatment was carried out and hot meals were distributed.

MALAWI COMMAND

Command leaders:
Majors Godfrey and Diane Payne

Officer Commanding:
Major Godfrey Payne (1 Jul 2007)

General Secretary:
Major Francis Nyambalo (1 Feb 2007)

Command Headquarters: PO Box 51140, Limbe, Malawi

Tel: [265] 1 687105; fax: [265] 1 687031

The Salvation Army began operations in Malawi on 13 November 1967 and was granted official government recognition on 2 October 1973. The Malawi Division was part of the Zimbabwe Territory until 1988, when it was integrated into the Zambia Command, which was given territorial status and became known as the Zambia and Malawi Territory. The Army's work in Malawi has grown and developed and on 1 October 2002 it became a separate region. Further growth and expansion of the work in Malawi resulted in the region being elevated to command status on 1 February 2004.

Zone: Africa
Country included in the command: Malawi
'The Salvation Army' in Chichewa: Nkhondo ya Chipulumutso
Languages in which the gospel is preached: Chichewa, English, Lomwe, Sena, Tumbuka

SALVATIONISTS in Malawi rejoice in a continuing sense of God's guidance as they seek to keep the 'Vision for Mission' in the command.

The first review since Malawi was granted command status revealed numerical growth, the establishment of new openings from host corps, and the successful integration of community-based activities at corps level involving the total community. Two of the new openings are a direct result of integrated mission activities in the location of the centres.

After discussion took place with regard to the establishment of the command's own training college, approval has been sought for the first

session to be opened in 2008. To date there are 42 applicants at various stages of candidateship. The convening of an assessment seminar for all potential candidates, enabled personal interviews and teaching to take place.

An outcome of the ongoing in-service training was the commissioning of eight full-time envoys to the rank of captain. Commissioner Amos Makina (International Secretary for Africa) conducted the covenant and commissioning services.

The highlight of the year was the first-ever Command Congress, led by Chief of the Staff Commissioner Robin Dunster. A capacity congregation of 3,500 gathered in celebration

Some of Malawi's envoys who were commissioned to the rank of captain

and praise. It was the first time all divisions and districts had gathered at one venue – a fact that provided challenge and encouragement to the participants. Many decisions for Christ were recorded.

The command had great support from Harare City Corps Band (Zimbabwe) and the Zambia Territorial Youth Songsters. More than 3,000 Salvationists took part in a march of witness, led by a joint Malawi-Zimbabwe band.

STATISTICS

Officers 52 (active 48 retired 4) **Envoys** 4 **Cadets** 4 **Employees** 75
Corps 34 **Outposts** 12 **Outreach Units** 14 **New Openings** 40
Senior Soldiers 5,310 **Junior Soldiers** 873
Personnel serving outside command Officers 3

STAFF

Development Services: Mr Oswald Malunda
Education: Capt Alfred Banda
Finance: Maj George Nkhululu
Property: Maj George Nkhululu
Women's Ministries: Maj Diane Payne (CPWM)
Maj Jamiya Nyambalo (CSWM)

Youth and Candidates: Capt Robert Mtengowalira

DIVISIONS

Blantyre: PO Box 51749, Limbe;
 tel: 01 655 901; Maj Gerald Chimimba
Phalombe: PO Box 99, Migowi;
 tel: 01 481 216; Maj Chatonda Theu

DISTRICTS

Central and North: PO Box 40058, Kanengo,
 Lilongwe; tel: 01 716 869
Lower Shire: PO Box 35, Muona, Lower Shire;
 Capt Andson Namathanga

COMMUNITY DEVELOPMENT PROGRAMMES

Adult Literacy: Blantyre and Phalombe
 Divisions, Central and North and Lower Shire
 Districts
Community Counselling: Bangwe, Gooke,
 Migowi, Nguludi
Feeding/Food for Work: Bangwe, Blantyre,
 Migowi, Nguludi
HIV/Aids Home-based Care: Bangwe, Migowi,
 Nguludi, Nsanje
Orphans and Vulnerable Children: Blantyre and
 Phalombe Divisions, Central and North and
 Lower Shire Districts

SOCIAL SERVICES

Hans Andersen Memorial Youth Centre: Mchinji

171

MEXICO TERRITORY

Territorial leaders:
Colonels Olin O. and Dianne Hogan

Territorial Commander:
Colonel Olin O. Hogan (1 Oct 2001)

Chief Secretary:
Major Josué Cerezo (1 Apr 2004)

Territorial Headquarters: San Borja #1456, Colonia Vértiz Narvarte, Delegación Benito Juárez, México 03600, DF

Postal address: Apartado Postal 12-668, México 03020, DF

Tel: [525] 5575-1042; 5559-5244/9625; fax: [525] 5575-3266; email: mexico@salvationarmy.org

In 1934, a group known as the Salvation Patrol was commenced in Mexico by Alejandro Guzmán. In October 1937, he was presented with a flag by General Evangeline Booth at the USA Southern Territory Congress in Atlanta, Georgia. The Salvation Patrol then became absorbed into the international Salvation Army, operating under the supervision of DHQ in Dallas, Texas, later becoming part of the Latin America North Territory. On 1 September 1998 it was made a command in its own right and, on 1 October 2001, it became a territory.

Zone: Americas and Caribbean
Country included in the territory: Mexico
'The Salvation Army' in Spanish: Ejército de Salvación
Language in which the gospel is preached: Spanish

THE Mexico Territory continues to expand into new areas of the country in an effort to reach the least and the lost. One instance of this was a response to devastating hurricanes that struck Tapachula, Chiapas. This community was hit hard by flooding and high winds.

With 400 houses destroyed and as many families losing relatives, a decision was made to offer the Army's ministry of compassion and to preach Christ's concern for these distraught people. As a consequence there is now a Salvation Army-run home for children forced to live on the streets

because they lost family members in the floods.

In Cocotitlán, a community outside Mexico City, a building was donated and the Army began a work of service and spiritual development, with good success. Many other new openings were a testament to the spiritual fervour of the Mexican officers and soldiers.

The territorial theme for the year was 'Praying for Mexico' – an emphasis which has impacted the spiritual life and development of the Salvationists and resulted in a new passion to seek God and reach out to those eople who most need him.

After spending time in prayer, El
Arbolillo Corps sensed God's call to
go to the city dump and care for the
children who gain their livelihood and
daily food from the refuse left there.

Plans for the new year included the
opening of three new outposts and the
discipling of the new soldiers who had
been won for Christ.

A significant thrust has been in
serving people who are being trafficked
in the country. The territory is partner-
ing with the Canada and Bermuda
Territory and the USA in establishing a
fence of caring' which will provide a
care system for victims of sex trafficking on the American border.

The then International Secretary
for the Americas and Caribbean
Commissioner William Francis) led
a territorial seminar on human trafficking. Salvationists are addressing the
needs of people trapped in this evil
morass and also attempting to communicate with those who are at risk of
becoming victims.

The Salvation Army in Mexico is
ready to do what is necessary, when
necessary – to God's honour and glory.

STATISTICS

Officers 158 (active 129 retired 29) **Lieutenants**
7 **Cadets** (1st Yr) 7 (2nd Yr) 5 **Employees** 57
Corps 47 **Outposts** 15 **Institutions** 51
Senior Soldiers 1,710 **Adherents** 198 **Junior
Soldiers** 855

STAFF

Education: Maj Douglas Danielson
Finance: Maj Shirley Adams
Property: Maj James Hood
Social: Maj Sallyann Hood
Training: Maj Humberto García

Women's Ministries: Col Dianne C. Hogan
(TPWM) Maj Ruth Cerezo (TSWM)
Youth and Candidates: Maj Cecilia Rivera

DIVISIONS

Capital: Alicante No 88, Colonia Álamos
Delegación Benito Juárez, 03400 México, DF;
Apartado Postal 13-01, México, DF 07501;
tel: 5590-9220; fax: 5590-9603; Maj Douglas
Danielson

Northwest: Tamborel 601, Colonia Santa Rosa,
Chihuahua, CP31050; tel: (614) 1420-4002;
Maj Guadalupe Galván

Río Bravo: Lombardo Toledano #2709, Colonia
Alta Vista Sur, 64740 Monterrey, NL;
Apartado Postal 1097, 64000 Monterrey, NL,
México; tel: (81) 8359-5711;
fax: (81) 8359-9115; Maj Francisco Zuñiga

REGION

Southeast: Calle 19 No 116 X22 Y24,
Colonia México, Mérida, Yucatán 97128;
tel: (999) 944-6415; Maj Manuel Padilla

TRAINING COLLEGE

Calle Monte Albán #510, Colonia Independencia,
México 03630, DF; tel: (55) 5672-7986;
fax: (55) 5672-0608

SOCIAL SERVICES
Centre for Care of Persons in Transition

La Esperanza Centre: Labradores #85 Esquina
con Imprenta, 15270, México, DF;
tel: (55) 5789-1511; fax: 5702-8033

Children's Care Centres

Ciudad Juárez, Chih: Ulises Irigoyen #1674
Colonia Chaveña, CP 32060;
tel: (656) 1614-2828 (acc 50)

Chihuahua, Chih: Tamborel 601, Colonia Santa
Rosa, CP 31050; tel: (614) 1420-4002
(acc 70)

Culiacán, Sinaloa: Cuauhtémoc #40 Sur, Colonia
Las Vegas, Esquina Alba de Acosta, Cerca de
KZ4, CP 80090; tel: (667) 715-1043 (acc 27)

Matamoros, Tam: Calle Sonora #15 Esquina San
Pedro, Colonia Esperanza, CP 87310;
tel: (868) 810-1369 (acc 45)

Mexicali, BC: Avenida Aguascalientes #2300,
Colonia Santa Clara; tel: (686) 553-1194
(acc 30)

México, DF: Imprenta #225, Colonia Morelos,
CP 15270; tel: (55) 5789-0554;
fax: (55) 5702-3666 (acc 30)

Nuevo Laredo, Tam: Avenida Santos Degollado

#1217, Sector Centro, CP 8800;
tel: (867) 712-1455 (acc 30)
Reynosa, Tam: Allende #465 Poniente, Colonia
Centro, CP 88500; tel: (899) 922-5463 (acc 75)
San Luis Potosí, SLP: Bolívar #1426 Barrio
San Miguelito, CP 78339; tel: (444) 815-4530
(acc 30)
Tampico, Tam: Avenida Central #501, Colonia
Moctezuma, CP 89250; tel: (833) 212-0365
(acc 55)
Tapachula, Chiapas: Avenida 11 Sur #44,
Colonia 16 de Septiembre, entre la 18y20,
Oriente; tel: (962) 625-6733 (acc 50)
Tijuana, BC: Calle Aquiles Serdán #11585,
Colonia Libertad, Parte Baja,CP 22300;
tel: (664) 683-2694 (acc 85)
Torreón, Coah: Calle 21, #373 Nte, CP 27000;
tel: (871) 7136-023 (acc 65)
Villahermosa, Tab: Calle Fco Sarabia #304,
Colonia Segunda del Águila, CP 86080;
tel: (993) 315-2694 (acc 30)

Children's Homes

Acapulco, Gro: Avenida de los Cantiles #16,
Fraccionamiento Mozimba, CP 39460;
tel: (744) 446-0359 (acc 90)
Chihuahua, Chih: Tamborel #601, Colonia
Santa Rosa, CP 31050; tel: (614) 420-4002
(acc 70)
Coatzacoalcos, Ver: Gutiérrez Zamora #1120
Colonia Centro, CP 96400;
tel: (921) 214-5923 (acc 50)
Cuernavaca, Mor: Avenida Atlacomúlco, #124,
Colonia Acapantzingo, CP 62440;
tel: (777) 312-8207/ 8238 (acc 45)
Culiacán, Sin: Chuahutémoc #40 Sur, Colonia
Las Vegas, Esquina Alba de Acosta, Cerca de
KZ4, CP 80090; tel: (667) 715-1043 (acc 27)
Guadalajara, Jal: Calzada Revolución #2011,
Sector Reforma, CP 44800; tel: (33) 3635-4192
(acc 100)
Matamoros, Tam: Calle Sonora #15 Esquina
San Pedro, Colonia Esperanza, CP 87310;
tel: (868) 810-1369 (acc 30)
Mazatlán, Sin: Calle Ángel Flores s/n, Colonia
El Venadillo CP 82129; tel: (669) 980-7609
(acc 30)
Mérida, Yuc: Calle 103, #506 Ax 62, Colonia
Delio Moreno Cantón, CP 97268;
tel: (999) 928-5153 (acc 30)
México, DF: Avenida Encino Grande #550,
Tetelpán, VAO, CP 17000; tel: (55) 5585-0144
(acc 120)
Nuevo Laredo, Tam: Avenida Santos Degollado
1217, CP 88000; tel: (867) 712-1455 (acc 30)
Puebla, Pue: Calle 16 Sur #704 Colonia Analco

Centro, CP 72000; tel: (222) 242-6047 (acc 35)
Reynosa, Tam: Allende #465 Poniente, Colonia
Centro, CP 88500; tel: (899) 922-5463;
fax: (899) 930-9028 (acc 25)
Saltillo, Coah: Durazno #354, Colonia del Valle,
CP 25000; tel: (844) 436-2005 (acc 40)
San Luis Potosí, SLP: Bolívar #1426, Barrio San
Miguelito, CP 78339; tel: (444) 815-4530
(acc 30)
Tampico, Tam: Avenida Central #501 Colonia
Moctezuma, CP 89250; tel: (833) 212-0365
(acc 55)
Torreón, Coah: Calle 21, #373 Nte, CP 27000;
tel: (871) 7136-023 (acc 50)
Veracruz, Ver: Revillagiegdo #1507, Colonia
México, CP 91756; tel: (229) 934-1927 (acc 50)
Villahermosa, Tab: Calle Fco Sarabia #304,
Colonia Segunda del Águila, CP 86080;
tel: (993) 315-2694 (acc 30)

Clinic and Dispensary

México DF: Clínica de Salud Mental, Calle
Imprenta #221 Colonia Morelos, CP 15270;
tel: (55) 5794-1994

Feeding Centres (Senior Citizens and Children)

Alvarado, Ver: Ignacio Ramírez #87, CP 95250,
Apartado Postal 1; tel: (297) 973-2191 (acc 160)
Can Cún: Avenida Talleres entre 109 y 111
región 94, Manzana 80 Lote 28, Can Cún,
Quintana Roo; tel/fax: (998) 840-1074
(acc 30)
Culiacán, Sin: Chuahutémoc #40 Sur, Colonia
Las Vegas, Esquina Epitacio Alba de Acosta,
Cerca de KZ4, CP 80090; tel: (667) 715-1043
(acc 30)
Genaro Vázquez: Manzana Heroica Lote 13,
Colonia Genaro Vázquez, Monterrey, Nuevo
Léon (acc 100)
Mexicali, BC: Avenida Aguascalientes #2300,
Colonia Santa Clara, CP 21110;
tel: (686) 553-1194 (acc 50)
México, DF (Corps #3): Norte 68 #3742,
Colonia M. de Río Blanco, CP 07880;
tel: (55) 5751-3598 (acc 60)
México, DF (Corps #6): Calle 12 #68 Esquina
Avenida Pantitlán, Colonia Provenir, CP 57430,
Netzahualcoyotl, Estado de México;
tel/fax: (55) 5200-1839 (acc 30)
Monclova, Coah: Benjamín Garza #1221,
Colonia Primero de Mayo, CP 25760;
tel: (866) 631-3502 (acc 50)
Monterrey, NL: Carvajal y de la Cueva #1716
Nte, Colonia Primero de Mayo, CP 64580;
tel: (81) 8375-0379 (acc 80)

Nogales, Sonora: Calle San Juan #191, Colonia
Benit Juárez, CP 84015; tel/fax: (631) 312-4647
(acc 60)

Puerto Vallarta: Sonora 232 Colonia Mojoneras,
Puerto Vallarta, Jalisco 48300;
tel: (322) 290-1587 (acc 50)

Sabinitas, NL: Calle Plutarco Elías Calles #401,
Colonia 6 de Marzo, Guadalupe, NL 67160;
tel: (81) 8299-5981 (acc 75)

Saltillo, Coah: Sosténes Rocha 170, Colonia
Chamizal, CP 25180; tel: (844) 135-3458
(acc 80)

San Juan Ixhuatepec: Edo de México,
Tenochtitlan #10, Administración San Juan
Ixhuatepec, Tlanepantla, Edo de México,
CP 54180; tel: (55) 5715-0649 (acc 80)

Tijuana, BC: Calle Aquiles Serdán #11585,
Colonia Libertad, Apartado Postal
5-G; tel: (664) 683-2694 (acc 45)

Toluca, Edo de México: Calle Pangue
Iztaccihuati #3, Colonia Parques Nacionales,
Toluca, Edo de México 50100;
tel: (722) 278-7335 (acc 25)

Xochitepec: Calle Hidalgo S/N esquina Jalisco,
Colonia Lázaro Cárdenas, Xochitepec,
Morelos 6279o; tel/fax: (777) 361-3628
(acc 30)

Feeding Centre (Men)

Mexicali, BC: Avenida Aguascalientes #2300,
Colonia Santa Clara, CP 21110;
tel: (686) 553-1194 (acc 50)

Night Shelters (Men)

Mexicali, BC: Avenida Aguascalientes #2300,
Colonia Santa Clara, CP 21110;
tel: (686) 553-1194 (acc 50)

México, DF: La Esperanza, Labradores #85,
Esquina con Imprenta, Colonia Morelos,
México 15270 DF; tel: (55) 5789-1511
(acc 125)

Monterrey, NL: Carvajal y de la Cueva #1716
Nte, Colonia Primero de Mayo, CP 64580;
tel: (81) 8375-0379 (acc 80)

Piedras Negras, Coah: Victoria #805 Nte,
Colonia Centro CP 26030; tel: (878) 782-2707
(acc 50)

Tijuana, BC: Calle Aquiles Serdán #11585,
Colonia Libertad, Porte Baja, CP 22300; tel:
(664) 683-2694 (acc 45)

Vocational Training Centre

México DF: Labradores #85 Esq Con
Imprenta, Colonia Morelos, CP 15270;
tel: (55) 5789-1511

COMMITMENT AT THE CROSS

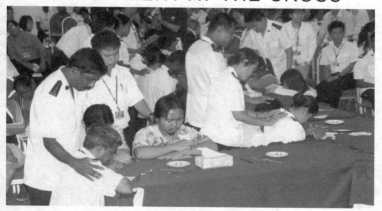

Singapore, Malaysia and Myanmar Territory: Delegates to the
territory's first-ever Mission For Vision Convention, held in Port Dickson,
Malaysia, kneel at a cross-shaped mercy seat. Many prayerfully signed
commitment cards as they rededicated themselves to God.

THE NETHERLANDS AND CZECH REPUBLIC TERRITORY

Territorial leaders:
Commissioners Roy and Arda Frans

Territorial Commander:
Commissioner Roy Frans
(1 Jul 2007)

Chief Secretary:
Lieut-Colonel Theo Wolterink
(1 Aug 2007)

Territorial Headquarters: Spoordreef 10, 1315 GN Almere, The Netherlands

Tel: [31] (36) 5398111; fax: [31] (36) 5331458; email: ldhnl@legerdesheils.nl;

web sites: www.legerdesheils.nl; www.armadaspasy.cz

Captain and Mrs Joseph K. Tyler, English officers, and Lieutenant Gerrit J. Govaars, a gifted Dutch teacher, commenced Salvation Army work in the Gerard Doustraat, Amsterdam, on 8 May 1887. Operations soon spread throughout the country and reached Indonesia (then The Netherlands East Indies) in 1894. Further advances were made in 1926 in Surinam and in 1927 in Curaçao.

Salvation Army operations in Czechoslovakia commenced in 1919, the pioneer being Colonel Karl Larsson. Evangelistic and social activities were maintained until suppressed in June 1950. After the opening of the central European borders, The Salvation Army's work was re-established and The Netherlands Territory was asked to take charge of the redevelopment. By the end of 1990 centres were reopened in Havirov, Prague, Brno and Ostrava and the work has grown steadily since then.

On 1 February 2002, the territory was renamed The Netherlands and Czech Republic Territory.

Zone: Europe
Countries included in the territory: Czech Republic, The Netherlands
'The Salvation Army' in Dutch: Leger des Heils; in Czech: Armáda Spásy
Languages in which the gospel is preached: Czech, Dutch
Periodicals: *Dag In Dag Uit*, *Heils-en Strijdzangen*, *InterCom*, *Strijdkreet*, *VoorWerk* (all Dutch), *Prapor Spásy* (Czech)

FOR many years Lieut-Colonel Alida Bosshardt, OF, was the face of The Salvation Army in The Netherlands – and its inspiration. When she was promoted to Glory on 25 June 2007, the whole country mourned.

News of her death immediately impacted the media; the Army was constantly featured in the press and on radio and television. The funeral could have been classed as of 'State' proportions, with police in full ceremonial dress and the streets of Amsterdam lined with thousands of people.

The Queen's representative, the Prime Minister and former Prime Minister, along with many celebrities and notable personalities, attended the crowded service in the Koningskerk (The King's Church) in the centre of Amsterdam. The Mayor paid tribute to Lieut-Colonel Bosshardt as 'The Angel of Amsterdam'.

The service was broadcast live on television and edited repeats were featured for many days following the event.

Around the territory, many corps have used new and old ways of moving out into the community. Examples include the formation of a shanty choir – a male voice choir which sings old Salvation Army songs in sea shanty style; a girls' song-and-dance group; 40 people participating in a brass band for ex-Salvationists and non-Christians who want to play Salvation Army music; Youth Alpha; Connect 45 – a new youth programme; the start of a new Salvation Army scouting group; the launch of the 'Real Life' emphasis – The Salvation Army for a new generation; and prayer-walking through local neighbourhoods.

The Soldiers and Adherents Course, a strong feature of the territory's education and training programme, celebrated its 20th anniversary. More than 170 people met at Belmont Conference Centre for a training day under the theme 'The Old Word in a New Language'.

Clients of the Social Services were encouraged to participate in an art exhibition and produced more than 70 pieces of art. Some were featured in the *2007 Salvation Army Diary*. A collection of the art was also exhibited at the Ministry of Health, Employment and Social Affairs building, the display being opened by the State Secretary.

Launched three years ago, a soup book containing many original recipes has proved very successful. The first print run sold out and a second edition is now in shops. The La Ruche Restaurant in the town of Ede features soups from the book and all profits go to The Salvation Army. The Army received a top advertising award for the book.

The Salvation Army in the Czech Republic, working with the homeless, joined with other organisations to mark the International Day Against Poverty. Representatives of municipal and regional authorities, and the media, attended the event. Many of the Army's centres for the homeless arranged exhibitions of their work.

STATISTICS
Officers 388 (active 172 retired 220) **Employees** 4,226
Corps 73 (99 local service centres) **Business Units** 17 (187 local service centres)
Senior Soldiers 4,446 **Adherents** 1,206 **Junior Soldiers** 530

STAFF
The Salvation Army Church
Field: Maj Johan C. J. van Vliet
Field Programme Support (incl Youth and Adult Ministries): Major Arie van Dijk
Candidates: Maj Tineke van de Wetering
Editor-in-Chief: Mr Rudi Tinga
Education and Training: Maj Jeanne van Hal
Finance and International Projects: Envoy Harm Slomp
Finance, Accommodation and Dataprocessing: Mr Bert Barink

Music: Mr Roel van Kesteren
Officers' Affairs: Lt-Col Tineke Wolterink
Adult Ministries: see Field Programme Support
Women's Ministries: Comr Arda Frans (TPWM)
Lt-Col Tineke Wolterink (TSWM)
Youth: see Field Programme Support

DIVISIONS

Central: Piccolostraat 13, 1312 RC Almere;
tel: (36) 536 51 06; Maj Elsje Klarenbeek
North/East: Gein 27, 8032 BB Zwolle;
tel: (38) 452 67 13; fax: (38) 452 67 19;
Maj Teunis Scholtens
South: Wittebrem 22, 3068 TM Rotterdam;
tel: (10) 4557921; Maj Johannes A. den
Hollander

THE SALVATION ARMY MAIN FOUNDATION
Board of Administration
Chairman: Comr Roy Frans (TC)

Staff
Secretary: Lt-Col Theo Wolterink (CS)
Financial Sec: Envoy Harm Slomp
Managing Director: Envoy Harm Slomp (interim)

THE SALVATION ARMY SERVICES FOUNDATION
Board of Administration
Chairman: Comr Roy Frans (TC)
Vice-Chairman: Lt-Col Theo Wolterink (CS)
Official (non-voting) Sec: Maj Henny van Pelt
Members: Mrs L. M. Welschen-van der Hoek;
Mr G. L. Telling

Staff
Managing Director: Envoy Harm Slomp
Communications:
Domestic Affairs Staff/Personnel: Mr Arie M.
Rietveld
Fund-Raising and Marketing:
Financial and Economics: Mr Peter van der
Kist
Recycling: Capt Robert Paul Fennema
Sales and Supplies: Capt Robert Paul Fennema

RECYCLING SERVICES

Ettenseweg 6a, 4706 PB Roosendaal;
tel: (165) 376055; fax: (165) 376056
Depot: Hattem
Service Centres: Amsterdam, Dordrecht

SALES AND SERVICES (ReShare BV)
Spoordreef 10, 1315 GN Almere;
tel: (36) 539 82 08; fax: (36) 539 81 67

THE SALVATION ARMY FUND-RAISING FOUNDATION
Board of Administration
Chairman: Comr Roy Frans (TC)
Vice-Chairman: Lt-Col Theodoor Wolterink (CS)
Official (non-voting) Sec: Maj Hendrik van Pelt
Members: Mrs A. M. A. Bartels-Koene,
Mrs F. H. van Ham-Laning, Mr C. Hendriks,
Drs C. Bremmer, Mr J. de Widt, Mr F. B. A.
M. van Oss

Staff
Managing Director: Envoy Harm Slomp (interim)

*All activities of the Foundation are to be executed
by The Salvation Army Services Foundation.*

THE SALVATION ARMY FOUNDATION FOR WELFARE AND HEALTH CARE
Care for the Homeless (total acc 3,666): night
shelter (acc 649); day care (acc 772); 24-hour
shelter (acc 1,255); young people (acc 198);
supervised living (acc 792)
Substance Misuse Services (total acc 36):
residential (acc 20); supervised living (acc 16)
Probation Services (total capacity 937):
ambulatory programmes (718); day training
centres (acc 74); remand probation homes
(acc 105)
Health Care and Care for the Elderly (total
capacity 1,439): permanent stay (acc 381);
temporary stay (incl medical care of homeless)
(acc 217); day care (acc 41); ambulatory
programmes (incl home care) (555);
supervised living (acc 245)
Care for Children and Young People (total
acc 402): residential care (acc 313); day care
(acc 89)
Prevention and Social Rehabilitation Services
(total acc 877): ambulatory programmes
(acc 579); work coaching (acc 224); day care
(incl play groups) (acc 74)

Board of Administration
Chairman: Comr Roy Frans (TC)
Vice-Chairman: Lt-Col Theo Wolterink (CS)
Sec/Treasurer: Envoy Harm Slomp
Members: Envoy G. P. W. Jansen, Mr L. H. van
den Heuvel, Mr H. N. Hagoort, Mr F. van der
Meulen, Mrs. W. W. J. van Dalen-Schiphorst

Staff
Managing Director: Lt-Col Christina A. Voorham
Deputy Director: Mr Hermanus M. van
Teijlingen

The Netherlands and Czech Republic Territory

Administration and Information: Mr Johannes C. van Voorst, Mr Aart Hulleman
Issue Managers: Mr Marinus A. J. Timmer, Mr Josephus J. Sesink, Mr Jeroen Hoogteijling, Rev Johannes J. Blom
Information Manager: Mrs Gerdine van Harten
Controller:
Main Office: Spoordreef 10, 1315 GN Almere; tel: (36) 539 82 50; fax: (36) 534 07 10

Probation Services Leger des Heils Jeugdzorg & Reclassering
Central Office: Nieuwegracht 94, 3512 LX Utrecht; tel: (30) 232 64 70

Goodwill Centres, Amsterdam
Information: Rode Kruisstraat 24b, 1025 KN Amsterdam; tel: (20) 630 11 11

Goodwill Work, The Hague
Information: St Barbaraweg 4, 2516 BT Den Haag; tel: (70) 311 55 40

Centres for Living, Care and Welfare
Central Region
Information: Jan van Eijklaan 2-6, 3723 BC Bilthoven; tel: (30) 274 91 21
Northern Region
Information: Kwinkenplein 10-A, 9712 GZ Groningen; tel: (50) 317 26 70
South-Western Region
Information: Kromhout 110, 3311 RH Dordrecht; tel: (78) 632 07 00
Northern Holland
Information: Mariettahof 25, 2033 WS Haarlem; tel: (23) 553 39 33
Flevoland Province
Information: Spoordreef 12, 1315 GN Almere; tel: (36) 549 68 00
Gelderland-East Province (incl substance misuse services)
Information: Wilmersdorf 9, 7327 AD Apeldoorn; tel: (55) 53 80333
Limburg/Brabant
Information: Mariastraat 13, 6211 EP Maastricht; tel: (43) 350 33 84
Overijssel
Information: Eiffelstraat 1 – 117, 8013 RT Zwolle; tel. (38) 467 19 40
Twente/Achterhoek
Information: Molenstraat 30, 7514 DJ Enschede; tel: (53) 475 40 60
Veluwe/IJsselstreek
Information: Koekoeksweg 2C, 8084 M 't Harde; tel: (525) 65 96 90

Centre for Social Services, Rotterdam
Information: Kooikerweg 28, 3069 WP Rotterdam; tel: (10) 222 98 88

Child Care Centre, Utrecht/'t Gooi
UJL: Prins Frederiklaan 201, 3818 KC Amersfoort; tel: (33) 467 80 70

Hotel and Conference Centre 'Belmont'
Goorsteeg 66, 6718 TB Ede; tel: (31) 848 23 65 (50 twin-bedded rooms, 14 conference rooms acc varying from 12-375, during summer 96 extra beds available, in tents acc 160)

CZECH REPUBLIC

Officer-in-charge: Maj Pieter H. Dijkstra (18 Jun 2003)

National Headquarters: Petrzilkova 2565/23, 158 00 Praha 5; tel/fax: (00420) 251 106 424; email: info@armadaspasy.cz; web site: www.armadaspasy.cz

STATISTICS
(not included in statistics of The Netherlands)
Officers 20 **Envoys** 4 **Cadets** (1st Yr) 2 **Employees** 335
Corps 8 **Community Centres** 15 **Institutions** 17
Senior Soldiers 80 **Adherents** 49 **Junior Soldiers** 14

STAFF
Asst Leader: Maj Alida N. A. Dijkstra-Voorn
Asst to the Leaders: Pavla Vopeláková
National Director for Institutional Social Work: Envoy Premysl Kopecek
Asst to National Director for Institutional Social Work: Envoy Marta Kopecková
Training: Maj Philippa Smale
Finance: Mrs Hana Kosová

CENTRES
Hostels for Men and Women and Night Shelters
Brno: Mlýnská 25, 602 00 Brno; tel: 543 212 530 (acc 136)
Krnov: Csl armády 837 bcd, 794 01 Krnov; tel: 554 612 296 (acc 85, includes mothers and children)
Opava: Nákladní 24, 746 01 Opava; tel: 553 712 984 (acc 48)
Prague: Tusarova 60, 170 00 Praha 7; tel: 220 184 000 (acc 220)

The Koningskerk (The King's Church) in the centre of Amsterdam is crowded for the funeral service of Lieut-Colonel Alida Bosshardt, OF – the most famous Salvation Army officer in The Netherlands. For many years she had worked and lived among prostitutes and poor families in the city's red light district. The Mayor of Amsterdam paid tribute to her as 'The Angel of Amsterdam'. The service was broadcast live on television and edited repeats were featured for several days following the event.

Hostels for Men and Night Shelters

Havírov:
  Hostel, Na spojce 2, 736 01 Havírov;
    tel: 596 810 197 (acc 35)
  Night Shelter, Pod Svahem 1, Havírov- Šubark;
    tel: 596 881 007 (acc 24)
Karlovy Vary: Nákladní 7, 360 05 Karlovy Vary;
    tel: 353 569 267 (acc 45)
Opava: Nákladní 24, 746 01 Opava;
    tel: 553 712 984 (acc 48)
Ostrava: U Novych Válcoven 9, 709 00 Ostrava-
    Mariánské Hory; tel: 596 620 650 (acc 114)
Šumperk: Vikyrovicka 1495, Šumperk-Luže;
    tel: 583 224 634 (acc 35)

Homes for Mothers and Children

Havírov: Dvoráková 21/235, 736 01 Havírov;
    tel: 596 810 221 (acc 18 mothers plus children)
Krnov: Csl armády 837 bcd, 794 01 Krnov;
    tel: 554 612 296 (acc 85, includes hostel for
    men and women)
Ostrava: Gen Píky 25, Ostrava-Fifejdy 702 00;
    tel: 596 611 962 (acc women 30, mothers 10
    and 15-20 children)
Opava: Rybárská 86, 746 01 Opava;
    tel: 553 712 984 (acc mothers 11 children 33)

Alternative Punishment Programme

Opava: Nákladní 24, 746 01 Opava;
    tel: 553 712 984

Farm Rehabilitation Project

747 24 Strahovice 1; mobile: 737 215 396 (acc 4)

Elderly Persons Project

Ostrava-Kuncicky: Holvekova 38, 710 00
    Ostrava-Kuncicky; tel: 596 237 151 (acc 40)

Youth Centre

Brno-Bystrc: Kubickova 23, 635 00 Brno-Bystrc;
    tel: 546 221 756

Prison Work

Prague: Petržilkova 2565/23, 158 00 Praha 5;
    tel/fax: (00420) 737 215 427

NEW ZEALAND, FIJI AND TONGA TERRITORY

Territorial leaders:
Commissioners Garth and Merilyn McKenzie

Territorial Commander:
Commissioner Garth McKenzie
(1 June 2004)

Chief Secretary:
Colonel Robin Forsyth (1 June 2004)

Territorial Headquarters: 204 Cuba Street, Wellington, New Zealand

Postal address: PO Box 6015, Wellington 6001, New Zealand

Tel: [64] (04) 384 5649; fax: [64] (04) 802 6258; web site: www.salvationarmy.org.nz

On 1 April 1883 Salvation Army activities were commenced at Dunedin by Captain George Pollard and Lieutenant Edward Wright. Social work began in 1884 with a home for ex-prisoners. Work was begun officially in Fiji on 14 November 1973 by Captain Brian and Mrs Beverley McStay, and in Tonga on 9 January 1986 by Captain Tifare and Mrs Rebecca Inia.

Zone: South Pacific and East Asia
Countries included in the territory: Fiji, New Zealand, Tonga
'The Salvation Army' in Maori: Te Ope Whakaora
Languages in which the gospel is preached: English, Fijian, Hindi, Korean, Maori, Rotuman, Samoan, Tongan and Vietnamese
Periodical: *War Cry*

THE Territorial Strategic Mission Plan (2006-2010) increasingly drives The Salvation Army's activities and emphases.

Four goals provide a unifying focus, supporting the territory's mission of 'Caring for People, Transforming Lives and Reforming Society through God in Christ by the Holy Spirit's power': to grow all Salvationists as dynamic disciples; increase the number of new soldiers; take significant steps towards the eradication of poverty; be a connected, streamlined

mission-focused Army.

Twenty months of unbroken 24-7 prayer ran into October 2006 with 'New Zeal', an event that featured worship and teaching from local and international speakers. 24-7 prayer has become part of the regular rhythm of corps life in many places, with one New Zealand corps establishing the first 24-7 Prayer 'Boiler Room' in the southern hemisphere.

Tonga's new divisional headquarters was damaged in rioting at the close of 2006, just a few days before the building's official dedication. The Salvation Army was a force for peace, protecting a group of Chinese nationals under threat by some rioters, and found many other opportunities to minister to people in need.

The territory hosted the South Pacific and East Asia College for Officers at Booth College of Mission, Wellington (14 February - 12 March 2007). Twenty-nine delegates, including three translators, from 12 countries explored the themes of justice, mercy and faith.

Fair Trade products are promoted, and the Social Policy and Parliamentary Unit resources Salvationists and decision-makers on matters of social justice. Preventing human trafficking is high on the agenda, as is raising the level of public debate about rehabilitation in prisons and alternative punishment. The territory entered into a contract with the New Zealand Government to assist newly released prisoners who have few social supports.

Child sponsorship goes from strength to strength. Young people from Waitakere Corps (New Zealand) began by sponsoring one boy from Fiji in April 2002. The corps now sponsors 21 children around the world. In Tonga, a Sponsorship Church Parade saw 30 children and their families attend a special service. The desire is to not only care for these children but disciple them as well.

Young people took up the challenge to 'Make Change for Fiji and Tonga' by raising money for mission work in those Pacific Islands. This will be presented at a tri-territorial youth congress scheduled to take place in January 2008.

The territory has rolled out a database system called SAMIS (Service and Mission Information System) to keep track of people helped and services provided. This helps with the efficiency and effectiveness of service delivery and tracks outcomes related to discipleship.

There are promising signs of numerical growth as Salvationists across the territory work together as a united mission team. The territory has a big vision, big goals have been set, but ours is a big God!

STATISTICS

Officers 539 (active 346 retired 193) **Cadets** (1st Yr) 12 (2nd Yr) 7 **Employees** 2,779
Corps 93 **New Plants** 7 **Outposts** 3 **Mission Teams** 1 **Recovery Churches** 9 **Institutions** 65
Senior Soldiers 5,603 **Adherents** 1,610 **Junior Soldiers** 571
Personnel serving outside territory Officers 15 Layworkers 2

STAFF

Book Production: Maj Harold Hill
Moral and Social Issues Council: Maj Harold Hill
Overseas Development Consultant: Maj Daryl Crowden
Social Policy and Parliamentary Unit: Maj Ian Kilgour
Territorial Events Co-Ordinator: Mr David Smith

Business Administration: Maj Bruce Vyle
Audit: Mr Graeme Tongs
Finance: Capt Richard Morris
Information Technology: Mr Mark Bennett
Property: Mr Ian McLaren
Public Relations and Communications: Maj David Bennett
Trade: Maj Roger Horton

Personnel: Lt-Col Wilfred Arnold
  Asst (Admin): Maj Margaret Ousey
  Asst (Pastoral Care): Lt-Col Margaret Arnold
  Asst (Overseas Service): Maj Elaine Vyle
  Human Resources: Mr Paul Geoghegan
  Booth College of Mission:
    Principal: Maj Robert Donaldson
    School for Bible and Mission: Maj Garth Stevenson
    Centre for Leadership Development: Maj Robert Donaldson
    Education Consultant and Registrar: Maj Kingsley Sampson

Programme: Maj Ross Gower
  Asst: Maj Annette Gower
  Social Programme: Maj Campbell Roberts
  Creative Ministries and National Youth Bandmaster:
    Youth: Maj Barry Keane
    Candidates: Maj Janine Donaldson
    Planned Giving: Maj Sandra Mellsop
    SpiritSong: Vocal Leader Denise Hewitt
    Children's Ministries: Capt Jennifer Morris

Women's Ministries: Comr Merilyn McKenzie (TPWM) Col Shona Forsyth (TSWM)

DIVISIONS

Central: 204 Cuba St, PO Box 6421, Wellington 6141; tel: (04) 384 4713; fax: (04) 802 6267; email: cdhq@nzf.salvationarmy.org; Maj Rod Carey

Midland: 12 Vialou St, PO Box 500, Hamilton 3240; tel: (07) 839 2242; fax: (07) 839 2282; email: Midland_dhq@nzf.salvationarmy.org; Maj Lindsay Chisholm

Northern: 369 Queen St, PO Box 5035, Auckland 1001; tel: (09) 379 4150; fax: (09) 379 4152; email: ndhq@nzf.salvationarmy.org; Maj Brian Peddle

Southern: 71 Peterborough St, PO Box 25-207, Christchurch 8001; tel: (03) 377 0799; fax: (03) 377 3575; email: southern@nzf.salvationarmy.org; Maj Lyndon Buckingham

FIJI DIVISION

Headquarters: PO Box 14412, Suva, Fiji; tel: [679] 331 5177; fax: [679] 330 3112
Divisional Commander: Maj Gordon Daly; email: dhq_fiji@nzf.salvationarmy.org
Corps 10 Corps Plants 2 Outposts 4

Community and Family Services:
  Eastern: Grantham Rd, Suva; tel: (679) 337 2122

  Western: 38 Sukanaivalu Rd, Lautoka; tel: (679) 664 5471
Family Care Centres:
  Labasa: Sarwan Singh St, Nasea; tel: (679) 881 1898 (acc 16)
  Lautoka: 160 VM Pillai Rd, Rifle Range; tel: (679) 665 0952 (acc 16)
  Suva: 21 Spring St, Toorak; tel: (679) 330 5518 (acc 18)
Court and Prison Officers:
  Suva; tel: (679) 337 2122
  Lautoka; tel: (679) 665 0952/664 5471
Farm Project: Farm 80, Lomaivuna; tel: (679) 359 3679
Girls' Home: Mahaffy Dr, Suva; tel: (679) 331 3318 (acc 20)
Raiwai Hostel: (Hostel for young male tertiary students) Grantham Rd, Suva; tel: (679) 338 7438 (acc 20)
Red Shield House: (Hostel for young females) 37 Moala St, Suva; tel: (679) 338 1347 (acc 8)
Sewing Skills Programmes:
  Labasa: Lot 2 Batinikama, Siberia Rd; tel: (679) 881 4822
  Lautoka: 38 Sukanaivalu Rd, Waiyavi; tel: (679) 666 3712
  Suva: 50 MacGregor Rd; tel: (679) 3307 746
Tiny Tots Kindergartens:
  Ba: 6 Old Kings Rd, Yalalevu; tel: (679) 667 0155 (acc 15)
  Labasa: Lot 2 Batinikama, Siberia Rd; tel: (679) 881 4822 (acc 15)
  Lautoka: Waiyavi Centre, 38 Sukanaivalu Rd, Waiyavi; tel: (679) 666 3712 (acc 50)
  Lomaivuna: Farm 80; tel: (679) 360 1238
  Nadi: Lot 30-31, Goundar St; tel: (679) 670 0405 (acc 15)
  Suva Central: 56 MacGregor Rd; tel: (679) 330 7746 (acc 30)

School for Officer Training and Leadership Training
  tel: (679) 330 7749; fax: (679) 330 7010; email: SFOT_FIJI@nzf.salvationarmy.org

TONGA REGION

Regional Headquarters: Mossimani Building, Cnr Hala Fatafehi and Mateialona, Nuku'alofa, Tonga; tel: [676] 23-760, 27-835; email: rhq_tga@nzf.salvationarmy.org
Regional Commander: Maj Rex Johnson
Corps 4 Corps Plant 1

Social Services Centre: Vaha'akolo Rd, Longolongo, Nuku'alofa, Tonga
Court and Prison Work: Nuku'alofa

Addiction Programme: PO Box 1035,
Nuku'alofa; tel: (676) 23760;
email: rhq_tga@nzf.salvationarmy.org

Kindergartens:
Sopu, Nuku'alofa; tel: (676) 26370 (acc 30)
Kolovai; tel: (676) 11737 (acc 20)

Mobile Health Clinic: Popua Community

BOOTH COLLEGE OF MISSION (BCM)
**School for Officer Training (SFOT); Centre
for Leadership Development; School of
Bible and Mission:** 20 William Booth Grove,
Upper Hutt, PO Box 40-542, Upper Hutt;
tel: (04) 528 8628; fax: (04) 527 6900
Principal, BCM and SFOT: Maj Robert
Donaldson

FAMILY TRACING SERVICE
PO Box 6015, Wellington 6015;
tel: (04) 382 0710; fax: (04) 802 6257;
email: familytracing@nzf.salvationarmy.org

FARM
Jeff Memorial Farm, Kaiwera RD 2, Gore;
tel: (03) 205 3572

INDEPENDENT LIVING UNITS
Ashburton: Wilson Court, 251-255 Tancred St
(units 3)
Auckland: 353 Blockhouse Bay Rd (units 19)
Bell Block: Bingham Court, 46 Murray St
(units 10)
Blenheim: 35 George St (units 7)
Carterton: 204 High St South (units 8)
Christchurch: 794 Main North Rd, Belfast
(units 10)
Gisborne: Edward Murphy Village,
481 Aberdeen Rd (units 30)
Hamilton: Nawton Village, 57 Enfield St
(units 40)
Kapiti: 41 Bluegum Rd, Paraparaumu Beach
(units 18)
Mosgiel: Elmwood Retirement Village,
22 Elmwood Dr (units 30); 17 Cedar Cres
(units 30)
Oamaru: Glenside, 9 Arthur St (units 12)
Papakura: 91 Clevedon Rd (units 6)
Wellington: Summerset Units, Newtown: 182a
Owen St (units 11); 210, 212, 214 Owen St
(units 3); 226 Owen St (units 9)

OFFICERS' ACCOMMODATION
(under THQ)
Auckland: 9 Willcott St (units 6); 6d Liston St,
Northcote (unit 1); 19 Splendour Cl, Henderson
(unit 1); 10 Sydenham Rd, Mt Eden (unit 1)

Wellington: 176, 176a, 178, 178a Queens Dr,
Lyall Bay (units 4)

YOUTH CAMPS AND CONFERENCE CENTRES
Blue Mountain Lodge Christian Adventure
Centre: RD 1, Owhango, National Park;
tel: (07) 892 2630;
web site: www.bluemountainlodge.co.nz

SOCIAL SERVICES (under THQ)
Addiction and Supportive Accommodation Services
National Office: Level 2, 369 Queen St, PO Box
7342, Wellesley St, Auckland 1141;
tel: (09) 369 5143; fax: (09) 377 1249;
National Manager: Maj Lynette Hutson
email: lynette_hutson@nzf.salvationarmy.org

**Bridge Programme: Community and
Residential Programmes (Treatment of
Alcohol and Drug Dependency)**
Auckland Bridge Centre: PO Box 56-442,
7-15 Ewington Ave, Mt Eden, Auckland 1446;
tel: (09) 630 1491; fax: (09) 630 8395;
email: akbridge@xtra.co.nz (acc assessment 21,
treatment 16, day clients 7)
Manukau Bridge Centre: 16b Bakerfield Place,
PO Box 56 442, Manukau City;
tel: (09) 261 0887; fax: (09) 263 9325;
email: mkbridge@xtra.co.nz
Waitakere Bridge Centre: 17 James Laurie St,
PO Box 69 005, Glendene, Waitakere City;
tel: (09) 835 4069; fax: (09) 835 4690;
email: wkbridge@xtra.co.nz
Whangarei: Northland Bridge, PO Box 1746,
115 Bank St; tel: (09) 430 7500;
fax: (09) 430 7501
Christchurch: The Bridge Programme: PO Box
9070, Addington, 35 Collins St;
tel: (03) 338 4436; fax: (03) 338 4312 (acc 26)
Waikato: Bridge Programme: 25 Thackeray St,
Wellington: 22-26 Riddiford St, PO Box 6033,
Wellington; tel: (04) 389 6566;
fax: (04) 389 7110 (acc 24)
Dunedin: 44a Filleul St; tel: (03) 477 9853;
fax: (03) 477 1493 (acc 8)
Invercargill: 110 Leven St, PO Box 74;
tel: (03) 218 3094;

**Oasis Centres: Treatment Centres for
Gambling**
Auckland: PO Box 41-309, St Lukes, 726 New
North Rd; tel: (09) 846 0660;
fax: (09) 846 0440
Christchurch: PO Box 9070, Addington,

126 Bealey Ave; tel: (03) 365 9659;
fax: (03) 365 7585; email: oasisch@xtra.co.nz
Dunedin: 44 Filleul St; tel: (03) 477 9852;
fax: (03) 477 1493
Hamilton: 2nd Floor, Cecil House, Garden Pl;
Postal address: 25 Thackeray St;
tel: (07) 839 7053; fax: (07) 839 4428
Queenstown: 29 Camp St, PO Box 887,
Queenstown; tel: (03) 442 5103;
fax: (03) 442 9644
Wellington: 26 Riddiford St, PO Box 6033;
tel: (04) 389 6566; fax: (04) 389 7110

Community Addictions Programme

Invercargill: Social Service Centre, PO Box 74,
Cnr Gala and Leven Sts;
tel/fax: (03) 218 3094
Kaitaia: PO Box 391, 100 Commerce St;
tel: (09) 408 3362; fax: (09) 408 3365
Tauranga: PO Box 164, 375 Cameron Rd;
tel: (07) 578 5505; fax: (07) 578 4536

Supportive Accommodation Services

Auckland: Epsom Lodge: PO Box 26-098,
18 Margot St, Epsom, Auckland 1344;
tel: (09) 524 5675; fax: (09) 524 9604
(acc men 90)
Christchurch: Addington Social Services Centre:
PO Box 9057, 62 Poulson St, Addington,
Christchurch 8002; tel: (03) 338 5154;
fax: (03) 338 4390 (acc 90)
Invercargill: PO Box 74, Cnr Gala and Leven
Sts; tel/fax: (03) 218 3094 (acc 35)
Temuka: Bramwell Booth House (Intellectual
Disability): PO Box 57, Milford Rd;
tel: (03) 615 9570; fax: (03) 615 9571 (acc 18)
Wellington: (Intellectual Disability) PO Box
6033, 26 Riddiford St; tel: (04) 389 0594;
fax: (04) 389 1130 (acc 12)

Reintegration Services

Christchurch: 62 Poulson St, PO Box 9057,
Addington, Christchurch 8002;
tel: (03) 338 2643; fax: (03) 338 4390
Wellington: PO Box 40542, Upper Hutt 5140;
tel: (04) 529 7701; fax: (04) 527 6900

Mothercraft Centre

Bethany: 35 Dryden St, Grey Lynn, Auckland
1002; tel: (09) 376 1324; fax: (09) 376 1307;
web site: www.bethanycentre.org.nz
(acc antenatal 14, mothers and babies 7)

Employment Plus

National Office: 204 Cuba St, PO Box 6015,
Wellington 6001; tel: (04) 382 0714;

fax: (04) 382 0711; toll free: 0800 437 587
National Manager: Mr George Borthwick;
email: g.borthwick@eplus-salvationarmy.
org.nz
National Mission Directors: Majs Merilyn
and Kevin Goldsack; email:
merilyn_goldsack@nzf.salvationarmy.org.nz;
kevin_goldsack@nzf.salvationarmy.org.nz
Finance Service Bureau: 12 Vialou St, PO Box
5347, Frankton, Hamilton; tel: (07) 834 3195;
fax: (07) 834 3198

Regions

Central: 148 Manchester St, PO Box 569,
Fielding; tel: (06) 323 9017; fax: (06) 323 9620;
email: a.adams@eplus-salvationarmy.org.nz
Midland: 12 Vialou St, PO Box 5139, Hamilton;
tel: (07) 834 3198; fax: (07) 838 0376; email:
t.mcloughlin@nzf.salvationarmy.org.nz;
p.rodgers@eplus-salvationarmy.org.nz
Northern: 12 Kaka St, PO Box 1524, Whangarei;
tel: (09) 438 4470; fax: (09) 438 6500;
email: a.carrington@eplus-salvationarmy.org.nz
Southern: 160 Crawford St, Dunedin, PO Box 784,
Dunedin; tel: (03) 476 7111; fax: (03) 476 7188;
email: b.lee@eplus-salvationarmy.org.nz;
d.dixon@eplus-salvationarmy.org.nz

Services for Older People

National Office: 204 Cuba St, PO Box 6015,
Wellington 6001; tel: (04) 382 0742;
fax: (04) 382 0711

Home Care

Business Centre: 71 Seddon Rd, PO Box 9417,
Hamilton; tel: (07) 834 3967;
fax: (07) 834 8156;
email: homecare.hamilton@xtra.co.nz
Service Centres: Auckland (2), Hamilton,
Paeroa, Tauranga

SOCIAL SERVICES (under DHQ)
Community Ministries

Aranui: 32 Portsmouth St; tel/fax: (03) 388 1072
Auckland City: PO Box 27-153, 691 Mt Albert
Rd, Royal Oak; tel: (09) 625 7940;
fax: (09) 625 6045
Blenheim: Cnrs George and Henry Sts, Blenheim;
tel: (03) 578 0862; fax: (03) 578 0990
Christchurch: PO Box 1015, 32 Lichfield St;
tel: (03) 366 8128; fax: (03) 366 8295
Dunedin: 44a Filluel St; tel: (03) 477 9852;
fax: (03) 477 1493
Feilding: 124 Manchester St; tel: (06) 323 4718;
email: feilding_corps@nzf.salvationarmy.org
Foxton: Avenue Rd; tel: (06) 363 8669;
email: foxton_corps@nzf.salvationarmy.org

Gisborne: PO Box 1086, 389 Gladstone Rd;
tel: (06) 868 9468; fax: (06) 868 1395;
email: Gisborne_corps@nzf.salvationarmy.org

Gore: 21 Irwell St; tel: (03) 208 4443

Hamilton: The Nest, PO Box 8020, Cnr Ohaupo
Rd and Kahikatea Dr; tel: (07) 843 4509;
fax: (07) 843 3865; incl Mary Bryant Family
Home, 24 Ohaupo Rd; tel: (07) 843 4509;
email: nest_cfs@nzf.salvationarmy.org (acc 8)

Hastings: PO Box 999, Cnr Warren St and Ave
Rd; tel: (06) 876 5771; fax (06)870 9331;
email: hastings_corps@nzf.salvationarmy.org

Hornby: 23 Manurere St, Hornby, Christchurch
4; tel: (03) 349 6268; fax: (03) 349 6268

Hutt City: Cnr Kings Cres and Cornwall St,
PO Box 30745, Lower Hutt; tel: (04) 570 0273;
fax: (04) 570 0274;
email: huttcity_corps@nzf.salvationarmy.org
web site: www.sacrossroads.org.nz

Invercargill: PO Box 252, Tay St;
tel/fax: (03) 214 0223

Linwood: 177 Linwood Ave; tel: (03) 389 3723

Manukau City: PO Box 76-075, 16b Bakerfield Pl,
Manukau City; tel: (09) 262 2332;
fax: (09) 262 4103

Motueka: PO Box 85, Motueka; tel: (03) 528 9338;
fax: (03) 528 9642

Napier: PO Box 3086, 56 Tait Dr;
tel: (06) 844 4941; fax: (06) 844 8483:
email: napier_corps@nzf.salvationarmy.org

Nelson: 57 Rutherford St, PO Box 22;
tel: (03) 548 4807; fax: (03) 548 4810

North Shore City: 407 Glenfield Rd, Glenfield,
Auckland, PO Box 40555, Glenfield;
tel: (09) 441 2554; fax: (09) 441 7599

North Taranaki: PO Box 384, Cnr Powderham
and Dawson Sts, New Plymouth;
tel: (06) 758 9338; fax (06) 758 2325;
email:
northtaranaki_corps@nzf.salvationarmy.org

Palmerston North: 431 Church St, PO Box 869,
Palmerston North; tel: (06) 358 7455;
fax: (06) 358 2314; email: palmerston-
north_cfs@nzf.salvationarmy.org

Porirua East: PO Box 53-025, Cnr Warspite Ave
and Fantame St; tel: (04) 235 6266;
fax: (04) 235 6482;
email: porirua_cfs@nzf.salvationarmy.org

Queenstown: PO Box 887, Camp St;
tel: (03) 442 5103; fax: (03) 442 9644

Rotorua: 1115 Haupapa St; tel: (07) 348 8113;
fax: (07) 346 8075; email:
rotorua_cfs@nzf.salvationarmy.org

Sydenham: 17 Southampton St;

tel: (03) 331 7483; fax: (03) 332 8395

Tauranga: 375 Cameron Rd; tel: (07) 578 5505;
fax: (07) 578 4536; email: tauran-
ga_corps@nzf.salvationarmy.org

Timaru: 206 Wai-iti Rd, Timaru;
tel/fax: (03) 684 7139

Tokoroa: PO Box 567; tel: (07) 886 9812;
fax 886 9512; email:
tokoroa_cfs@nzf.salvationarmy.org

Upper Hutt: 695 Fergusson Dr; tel: (04) 528 6745;
email: upper_hutt_corps@nzf.salvationarmy.org

Wairarapa: PO Box 145 Carterton, 204-210 High
St South, Carterton; tel: (06) 379 7176;
fax: (06) 379 6109; email: wairara-
pa_corps@nzf.salvationarmy.org

Waitakere City: PO Box 21-708 Henderson,
7-9 View Rd; tel: (09) 837 4471;
fax: (09) 837 1246

Wellington: 26 Riddiford St, Newtown;
tel: (04) 389 0594; fax: (04) 389 1130;
Counselling Service: 26 Riddiford St, Newtown;
tel: (04) 389 0594; fax: (04) 389 1130;
email: wellingtoncfs@nzf.salvationarmy.org
Youth Services: 1 Ghuznee St;
tel: (04) 384 6119; fax: (04) 384 6115

Early Childhood Education Centres

Gisborne: 'Noah's Young Ones': PO Box 1086,
389 Gladstone Rd, Gisborne;
tel: (06) 868 9468; fax: (06) 868 1395
(roll 24)

Hamilton: The Nest Educare: PO Box 8020,
Cnr Ohaupo Rd and Kahikatea Dr;
tel: (07) 843 4066; fax: (07) 843 3865
(roll 50)

Masterton: Cecilia Whatman Early Childhood
Education Centre: 132-140 Ngaumutawa Rd;
tel: (06) 378 7316 (roll 50)

Upper Hutt: William Booth Educare:
PO Box 40-542 Upper Hutt;
tel: (04) 528 8628 527 6929 (roll 25)

Waitakere: Kidz Matter 2US: PO Box 21-708,
Henderson; tel: (09) 837 4471;
fax: (09) 837 1246 (roll 25)

Wellington: Britomart ECEC: 126 Britomart St,
Berhampore, Wellington 6002;
tel: (04) 389 9781 (roll 28)

COURT AND PRISON SERVICE

National Consultant: 1a Sproston Ave, Ellerslie,
Auckland; tel: (09) 262 2332;
fax: (09) 262 4103; mobile: 027 478 9758

Auckland: PO Box 27 153, Mt Roskill;
tel: (09) 916 9267; fax: (09) 309 9751

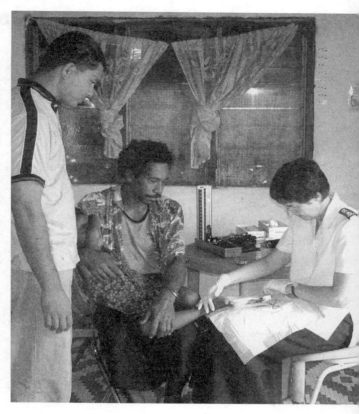

New Zealand officer Major Tanya Dunn, a registered nurse, holds a health clinic in Tonga while stationed on those islands as Regional Health Officer. A mobile bus funded by women's ministries groups in New Zealand means The Salvation Army can attend to the health needs of more people living in extremely poor areas of Tonga.

Alexandra: 21 Aronui Rd; tel: (03) 448 9436

Blenheim: PO Box 417; tel: (03) 578 0862; fax: (03) 578 0990

Christchurch: PO Box 25 207; tel: (03) 377 0799; fax: (03) 377 3575

Dunedin: 44a Filleul St; tel: (03) 477 9852; fax: (03) 477 1493; mobile: 027 496 7194

Gore: 21 Irwell St; tel/fax: (03) 208 4443

Hamilton: tel: (07) 843 4509; fax (07) 843 3865; mobile: 027 280 9673

Invercargill: 14 Trent St; tel/fax: (03) 217 1131

North Shore: PO Box 40 034, Glenfield; tel: (09) 441 2554; fax (09) 441 7599

Manukau: PO Box 76 075; tel/fax: (09) 252 3473; mobile: (027) 478 4429

Kaitaia: PO Box 391; tel: (09) 408 3362; fax (09) 408 3362

Lower Hutt/Upper Hutt: PO Box 31 363, Lower Hutt; tel: (04) 389 0594; fax: (04) 389 1130

Palmerston North: PO Box 869; tel/fax: (06) 353 3459

Porirua: PO Box 53 025, Porirua East; tel: (04) 914 3260; fax (04) 914 3262

Timaru: 206 Wai-iti Rd; tel/fax: (03) 684 7139

Waitakere: mobile (027 2430586

Wellington: PO Box 5094; tel: (04) 918 8063; fax (04) 918 8098

Westport: tel: (03) 789 8085; fax: (03) 789 8058

Whangarei: tel: (09) 983 5460

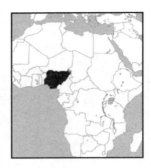

NIGERIA TERRITORY

Territorial leaders:
**Commissioners Jean B. and
Véronique Ludiazo**

Territorial Commander:
Commissioner Jean B. Ludiazo
(1 Feb 2007)

Chief Secretary:
Lieut-Colonel Festus Oloruntoba (1 Sep 2007)

Territorial Headquarters: 6 Shipeolu St, Igbobi, Shomolu, Lagos

Postal address: Box 3025, Shomolu, Lagos, Nigeria

Tel/fax: [234] (1) 774 9125; email: Nigeria@NIG.salvationarmy.org

Salvation Army operations began in Nigeria in 1920 when Lieut-Colonel and Mrs George H. Souter landed in Lagos, to be followed later by Staff-Captain and Mrs Charles Smith, with 10 West Indian officers.

Zone: Africa
Country included in the territory: Nigeria
'The Salvation Army' in Yoruba: Ogun Igbala Na; in Ibo: Igwe Agha Nzoputa; in Efik: Nka Erinyana; in Edo: Iyo Kuo Imienfan; in Urhobo: Ofovwi re Arhc Na; in Hausa: Soldiogi Cheta
Languages in which the gospel is preached: Edo, Efik/Ibibio, English, Hausa, Ibo, Ijaw, Calabari, Tiv, Urhobo, Yoruba
Periodicals: *Salvationist, The Shepherd, The War Cry*

GREAT blessing, encouragement and challenge came from the visit of Commissioners Amos and Rosemary Makina (International Secretary, Africa, and Zonal Secretary for Women's Ministries). As Salvationists gathered in rallies and officers' councils, the presence of the Holy Spirit was a living experience.

The centenary year of the Home League was commemorated with week-long celebrations that included public lectures, symposia, a drama on child abuse and human trafficking – even a fun fair. The WWW slogan

– 'While Women Weep' – was prominently and frequently displayed.

The presentation of nine cadets at the training college was a 'life-giving' Sunday for the territory. The young and dynamic four couples and single cadet in the Witnesses for Christ Session were enthusiastically welcomed.

One of the biggest meetings in the year under review was the Territorial Men's Fellowship Congress held at Akure, in Ondo State. The State Governor was represented by his deputy, who declared the congress open and with other State Cabinet members joined in the opening worship. The congress brought together men of different status in life; many testified that it was a time of spiritual refreshment.

Salvationists from across the country gathered to bid farewell to Commissioners Stuart and Hope Mungate, who had been outstanding territorial leaders. Every effort is being made by new leaders Commissioners Jean and Véronique Ludiazo to ensure the achievement of the territory's faith goals and themes: 'Mission and Vision'; 'Press on Church Planting'; 'The Great Commission – not Great Omission'.

Issues relating to the territory's growth and development were identified at the Divisional Leaders Conference conducted by the territorial commander and the way forward was fashioned according to the Holy Spirit's guidance.

A leadership development seminar led by Commissioner Linda Bond (Secretary for Spiritual Life Development, IHQ) brought together 25 officers of various ranks and appointments, for whom it proved a rewarding experience.

It was thrilling for the territory to welcome Colonel Robert Redhead from Canada, to lead the Territorial Music Conference. This week-long event was rounded off with a festival, with Salvationists and non-Salvationists alike being attracted by the ministry of Christian music.

STATISTICS

Officers 422 (active 337 retired 85) **Cadets** 9 **Employees** 400
Corps 173 **Societies and Outposts** 169 **Institutions** 19 **Schools** 41 **Clinics** 19

Senior Soldiers 27,811 **Adherents** 3,996 **Junior Soldiers** 8,850
Personnel serving outside territory Officers 4

STAFF

Business Administration: Maj Friday Ayanam
Editor/Literary: Maj Lydia Omokaro
Extension Training Officer: Capt Michael Olatunde
Field Programme: Maj Joseph Akpan
Personnel: Maj Cornelius K. Ajubiga
Prison Chaplain: Maj Benson Erhuwumnsee
Property: Lazarus Akpadiaha
Public Relations: Maj O. Mgbebuihe
Social: Maj Ebenezer O. Abayomi
HIV/Aids: Maj G. Omokaro
Sponsorship: Maj Comfort Abayomi
Training: Maj Chika B. Ezekwere
Women's Ministries: Comr Véronique Ludiazo (TPWM) Lt-Col Gloria Oloruntoba (TSWM) Maj Caroline Ajubiga (THLS) Maj Mary Adejoro (TLOM), Maj Patience Akpan (Development and Young Women's Sec)
Youth and Candidates: Maj Maurice Akpabio

DIVISIONS

Akwa Ibom Central: c/o Afia Nisit PA, via Uyo; Maj Etim Udo
Akwa Ibom East: PO Box 20, Ikot Ubo, via Eket; Maj Edet Essien
Akwa Ibom South West: c/o Abak PO Box 23, Abak; Capt Udoh Uwak
Akwa Ibom West: PO Box 47, Etinan; Maj Smart Umoh
Anambra East: Umuchu; Maj Edwin Okorougo
Anambra West: 5 Urenebo St, Housing Estate, PO Box 1168, Onitsha, Anambra State; Maj Stephen Uzoho
Ibadan: PO Box 261, Ibadan, Oyo State; Capt Michael Sijuade
Imo Central: based at Orogwe-Owerri; Maj Paul Onyekwere
Lagos: PO Box 2640, Surulere, Lagos State; Maj Patrick Orasibe
Ondo/Ekiti: PO Box 51, Akure, Ondo State; Maj Michael Oyesanya

DISTRICTS

Abia: 2-8 Market Rd, PO Box 812, Aba, Abia State; Maj Simon Ekpendu
Badagry: PO Badagry, Lagos State; Maj Joseph Ogunde
Cross River: PO Box 11, Calabar, Cross River State; tel: (087) 220284; Maj Samuel Edung
Edo/Delta: PO Box 108, Benin City, Edo State; Maj Emmanuel Agazie

Egba: PO Box 46, Ado Odo, Ogun State;
Maj Raphael Ogundahunsi
Imo North: PO Box 512, Akokwa;
Maj Bramwell Anozie
Northern: PO Box 512, Jos, Plateau State;
Maj Paul Dim
Rivers: PO Box 1161, Port Harcourt, Rivers
State; Capt Joseph Mbagwu

SECTIONS
Akwa Ibom South East: PO Box 25 Ikot Abasi;
Maj Kennedy Inyang
Enugu/Ebonyi: Enugu, PO Box 1454,
4 Moorehouse St, Ogui, Enugu State;
Maj Godspower Sampson

TRAINING COLLEGE
4 Shipeolu St, Shomolu, Igbobi, Lagos
(PO Box 17); tel: (01) 774 9125

SOCIAL SERVICES
Corps-based Prison Ministry
Afaha Eket Corps Prison Work, Agbor Corps,
Badagry Prison Work, Benin Central Prison
Work, Ibadan Central Corps, Port Harcourt
Corps Prison Team

THQ-based Prison Ministry
Badagry Prison, Ikoyi Prison, Kirikiri Maximum
Security, Kirikiri Minimum Security, Kirikiri
Women's Prison

HIV/Aids Action Centre and Voluntary Counselling and Testing Centre
11 Odunlami St, PO Box 125, Lagos

Medical Centres
Ado Odo Medical Centre: Ado Odo Corps,
PO Box 46, Ado Odo, Ogun State (acc 2)
Gbethromy Training and Medical Centre:
c/o Badagry PO, Badagry, Lagos State (acc 8)
Iyara Health Centre: c/o Ado Irele, Ondo State
(acc 3)
Lagos Central Corps Clinic: 11 Odunlami St,
PO Box 125, Lagos State (acc 2)
Nda Nsit Clinic/Maternity: Nda Nsit Corps,
via Uyo, Akwa Idom State (acc 2)
Nkoro Corps Mobile Clinic: Nkoro Corps,
via Boni PO Box, Rivers State (acc 4)
Ubrama Health Centre/Clinic: Ubrama PO Box
Ahoada Alaga, Rivers State
Umucheke Corps Clinic: via Uruala PO, Ideato
L/G. A., Imo State (acc 4)

Social Centres/Institutions/Programmes
Akai Children's Home: PO Box 1009, Eket,

Akwa Ibom State (acc 35)
Benin Rehabilitation Centre: 20A First East
Circular Rd, PO Box 108, Benin City,
Edo State (acc 17)
Oji River Rehabilitation Centre: Oji River PO,
via Enugu, Enugu State (acc 64)
Orphans/Vulnerable Centre/Orphans Psycho-
Social Centre – Akai: PO Box 1009, Eket
Akwa Ibom State

SCHOOLS
Nursery
Aba Corps, Agbor Corps, Akai Corps, Akokwa
Corps, Amauzari Corps, Benin Corps,
Ibughubu Corps, Ikot Inyang Eti, Ile Ife
Corps, Ivue Corps, Jos Corps, Mpape Corps,
Onitsha Corps, Osumenyi Corps, Somorika
Corps, Suleja, Umucheke Corps, Umuchu
Corps, Umudike Corps

Primary
Aba Corps, Akai, Amauzari Corps, Benin Corps,
Ile Ife, Ikot Inyang Eti, Ivue Corps, Jos Corps,
Mpape Corps, Onitsha Corps, Somorika Corps,
Suleja

VOCATIONAL TRAINING CENTRES
Afia Nsit-Nsit VTC: Afia Nsit-Nsit Corps,
PO Box 8, Afia Nsit Urua Nko, Akwa Ibom
State (acc 8)
Abak Training Centre: Abak Corps, PO Box 23,
Abak, Akwa Ibom State (acc 4)
Amauzari VTC: Amauzari Corps, via Owerri PO,
Imo State (acc 4)
Enugu VTC: Enugu Corps, 4 Moorhouse St,
PO Box 1454, Ogui, Enugu State (acc 6)
Ibesit Training Centre: Ibesit Corps, Anang PA,
Ukanafun LGA, Akwa Ibom State (acc 3)
Ikot Okobo Training Centre: PO Box 493, Eket,
Akwa Ibom State (acc 156)
Ilesha VTC: Ilesha Corps, PO Box 91, Ilesha,
Oyo State (acc 30)
Ile-Ife VTC: Ile-Ife Corps, PO Box 113, Ile-Ife,
Oyo State
Orogwe VTC: Orogwe Corps, via Owerri PO,
Imo State (acc 235)
Supare VTC: Supare Corps, PMB 257,
via Ikare Akoko, Ondo State (acc 30)
Umuogo VTC: Umuogo Corps, c/o Amuzu PA,
via Owerri, Imo State (acc 8)

NORWAY, ICELAND AND THE FÆROES TERRITORY

Territorial leaders:
Commissioners Carl and Gudrun Lydholm

Territorial Commander:
Commissioner Carl Lydholm (11 Jul 2005)

Chief Secretary:
Lieut-Colonel Clive Adams (1 Jul 2007)

Territorial Headquarters: Kommandør T I Øgrims plass 4, 0165 Oslo, Norway

Postal address: Box 6866, St Olavs Plass, 0130 Oslo, Norway

Tel: [47] 22 99 85 00; fax: [47] 22 20 84 49; email: nor.leadership@frelsesarmeen.no

Web site: www.frelsesarmeen.no

Commissioners Hanna Ouchterlony and George Scott Railton with Staff-Captain and Mrs Albert Orsborn 'opened fire' in Oslo (Kristiania) on 22 January 1888. Work began in Iceland on 12 May 1895, pioneered by Adjutant Christian Eriksen, Captain Thorstein Davidsson and Lieutenant Lange, and spread to The Færoes in 1924.

Zone: Europe
Countries included in the territory: Iceland, Norway, The Færoes
'The Salvation Army' in Norwegian: Frelsesarmeen; in Icelandic: Hjálpraedisherinn; in Færoese: Frelsunarherurin
Languages in which the gospel is preached: Færoese, Icelandic, Norwegian
Periodicals: *Herópid* (Icelandic), *FAbU nytt, Krigsropet, Frelsesofficeren* (Norwegian)

THERE was a new venue for the annual congress. After being held in a huge sports hall for many years, the event was moved to a large church in Oslo, and with gatherings for all generations taking place under the same roof there was a strong spirit of unity.

Around 1,200 Salvationists and friends almost filled the church for the series of meetings around the theme 'Being Together'. General Shaw Clifton and Commissioner Helen Clifton brought inspiration with their preaching and presence, and the mercy seat was used by large numbers of people in each gathering.

The training college welcomed 11 new cadets representing all three countries in the territory; four came from the Faroes, the smallest country (about 50,000 inhabitants). A Bible school offering one-year studies in connection with the training college was opened and students have been studying alongside the cadets.

Plans are going ahead to develop a Salvation Army academy, gathering all the territory's education programme at one location.

A cooperation with two different faculties of theology was developed at the training college for accredited studies. One of these – 'The Salvation Army, its History, Theology and Spirituality' – was taught with non-Salvationist students coming to the training college; the other – 'Diakonia (The Service of Christ)' – was taught at the University of Oslo, where cadets were in attendance.

Teaching staff were from both the university and The Salvation Army. This cooperation was extended to officers' continuing education.

The territory's group of 209 scouts who travelled to The Netherlands for a Salvation Army scouts' and guides' world jamboree found new friends and inspiration for the future of scouting. An exchange programme for youth resulted in three young people from Peru and two from Norway working and living together for a year (six months in each country) to deepen understanding of their different cultures.

'Solheimsviken' – the corps that was started in 2001 in a troubled area of Bergen – was given a prize from the local authorities for its idealistic youth work that helped reduce the crime rate among youths in the area.

The territory also received a reputation award, rating The Salvation Army above all government institutions, other organisations and non-governmental organisations.

A renewed focus on sports ministry was the outcome of the territory's mission team participating in the FIFA World Cup events in Germany.

A consultation process to find the future direction and goal for the Army's mission and work began with a day's gathering of representatives from the whole territory – officers, soldiers, and employees. This was followed by an extended leaders' conference before the customary leaders' conference. The process proved so successful it will continue in coming years.

STATISTICS
Officers 436 (active 194 retired 242) **Cadets** 1 **Employees** 1,975
Corps 115 **Outposts** 289 **Institutions** 37 (including slum posts) **Centre for Deaf and Blind** 1 **Industrial Centres/Second-hand Shops** 45
Senior Soldiers 5,680 **Adherents** 1,223 **Junior Soldiers** 60
Personnel serving outside territory Officers 24

STAFF
Sec for Business Administration: Maj Jan Risan
Financial Sec: Maj Jan Peder Fosen
Chief Accountant: Mr Egil Hognerud
Communication/Information/Marketing: Mr Andrew Hannevik
Missionary Projects: Maj Eli Nodland Hagen
Property: Mr Dag Tellefsen
'Sally Ann' – Fair Trade:
  Sally Ann Norway Ltd:
    email: sallyann@sallyann.no
    web site: www.sallyann.no
    Manager: Mrs Sissel Skogly
    Chair of Board: Maj Jan Risan
    Shop: Kirkeveien 62, 0330 Oslo; Ingrid Elisabeth Hagen (shop manager)

Sec for Personnel: Maj Lise O. Luther

Sec for Field Programme: Maj Jan Øystein Knedal
  Asst Sec for Field Programme: Maj Bernt Olaf Ørsnes
Community: Maj Birgit T. Fosen
Music: Maj Jan Harald Hagen
Over 60s: Maj Leif-Erling Fagermo

Norway, Iceland and The Færoes Territory

Study: Mr Eiliv Herikstad
Territorial Band: B/M John Philip Hannevik
Youth: Maj Lisbeth Welander

Women's Ministries: Comr Gudrun Lydholm
(TPWM) Lt-Col Marianne Adams (TSWM)
Maj Brit Knedal (Home and Family)

Sec for Social Services: Maj Elisabeth Henne
Alcohol and Drug Rehabilitation:
Maj Hildegard A. Ørsnes
Children and Family Homes: Mrs Lindis Evja
Day Care Centres for Children: Mrs Anne-
Dorthe Nodland Aasen
Investigation: Maj Erling Levang
Work Rehabilitation and Recycling: Mr Thor
Fjellvang

THQ
Executive Sec for TC: Maj Inger Marit
Nygård
Editor: Mrs Hilde Dagfinrud Valen
Training: Maj Gro Merete Berg

DIVISIONS

Central: Borggt 2, PO Box 2869, Tøyen, 0608
Oslo; tel: 23 24 49 20; fax: 23 24 49 21;
Maj Frank Gjeruldsen
Eastern: Kneika 11, PO Box 40, 3056
Solbergelva; tel: 32 87 12 90; fax: 32 87 12 01;
Maj Arne Undersrud
Midland: Knausv 12, Smeby, PO Box 3002,
2318 Hamar; tel: 62 52 21 83; fax: 62 54 91 08;
Maj Brith-Mari Heggelund
Northern: Bjørkvn 12, PO Box 8255 Jakobsli,
7458 Trondheim; tel: 73 57 14 20;
fax: 73 57 16 93; Maj Solfrid Bakken
North Norway: Skolegt 6, PO Box 177,
9252 Tromsø; tel: 77 68 83 70; fax: 77 68 81 51;
Maj Paul-William Marti
Western: Kongsgt 50, PO Box 553,
4003 Stavanger; tel: 51 56 41 60;
fax: 51 56 41 61; Maj Per Arne Pettersen

TRAINING COLLEGE

1385 Asker: Brendsrudtoppen 40; tel: 66 76 49 70;
fax: 66 76 49 71

UNDER THQ
Jeløy Folk High School
1516 Moss: Nokiavn 30b, Folk High School;
tel: 69 91 10 70; fax: 69 91 10 80

ICELAND REGION

Kirkjurstræti 2, IS 121 Reykjavik;
tel: (354)561 3203, fax: (354) 561 3315; Maj
Anne Marie Reinholdtsen

Convalescent Home: Skólabraut 10, PO Box
115, IS-172 Seltjarnarnes; tel: [354] 561 2090;
fax: [354] 561 2089
Guest Home: PO Box 866, IS-121 Reykjavik;
tel: [354] 561 3203; fax: [354] 561 3315

THE FÆROES DISTRICT
(under THQ)
Torsgøta 19, PO Box 352, FO-110 Torshavn,
Færøyene; tel: (00298) 31 21 89;
fax: (00298) 31 41 89; Maj Samuel Jakob
Joensen
Hostel: FO-100 Torshavn, N Winthersgt 3;
tel: (00298) 31 73 93

SOCIAL SERVICES
Head Office: Kommandør T I Øgrims plass 4
0165 Oslo; tel: 22 99 85 00; fax: 22 99 85 84

Childrens' and Youths' Homes
3028 Drammen: Bolstadhagen 61;
tel: 32 20 45 80; fax: 32 20 45 81
1441 Drøbak: Nils Carlsensgt 31;
tel: 64 90 51 30; fax: 64 91 51 31
1112 Oslo: Nordstrandsvn 7; tel: 23 16 89 10;
fax: 22 29 20 85
2021 Skedsmokorset: Flesvigs vei 4;
tel: 63 87 44 19; fax: 63 87 41 77
4011 Stavanger: Vidarsgt 4; tel: 51 52 11 49;
fax: 51 52 66 31
7037 Trondheim: Øystein Møylas veg 20 B;
tel: 73 95 44 33, fax: 73 95 44 39
1540 Vestby: Soldammen, Svingen;
tel: 64 98 04 70; fax: 64 98 04 71

Day Care Centres for Children
1385 Asker: Brendsrudtoppen 60; tel: 66 78 74 86;
fax: 66 79 02 64
5011 Bergen: Skottegt 16; tel: 55 23 08 83;
fax: 55 23 47 45
1441 Drøbak: Nils Carlsensgt 31; tel: 64 93 15 09;
fax: 64 93 15 73
0664 Oslo: Regnbuevn 2C; tel: 23 03 93 30,
fax: 23 03 93 39

Family Centres
3023 Drammen: Home-Start Family Contact,
Landfalløya 78; tel: 32 83 39 93;
fax: 32 89 74 72
0487 Oslo: Kapellvn 61; tel: 22 09 86 20,
fax: 22 09 86 21

Nursing Homes
0661 Oslo: Ensjøtunet, Malerhaugvn 10b;
tel: 22 57 66 30; fax: 22 67 09 34

Old People's Welfare Centre

0661 Oslo: Malerhaugvn 10b; tel: 22 57 66 30;
fax: 22 67 09 34

Slum and Goodwill Centres

6005 Ålesund: Giskegt 27; tel: 70 12 18 05;
fax: 70 12 18 05

5808 Bergen: Ladegårdsgt 21; tel: 55 56 34 70;
fax: 55 56 34 71

0656 Oslo: Borggt 2; tel: 23 03 74 494004

Hostels

5812 Bergen: Bakkegt 7; tel: 55 30 22 85,
fax: 55 30 22 90

5054 Bergen: Bjørnsonsgt 4; tel: 55 20 56 00;
fax: 55 20 56 01

8001 Bodø: Kongensgt 16; tel: 75 52 23 38;
fax: 75 52 23 39

5501 Haugesund: Sørhauggt 215;
tel: 52 72 77 01; fax: 52 72 35 30

0561 Oslo: Heimen, Heimdalsgt 27 A;
tel: 23 21 09 60; fax: 22 68 00 98

0656 Oslo: Schweigaardsgt 70; tel: 23 24 39 00;
fax: 23 24 39 09

0354 Oslo: Sporveisgt 33; tel: 22 95 73 50;
fax: 22 95 73 51

3111 Tønsberg: Farmannsvn 26; tel: 33 31 54
09; fax: 33 31 07 74

7041 Trondheim: Furulund, Lade Allè 84;
tel: 73 90 70 30; fax: 73 90 70 40

**Rehabilitation Homes for Alcoholics/Drug
Addicts**

1900 Fetsund: The Door of Hope, Falldalsvn
411; tel: 63 88 79 60; fax: 63 88 79 61

4017 Stavanger: Auglendsdalen 64;
tel: 51 82 87 00; fax: 51 82 87 82

**Day Care Centres (Alcoholics/Drug
Addicts)**

0187 Oslo: Urtegaten 16 A/C; tel: 23 03 66 80;
fax: 23 03 66 81

7012 Trondheim: Hvedingsveita 3;
tel: 73 52 09 00; fax: 73 51 03 97

Health Clinic for Drug Addicts

0650 Oslo Borggt 2, tel: 22 08 36 70
0187 Oslo Urtegt 16 A/C; tel: 22 67 43 45

Prison Work

0666 Oslo, Ole Deviksv 20; tel: 23 06 92 35,
fax: 22 65 57 74

Home for Prisoners

0666 Oslo, Ole Deviksv 20; tel: 23 06 92 35;
fax: 22 65 57 74

**Work Rehabilitation and Recycling
Centres (FRETEX)**

(including 45 second-hand shops)

5852 Bergen: Sandalsringen 3; tel: 55 92 59 00;
fax: 55 92 59 10

3036 Drammen: Kobbevikdalen 71;
tel: 32 20 83 50; fax: 32 20 83 51

3550 Gol: Sentrumsvn. 63; tel: 32 07 98 80;
fax: 32 07 98 81

9406 Harstad: Storgt 34; tel: 77 00 24 77;
fax: 77 00 24 71

7080 Heimdal: Heggstadmyra 2; tel: 72 59 59 15;
fax: 72 59 59 19

9900 Kirkenes: Pasvikvn 2; tel: 78 97 02 40;
fax: 78 97 02 41

2615 Lillehammer: Storgt 91; tel: 61 24 65 50;
fax: 61 24 65 51

0668 Oslo: Ole Deviksvei 20; tel: 23 06 92 00;
fax: 23 06 92 01

3735 Skien: Bedriftsvn 58; tel: 35 59 89 44;
fax: 35 59 57 44

4033 Stavanger: Midtgårdvn 22; tel: 51 95 13 00;
fax: 51 95 13 01

9018 Tromsø: Skattøravn 39; tel: 77 67 22 88;
fax: 77 67 22 87

6002 Ålesund: Korsegt 6; tel: 70 12 71 75;
fax: 70 12 71 75

Second-hand Shops:
Ålesund (2), Bergen (5), Bryne, Drammen (2),
Fredrikstad, Gol, Harstad, Haugesund,
Jørpeland, Kirkenes, Kristiansand, Levanger,
Lillehammer, Lillestrøm, Lyngdal, Molde,
Moss, Ølen, Oslo (5), Sandnes (2), Sandvika,
Sarpsborg, Skien , Stavanger (3), Tromsø,
Trondheim (5), Tønsberg, Voss; Art Galleri in
Bergen

**The territory received a reputation award, rating The
Salvation Army above all government institutions, other
organisations and non-governmental organisations**

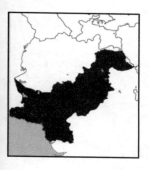

PAKISTAN TERRITORY

Territorial leaders:
Colonels Robert and Marguerite Ward

Territorial Commander:
Colonel Robert Ward (1 Feb 2008)

Chief Secretary:
Lieut-Colonel Yusaf Ghulam (1 Oct 2007)

Territorial Headquarters: 35 Shahrah-e-Fatima Jinnah, Lahore

Postal address: PO Box 242, Lahore 54000, Pakistan

Tel: [92] (42) 758 1644/756 9940; fax: [92] (42) 757 2699

The Salvation Army began work in Lahore in 1883 and was eventually incorporated under the Companies Act of 1913 on 9 October 1968.

Zone: South Asia
Country included in the territory: Pakistan
Languages in which the gospel is preached: English, Punjabi, Pashto, Urdu
Periodicals: *Home League Quarterly, The War Cry* (in Urdu)

THROUGHOUT its history, The Salvation Army in Pakistan has never stopped growing. Now, as the territory is preparing to celebrate 125 years of ministry, the landmark figure of 60,000 senior soldiers has been reached.

Add to that total the thousands of children, adherents and Home League members who call The Salvation Army their church, and a clear picture emerges of a strong community of faith for whom belonging to the Army defines identity and purpose.

Its presence in nearly 700 communities puts The Salvation Army very much in touch with the reality of people's lives in Pakistan. The officers live with their people; strong relationships exist, affording a unique position to influence the development of individuals and communities. The gospel's

power is evident in the lives of more than 7,000 first-time seekers recorded during the year.

In the north of the country Salvationists continued to assist communities to rebuild following the devastating earthquake of October 2005. Targeting 40 remote hamlets in the mountains surrounding Balakot, a team of officers led by Captain MacDonald Chandi (Territorial Emergency Services Coordinator) delivered more than 4,000 quilts and 3,500 iron roofing-sheets to the struggling communities.

More than 1,350 families benefited from the programme, and in addition to offering this much-needed material help a process of community-based trauma counselling was begun.

The territory records its gratitude to

the international Salvation Army for wonderful assistance in the earthquake relief and rehabilitation work. Numerous territories have contributed financially and many individuals have willingly joined the relief teams or offered technical support.

The Executive Officers Conference decided to place renewed emphasis on corps-based literacy training and job-creation. This was in response to a survey of some 90,000 adults and children in Salvation Army communities, which confirmed the picture of an Army where a majority of its members belong to the poorest segments of society.

Already a number of corps have commenced literacy classes and the territory is planning to start production for 'Sally Ann', The Salvation Army's international Fair Trade network.

Commissioner John Nelson (retired), a former Territorial Commander of Pakistan, returned to the territory as Acting Chief Secretary for three months. This followed the retirement of Lieut-Colonels Cedric and Barbara Sharp, who were thanked for many years of service in Pakistan, most recently as CS and Territorial Secretary for Women's Ministries.

Commissioner Nelson also conducted the retirement of Commissioners Gulzar Patras and Sheila Gulzar and the installation of the new territorial leaders, Colonels Bo and Birgitte Brekke. Just a year later, the territory was shocked by the sudden promotion to Glory of Colonel Bo Brekke on 27 September 2007.

STATISTICS

Officers 378 (active 296 retired 82) **Cadets** (1st Yr) 22 **Candidates** (as corps leaders) 6 **Employees** 188
Corps 130 **Societies** 559 **Institutions** 7 **Schools** 3 **Training and Resource Centres** 5
Senior Soldiers 60,062 **Adherents** 12,317 **Junior Soldiers** 14,629

STAFF

Editor: Capt Raja Azeem Zia
Emergency Services: Capt MacDonald Chandi
Field: Maj Samuel Tari
Finance: Maj Britt Alhbin
Human Resources Development:
Projects: under CS
   Project Area Coordinators: Maj Bernice Rehmat (Lahore) Capt Sabir Shaffi (Faisalabad)
Property:
Social Services:
Training: Maj Geoff Webb
   Mission Training and Education Centre: Maj Kalie Webb (Director)
Women's Ministries: Col Marguerite Ward (TPWM) Lt-Col Rebecca Yusaf (TSWM)
Youth: Maj Khuram Shahzada
   Candidates: Maj Victoria Khuram

DIVISIONS

Faisalabad: Jamilabad Jamia Salfia Rd, Faisalabad; tel: (411) 753586; Maj Shafqat Masih
Islamabad: William Booth Village, Khana Kak (Majaraj Plaza) Iqbal Town, Islamabad; mobile: 0300 5244618; Capt Washington Daniel (Div Officer)
Jaranwala: Water Works Rd, nr Telephone Exchange, Jaranwala; tel: (468) 312423; Lt-Col Morris John
Jhang: Yousaf Shah Rd, Jhang Saddar; tel: (471) 611589; Capt Michael Gabriel (Div Officer)
Karachi: 78 NI Lines, Frere St, Saddar, Karachi 74400; tel: (21) 225 4260; Lt-Col Zarina Viru
Khanewal: Chak Shahana Rd, Khanewal 58150; tel: (692) 53860; Maj Walter Emmanuel
Lahore: The Salvation Army, Bahar Colony, Kot Lakhpat, Lahore; tel: (42) 583 4568; Maj Samuel Barkat
Sahiwal: Karbala Rd, Sahiwal; tel: (441) 66383; Capt Haroon Ghulam (Div Officer)
Sheikhupura: 16 Civil Lines Rd, Qila, Sheikhupura; tel: (4931) 56521; Maj Salamat Masih

DISTRICT

Hyderabad: Bungalow No 9, 'E' Block, Unit
No 11, Latifabad 11, Hyderabad;
tel: (221) 813445; Maj Javed Yousaf

TRAINING COLLEGE

Ali Bridge, Canal Bank Rd North,
Tulspura, Lahore; tel: (42) 658 2450;
email: sacollege@cyber.net.pk

CONFERENCE CENTRE

Lahore: 35 Shahrah-e-Fatima Jinnah,
PO Box 242, Lahore 54000; tel: (42) 758 1644
ext 338

MISSION TRAINING AND EDUCATION CENTRE

Ali Bridge, Canal Bank Rd North, Tulspura,
Lahore; tel: (42) 658 2450

SOCIAL SERVICES

Boarding Hostels

Boys

Jhang: Yousaf Shah Rd, Jhang Saddar;
tel: (471) 624763 (acc 70)

Girls

Lahore: 35 Shahrah-e-Fatima Jinnah, PO Box 242,
Lahore 54000; tel: (42) 756 9940 (acc 60)
Sheikhupura: 16 Civil Lines, Quilla,
Sheikhupura; tel: (56) 378 4378 (acc 50)

Children's Home

Karachi: Site Metroville, PO Box 10682,
Karachi 75700; tel: (21) 665 0513 (acc 50)
Lahore: Joyland, 90-B Block, Model Town,
Lahore; tel: (42) 585 0190 (acc 60)

EDUCATION

Schools

Azam Town Secondary School, Street 6, 100
Foot Rd, Azam Town, Karachi 75460; tel:
(21) 538 4223
Shantinagar Educational Institute: Chak No
72/10-R, Shantinagar; tel: (692) 52985
Tibba Coaching Centre: Chak No 72/10-R,
Tibba, Shantinagar; tel: (692) 52985

REHABILITATION CENTRES FOR DISABLED

Lahore: Manzil-e-Shifa, 35 Shahrah-e-
Fatima Jinnah, PO Box 242,
Lahore 54000; tel: (42) 756 9940
Karachi: Manzil-e-Umead, PO Box
10735, Site Metroville,
Karachi 75700; tel: (21) 665 0434

Widows receive quilts and
men take home metal sheets
as Salvation Army relief
teams distribute winter relief
resources to people from
remote mountain villages of
northern Pakistan struggling
to recover from a devastating
earthquake. The Pakistan
military assisted The
Salvation Army in delivering
more than 4,000 quilts and
3,500 iron roofing-sheets to
the struggling communities.

PAPUA NEW GUINEA TERRITORY

Territorial Commander:
Colonel Andrew Kalai (1 Jun 2005)

Chief Secretary:
Lieut-Colonel James Condon
(1 Sep 2004)

Territorial Headquarters: Angau Dr, Boroko, National Capital District

Postal address: PO Box 1323, Boroko, NCD, Papua New Guinea

Tel: [675] 325-5522/5507; fax: [675] 323 3282

The Salvation Army officially commenced in Papua New Guinea on 31 August 1956 and the first meeting was conducted on Sunday 21 October at the Royal Police Constabulary Barracks in Port Moresby. The first officers appointed to the work there were Major and Mrs Keith Baker and Lieutenant Ian Cutmore. On 4 July 1994, after 38 years as part of the Australia Eastern Territory, Papua New Guinea became an independent command and on 9 December 2000 was elevated to territory status.

Zone: South Pacific and East Asia
Country included in the territory: Papua New Guinea
Languages in which the gospel is preached: English, Hiri Motu, Pidgin and many local languages
Periodicals: *Tokaut*

THE 50th anniversary of Salvation Army work in Papua New Guinea was celebrated with a territorial congress in November 2006, with General Shaw Clifton and Commissioner Helen Clifton as guest leaders. In total more than 30,000 people attended the gatherings.

Among the 40-plus overseas visitors returning to PNG for the celebrations was one of the pioneering officers from Australia, Commissioner Ian Cutmore (retired), with Commissioner Nancy Cutmore.

An historic moment came when Sir Brian Bell was admitted to the Order of Distinguished Auxiliary Service by the General. It was the first time this award had been given in PNG.

Sir Brian has been a leading businessman in Papua New Guinea for nearly 60 years and a charter member of the original Salvation Army Advisory Board that was formed in 1984. He has served as the board's chairman for the past 15 years, during which time he has overseen the raising of large sums of money for Salvation Army use.

The congress saw the launch of the book *Salvation Assault – the History of The Salvation Army in Papua New Guinea*, written by Major Allen Satterlee. Another book on the life of the first soldier in PNG, Kei Geno, was launched by his family.

The commissioning of 12 cadets of the Visionaries Session also took place.

The work of saving souls is progressing, particularly in the Wewak region in the north of the country. The Salvation Army has been in this region for only five years but already has established 13 churches/fellowships, and more villages are wanting the Army to begin work in their communities.

Following the volcanic eruption on Manam Island in December 2004, the displaced people had to move to Pottsdam on the north of the main island of PNG. The Salvation Army now has a fellowship established there, and 11 of their number travelled to Lae for the Women's Bible Convention.

A new ministry was formally launched in Port Moresby. The Settlement Ministry Team of officers and lay people focuses primarily on settlement areas in and around Port Moresby, ministering in particular to children and youth but also starting men's and women's activities.

Expansion of the high school in Port Moresby continues, with a further grade being added. New classrooms were built for the primary school, high school and FODE (Flexible, Open and Distance Education) centre at the THQ compound in Boroko.

The territory gives praise to God for continued progress. Further growth is limited only by lack of resources.

STATISTICS

Officers 181 (active 160 retired 21) **Cadets** (1st Yr) 12 (2nd Yr) 10 **Employees** 233

Corps 51 **Outposts** 68 **Institutions** 3 **Motels** 2 **Hostels** 2 **Schools** 5 **Health Centre** 1 **Health Sub Centres** 2 **Community Health Posts** 17 **Counselling Centres** 8

Senior Soldiers 5,859 **Adherents** 2,186 **Junior Soldiers** 1,320

STAFF

Business Administration:
Personnel: Capt Margaret McLeod
Programme:
Leadership Development: Maj Lapu Rawali
Property: Maj Drew Ruthven
Public Relations and Planned Giving: Capt Soddy Maraga
SALT: Capt Borley Yanderave
Training: Maj James Cocker
Women's Ministries: Lt-Col Jan Condon (TSWM)
Youth: Capt Christian Goa

DIVISIONS

North Coastal: PO Box 667, Lae, Morobe Province; tel: 472 0905, fax: 472 0897; Maj Sere Kala

North Eastern: PO Box 343, Kainantu, Eastern Highlands Province; tel/fax: 737 1220; Maj Mais Kihi

North-Western: PO Box 365, Goroka, Eastern Highlands Province; tel: 732 1382; fax: 732 1218; Capt David Temine

South Eastern: Kwikila, Central Province (mail to PO Box 1323, Boroko, National Capital District); mobile: 698 5966; Maj Kabona Rotona

South Western: PO Box 4227, Boroko, National Capital District; tel: 321 6005; fax: 321 6008; Maj Heather Gill (acting)

Gulf Regional Office: PO Box 132, Kerema, Gulf Province; tel/fax: 648 1384; Capt Haro Gomara

OFFICER TRAINING COLLEGE

PO Box 5355, Boroko, National Capital District; tel: 323 0553; fax: 325 6668

SALT CENTRE

PO Box 343, Kainantu, Eastern Highlands Province; tel: 737 1125

EDUCATION SERVICES

Boroko FODE Centre (acc 240)
Boroko Primary School (acc 740)
SA High School, Boroko (acc 60 – Grade 9 and 10 only)
Lae Primary School (acc 210)

Community Health Workers Training School

Private Mail Bag 3, Kainantu, Eastern Highlands Province; tel: 737 1404 (acc 50)

Children from a settlement area in Kaugere enjoy ministry from the new Settlement Ministry Team established in Port Moresby

HOSTELS AND MOTELS

Goroka Motel: PO Box 365, Goroka, Eastern
  Highlands Province; tel: 732 1382;
  fax: 732 1218 (family units 2, double units 4,
  house 1)
The Elphick Motel: PO Box 637, Lae,
  Morobe Province; tel: 472 2487;
  fax: 472 7487 (acc double rooms 8)
Koki Centennial House: (single women)
  (acc double rooms 24)

SOCIAL PROGRAMME
Community Services and HIV/Aids

Courts and Prison Ministry, Missing Persons,
  Welfare Feeding Projects
Jim Jacobsen Centre: PO Box 901, Lae, Morobe
  Province; tel/fax: 472 1117
House of Hope (Ela Beach Care and Counselling
  Centre); tel: 320 0389

DEVELOPMENT SERVICES

Onamuga Development Project: Private Mail
  Bag 3, Kainantu, Eastern Highlands Province
Literacy Programmes: each division

HEALTH SERVICES

North Coastal: PO Box 667 Lae, Morobe
  Province; tel: 472 0905, fax 472 0897
  Community Health Posts: Pongani, Waru
North Eastern: Private Mail Bag 3, Kainantu,
  Eastern Highlands Province; tel/fax: 737 1279
  Onamuga Health Centre (acc 35)
  Health Sub Centre: Misapi
  Community Health Posts: Barokira, Kokopi,
  Norikori, Pitanka, Yauna
North Western: PO Box 365, Goroka, Eastern
  Highlands Province; tel: 732 1382;
  fax: 732 1218
  Community Health Posts: Kamila, Kwongi
South Eastern: PO Box 1323, Boroko, National
  Capital District; Health Sub Centre: Boregaina
  (acc 10)
  Community Health Posts: Dirinomu,
  Kokorogoro, Kwaipo, Matairuka, Meirobu
South Western: PO Box 4227, Boroko, National
  Capital District; tel: 321 6000
  Community Health Posts: Ilavapari, Lapari,
  Sogeri

THE PHILIPPINES TERRITORY

Territorial leaders:
Colonels Malcolm and Irene Induruwage

Territorial Commander:
Colonel Malcolm Induruwage (2 Apr 2006)

Chief Secretary:
Lieut-Colonel Graham Durston (1 May 2006)

Territorial Headquarters: 1414 Leon Guinto Sr St, Ermita, Manila 1000

Postal address: PO Box 3830, Manila 1099, The Philippines

Tel: [63] (2) 524 0086/88; fax: [63] (2) 521 6912; PR Dept: [63] (2) 536 3068;
email: saphl1@phl.salvationarmy.org

The first Protestant preaching of the gospel in The Philippines was done by Major John Milsaps, a chaplain appointed to accompany US troops from San Francisco to Manila in July 1898. Major Milsaps conducted open-air and regular meetings and led many into a saving knowledge of Jesus Christ.

The advance of The Salvation Army in The Philippines came at the initiative of Filipinos who had been converted through contact with The Salvation Army in Hawaii, returned to their homeland and commenced meetings in Panay, Luzon, Cebu and Mindanao Islands during the period 1933-37. On 6 June 1937 Colonel and Mrs Alfred Lindvall officially inaugurated this widespread work.

The Salvation Army Philippines was incorporated in 1963 as a religious and charitable corporation under Company Registration No 24211. The Salvation Army Social Services was incorporated in 1977 as a social welfare and development corporation under Company Registration No 73979 and The Salvation Army Educational Services was incorporated in 2001 as an educational corporation under Company Registration No A200009937.

Zone: South Pacific and East Asia
Country included in the territory: The Philippines
'The Salvation Army' in Filipino: Hukbo ng Kaligtasan; in Ilocano: Buyot ti Salakan
Languages in which the gospel is preached: Antiqueño (Kinaray-a), Bagobo, Bicolano, Cebuano, English, Hiligaynon (Ilonggo), Ilocano, Korean, Pangasinan, Filipino (Tagalog), T'boli, Waray
Periodicals: *Home League Programme Aids, The War Cry*

THE 2006 theme 'Christian Believers of One Heart and Mind' encouraged Filipino Salvationists to grow in a more unified understanding of Salvation Army doctrine and practice. Relevant faith education was given in reinstituted soldiers' meetings.

Seminars on stress debriefing and trauma counselling were facilitated, particularly to address overseas Filipino workers (OFWs) who had been repatriated from the Israeli/Lebanon war zone. An estimated 30,000 Filipino workers faced displacement and loss of jobs.

The Salvation Army's response to the needs of the OFWs, specifically domestic helpers, was recognised by the Philippines Government. Evacuees were given food parcels, wheelchairs and medications as well as trauma counselling by Salvation Army workers. Ongoing support was offered in the form of micro-loans to set up small businesses.

A number of devastating typhoons hit The Philippines from June to December 2006, the worst of which were super typhoons Milenyo and Reming. The latter caused heavy loss of life, including more than 1,000 people in the Bicol Province where Salvation Army emergency services gave intensive relief. The teams travelled by *bancas* (canoes) to get to a small island off the coast where no other aid reached.

The preaching of God's message was integral in these compassionate acts as people found inner peace amid the tragedy they experienced.

The territory purchased properties that will be essential to its mission in future years. A generous legacy enabled the buying of land in Asingan for the development of educational services in that centre. More than 200 children are being educated in this school.

The congregation at Merville Society rejoiced over its new set of buildings dedicated to God's glory in November 2006. Generous financial support for this project came from USA Eastern and USA Central Territories.

A prime lot for the new site of THQ has been bought with the aid of USA Western Territory.

The year 2007 marked the territory's jubilee celebrations – 70 years of making Christ known throughout the archipelago. 'Go, Search for the Lost' was the year's theme, which was launched at divisional and cluster centres during special New Year's Day rallies.

The theme was also highlighted at the commissioning of the five cadets of the Heralds of the Good News Session. They were commissioned by Chief of the Staff Commissioner Robin Dunster, who had worked closely with them when she was Territorial Commander, The Philippines.

During her visit the Chief also led the first Territorial Officers' Councils since 2000. Some 220 active and retired officers met for two days and experienced a wonderful time of reunion and blessing. In the same week the first-ever Gospel Arts Camp had an overwhelming response as 189 young people registered for the five-day event.

STATISTICS

Officers 222 (active 178 retired 39) **Cadets** 12 **Envoys/Lieutenants** 7 **Employees** 53
Corps 78 **Societies/Outposts/Outreaches/ New Plants** 84 **Institutions** 2 **Social Centres** 23
Senior Soldiers 5,910 **Adherents** 3,122 **Junior Soldiers** 1,883
Personnel serving outside territory Officers 9 Lay workers 2

STAFF

Sec for Business Administration: Maj Dina Ismael
Christian Bookstore: Mr Lemuel Aguirre
Finance: Capt Estelita Bautista
Information Technology: Mr Victor Benganan Jr
Internal Auditor: Capt Jovita Padayao
Property Administrator: Alfredo Agpaoa Jr

The Philippines Territory

Territorial Planned Giving Director:
Maj Florante Parayno

Sec for Personnel Administration:
Candidates and Silver Star: Capt Melinda
Casidsid
Training and Development: Maj Elnora
Urbien

Sec for Programme Administration:
Maj Leopoldo Posadass
Corps Programme: Capt David Casimero
Educational Services Coordinator: Maj Elnora
Urbien
Sponsorships and Scholarship: Maj Evelyn
Posadas
Youth and Children: Capt Quintin Casidsid
Gospel Arts Coordinator: Mr Nic Bagasol Jr
Community Services Coordinator: Ms Airene
Margarette B. Lozada
Legal Consultant: Mr Paul Stephen
Salegumba
THQ Chaplain/Asst to Administration:
Maj Florida Oalang
Training: Capt David Oalang

Women's Ministries: Col Irene Induruwage
(TPWM) Lt-Col Rhondda Durston (TSWM)
Capt Ruby Casimero (Family and Women's
Development)

DIVISIONS

Central Philippines: 20 Senatorial Dr,
Congressional Village, Project 8, Quezon
City; tel: (02) 453 8208/929 6312;
email: Central@phl.salvationarmy.org;
Maj Virgilio Menia
Mindanao Island: 344 NLSA Rd, Purok
Bayanihan, San Isidro, Lagao 9500 General
Santos City; tel: (083) 553 5956;
email: Mid@phl.salvationarmy.org;
Maj Myline Joy Flores
Northern Luzon: Doña Loleng Subd
Nancayasan, 293 Urdaneta, Pangasinan;
tel: (075) 568 2310;
email: Northern@phl.salvationarmy.org;
Maj Alexander Genabe
Visayas Islands: 731 M. J. Cuenco Ave,
Cebu City; tel: (032) 416 7126;
tel/fax: (032) 416 7346;
email: Vid@phl.salvationarmy.org;
Maj Ronaldo Banlasan

TRAINING COLLEGE

Pantay Rd, Sitio Bukal Brgy, Tandang Kutyo,
Tanay, Rizal; tel: (02) 654 2909;
fax: (02) 654 2895

UNDER THQ
Sponsorship/Scholarship Programme, Missing
Persons/Family Tracing Service, Emergency
Disaster Relief

SOCIAL SERVICES
Residential Social Centres
(Abused girls/children)
Bethany Home: 20 Senatorial Dr, Congressional
Village, Project 8, Quezon City (acc 40)

(Street children)
Joyville Home: Pantay Rd, Sitio Bukal, Tanay,
Rizal (acc 25)

Learning Centres
Asingan Educational Services Inc: Bautista St,
Poblacion, 2439 Asingan, Pangasinan
Iloilo: Arroyo St, 5000 La Paz, Iloilo City

Child Care Centres
Bagong Silang: Phase 78-81K6, Lot 3A,
Package 3, Bagong Sitang Tala, Caloocan City
Bulalacao: Bulalacao, 5214 Oriental Mindoro
Caloocan: Cor Langaray, Dagat-dagatan Ave,
Caloocan City
Cebu: 731 M. J. Cuenco Ave, 6000 Cebu City
Dagupan: Puelay District, 2400 Dagupan City
Davao: Blk 14, Lot 10, Kingfisher St, RPJ
Village II, Seaside Subd, Matina Aplaya,
Matina, 8000 Davao City
General Santos: 344 NLSA Rd, Purok Bayanihan,
San Isidro, Lagao, 9500 General Santos City
Laoag: 50 Buttong, 2900 Laoag City, Ilocos Norte
Legazpi: 332 San Roque, Governor St, San
Roque, Legazpi City
Mariveles: Porto del Sur, National Rd, 2105
Mariveles, Bataan
Olongapo: Camia St, Sta Rita, 2200 Olongapo
City
Quezon City 1: 115 Batanes St, San Isidro Gals,
Quezon City
Quezon City 2: 20 Senatorial Dr, Congressional
Village, Project 8, Quezon City
Signal Village: Daisy St, Zone 6, Signal Village,
Taguig, Metro Manila
Sta Barbara: 20 Poblacion Norte, 2419 Sta
Barbara, Pangasinan
Tondo: 18215 Velasquez St, 1012 Tondo, Manila

Nutrition, Feeding and Day Care Centres
Dasmarinas: Blk 11, Lot 6, San Antonio de
Padua II Area E, DBB, Dasmarinas, Cavite
Makati: 3493 Honda St, Pinagkaisahan, 1200
Makati City
Signal Village: Daisy St, Zone 6, Signal Village,
Taguig, Metro Manila

The Philippines Territory

Dormitories for Students and Working Women

Baguio: 35-37 P. Guevarra St, Aurora Hill, 2600 Baguio City (acc 50)

Lapu-Lapu: Gun-ob, Lapu-lapu City (acc 12)

Makati: 3493 Honda St, Pinagkaishan, 1200 Makati City (acc 12)

Quezon City 1: 67 Batanes St, Galas, Quezon City (acc 12)

San Jose Mindoro: 3090 Roxas St, Doña Consuelo Subd, 5100 San Jose, Occidental Mindoro (acc 12)

Programmes for Minorities

Bamban: c/o San Jose Corps, 3090 Roxas St, Doña Consuelo Subd, Occidental Mindoro

Bulalacao: Bulalacao, 5214 Oriental Mindoro

Lake Sebu: T'boli Village, Lake Sebu

Wali: Bo Wali, Maitum, Saranggani Province

Skills Training

Lapu-lapu: Gun-ob 6015, Lapu-lapu City

Livelihood Support

Ansiray Fishcages: Ansiray, 5100 San Jose, Occidental Mindoro

Badipa: Bayaoas, Urdaneta, Pangasinan

Bautista: Nibaliw Norte, 2424 Bautista, Pangasinan

Bagong Silang: Phase 7B-Blk 6, Lot 3A Package 3, Bagong Silang, Tala quezon City

Bamban Carabao Raising: 3090 Roxas St, Doña Consuelo Subd, 511 San Jose, Occidental Mindoro

Bella Luz Cooperative Store: Brgy Bella Luz, 3318 San Mateo, Isabela

Bulalacao: Bulalacao 5214, Oriental Mindoro

Cabayaoasan Agricultural Cooperative: Cabayaoasan, 2413 Mangatarem, Pangasinon

Cacutud: 34-B Misael St, Diamond Subd, Balibago, Angeles City

Camangaan Agricultural Cooperative: Bo Camangaan, Rosales, 2442 Pangasinon

Cebu Central: 731 M. J. Cuenco Ave, Cebon City 6000

Dagupan: Puelay District, 2400 Dagupan City

General Santos: 344 NLSA Rd, Purok Bayanihan, San Isidoro, Lagao 9500, General Santos City

Iligan: Purok 5A Tambo, 9200 Iligan City, Lanao del Norte

Lake Sebu Tinalak Weaving: 9512 Poblacion, Lake Sebu, South Cotabuto

Legaspi: Governor St, 332 San Roque, Legaspi City

Liloan: Catherine Booth Development Centre, Tayud, Liloan, 6002 Cebu City

Lopez Quezon Carabao Raising: Abines St, Talolong Lopez, Quezon

Lourdes Carabao Raising: Barangay Lourdes, Lopez, Quezon

Magsaysay: Burgos St, Magsaysay, Occidental Mindoro

Malingao: Bo Malingao, Tubod, 9202 Lanao del Norte

Manila Central: 1414 Leon Guinto Sr St, 1000 Ermita, Manila

Mariveles: Porto del Sur, National Rd, 2105 Mariveles, Bataan

Merville: 128 Sitio Malaya, Brgy Merville, Paranaque City

Nasukob: Nasukob, 5214 Bulalacao, Oriental Mindoro

Orani: 163 Calero St, Orani, 2112 Bataan

Ozamis: Carmen Annex, 7200 Ozamis City

Pahanocoy Tricycad: Florence Ville Subd, Pahanocoy, 6100 Bacolod City

Pasay: 511 Inocencio St, Pasay City

Sampaloc: Sitio, Hinadiongan, Sampaloc, Tanay, Rizal 1080

San Jose Mindoro: 3090 Roxas St, Doña Consuelo Subd, 511 San Jose, Occidental Mindoro

Signal Village: Daisy St, Zone 6, Signal Village, Taguig, Metro Manila

Sta Ana: 2439 Asingan, Pangasinan

Wali: Wali, Maiturn, 9515 Saranggani Province

Agricultural Assistance

Bella Luz: Barangay Bella Luz, 3318 San Mateo, Isabela

Nasukob Agricultural Loan: Nasukob, 5214 Bulalacao

Santa Agricultural Loan: Mabibila Sur, Santa, Ilocos Sur

Wali: Bo Wali, Maitum, Saranggani Province

Micro-Enterprise Credit Projects

Almacen: Barangay Almacen, 2111 Hermoza, Bataan

Ansiray: 5100 San Jose, Occidental Mindoro

Badipa: Bayaoas, Urdaneta, Pangasinan

Bautista: Nibaliw Norte 2424 Bautista, Pangasinan

Bulalacao: Bulalacao 5214, Oriental Mindoro

Cacutud: 34-B Misael St, Diamond Subd, Balibago, Angeles City

Cebu Central: 731 M. J. Cuenco Ave, Cebon City 6000

Dagupan: Puelay District, 2400 Dagupan City

Davao: Block 14 Lot 10, Kingfisher St, RPJ Village II, Seaside Subdivision Matina Aplaya, Matina 8000, Davao City

General Santos: 344 NLSA Rd, Purok Bayanihan,

Cadets of the Heralds of the Good News Session in The Philippines are commissioned as Salvation Army officers by Chief of the Staff Commissioner Robin Dunster

San Isidoro, Lagao 9500 General Santos City
Iligan: Purok 5A Tambo, 9200 Iligan City, Lanao del Norte
Lake Sebu: 4512 Poblacion, Lake Sebu, South Cotabato
Legaspi: Governor St, 332 San Roque Legaspi City
Liloan: Catherine Booth Development Center, Tayud, Liloan, 6002 Cebu City
Magsaysay: Burgos St, Magsaysay, Occidental Mindoro
Malingao: Bo Malingao, Tubod, 9202 Lanao del Norte
Manila Central: 1414 Leon Guinto Sr, St 1000 Ermita, Manila
Mariveles: Porto del Sur, National Rd, 2105 Mariveles, Bataan
Merville: 128 Sitio Malaya, Brgy Merville, Paranaque City
Nasukob: Nasukob 5214 Bulalacao, Oriental Mindoro
Orani: 163 Calero St, Orani, 2112 Bataan
Ozamis: Carmen Annex, 7200 Ozamis City
Pasay: 511 Inocencio St, Pasay City
Sampaloc: Sitio, Hinadiongan, Sampaloc, Tanay, Rizal 1080
San Jose Mindoro: 3090 Roxas St, Doña Consuelo Subd, 511 San Jose, Occidental Mindoro
Signal Village: Daisy St, Zone 6, Signal Village, Taguig, Metro Manila
Sta Ana: 2439 Asingan, Pangasinan
Wali: Wali, Maiturn, 9515 Saranggani Province

Water Systems
Bulalacao: Bulalacao, 5214 Oriental Mindoro
Camangaan: Bo Carmangaan, Rosales 2442, Pangasinon
Lopez: San Vicente St, Barangay Magsaysay, Lopez, Quezon
Lourdes: Barangay Lourdes, Lopez, Quezon

Mariveles: Porto del Sur, National Rd, 2105 Mariveles, Bataan
Nasukob: Nasukob, 5214 Bulalacao, Oriental Mindoro
Palili: c/o The Salvation Army, 163 Calero St, Orani 2112, Bataan
Sampaloc: Sitio, Hinadiongan Sampalac Tanay, Rizal 1080
Upper Katalicanan: c/o Midsayap Corps, Poblacion 8, Midsayap 9410, North Cotabato

Housing Project
Lopez, Quezon: Abines St, Talolong, Lopez, Quezo

Anti-Human Trafficking Projects
Bacolod; Cebu; Darapuay; Dasmarinas; Davao; Diamond/Cacutud; General Santos; Iligan; Laoag; Lapu-Lapu; Mariveles Corps; Olongapo; Orani; Pasay; Quezon City 2; Sinamar; San Jose Mindoro

HEALTH
Barangay Health Workers in Rural Corps
Botica sa Barangay
Cabayaosan Corps: Cabayaosan, Mangataram Pangasinan
San Jose Occidental Mindoro: 3090 Roxas St, Doña Consuelo Subd, San Jose Occidental Mindoro

HIV/Aids Programmes
Ansiray; Bacolod; Bella Luz; Bulalacao; Cantamuak; Cebu; Dagupan; Darapuay; Dasmarinas; Davao; Diamond/Cacutud; Diffun; General Santos; Iligan; Lake Sebu; Laoag; La Paz; Lapu-Lapu; Lebe; Legaspi; Mariveles Nasukob; Olongapo; Orani; Pandanan; San Jose Antique; San Jose Mindoro; Santiago; Sinamar; Tacloban; Tondo; Urdaneta; Villa Ros; Wali

PORTUGAL COMMAND

Command leaders:
Majors Alberto and Maria José Serém

Officer Commanding:
Major Alberto Serém (1 Sep 2006)

Command Headquarters: Rua Dr Silva Teles, 16, 1050-080 Lisboa

Postal address: Apartado 14109, 1064-002 Lisboa, Portugal

Tel: [351] (21) 780 2930; fax: [351] (21) 780 2940;

email:Portugal_Command@POR.salvationarmy.org; web site: www.exercitodesalvacao.pt

On 25 July 1971, official recognition was given to the first corps established in Portugal. The work was started in the northern city of Porto by a group of evangelical Christians. On 28 January 1972, Major and Mrs Carl S. Eliasen arrived in Lisbon to start work there and to supervise the existing activities.

On 4 July 1974 The Salvation Army was recognised by the Ministry of Justice as a religious and philanthropic organisation. All social activities are incorporated in Centro Social do Exército de Salvação which was constituted in Portugal on 26 March 1981 (Public Utility Register 16/82 dated 10 March 1982). On 8 March 2007 The Salvation Army was registered as a Collective Religious Person (the legal term for a church).

Zone: Europe
Country included in the command: Portugal
'The Salvation Army' in Portuguese: Exército de Salvação
Language in which the gospel is preached: Portuguese

SINCE opening its work in Portugal in the early 1970s, The Salvation Army has been officially recognised as a religious and philanthropic organisation. But, with the advent of a newly approved law, a major development took place on 8 March 2007 when The Salvation Army was registered as a Collective Religious Person (the legal term for a church).

As well as benefiting from a number of fiscal privileges, the Army has gained a higher level of legal status and national respect, giving it parity with other established churches.

The summer air was filled with Army music when the Alabama-Louisiana-Mississippi Divisional Youth Band (USA Southern) toured the country, giving concerts in several places which had never received a Salvation Army visit. The welcome was warm and spontaneous, and many people listened attentively to the gospel.

After the tour, a small group stayed to give instruction and support at the National Music School – always a highlight of the year.

When more than 50 young people attended the New Year Retreat, most of them 'nailed' 'old things' to a cross and received new power from God for the year just starting. The young people's commitments to the

Lord were sincere and vibrant.

The centenary of the Home League was celebrated during Women's Week in February 2007. A 'WWW2007' logo was used in the re-launching of women's ministries in the command. A significant number of new home league members were enrolled. Women's groups are developing in different areas, with computer classes and outings being among the features.

March saw the beginning of the command's Multi-ethnic Ministries, aiming at taking the gospel to the many Africans who make Portugal their home or are passing through.

STATISTICS
Officers active 15 **Employees** 118
Mission Areas with Corps 5 **Institutions** 7
Senior Soldiers 79 **Adherents** 52 **Junior Soldiers** 18
Personnel serving outside command Officers 4

STAFF
Finance: Maj Peter Robertson
Public Relations: Maj Pedro Neves
Social: Dra Sandra Martins Lopes
Women's Ministries: Maj Maria José Serém (CPWM)

SOCIAL SERVICES
Children's Home
Centro de Acolhimento Novo Mundo, Ave Desidério Cambournac, 14, 2710-553 Sintra; tel: 219 244 239; fax: 219 249 688 (acc 14)

Clothing and Food Distribution Centre
Rua Escola do Exército, 11-B, 1150-143 Lisboa; tel: 213 528 137; fax: 213 160 732

Thrift Shop
Chelas: Rua Rui de Sousa, Lote 65 A-Loja C, 1900-802 Lisboa

Day Centres for the Elderly and Home Help Services
Colares: Av dos Bombeiros Voluntários, Várzea de Colares, 2705-180 Sintra; tel: 219 288 450; fax: 219 288 458
Lisboa: Rua Capitão Roby, 19 (Picheleira), 1900-111 Lisboa; tel: 218 409 108; fax: 218 409 112
Porto: Av Vasco da Gama, 645, Lojas 1 e 2, Ramalde, 4100-491 Porto; tel: 226 172 769; fax: 226 171 120

Eventide Homes
Nosso Lar: Av dos Bombeiros Voluntários, Várzea de Colares, 2705-180 Colares; tel: 219 288 450; fax: 219 288 458 (acc 30)
Marinel: Rua das Marinhas, 13, Tomadia, Praia das Maçãs, 2705-313 Colares; tel: 219 288 480; fax: 219 288 481 (acc 50)

Night Shelter for the Homeless
Rua da Manutenção, 7 (Xabregas) – 1900-318 Lisboa; tel: 218 680 908; fax: 218 680 913 (acc 75)

HOLIDAY AND CONFERENCE CENTRES
Casa Marinel, Av José Félix da Costa, 9, Praia das Maçãs – 2705-312 Colares (Information from CHQ)
Vivenda Boa Nova, Rua do Vinagre, 9, 2705-354 Colares; tel: 219 291 718 (Holiday bookings to CHQ)

A new senior soldier and two adherents are enrolled at Castelo Branco, during second anniversary celebrations of the command's newest corps

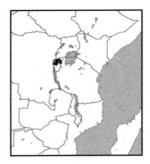

RWANDA REGION

Regional leaders:
Majors Stephen and Grace Chepkurui

Regional Commander:
Major Stephen Chepkurui
(1 Feb 2007)

Regional Headquarters: Plot 319, Kimihurura Mutekano, Zone 0057, Kigali

Postal address: PO Box 812, Kigali, Rwanda

Tel: [250] 587639; fax: [250] 511812; email: Rwanda@rwa.salvationarmy.org

As a result of civil war and genocide in Rwanda, The Salvation Army became actively involved in relief work in September 1994. Operations were concentrated in Kayenzi Commune, part of the Gitarama Prefecture. Following mission work by officers from Zaïre, Uganda and Tanzania in 1995, officers were appointed from Congo (Brazzaville) to develop corps and mission work in Kayenzi Commune. Kayenzi Corps officially began its ministry on 5 November 1995.

In 1983, Justin Lusombo-Musese (a Congolese born in Burundi) was introduced by a friend to some of William Booth's writings and learned about The Salvation Army's early history. Justin and the friend were so enthused they decided to become members of the Army. Over the ensuing years they persistently requested International Headquarters to start Army operations in Burundi, and on 5 August 2007 the work was officially recognised with the warranting of Justin Lusombo-Musese and his wife Justine Fatouma as auxiliary-captains. The Rwanda Region's leadership will give guidance and support to future development in Burundi.

Zone: Africa
Countries included in the region: Burundi, Rwanda
The Salvation Army in Kinyarwanda: Ingabo Z'Agakiza
Languages in which the gospel is preached: English, French, Kinyarwanda, Kirundi, Kiswahili

GOD continues to bless his work in Rwanda. This is seen particularly in evangelical ministry and social work being undertaken jointly by officers and local officers.

The Salvation Army assisted in resettling 70 Rwandan families who returned to their native land from Tanzania, where they had lived as refugees for many years. The project funded through the International Emergency Services, IHQ, provides clean water and sanitation to all the families, so helping to transform the lives of some of Rwanda's most marginalised people.

In the village of Gituro the district mayor and government officials were present to officially open and dedicate a water pump and community shelter. During his opening speech the mayor pronounced Gituro to be a 'Salvation Army village'. He has ordered the allocation of land to the Army for future community development.

Before the Gituro pump was opened the women and children walked seven kilometres to collect stagnant, brown,

A water pump is made operational in the village of Gituro. During his speech the district mayor pronounced Gituro to be a 'Salvation Army village'. He has ordered the allocation of land to the Army for future community development.

contaminated water. They now have a source of clear, clean, safe water just 600 metres away.

In parallel with this water project, the Army is funding the building of 70 pit latrines, one for each family.

A three-year project funded by Switzerland, Austria and Hungary Territory is providing skimmed and powdered milk to mothers and malnourished children. At seven centres 14 helpers trained by health personnel assist the beneficiaries in the proper handling of the milk.

The Salvation Army continues to support young children who are at risk of dropping out of school to become street beggars. By paying fees direct to the school bank account, regional headquarters provides 75 per cent of a child's school fees and, in cases where parents are unable to raise any money, the full amount is paid.

The Africa Regional Team has helped transform young people into agents of change in society. Trained youth leaders known as Frontiers go into villages to encourage the community to respond to their own needs and be able to find solutions to their problems. They also attend and participate in communal activities.

STATISTICS

Officers 17 **Lieutenants** 8 **Auxiliary-Captains** 2 **Employees** 29

Corps 7 **Outreach Unit** 1 **Outposts** 6 **Pre-School Facility** 2 (acc 170)

Senior Soldiers 883 **Adherents** 295 **Junior Soldiers** 570

STAFF

Women's Ministries: Maj Grace Chepkurui (RPWM)

Regional Sec: Maj Daniel Moukoko

Education: Capt Dancile Ndagijimana
Finance: Maj Daniel Moukoko
Projects: Maj Arschette Moukoko
Public Relations: Capt Emmanuel Ndagijimana
Youth: Capt Emmanuel Ndagijimana

DISTRICT

Kayenzi: PO Box 812 Kigali; Capt Celestin Ayabagabo; mobile: 250 08587988

BURUNDI

Ruhero II, Boulevard de l'Independence, Parcelle No 1416, Bujumbura, Burundi; Aux-Capt Justin Lusombo-Musese; email: lusombo@yahoo.com; mobile: 257 79996148

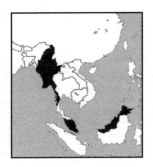

SINGAPORE, MALAYSIA AND MYANMAR TERRITORY

Territorial leaders:
Colonels David and Grace Bringans

Territorial Commander:
Colonel David Bringans (1 Mar 2003)

Chief Secretary:
Lieut-Colonel Keith Burridge (1 Jul 2007)

Territorial Headquarters: 20 Bishan St 22, Singapore 579768

Postal address: Ang Mo Kio Central, PO Box 640, Singapore 915605

Tel: [65] 6555 0188; fax: [65] 6552 8542; web site: www.salvationarmy.org.sg

In May 1935 Salvation Army work began in Singapore. It spread to Penang (1938), Melaka and Ipoh (1940), Kuching (Sarawak) (1950), Kuala Lumpur (1966) and Kota Kinabalu (Sabah) (1996).

'The General of The Salvation Army' is a 'corporation sole' by The Salvation Army Ordinance 1939 in the Straits Settlements; by The Salvation Army (Incorporation) Ordinance 1956 in the Federation of Malaya; and by the Missionary Societies Order 1957 in the Colony of Sarawak.

Adjutant Taran Das (Reuben Moss), who was attached to the Lahore headquarters in India, was appointed to open the work in Burma (now Myanmar) by Commissioner Booth Tucker in January 1915. Myanmar Salvationists have, since 1966, developed their witness and service despite the restriction on reinforcements from overseas. In 1994 Myanmar was joined to the Singapore and Malaysia Command. The command was elevated to territory status on 1 March 2005.

Zone: South Pacific and East Asia

Countries included in the territory: Malaysia, Myanmar, Singapore

'The Salvation Army' in Chinese: (Mandarin) Chiu Shi Chen, (Cantonese) Kau Shai Kwan, (Amoy, Hokkien) Kiu Se Kun; Bahasa: Bala Keselamatan; Myanmar: Kae Tin Chin Tat; Tamil: Retchania Senai

Languages in which the gospel is preached: Burmese, Chin (Mizo, Zahau, Dai), Chinese (Amoy, Cantonese, Hokkien, Mandarin), English, Bahasa, Malay, Tamil, Telegu

Periodical: *The War Cry*

GOD continues to work in the lives of people throughout the territory. Every corps and centre is encouraged to find ways to 'Advance … in Vision For Mission and Passion For People'.

The territory's first-ever Mission For Vision Convention was held in Port Dickson, Malaysia (30 May-4 June 2006) with 456 people of all ages attending from all parts of Singapore, East and West Malaysia and other countries. There were 22 delegates from Myanmar.

The international guests included Commissioners Earle and Wilma Maxwell (retired) from Australia and Commissioner Linda Bond (IHQ). Others came from India, Indonesia,

Kenya, Taiwan and the USA. Translation was provided in English, Tamil, Chinese, Bahasa and Burmese.

Sessions included Bible study, 'Worship and the Word', family worship and an all-night of powerful prayer in different styles and languages.

Other features were 'Wise Women', the highlight being *The World's Greatest Romance* – Carol Jaudes's dramatic presentation of the life of General Evangeline Booth; 'Mighty Men' – teaching by Commissioner Earle Maxwell on the lives of seven of Jesus' disciples; 'The Amazing Mission Race' in which teams aimed to complete mission-oriented tasks; 'Youth Alive' ; and the 'Holiday Trek' programme for 72 children run by Scripture Union Singapore. Eight children accepted Jesus for the first time.

Inspired and challenged to do more to build God's Kingdom, delegates returned to their corps armed with a greater depth and knowledge of God and The Salvation Army.

On 17 June 2006, Territorial Commander Colonel David Bringans, Mr S. Dhanabalan (Territorial Advisory Board Chairman) and Mr Laurence Lien of the Lien Foundation, who provided funding, opened the Peacehaven Nursing Home Dementia Hope Resident Living Area. Accommodating 34 people, it is the first residential hostel of its kind in Singapore for those suffering mild dementia.

Six cadets of the Heralds of the Good News Sessions were commissioned as officers by the TC (two in Singapore on 19 November 2006 and four in Myanmar on 17 March 2007).

The West Malaysian Peninsular suffered heavy flooding toward the end of 2006. Some 120,000 people were displaced and 17 killed. Relief supplies such as food, sleeping mats/blankets, clothing and cleaning provisions were gratefully received by people affected in areas helped by the Army. School uniforms, books and fees were also provided in some places.

Aid was distributed when parts of Sabah (East Malaysia) were also flooded.

STATISTICS
Officers 131 (active 119 retired 12) **Lieutenants** 4 **Cadets** 12 **Employees** 721
Corps 50 **Outposts** 14 **Institutions** 16 **Kindergarten** 2 **Day Care Centres** 18
Senior Soldiers 2,441 **Adherents** 478 **Junior Soldiers** 448

STAFF
Editor: Col Grace Bringans
Finance: Mdm Koh Guek Eng
Human Resources: Mrs Toh-Chia Lai Ying
Programme: Capt Ian Robinson
Property: Mr John Ng
Public Relations: Mr Gregory Lee
Projects: Lt-Col Keith Burridge
Training: Maj Kong Chew (Bob) Lee
Women's Ministries: Col Grace Bringans (TPWM) Lt-Col Beryl Burridge (TSWM)
Youth and Candidates: Capt Hary Haran

SCHOOL FOR OFFICER TRAINING (SINGAPORE AND MALAYSIA)
500 Upper Bukit Timah Rd, Singapore 678106; tel: 6349 5333

SINGAPORE
Children's Homes
Gracehaven: 3 Lorong Napiri (off Yio Chu Kang Rd), Singapore 547528; tel: 6488 1510 (acc 160)
The Haven: 350 Pasir Panjang Rd, Singapore 118692; tel: 6774 9588/9 (acc 50)

Day Care Centres for Children
Ang Mo Kio Child Care Centre: Blk 610 Ang

211

Mo Kio Ave 4, #01-1227 Singapore 560610;
tel: 6452 4862 (acc 89)
Bukit Batok East Child Care Centre: Blk 247
Bukit Batok East Ave 5, #01-86 Singapore
650247; tel: 6562 4976 (acc 73)
Bukit Batok West Child Care Centre: Blk 415
Bukit Batok West Ave 5, #01-264 Singapore
650415; tel: 6567 2050 (acc 91)
Bukit Panjang Child Care Centre: Blk 402
Fajar Rd, #01-217 Singapore 670402;
tel: 6760 2624 (acc 82)
Bukit Panjang Family Service Centre: Blk 404
Fajar Rd, #01-267 Singapore 670404;
tel: 6763 0837 (acc 98)
Pasir Ris Child Care Centre: Blk 427 Pasir Ris
Dr 6, #01-43 Singapore 510427;
tel: 6582 0286 (acc 76)
Tampines Child Care Centre: Blk 159
Tampines St 12, #01-95 Singapore 521159;
tel: 6785 2976 (acc 90)

Day Care Centres for the Elderly

Bedok Multiservice Centre for the Elderly:
Blk 121, #01-161 Bedok North Rd, Singapore
460121; tel: 6445 1630 (acc 65)
Bedok Rehabilitation Centre: Blk 121, #01-163
Bedok North Rd, Singapore 460121;
tel: 6445 1630 (acc 35)

Family Support Services

Blk 42, Beo Cresc, #01-95 Singapore 160042;
tel: 6273 7207

Hostels

Foreign Nurses' Hostel: 20 Bishan St 22,
Singapore 579768; tel: 6452 4975
Foreign Students' Hostel: 500 Upper Bukit Timah
Rd, Singapore 678106; tel: 6349 5344 (acc 80)
Peacehaven Nurses' Hostel: 9 Upper Changi Rd
North, Singapore 507706; tel: 6546 5678
(acc 100)
Young Women's Hostel: The Haven, 350 Pasir
Panjang Rd, Singapore 118692;
tel: 6774 9588/9 (acc 10)

Nursing Home

Peacehaven, 9 Upper Changi Rd North,
Singapore 507706; tel: 6546 5678 (acc 374)

Prison Support Services

7 Upper Changi Rd North, Singapore 507705;
tel 6546 7788 ext 4052

Red Shield Industries

309 Upper Serangoon Rd, Singapore 347693;
tel: 6288 5438

Youth Development Centre

Blk 65 Kallang Bahru, #01-305 Singapore
330065; tel: 6291 6303; under Territorial
Youth Dept

Corps Community Services

Balestier Corps and Community Services:
48 Martaban Rd, Singapore 328664;
tel: 6253 1433
Changi Corps and Community Centre: 7 Upper
Changi Rd North, Singapore 507705;
tel: 6546 5827

EAST MALAYSIA
Boys' Home

Kuching Boys' Home: Jalan Ban Hock, 93100,
Kuching, PO Box 547, 93700 Kuching,
Sarawak, Malaysia; tel: (082) 24 2623 (acc 35)

Children's Home

Kuching Children's Home: 138 Jalan Upland,
93200 Kuching, PO Box 106, 93700 Kuching,
Sarawak, Malaysia; tel: (082) 24 8234 (acc 60)

Day Care Centres for Children

Kuching Kindergarten: Sekama Rd 93300,
Kuching Sarawak, Malaysia, PO Box 44,
93700 Kuching Sarawak, Malaysia;
tel: (082) 333981 (acc 120)
Rainbow Centre: 588B Lucky Garden, Tanjong
Batu Rd, 97000, Bintulu Sarawak, PO Box
1701, 97010 Bintulu Sarawak, Malaysia;
tel: (086) 313842 (acc 35)

Corps Community Services

Bintulu Corps and Community Services: Lot 216,
2nd Floor BDA Shophouse, 16 Jalan Tanjong
Batu, 97000 Bintulu; tel: (086) 315 843
Kota Kinabalu Corps and Community Services:
20-2 Block A Inanam Business Ctr, Batu 6,
Jalan Tuaran, 88450 Kota Kinabalu, Sabah,
PO Box 14234, 88848 Kota Kinabalu, Sabah,
Malaysia; tel: (088) 433766
Kuching Corps and Community Services: Jalan
Ban Hock, 93100 Kuching, Sarawak,
Malaysia; tel: (082) 242623

Red Shield Industries

Ground – 1st Flr, 1 Jalan Ang Cheng Ho, 93100
Kuching; tel: 082 410564

WEST MALAYSIA

Liaison and Public Relations Office: 26-1 Jalan
Puteri, 4/2 Bandar Puteri, 47100 Puchong,
Selangor Darul Ehsan, Malaysia;
tel (06) 8061 4929

Boys' Homes
Ipoh Boys' Home: 4367 Jalan Tambun, 31400 Ipoh, PO Box 221, 30720 Ipoh, Perak, Malaysia; tel: [60] (05) 545 7819 (acc 60)
Lighthouse Boys' Home: 346-G Taman Yong Pak Kian, Ujong Pasir 75050 Melaka, Malaysia; tel: (06) 283 2101 (acc 25)

Centre for Special Children
Hopehaven Centre for Special Children: 321 Jalan Parameswara, 75000 Melaka, Malaysia; tel: [60] (06) 283 2101 (acc 100)

Children's Homes
Ipoh Children's Home: 255 Kampar Rd, 30250 Ipoh, Perak, Malaysia; tel: (05) 254 9767; fax: (05) 242 9630 (acc 50)
Penang Children's Home: 8A Logan Rd, 10400 Penang, Malaysia; tel: (04) 227 0162 (acc 58)
Lighthouse Children's Home: 321 Jalan Parameswara, 75000 Melaka, Malaysia; tel: (06) 283 2101 (acc 35)

Day Care Centres for Children
Batang Melaka Day Care Centre: J7702 Main Rd, 77500 Batang Melaka, Malaysia; tel: (06) 446 1601 (acc 80)
Banting Day Care Centre: 30 Jalan Cendana 15, Taman Mihhibah, Banting 42700 (acc 50)
Kuala Lumpur Kindergarten: 1 Lingkungan Hujan, Overseas Union Garden 58200 KL, Malaysia; tel: (03) 7782 4766 (acc 100)
Little Lambs Day Care Centre for Needy Children: 321 Jalan Parameswara, 75000 Melaka, Malaysia; tel: (06) 283 2101 (acc 20)

Homes for the Aged
Joyhaven Home for the Elderly: 1 Jalan 12/17, Seksyen 12, 46200 Petaling Jaya, Selangor, Malaysia; tel: (03) 7958 6257 (acc 25)
Perak Home for the Aged: Jalan Bersatu, Jelapang, 30020 Ipoh, Perak, Malaysia; tel: (05) 526 2108 (acc 55)

Red Shield Industries
No 30, Jalan TPP 1/12, Taman Perindustrian Puchong Batu 12, Jalan Puchong, 47100 Puchong, Selangor Darul Ehsan, Malaysia; tel: (03) 8061 4757

Rehabilitation Centre
Chang T'en Men's Shelter, 46 Kg Bandar Hilir, Bandar, Melaka, Malaysia; tel: (06) 283 2101 (acc 20)

Corps Community Services
Batang Melaka Corps and Community Services: J7702 Main Rd, Batang Malaka, 77500 Selander, Melaka West Malaysia; tel: (06) 4461601
Puchong Community Services: 26-1 Jalan Puteri 4/2, Bandar Puteri 47100, Puchong, Selangor, Malaysia; tel: (03) 8061 4929
Melaka Corps and Community Services: 321 Jalan Parameswara, 75000 Melaka, Malaysia; tel: (06) 283 1203

MYANMAR REGION
Headquarters: 176-178 Anawrahta St, Botahtaung, East Yangon 11161, Myanmar; Postal address: GPO Box 394, Yangon, Myanmar; tel: [95] (1) 294267/293307; fax: [95] (1) 298067
Regional Officer: Maj James Aaron

DISTRICTS
Tahan: District Office: D-group, Tahan, Kalemyo; tel: [95] (73) 21396
Tamu: District Office: Kanan Corps, Kanan Township

SCHOOL FOR OFFICER TRAINING (Myanmar)
50 Byaing Ye O Zin St, Tarmway, Yangon, Myanmar; tel: [95] (1) 543694

Boys' Home
406 Banyadala Rd, Tarmway, Yangon, Myanmar (acc 50)

Children's Home
50 Bago Rd, Pyu, Myanmar (acc 50)

Girls' Home
50 Byaing Ye O Zin St, Tarmway, Yangon, Myanmar (acc 50)

Day Care Centre for Children
Tarmway Corps

❛ Inspired and challenged to do more to build God's Kingdom, delegates returned to their corps armed with a greater depth and knowledge of God **❜**

SOUTH AMERICA EAST TERRITORY

Territorial leaders:
Colonels Nestor and Rebecca Nuesch

Territorial Commander:
Colonel Nestor Nuesch (1 Dec 2006)

Chief Secretary:
Lieut-Colonel Luis E. Castillo (1 Apr 2004)

Territorial Headquarters: Avda Rivadavia 3257 (C1203AAE), Buenos Aires, Argentina

Postal address: Casilla de Correos 2240 (C1000WAW) Buenos Aires, Argentina

Tel/fax: [54] (11) 4864-9321/9348/9491/1075; email: ejersaljefatura@SAE.salvationarmy.org;

web site: www.ejercitodesalvacion.org.ar

Four officers, who knew no Spanish, established The Salvation Army in Buenos Aires in 1890. Operations spread to other South American nations, of which Paraguay (1910), Uruguay (1890) and Argentina now comprise the South America East Territory.

The Salvation Army was recognised as a juridical person in Argentina by the Government Decree of 26 February 1914 (No A 54/909); in Uruguay by the Ministry of the Interior on 17 January 1917 (No 366537); and in Paraguay by Presidential Decree of 28 May 1928 (No 30217).

Zone: Americas and Caribbean
Countries included in the territory: Argentina, Paraguay, Uruguay
'The Salvation Army' in Spanish: Ejército de Salvación
Language in which the gospel is preached: Spanish, Korean, Guaraní
Periodicals: *El Cruzado*, *El Oficial*, *El Salvacionista*, *El Mensajero* (Women's Ministries magazine)

UNDER the leadership of then territorial leaders Colonels Peder and Janet Refstie, showers of blessings fell upon 112 officers in the Argentinian mountains while attending their retreat (21-24 November 2006). With the theme 'Seeking the Face of Jesus', all were encouraged and strengthened in their spiritual lives and ministry.

The installation of Colonels Nestor and Rebecca Nüesch as the territorial leaders (7 December) was conducted by Commissioner William Francis (then International Secretary for the Americas and Caribbean) and Commissioner Marilyn Francis. The visiting speakers brought not only a sense of dignity and importance to the occasion but also an awareness of God's presence as the incoming leaders were charged with their new responsibilities.

Two days later the territorial commander conducted the commissioning of five cadets of the Heralds of the Good News Session – an exciting occasion.

The excitement of the Army spirit continued as Buenos Aires Division celebrated 'Salvationist Week' (11-17 December) in downtown Buenos Aires. Many officers and soldiers participated in music, singing and fund-raising for Salvation Army social work.

The Home League's traditional four-fold programme – worship, education, fellowship, service – continues to be the main territorial emphasis of women's ministries, so it was very pleasing that Norway sponsored Baby Song training seminars in Montevideo and Salto.

However, women's ministries have a varied and sometimes unusual expression within the territory, such as teaching skills in haircutting, dressmaking and electrical home appliance repairs.

Two new home leagues have been started – in the Argentinian city of Pigué and in the town of Rivera (Uruguay).

While spiritual showers continued to fall upon the territory, it was most unexpected that April showers would bring torrential floods to the city of Rosario in Santa Fe Province (Argentina). For six days Salvation Army personnel assisted flood victims with food, housing, whatever material goods could be obtained and, most importantly, spiritual encouragement during their time of crisis.

STATISTICS

Officers 147 (active 117 retired 30) **Cadets** 8 **Employees** 117
Corps 41 **Outposts** 19 **Institutions** 41
Senior Soldiers 1,606 **Adherents** 604 **Junior Soldiers** 583

STAFF

Personnel: Maj Ricardo Bouzigues
Programme: Maj Raúl Bernao
Business Administration: Maj Lidia Saavedra
Women's Ministries: Col Rebecca Nuesch
(TPWM) Lt-Col Aída Castillo (TSWM)
Maj Lidia Bernao (TLOMS) Lt-Col Evangelina
Luriaud (SSF)

Education: Maj Ricardo Bouzigues
Finance: Sergio Cerezo (Accountant in charge)
Legal: Rene Menares
Music and Gospel Arts: S/L Omar Pérez
Projects/Sponsorship/Missing Persons: Claudia
Franchetti
Property: Rolando Ramírez
Public Relations: Maj Raúl Bernao
Red Shield/Thrift Store Operations:
Lt-Col Jorge Páez
Social: Maj Eduardo Baigorria
Supplies: Maj Lidia Saavedra
Training: Maj John Mowers
Youth and Candidates: Maj Wendy Johnstone

DIVISIONS

Buenos Aires: Avda Rivadavia 3257 – Piso 2
(C1203AAE), Buenos Aires, Argentina;
tel: (011) 4861 1930/9499; Maj Pablo Nicolasa
Central Argentina: Urquiza 2142, (S2000AOD)
Rosario Pcia de Santa Fe, Argentina;
tel/fax: (0341) 425 6739; Maj Carlos Bembhy
Uruguay: Hocquart 1886, (11800) Montevideo,
Uruguay; tel: (598) (2) 409 7581; Maj Bartolo
Aguirre

DISTRICTS

Paraguay and Northeast Argentina: Dr Hassler
y MacArthur 4402, Casilla 92, Asunción,
Paraguay; tel/fax: 595 (21) 608 584;
Maj Danton Moya
Southern Argentina: Moreno 763 (B8000FWO)
Bahía Blanca, Pcia de Buenos Aires;
tel/fax: (0291) 4533 642; Maj Dorcila Soza

TRAINING COLLEGE

Avda Tte Gral Donato Álvarez 465/67,
(C1406BOC) Buenos Aires;
tel/fax: (011) 4631 4815

COMMUNITY AND DAY CARE CENTRES

Argentina: Pellegrini 376, (E3200AMF)
Concordia (Entre Ríos); tel: (0345) 421 1751
(acc 30)
Uruguay: Sarandí 1573, (60,000) Paysandú;
tel: (72) 22709 (acc 30)

CONFERENCE CENTRES AND YOUTH CAMP
Argentina

Parque General Jorge L. Carpenter, Avda Benavídez, (Paraguay y Uruguay) (1619) Benavídez, Pcia de Buenos Aires; tel: (03488) 458644

Betel, Arruabarrena 1659, (X5174GKG) Huerta Grande, Córdoba; tel: (03548) 423747

Parque El Oasis, Ruta 14 Km 7 Camino Público a Rosario – Zona Rural (Santa Fe); tel: (0341) 495 0003

SOCIAL SERVICES
Counselling and Labour Exchange
Argentina: Loria 190, (C1173ACD) Buenos Aires; tel: (011) 4865 0074

Boys' Home
Uruguay: El Lucero, J. M. Blanes 62, (50,000) Salto; tel: (732) 32740 (acc 30)

Children's Homes (mixed)
Argentina: Evangelina, Monroe 1166, (B1878IPP) Quilmes, Pcia de Buenos Aires; tel: (011) 4253 0623 (acc 32)

Paraguay: El Redil, Dr Hassler y MacArthur, Asunción; tel: [595] (21) 600 291 (acc 40)

Eventide Homes
Argentina

Catalina Higgins Home, Calle Mitre, 54 No 2749, (1650) Villa Maipú, San Martín, Pcia de Buenos Aires; tel: (011) 4753 4117 (acc 54)

Eliasen Home, Primera Junta 750 (B1878IPP) Quilmes, Pcia de Buenos Aires; tel: (011) 4254 5897 (acc 37)

Uruguay: El Atardecer, Avda Agraciada 3567, (11800) Montevideo; tel: (2) 308 5227/309 5385 (acc 75)

Industrial Homes
Argentina

Avda Sáenz 580, (C1437DNS) Buenos Aires; tel: (011) 4911 7561/0781/7585

Amenábar 581, (S2000OQK) Rosario; tel: (0341) 482 0155

O'Brien 1272/84, (C1137ABD) Buenos Aires; tel: (011) 4305 5021

Salta 3197, Barrio San Javier, (H3500BOF) Resistencia; tel: (03722) 466 529

Night Shelters
(Men)
Argentina

Alberdi 773 bis, (S2000AOD) Rosario, Pcia de Santa Fe; tel: (0341) 425 0861 (acc 20)

Copahué 2032, (C1288ABB) Buenos Aires; tel: (011) 438 6750 (acc 75)

Godoy Cruz 352, (M5500GOQ) Mendoza, Pcia de Mendoza; tel: (0261) 429 6113 (acc 24)

Maza 2258 (C1240ADV) Buenos Aires; tel: (011) 4912 0843 (acc 86)

(Women and Children)
Argentina

José I. Rucci 1231, (B1822CJY) Valentín Alsina, Pcia de Buenos Aires; tel: (011) 4228 4328 (acc 34)

O'Brien 1272, (C1137ABD) Buenos Aires; tel: (011) 4304 8753 (acc 38)

Students' Homes
Argentina

Bat de Junín 2921, (S3000ASQ) Santa Fe; tel: (0342) 452 0563 (acc 28)

Calle 4, No 711, (1900) La Plata, Pcia de Buenos Aires; tel: (0221) 483 6152 (acc 16)

Félix Frías 434/6, (X5000AHJ) Córdoba; tel: (0351) 423 3228 (acc 15)

San Martín 964 (U9100BET) Trelew, (Chubut); tel: (02965) 433 125 (acc 20)

Women's Residence
Argentina: Esparza 93, (C1171ACA) Buenos Aires; tel: (011) 4861 3119 (acc 56)

Primary School
Argentina: EEGB No 1027 Federico Held, Barrio ULM, (3730) Charata, Pcia del Chaco; tel: (03731) 421 292 (acc 450)

Medical Clinic
Paraguay: Héroes de la Independencia y Vietnam, Villa Laurelty, San Lorenzo; tel: [595] 21 577 082

‘ Women's ministries have a varied and sometimes unusual expression within the territory, such as teaching skills in haircutting, dressmaking and electrical repairs ’

SOUTH AMERICA WEST TERRITORY

Territorial leaders:
Colonels Jorge and Adelina Ferreira

Territorial Commander:
Colonel Jorge Ferreira (1 Feb 2007)

Chief Secretary:
Lieut-Colonel Susan McMillan (1 Jul 2003)

Territorial Headquarters: Avda España 44, Santiago, Chile

Postal address: Casilla 3225, Santiago 1, Chile (parcels/courier service: Avenida Espana No 44, Santiago Centro, Santiago, Chile)

Tel: [56] (2) 671 8237/695 7005; fax: [56] (2) 698 5560

email: southamericawest@salvationarmy.org

Salvation Army operations were commenced in Chile soon after the arrival of Brigadier and Mrs William T. Bonnet to Valparaíso on 1 October 1909. The first corps was opened in Santiago on 28 November, with Captain David Arn and Lieutenant Alfred Danielson as officers. Adjutant and Mrs David Thomas, with Lieutenant Zacarías Ribeiro, pioneered in Peru in March 1910. The work in Bolivia, started in December 1920, was planned by Brigadier Chas Hauswirth and established by Adjutant and Mrs Oscar E. Ahlm. Quito saw the Army's arrival in Ecuador on 30 October 1985 under the command of Captain and Mrs Eliseo Flores Morales.

Zone: Americas and Caribbean

Countries included in the territory: Bolivia, Chile, Ecuador, Peru

'The Salvation Army' in Aymara: Ejercitunaca Salvaciananaca; in Quechua: Ejercituman Salvacionman; in Spanish: Ejército de Salvación

Languages in which the gospel is preached: Aymara, Quechua, Spanish

Publications: *El Grito de Guerra* (*The War Cry*), *El Trebol* (Women's Ministries annual magazine and programme aids)

WITH a territorial theme of 'Because Your Word ... Challenges Me to Serve', Salvationists were mobilised to find new and better ways of serving Christ and their fellow men and women.

An emphasis was placed on uniting corps and social work, involving soldiers in the ministry of Salvation Army social service centres to a greater extent, and bringing those centres' clients into a relationship with corps fellowships – the body of Christ.

It was with great joy and hope that the territory inaugurated its Enterprise Development (recycling) programme. Two stores and a warehouse are contributing to this operation, with plans for two more stores in the near future.

In Chile, The Salvation Army was privileged to be awarded six contracts by the government to open and operate infant care centres. This was part of a government election promise to open

217

800 such centres in the country by the end of 2006.

The Army's six centres are model infant care centres being operated by corps. In one case the centre is the tip of the lance for a Salvation Army operation in a new community.

Santiago's ecumenical community honoured the first Salvation Army 'martyr' – Lieutenant Per Alfred Danielsson, a Swedish officer who helped begin the Army's work in this territory but died at a young age. He was recognised at the Reformation Day celebration (28 October 2006) as one of the early evangelical missionaries who opened the way for the evangelical Church that now serves Chile.

In Ecuador, a human trafficking project has included educating community leaders to encourage their people to recognise the dangers of trafficking. In addition, a home was opened for pregnant teens, many of whom have been victims of trafficking.

Two more outposts were opened in Bolivia, in communities very needful of the Army's presence. Both are doing well, one with the help of an international sponsorship agency to provide an after-school care centre for 150 children.

Peru celebrated 96 years of Salvation Army ministry in that country with a divisional congress. Commissioners Carl and Gudrun Lydholm (territorial leaders for Norway, Iceland and The Færoes) were the special guests and brought blessing to their Peruvian comrades.

After the launch of the 2007 theme – 'Because Your Word ... Sends Me Forth in Mission' – the first territorial event of the year was the Executive Officers Conference, with Lieut-Colonel Lyell Rader (USA Eastern Territory) as guest Bible teacher. His inspiring lectures set the tone for the year's emphasis.

STATISTICS
Officers 294 (active 262 retired 32) **Cadets** (1st Yr) 11 (2nd Yr) 6 **Employees** 824
Corps 84 **Outposts** 18 **Schools 15 After School/ Community Centres** 35 **Hospital** 1 **Kindergartens** 28 **Institutions** 22
Senior Soldiers 3,891 **Adherents** 466 **Junior Soldiers** 1,775

STAFF
Business Administration: Maj María de Alarcón
Personnel: Maj David Alarcón
Programme: Maj Antonio Arguedas
Women's Ministries: Col Adelina de Ferreira (TPWM)

Education: Lt-Col Luis Aguilera
Schools: Maj Elizabeth de Negrete
Finance and Legal: Maj María de Alarcón
Public Relations and Property: Maj María Flores
Social and Sponsorship: Capt Paulina de Márquez
Strategic Planning: Maj Eliseo Flores
Trade: Capt Manuel Márquez
Literary and Editor, *The War Cry*: Maj Lilian de Arguedas
Training: Maj Ángela de García
Candidates: Maj Lilian de Arguedas
Enterprise Development: Maj Domingo Negrete

DIVISIONS
Bolivia Altiplano: Calle Cañada Strongest 1888, Zona San Pedro, Casilla 926, La Paz, Bolivia; tel: 591 (2) 249-1560; fax: 591 (2) 248-5948; Maj Eliseo Flores
Bolivia Central: Calle Rico Toro 773 Zona Queru Queru, Casilla 3594, Cochabamba; tel: 591 (4) 4454281 - 4454337; fax: 591 (4) 411-5887; Maj Franklin Abasto
Chile Central: Agustinas 3020, Casilla 3225, Santiago 1; tel/fax: 56 (2) 681-4992/681-5277; Maj Cecilia Bahamonde

Chile South: Av Caupolicán 990, Casilla 1064, Temuco; tel: 56 (45) 215-850; fax: 56 (2) 271-425; Maj Juan Carlos Alarcón

Ecuador: Tomas Chariove N49-144 y Manuel Valdivieso, El Pinar, Casilla 17 10.7179, Quito; tel/fax: 593 (2) 243-5422/244-7829; Maj Jaime Herrera

Peru: Calle Zaragoza 215, Urbanización Parque San Martín, Pueblo Libre, Lima 21, Apartado 690, Lima 100; tel: 51 (1) 463-1149, 463-1441; fax: 51 (1) 261-4694; Maj Alex Nesterenko

DISTRICT

Chile North: Sucre 866, Casilla 310, Antofagasta; tel: 56 (55) 280-668; fax: 56 (55) 224-094; Maj Luis Cisternas

TRAINING COLLEGE

Escuela de Cadetes: Coronel Souper 4564, Santiago, Chile; tel: 56 (2) 776-2425/ 776-0865; fax: 56 (2) 779-9187

SALVATION ARMY CAMP GROUNDS

Bolivia

Chaparé, Chimoré: Población Chimoré, Chaparé

Eben-Ezer: Los Yungas, Puente Villa, Comunidad Tarila, Provincia Nor Yungas

Chile

Arica: Parcela 16, Calle San Martín, Villa la Frontera, Arica

El Complejo Angostura: Panamericana Sur Km 55, Sur de Santiago; tel: 591 (2) 825-0398

EDUCATIONAL WORK

BIBLE INSTITUTE

Prolongación Illampu 188, Zona San Pedro, La Paz, Bolivia; tel: 591 (2) 231-1189 (acc 20)

VOCATIONAL MINISTRIES

Bolivia

Lindgren: Murillo 434, Barrio Central Viacha, La Paz; tel/fax: 591 (2) 280-0969 (acc 200)

William Booth: Sucre 909, Oruro; tel/fax:591 (2) 525-1369 (acc 480)

SCHOOLS

Bolivia

Villa Cosmos: Uraciri Patica 2064, Barrio Cosmos 79, Unidad Vecinal C; tel: 591 (2) 288-0118 (acc 175)

William Booth: Sucre 909, Oruro; tel/fax: 591 (2) 525-1369 (acc 800)

Chile

Arica: Av Cancha Rayada 3839, Segunda Etapa, Poblacion Cardenal Silva Henriquez, Casilla 203, Arica; tel/fax: 56 (58) 211-100 (acc 678)

Calama: Aníbal Pinto 2121, Calama; tel/fax: 56 (55) 311-216/345-802 (acc 1,155)

Catalina Booth: Irene Frei 2875, Villa Esmeralda, Calama; tel/fax: 56 (55) 312-608 (acc 800)

Naciones Unidas: Séptimo de Línea 148, Población Libertad, Puerto Montt; tel/fax: 56 (65) 254-047/251-918, 56 (2) 6431875 (acc 1,320)

Pudahuel: Mapocho 9047, comuna de Pudahuel, Casilla 3225, Santiago (acc 176)

William Booth: Zenteno 1015, Osorno; tel: 56 (64) 247-449; tel/fax: 56 (64) 233-141 (acc 720)

Peru

Eduardo Palací: Av Progreso 1032, Urb San Gregorio, Vitarte; tel/fax: 51 (1) 356-0297 (acc 500)

Miguel Grau: Av 29 de Diciembre 127, Trujillo; tel/fax: 51 (44) 255-571 (acc 320)

Ecuador: Calle H 1 393 Morales, Urbanización Las Orquídeas, Casilla 1710-7179 Cayambe; tel: 593 (2) 211-0196 (acc 300)

Pre-Primary Schools

Chile

El Bosque: Las Vizcachas 858, Población Las Acacias, El Bosque, Santiago; tel: 56 (2) 529-4242 (acc 45)

Refugio Feliz: Calle Mapocho 9047, Comuna de Pudahuel, Casilla 3225, Santiago; tel: 56 (2) 788-0035 (acc 90)

MEDICAL WORK

Bolivia

Harry Williams Hospital: Av Suecia 1038-1058, Zona Huayra K'assa, Casilla 4099, Cochabamba; tel: 591 (4) 422-7778; fax: 591 (4) 423-1601 (acc 27)

Community Extension Programme: Av Suecia 1038-1058, Zona Huayra K'assa, Casilla 4099, Cochabamba; tel: 591 (4) 422-7778; fax: 591 (4) 423-1601

Mobile Clinic: Av Suecia 1038-1058, Zona Huayra K'assa, Casilla 4099, Cochabamba; tel: 591 (4) 422-7778; fax: 591 (4) 423-1601

Ecuador

Dental Clinic, Quito Sur: Calle Apuela s 25-182 y Malimpia, Santa Rita, Casilla 17.107179; tel: 593 (2) 284-5529

Integral Health Centre, Esmeraldas: Calles Uruguay y Ecuador, Barrio Las Américas, Esmeraldas; tel: 593 (6) 271-0439

Community Health Programme (Rural Areas): Pimampiro, administered by DHQ, Tomás Chariove N49-144 y Manuel Valdivieso, El Pinar, Casilla 17,10.7179, Quito; tel/fax: 593 (2) 243-5422/244-7829

SOCIAL WORK

Social Welfare Office: Herrera 151, Santiago, Chile; tel: 56 (2) 681-2138

Men's Shelters

Bolivia: Calle Prolongación Illampu 188, Zona San Pedro, La Paz, Casilla 926, La Paz; tel: 591 (2) 231-1189 (acc 100)

Chile

Antofagasta: Calle Prat 1045, Casilla 917 Antofagasta; tel: 56 (55) 223-847 (acc 50)

Valparaíso: Calle Villagrán 9, Casilla 1887 Valparasío; tel: 56 (32) 221-4946 (acc 170)

Peru: Calle Colón 138/142, Apartado 139 Callao; tel: 51 (1) 429-3128 (acc 62)

Transit House (Women)

Chile: Calle Zenteno 1499, Santiago, Casilla 3225, Santiago; tel: 56 (2) 554-1767 (acc 16)

Pregnant Teens Refuge

Ecuador: Manta, Avda 201 entre calles 116 y 117, Barrio La Paz, Casilla 13-05-149; tel: 593 (5) 292-0147 (acc 40)

Student Residence Halls
Bolivia

'Dr María J. Saavedra' (girls): Villa 8 de Diciembre, Calle Rosendo Gutiérrez 120, Barrio Alto Sopocachi, Casilla 926, La Paz; tel: 591 (2) 241-0470 (acc 10)

'Remedios Asín' (girls): Cañada Strongest #1888, Casilla 926, La Paz; tel: 591 (2) 248-0502 (acc 55)

'Tte-Coronel Jorge Nery Torrico' (boys): Calle Junin 496, Entre 6 de Octubre y Potosí, Oruro (acc 24)

'Tte-Coronel Rosa de Nery' (girls): Calle Lanza S-0555, Casilla 3198, Cochabamba; tel: 591 (4) 422-6553/1491 (acc 40)

Chile

'Casa Betania' (boys): Calle Sucre 866, Casilla 310, Antofagasta; tel: 56 (55) 284-763 (acc 30)

'El Faro' (boys): Calle Santiago Concha 1333,

Casilla 3225, Santiago 21; tel: 56 (2) 555-3406 (acc 24)

Peru

'Catalina Booth' (girls): Jirón Huancayo 245, Apartado 690, Lima 100; tel: 51 (1) 433-8747 (acc 28)

'Las Palmeras': Jirón Amoraca 212, Distrito Morales Tarapoto, San Martín, Apartado 88, Tarapoto, San Martín; tel: 51 (94) 527-540 (acc 20)

Children's Homes
Bolivia

Evangelina Booth Girls' Home, Francisco Viedma 1054, Villa Montenegro, Casilla 542, Cochabamba; tel: 591 (4) 424-1560 (acc 40)

Maria Remedios Asin Boys' Home, Calle Murillo 436, Barrio Central Viacha, Casilla 15084, La Paz; tel/fax: 591 (2) 280-0404 (acc 70)

Oscar Ahlm's Boys' Home, Km 19 Carretera a Oruro/Camino a Comunidad Thiomogo, San Jorge, Vinto Casilla 542, Cochabamba; tel: 591 (4) 435-6264 (acc 45)

Chile

El Broquel Girls' Home: 12 Poniente 8390, La Granja, Casilla 3225, Santiago 1; tel/fax: 56 (2) 541-6079 (acc 40)

El Redil Boys' Home: Calle Arzobispo Valdivieso 410, Casilla 61, Llo Lleo; tel: 56 (35) 282-054 (acc 60)

Los Copihues Girls' Home: Calle Los Sauces 0202, Población Las Quilas, Casilla 1064, Temuco; tel: 56 (45) 234-028/275-008 (acc 60)

Tte-Coronel Helmuth Hühner Boys' Home: Av Arturo Allessandri 6342, Lo Valledor, Pedro Aguirre Cerda, Casilla 3225, Santiago 1; tel: 56 (2) 521-5575 (acc 69)

Eventide Home

Chile: Otoño Dorado, Av La Florida 9995, La Florida; tel: 56 (2) 287-5280; tel/fax: 56 (2) 287-1869 (acc 40)

Day Care Centres for the Aged

Chile: Berlín 818, Población Los Lagos, Angol; tel: 56 (45) 712-583 (acc 20)

Ecuador: Calle Montalvo 220 Cayambe; tel: 593 (2) 236-1273 (acc 60)

Day Nurseries/Kindergartens
Bolivia

Catalina Booth: Lanza S-0555, Zona Central, Casilla 542, Cochabamba; tel: 591 (4) 449-3258 (acc 150)

Cuerpo Central Santa Cruz: Calle Corumba 2360
(Esq Calle Cañada Larga) Barrio Lazareto,
Casilla 2576, Santa Cruz; tel: 591 (3) 346-3531
(acc 30)

La Roca: Calicanto, Casilla 3596, Cochabamba;
tel: 591 7039 1241 (acc 45)

Mi Casita: Calle J. Mostajo s/n, Zona El Temporal,
Cochabamba; tel: 591 (4) 445-0809 (acc 70)

Nueva Vida: Uv 133 – Final Avenida Santos
Dumont, Barrio Santa Fe de Palmasola,
Manzana 28, Casa 2, Casilla 4819, Zona Sur
Santa Cruz; tel: 591 (3) 356-9760 (acc 100)

Refugio de Amor: Villa 8 de Diciembre, Calle
Rosendo Gutiérrez 120, Barrio Alto Sopocachi,
Casilla 926, La Paz; tel: 591 (2) 2410470 (acc 50)

Wawasninchej: Av Suecia 1083, Zona Huayra
K'assa, Casilla 542, Cochabamba;
tel: 591 (4) 422-4808 (acc 56)

Chile:

Arca de Noé: El Fundador 13678, Población
Santiago de la Nueva Extremadura, La Pintana,
Casilla 3225, Santiago 1 (acc 18)

Catalina Booth: Hipólito Salas 760, Concepción;
tel: 56 (41) 223-0447 (acc 24)

Faro de Angeles: Calle Santa Martha 443, Cerro
Playa Ancha, Casilla 1887, Valparaíso;
tel: 56 (32) 228-1160 (acc 100)

'Gotitas': Avda Carlos Condell 1535, Los Salares,
Casilla 436, Copiapó; tel: 56 (52) 216-099
(acc 80)

'Las Estrellitas': Esmeralda 862, Casilla 134,
Iquique; tel/fax: 56 (57) 42135 (acc 18)

La Estrellita: Maipú 284, Maipú, Casilla 3225,
Santiago 1; tel: 56 (2) 531-2638 (acc 55)

Lautarito: Castro 5193, Población Lautaro,
Casilla 581, Antofagasta; tel: 56 (55) 380-719
(acc 70)

Neptuno: Los Aromos 833, Lo Prado, Casilla
3225, Santiago 1; tel: 56 (2) 773-5154 (acc 60)

Nido Alegre: Calle Santa Petronila 1048, Quinta
Normal, Casilla 3225, Santiago 1;
tel: 56 (2) 773-8554 (acc 96)

Padre las Casas: Calle los Misioneros #1354,
Comuna de Padre las Casas, Temuco (acc 20)

Puente Alto: Santo Domingo 90, Comuna Pte
Alto, Casilla 3225, Santiago 1;
tel: 56 (2) 419-0110/850-3331 (acc 75)

Rancagua: Iquique 24, esquina Bolivia, Población
San Francisco, Rancagua; tel: 56 (72) 239-028
(acc 18)

Rayito de Luz: Picarte 1894, Valdivia;
tel/fax: 56 (63) 214-404 (acc 120)

Rayitos de Sol: Av Brasil 73, Casilla 3225,
Santiago 1; tel: 56 (2) 699-3595;
fax: 56 (2) 688-4755 (acc 100)

Ecuador

Arca de Noe: Avda 201, entre calles 116 y 117,
Barrio La Paz, Casilla 13-05-149, Manta;
tel: 593 (5) 292-0147 (acc 80)

Gotitas de Miel: Montalvo 220, Cayambe, Casilla
17.1071.79, Quito; tel: 593 (2) 236 1273
(acc 100)

La Colmena: Calle Pomasqui 955 y Pedro
Andrade, La Colmena, Casilla 17.1071.79,
Quito; tel: 593 (2) 258 1081, 228 4776
(acc 60)

Mi Casita: Apuela S25-182 y Malimpia, Santa
Rita, Casilla 17.1071.79, Quito;
tel: 593 (2) 284-5529 (acc 40)

'Mi Hermoso Redil': Urbanización Sierra
Hermosa, Calle 5, lotes 237-239, Parroquia de
Carapungo, Quito;   tel: 593 (2) 282-6835
(acc 40)

Nueva Esperanza: Av Martha de Roldós km 5½,
Via Daule, Casilla 09.01.10478, Guayaquil;
tel: 593 (4) 300-0842 (acc 40)

Pedacito de Cielo: Calles Uruguay y Ecuador,
Barrio Las Américas, Esmeraldas;
tel: 593 (06) 2710-439 (acc 150)

Food Aid Programme

Chile: Oscar Bonilla 2, Calle Ejército 721,
Ancud; tel: 56 (65) 622-045 (acc 80)

Peru

Chiclayo: PP.JJ. Sto Toribio de Mogrovejo,
MZ 'I' Lote 6 (primer sector);
tel: 51 (74) 201-883 (acc 100)

'El Porvenir': Calle Synneva Vestheim 583,
Caserío El Porvenir, Provincia Rioja, Dpto
San Martín (community phone) (acc 30)

Tacna: Av Los Pintores 575, Urb Las Begonias,
'Cono Sur Este', Apartado 806, Tacna;
tel: 51 (52) 400-612 (acc 80)

Community Day Centres/School-Age Day Care Centres (attached to corps/outposts)

Bolivia

Achachicala, La Paz (acc 291)
Batallón Colorados, Sucre (acc 60)
Corqueamaya, La Paz (acc 70)
El Tejar, La Paz (acc 100)
El Temporal, Cochabamba (acc 75)
'El Vergel' Nutritional Programme, Chaparé
(acc 40)
Huayra K'assa, Cochabamba (acc 50)
La Chimba, Cochabamba (acc 80)
Lacaya, La Paz (acc 75)
Pacata, Cochabamba (acc 35)
Parotani, Cochabamba (acc 60)

Salvationists in South America West live out their territorial slogan 'Because Your Word ... Challenges Me to Serve' as a cadet provides a homeless man in Santiago, Chile, with a hot meal and THQ staff and Folklore Choir prepare to bring Christmas cheer to hospital patients

Pockonas, Sucre (acc 50)
Potosí, (acc 30)
Primero de Mayo, Santa Cruz (acc 50)
Tarija (acc 50)
Tiahuanacu, La Paz (acc 100)
Viacha, La Paz (acc 400)
Villa Canteria, Potosí (acc 150)
Villa Cosmos, La Paz (acc 300)
Villa Fátima, La Paz (acc 80)
Zona Este de Oruro, Oruro (acc 300)

Chile
Las Acacias, Santiago (acc 50)
Martha Brunet, Santiago (acc 50)
Nueva Extremadura, Santiago (acc 40)
Puente Alto, Santiago (acc 75)

Ecuador
El Rancho, Quito (acc 120)
Gotitas de Miel, Quito (acc 50)
Mi Casita, Quito (acc 120)
Nido Alegre, Quito (acc 130)

Nueva Esperanza, Guayaquil (acc 140)

Peru
Buenos Aires (acc 50)
La Esperanza, Trujillo (acc 40)
San Martín de Porras, Lima (acc 40)
Tacna (acc 80)
Vitarte, Lima (acc 80)

Enterprise Development
Warehouse: Coronel Souper 4564, Estación Central, Casilla 3225, Santiago 1, Chile; tel: 562 764 1917

Family Intervention Centre
Av Alemania 3510, Hualpencillo, Talcahuano, Casilla 1171, Concepción, Chile: tel/fax: 56 (41) 434-410 (acc 150)

Tailoring Workshop and Sewing Centre
Talle de Costura SPS, Calle Apuela S25-182 y Malimpia, Santa Rita, Casilla 17.1071.79, Quito, Ecuador; tel: 593 (2) 284-5529

SOUTHERN AFRICA TERRITORY

Territorial leaders:
Commissioners Trevor and Memory Tuck

Territorial Commander:
Commissioner Trevor Tuck (1 Jun 2005)

Chief Secretary:
Lieut-Colonel Joash Malabi (1 Feb 2007)

Territorial Headquarters: 119-121 Rissik Street, Wanderers' View, Johannesburg 2001

Postal address: PO Box 1018, Johannesburg 2000, South Africa

Tel: [27] (011) 718 6700; fax: [27] (011) 718 6790;

email: CS_SouthernAfrica@SAF.salvationarmy.org; web site: www.salvationarmy.co.za

On 4 March 1883 Major and Mrs Francis Simmonds with Lieutenant Alice Teager 'opened fire' in Cape Town. Other officers were sent to the island of St Helena in 1886 to consolidate work commenced (in 1884) by Salvationist 'Bluejackets'. Social services began in 1886. The Army's first organised ministry among the African people was established in 1888 in Natal and, in 1891, in Zululand. Evangelistic effort in Mozambique, pioneered in 1916 by African converts, was officially recognised in 1923.

Zone: Africa

Countries included in the territory: Lesotho, Mozambique, Namibia, St Helena, South Africa, Swaziland

'The Salvation Army' in Afrikaans: Die Heilsleër; in IsiXhosa: Umkhosi wo Sindiso; in IsiZulu: Impi yo Sindiso; in Portuguese: Exército de Salvação; in SeSotho: Mokhosi oa Poloko; in SiPedi: Mogosi wa Pholoso; in Tshivenda: Mbi ya u Tshidza; in Tsonga: Nyi Moi Yoponisa

Languages in which the gospel is preached: Afrikaans, English, Portuguese, SeSotho, Shangaan, SiPedi, Tsonga, Tswana, Tshivenda, IsiXhosa, IsiZulu

Periodicals: *Echoes of Mercy, Home League Highlights, Home League Resource Manual, Outer Circle Newsletter, SAMF Newsletter, The Reporter, The War Cry*

TERRITORIAL leaders Commissioners Trevor and Memory Tuck continued their territorial vision of 'Together with Christ in Mission' by holding a further three mission conferences early in 2007 for all leaders. Bible conventions took place in three divisions during 2006 and early 2007.

The territory considered it a privilege to send two officers to Germany for the FIFA Soccer World Cup 2006. They were part of an international team of eight Salvation Army evangelists based for two weeks in Gelsenkirchen. Two delegates attended the Roots Conference held in the USA.

Retired General Paul Rader and Commissioner Kay Rader visited the territory during June 2006. Other visitors were Commissioners Max and Lenora Feener (USA Southern), who conducted the opening and dedication of a new regional headquarters building in Maputo, Mozambique (February

2007). This project was financed by USA Southern Territory.

In August 2006 the territory hosted the Army's second International Theology and Ethics Symposium. The General brought an opening greeting and gave the Bible message during Sunday morning worship.

During the latter part of 2006 a team of four officers was assigned to visit Namibia to investigate the possibility of re-establishing The Salvation Army in that country. Shortly after the beginning of the Second World War the Army's work closed in South West Africa (Namibia).

In his book *Salvation Safari* (published in 1985), Colonel Brian Tuck wrote: 'Whilst there may have been real reasons why the Army "could do no mighty works" in South West Africa, the failure to accept the risk of going back needs to be righted by future generations of Salvationists.'

The territory decided the time was right for a possible return and sent an investigatory party. Team members agreed it had been a fruitful exploration and that the harvest is ready.

Following the visit of the General's Representative for Global Evangelisation, Colonel Dick Krommenhoek, during February 2007, the General approved the recommendation to commence work in Namibia.

A number of leadership changes included Lieut-Colonels Joash and Florence Malabi (from Kenya) being welcomed as Chief Secretary and Territorial Secretary for Women's Ministries respectively.

STATISTICS

Officers 327 (active 222 retired 105) **Auxiliary-Captains** 12 **Lieutenants** 10 **Cadets** 7 **Employees** 510

Corps 235 **Corps Plants, Societies and Outposts** 96 **Mission Team** 1 **Schools** 3 **Hospitals** 2 **Institutions** 25 **Day Care Centres** 18 **Goodwill Centres** 7 **Recycling Stores** 4 **Nursery Schools** 3

Senior Soldiers 29,226 **Adherents** 1,741 **Junior Soldiers** 4,767

STAFF

Business Administration: Maj Timothy Mabaso
Child Sponsorship: Maj Eva Marseille
Ecumenical: Maj Paul Khantsi
Editor: Maj Eva Marseille
Education: Maj Mercy Mahlangu
Family Health: Maj Lenah Jwili
Family Tracing: Lt-Col Veronica Trollip
Finance: Maj Gerrit Marseille
Health Services: Capt (Dr) Felicia Christians
HIV/Aids Ministries: Maj Lenah Jwili
Information Technology: Capt Jonathan Payne
Personnel: Maj William Langa
Programme: Maj Barry Schwartz
Projects: Mr Gavin Blackwood
Property: Maj Andrew Moholoagae
Public Relations: Maj Harry Fillies
Trade: Mrs Helen Tuck
Training: Maj Alistair Venter (S Afr) Capt Mario Nhacuba (Mozambique)
  Candidates: Maj Alistair Venter
Women's Ministries: Comr Memory Tuck (TPWM) Lt-Col Florence Malabi (TSWM) Maj Flemah Mabaso (LOM/SAMF)
Youth: Capt Stephen Malins

REGION

Mozambique: Ave Armando Tivane 849, Maputo, Mozambique;
tel: [258] 1 487 422/423; fax: [258] 1 487 408;
Regional Sec: Maj Célestin Pululu

DIVISIONS

Central: PO Box 756, Rosettenville, Johannesburg 2130; tel: (011) 435-0267; fax: (011) 435-2835; Maj Albert Shekwa
Eastern Cape: PO Box 12514, Centralhill, Port Elizabeth 6006; tel: (041) 585-5363; fax: (041) 586-3521; Maj Daniel Kasuso
Eastern Kwa Zulu/Natal: PO Box 1267, Eshowe 3815; tel: (035) 474-1132; fax: (035) 474-1132
Mid Kwa Zulu/Natal: PO Box 100061, Scottsville, Pietermaritzburg 3209;

tel: (033) 386-3881; fax: (033) 386-8019;
Maj Jabulani Khoza

Mpumalanga/Swaziland: PO Box 1571,
Nelspruit 1200; tel/fax: (013) 741-2869;
Maj Ivy Mntambo

Northern: PO Box 3549, Louis Trichardt 0920;
tel/fax: (015) 963-6145; Maj Johannes
Raselalome

Northern Kwa Zulu/Natal: PO Box 923,
Vryheid 3100; tel: (034) 982-3113;
fax: (034) 983-2882; Maj Bennie Harms

Western Cape: PO Box 13079, Mowbray,
Cape Town 7705; tel: (021) 689-8915;
fax: (021) 689-3023; Maj Lindsay Rowe

St Helena: The Salvation Army, Jamestown,
Island of St Helena, South Atlantic Ocean;
tel: 09 (290) 2703; fax: 09 (290) 2052

COLLEGES FOR OFFICER TRAINING

South Africa: PO Box 32902, Braamfontein 2017;
tel: (011) 718 6762

Mozambique: Rua Hospital de Bagamoio 1360,
(Post Box) CP 4099, Maputo;
tel: [258] 01 471421

DAY CARE CENTRES FOR PRE-SCHOOL CHILDREN

Central: Benoni, Eldorado Park, Galashewe,
Katlehong, Lethlabile, Mangaung

Mpumalanga/Swaziland: Barberton,
Emangweni, Pienaar

Mid Kwa Zulu/Natal: Hammarsdale, Imbali,
Kwa Mashu, Umlazi

Northern: Messina

Northern Kwa Zulu/Natal: Ezakheni,
Madadeni, Mondlo, Ulundi, Vryheid

Western Cape: Bonteheuwel, Mitchells
Plein, Manenburg

DAY CARE CENTRES FOR SENIOR CITIZENS

Central: Benoni, Kimberley, Krugersdorp,
Pretoria, Vereeniging

Eastern Cape: East London, Port Elizabeth

Mid Kwa Zulu/Natal: Pietermaritzburg

Western Cape: Goodwood

GOODWILL CENTRES

Benoni West 1503: Benoni Goodwill Centre,
PO Box 17299

East London, Vincent 5217: Hind House,
PO Box 13012

Kimberley 8300: Kimberley Goodwill Centre,
PO Box 1691

Krugersdorp 1740: Family Mission Centre,
PO Box 351

Pietermaritzburg, Scottsville 3209: Hope
Goodwill House, PO Box 100-213

Vereeniging 1930: Sally Ann Cottage,
PO Box 2090

HEALTH SERVICES

Booth Hospital: 32 Prince St, Oranjezicht, Cape
Town 8001; tel: (021) 465-4896/46 (acc 84)

Mountain View Hospital: PO Salvation 3110,
via Vryheid, Natal; tel: (034) 967-1544 (acc 88)

Msunduza Community and Primary Health Care
Centre and Mbuluzi Clinic: Box 2543,
Mbabane, Swaziland; tel: (268) 404-5243

Community Care Clinics:
Barkerville (Mount Frere), Gumtree, Mahlahleni,
Mooiplaas, Mvusi (Mount Frere), Ombimbini,
Squwbezi

RETIRED OFFICERS RESIDENCES

Doonside 4135: Sunset Lodge, 10 World's
View Cl, World's View

Emmarentia 2029: Emmarentia Flats, PO Box
85214, Johannesburg; tel: (011) 646-2126

Orlando 1804: Ephraim Zulu Flats, PO Box 49;
tel: (011) 982-1084

SOCIAL SERVICES

Crèches

Bridgman Crèche: PO Box 62, Kwa Xuma 1868;
88, 3b White City, Jabavu 1856;
tel: (011) 982-5574 (acc 140)

Carl Sithole Crèche: Carl Sithole Centre, PO Box
180, Orlando 1804; tel: (011) 986-7417 (acc 40)

Children's Homes

Bethany: Carl Sithole Centre, Klipspruit, PO Box
180, Orlando 1804; tel: (011) 986-7417
(acc children 6-18 yrs 110)

Bethesda: Zodwa's House, Carl Sithole Centre,
PO Box 180, Orlando 1804, Soweto
(acc children 2-6 yrs 32)

Ethembeni (Place of Hope): 63 Sherwell St,
Doornfontein, Johannesburg 2094;
tel: (011) 402-8101 (acc children 0-3 yrs 60)

Firlands: Fourth Ave, PO Box 44291, Linden
2104; tel: (011) 782-5556/7 (acc children 3-18
yrs 60)

Joseph Baynes House: 89 Trelawney Rd,
Pentrich, PO Box 212275, Oribi 3205, Natal;
tel: (033) 386-2266 (acc children 0-18 yrs 72)

Strathyre: Eleventh Ave, Dewetshof, PO Box
28240, Kensington 2101, Johannesburg;
tel: (011) 615-7327/7344 (acc children 3-18
yrs 50)

Commissioner Trevor Tuck (TC) addresses the officers who were to visit Namibia to investigate the possibility of re-establishing The Salvation Army in that country

Community Programme

Thusanong/Osizweni: Home-based Community Care and Counselling Programme, Carl Sithole Centre, Klipspruit, Soweto, PO Box 180, Orlando 1804; tel: (011) 986-7417

Street Children's Home

Musawenkosi: PO Box 14794, Madadeni Township 2951 (acc boys 7-18 yrs 16)

Eventide Home (men)

Beth Rogelim: Cape Town 8005, 22 Alfred St; tel: (021) 425-2138 (acc 52)

Eventide Homes (men and women)

Emmarentia: Johannesburg, PO Box 85214, Emmarentia 2029, 113 Komatie Rd; tel: (011) 646-2126 (acc 40)

Ephraim Zulu Senior Citizen Centre: Orlando 1804, PO Box 49; tel: (011) 982-1084 (acc 100)

Salisbury House: East London, 19 Rhodes St, PO Box 18380; tel: (011) 722-4454

Sunset Lodge: Doonside, 4135, 10 World's View Cl, PO Box 53, World's View, 4125, South Coast, Natal; tel: (031) 903-3139 (acc 76)

Thembela: Durban 4001, 68 Montpelier Place; tel: (031) 321-6360 (acc 53)

Homes for Abused Women

Cape Town 8000: Care Haven, PO Box 38186, Gates Ville 7766; tel: (021) 638-5511; fax: (031) 637-0226; email: careaid@iafrica.co.za (acc 18 women, 60 children)

Durban: Family Care, PO Box 47122, Greyville 4023; tel: (031) 309-1395 (acc 45)

Port Elizabeth: Haven of Hope Home, PO Box 2304, North End 6056; tel: (041) 373-4317 (acc 32)

Pretoria: Beth Shan, PO Box 19713, Pretoria West 0117 (acc 15 women)

Men's Homes

Bloemfontein Men's Home: 23 Fountain St, Bloemfontein 9301; tel: (051) 447-2626 (acc 28)

Beth Rogelim: 22 Alfred St, Cape Town 8005; tel: (021) 425-2138 (acc 100)

Durban Men's Home: 150 Berea Rd, Durban 4001; tel: (031) 201-7922/2404 (acc 66)

Rehabilitation Centres

Hesketh King Treatment Centre: PO Box 5, Elsenburg 7607, Cape; tel: (021) 884-4600 (acc 60)

Mountain Lodge: PO Box 168, Magaliesburg 2805 (acc 60)

Social Centres

Durban Family Care Centre: PO Box 47122, Greyville, Durban 4023; tel: (031) 309-1395 (acc 70)

Haven of Hope Home: PO Box 2304, North End, Port Elizabeth 6056; tel: (041) 373-4317 (acc 60)

Johannesburg Social Services: Simmonds St Ext, Johannesburg 2001; tel: (011) 832-1227; fax: (011) 833-6259 (acc 56)

Pretoria Family Care Centre: PO Box 19713, Pretoria West 0117; tel: (012) 327-3005 (acc 80)

SCHOOLS

Bethany Combined School: Carl Sithole Centre, PO Box 180, Orlando 1804; tel: (011) 986-7417

Mathunjwa High School: PO Box 923, Vryheid 3100

William Booth Primary School: Mountain View, PO Salvation 3110; tel: (034) 967-1533

YOUTH TRAINING CENTRE

Mission House, 162 High St, Rosettenville 2130; tel/fax: (011) 435-1822

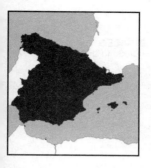

SPAIN COMMAND

Command leaders:
Majors F. Bradford and Heidi Bailey

Officer Commanding:
Major F. Bradford Bailey (1 Aug 2005)

Command Headquarters: Hermosilla 126 Lc 1, 28028 Madrid

Postal address: Ejército de Salvación, c/ Hermosilla, 126 Local 1, 28028 Madrid, Spain

Tel: [34] 91 356 6644; fax: [34] 91 361 4782; email: Spain_Command@SPA.salvationarmy.org

Following the appointment of Captain and Mrs Enrique Rey to La Coruña on Ascension Day 1971, it was announced on 24 December 1971 that The Salvation Army had been granted the status of a Legal Person, enjoying full legal rights in the country and permitted to carry on its work without let or hindrance.

Zone: Europe
Country and autonomous communities included in the territory: Canary Islands, Mallorca, Spain
'The Salvation Army' in Spanish: Ejército de Salvación
Languages in which the gospel is preached: English (Mallorca, Denia), Filipino, Spanish

THE Salvation Army in Spain has celebrated 35 years of dedicated service and continues to have tremendous potential for purposeful and long-lasting growth.

In 2006 the Evangelical Church population grew to more than 350,000 of a total of over 40 million inhabitants. So while the challenge is awesome, Salvationists nevertheless have a clear picture of The Salvation Army's mission in their country.

Focused on and motivated by the theme 'Committed to the Content of The Word', the command celebrated a year for the recruitment of 41 new soldiers. Barcelona Corps recorded a historic enrolment of 25 uniformed soldiers at one time.

Madrid Central Corps marked its 30th anniversary with a weekend of celebrations at which soldiers and friends from the city's three corps gathered together. In the Sunday morning meeting more than 40 people – adults and children – signed a commitment card to pledge their future service to the Lord through The Salvation Army.

The command continues to discover ways to network with like-minded social service organisations in an effort to assist thousands of immigrants who make their way to Spain, looking for a better life. This situation provides opportunities to befriend and serve this disadvantaged, isolated and vulnerable group.

As a founding member and active contributor of 'Diaconia Madrid', The

Salvation Army in Spain has been invited to apply for local and national government funding being released to implement and develop social action strategies that deal with the complex issue of immigration.

The fact that The Salvation Army has made positive inroads into the Latin American immigrant population places it as one of the principle players in implementating innovative social ministry initiatives.

STATISTICS

Officers 33 (active 31 retired 2) **Employees** 26
Corps 11 **Outposts** 5 **Institution** 1
Senior Soldiers 357 **Adherents** 57 **Junior Soldiers** 74
Personnel serving outside command Officers 2

STAFF

Women's Ministries: Maj Heidi Bailey (CPWM)
Business Administration: Maj Ambrosio Aycón
Programme and Evangelism: Maj Juan José Arias
Asst Programme and Evangelism Officer: Maj Belinda Arias
Accountant: Fausta Gonzales
Evangelical Training: Capts Shane and Pauline Gruer-Caulfield
Projects: Maj Heidi Bailey

SOCIAL SERVICES
Food and/or Clothing Distribution Centres

Alicante 03002: Avda de Denia 45, B°5 PB Dcha, Edif Montreal (known as 'La Pirámide)
Barcelona 08024: c/ del Rubí 18
Denia, Alicante 03700: c/ San José 14 B
La Coruña 15010: c/ Francisco Añón 9
Las Palmas 35014: Plaza de los Ruiseñores, Local 8 alto, Miller Bajo
Madrid 28028: c/ Hermosilla, 126, Local 4
Madrid 28038: Avda Rafael Alberti, 18 Bis
Mallorca 07015: Cala Mayor, Avda Joan Miró 285
Tenerife 38006: c/ Marisol Marín 10
Valdemoro-Madrid 28340: c/Bretón de los Herreros 10

Emergency Feeding Kitchens

Alicante 03700: 45, B°5 PB Dcha, Edif Montreal (known as 'La Pirámide)
Barcelona 08024: c/ del Rubí 18
La Coruña 15010: c/ Francisco Añón 9

Thrift Shops 8

Eventide Home (men and women)

Finca El Apostolado, Vereda del Alquitón 9, Arganda del Rey, Madrid 28500 (acc 35)

CONFERENCE, RETREAT AND HOLIDAY CENTRE

Camp Sarón, Partida Torre Carrals 64, 03700 Denia, Alicante; tel: 96 578 2152; fax: 96 643 1206; web site: www.campsaron.com (acc 61)

Spanish Salvationists provide food and clothing for homeless people during the street night patrol in Alicante

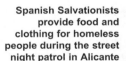

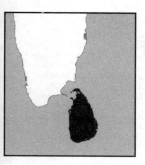

SRI LANKA TERRITORY

Territorial leaders:
Colonels Lalzamlova and Nemkhanching

Territorial Commander:
Colonel Lalzamlova (1 Jun 2006)

Chief Secretary:
Lieut-Colonel Edward Daniel (1 May 2004)

Territorial Headquarters: 53 Sir James Peiris Mawatha, Colombo 2

Postal address: PO Box 193, Colombo, Sri Lanka

Tel: [94] (11) 232 4660/233 2159; fax: [94] (11) 243 6065; web site: www.sri.salvationarmy.org

Salvation Army work began in Ceylon (now Sri Lanka) on 26 January 1883 under the leadership of Captain William Gladwin. 'The General of The Salvation Army' is a corporation Sole by Ordinance No 11 of 1924.

Zone: South Asia
Country included in the territory: Sri Lanka
'The Salvation Army' in Sinhala: Galavime Hamudava; in Tamil: Ratchaniya Senai
Languages in which the gospel is preached: English, Sinhala, Tamil
Periodical: *Yudha Handa (The War Cry)*

THE Salvation Army in Sri Lanka moves forward, focusing its role on nation-building. Drawing strength from God, Salvationists are vibrant witnesses as they reach out to needs in their communities.

Nearly 280 houses were handed over to tsunami-affected families. Further construction work is in progress. Livelihood and community development training has been given. Foster care for children and psycho-social counselling are being implemented.

Invaluable financial support was provided by Salvationists in Canada, The Netherlands, New Zealand, Australia , Hong Kong and SAWSO (Salvation Army World Service Office).

Through the Women's Ministries Department training in sewing and spoken English was provided respectively to 374 and 159 women. Computer training centres were opened at Dias Place, Matale and Hikkaduwa Corps.

With funds from the World Bank and UNAIDS, the HIV/Aids Department arranged an observation study visit to Thailand. Twenty-two health providers from four main government hospitals across the island formed the team with two from The Salvation Army, who co-ordinated the visit.

Personnel and spiritual development go hand in hand – as seen in 'Servant Leadership' training sessions; a Brengle Institute funded by Sri Lanka's partner in mission, the USA Eastern Territory; the Women's Ministries programme visit to India Eastern; and a micro-credit workshop.

The visit of General Shaw Clifton and Commissioner Helen Clifton was a source of great encouragement. In one of the meetings a host of Salvationists encircled the General as they came to the mercy seat to rededicate their lives to God. Forty-three young people committed themselves for full-time service as officers.

The Army's world leaders were received by the Prime Minister, the Honourable Ratnasiri Wickramanayake, who expressed his appreciation of Salvation Army work in Sri Lanka.

A new home for elderly women at Rajagirya was opened and dedicated by the General. It was named after the late Colonel Iris Perera as a tribute to the life and service of the wife of Sri Lanka's first national territorial commander.

Five cadets of the Heralds of the Good News Session were commissioned as officers and five 'Witnesses for Christ' were welcomed to the training college.

At Rambukanna Conference Centre 56 corps cadets enjoyed a camp themed 'Building Up'. A four-day music school organised by the Youth Department was attended by 91 youths and officers.

Major Anura Withana, Editor of *Yudhha Handa* (*The War Cry*), received a Christian Media Society award in recognition of his endeavours in promoting Christian television and radio programmes. The award was presented by the Speaker of the Sri Lankan Parliament.

STATISTICS
Officers 149 (active 101 retired 48) **Cadets** 8 **Employees** 151
Corps 44 **Corps Plants** 8 **Social Homes** 7 **Hostels** 7 **Community Centres** 5 **Day Care Centres** 7 **Health Centre** 1 **Conference Centre** 1
Senior Soldiers 3,546 **Adherents** 747 **Junior Soldiers** 534
Personnel serving outside territory Officers 2

STAFF
Candidates: Capt Rohini Hettiarachchi
Community Development: Maj Noel Lapeña
Community Relations and Resource Development:
Editorial: Maj Anura Vithana
Field, Community Services, Evangelism and Ecumenical Relations: Maj P. Anthony Fernando
Finance: Maj Juppalli Zachariah
HIV/Aids Programme: Mrs Swarna De Silva
Information Technology: Miss Coojanie Heendeniya
Leadership Development: Maj Chandralatha Jayaratnasingham
Projects: Maj Colleen Marshall
Property: Maj Ian Marshall
Social Services and Sponsorship: Maj Marilou Lapeña
Training: Maj Nihal Hettiarachchi
Tsunami Resconstruction Programme: Maj Packianathan Jayaratnasingham
Women's Ministries: Col Nemkhanching (TPWM) Lt-Col Lalitha Daniel (TSWM)
Youth: Maj A. Newton Fernando

DIVISIONS
Rambukkana: Mawanella Rd, Rambukkana; tel: (035) 226 5179; email: salrambu@sltnet.lk; Maj Sarukkalige Chandrasiri
Western: 53 Sir James Peiris Mawatha, Colombo 2; tel: (11) 232 4660 ext 270; Maj Alister Philip

DISTRICTS
Kandy: 26 Srimath Bennet Soysa Veediya, Kandy; tel: (08) 223 4804; Capt Ranjith Senaratne
Northern: 295 Kandy Rd, Arialai Jaffna; mobile: 077 6421484; Maj Newton Jacob

SECTIONS
Eastern: 135 Trincomalee St, Batticaloa; tel: (065) 222 4558; fax: (065) 222 4768 (AST Link Communication & Agency Post

Office – Batticaloa); Capt M. Puvanendran
Southern: Weerasooriya Watte, Patuwatha-
Dodanduwa; tel: (091) 227 7146

TRAINING COLLEGE
77 Ananda Rajakaruna Mawatha, Colombo 10;
tel: (11) 268 6116; email: lankatg@sltnet.lk

SOCIAL SERVICES
Children's Homes
Batticoloa Girls' Home: 135 Trincomalee St,
Batticaloa; tel: (065) 222 4558 (acc 16)
Dehiwela Girls' Home: 12 School Ave,
Dehiwela; tel: 271 7049 (acc 50)
Rajagiriya Boys' Home: Obeysekerapura,
Rajagiriya; tel: 286 2301 (acc 30)
Shalom Children's Home and Centre: Kandy Rd,
Kaithady, Jaffna; mobile: 0777 218762
(acc boys 16, girls 22, remandees 10)
Sunshine House: 127 E. W. Perera Mawatha,
Colombo 10 (acc remandees 34)
Swedlanka Boys' Home: South Pallansena Jaya
Mawatha, Kochchikade; tel: (031) 227 7964
(acc 25)
The Haven: 127, E. W. Perera Mawatha,
Colombo 10; tel: 269 5275 (acc babies 10,
children 10)

Hostels
Dehiwela Eventide Home for Women: 8 School
Ave, Dehiwela; tel: 272 8542 (acc 34)
Hope House Home for Employed Disabled Men:
11 Sir James Peiris Mawatha, Colombo 2;
tel: (11) 232 4660 ext 200 (acc 12)
Ladies' Hostel (1): 18 Sri Saugathodaya Mawatha,
Colombo 2; tel: (11) 254 4004 (acc 82)
Ladies' Hostel (2): 30 Union Pl, Colombo 2:
tel: (11) 242 1318 (acc 78)
Rajagiriya Elders' Home and Iris Perera Home:
1700 Cotta Rd, Rajagiriya; tel: 288 5947
(acc men 8, women 6, destitute men 12,
destitute women 6, working girls 24)
Rawathawatte Hostel for Women: 14 Charles Pl,
Rawathawatte, Moratuwa; tel: 421 3018
(acc working girls 28)
The Haven: 127 E. W. Perera Mawatha,
Colombo 10; tel: 269 5275 (acc unwed mothers
14, elderly women 10, rehabilitation 10)

Community Centres
Dias Place: 16, Dias Place, Colombo 11;
tel: 242 3912
Hope House: 11 Sir James Peiris Mawatha,
Colombo 2; tel: (11) 232 4660 ext 200
Matale: 147 Trincomalee St, Matale;
tel: (066) 223 0844

Rambukkana: Mawanella Rd, Rambukkana;
tel: (035) 226 5179
Weerasooriya Centre: 88 Weerasooriya Watta,
Patuwatha, Dodanduwa; tel: (091) 227 7146

Child Day Care Centres
Amparai: Main Rd, Amparai; tel: (063) 222 3779
Kudagama: Kudagama, Dombemada
Hewadiwela: Hewadiwela; tel: (035) 226 6785
Madampe: Madampe (NWP); tel: (032) 224 7285
Talampitiya: Mahagama, Kohilagedera,
Talampitiya; tel: (037) 223 8278
Wattegama: 34 Nuwaratenne Rd, Wattegama;
tel: (060) 280 3319

HEALTH SERVICES
HIV/Aids Community Counselling Programme:
53 Sir James Peiris Mawatha, Colombo 2;
tel: (11) 232 4660 ext 208
Counselling and Counselling Training Centre:
Colombo
Physiotherapy Unit: Colombo; tel (11) 232 4660
ext 204

KALUTARA ESTATE AND CAMP CENTRE
Galapatha, Kalutara

TSUNAMI RECONSTRUCTION PROGRAMMES
Hikkaduwa, Southern Section: Weerasooriya
Conference Centre, Weerasooriya Watte,
Pathuwatha, Dodanduwa-Hikkaduwa;
tel: (091) 227 7146
Jaffna, Northern District: 77 Rasavinthottam,
off Kandy Rd, Jaffna; tel/fax: (021) 222 5745

CONFERENCE CENTRES
Rambukkana Conference Centre for Camp:
Mawanella Rd, Rambukkana;
tel: (035) 2265179
Weerasooriya Conference Centre: Weerasooriya
Watta, Patuwatha, Dodanduwa-Hikkaduwa;
tel: (091) 227 7146

❛ Drawing strength from God, Salvationists are vibrant witnesses as they reach out to their communities ❜

231

SWEDEN AND LATVIA TERRITORY

Territorial leaders:
Commissioners Victor and Roslyn Poke

Territorial Commander:
Commissioner Victor Poke (1 Nov 2006)

Chief Secretary:
Lieut-Colonel Kristina Frisk (1 Aug 2006)

Territorial Headquarters: Östermalmsgatan 71, Stockholm, Sweden

Postal address: Box 5090, SE 102 42 Stockholm, Sweden

Tel: [46] (08) 562 282 00; fax: [46] (08) 562 283 91; email: fralsningsarmen@fralsningsarmen.se;

web site: www.fralsningsarmen.se

Commissioner Hanna Ouchterlony, inspired by the first Army meeting held on Swedish soil in Värnamo in 1878 led by the young Chief of the Staff, Bramwell Booth, began Salvation Army work in a Stockholm theatre on 28 December 1882. The first women's home and a men's shelter were opened in 1890. Work among deaf and blind people was inaugurated in 1895. The Salvation Army was re-established in Latvia on 18 November 1990 and two months later, on 23 January 1991, The Salvation Army in Latvia became a juridical person. On 15 November 1994 the Sweden Territory was renamed the Sweden and Latvia Territory.

Zone: Europe
Countries included in the territory: Latvia, Sweden
'The Salvation Army' in Swedish: Frälsningsarmén; in Latvian: Pestíšanas Armija
Languages in which the gospel is preached: Latvian, Russian, Swedish
Periodicals: *FA-musikant*, *Stridsropet*, *William*

AS a result of the 'Eldsflamman' ('The Flame') prayer chain staging prayer weekends at 14 corps, a number of prayer groups were established around the territory. During 2006 a scriptural theme emerged for the territory – 'Seek the peace and prosperity of the city to which I have sent you' (Jeremiah 29:7 paraphrased).

During the national elections, then Territorial Commander Commissioner Hasse Kjellgren appeared on national television calling all parties to be aware of community and family needs.

A Challenge Weekend for youths from 16 years of age, held at the National Youth Centre, Dragudden, was titled 'Here but Further'. Around 200 young people and youth leaders gathered for a new year festival in Gothenburg. A national camp at Öland attracted 360 children and youths.

In Örebro, a second series of retreats was held for all corps leaders in the territory, aimed to strengthen and encourage them in their ministry.

Divisional congresses took place in Umeå and Malmö.

Every day during the European Athletics Championships in Gothenburg, Salvationists spent several hours evangelising in the city centre.

Refugee children arriving in Sweden without parents or relatives have been received at the Salvation Army youth housing in Jönköping. There is room for five children or youths.

After noticing that several children often arrived at school tired and without having had breakfast, the corps in Malmö has set up a breakfast café every Friday for 25 schoolchildren.

The Salvation Army's 'Homeless Campaign 2006' was awarded two advertising prizes – the Keys of Gold. The first Salvation Army Fair Trade shop was opened in Stockholm.

Men and women took part in 'Days to Enjoy God's Creation', arranged by the Home and Family Department, and Smålandsgården hosted a women's weekend titled 'Appetite for Life – Appetite for Creating'. Mothers with children joined together at Lännersta Guest and Conference Centre, under the theme 'Single … Unique'.

Halmstad Corps arranged a summer conference titled 'To Build Deeply', with participants from around the country. Bauska Corps in Latvia organised a camp for families; about 50 people gathered at the Salvation Army summer centre outside Liepaja.

The fourth volume of the history of The Salvation Army in Sweden, written by Commissioner Sven Nilsson (retired), was published. The book covers the period 1981-2003.

After the success of *The Cook Book* – a collection of recipes from well-known Swedes, published to raise funds for The Salvation Army – *The Porridge Book* has now been edited.

STATISTICS

Officers 407 (active 178 retired 229) **Cadets** (2nd Yr) 10 **Employees** 1,879
Corps 163 **Outposts** 56 **Goodwill Centres** 14 **Institutions** 18 **Hotels/Guest Homes** 2 **Centres for Deaf and Blind** 7 **Community and Family Services** 20
Senior Soldiers 5,606 **Adherents** 733 **Junior Soldiers** 227
Personnel serving outside territory Officers 8

STAFF

Training: Maj Mona Stockman (Training College)
  Mr and Mrs Peter and Rut Baronowsky (FAFI)
  Majs Kjell and Ann-Christine Karlsten (Saved2Save)
  Mr Magnus Wetterberg (People's High School)

Sec for Business Administration: Maj Bert Åberg
Finance: Capt Elisabeth Beckman
Legacies: Lt-Col Ing-Britt Hansson
Personnel: Mrs Eva Malmberg
Property: Maj Bert Åberg
Trade: Mrs Kai Kjäll-Andersson

Sec for Communications: Comr Roslyn Poke
Media Sec: Mr Anders Östman
Fundraising: Mr Mats Wiberg
International Development/Child Sponsorship: Mr Christian Lerne
Marketing: Jan Kempe
'Sally Ann' – Fair Trade:
  Sally Ann Sverige AB:
    email: sallyann@fralsningsarmen.se
    web site: www.sallyann.se
    Manager: Mr Lars Beijer
    Chairman of Board: Mr Christer Hagman
    Shop: Nytorgsgatan 27, 116 40 Stockholm;
    Ida Nordenberg (shop manager)

Asst Sec for Field/Programme: Maj Kenneth Nordenberg
Music: Mr Lars-Otto Ljungholm
Candidates: Maj Mona Stockman
Youth: Maj Kjell Karlsten

Women's Ministries: Comr Roslyn Poke (TPWM) Maj Ingrid Albinsson (TH&FS)

Sec for Social Services: Maj Britt-Marie Alm
Children and Families: Maj Kenneth Karlsson
(Asst Soc S Sec)
Community and Families: Maj Ingelise Linck
Rehabilitation: Capt Sonja Blomberg

DIVISIONS

Göteborg: Järntorgsgatan 8, 413 01 Göteborg;
tel: (031) 10 29 40; fax: (031) 10 29 43;
Maj Kjell Olausson
Jönköping: V. Storgatan 21, 3 tr, PO Box 295,
551 14 Jönköping; tel: (036) 16 31 60;
fax: (036)12 83 65; Col Kehs David Löfgren
Örebro: Kungsgatan 24, 702 24 Örebro;
tel: (019) 14 29 48; fax: (019) 611 47 41;
Maj Per-Olof Larsson
Umeå: Bölevägen 17A, 904 31 Umeå;
tel: (090) 13 50 47; fax: (090) 13 81 77;
Maj Christian Paulsson

TRAINING
Training College
Frälsningsarméns Bibel och Officersinstitutesz,
Ågestagården, Bonäsvägen, 123 52 Farsta;
tel: (08) 562 281 50; fax: (08) 562 281 70

Training, Development Institute – FAFI
Ormingeplan 2, PO Box 2143, 132 02
Saltsjö-Boo; tel/fax: (08) 747 12 15;
web site: www.fralsningsarmen.se/fasi;
email: fasi@fralsningsarmen.se

Saved2Save – Training School
Mellangatan 21, 621 56 Visby;
tel: (0498) 21 58 90;
web site: www.saved2save.com;
email: info@saved2save.com

People's High Schools
Ågesta Folkhögskola: Bonäsvägen 5,
123 52 Farsta; tel: (08) 562 281 00;
fax (08) 562 281 20
Älvsjö Bransch: Älvsjö Gårdsväg 9,
125 30 Älvsjö; tel: (08) 647 52 77;
fax: (08) 556 233 15

CONFERENCE CENTRE/GUEST HOME
Smålandsgården, Örserum, 563 91 Gränna;
tel: (0390) 300 14; fax: (0390) 304 17
(acc 67)

SOCIAL SERVICES
Head Office: Östermalmsgatan 71, PO Box
5090, 102 42 Stockholm; tel: (08) 562 282 00;
fax: (08) 562 283 98

Family Tracing Service: PO Box 5090, 102 42
Stockholm; tel: (08) 562 283 75;
fax: (08) 562 283 98

Conference Centre/Guest Home:
'Lännerstahemmet', Djurgårdsvägen 7, 132 46
Saltsjö-Boo; tel: (08) 715 11 58;
fax: (08) 747 11 76

Work Among Alcoholics
Treatment Centre for Substance Abusers
'Kurön', 178 92 Adelsö; tel: (08) 560 518 80;
fax: (08) 560 514 05 (acc 63)

Rehabilitation Centres
Göteborg: 'Lilla Bommen', S:t Eriksgatan 4,
411 05 Göteborg; tel: (031) 60 45 56;
fax: (031) 711 83 67 (acc 63)
Göteborg: 'Nylösegården', Skaragatan 3,
415 01 Göteborg; tel: (031) 25 59 59;
fax: (031) 21 99 86 (acc 20)
Örebro: 'Gnistan', Bruksgatan 13, 702 20
Örebro; tel: (019) 32 38 40;
fax: (019) 32 37 72 (acc 11)
Stockholm: 'Värtahemmet', Kolargatan 2;
115 42 Stockholm; tel: (08) 545 835 00;
fax: (08) 545 835 07 (acc 42)
Stockholm Tyresö: 'Källan', Wättingegårdsväg
1, 135 40 Tyresö; tel: (08) 448 73 50;
fax: (08) 448 73 59 (acc 20)
Sundsvall: 'Klippangården', Fredsgatan 38,
852 38 Sundsvall; tel: (060) 17 31 74;
fax: (060) 17 52 10 (acc 16)
Uppsala: 'Sagahemmet', Storgatan 2 A, 753 31
Uppsala; tel: (018) 10 08 01;
fax: (018) 12 12 39 (acc 26)

Night Shelters
Örebro: 'Gnistan', Bruksgatan 13, 702 20 Örebro;
tel: (019) 32 38 40; fax: (019) 32 37 72
(acc 10)
Stockholm: 'Midsommarkransen',
Midsommarslingan 1-3, 126 32 Hägersten;
tel: (08) 19 13 30; fax: (08) 744 20 78 (acc 27)
Uppsala: 'Sagahemmet', Storgatan 2 A, 753 31
Uppsala; tel: (018) 10 08 01; fax: (018) 12 12 39
(acc 10)

Drop-in Centre
Stockholm: Bergsundsstrand 51, 117 38
Stockholm; tel: (08) 34 85 98;
fax: (08) 31 97 85

Harbour Light Corps
'Fyrbåkskåren', S:t Eriksgatan 4, 411 05
Göteborg; tel: (031) 19 82 18

A young girl helps celebrate 125 years of The Salvation Army in Switzerland

Jesus, friend of little children,
Be a friend to me;
Take my hand and ever keep me
Close to thee.
Step by step, O lead me onward,
Upward into youth;
Wiser, stronger, still becoming
In thy truth.

Song Book of The Salvation Army, 842

Aboriginal children at a sports clinic in Australia Eastern are welcomed by Territorial Sports Ministry Director Adrian Kistan

Happy children in The Salvation Army's care in Shishu Niloy, Bangladesh

Top: Young people celebrate Easter in Brazil

Left: Face-painting at a children's event in USA Central Territory

Below: Italian children learn about Jesus in a Sunday school class in Rome

Prayertime during a children's meeting at the United Kingdom Territory's holiday fellowship week in Bognor Regis

Young people take part in the opening of a new outpost in Villa Canteria, Potosi, Bolivia (South America West Territory)

Sweden and Latvia Territory

Advisory Service
Uppsala: 'Brobygget', S:t Persgatan 20,
753 20 Uppsala; tel: (018) 71 05 44;
fax: (018) 14 84 59

Work Among Children and Families
Pre-Schools
Jönköping: 'Vårsol', Von Platensgatan 10,
553 13 Jönköping; tel: (036) 71 15 02;
fax: (036) 71 21 90 (acc 17)
Umeå: 'Krubban', Måttgränd 74, 906 24
Umeå; tel: (090) 18 05 90;
fax: (090) 18 27 88 (acc 18)
Västra Frölunda: 'Morgonsol', Poppelgatan 11;
PO Box 5003, 426 05 Västra Frölunda;
tel/fax: (013) 29 10 29 (acc 34)

School and Treatment Centre for Adolescents
'Sundsgården', 179 96 Svartsjö;
tel: (08) 560 428 21; fax: (08) 560 425 00
(acc 27)

Treatment Centre for Families
'FAM-Huset', Hagvägen 1, 513 32 Fristad;
tel: (033) 21 01 62; fax: (033) 21 01 63
(acc adults 8, babies 8)

Emergency Diagnostic and Short-term Treatment Centre
'Vårsol', Von Platensgatan 10, 553 13

Jönköping; tel: (036) 16 74 58;
fax: (036) 71 21 90 (acc 6)

Group Homes for Adolescents
Jönköping: 'Vårsols Ungdomsboende', V:a
Storgatan 21, 553 15 Jönköping;
tel: (036) 17 32 75; fax: (036) 17 32 74 (acc 6)
Stockholm: 'Locus', Grev Turegatan 66, 114 38
Stockholm; tel: (08) 667 21 82;
fax: (08) 667 21 87 (acc 14)

Family Centre with Advisory Service
'Vårsols Familjecenter', V:a Storgatan 21, 553
15 Jönköping; tel: (036) 17 32 72;
fax: (036) 17 32 74

Salvation Army Refugee Aid
Jönköping SARA

Vacation Centres for Children
Gävle: 'Rörberg', Hedesundavägen 89, 818 91
Valbo; tel: (026) 330 19 (acc 15)
Luleå: Sunderbyvägen 323, 954 42 Södra
Sunderbyn; tel: (0920) 26 57 25 (acc 15)
Malmö: Klockarevägen 20, 236 36 Höllviken;
tel: (040) 45 05 24 (acc 15)

Work Among Families and Elderly People
Centre for Elderly People
'Dalen', Storgatan 14, 571 31 Nässjö;
tel: (0380) 188 11 (acc 20)

New soldiers
enrolled at Riga 1
Corps in Latvia are
pictured with their
corps officer,
Lieutenant Sarah
Ilsters (far right)

Sweden and Latvia Territory

Community and Family Services
Gävle: Hedesundavägen 89, 818 91 Valbo; tel/fax: (026) 330 28
Göteborg: Brämareg 7, 417 04 Göteborg; tel: (031) 23 80 00
Göteborg: S. Allégatan 9, 413 01 Göteborg; tel: (031) 711 36 27
Halmstad: Snöstorpsv 52, PO Box 4065, 300 04 Halmstad; tel: (035) 10 53 48; fax: (035) 15 72 05
Jönköping: V:a Storgatan 21, 553 15 Jönköping; tel: (036) 71 42 67
Linköping: Badhusgatan 6 A, 582 22 Linköping; tel: (013) 12 14 12
Luleå: Köpmangatan 52a, 9972 34 Luleå; tel: (0920) 188 75
Malmö: Hyregatan 3 C, PO Box 171 58, 200 10 Malmö; tel: (040) 30 25 18; fax: (040) 23 12 88
Norrköping: Vattengatan 5, 602 20 Norrköping; tel: (011) 12 22 28; fax: (011) 12 53 19
Stockholm: 'Elisabetgården', Observatoriegatan 4, 113 29 Stockholm; tel: (08) 30 49 80; fax: (08) 34 71 37
Umeå: Sveagatan 3 B, 903 27 Umeå; tel: (090) 13 76 16
Uppsala: S:t Persgatan 20, 753 20 Uppsala; tel: (018) 71 05 44; fax: (018) 14 84 59
Västerås: Hantverkargatan 3, PO Box 430, 721 08 Västerås; tel: (021) 14 65 78; fax: (021) 13 88 50
Örebro: Kungsgatan 24, 702 24 Örebro; tel/fax: (019) 18 74 32

Drop-in Centres
Göteborg: Brämareg 7, 417 04 Göteborg; tel: (031) 23 80 00
Göteborg: S Allégatan 9, 413 01 Göteborg; tel: (031) 711 36 27
Uppsala: S:t Persgatan 20, 753 20 Uppsala; tel: (018) 71 05 44; fax: (018) 14 84 59
Västerås: Hantverkargatan 3, PO Box 430, 721 08 Västerås; tel: (021) 14 65 78; fax: (021) 13 88 50

Recreation Centres for Elderly People
Malmö: 'Furubo', Klockarevägen 22, 236 36 Höllviken; tel: (040) 45 39 13
Norrköping: 'Ro', Rovägen 2, 610 24 Vikbolandet; tel: (0125) 500 56

Work Among Disabled People and Multicultural Ministries
Deaf and Blind People
Göteborg: S Allég 9, 413 01 Göteborg; tel: (031) 51 54 79

Luleå: Åkerbärsstigen 11, 974 52 Luleå
Malmö: Hyregatan 3 A, 211 21 Malmö; tel: (040) 611 78 57
Stockholm: Observatoriegatan 4, 113 29 Stockholm; tel: (08) 31 22 53
Umeå: Sveagatan 3 B, 903 27 Umeå; tel: (090) 17 84 02
Örebro: Kungsgatan 24, 702 24 Örebro; Örnsköldsvik: Postbox 280, 891 26 Örnsköldsvik; tel: (0660) 163 66

Multicultural Ministries
'Akalla', Sibeliusgången 6, 164 73 Kista; tel: (08) 750 62 16; fax: (08) 751 71 61

Second-hand Shops
Head office: Stensätravägen 3B, 127 39 Skärholmen; tel: (08) 563 169 50; fax: (08) 563 169 60
Shops: Borås, Eskilstuna, Falun, Göteborg (2), Halmstad, Jönköping, Karlstad, Linköping, Luleå, Malmö (2), Motala, Norrköping, Skellefteå, Stockholm (6), Sundbyberg, Sundsvall, Umeå, Uppsala (2), Västerås, Örebro

LATVIA REGION (UNDER THQ)
Regional Headquarters: Bruninieku iela 10A, LV 1001 Riga; tel: [371] 731 00 37; fax: [371] 731 52 66; email: info@pestisanasarmija.lv; web site: www.pestisanasarmija.lv
Regional Commander: Maj Göran Larsson
Training: Maj Chris Larsson

STATISTICS
Officers 8 (active 7 retired 1) **Envoys** 5 **Employees** 79
Corps 7 **Outposts** 5 **Institutions** 4

SOCIAL SERVICES
Leontine Gorkša Childrens' Home: Agenskalna iela 3, LV 1007 Riga; tel: [371] 760 17 00
Maternity and Child Health Centre: Bruninieku iela 10A, LV 1001 Riga; tel: [371] 727 13 84
'Patverums' Day Centre for Children at Risk: Bruninieku iela 10 A, LV 1001 Riga; tel: [371] 731 14 63
Skangale School Home: Liepa pag, Césu rajons, LV 4128 Liepa; tel: [371] 410 22 20; fax: [371] 410 22 21

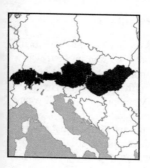

SWITZERLAND, AUSTRIA AND HUNGARY TERRITORY

Territorial leaders:
**Commissioners Kurt Burger and
Alicia Burger-Pedersen**

Territorial Commander:
Commissioner Kurt Burger (1 Sep 2007)

Chief Secretary:
Lieut-Colonel Franz Boschung (1 Oct 2007)

Territorial Headquarters: Laupenstrasse 5, Bern, Switzerland

Postal address: Die Heilsarmee, Postfach 6575, 3001 Bern, Switzerland

Tel: [41] (31) 388 05 91; fax: [41] (31) 388 05 95; email: info@swi.salvationarmy.org

web sites: www.heilsarmee.ch; www.armeedusalut.ch; www.salvationarmy.ch

On 10 December 1882 Salvation Army operations were commenced in the Salle de la Réformation, Geneva, by the Maréchale, Catherine Booth, and Colonel Arthur S. Clibborn. Bitter opposition was encountered but now the Army is recognised as an evangelical and social force throughout the Confederation. The Salvation Army's constitution consists of Foundation Salvation Army Switzerland; Cooperative Salvation Army Social Organisation; Salvation Army Immo Ltd.

Work first commenced in Austria on 27 May 1927 in Vienna. Unofficial meetings had been held earlier, but the official opening was conducted by Lieut-Commissioner Bruno Friedrich and Captain Lydia Saak was the officer-in-charge. 'Verein der Heilsarmee' was legally recognised by the Austrian Federal Ministry on 8 May 1952.

The Salvation Army's operations in Hungary were commenced on 24 April 1924 by Colonel Rothstein with two German women-officers. The evangelistic and social activities were maintained until suppressed in 1950. After the opening of the central European borders, The Salvation Army was officially re-established on 3 November 1990 by General Eva Burrows.

Zone: Europe

Countries included in the territory: Austria, Hungary, Switzerland

'The Salvation Army' in German: Die Heilsarmee; in French: Armée du Salut; in Hungarian: Az Üdvhadsereg; in Spanish: Ejército de Salvación

Languages in which the gospel is preached: French, German, Hungarian, Spanish

Periodicals: *Espoir* (French), *Dialog* (German), *Dialogue* (French), *IN* (French and German), *Just 4 U* (French), *Trialog* (German), *Klecks* (German)

JANUARY 2007 saw the start of a year of thanksgiving as the territory celebrated 125 years of The Salvation Army in Switzerland.

The main objectives were defined as: ***Thanksgiving:*** to God and to all people who have contributed to making The Salvation Army the movement it is today; ***Encouragement:*** to motivate for the common task; ***Strengthening:*** a strong belief for a bright future.

One of the jubilee activities was for

237

all corps and institutions to hold a brunch on Saturday 17 March, to which people from the neighbourhood would be invited. Nationally, more than 15,000 people attended. Extensive and very positive media coverage was given to this event.

In May the General and Commissioner Helen Clifton led the main 125th anniversary celebrations in the capital city, Bern, where a congress was followed by traditional Ascension Day meetings.

In the second half of 2006 it had been decided to hold a 24/7 prayer event during the 365 days of the jubilee year. Trial weeks were successfully held in each division in October and the 'Prayer Marathon' started on the last weekend of January 2007. All weeks were very quickly booked and it was enthusistically anticipated that this project would be a complete success.

The training of officers is undergoing some fundamental changes. Cadets will gain a Diploma in Christian Leadership which will count towards a Bachelor degree if they wish to continue studying after training.

The territory faces a serious issue as the number of candidates is very low, but it is hoped that the new programme will attract more Salvationists willing to commit their lives to full-time service for God as officers.

In May 2006 Commissioner Linda Bond (International Secretary for Spiritual Life Development) led a series of conferences and the annual congress in Zurich. The congress theme was 'Belief and Action' and all participants received a white wristband with this motto written on it. It was a way to express The Salvation Army's solidarity with the 'Stop Poverty!' campaign. Many people are still wearing the white bands.

From January 2006 the territory has been operating a strategy board which, chaired by the territorial commander, serves as the ultimate executive body of The Salvation Army in Switzerland. This new structure with a separation of powers fits perfectly with the increasing necessity for transparency and good corporate governance to which charities in Switzerland have to adhere.

STATISTICS

Officers 416 (active 191 retired 225)
  Lieutenants 7 **Cadets** (1st Yr) 4 (2nd Yr) 4 (3rd Yr) 4 **Employees** 1,350
Corps 68 **Outposts** 20 **Institutions** 39 **Thrift Stores** 26
Senior Soldiers 3,101 **Adherents** 770 **Junior Soldiers** 427
Personnel serving outside territory Officers 17 Layworkers 2

STAFF

Dept of Evangelisation: Maj Fritz Schmid
Society and Family: Comr Alicia Burgur-Pedersen (TPWM) Lt-Col Hanny Boschung (TSWM) Maj Christianne Winkler (Coordinator, Women's Groups)
Music and Gospel Arts: Sgt Phillip Manger
Youth: Capt Thomas Bösch

Dept of Social Work: Sgt Erhard Meyner
Social French Part: Mr Michel Bonjour
Social German Part: Mr Christian Rohrbach
Prison Work: Maj Samuel Winkler
Family Tracing: Maj Neil Bannister
Refugees: Mr Jakob Amstutz
Thrift Stores: Mr David Küenzi

Dept of Personnel: Maj Marianne Meyner
Candidates: Maj Daniela Zurbrügg
Training: Maj Hervé Cachelin
Personnel Administration: Sgt Christian Hefti

Dept of Finance and Business Administration:
Sgt Philip Bates
Finance + Controlling Evangelisation:
Maj Peter Zurbrügg
Finance + Controlling THQ: Sgt Kenneth Hofer
Finance + Controlling Social: Mr Michael
Lippuner
Property: Mr Marc Hendry
Mission & Development: Sgt Markus Muntwiler

Dept of Communication: Sgt Pierre Reift
Editor and Publishing: Mr Hans-Christoph
Inniger
Information Technology: Mr Martin Schweizer
Fundraising: Mr Bernhard Stegmayer
Museum and Archives: Maj Heidi Scheurer
Trade Shop: Mrs Hanni Butler

DIVISIONS

Bern: Gartenstrasse 8, 3007 Bern;
tel: (031) 380 75 45; fax: (031) 380 75 42;
Maj Walter Bommeli
Division Romande: Rue de l'Ecluse 16, 2000
Neuchâtel; tel: (032) 729 20 81; Maj Jacques
Donzé
Nordwestschweiz : Breisacherstrasse 45,
4057 Basel; tel: (061) 691 11 50;
fax: (061) 691 12 59; Maj Hans Knecht
Ost-Division: Eidmattstrasse 16, 8032 Zürich;
tel: (044) 383 69 70; fax: (044) 383 52 48;
Maj Allan Hofer

SCHOOL FOR OFFICER TRAINING
4012 Basel, Habsburgerstrasse 15, Postfach 410,
CH-4012 Basel; tel: (061) 387 91 11;
fax: (061) 381 77 63

SOCIAL WORK
Social Services Advice Bureaux
4053 Basel: Frobenstrasse 18; tel: (061) 272 00 07;
fax: (061) 273 29 00
3007 Bern: Gartenstrasse 8; tel: (031) 380 75 40;
fax: (031) 380 75 42
2503 Biel-Bienne: Oberer Quai 12;
tel: (032) 322 53 66; fax: (032) 322 60 64
1018 Lausanne: Rue de la Borde 22;
tel: (021) 646 46 10
8400 Winterthur: CASA, Wartstrasse 9;
tel: 052 202 77 80
8026 Zürich: Müllerstrasse 87;
tel/fax: (044) 298 90 60
8032 Zürich: Eidmattstrasse 16;
tel: 044 422 79 00

Adult Rehabilitation Centres
1201 Genève: Centre-Espoir, Rue Jean-Dassier 10;

tel: (022) 338 22 00; fax: (022) 338 22 01
(acc 109)
3098 Köniz: Buchseegut, Buchseeweg 15;
tel: (031) 970 63 63; fax: (031) 970 63 64
(acc 44) (with gardening and workshop)
1003 Lausanne: Avenue Ruchonnet 49;
tel: (021) 310 40 40; fax: (021) 310 40 42
(acc 23)
1005 Lausanne: La Résidence, Place du Vallon 1a;
tel: (021) 320 48 55; fax: (021) 310 39 34
(acc 38)
5022 Rombach (Aarau): Obstgarten,
Bibersteinstrasse 54; tel: (062) 839 80 80;
fax: (062) 839 80 89 (acc 34)
2024 St-Aubin: Le Devens, Socio-medical Home;
tel: (032) 836 27 29; fax: (032) 836 27 28
(acc 34)
9205 Waldkirch: Hasenberg; tel: (071) 434 61 61;
fax: (071) 434 61 71 (acc 44) (agriculture and
workshop)

Community Centres
Eidmattegge, Zürich; Gelber Stern, Zürich;
Genève; Open Heart, Zürich.

Emergency Shelters
1201 Genève: Accueil de Nuit, Chemin Galiffe 4;
tel: (022) 338 22 00; fax: (022) 338 22 01
(acc 40)
1005 Lausanne: La Marmotte, Place du Vallon 1a;
tel: (021) 320 48 55; fax: (021) 310 39 34
(acc 28)

Holiday Flats
3715 Adelboden: Chalet Bethel;
tel: (033) 673 21 62 (acc 20)

Homes for the Aged
3013 Bern: Lorrainehof, Lorrainestrasse 34;
tel: (031) 330 16 16; fax: (031) 330 16 00
(acc 52 + 10 flats) (health care)
1814 La Tour-de-Peilz: Le Phare-Elim, Avenue
de la Paix 11; tel: (021) 977 33 33;
fax: (021) 977 33 90 (acc 44) (health care)
1201 Genève: Résidence Amitié (health care),
Rue Baudit 1; tel: (022) 919 95 95;
fax: (022) 740 30 15 (acc 52) (health care)
2000 Neuchâtel: Le Foyer, Rue de l'Ecluse 18;
tel: (032) 729 20 20 (acc 30) (health care)

Homes for Children
8344 Bäretswil: Sunnemätteli Home for
Handicapped Children; Wirzwil;
tel: (044) 939 11 88; fax (044) 979 10 45
(acc 16)
4054 Basel: Kinderheim Holee, c/o Felix Platter

Spital, Hegenheimerstrasse 166;
tel: (061) 301 24 50; fax: (061) 301 24 44
(acc 23)

8932 Mettmenstetten: Kinderheim Paradies;
tel: (044) 768 58 00; fax: (044) 768 58 19
(acc 23)

3110 Münsingen: Kinderwohnheim Sonnhalde,
Standweg 7; tel: (031) 721 08 06;
fax: (031) 721 42 72 (acc 24)

Day Care Centres
Genève; Kreuzlingen; St-Aubin; Zürich.

Hostels for Men
4058 Basel: Rheinblick, Rheingasse 80;
tel/fax: (061) 681 21 30 (acc 48)

8004 Zürich: Dienerstrasse 76;
tel: (044) 298 90 80; fax: (044) 242 41 71
(acc 26)

8005 Zürich: Geroldstrasse 27;
tel: (043) 204 10 20; fax: (043) 445 70 21
(acc 25)

Hostels for Men and Women
3006 Bern: Passantenheim, Muristrasse 6;
tel: (031) 351 80 27; fax: (031) 351 46 97
(acc 43)

2503 Biel: Haus am Quai, Oberer Quai 12;
tel: (032) 322 68 38; fax: (032) 322 60 64
(acc 24)

3600 Thun: Passantenheim, Waisenhausstrasse 26;
tel: (033) 222 69 20 (acc 15)

8400 Winterthur: Wartstrasse 40-42;
tel: (052) 212 64 75 (acc 30)

8026 Zürich: Molkenstrasse 6; tel: (044) 298 90 00;
fax: (044) 242 38 97 (acc 86)

Hostel for Women
4058 Basel: Frauenwohnheim Rheinblick,
Alemannengasse 7; tel: (061) 681 34 70;
fax: (061) 681 34 72 (acc 37)

Young Women's Residence
4059 Basel: Schlössli, Eichhornstrasse 21;
tel: (061) 335 31 10; fax: (061) 335 31 29
(acc 12)

Refugee Work
Main office: 3008 Bern, Effingerstrasse 67;
tel: (031) 380 18 80; fax: (031) 398 04 28
(9 centres, 4 coordination offices)

Social Flats
3007 Bern: Begleitetes Wohnen, Gartenstrasse 8;
tel: (031) 380 75 41; fax: (031) 380 75 42
(38 flats)

HOTELS
4055 Basel: Bed and Breakfast,
Habsburgerstrasse 15; tel: (061) 387 91 11;
fax: (061) 381 77 63

1204 Genève: Bel' Espérance, Rue de la
Vallée 1; tel: (022) 818 37 37;
fax: (022) 818 37 73 (65 beds, 40 rooms)

3852 Ringgenberg: Guesthouse,
Vordorf 264; tel: (033) 822 70 25;
fax: (033) 822 70 74 (24 beds, 12 rooms)

YOUTH CENTRES
Under THQ
3715 Adelboden (acc 75)

Under DHQ
Basel Division: 4462 Rickenbach, Waldegg
(acc 100)

Division Romande: 1451 Les Rasses (acc 150)

Ost-Division: 8712 Stäfa (acc 55)

AUSTRIA
City Command: AT-1020 Vienna Salztor-
Zentrum, Grosse Schiffgasse 3;
tel: [43] (1) 214 48 30; fax: [43] (1) 214 48 30 55;
Maj Hans-Marcel Leber

Hostel for Men
AT-1020 Vienna: Salztor-Zentrum, Grosse
Schiffgasse 3; tel: [43] (1) 214 48 30;
fax: [43] (1) 214 48 30 55 (acc men 60,
sheltered housing 42, external flats 21)

HUNGARY REGION
Regional Headquarters: Bajnok utca 25,
HU-1063 Budapest VI, Hungary;
tel: [36] (1) 332 3324; fax: [36] (1) 373 0010
Regional Officer: Maj Ruth Tschopp

Hostel for Men
'Új Remenység Háza', HU-1086 Budapest VIII,
Dobozi utca 29; tel: [36] (1) 314 2775;
fax: [36] (1) 303 9318 (acc 98)

Hostel for Women
'A Válaszút Háza', HU-1171 Budapest XVII,
Lemberg utca 38-42; tel: [36] (1) 259 1095;
fax: [36] (1) 253 5473 (acc 24)

Refuge for Maltreated Women and Children
'Fény Házá', IV utca 16, HU-1172 Budapest XVII;
tel/fax: [36] (1) 257 9461 (acc mothers with
children 5)

TAIWAN REGION

Regional Commander:
Major Fona Ling (1 Jul 2005)

Regional Headquarters: 273/3F Tun Hwa South Road, Section 2, Da-an District, Taipei 106

Postal address: PO Box 44-100, Taipei, Taiwan

Tel: [886] (02) 2738 1079/1171; fax: [886] (02) 2738 5422; email: taiwan@taw.salvationarmy.org

Pioneered in 1928 by Colonel Yasowo Segawa, Salvation Army work in Taiwan was curtailed by the Second World War. Following initiatives by American servicemen Leslie Lovestead and Robert McEaneney, operations were officially re-established in October 1965 by Colonel and Mrs George Lancashire. Formerly linked with Hong Kong, it became a separate region on 1 January 1997.

Zone: South Pacific and East Asia
Country included in the region: Taiwan
'The Salvation Army' in Taiwanese (Hokkien): Kiu Se Kuen; in Mandarin: Chiu Shih Chun
Languages in which the gospel is preached: English, Hakka, Mandarin, Taiwanese (Hokkien)
Periodicals: *Taiwan Regional News*

THE theme of the year – 'Germination' – expressed the region's anticipation as it focused on corps growth. Seminars were held to equip officers with varied evangelistic methods. These included the Alpha Course and 'Seven Blessings'; delegates also participated in a 'Ministries to the Grassroots' workshop.

This training programme led to each corps using at least one of the methods they considered appropriate to their local community. It is the prayer that The Salvation Army's forces will now be strengthened by an increase in converts.

Musicians from Tai Hang Tung Corps (Hong Kong) visited Taipei for Christmas 2006. They presented attractive gospel messages in open-air meetings and gave effective community ministry in serving Christmas dinners to elderly people.

Powerful messages stirred up a passion for evangelism and holy living when Commissioner Verna Skinner (retired), guest speaker from Australia, led the Easter campaign. In youth councils she encouraged young people to witness for Christ and choose strong values for their lives.

Mother's Day was a wonderful time of fellowship spent at a farm. All corps came together for united worship and a family outing, which afforded an excellent opportunity to reach out to relatives and friends.

A donation from the USA helped to

complete the building of an activity hall at Puli Community Development Centre.

An historic ecumenical event was witnessed when the first united World Day of Prayer meeting was held with the Quakers at Puli Corps, in the geographical centre of Taiwan.

During the year under review delegates from the region attended a united women's ministries camp in Hong Kong and the Cascade Divisional Music Camp (USA Western Territory).

STATISTICS
Officers 16 (active 14 retired 2)
Corps 5 **Outreach Centre** 1 **Social Services Centres** 4

Senior Soldiers 191 **Adherents** 128 **Junior Soldiers** 41

STAFF
Women's Ministries: Maj Fona Ling, Chan Suet-fong (RPWM)
Youth and Social: Capt Sara Tam Mei-sun

SOCIAL SERVICES
Homeless
Taipei Homeless Caring Centre: c/o 1/F, No 42, Lane 65, Chin Si St., Taipei 103

Youth
Puli Youth Services Centre: No 302-1, Chung San Rd, Sec 1, Puli Town, Nantou County 545 (acc 40)
Puli Youth Hostel for Boys: Joshua Home, 4/F Room 2, No 15 Lane 261, Zhong Hwa Rd, Puli Town, Nantou County 545

COMMUNITY SERVICES
Puli Community Development Centre: c/o No 62-1, Shueitou Rd, Puli Town, Nantou County 545

REPLANTING CROPS IN KOREA

Help with the restoration and replanting of farm crops is given after unprecedented torrential summer rains in Korea during July 2006. The Salvation Army also assisted in flood relief by repairing damaged properties and providing meals and basic living necessities.

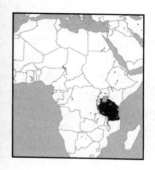

TANZANIA COMMAND

(Tanzania Territory from 1 Feb 2008)

Command leaders:
**Lieut-Colonels Hezekiel and
Mirriam Mavundla**

Officer Commanding:
Lieut-Colonel Hezekiel Mavundla
(1 Feb 2007)

General Secretary:
Major Benjamin Mnyampi (1 Feb 2007)

Command Headquarters: Kilwa Road, Dar es Salaam

Postal address: PO Box 1273, Dar es Salaam, Tanzania

Tel/fax: [255] (22) 2850468/2850542; web site: www.salvationarmy.org/tnz/www.tnz.nsf

Adjutant and Mrs Francis Dare began Salvation Army work in Tabora, Tanzania (formerly known as Tanganyika), in November 1933, as part of the East Africa Territory. In 1950, at the request for assistance from the Colonial Governor, The Salvation Army set up Mgulani Camp, where the Tanzania Headquarters is now located. Tanzania became a separate command on 1 October 1998.

Zone: Africa
Country included in the command: Tanzania
'The Salvation Army' in Kiswahili: Jeshi la Wokovu
Languages in which the gospel is preached: Kiswahili and various tribal languages

SALVATIONISTS continue to see opportunities for the expansion of God's Kingdom, and every effort is made towards achieving this. The Salvation Army was able to enter two new regions, namely Kigoma and Shinyanga.

The command aims to take the gospel to all the regions of Tanzania. Four outposts were upgraded to corps status.

The command review was carried out by Commisssioners Amos and Rosemary Makina (International Secretary and Zonal Secretary for Women's Ministries, Africa). An analysis of statistics indicates encouraging growth in the number of soldiers, cadets, officers and meeting attendance. There is an increase in the number of Salvationists desiring to become officers but the educational standard needs to be raised.

The production of Kiswahili lesson books for Sunday schools and junior soldiers is a major breakthrough that will support the ministry tremendously. Work has started on a Kiswahili corps cadet lesson book.

The flexible training programme continued for the eight couples who are corps leaders. They received copies of *The Salvation Army Ceremonies Book* and were authorised to use these in conducting ceremonies. This should slightly speed up enrolments. Their three years' training is completed in 2008.

During the year under review there were changes in the command's leadership. Lieut-Colonels Hezekiel and Mirriam Mavundla and Majors Benjamin and Grace Mnyampi are the third team of leaders since Tanzania became a command in 1998.

STATISTICS

Officers 113 (active 105 retired 8) **Cadets** 13
Employees 155
Corps 65 **Outposts** 64 **Schools** 2 **Day Care Centres** 17 **Hostel** 1
Senior Soldiers 4,566 **Junior Soldiers** 1,835
Personnel serving outside command Officers 4

STAFF

Education: Maj Lynda Levis
Field: Maj Frazer Chalwe
Finance: Mr Colin Foster (Administrator)
Projects Officer: Mr Frederick Urembo
Property: Maj Frazer Chalwe
Social Services: Mr Frederick Urembo
Sponsorship: Mrs Ann Foster
Training: Maj Herman Mbakaya
Women's Ministries: Lt-Col Mirriam Mavundla (CPWM) Maj Grace Mnyampi (CSWM) Maj Rhodina Chalwe (LOMS/SAMF)
Youth and Candidates: Maj Joy Paxton

DIVISIONS

Mbeya: PO Box 1214, Mbeya;
tel: (025) 2560009; Maj Samwel Mkami
Tarime: PO Box 37, Tarime;
tel: (028) 2690095; Maj Hubert Ngoy

DISTRICTS

Coastal: PO Box 7622, Dar es Salaam;
tel: (022) 2860365; Maj Isaac Pepete
Mwanza: PO Box 11267, Mwanza;
tel: (028) 40123; Maj Yohana Msongwe
Serengeti: PO Box 28, Mugumu;
tel: (028) 2621434; Maj Daniel Simwali

TRAINING COLLEGE
PO Box 1273, Dar es Salaam

AGRICULTURE DEVELOPMENT PROGRAMME
PO Box 1273, Dar es Salaam

EDUCATIONAL WORK
Primary School for the Physically Handicapped
Matumaini School, PO Box 1273, Dar es Salaam; tel: (022) 2851861 (acc 175)

Secondary School
Itundu School, PO Box 2994, Mbeya

Secretarial College
Shukrani Secretarial College, PO Box 555, Mbeya; tel: (00255) (0)25 2504404; fax: (00255) (0)25 2500202

SOCIAL SERVICES
Community-Based Rehabilitation/Inclusive Education: Dar es Salaam, Mbeya, Tabora
HIV/Aids Community Counselling Services: Coastal, Mbeya, Mwanza, Serengeti, Tarime
Kwetu Counselling and Psycho-Social Support Services: PO Box 1273, Dar es Salaam
Mbagala Girls' Home: PO Box 1273, Dar es Salaam
Mgulani Hostel and Conference Centre: PO Box 1273, Dar es Salaam; tel: (022) 2851467 (acc 110)
Vocational Training Workshop: PO Box 1273, Dar es Salaam
Water & Sanitation Services: Serengeti and Tarime

WOMEN'S COMMUNITY DEVELOPMENT PROGRAMMES
Mbeya, Mwanza, Serengeti, Tabora, Tarime

❟ An analysis of statistics indicates encouraging growth in the number of soldiers, cadets, officers and meeting attendance ❟

UGANDA COMMAND

Command leaders:
Majors Moses and Sarah Wandulu

Officer Commanding:
Major Moses Wandulu (1 Jul 2007)

General Secretary:
Major Stephen Moriasi (1 Jul 2007)

Command Headquarters: Plot 78-82 Lugogo Bypass, Kampala

Postal address: PO Box 11776, Kampala, Uganda

Tel: [256] 41 533901; fax: [256] 41 534968; Kampala mobile: [256] 782 855556

The Salvation Army opened fire in Uganda in 1931 when Captain and Mrs Edward Osborne unfurled the flag in Mbale, as part of the East Africa Territory. Uganda became a separate command on 1 November 2005.

Zone: Africa
Country included in the command: Uganda
'The Salvation Army' in Kiswahili: Jeshi La Wokovu; in Kiganda: Eje Liobulokozi
Languages in which the gospel is preached: English, Kiswahili, Kiganda and a number of tribal languages

GOD'S Spirit is at work in Uganda! New soldiers have been enrolled and a number of centres opened. The addition of these centres meant finding new leaders to assist the officers in their preaching and teaching ministry. Happily, several prospective officers have been identified and are now in positions of leadership while undergoing distance-learning.

Two Ugandan cadets joined the training college in Kenya Territory for a two-year training period. Seven lieutenants are undertaking training within Uganda under the direction of the command's new director of training. They receive two weeks' tuition at the training centre every two months, followed by six weeks'

practical training in their appointments.

Areas of new work were established, including vocational training centres, several schools-based projects and the provision of water in a number of centres. Officers' quarters and corps halls were improved in several places. A new Command Headquarters office/ accommodation unit was opened in early 2007.

One officer and an employee travelled to southern Sudan to ascertain possible links which will assist in enabling the command to open Salvation Army work in that country.

Through UNICEF funding, work in northern Uganda has continued in assisting hundreds of families in internally displaced people's camps.

International Emergency Services volunteers from different parts of the world have helped in providing care for these vulnerable people.

Much of the Army's work in Uganda involves assisting youth and children. The sponsorship programme that supports this ministry continues to expand.

STATISTICS
Officers 54 (active 51 retired 3) **Cadets** 4
Employees 94
Corps 24 **Outposts** 49 **Outreach Centres** 2
Pre-primary Schools 2 **Day-care Centre** 1
Primary Schools 10 **Vocational Centres** 2
Institutions 3
Senior Soldiers 3,745 **Junior Soldiers** 2,918

STAFF
Social Services and Training: Maj Rachel Tickner
Women's Ministries: Maj Sarah Wandulu (CPWM) Maj Rose Moriasi (CSWM)

DIVISION
Eastern: PO Box 168, Tororo; Maj Eliud Nabiswa

DISTRICTS
Central-West: PO Box 73, Kigumba via Masindi; tel: 046-523672; Maj Joseph Wandulu
Southern: PO Box 2012, Busia; tel: 043-251296; Capt Emmanuel Sichibona

TRAINING CENTRE
Attached to THQ

SOCIAL SERVICES
Children's Home
PO Box 48, Tororo; tel: 045-45244 (acc 54)

Community Centre
PO Box 11776, Kampala; tel: 041-532517

Home for Children with Physically Disabilities
PO Box 1186, Kampala; tel: 041-542409 (acc 30)

Vocational Training Workshops
PO Box 11776, Kampala; PO Box 13, Lira

PROJECTS
Emergency Outreach to Internally Displaced People
PO Box 13, Lira; tel: 047-320873

Emergency Support for Early Childhood Development
PO Box 1227, Gulu; tel: 047-135828

'Peace for African Child' (Education Programme)
PO Box 11776, Kampala

SAU-OVC Programme
HIV/Aids Education for Orphans and Vulnerable Children:
PO Box 11776, Kampala; tel: 041-533113

WORTH Programme
Income Generation for Women:
PO Box 2214, Mbale; tel: 045-79295

Trainees in a carpentry class at one of the vocational training workshops in Kampala

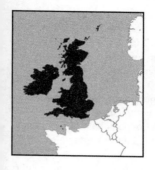

UNITED KINGDOM TERRITORY WITH THE REPUBLIC OF IRELAND

Territorial leaders:
Commissioners John and Elizabeth Matear

Territorial Commander:
Commissioner John Matear (2 Apr 2006)

Chief Secretary:
Lieut-Colonel William Cochrane
(1 Aug 2006)

Territorial Headquarters: 101 Newington Causeway, London SE1 6BN, UK

Tel: [44] 20 7367 4500; email: thq@salvationarmy.org.uk;
web site: www.salvationarmy.org.uk

The foundation of the territory dates from the earliest formation of The Salvation Army prior to the adoption of that title in 1878 when the Founder, William Booth, took charge of a mission to the East End of London in July 1865. Certain UK corps were first established as Christian Mission stations.

Throughout the Army's history its work in this geographical area has been organised in a variety of forms and territories but before 1990 these were all part of International Headquarters administration. However, on 1 November 1990 a restructuring occurred so that now the United Kingdom Territory is separate from International Headquarters and under a single command similar to that of the Army's other territories.

Zone: Europe
Countries included in the territory: Channel Islands, Isle of Man, Republic of Ireland, United Kingdom of Great Britain and Northern Ireland
Languages in which the gospel is preached: English, Korean, Urdu, Welsh
Periodicals: *Kids Alive!, Salvationist, The War Cry*

IN his new year message for 2007, Territorial Commander Commissioner John Matear wrote: 'Our work is Kingdom work – nothing more, nothing less and nothing else! If we are humble, obedient and totally dependent on God then he will continue to work through us for his glory.'

The Territorial Congress in Harrogate in October 2006 provided evidence both of the continuing work and Salvationists' motivation, with celebration, worship, and personal and corporate commitment.

Away from the large gatherings, innovative outreach ventures were making an impact on communities, often through young people. The newly planted centre of Goldthorpe, for example, provided a support network through text messaging.

A 'youth zone' was created in a

problem suburb of south Leicester to encourage young people to be a positive influence in their neighbourhood. In Raynes Park, south London, the A2B Rock School worked with socially excluded young people.

The territorial youth programme ALOVE kicked off its 'Essential' scheme in September 2006, placing trainees for a year in frontline mission situations across the territory.

Meanwhile, 2007 saw the centenary of the foundation of the Home League, and a wide range of imaginative programmes now operates in the territory under the umbrella of Adult and Family Ministries.

The year 2007 also marked the 200th anniversary of the abolition of the Slave Trade Act. The Salvation Army in the UK and Ireland was deeply engaged in raising awareness of its 21st-century equivalent – human trafficking – and other kinds of social deprivation.

A refuge for endangered women and children in Birmingham was opened by the Earl and Countess of Wessex in May 2006, and the similar Glen Alva centre in Belfast was opened by Peter Hain, MP (Secretary of State for Northern Ireland) in September.

In January 2007 the Princess Royal officially reopened the extended Riverside House Centre for Homeless Men in London's Docklands, while April saw the reopening of Hopetown Centre for Women in the same district and Cambria House Resettlement Centre in Camden.

Other new social service facilities included Logos House in Bristol opened in June 2006, a new unit for rough sleepers in Belfast's Centenary House in March 2007, and in October 2006 a ground-breaking drug detox unit attached to Greig House in Tower Hamlets, London, catering primarily for the Bangladeshi community.

There were other innovations in social outreach. In June 2006 Rochester Row Outreach Centre, Westminster, hosted a jobs fair specifically for homeless people, and in March 2007 the Penzance Project in Cornwall announced it was to open a residential treatment centre 'for people with chaotic lifestyles'.

The territory also announced in February 2007 its intention to explore the provision of Employment Services in partnership with Tomorrow's People.

Salvation Army relief was on hand in emergencies, including a tornado in north London (November 2006), the Cumbria rail crash (February 2007) and a minor earthquake in Folkestone (April 2007).

Regular national events continued to attract, particularly the Roots convention in May 2006 with 3,500 delegates considering the theme 'Metamorphosis'. The event also saw the launch of the Deeper Read Book Club promoted through the pages of *Salvationist*.

Among many musical highlights of the year was the release in October 2006 of *The Quiet Heart*, a CD of classic Salvation Army choral music recorded by the world-renowned King's Singers.

Changes were evident, with Balvonie Conference Centre in Scotland being closed in May 2006, while early in 2007 Salvationist Publishing and Supplies relocated from London to Wellingborough.

The role of communications technology grew again, with yet more resources being delivered via the internet or on CD-ROM, and fundraising initiatives with partners such as eBay.

In April 2007 Commissioner Betty Matear became Moderator of the Free Churches and a president of Churches Together in England. The first Salvationist to hold the office of Moderator of the Free Churches, she was inducted in a public ceremony at William Booth College.

THE SALVATION ARMY TRUSTEE COMPANY

Registered Office: 101 Newington Causeway, London SE1 6BN

THE SALVATION ARMY (REPUBLIC OF IRELAND)

Registered Office: PO Box 2098, Dublin 1, Republic of Ireland

STATISTICS

Officers 2,788 (active 1,321 retired 1,467) **Cadets** (1st Yr) 27 (2nd Yr) 32 **Employees** 5,302

Corps/Outreach Centres/New Plants 754 **Social Service Centres** 113 **Red Shield Clubs** 23 **Mobile Units for Servicemen** 10

Senior Soldiers 34,222 **Adherents** 10,350 **Junior Soldiers** 5,684

Personnel serving outside territory Officers 92 Layworkers 12

STAFF

Women's Ministries: Comr Elizabeth Matear (TPWM) Maj Joan Parker (TSWM/Asst CS)
TC's Representative in Scotland: Comr Keith Banks
TC's Associate Representative in Scotland: Comr Pauline Banks

Asst Chief Sec: Lt-Col Roland Sewell (Special Services)
Executive Sec to Territorial Leadership: Maj Clifford Ashworth
Sec for Administrative Review: Maj Michael Parker
International Staff Band: B/M Stephen Cobb
International Staff Songsters: S/L Mrs Dorothy Nancekievill

Sec for Business Administration: Maj John Wainwright
Asst Sec for Business Administration (Risk and Research): Mr David Rice
Asst Sec for Business Administration (Business Operations): Maj Margaret Stredwick
Company Sec: Maj Alan Read
Finance: Maj David Hinton
Internal Audit: Mr Phil Goss
Property: Mr Mark Johnston-Wood
Strategic Information: Dr David Clayden
SAGIC: Mr John Mott
Trade: Mr Trevor Caffull

Sec for Communications: Lt-Col Royston Bartlett
Editor-in-Chief and Publishing Sec: Maj Christine Clement
Editors: Maj Christine Clement (*Salvationist*) Maj Nigel Bovey (*The War Cry*) Mr Justin Reeves (*Kids Alive!*)
Head of Media: Cathy Le Feuvre
International Heritage Centre and Schools and Colleges Information Unit: Maj Stephen Grinsted (Director)
Marketing and Fundraising: Mr Julius Wolff-Ingham

Sec for Personnel: Maj George Pilkington
Asst Sec for Personnel: Maj Christine Barr
Asst Sec for Personnel (Development): Maj Sylvia Hinton
Child Protection: Mr Dean Juster
Human Resources (Employees): Miss Irene Lovely
Overseas Services Sec: Maj Elizabeth Burns
Pastoral Care Unit: Maj Colin Cowdery
Retired Officers Sec: Maj Ruth Downey

Sec for Programme: Maj Ian Barr
Anti-Trafficking Response: Lt-Col Dawn Sewell
Employment Services: Lt-Col Roland Sewell
Evangelism: Maj Paul Main
Adult and Family Ministries: Maj Janice Williams

Children's and Youth Ministries: Maj Roger Batt (TYS) Mr Russell Rook (ALOVE)
Mission Development Unit: Maj Jenine Main
Music Ministries: B/M Stephen Cobb
International Development: Mr Duncan Parker
Family Tracing: Maj Mike Sebbage
Research and Development: Dr Mike Emberson
Social Services: Maj Ian Harris (Director)
  Compliance and Monitoring: Maj Paul Hardy
  Red Shield Defence and Emergency Services: Maj Malcolm Watkins
Special Events: Mr Melvin Hart

WILLIAM BOOTH COLLEGE

Denmark Hill, London SE5 8BQ;
  tel: (020) 7326 2700; fax: (020) 7326 2750
  Principal: Capt Norman Ord
  Associate Principal: Capt Christine Ord
  Directors of School for Officer Training:
    Training Programme: Maj Karen Shakespeare
    Spiritual Programme: Capt Gordon Cotterill
  Director of School for In-Service Training and Development: Maj Judith Payne
  Territorial Candidates Director: Maj Mark Herbert

INTERNATIONAL HERITAGE CENTRE (including The William Booth Birthplace Museum, Nottingham) AND SCHOOLS AND COLLEGES INFORMATION UNIT

Denmark Hill, London SE5 8BQ;
  tel: (020) 7737 3327; fax: (020) 7737 4127;
  email: heritage@salvationarmy.org.uk

SCOTLAND SECRETARIAT

12a Dryden Rd, Loanhead, Midlothian EH20 9LZ;
  tel: (0131) 440 9100; fax: (0131) 440 9111;
  Scotland Sec: Maj Robert McIntyre

DIVISIONS

Anglia: 2 Barton Way, Norwich NR1 1DL;
  tel: (01603) 724 400; fax: (01603) 724 411;
  Maj Alan Burns
Central North: 80 Eccles New Rd, Salford, Gtr Manchester M5 4DU; tel: (0161) 743 3900;
  fax: (0161) 743 3911; Maj Melvyn Jones
Central South: 16c Cowley Rd, Uxbridge, Middlesex UB8 2LT; tel: (01895) 208800;
  fax: (01895) 208811; Maj Christine Bailey
East Midlands: Paisley Grove, Chilwell Meadows Business Park, Nottingham NG9 6DJ;
  tel: (0115) 983 5000; fax: (0115) 983 5011;
  Maj Jonathan Roberts
East Scotland: 12a Dryden Rd, Loanhead,

Midlothian EH20 9LZ; tel: (0131) 440 9100;
  fax: (0131) 440 9111; Maj Robert McIntyre
Ireland: 12 Station Mews, Sydenham, Belfast BT4 1TL; tel: (028) 9067 5000;
  fax: (028) 9067 5011; Maj David Jackson
London Central: 2nd Floor, 33/35 Kings Exchange, Tileyard Road, London N7 9AH;
  tel: (020) 7619 6100; fax: (020) 7619 6111;
  Maj Ray Irving
London North-East: Maldon Rd, Hatfield Peverel, Chelmsford, Essex CM3 2HL;
  tel: (01245) 383 000; fax: (01245) 383 011;
  Maj Michael Highton
London South-East: 1 East Court, Enterprise Rd, Maidstone, Kent ME15 6JF;
  tel: (01622) 775000; fax: (01622) 775011;
  Maj Anthony Cotterill
North Scotland: Deer Rd, Woodside, Aberdeen AB24 2BL; tel: (01224) 496000;
  fax: (01224) 496011; Maj Martin Hill
North-Western: 16 Faraday Rd, Wavertree Technology Park, Liverpool L13 1EH;
  tel: (0151) 252 6100; fax: (0151) 252 6111;
  Maj Marion Drew
Northern: Balliol Business Park West, Newcastle upon Tyne NE12 8EW; tel: (0191) 238 1800;
  fax: (0191) 238 1811; Maj Melvin Fincham
South and Mid Wales: East Moors Rd, Ocean Park, Cardiff CF24 5SA; tel: (029) 2044 0600;
  fax: (029) 2044 0611; Maj Peter Moran
South-Western: 6 Marlborough Court, Manaton Close, Matford Business Park, Exeter, Devon EX2 8PF; tel: (01392) 822100;
  fax: (01392) 822111; Maj Clifford Bradbury
Southern: 6-8 Little Park Farm Rd, Segensworth, Fareham, Hants PO15 5TD; tel: (01489) 566800;
  fax: (01489) 566811; Maj Neil Webb
West Midlands: 102 Unett St North, Hockley, Birmingham B19 3BZ; tel: (0121) 507 8500;
  fax: (0121) 507 8511; Maj Samuel Edgar
West Scotland: 4 Buchanan Court, Cumbernauld Rd, Stepps, Glasgow G33 6HZ;
  tel: (0141) 779 5000; fax: (0141) 779 5011;
  Maj Ivor Telfer
Yorkshire: 1 Cadman Court, Hanley Rd, Morley, Leeds LS27 0RX; tel: (0113) 281 0100;
  fax: (0113) 281 0111; Maj William Heeley

CONFERENCE CENTRES

Carfax: Bath BA2 4BS; tel: (01225) 462089
St Christopher's (small): 15 Sea Rd, Westgate-on-Sea, Kent; tel: (01843) 831875
Sunbury Court (incl Recreation Centre and Log Cabin): Lwr Hampton Rd, Sunbury-on-Thames, Middlesex TW16 5PL;
  tel: (01932) 782196

CONFERENCE AND YOUTH CENTRE

Sunbury Court, Log Cabin and Recreational Centre: Lwr Hampton Rd, Sunbury-on-Thames, Middlesex TW16 5PL; tel: (01932) 782196

SELF-CATERING ACCOMMODATION

Caldew House: Sebergham, Cumbria; tel: (01225) 462089 (large house)

Hulham Cottage: Exmouth, Devon; tel: (01225) 462089 (2 flats)

St Christopher's: Westgate-on-Sea, Kent; tel: (01843) 831875 (5 flats)

Sunbury Court, Log Cabin and Recreational Centre: Lower Hampton Rd, Sunbury-on-Thames, Middlesex TW16 5PL; tel: (01932) 782196

FAMILY TRACING SERVICE

101 Newington Causeway, London SE1 6BN; tel: (020) 7367 4747; fax: (020) 7367 4723

FARM

Hadleigh: Castle Lane, Hadleigh, Benfleet, Essex; tel: (01702) 558550

HOTELS

Bath: Carfax Hotel, Gt Pulteney St, Bath BA2 4BS; tel: (01225) 462089

Bournemouth: Cliff House, 13 Belle Vue Rd, Bournemouth, Dorset BH6 3DA; tel: (01202) 424701 (office); (01202) 425852 (guests)

Westgate-on-Sea: St Christopher's, 15 Sea Rd, Westgate-on-Sea, Kent CT8 8SA; tel: (01843) 831875

INSURANCE CORPORATION

The Salvation Army General Insurance Corporation Ltd, Faith House, 23-24 Lovat Lane, London EC3R 8EB; tel: 0845 634 0260; fax: 0845 634 0263

PASTORAL CARE UNIT

Administration and Seminar Centre (inc Trauma Care Programme): 432 Forest Rd, Walthamstow, London E17 4PY; tel: (020) 8509 1803; fax: (020) 8520 3755; Helpline tel: (020) 8509 1803; After-office hours tel: 0779 699 1579

Counselling Services: 1 Water Lane, Stratford, London E15 4LU; tel: (020) 8536 5480; fax: (020) 8536 5489; Maj Philip Packman

Pastoral Support:

London Central, London North-East, UKT personnel departing/arriving from overseas; tel: (020) 8509 1803

Central South, London South-East, Southern, South-Western; tel: (01895) 252794

Central North, North-Western, South and Mid Wales, West Midlands; tel: (01282) 697378

Northern, Yorkshire, East Midlands, Anglia: tel: (0113) 253 7205

Scotland and Ireland: tel: (01506) 854474

TRADE (SP&S LTD)

Head Office (and shop): 66-78 Denington Rd, Denington Industrial Estate, Wellingborough, Northants NN8 2QH; tel: (01933) 445445 (mail order); fax: (01933) 445415

Shop: 1 Tiverton St, London SE1 6NT

TRADING (THE SA TRADING CO LTD)

66-78 Denington Rd, Denington Industrial Estate, Wellingborough, Northants NN8 2QH

Textile Recycling Division: tel: (01933) 441086; fax: (01933) 445449; email: TA102@dial.pipex.com

Charity Shops Division: tel: (01933) 441807; fax: (01933) 442942; email: cpsatco@compuserve.com

SOCIAL SERVICES DEPARTMENT

Centres for Elderly People

Bath: Smallcombe House, Bathwick Hill, BA2 6EJ; tel: (01225) 465694; fax: (01225) 465769 (acc men and women 31, sheltered flat 1)

Buxton: The Hawthorns, Burlington Rd, SK17 9AR; tel: (01298) 23700; public call box: (01298) 24955; fax: (01298) 73624 (acc 34)

Coventry: Youell Court, Skipworth Rd, Binley CV3 2XA; tel (024) 76561300; fax: (024) 76561306 (acc 40)

Edinburgh:

Davidson House, 266 Colinton Rd, EH14 1DT; tel: (0131) 441 2117 (acc 40)

Eagle Lodge, 488/1 Ferry Rd, EH5 2DL; tel: (0131) 551 1611; fax: (0131) 552 5673 (acc 32)

Glasgow: Eva Burrows Day Centre, Clyde Place, Halfway, Cambuslang G72 7QT; tel: (0141) 646 1461 (acc 32, day centre places 24)

Hassocks: Villa Adastra, 79 Keymer Rd, BN6 8QH; tel: (01273) 842184 (office); (01273) 845299 (residents) (acc 40, day centre places 20)

Holywood: The Sir Samuel Kelly Memorial Home, 39 Bangor Rd, Co Down BT18 0NE; tel: (028) 9042 2293; fax: (028) 9042 7361 (acc 40)

London:

Alver Bank, 17 West Rd, Clapham SW4 7DL;
tel: (020) 7627 8061 (office);
(020) 7428 1119 (residents) (acc 27)

Glebe Court, 2 Blackheath Rise, Lewisham
SE13 7PN; tel: (020) 8297 0637 (office);
(020) 8463 0508 (residents);
fax: (020) 8852 7298 (acc 42)

Rookstone, Lawrie Park Cres, Sydenham
SE26 6HH; tel: (020) 8778 0317 (office);
(020) 8778 0314 (residents);
fax: (020) 8778 5822 (acc 32)

North Walsham: Furze Hill House,
73 Happisburgh Rd, NR28 9HD;
tel: 01692 503164 (acc 40, day centre
places 22)

Nottingham: Notintone House, Sneinton Rd,
NG2 4QL; tel: (0115) 950 3788;
public call box: (0115) 950 2060 (acc 40)

Prestwich: Holt House, Headlands Dr, Hilton
Lane, Gtr Manchester M25 9YF;
tel: (0161) 773 0220 (office); (0161) 798 5860
(residents); fax: (0161) 798 6428 (acc 32)

Sandridge: Lyndon, 2 High St, Sandridge,
St Albans AL4 9DH; tel: (01727) 851050 (acc
32)

Southend-on-Sea: Bradbury Home, 2 Roots
Hall Drive, SS2 6DA; tel: (01702) 435838
(acc 34)

Tunbridge Wells: Sunset Lodge, Pembury Rd,
TN2 3QT; tel: (01892) 530861 (office);
(01892) 533769 (residents) (acc 27)

Weston-super-Mare: Dewdown House,
64 Beach Rd, BS23 4BE; tel: (01934) 417125
(acc 40)

Centres for Families (Residential)

Belfast:

Glen Alva, 19 Cliftonville Rd, BT14 6JN;
tel: (028) 9035 1185 (acc family units 20,
max 77 residents)

Thorndale Parenting Assessment/Family Centre,
Duncairn Ave, Antrim Rd, BT14 6BP;
tel: (028) 9035 1900 (acc family units 34,
single bedsits 4, max 125 residents)

Leeds: Mount Cross, 139 Broad Lane, Bramley
LS13 2JP; tel: (0113) 257 0810 (acc flats 28,
max 78 residents)

Portsmouth: Catherine Booth House,
1 Aylward St, PO1 3PH; tel: (023) 9273 7226
(acc family units 15, max 40 residents)

Refuge from Domestic Violence (women with children)

Birmingham: Shepherd's Green House; address

and telephone confidential; contact via West
Midlands DHQ (acc 16 families, 4 single
women)

Centres for People with Learning Difficulties

Kilbirnie: George Steven Centre, Craigton Rd,
KA25 6LJ

Plymouth: Pilgrim House, Courtfield Rd,
PL3 5BB; tel: (01752) 660302

Stoke: Lovatt Court, Lovatt St, Stoke-on-Trent
ST4 7RL; tel: (01782) 415621

Centres for the Single Homeless

Accrington: Accrington H20, Russia St,
BB5 1SG; tel: (01254) 389157 (acc 11)

Belfast:

Centenary House, 2 Victoria St, BT1 3GE;
tel: (02890) 320320 (acc direct access 80)

Calder Fountain (attached to Centenary House)
(registered care 28, resettlement 12)

Birmingham: William Booth Lane, B4 6HA;
tel: (0121) 236 6554; (0121) 236 7135 (office)
(acc 74)

Blackburn: Bramwell House, Heaton St,
BB2 2EF; tel: (01254) 677338 (acc 54)

Bolton: Gilead House, Duke St, BL1 2LU;
tel: (01204) 394499 (acc 69 + 2 flats)

Bradford: Lawley House, 371 Leeds Rd,
BD3 9NG; tel: (01274) 731221 (acc direct
access 51, resettlement 12)

Braintree: New Direction Centre, David
Blackwell House, 25-27 Bocking End,
CM7 9HB; tel: (01376) 553373 (acc 14)

Bristol: Logos House, Little George St, BS2 9EL;
tel: (0117) 955 2821 (acc 69)

Cardiff: Ty Gobaith, 240 Bute St, CF1 5TY;
tel: (029) 2048 0187 (acc 50)

Cardiff: Northlands, 202 North Rd, CF4 3XP;
tel: (029) 2061 9077 (acc 26)

Coventry: 1 Lincoln St, CV1 4JN;
tel: (024) 7625 1477 (acc 99)

Darlington: Tom Raine Court, Coburg St,
DL1 1SB; tel: (01325) 489242 (acc 37)

Dublin: Granby Centre, 9-10 Granby Row,
Dublin 1, Eire; tel: [353] (1) 872 5500
(acc units 106)

Dundee:

Strathmore Lodge, 31 Ward Rd, DD1 1NG;
tel: (01382) 225448 (acc 39)

Burnside Mill, Milnes East Wynd, DD1 5BA
(acc 20)

Edinburgh:

Ashbrook, 492 Ferry Rd, EH5 2DL;
tel: (0131) 552 5705 (acc 24)

The Pleasance, EH8 9UE; tel: (0131) 556 3957 (acc 37)

Glasgow:

Hope House, 14 Clyde St, G1 5JH; tel: (0141) 552 0537 (acc 98)

Wallace of Campsie House, 30 East Campbell St, G1 5DT; tel: (0141) 552 4301; fax: (0141) 552 5910 (acc 52)

William Hunter House, 70 Oxford St, G5 9EP; tel: (0141) 429 5201 (acc 43)

Grimsby: Brighowgate, DN32 0QW; tel: (01472) 242648 (acc 46)

Hull: William Booth House, 2 Hessle Rd, HU1 2QQ; tel: (01482) 225521 (acc 113)

Huntingdon: Kings Ripton Court, Kings Ripton Rd, PE17 2NZ; tel: (01480) 423800 (acc 36)

Inverness: Huntly House, 1-2 Huntly Pl, IV3 6HA; tel: (01463) 234123 (acc 26); includes Huntly House Resettlement Project; tel: (01463) 234123 (21 spaces)

Ipswich: Lyndon House, 107 Fore St, IP4 1LS; tel: (01473) 251070 (acc 39)

Isle of Man: David Gray House, 6 Drury Tce, Douglas, IM2 3HY; tel: (01624) 662814 (acc 4)

Leamington Spa: Eden Villa, 13 Charlotte St, CV31 3EB; tel: (01926) 450708 (acc 11)

Leeds: Spring Grove, 139 Broad Lane, Bramley, LS13 2JP; tel: (0113) 257 7552 (acc 6)

Liverpool:

Ann Fowler House, Fraser St, L3 8JX; tel: (0151) 207 3815 (acc 38)

Darbyshire House, 380 Prescot Rd, L13 3DA; tel: (0151) 228 0925 (acc 45)

London:

David Barker House, Blackfriars Rd, SE1 (acc 40)

Booth House, 153-157 Whitechapel Rd, E1 1DF; tel: (020) 7247 3401 (acc 150)

Cambria House, 37 Hunter St, WC1N ; tel: (020) 7837 1654 (acc 48)

Edith Road, 10-12 Edith Rd, Hammersmith, W14 9BA; tel: (020) 7603 1692 (acc 25)

Edward Alsop Court, 18 Great Peter St, Westminster, SW1 2BT; tel: (020) 7233 0296 (acc 108)

Hopetown, 60 Old Montague St, Whitechapel, E1 5LF; tel: (020) 7377 6429 (acc 116)

Riverside House, 20 Garford St, West India Dock Rd, E14 8JG; tel: (020) 7987 1520 (acc 51)

Manchester: 1 Wilmott St, Chorlton-on-Medlock, M15 6BD; tel: (0161) 236 7537 (acc 113)

Newcastle upon Tyne:

39 City Rd, NE1 2BR; tel: (0191) 233 9150 (acc 66)

Cedar House, Denmark St, Byker, NE6 2UH; tel: (0191) 224 1509 (acc direct access 18, resettlement flats 6)

Nottingham:

Acorn Lodge, Campbell St, NG3 1GZ (acc 12)

Sneinton House, 2 Boston St, NG1 1ED; tel: (0115) 950 4364 (acc 70)

Penzance: Chy Govenek, 9 Penare Rd (acc 8)

Perth: 16 Skinnergate, PH1 5JH; tel: (01738) 624360 (acc 36)

Plymouth: Devonport House and Zion House, Park Ave, PL1 4BA; tel: (01752) 562170/564545 (acc 72)

Reading: Willow House, Willow St, RG1 6BD; tel: (0118) 959 0681 (acc 38)

Rochdale: Providence House, High St, OL12 0NT; tel: (01706) 645151 (acc 73)

St Helens: Salisbury House, Parr St, WA9 1JU; tel: (01744) 744800 (acc 68)

Salford: James St (off Oldfield Rd), M3 5HP; tel: (0161) 831 7020/7040 (acc 38)

Sheffield: 161 Fitzwilliam St; Office and Postal Address: 126 Charter Row, S1 4HY; tel: (0114) 272 5158 (acc 51)

Skegness: Witham Lodge, Alexandra Rd, PE25 3TL; tel: (01754) 899151 (acc 30)

Southampton: Mountbatten Centre, 57 Oxford St, SO14 3DL; tel: (023) 8033 3508/8063 7259

Stoke-on-Trent: Vale St, ST4 7RN; tel: (01782) 744374 (acc 64 + 4 training flats)

Sunderland: Swan Lodge, High St East, SR1 2AU; tel: (0191) 565 5411 (acc 65)

Swindon: Booth House, 1 Spring Close, SN1 2BF; tel: (01793) 401830 (acc 50)

Warrington: James Lee House, Brick St, Howley, WA1 2PD; tel: (01925) 636496 (acc 54)

Children's Homes/Centres (Residential)

Dublin:

Lefroy Night Light, 12-14 Eden Quay, Dublin 1, Eire; tel: [353] (1) 874 3762 (acc 7 overnight emergency beds)

Lefroy Support Flats, 12-14 Eden Quay, Dublin 1, Eire; tel: [353] (1) 874 3762 (acc 7)

Leeds: Spring Grove, 139 Broad Lane, Bramley, LS13 2JP; tel: (0113) 257 7552 (acc 6 female care leavers)

London: The Haven, Springfield Rd, SE26 6HG; tel: (020) 8659 4033/4 (acc 12)

Day Care and Contact Centres for Children

Leeds: Copper Beech Day Nursery, 137 Broad Lane, Bramley, LS13 2JP; tel: (0113) 256 5820 (registered for 62)

There are a further 7 Day Nurseries, 25 Pre-schools/ Playgroups, 2 Crèches, 12 Out-of-

*school Clubs and 8 Child Contact Centres
attached to social centres and corps*

Domiciliary Care (elderly)
Community Care Service (Angus): 24 West
High St, Forfar, DD8 1BA; tel: (01307) 469393

Drop In Centres
Edinburgh: 77 Bread St, EH3 9AH;
tel: (0131) 228 5351
Glasgow: Laurieston Centre, 39 South Portland
St, G5 9JL; tel: (0141) 429 6533
London: 97 Rochester Row, SW1P 1LJ;
tel: (020) 7233 9862
Norwich: Pottergate Arc, 28 Pottergate,
NR2 1DX; tel: (01603) 663496
Southampton: H2O Project, Princess St, Northam,
SO14 5RP; tel: (023) 8022 4632

Employment Training Centres
Hadleigh: Castle Ave, Castle Lane, Hadleigh,
Benfleet, Essex SS7 2AS; tel: (01702) 552963
Norwich: Employment 2000, Calvert St;
tel: (01603) 761175

Night Shelter
Dublin: Cedar House, Marlborough Pl, Dublin 2,
Eire; tel: [353] (1) 873 1241 (acc 48)

Outreach Teams
Bristol: Logos House, Bridge Project, Little
George St, BS2 9EL; tel: (0117) 955 2821
Cardiff: Bus Project, Ty Gobaith, 240 Bute St,
CF1 5TY; tel: (029) 2048 0187
London: Faith House, 11 Argyle St, King's
Cross, WC1H 8EJ; tel: (020) 7837 5149
York: Homeless Prevention/Resettlement,
Gillygate, YO31 7EA; tel: (01904) 630470

Prison Ministries
Prison Ministries Officer, 101 Newington
Causeway, London SE1 6BN;
tel: (020) 7367 4866

Probation Hostel
Isle of Man: David Gray House, 6 Drury Tce,
Douglas, IM2 3HY; tel: (01624) 662814
(acc 9)

Red Shield Services
UK THQ: 101 Newington Causeway, London
SE1 6BN; tel: (020) 7367 4851
HQ Germany: SAHQ/CVWW, Block 1, NAAFI
Complex, BFPO 15; tel: [49] (5221) 24627

Sheltered Housing
London: Alver Bank, 17 West Rd, Clapham,
SW4 7DL; tel: (020) 7627 8061 (acc single 6,
double 2)
Tunbridge Wells: Charles Court, Pembury Rd,
TN2 3QY; tel: (01892) 547439 (acc single 9,
double 8)

Addiction Service
Bristol: Bridge Project, Little George St, BS2 9EL;
tel: (0117) 955 0074 (acc 32)
Cardiff: Bridge Project, Ty Gobiath, 240 Bute St,
CF1 5TY; tel: (029) 2048 0187 (acc 23)
Dublin: York House, Alcohol Recovery Unit
(inc short-term intervention), Longford St
Little, Dublin 2, Rep of Ireland;
tel: (00 353-1) 476 3337 (acc 24)
Greenock: Fewster House, 10 Terrace Rd,
PA15 1DJ; tel: (01475) 721572 (acc 34)
Highworth: Gloucester House, 6 High St,
Swindon, SN6 7AG; tel: (01793) 762365
(acc 12, Halfway House 3, day programme 4)
London:
Greig House, 20 Garford St, West India Dock Rd,
E14 8JG; tel: (020) 7987 5658 (acc 25)
Riverside House 'Specialist' Homeless Centre for
People with Addiction Issues, 20 Garford St,
West India Dock Rd, E14 8JG;
tel: (020) 7068 0950 (acc 31)
Riverside House Harbour Recovery Project (inc
detoxification), 20 Garford St, West India
Dock Rd, E14 8JG; tel:(020) 7068 0950 (acc 8)
Stirling: Harm Reduction Service, SA Hall,
Drip Rd, FK8 1RA; tel: (01786) 448923

Offering Hope to Trafficked Women
The Jarrett Community

Biomedical Services
Biomedical Support Services are provided across
social work disciplines in partnership with the
University of Kent, Canterbury

❜ Our work is Kingdom work – nothing more, nothing less and
nothing else! If we are humble, obedient and totally dependent
on God then he will continue to work through us for his glory.

Commissioner John Matear (TC)

THE UNITED STATES OF AMERICA

National leaders:
Commissioners Israel L. and Eva D. Gaither

National Commander:
Commissioner Israel L. Gaither (1 May 2006)

National Chief Secretary:
Lieut-Colonel David Jeffrey (1 Jul 2007)

National Headquarters: 615 Slaters Lane, PO Box 269, Alexandria, VA 22313-0269, USA

Tel: [1] (703) 684 5500; fax: [1] (703) 684 3478;
web site: www.salvationarmyusa.org

The Salvation Army began its ministry in the United States in October 1879. Lieutenant Eliza Shirley left England to join her parents who had migrated to America earlier in search of work. She held meetings that were so successful that General William Booth sent Commissioner George Scott Railton and seven women officers to the United States in March 1880 to formalise the effort. Their initial street meeting was held on the dockside at Battery Park in New York City the day they arrived.

In only three years, operations had expanded into California, Connecticut, Indiana, Kentucky, Maryland, Massachusetts, Michigan, Missouri, New Jersey, New York, Ohio and Pennsylvania. Family services, youth services, elderly services and disaster services are among the many programmes offered in local communities throughout the United States, in Puerto Rico, the Virgin Islands, the Marshall Islands and Guam.

The National Headquarters was incorporated as a religious and charitable corporation in the State of New Jersey in 1982 as 'The Salvation Army National Corporation' and is qualified to conduct its affairs in the Commonwealth of Virginia.

Zone: Americas and Caribbean
Periodicals: *The War Cry, Word & Deed – A Journal of Theology and Ministry, Women's Ministries Resources, Young Salvationist*

ON 1 May 2006 Commissioners Israel L. and Eva D. Gaither assumed leadership responsibilities as the USA National Commander and National President of Women's Ministries respectively.

Within weeks of their taking office, the national leaders' first visit was to the Hurricane Katrina stricken Gulf Coast to offer support to victims and Salvation Army personnel.

Recognised as a key leader in linking biblical faith and values in service to the poor, The Salvation Army became one of the founders in the public launching of Christian Churches Together.

The Brengle Holiness Institute and the National Soldiers Seminar on Evangelism forums were conducted for the deepening of the Salvationist's spiritual life and commitment to the Army's mission.

Christmas 2006 was another record-setting year with $117,225,080 donated to the annual Red Kettle Appeal.

Citizens of the USA continue to provide the mission of The Salvation Army with unprecedented financial and voluntary support.

NATIONAL STATISTICS
(incorporating all USA territories)
Officers 5,374 (active 3,526 retired 1,848) **Cadets** (1st Yr) 110 (2nd Yr) 119 **Employees** 59,427
Corps 1,275 **Outposts** 29 **Institutions** 800
Senior Soldiers 83,798 **Adherents** 16,669 **Junior Soldiers** 26,333

STATISTICS
(National Headquarters)
Officers (active) 26 **Employees** 65 **SAWSO Employees** 19

STAFF
Women's Ministries: Comr Eva D. Gaither

(NPWM) Lt-Col Barbara Jeffrey (NSWM, NRVAVS); fax: (703) 684 5511
Asst Nat Chief Sec: Maj Sandra Defibaugh
Nat Treasurer and Nat Sec for Business Administration: Lt-Col John Falin
Nat Sec for Personnel: Lt-Col Judy Falin
Nat Sec for Programme: Maj Gary Miller; fax: (703) 519 5880
Nat Social Services Sec: Maj Ronald Foreman fax: (703) 519 5889
Nat Community Relations and Development Sec: Maj George Hood; fax: (703) 684 5538
Nat Editor-in-Chief and Literary Sec: Maj Edward Forster; fax: (703) 684 5539
Salvation Army World Service Office (SAWSO): Lt-Col Daniel L. Starrett, jr; fax: (703) 684 5536

ARCHIVES AND RESEARCH CENTRE
Email: Archives@usn.salvationarmy.org

USA National Commander Commissioner Israel L. Gaither welcomes former President George H. W. Bush and former First Lady Barbara Bush in Houston, Texas, where the former president and his wife were volunteering as Salvation Army bell-ringers during the 2006 Red Kettle Christmas Appeal

First Lady Laura Bush addresses the National Advisory Organisations Conference in Dallas, Texas

USA CENTRAL TERRITORY

Territorial leaders:
Commissioners Kenneth and Joy Baillie

Territorial Commander:
Commissioner Kenneth Baillie (13 Nov 2002)

Chief Secretary:
Lieut-Colonel Paul R. Seiler (1 Jul 2006)

Territorial Headquarters: 10 W Algonquin Rd, Des Plaines, IL 60016-6006, USA

Tel: [1] (847) 294-2000; fax: [1] (847) 294-2295; web site: www.usc.salvationarmy.org

The Salvation Army was incorporated as a religious and charitable corporation in the State of Illinois in 1913 as 'The Salvation Army' and is qualified to conduct its affairs in all of the states of the territory.

Zone: Americas and Caribbean
USA states included in the territory: Illinois, Indiana, Iowa, Kansas, Michigan, Minnesota, Missouri, Nebraska, North Dakota, South Dakota, Wisconsin
'The Salvation Army' in Spanish: Ejército de Salvación; in Swedish: Frälsningsarmén
Languages in which the gospel is preached: English, Korean, Laotian, Russian, Spanish, Swedish
Periodical: *Central Connection*

THE territory continued looking outward into the world – meeting needs at home and beyond in the name of Christ, supported by generous giving and effective stewardship.

A new record high was set for youth summer mission team participants: 19 served on teams in Argentina, India and Kenya; 14 served territorially, and four interns served in Latvia and Ukraine. A young Salvationist from a 'partners in mission' territory (Eastern Europe) participated for the first time.

Adult short-term missions were reintroduced. Seven people spent two weeks in Germany assisting Hanover Corps with Christmas ministries and fundraising. Twenty people (men the first week, young people the second) renovated a children's home in Jamaica.

Child sponsorship reached a record annual high – more than $131,000 for 470 sponsorships. Two cadets from Zimbabwe joined the God's Fellow Workers Session at the college for officer training.

In addition to a continued territorial emphasis on 'Discipleship Training' courses, Sweden began using the materials and a course was taught in Mexico (the Spanish translation being made available for free to other territories).

A territorial training seminar on

discipleship, outreach and the Bible was held.

The first six finalists qualified to build a Salvation Army Ray and Joan Kroc Corps Community Centre were announced: Grand Rapids, Michigan; Green Bay, Wisconsin; Quincy, Illinois; Detroit, Michigan; Omaha, Nebraska; and St Joseph County, Indiana.

The nation's largest adult rehabilitation centre was dedicated by National Commander Commissioner Israel L. Gaither in Detroit. Chicago's mayor helped dedicate a large, new red shield centre and corps serving a low-income area.

The territorial social services certification programme, along with 17 social service and child care programmes, received accreditation from external organisations.

USA national leaders Commissioners Israel L. and Eva D. Gaither were special guests at the territory's 'LeadingEdge' congress and commissioning weekend. Local leadership, discipleship and world missions were emphasised. The giving of $6.8 million to the international Self-Denial World Mission Fund thrilled the 3,100 delegates.

Twenty-seven cadets of the Visionaries Session were commissioned as officers. A winter candidate recruitment weekend attracted more than 70 participants.

'The Gospel According to Hollywood' was the newest worship series produced by the Territorial Music and Gospel Arts Department.

The Chicago Staff Band (celebrating its 100th year in 2007) toured Australia Southern Territory. More than 220 delegates studied music, worship arts and the Bible at the Central Music Institute.

In an ongoing response to last year's Gulf Coast hurricanes, deployment of emotional and spiritual care teams continued. More than 8,000 people have received disaster response training; select individuals were trained for international deployment. The Indiana Division's disaster services director served an extended assignment in Uganda's refugee camps.

Disaster services responded to deadly heatwaves and severe ice, snow and rain storms (some with tornadoes, gale winds and flooding) that killed or injured dozens and left immense property damage in the territory.

Nearly 600 Central and Southern Territory youth attended the 'Xplore 2006' jamboree. Meaningful activities, devotionals and speakers drew campers closer to God. The ever-popular Central Bible and Leadership Institute helped Salvationists of all ages grow in faith.

STATISTICS

Officers 1,196 (active 755 retired 441) **Cadets** (1st Yr) 26 (2nd Yr) 24 **Employees** 12,241
Corps 269 **Institutions** 134
Senior Soldiers 18,301 **Adherents** 3,211 **Junior Soldiers** 4,597
Personnel serving outside territory Officers 28

STAFF

Personnel: Lt-Col William Harfoot
Programme:
Business: Lt-Col Mickey L. McLaren

Adult Rehabilitation Centres: Maj Graham
  Allan
Audit: Maj David Clark
Candidates: Majs Andrew S. and Cheryl Miller
Community Relations and Development:
  Majs Ralph and Susan Bukiewicz
Corps Mission and Adult Ministries:
  Maj Joseph Wheeler
Evangelism and Corps Growth: Capt Carol J.
  Lewis
Finance: Maj Robert Doliber
Information Technology: Mr Ronald E. Shoults
Legal and Legacy: Maj James C. Hoskin
  (designate)
Music and Gospel Arts: B/M William F.
  Himes, jr, OF
Officer Resource and Development:
  Lt-Col Susan Harfoot
Pastoral Care Officers: Majors Larry and
  Margo Thorson
Property: Maj David Corliss
Resource Connection Dept: Mr Robert Jones
Risk Management: Maj Norman R. Nonnweiler
Social Services: Maj Richard E. Vander Weele
Training: Maj Jeffrey Smith
Women's Ministries: Comr Joy Baillie (TPWM)
  Lt-Col Carol Seiler (TSWM) Maj Mary
  Corliss (TCCMS/TMFS)
Youth: Majs Robert and Collette Webster

DIVISIONS

Eastern Michigan: 16130 Northland Dr,
  Southfield, MI 48075-5218;
  tel: (248) 443-5500; Maj Norman S. Marshall
Heartland: 401 NE Adams St, Peoria,
  IL 61603-4201; tel: (309) 655-7220;
  Maj Charles Smith
Indiana: 3100 N Meridian St, Indianapolis,
  IN 46208-4718; tel: (317) 937-7000;
  Maj Richard Amick
Kansas and Western Missouri: 3637
  Broadway, Kansas City, MO 64111-2503;
  tel: (816) 756-1455; Lt-Col Theodore J.
  Dalberg
Metropolitan: 5040 N Pulaski Rd, Chicago, IL
  60630-2788; tel: (773) 725-1100;
  Lt-Col David E. Grindle
Midland: 1130 Hampton Ave, St Louis, MO
  63139-3147; tel: (314) 646-3000;
  Maj Lonneal Richardson
Northern: 2445 Prior Ave, Roseville, MN
  55113-2714; tel: (651) 746-3400; Maj Daniel
  Sjogren
Western: 3612 Cuming St, Omaha,
  NE 68131-1900; tel: (402) 898-5900;
  Maj Merle Heatwole

Western Michigan and Northern Indiana:
  1215 E Fulton, Grand Rapids, MI 49503-
  3849; tel: (616) 459-3433; Maj James Nauta
Wisconsin and Upper Michigan: 11315 W
  Watertown Plank Rd, Wauwatosa, WI
  53226-0019; tel: (414) 302-4300; Maj Robert
  E. Thomson, jr

COLLEGE FOR OFFICER TRAINING
700 W Brompton Ave, Chicago, IL 60657-1831;
  tel: (773) 524-2000

SOCIAL SERVICES
Adult Rehabilitation Centres
Chicago (Central), IL 506 N Des Plaines St;
  tel: (312) 738-4367 (acc 200)
Chicago (North Side), IL 60614: 2258 N
  Clybourn Ave; tel: (773) 477-1771 (acc 135)
Davenport, IA 52806: 4001 N Brady St;
  tel: (563) 323-2748 (acc 80)
Des Moines, IA 50309-4897: 133 E Second St;
  tel: (515) 243-4277 (acc 58)
Flint, MI 48506: 2200 N Dort Highway;
  tel: (810) 234-2678 (acc 122)
Fort Wayne, IN 46802: 427 W Washington Blvd;
  tel: (260) 424-1655 (acc 55)
Gary, IN 46402: 1351 W Eleventh Ave;
  tel: (219) 882-9377 (acc 98)
Grand Rapids, MI 49507-1601: 1491 S Division
  Ave; tel: (616) 452-3133 (acc 110)
Indianapolis, IN 46202-3915: 711 E Washington
  St; tel: (317) 638-6585 (acc 97)
Kansas City, MO 64106: 1351 E 10th St;
  tel: (816) 421-5434 (acc 132)
Milwaukee, WI 53202-5999: 324 N Jackson St;
  tel: (414) 276-4316 (acc 93)
Minneapolis, MN 55401-1039: 900 N Fourth St;
  tel: (612) 332-5855 (acc 125)
Omaha, NE 68131-2642: 2551 Dodge St;
  tel: (402) 342-4135 (acc 98)
Rockford, IL 61104-7385: 1706 Eighteenth Ave;
  tel: (815) 397-0440 (acc 80)
Romulus, MI 48174-4205: 5931 Middlebelt;
  tel: (734) 729-3939 (acc 111)
St Louis, MO 63108-3211: 3949 Forest Park
  Blvd; tel: (314) 535-0057 (acc 102)
South Bend, IN 46601-2226: 510-18 S Main St;
  tel: (574) 288-2539 (acc 52)
Southeast, MI: (acc 311)
  Main Campus: 1627 W Fort St, Detroit,
    MI 48216; tel: (313) 965-7760;
    toll-free: (866) GIVE-TOO
  North Campus: 118 W Lawrence, Pontiac,
    MI 48341; tel: (248) 338-9601
Springfield, IL 62703-1003: 221 N 11th St;
  tel: (217) 528-7573 (acc 89)

259

Waukegan, IL 60085-6511: 431 S Genesee St;
  tel: (847) 662-7730 (acc 100)

UNDER DIVISIONS
Emergency Lodges
Alton, IL 62002: 525 Alby
Ann Arbor, MI 48108: 3660 Packard Rd
Appleton, WI 54914: 124 E North St
Belleville, IL 62226: 4102 W Main St
Benton Harbor, MI 49022: 645 Pipestone St
Bloomington, IL 61701: 212 N Roosevelt
Champaign, IL 61820: 119-123 E Univ Ave
Chicago, IL 60640: 800 W Lawrence
Columbia, MO 65203: 602 N Ann St
Davenport, IA 52803-5101: 301-307 W 6th St
Decatur, IL 62525: 229 W Main St
Detroit, MI 48208-2517: 3737 Lawton
Grand Island, NE 68801-5828; 818 W 3rd St
Grand Rapids, MI 49503: 143 Lakeside Dr SE
Hillsboro, IL 62049: Box 356
Hutchinson, KS 67504-0310: 200 S Main
Independence, MO 64050-2664: 14704
  E Truman Rd
Indianapolis, IN 46204: 540 N Alabama St
Iron Mountain, MI 49801: 114 W Brown St
Jefferson City, MO 65101: 907 Jefferson St
Kankakee, IL 60901: 148 N Harrison
Kankakee, IL 60901: 541 E Court Ave
Kansas City, KS 66102: 1201½ Minnesota
LaCrosse, WI 54601: 223 N 8th St
Lafayette, IN 47904-1934: 1110 Union St
Lawrence, KS 66044: 946 New Hampshire St
Madison, WI 53703: E 630 Washington Ave E
Mandan, ND 58554: 100 6th Ave SE
Mankato, MN 56001-2338: 700 S Riverfront Dr
Milwaukee, WI 53205: 1730 N 7th St
Monroe, MI 48161: 815 E 1st St
O'Fallon, MO 63366-2938: 1 William Booth Dr
Olathe, KS 66061: 400-402 E Santa Fe
Omaha, NE 68131: 3612 Cuming St
Peoria, IL 61603: 417 NE Adams St
Peoria, IL 61603: 414 NE Jefferson St
Quincy, IL 62301: 400 Broadway
Rockford, IL 61104: 1706 18th Ave E
St Cloud, MN 56304: 619 E St Germain St
St Joseph, MO 64501: 618 S 6th St
St Louis, MO 63132: 10740 W Page Ave
St Louis, MO 63108: 3744 Lindell Blvd
Sheboygan, WI 53081: 710 Pennsylvania Ave
Sioux Falls, SD 57103-0128: 800 N Cliff Ave
Somerset, WI 54025: 203 Church Hill Rd
Springfield, IL 62702: 530 N 6th
Springfield, MO 65802: 1707 W Chestnut
  Expwy
Warren, MI 48091: 24140 Mound Rd
Waterloo, IA 50703: 218 Logan Ave

Waterloo, IA 50703: 229 Logan Ave
Waterloo, IA 50703: 603 S Hanchett Rd
Waukesha, WI 53188: 445 Madison St
Wichita, KS 67202-2010: 350 N Market

Senior Citizens' Residences
Chicago, IL 60607: 1500 W Madison
Columbus, IN 47201: 300 Gladstone Ave
Grandview, MO 64030: 6111 E 129th St
Indianapolis, IN 46254-2738: 4390 N High
  School Rd
Kansas City, KS 66112: 1331 N 75th St
Minneapolis, MN 55403-2116: 1421 Yale Pl
Oak Creek, WI 53154: 150 W Centennial Dr
Oak Creek, WI 53154: 180 W Centennial Dr
Omaha, NE 68131: 923 38th St
St Louis, MO 63118: 3133 Iowa St

Harbour-Light Centres
Chicago, IL 60607: 1515 W Monroe St;
  tel: (312) 421-5753
Clinton Township, MI 48043: 42590 Stepnitz
Detroit, MI 48201: 3737 Lawton;
  tel. (313) 361-6136
Indianapolis, IN 46222: 2400 N Tibbs Ave;
  tel: (317) 972-1450
Minneapolis, MN 55403: 1010 Currie;
  tel: (612) 338-0113
Monroe, MI 48161: 3580 S Custer
St Louis, MO 63188: 3010 Washington Ave

Substance Abuse Centres
Detroit, MI 48216: 3737 Humboldt
Grand Rapids, MI 49503: 72 Sheldon Blvd SE:
  tel: (616) 742-0351
Kansas City, KS 66101: 1200 N 7th St;
  tel: (913) 342-5500
Kansas City, MO 101 W. Linwood;
  tel: (816) 756-2769
Kansas City, KS 66102: 1203 Minnesota Ave;
  tel: (913) 281-5060
Kansas City, KS 66102: 1019 Waterway Dr;
  tel: (913) 342-2173

Transitional Housing
Appleton, WI 54914: 105 S Badger Ave
Brainerd, MN 56401: 208 S 5th St
Champaign, IL 61820: 502 N Prospect
Duluth, MN 55806: 215 S 27th Ave W
Grand Forks, ND 58203: 1600 Univ Ave
Green Bay, WI 54301: 626 Union Ct
Jefferson City, MO 65101: 907 Jefferson St
Joplin, MO 64801: 320 E 8th St
Kansas City, MO 64111: 101 W Linwood Blvd
Kansas City, MO 64127: 6935 Bell Rd
Lawrence, KS 66044: 946 New Hampshire

Young musicians focus on a rehearsal at the Central Music Institute. The camp setting allows for serious music instruction in a relaxing atmosphere.

Milwaukee, WI 53208: 3120 W Wisconsin Ave
Minneapolis, MN 55403: 1010 Currie
New Albany, IN 47151: 2300 Green Valley Rd
Omaha, NE 68131: 3612 Cuming St
Rochester, MN 55906: 20 First Ave NE
Rockford, IL 61104: 416 S Madison
Steven's Point, WI 54481: 824 Fremont
St Louis, MO 63118: 2740 Arsenal
Sioux Falls, SD 57103-0128; 800 N Cliff Ave
Springfield, MO 65802: 10740 W Chestnut
  Expwy
Waterloo, IA 50703: 149 Argyle St
Wausau, WI 54401-4630: 113 S Second St
Wichita, KS 67202-2010: 350 Market

Child Day Care

Benton Harbor, MI 49023: 1840 Union St
Bloomington, IN 47404-3966: 111 N Rogers St
Chicago, IL 60607: 1515 W Monroe
Columbia, MO 65203: 1108 W Ash
DeKalb, IL 60115-0442: 830 Grove St
Emporia, KS 66801: 327 Constitution St
Fond du Lac, WI 54936: 237 N Macy St
Kansas City, KS 66117: 500 N 7th St
Kansas City, MO 64111: 500 W 39th St
Kokomo, IN 46902: 1105 S Waugh St
Lansing, MI 48901-4176: 525 N Pennsylvania
  Ave
Leavenworth, KS 66048: 600 Walnut
Madison, WI 53703: 630 Washington Ave
Menasha, WI 54911: 1525 Appleton Rd
Mishawaka, IN 46544: 1026 Dodge Ave
Oak Creek, WI 53154: 8853 S Howell Ave
Olathe, KS 66051: 420 E Santa Fe
Omaha, NE 68131: 3612 Cuming St
Pekin, IL 61554: 243 Derby St

Peoria, IL 61603: 210 Spalding Ave
Plymouth, MI 48170: 9451 S Main St
Rockford, IL 61101: 210 N Kilburn
Rockford, IL 61104: 220 S Madison
Royal Oak, MI 48073: 3015 N Main St
Saginaw, MI 48602: 2030 N Carolina St
St Louis, MO 63118: 3740 Marine Ave
St Paul, MN 55102: 401 W 7th St
Sheboygan, WI 53081: 1116 Huron St
Topeka, KS 66601: 1320 E 6th St
Traverse City, MI 49685-0063: 1239 Barlow St

Emergency Diagnostic and Short-term Treatment Centre

Edwin Denby Memorial Children's Home:
  20775 Pembroke Ave, Detroit, MI 48219;
  tel: (313) 537-2130 (acc 40)
Wilcox Residential Programs: North Platte,
  NE 69101-2268, 1121 W 18th St;
  tel: (308) 534-4164

Youth Group Homes

North Platte, NE 69101-2258: 1121 W 18th St
Omaha, NE 68131-1998: 3612 Cuming St

Emergency Shelter Care of Children

Kansas City, MO 64111: 101 W Linwood
  Blvd
North Platte, NE 69101: 704 S Welch Ave
Oak Park, IL 60302-1713: 924 N Austin
Omaha, NE 68131: 3612 Cuming St
St Paul, MN 55108-2542: 1471 Como Ave W
Wichita, KS 67202-2010: 350 N Market

Head Start Programmes

Chicago, IL 60651: 4255 W Division
Chicago, IL 60612: 20 S Campbell

USA Central Territory

Chicago, IL 60644: 500 S Central
Chicago, IL 60620: 9211 S Justine
Chicago, IL 60651: 1345 N Karlov
Chicago, IL 60607: 1 N Ogden
Chicago, IL 60621: 845 W 69th St
Omaha, NE 68131-1998: 3216 Cuming St
Saginaw, MI 48602: 2030 N Carolina St

Homes (each of the following have facilities for unmarried mothers)

Detroit, MI 48219-1398: 20775 Pembroke Ave
Grand Rapids, MI 49503: 1215 E Fulton St;
  tel: (616) 459-9468 (Kindred homes)
Omaha, NE 68131-1998: 3612 Cuming St

Latchkey Programmes

DeKalb, IL 60115-0442: Camp 'I Can Do It'
DeKalb, IL 60115-0442: 830 Grove St
Evanston, IL 60201-4414: 1403 Sherman Ave
Gary-Merrillville, IN 46408-4420: 4800
  Harrison St
Huntingdon, IN 46750: 1424 E Market St
Huron, SD 57350: 237 Illinois St SW
Indianapolis, IN 46203-1944: 1337 Shelby St
Kokomo, IN 46902: 1101 S Waugh
Jacksonville, IL 62650: 331 W Douglas St
Minneapolis, MN 55411: 3000 W Broadway
Newton, IA 50208: 301 N 2nd Ave E
North Platte, NE 69101: 421 E 6th St
Omaha, NE 68131: 3612 Cuming St
Pekin, IL 61554: 243 Derby St
Royal Oak, MI 48073: 3015 N Main Sts
Springfield, MO 65802: 1707 W Chestnut
  Expway
St Louis, MO 63113: 2618 N Euclid Ave
St Louis, MO 63143: 7701-15 Rannells Ave
Wyandotte, MI 49192-3498: 1258 Biddle Ave

Residential Services for Mentally Ill

Omaha, NE 68131: 3612 Cuming St

Permanent and/or Supportive Housing

Coon Rapids, MN 55433: 10347 Ibis Ave
Jefferson City, MO 65101: 907 Jefferson St
Joplin, MO 64801: 320 E 8th St
Lansing, MI 48912: 525 N Pennsylvania
Minneapolis, MN 55403: 53 Glenwood Ave
St Louis, MO 63103: 205 N 18th St
St Paul, MN 55108: 1471 Como Ave W

Permanet and/or Supportive Housing

Coon Rapids, MN 55443: 10347 Ibis Ave
Jefferson City, MO 65101: 907 Jefferson St
Joplin, MO 64801: 320 E. 8th St
Lansing, MI 48912: 525 N Pennsylvania
Minneapolis, MN 55403: 53 Glenwood Ave
St Louis, MO: 205 N 18th St
St Paul, MN 55108: 1471 Como Ave W

Foster Care

Wichita, KS 67202: Kock Center, 350 N Marat

Medical/Dental Clinics (SA owned and occupied)

Grand Rapids, MI 49503: 1215 E Fulton St
Rochester, MN 55906: 20 1st Ave NE
Sheboygan, WI 53081: 710 Pennsylvania Ave

UNDER THQ

Conference Centre: 10 W Algonquin, Des
  Plaines, IL 60016-6006

*In addition, a number of fresh-air camps, youth
centres, community centres, red shield clubs, day
nurseries, family service and emergency relief
bureaux are attached to corps and divisions.*

Children give a helping hand in filling 'military care packages'. Salvationists and friends in several USA Central Territory divisions prepared thousands of these packages for shipment to US military personnel based overseas.

USA EASTERN TERRITORY

Territorial leaders:
Commissioners Lawrence R. and Nancy A. Moretz

Territorial Commander:
Commissioner Lawrence R. Moretz
(13 Nov 2002)

Chief Secretary:
Lieut-Colonel Larry Bosh (1 Jul 2006)

Territorial Headquarters: 440 West Nyack Road, PO Box C-635, West Nyack, New York 10994-1739, USA

tel: [1] (845) 620-7200; fax: [1] (845) 620-7756; web site: www.salvationarmy-usaeast.org

The Salvation Army was incorporated as a religious and charitable corporation in the State of New York in 1899 as 'The Salvation Army' and is qualified to conduct its affairs in all of the states of the territory.

Zone: Americas and Caribbean

USA states included in the territory: Connecticut, Delaware, Kentucky, Maine, Massachusetts, New Hampshire, New Jersey, New York, Ohio, Pennsylvania, Rhode Island, Vermont

Other countries included in the territory: Puerto Rico, Virgin Islands

'The Salvation Army' in Korean: Koo Sei Kun; in Norwegian: Frelsesarmeen; in Spanish: Ejército de Salvación; in Swedish: Frälsningsarmén

Languages in which the gospel is preached: Creole, English, Korean, Laotian, Portuguese, Russian, Spanish, Swedish

Periodicals: *¡Buenas Noticias!* (Spanish), *Cristianos en Marcha* (Spanish), *Good News!*, *Good News!* (Korean), *Priority!*, *Ven a Cristo Hoy* (Spanish)

THE third Mission and Ministries Forum (MMIII) ascended to new heights. Exactly 100 officers – all within their first seven years of commissioned service – convened at Camp Ladore for an intensive 48 hours. Under the ministry of the territorial leaders and cabinet members, delegates sharpened their understanding of the Army's mission.

On 9 June 2006 Territorial Commander Commissioner Lawrence Moretz commissioned 56 new officers of the Visionaries Session. Fifty were cadets who had been through training; six were auxiliary-captains becoming full captains.

Challenging the Visionaries to return to street evangelism as a primary strategy for winning souls for Christ, Commissioner Nancy Moretz said: 'God has not called the Visionaries to bore, boss or even blog people into his Kingdom. Let's get back to the street!'

Whilst Commissioning Sunday was a decidedly multicultural day in the history of the territory, the previous day had seen the first-ever territorial Hispanic celebration, where people of all ages and national backgrounds came to praise God and learn more of him in their own language.

June 9 was also the day when the territory officially launched its 24-7/SA Prayer initiative. Nearly 80 people gathered in Railton Hall at Territorial Headquarters to commence a year of non-stop prayer.

Major Janet Munn (Territorial Ambassador for Prayer and Spiritual Formation), who appeared on a DVD explaining the 24-7 process, reminded everyone that God gets people praying before he makes a major move on earth.

The prayer year began with two weeks at THQ but the first 'field exercise' in praying around the clock came during summer camps. At Camp Ladore, a week of prayer began with the blast of a ram's horn in the middle of the lake. From Old Orchard Beach to Star Lake Music Camp, campers filled prayer rooms.

Prayer continued beyond four walls of a room. The Territorial Arts Ministry Team (TAM) took prayer to the streets, laying-on hands and praying over a school in New York City's Greenwich Village. Officers from the Ambassadors of the King Session, celebrating their 55th reunion at Old Orchard Beach, stood on the pavilion platform, held hands with young War College students and earnestly prayed for them.

Commissioner Christine MacMillan

(then TC, Canada and Bermuda) delivered a series of powerful messages during the first weekend of Old Orchard Beach Camp. Among other things, she called for the Army to engage in prayer and in a mission of 'inconvenience'.

On 8 September, at Centennial Memorial Temple in New York City, the territory welcomed 37 cadets of the God's Fellow Workers Session. They were a diverse group: from the United Kingdom, Colombia, Peru, Congo, the Dominican Republic, Guyana, Haiti, and the United States (with every USA Eastern division represented).

In June 2007, 8,000 delegates from the territory gathered in Hershey, Pennsylvania, for 'Mission Kaleidoscope Congress 2007' led by the General and Commissioner Helen Clifton. Every major meeting was filled with spectacular audio and visual effects. The audience saw the Army's flag unfurling into a kaleidoscope of patterns and pictures, revealing the Army's multifaceted ministry.

Others Press®, a new imprint of the USA Eastern Territory, launched two books – *Heartwork of Hope: A Directed Journal* by Major JoAnn Shade; and *Symbala's River* by Major Stephen Kelly.

PrimeTime®, the faith-based after-school programme for children aged 6-14, has partnered with Scripture Union to assist its children's ministry. Various church groups around the country and across denominations are using this programme to attract unchurched children.

STATISTICS

Officers 1,719 (active 1,113 retired 606) **Cadets** 76 **Employees** 11,962

Corps 397 **Outposts** 4 **Institutions** 144 **Senior Soldiers** 20,780 **Adherents** 7,452 **Junior Soldiers** 8,015

Personnel serving outside territory Officers 25 Layworker 1

STAFF

Personnel: Maj Mark W. Tillsley
Programme: Maj Richard J. Munn
Business: Maj James W. Reynolds
Asst Chief Sec: Lt-Col Tito E. Paredes
Territorial Ambassadors for Evangelism: Lt-Cols Howard and Patricia Burr
Territorial Ambassadors for Holiness: Majs David and Jean Antill
Territorial Ambassador for Prayer/Spiritual Formation: Maj Janet M. Munn
ARC Commander: Lt-Col Timothy Raines
Audit: Maj John Cramer
Community Relations/Development: Maj Karla Clark
Education: Maj Edward Russell
Finance: Maj Glenn C. Bloomfield
Information Technology: Mr Paul Kelly
Legal: Maj Thomas V. Mack
Literary: Linda D. Johnson
Mission and Culture: Maj William R. Groff
Music: B/M Ronald Waiksnoris
New York Staff Band: B/M Ronald Waiksnoris
Territorial Songsters: S/L William Rollins
Officers' Services/Records: Maj Peter H. Stritzinger
Pastoral Care and Spiritual Special: Lt-Col R. Eugene Pigford
Property/Mission Expansion: Maj Hubert S. Steele III
Risk Management: Mr Samuel C. Bennett
Social Services: Maj John Cheydleur
Supplies/Purchasing: Maj Frank Klemanski
Training: Maj Stephen Banfield
Women's Ministries: Comr Nancy A. Moretz (TPWM) Lt-Col Gillian Bosh (TSWM) Maj Sharon Tillsley (TMFS) Maj Eva Geddes (TCCM, TWAS) Lt-Col Susan Gregg (OCS)
Youth and Candidates: Maj Ivan Rock

DIVISIONS

Eastern Pennsylvania and Delaware: 701 N Broad St, Philadelphia, PA 19123; tel: (215) 787-2800; Lt-Col William R. Carlson
Empire State: 200 Twin Oaks Dr, PO Box 148, Syracuse, NY 13206-0148; tel: (315) 434-1300; Maj Donald W. Lance
Greater New York: 120 West 14th St, New York, NY 10011-7393; tel: (212) 337-7200; Maj Guy Klemanski
Massachusetts: 147 Berkeley St, Boston, MA 02116-5197; tel: (617) 542-5420; Maj William H. Bode
New Jersey: 4 Gary Rd, Union, NJ 07083-5598; tel: (908) 851-9300; Maj Donald Berry
Northeast Ohio: 2507 E 22nd St, 44115-3202, PO Box 5847, Cleveland, OH 44101-0847; tel: (216) 861-8185; Lt-Col William H. LaMarr
Northern New England: 297 Cumberland Ave, PO Box 3647, Portland, ME 04104; tel: (207) 774-6304; Maj David E. Kelly
Puerto Rico and Virgin Islands: 306 Ave De La Constitución 00901-2235, PO Box 71523, San Juan PR, 00936-8623; tel: (787) 999-7000; Capt Ricardo J. Fernandez
Southern New England: 855 Asylum Ave, PO Box 628, Hartford, CT 06142-0628; tel: (860) 543-8400; Maj William A. Bamford III
Southwest Ohio and Northeast Kentucky: 114 E Central Parkway, PO Box 596, Cincinnati, OH 45201; tel: (513) 762-5600; Maj Kenneth W. Maynor
Western Pennsylvania: 424 Third Ave, Pittsburgh, PA 15219; tel: (412) 394-4800; Maj Robert J. Reel

SCHOOL FOR OFFICER TRAINING

201 Lafayette Ave, Suffern, NY 10901-4798; tel: (845) 357-3501

THE SALVATION ARMY RETIREMENT COMMUNITY

1400 Webb St, Asbury Park, NJ 07712; tel: (732) 775-2200; Maj Jean Booth (Administrator) (acc 35)

SOCIAL SERVICES

Adult Rehabilitation Centres

(*Includes facilities for women*)

ARC Commander: Lt-Col Timothy Raines
Akron, OH 44311: 1006 Grant St, PO Box 1743; tel: (330) 773-3331 (acc 83)
Albany, NY 12206: 452 Clinton Ave, PO Box 66389; tel: (518) 465-2416 (acc 90)
Altoona, PA 16602: 200 7th Ave, PO Box 1405, 16603 (mail); tel: (814) 946-3645 (acc 39)
Binghamton, NY 13904: 3-5 Griswold St, tel: (607) 723-5381 (acc 62)
*Boston (Saugus), MA 01906: 209 Broadway Rte 1; tel: (781) 231-0803 (acc 125)
Bridgeport CT 06607: 1313 Connecticut Ave; tel: (203) 367-8621 (acc 50)

USA Eastern Territory

Brockton, MA 02301: 281 N Main St;
tel: (508) 586-1187 (acc 56)
Bronx, NY 10457: 4133 Park Ave;
tel: (718) 583-3500 (acc 108)
Brooklyn, NY 11217: 62 Hanson Pl;
tel: (718) 622-7166 (acc 136)
Buffalo, NY 14217-2587: 1080 Military Rd,
PO Box 36, 14217-0036; tel: (716) 875-2533
(acc 90)
Cincinnati, OH 45212: 2250 Park Ave, PO Box
12546, Norwood, OH 45212-0546;
tel: (513) 351-3457 (acc 175)
Cleveland, OH 44103: 5005 Euclid Ave;
tel: (216) 881-2625 (acc 159)
Columbus, OH 43215: 570 S Front St;
tel: (614) 221-4269 (acc 85)
*Dayton, OH 45402: 913 S Patterson Blvd;
tel: (937) 461-2769 (acc 74)
Erie, PA 16501: 1209 Sassafras St, PO Box 6176,
16512; tel: (814) 456-4237 (acc 50)
*Harrisburg, PA 17110: 3650 Vartan Way, PO Box
60095, 17106-0095; tel: (717) 541-0203 (acc 62)
*Hartford, CT 06132: 333 Homestead Ave,
PO Box 320440; tel: (860) 527-8106 (acc 110)
Hempstead, NY 11550: 194 Front St;
tel: (516) 481-7600 (acc 100)
Jersey City, NJ 07302: 248 Erie St;
tel: (201) 653-3071 (acc 75)
Mount Vernon, NY 10550: 745 S Third Ave;
tel: (914) 664-0800 (acc 80)
Newark, NJ 07101: 65 Pennington St, PO Box 815;
tel: (973) 589-0370 (acc 135)
New Haven, CT 06511: 301 George St, PO Box
1413, 06506; tel: (203) 865-0511 (acc 45)
*New York, NY 10036: 535 W 48th St;
tel: (212) 757-7745 (acc 140)
Paterson, NJ 07505: 31 Van Houten St, PO Box
1976, 07509; tel: (973) 742-1126 (acc 89)
*Philadelphia, PA 19128: 4555 Pechin St;
tel: (215) 483-3340 (acc 138)
Pittsburgh, PA 15203: 44 S 9th St;
tel: (412) 481-7900 (acc 127)
Portland, ME 04101: 30 Warren Ave, PO Box
1298, 04104; tel: (207) 878-8555 (acc 60)
Poughkeepsie, NY 12601: 570 Main St;
tel: (845) 471-1730 (acc 50)
*Providence, RI 02906: 201 Pitman St;
tel: (401) 421-5270 (acc 129)
*Rochester, NY 14611: 745 West Ave;
tel: (585) 235-0020 (acc 135)
San Juan, PR 00903: ARC, Fernández Juncos Ave,
Cnr of Valdés, Puerta de Tierra, PO Box 13814,
00908; tel: (787) 722-3301 (acc 36)
Scranton, PA 18505: 610 S Washington Ave,
PO Box 3064; tel: (570) 346-0007 (acc 62)
Springfield, MA 01104: 285 Liberty St, PO Box
1569, 01101-1569 (mail); tel: (413) 785-1921
(acc 70)
Staten Island, NY 10304: 2053 Clove Rd, PO Box
050169, 10305 (mail); tel: (718) 442-3080
(acc 39)
*Syracuse, NY 13224: 2433 Erie Blvd East;
tel: (315) 445-0520 (acc 100)
Toledo, OH 43602: 27 Moorish Ave, PO Box 355,
43697; tel: (419) 241-8231 (acc 60)
Trenton, NJ 08638: 436 Mulberry St, PO Box
5011; tel: (609) 599-9801 (acc 86)
Wilkes-Barre, PA 18702: 739 Sans Souci Parkway,
PO Box 728, 18703-0728; tel: (570) 823-4191
(acc 52)
*Wilmington, DE 19801: 107 S Market St;
tel: (302) 654-8808 (acc 81)
*Worcester, MA 01603: 72 Cambridge St;
tel: (508) 799-0520 (acc 115)

ATTACHED TO DIVISIONS
Adult Day Care
Buffalo, NY 14202: Golden Age Center,
950 Main St; tel: (716) 883-9800 (acc 300)
Carlisle, PA 17013: 20 East Pomfret St, PO Box
309; tel: (717) 249-1411
Cincinnati, OH 45210: 131 E 12th St;
tel: (513) 762-5693 (acc 25)
Lancaster, OH 43130: 228 Hubert Ave;
tel: (740) 687-1921 (acc 50)
Newport, KY 41072: 340 West 10th St,
PO Box 271; tel: (859) 291-8107 (acc 25)
Quincy, MA 02169-6932: 6 Baxter St;
tel: (617) 472-2345 (acc 27)
Syracuse, NY 13202: 749 S Warren St;
tel: (315) 479-1313

Extended In-home Service for the Elderly
Syracuse, NY 13202: 749 S Warren St;
tel: (315) 479-1309

Adult Rehabilitation
Kenmore, NY 14217: 1080 Military Rd;
tel: (716) 875-2533 (acc 90)

Day Care Centres
Akron, OH 44303: Child Development Center,
135 Hall St; tel: (330) 762-8177 (acc 43)
Boston, MA 02118: 1500 Washington St,
PO Box 180127; tel: (617) 536-5260 (acc 52)
Boston, MA 02124: 26 Wales St;
tel: (617) 436-2480 (acc 70)
Bronx, NY 10451: 425 E 159th St;
tel: (718) 742-2346 (acc 45)
Bronx, NY 10457: 2121 Washington Ave;
tel: (718) 563-1530 (acc 69)
Brooklyn, NY 11212: Day Care Center, 280
Riverdale Ave; tel: (718) 922-7661 (acc 100)

Brooklyn, NY 11212: Sutter Day Care and Family Day Care, 20 Sutter Ave; tel: (718) 773-3041/ (718) 735-6519 (acc 75 and 248)

Brooklyn, NY 11216: 110 Kosciusko St; tel: (718) 857-7264 (acc 39)

Brooklyn, NY 11221: 1151 Bushwick Ave; tel: (718) 455-0100 (acc 60)

Brooklyn, NY 11231: Family Day Care Redhook and Fiesta Day Care Center, 80 Lorraine St; tel: (718) 834-8755 (acc 62 and 65)

Cambridge, MA 02139: 402 Massachusetts Ave, PO Box 390647; tel: (617) 547-3400 (acc 28)

Cincinnati, OH 45202: 3501 Warsaw Ave; tel: (513) 251-1451 (acc 112)

Cleveland, OH 44103: 6010 Hough Ave; tel: (216) 432-0505 (acc 98)

Danbury, CT 06813-0826: 15 Foster St, PO Box 826; tel: (203) 792-7505 (acc 30)

Darby, PA 19023: 22 N Ninth St; tel: (610) 583-7202 (acc 25)

Hartford, CT 06105: 121 Sigourney St; tel: (860) 543-8488 (acc 69)

Hempstead, NY 11550: 65 Atlantic Ave; tel: (516) 485-4980 (acc 103)

Jersey City, NJ 07034: 562 Bergen Ave, PO Box 4237, Bergen Station; tel: (201) 435-7355 (acc 70)

Lexington, KY 40508: 736 W Main St; tel: (859) 252-7709 (acc 80)

Meriden, CT 06450-0234: 23 St Casimir Dr, PO Box 234; tel: (203) 235-6532 (acc 27)

Morristown, NJ 07960: 95 Spring St, PO Box 9150; tel: (973) 538-0543 (acc 95)

New York, NY 10034: 3732 10th Ave; tel: (212) 569-4300 (acc 63)

Philadelphia (Germantown), PA 19133: 2601 North 11th St; tel: (215) 225-2700 (acc 131)

Providence, RI 02905: 20 Miner St; tel: (401) 781-7238 (acc infant, pre-school and kindergarten 110)

Syracuse, NY 13202: Cab Horse Commons, 677 S Salina St; tel: (315) 479-1305

Syracuse, NY 13202: 749 S Warren St; tel: (315) 479-1334

Syracuse, NY 13202: University United Methodist Church Day Care, 324 University Ave; tel: (315) 426-1231

Syracuse, NY 13202: South Salina Street Infant Care Center, 667 S Salina St; tel: (315) 479-1329

Syracuse, NY 13207: Elmwood Day Care Center, 1640 S Ave; tel: (315) 701-2750

Syracuse, NY 13202: School Age Day Care, 749 S Warren St; tel: (315) 479-1334

Wilmington, DE 19899: 107 W 4th St; tel: (302) 472-0712 (acc 110)

Family Centres

Newark, NJ 07102: Newark Area Services Kinship Care, 45 Central Ave; tel: (973) 623-5959

Development Disabilities Services

Brooklyn, NY 11220: Centennial House, 426 56th St; tel: (718) 492-4415 (acc 9)

Brooklyn, NY 11237: Decade House, 315 Covert St; tel: (718) 417-1583 (acc 10)

Brooklyn, NY 11206: Millennium House, 13 Pulaski St; tel: (718) 222-0736 (acc 13)

Glendale, NY 11385: Glendale House, 71-29 70th St; tel: (718) 381-7329 (acc 13)

Jamaica, NY 11423: Family Care, 90-23 161st St; tel: (718) 206-9171 (acc 15)

Philadelphia, PA 19123: Developmental Disabilities Program, 701 N Broad St, Administrative Offices; tel: (215) 787-2804 (community homes 46, acc 100)

South Ozone Park, NY 11420: Hope House, 115-37 133rd St; tel: (718) 322-1616 (acc 9)

Springfield, OH 45501: Hand-in-Hand, 15 S Plum St; tel: (937) 322-3434

St Albans, NY 11412: Pioneer House, 104-14 186th St; tel: (718) 264-8350 (acc 12)

Evangeline Residence

New York, NY 10011: 123 W 13th St (Markle Memorial Residence); tel: (212) 242-2400; fax: (212) 229-2801 (acc 286)

Family Counselling

Boston, MA 02118: Family Service Bureau, 1500 Washington St; tel: (617) 236-7233; fax: (617) 236-0123

Bronx, NY 10458: Bronx Belmont Center for Families, 601 Crescent Ave; tel: (718) 329-5410

Bronx, NY 10453: Morris Heights Center for Families, 7 W Burnside Ave; tel: (718) 561-3190; fax: (718) 561-3856

Brooklyn, NY 11206: Bushwick Center for Families, 815 Broadway; tel: (718) 302-6921

Brooklyn, NY 11207: Williamsburg Center for Families, 295 Division St; tel: (718) 782-4587

Buffalo, NY 14202: Emergency Family Assistance, Family Court Visitation Program, Spouse Abuse Education Workshop, 960 Main St; tel: (716) 883-9800

Cincinnati, OH 45210: Cincinnati Family Service Bureau, 131 E 12th; tel: (513) 762-5660

Cincinnati, OH 45224: Cincinnati Family Service Bureau, 6381 Center Hill Ave; tel: (513) 242-9100

Covington, KY 41014: N Kentucky Family

Service Bureau, 1806 Scott Blvd;
tel: (859) 261-0835

Newport, KY 41072: N Kentucky Family Service
Bureau, 340 W 10th St; tel: (859) 491-5180

Rochester, NY 14604-4310: Rochester
Emergency Family Assistance, 70 Liberty Pole
Way, PO Box 41210; tel: (716) 987-9540

Syracuse, NY 13202: Family Services,
749 S Warren St; tel: (315) 479-3651

Syracuse, NY 13207: Family Place Visitation
Center, 350 Rich St; tel: (315) 474-2931

Foster Home Services

Allentown, PA 18102: Foster Care In-Home
Placement Services, Adoption Services and
Administrative Services, 344 N 7th St;
tel: (610) 821-7706

Brooklyn, NY 11207: Bushwick Homes for
Children, 815 Broadway; tel: (718) 302-6921

Jamaica, NY 11432: Jamaica Homes for
Children: 90-23 161st St, Rm 401;
tel: (718) 558-4486; fax: (718) 558-5799

Mineola, NY 11501: Nassau Therapeutic
Program: 85 Willis Ave; tel: (516) 746-1484;
fax: (516) 746-1488

New York, NY 10011: 132 W 14th St;
tel: (212) 807-6100; fax: (212) 620-3096

Group Homes for Adolescents

Bronx, NY 10451: Glover House, 301 E
162nd St; tel: (718) 992-4020 (acc men 12)

Bronx, NY 10469: North Bronx Group Home,
1268 Adee Ave; tel: (718) 515-6600
(acc men 12)

Fall River, MA 02720: Grace House/Gentle Arms
of Jesus Teen Living Center, 429 Winter St;
tel: (508) 324-4558 (acc 15)

Lefrak City, NY 11368: Lefrak City Group Home,
96-04 57th Ave, Apt 3K; tel: (718) 271-8318
(acc women 10)

Manhattan, NY 10027: Manhattan West Group
Home, 136 West 127th St; tel: (212) 678-6121
(acc men 12)

Manhattan, NY 10031: Manhattan East Group
Home, 241 East 116th St; tel: (212) 534-5455
(acc men 12)

New York, NY 10003: East Village Residence,
1 E 3rd St; tel: (212) 228-8306;
fax: (212) 253-1708 (acc 32)

New York, NY 10027: Lenox House, 131 W
132nd St; tel: (212) 334-1394 (acc men 12)

Harbour Light Centres

Boston, MA 02118: Adult Women's Program,
407-409 Shawmut Ave, PO Box 180130;
tel: (617) 536-7469 (acc 71)

Cleveland, OH 44115-2376: Harbor Light
Complex, 1710 Prospect Ave;
tel: (216) 781-3773 (acc 124)

Pittsburgh, PA 15233: 865 W North Ave;
tel: (412) 231-0500 (acc 50)

Hotels, Lodges, Emergency Homes

Akron, OH 44302: Booth Manor Emergency
Lodge, 216 S Maple St; tel: (330) 762-8481
ext 194 (acc 40)

Allentown, PA 18102: Hospitality House,
344 N 7th St; tel: (610) 432-0128 (acc 65)

Bellaire, OH 43906: 315 37th St;
tel: (740) 676-6810 (acc 20)

Boston, MA 02119: Roxbury Emergency
Shelter for Families, 23 Vernon St;
tel: (617) 427-6700/1 (acc 19)

Brooklyn, NY 11207: Bushwick Family
Residence, 1675 Broadway; tel: (718) 574-2701
(acc families 87)

Brooklyn, NY 11201: Brooklyn Drop-in Center
and Homeward Bound, 39-41 Bond St;
tel: (718) 935-0439 (acc 75)

Brooklyn, NY 11203: Kingsboro Men's Shelter,
681 Clarkson Ave; tel: (718) 363-7738
(acc 80)

Bronx, NY 10456: Franklin Women's Shelter
and Referral, 1122 Franklin Ave;
tel: (718) 842-9827 (acc 200)

Buffalo, NY 14202: 960 Main St, Emergency
Family Shelter; tel: (716) 884-4798 (acc 96)

Cambridge, MA 02139-0008: Day Drop-in Shelter
for Men and Women/Night Shelter for Men,
402 Mass Ave, PO Box 390647;
tel: (617) 547-3400 (acc 200/50)

Carlisle, PA 17013: Stuart House (Women's
Transitional Housing), 125-127 S Hanover St;
tel: (717) 249-1411 (acc 41)

Carlisle, PA 17013: Genesis House (Men's
Emergency Housing), 24 E Pomfret St;
tel: (717) 249-1411

Chester, PA 19013: Stepping Stone Program,
151 W 15th St; tel: (610) 874-0423 (acc 35)

Cincinnati, OH 45210: Emergency Shelter,
131 E 12th St; tel: (513) 762-5655 (acc 20)

Cleveland, OH 44115: Zelma George Family
Shelter, 1710 Prospect Ave;
tel: (216) 641-3712 (acc 110)

Concord, NH 03301: McKenna House (Adult
Shelter), 100 S Fruit St; tel: (603) 228-3505
(acc 29)

Dayton, OH 45402: Women and Children's
Homeless Shelter, 138 S Wilkinson St;
tel: (937) 228-8241 (acc 27)

Dayton, OH 45402: Men's Homeless Shelter,
624 S Main St; tel: (937) 228-8210 (acc 55)

East Northport, NY 11731: Northport Veterans' Residence, PO Box 300; tel: (631) 262-0601

East Stroudsburg, PA 18301: 226 Washington St; tel: (570) 421-3050

Elizabeth, NJ 07201: 1018 E Grand St; tel: (908) 352-2886 (acc 45)

Elmira, NY 14902: 414 Lake St, PO Box 293; tel: (607) 732-0314 (24-hour Domestic Violence Hotline); Victims of Domestic Violence Safe House (acc 15)

Elmira, NY 14901: Our House, 401-403 Division St; tel: (607) 734-0032 (acc 20)

Hartford, CT 06105: 225 S Marshall St; tel: (860) 543-8430 (Youth Shelter) (acc 14); tel: (860) 543-8423 (Family Shelter) (acc 27)

Jamestown, NY 14702: ANEW Center Shelter for Domestic Violence, Residential/Non-Residential Program, PO Box 368; tel: (716) 483-0830; 24-hour Hotline tel: (800) 252-8748

Johnstown, PA 15901: Emergency Shelter; tel: (814) 539-3110 (acc 24)

Laconia, NH 03801: The Carey House, 6 Spring St; tel: (603) 528-8086 (acc 30)

Lexington, KY 40508: Families, 736 W Main St; tel: (859) 252-7706 (acc 129)

Montclair, NJ 07042-2776: 68 N Fullerton Ave; tel: (973) 744-8666 (acc 18)

Newark, OH 43055: 250 E Main St; tel: (740) 345-3289 (acc 18)

New Britain, CT 06050: 78 Franklin Sq; tel: (860) 225-8491 (acc 25 men)

New York, NY 10022: Katrina Aid Today, 221 E 52nd St; tel: (212) 319-3081

Norristown, PA 19404: 533 Swede St; tel: (610) 275-9225 (acc 41)

Northport, NY 11768-0039: Northport Veterans' Residence, 79 Middleville Rd, Bldg 11, PO Box 300 (mail); tel: (631) 262-0601 (acc 87)

Perth Amboy, NJ 08862-0613: 433 State St; tel: (732) 826-7040 (acc men 40) (seasonal)

Philadelphia, PA 19107: Eliza Shirley House, 1320 Arch St; tel: (215) 568-5111 (acc 125)

Philadelphia, PA 19123: Red Shield Family Residence, 715 N Broad St; tel: (215) 787-2887 (acc 100)

Pittsburgh, PA 15219: Family Crisis Center, 424 Third Ave; tel: (412) 394-4819 (acc 40)

Pottstown, PA 19464: Lessig-Booth Family Residence, 137 King St; tel: (610) 327-0836 (acc 32)

Queens (Jamaica), NY 11435: Briarwood Family Residence, 80-20 134th St; tel: (718) 268-3395 (acc 91)

Street Outreach Project, 90-23 161st St (street

effort, not building bound); tel: (718) 523-3480

Queens (Long Island City), NY 11101: Borden Avenue Veterans' Residence, 21-10 Borden Ave; tel: (718) 784-5690 (acc 410)

Rochester, NY 14604-4310: Men's Emergency Shelter, Booth Haven, 70 Liberty Pole Way, PO Box 41210; tel: (585) 987-9500 (acc 39)

Rochester, NY 14604-4310: Women's Shelter, Hope House, 100 West Ave, PO Box 41210; tel: (585) 697-3430 (acc 19)

Rochester, NY 14604-4310: Safe Haven Emergency Shelter, 70 Liberty Pole Way, PO Box 21210; tel: (585) 987-9540 (acc 16)

San Juan, PR 00903: Homeless Shelter, Proyecto Esperanza, Fernández Juncos, Cnr Valdés; tel: (787) 722-2370

Schenectady, NY 12305: Evangeline Booth Home and Women's Shelter, 168 Lafayette St; tel: (518) 370-0276

Syracuse, NY: Parenting Center, 667 S Salina St; tel: (315) 479-1330

Syracuse, NY 13202: Emergency Lodge, 749 S Warren St; tel: (315) 479-1332

Trenton, NJ 08601: Homeless Drop In Center, 575 E State St; tel: (609) 599-9373

Waterbury, CT 06720: 74 Central Ave; tel: (203) 756-1718 (acc 29)

Waterbury, CT 06720: Youth Shelter, 140 Willow St; tel: (203) 756-3651 (acc 14)

West Chester, PA 19380: Railton House, 101 E Market St; tel: (610) 696-7434 (acc 17)

Wilkes Barre, PA 18701: Kirby Family House, 35 S Pennsylvania Ave; tel: (570) 824-8380 (acc 50)

Wilmington, DE 19899: Booth Social Service Center, 104 W 5th St; tel: (302) 472-0764 (acc 52)

Wooster, OH 44691: 24-Hour Open Door Emergency Shelter, 437 S Market St; tel: (330) 264-4704 (acc 56)

Zanesville, OH 43701: 515 Putnam Ave; tel: (740) 454-8953 (acc 35)

HIV Services

Bronx, NY 10458: 601 Crescent Ave; tel: (718) 329-5410; fax: (718) 329-5409

Bronx, NY 10453: 7 West Burnside Ave; tel: (718) 561-3190,; fax: (718) 367-6720

New York, NY 10011: 132 West 14 St; tel: (212) 352-5644; fax: (646) 335-6311

Homeless Youth and Runaways

Binghamton, NY 13901: Open Door Emergency Shelter, 127-131 Washington St; tel: (607) 722-0164

Rochester, NY 14604-1210: Genesis House,

35 Ardmore St, PO Box 41210;
tel: (585) 235-2600 (acc 14)
Syracuse, NY 13205: Barnabas House,
1912 S Salina St; tel: (315) 475-9720 (acc 8)
Syracuse, NY 13205: Booth House and Host
Home, 264 Furman St; tel: (315) 471-7628
(acc 8)

Transitional Housing Programme

Arlington, MA 02474-6597: Wellington House,
8 Wellington St (Single Resident Occupancy);
tel: (781) 648-2636 (acc 20)
Buffalo, NY 14202: 984 Main St;
tel: (716) 884-4798
Cincinnati, OH 45210: (families with children)
19 & 21 E 15th St; tel: (513) 762-5660
Cleveland, OH 44103: Railton House, 6000
Woodland; tel: (216) 361-6778 (acc 70)
Cleveland, OH 44115: Pass Program,
1710 Prospect Ave; tel: (216) 619-4727
(acc 91)
Cleveland, OH 44115: Project Share,
2501 E 22nd St; tel: (216) 623-7492 (acc 38)

Lancaster, PA 17603: 131 South Queen St;
tel: (717) 397-7565 (acc 21)
Philadelphia, PA 19103: Mid-City Apartments,
2025 Chestnut St; tel: (215) 569-9160 (acc 60)
Philadelphia, PA 19147: Reed House,
1320 S 32nd St; tel: (215) 755-6789 (acc 66)
Syracuse, NY 13205: Transitional Family
Apartments, 1482 S State St; tel: (315) 475-7663
Syracuse, NY 13205: Transitional Living Project
Apartments (youth), 1941 S Salina St;
tel: (315) 475-9720
Syracuse, NY 13205: Women's Shelter,
1704 S Salina St; tel: (315) 472-0947
West Chester, PA 19380: William Booth Initiative,
101 E Market St; tel: (610) 696-8746 (acc7)

Youth Service and Emergency Shelter

Hartford, CT: Youth Shelter Co-ed,
225 Marshall St; tel: (860) 543-8430
Syracuse, NY 13205: Barnabas, 1941 S Salina St;
tel: (315) 475-9744

Senior Citizens' Residences

Cincinnati, OH 45224: Booth Residence for the
Elderly and Handicapped, 6000 Townvista;
tel: (513) 242-4482 (acc 150)
New York, NY 10025: Williams Residence, 720
West End Ave; tel: (212) 316-6000;
fax: (212) 280-0410 (acc 367)
Philadelphia, PA 19139: Booth Manor, 5522
Arch St; tel: (215) 471-0500 (acc 50)
Philadelphia, PA 19131: Ivy Residence, 4051
Ford Rd; tel: (215) 871-3303 (acc 75)

**The General holds a small child as he issues a
challenge at the territorial congress**

**Hispanic Salvationists of USA Eastern Territory
meet in praise and worship**

USA SOUTHERN TERRITORY

Territorial leaders:
Commissioners Maxwell and Lenora Feener

Territorial Commander:
Commissioner Maxwell Feener
(1 Jul 2006)

Chief Secretary:
Lieut-Colonel Terry Griffin (2 Jul 2007)

Territorial Headquarters: 1424 Northeast Expressway, Atlanta, GA 30329-2088, USA

Tel: [1] (404) 728 1300; fax: [1] (404) 728 1392; web site: www.salvationarmysouth.org

The Salvation Army was incorporated as a religious and charitable corporation in the State of Georgia in 1927 as 'The Salvation Army' and is qualified to conduct all its affairs in all of the states of the territory.

Zone: Americas and Caribbean
USA states included in the territory: Alabama, Arkansas, Florida, Georgia, Kentucky, Louisiana, Maryland, Mississippi, North Carolina, Oklahoma, South Carolina, Tennessee, Texas, Virginia, West Virginia, District of Columbia
Languages in which the gospel is preached: English, Haitian-Creole, Korean, Laotian, Spanish, Vietnamese
Periodical: *Southern Spirit*

THE territory was blessed with a year of 'firsts' in many areas. The Territorial Communications Bureau was established in a location which afforded the bureau its own studio, production facilities and storage space. Communications to and throughout the territory now occur as events are happening. Also, the bureau is developing multimedia resources which will be available to the field as well as the nation.

In addition, all Salvation Army web sites in the territory are monitored to ensure compliance with international and national standards while more than 137 web operators have been trained.

The Territorial Planned Giving Section generates a total of more than $75 million. This undergirds the financial stability of the territory and allows the administration to respond to needs and opportunities with assurance.

Territorial Director of Planned Giving Lindsay Lapole has celebrated 20 years in that position and under his direction nearly $1.5 billion have been raised for Salvation Army services.

The Territorial Resource Development Section had an outstanding year

271

in raising more than $20 million throughout the territory. The territorial director and staff have developed ideas, formulae and techniques which are producing dramatic results.

Twenty-two capital campaign projects are in their feasibility or missional planning stage and another 59 are undergoing a thorough planning study. Nearly a quarter of a billion dollars are being sought in campaigns around the territory.

Volunteers are being recruited, trained and put to work. The territorial office works closely with divisional development directors and is an active resource in using this valuable asset.

The 2006 hurricane season was, thankfully, quiet. The 'big events' were replaced by the more typical compilation of tornadoes, floods, fires, man-made disasters as well as a few hurricanes. The territory responded to each with speed, competence and resources.

Two members of the THQ staff qualified as CEMs (Certified Emergency Managers). They join an elite group of fewer than 1,200 individuals with this professional designation in the entire country.

The territory hosted the National Youth Jamboree in July 2006. The same month saw the Territorial Music Institute, while June's events included the commissioning of the Visionaries Session and a music and gospel arts conference.

The installation of territorial leaders Commissioners Maxwell and Lenora Feener, the Territorial Bible Conference and the welcome of the God's Fellow Workers Session of cadets all took place in August 2006.

Other significant territorial events during the year under review included a youth workers' conference, the Youth Institute and the 'ROOTS South' convention.

STATISTICS

Officers 1,429 (active 970 retired 459) **Cadets** (1st Yr) 39 (2nd Yr) 43 **Employees** 16,864
Corps 347 **Societies/Outposts** 9 **Institutions** 251
Senior Soldiers 27,264 **Adherents** 2,717 **Junior Soldiers** 7,641
Personnel serving outside territory Officers 24

STAFF

Personnel: Lt-Col Donald Faulkner
Programme: Lt-Col Charles White
Business: Lt-Col H. Alfred Ward
Adult Rehabilitation Centres Command: Maj Larry White
Audit: Maj Eugene Broome
Community Relations and Development: Maj Ronald Busroe
Education: Maj Michael Reagan
Evangelism and Adult Ministries: Maj John White
Employee Relations: Mrs Brenda Klaas
Finance: Lt-Col David Mothershed
Legal: Lt-Col William Goodier
Multicultural Ministries: Maj Fernando R. Martinez
Music: Dr Richard E. Holz
Officers' Health Services: Maj Jeanne Johnson
Property: Mr Robert L. Taylor
Retired Officers: Maj Hilda Howell
Social Services: Mr Kevin Tompson-Hooper
Supplies and Purchasing: Maj Robert Bagley
Training: Maj Willis Howell
Women's Ministries: Comr Lenora Feener (TPWM) Lt-Col Linda Griffin (TSWM) Lt-Col Marian Faulkner (LOMS/Outreach) Lt-Col Mary Ward (TWAS)
Youth/Candidates: Capt Kelly Igleheart

DIVISIONS

Alabama-Louisiana-Mississippi: 1450 Riverside Dr, PO Box 4857, 39296-4857, Jackson, MS 39202; tel: (601) 969 7560; fax: (601) 969-9077; Maj John R. Jones, jr

USA Southern Territory

Arkansas and Oklahoma: 5101 N Pennsylvania Ave, PO Box 12600, 73157, Oklahoma City, OK 73112; tel: (405) 840 0735; fax: (405) 840 0460; Maj Henry Gonzalez

Florida: 5631 Van Dyke Rd, Lutz, FL 33558, PO Box 270848, 33688-0848, Tampa, FL; tel: (813) 962 6611; fax: (813) 962 4098; Maj R. Steven Hedgren

Georgia: 1000 Center Pl, NW, 30093, PO Box 930188, 30003 Norcross, GA 30003; tel: (770) 441-6200; fax: (770) 441-6214; Maj William Mockabee

Kentucky and Tennessee: 214-216 W Chestnut St, Box 2229, 40201-2229, Louisville, KY 40202; tel: (502) 583 5391; fax: (502) 625 1199; Maj John Needham

Maryland and West Virginia: 814 Light St, Baltimore, MD 21230; tel: (410) 347 9944; fax: (410) 539 7747; Maj Mark Bell

National Capital and Virginia: 2626 Pennsylvania Ave NW, PO Box 18658, Washington, DC 20037; tel: (202) 756 2600; fax: (202) 756 2660; Lt-Col William L. Crabson

North and South Carolina: 501 Archdale Dr, Box 241808, 28224-1808, Charlotte, NC 28217-4237; tel: (704) 522 4970; fax: (704) 522 4980; Maj Vernon Jewett

Texas: 6500 Harry Hines Blvd, PO Box 36607, 75235, Dallas, TX 75235; tel: (214) 956 6000; fax: (214) 956 9436; Maj Kenneth Johnson

SCHOOL FOR OFFICER TRAINING

1032 Metropolitan Pkwy, SW Atlanta, GA 30310; tel: (404) 753 4166; fax: (404) 753 3709

ATTACHED TO DIVISIONS
Alcoholic Rehabilitation

Dallas, TX 75235: 5554 Harry Hines Blvd (acc 90)
Fort Worth, TX 76103: 1855 E Lancaster (women only, acc 13)
Mobile, AL 36604: 1009 Dauphin St (acc 30)

Child Care Centres

Annapolis, MD 21403: 351 Hilltop Lane (acc 80)
Austin, TX 78701: 501 E 8th St (acc 28)
Austin, TX 78767: 4523 Tannehill Hill (acc 26)
Bradenton, FL 34205: 1204 14th Street W (acc 99)
Clearwater, FL 34625: 1625 N Belcher Rd (acc 70)
Charlottesville, VA 22204: 207 Ridge St (acc 50)
Decatur, AL 36604: 100 Austinville Rd SW
Fairfax, VA 22030: 4915 Ox Rd (acc 110)
Freeport, TX 77541-2620: 1618 Ave J (acc 85)
Hialeah, FL 33014: 7450 W 4th Ave (acc 147)
Irving, TX 75061: 250 E Grauwyler (acc 62)
Jacksonville, FL 32202: 318 N Ocean St (acc 125)

Lakeland, FL 33801: 835 N Kentucky (acc 45)
Louisville, KY 40203: 237 E Breckenridge (acc 42)
Lynchburg, VA 24501: 2215 Park Ave (acc 40)
Memphis, TN 38105: 696 Jackson Ave (acc 60)
Miami Sunset, FL 33143-1327: 8445 SW, 72nd St (acc 161)
Midland, TX 79703: 3500 Park Lane (acc 125)
Naples, FL 34104: 3180 Estey Ave (acc 53)
Nashville, TN 37207: 631 Dickerson Rd (acc 37)
Princeton, WV 24740: 300 Princeton Ave (acc 102)
Salisbury, MD 21804: 415 Oak St (acc 52)
San Antonio (Southside), TX 78211: 1034 Fenfield Ave (acc 92)
Winston-Salem, NC 27101: 1255 N Trade St (acc 10)

Children's Residential Care

Birmingham, AL 35212: Youth Emergency Services, 6001 Crestwood Blvd (acc 33)
St Petersburg, FL 33733: Sallie House Emergency Shelter, PO Drawer 10909

Family Resident Programme

Alexandria, VA 22301: 2525 Mt Vernon Ave (acc 40)
Amarillo, TX 79105: 400 S Harrison (acc 15)
Arlington, TX 76013: 711 W Border (acc 30)
Atlanta, GA 30310: 400 Luckie St NW (acc 56)
Austin, TX 78701: 501 E 8th St (acc 60)
Austin, TX 78767: 4523 Tannehill Ln (Women and Children Shelter) (acc 26)
Baltimore, MD 21030: 1114 N Calvert St (acc 75)
Beaumont, TX 77701: 1078 McFadden (acc 10)
Cambridge, MD 21613: 200 Washington St (acc 10)
Charlottesville, VA: 207 Ridge St NW (acc 36)
Chattanooga, TN 37403: 800 N McCallie Ave (acc 72)
Clearwater, FL 33756: 1527 East Druid Rd (acc 38)
Corpus Christi, TX 78401: 513 Josephine (acc 28)
Dalton, GA 30720: 1101 A North Thorton Ave (acc 24)
Ft Myers, FL 33901: 2163 Stella St (acc 28)
Fort Worth, TX 76103: 1855 E Lancaster Ave (acc 62)
Hagerstown, MD 21740: 534 W Franklin St (acc 30)
Harrisonburg, VA 22801: 895 Jefferson St (acc 72)
Hollywood, FL 33020: 1960 Sherman St (acc 140)
Houston, TX 77004: 1603 McGowen (acc 42)
Lakeland, FL 33801: 835 N Kentucky Ave (acc 45)

USA Southern Territory

Louisville, KY 40203: 209 E Breckinridge (acc 35)

Louisville, KY 40203: 817 S Brook St (acc 18)

Lynchburg, VA 24501: 2215 Park Ave (acc 22)

Memphis, TN 38105: 696 Jackson Ave (acc 120)

Naples, FL 34104: 3180 Estey Dr (acc 55)

Nashville, TN 37207-5608: 631 N 1st St (acc 53)

Newport News, VA 23602: 11931 Jefferson Ave (acc 30)

Norfolk, VA 23220: 2097 Military Highway, Chesapeake (acc 65)

Ocala, FL 34475: 320 NW 1st Ave (acc 24)

Orlando, FL 32804: 400 W Colonial Dr (acc 22)

Panama City, FL 32401: 1824 W 15th St (acc 48)

Parkersburg, WV 24740: 534-570 Fifth St (acc 32)

Pensacola, FL 32505: 1310 North S St (acc 24)

Richmond, VA 23220: 2 W Grace St (acc 52)

San Antonio, TX 78212: 515 W Elmira 78212 (acc 300)

Sarasota, FL 34236: 1400 10th St (acc 19)

Tampa, FL 33602: 1603 N Florida (acc 43)

Texarkana, TX 71854: 316 Hazel (acc 46)

Tyler, TX 75701: 633 N Broadway 75702

Washington, DC 20009: 1434 Harvard St NW (acc 60)

Wheeling, WV 26003: 140 16th St (acc 32)

Williamsburg, VA 7131: Merrimac Trail (acc 17)

Harbour Light Centres

Atlanta, GA 30313: 400 Luckie St (acc 242)

Houston, TX 77009: 2407 N Main St (acc 308)

Washington, DC 20002: 2100 New York Ave, NE (acc 207)

Senior Citizens' Centres

Arlington, TX 76013: 712 W Abrams

Beaumont, MS 1502: Bolton Ave

Birmingham, '614 Birmingham' AL 35203: 2410 8th Ave N

Brooklyn, MS: Carnes Rd

Dallas Cedar Crest, TX 75203: 1007 Hutchins Rd

Dallas Oak Cliff, TX 75208: 1617 W Jefferson Blvd

Dallas Pleasant Grove, TX 75217-0728: 8341 Elam Rd

Ft Worth, TX 76106: 3023 NW 24th St

Houston Aldine/Westfield, TX 77093: 2600 Aldine Westfield

Houston Pasadena, TX 77506: 45/6 Irvington Blvd

Houston Temple, TX 77009: 2627 Cherrybrook Ln 77502

Jacksonville, FL 32202: 17 E Church St

Lufkin, TX 75904: 305 Shands

Montgomery, AL 36107: 900 Bell St

Oklahoma City, OK 73129: 311 SW 5th St (includes 5 drop-in centres)

San Antonio Citadel, TX 78201: 2810 W Ashby Pl

San Antonio Hope Center, TX 78212: 521 W Elmira

Sarasota, FL 34236: 1400 10th St

Shreveport, LA 71163: 200 E Stoner

St Petersburg, FL 33713: 3800 9th Ave N

Washington (Sherman Ave), DC 20010: 3335 Sherman Ave NW

Washington (Southeast), DC 20003: 1211 G St SE

Senior Citizens' Residences

Atlanta, GA 30306: Wm Booth Towers, 1125 Ponce de Leon Ave NE (acc 99)

Charlotte, NC 28202-1727: Wm Booth Gardens Apts, 421 North Poplar St (acc 130)

Cumberland, MD 21502-0282: Wm Booth Tower, 220 Somerville Ave (acc 113)

Fort Worth, TX 76119-5813: Catherine Booth Friendship House, 1901 E Seminary Dr (acc 157)

Gastonia, NC 28054: Catherine Booth Garden Apts, 1336 Union Rd (acc 82)

High Point, NC 27263: William Booth Garden Apts, 123 SW Cloverleaf Place (acc 76)

Houston, TX 77009: Wm Booth Garden Apts, 808 Frawley (acc 62)

Ocala, FL 34470: Evangeline Booth Garden Apts, 2921 NE 14th St (acc 64)

Orlando, FL 32801: Wm Booth Towers, 633 Lake Dot Circle (acc 168)

Orlando, FL 32801: Catherine Booth Towers, 625 Lake Dot Circle (acc 125)

Pasadena, TX 77502: Evangeline Booth, 2627 Cherrybrook Ln. (acc 62)

San Antonio, TX 78201-5397: Wm Booth Gardens Apts, 2710 W Ashby Pl (acc 95)

Tyler, TX 75701: Wm Booth Gardens Apts, 601 Golden Rd (acc 132)

Waco, TX 76708-1141: Wm Booth Gardens Apts, 4200 North 19th (acc 120)

Waco, TX 76708-1141: Catherine Booth, N 19th

Service Centres

Alexander City, AL 35010: 823 Cherokee Rd

Americus, GA 31709: 204 Prince St

Bainbridge, GA 39819: 600 Scott St

Bay City, TX 77404: 1911 7th St

Borger, TX 79007-4252: 1090 Coronado Center Cir 79007-2502

Bogalusa, LA 70427: 400 Georgia Ave

Brownwood, TX 76801: 405 Lakeway

Bushnell, FL 33513: PO Box 25 (Sumter County)

Carrollton, GA 30112: 115 Lake Carroll Blvd

Carthage, MS 39051: 610 Hwy 16 West, Suite A

Cleburne, TX 76031: 111 S Anglin

Miami Area Commander Major Victor Valdes gives a media interview at the presentation of an emergency disaster services canteen by Federal Express

Columbia, MD 21045 (Howard County):
  PO Box 2877
Copperas Cove, TX 76522: 115 East Ave E
Corinth, MS 38835: 2200 Lackey Dr
Covington, GA 30014: 5193 Washington St
Culpeper, VA 22701: 14300 Achievement Dr
Douglas, GA 31533: 110 S Gaskin Ave
Dublin, GA 31021: 1617 Telfair St
Elberton, GA 30635: 262 N McIntosh St
Elizabethtown, KY 42701: 1006 N Mulberry
Enterprise, AL 366331: (Coffee County) 1919-B
  E Park Ave
Fernandina Beach, FL 32034: 191 Nassau Place
  (Nassau County)
Fort Payne, AL 35967: (Dekalb County)
  450 Gault Ave N
Frankline, VA, 23851: 50l N Main St
Fulton, MS 38843: 414 E Main St
Glen Burnie, MD 21061: 511 S Crain Hwy
Gonzales, LA 70737: 218 Bayou Narcisse
Guntersville, AL 35976: (Marshall County)
  1336 Gunter Ave
Haines City, FL 33844: 706 Jones Ave
Houma, LA 71270: 1414 E Tunnel Blvd.
Houston, MS 38851: 114 Washington St
Jackson, GA 30233 (Jackson/Butts County):
  178 N Benton St
Jacksonville Beach, FL 32240: 705 N 2nd St
  (Beaches Service Center)
Jasper, AL 35502: (Walker County) 207 20th St E
Kaufman, TX 75142: 305 W Fair
Lenoir, NC 28645: 108 Morganton Blvd
Lewisville, TX 75067: 207 Elm St 75057
McComb, MS 39648: 604 S. Magnolia Street
McDonough, GA 30253: 401 Race Track Rd
McGehee, AR 71670: (Desha County) 202 N 2nd
Milledgeville, GA 31061: 420 S Wilkinson St
Morganton, NC 28655: 420-B West Fleming Dr
Natchez, MS 39120: 175 Hwy 61 S
New Braunfels, TX 78130: 373 B Landa St
Newnan, GA 30264: 670 Jefferson St
Okmulgee, OK 74447-0123: 105-111 E 8th St
Oneonta, AL 35121: (Blount County)
  333 Valley Rd
Opelika, AL 36801: (Lee County) 720 Columbus
  Pkwy
Oxford, MS 38655: 1015 North Lamar St
Ozark, AL 36360: (Dale County) 154 E Broad St
Pontotoc, MS 38863: 187 Hwy 15 N

Putnam County, WV 25177: 720 North Winfield
  Rd, St Albans, WV
Sallisaw, OK: PO Box 292 Fort Smith, AR 72902
Scottsboro, AL 35768: (Jackson County) 1501
  W Willow St
Spencer, WV 25276: (Roane County)
  145 Main St
Starksville, MS 39759: 501 Hwy 12 W
St Albans, WV 25177: (Putnam County)
  720 N Winfield Rd
St Mary's, GA 31558: 1909 Osborne Rd
Sylacauga, AL 35150: (Talledega South) 100 E
  3rd St
Talladega, AL 35160: (Talledega North) 215 E
  Battle St
Tarpon Springs, FL 34689: 209 S Tarpon Ave
Thomasville, AL 36784: 122 W Wilson Ave
Troy, AL 36081: 509 Brundidge St
Vidalia, GA 30475: 204 Jackson St
Warrenton, VA 20186: 26 S Third St
Wellsburg, WV 26070: 491 Commerce St
Westminster, MD 21157: 300 Hahn Rd
Winchester, VA 22604: 300 Fort Collier Rd
Yadkinville, NC 27055: 748 N State St

Spouse House Shelters
Cocoa, FL: 919 Peachtree St 32922 (PO Box
  1540, 32923) (acc 16)
Panama City, FL 32401: 1824 W 15th St (PO Box
  540, 32412) (acc 12)

Port Richey, FL 34673: PO Box 5517 Hudson, FL 34674-5517 (acc 32)

Roanoke, VA 24016 (acc 60)

Thomasville, GA 31792: 208 South St (acc 9)

Warner Robins, GA 31093: 96 Thomas Blvd (acc 15)

SOCIAL SERVICES
Adult Rehabilitation Centres (including industrial stores)

Alexandria, VA 22312: Northern Virginia Center, 6528 Little River Turnpike (acc 120)

Atlanta, GA 30318-5726: 740 Marietta St, NW (acc 132)

Austin, TX 78745: 4216 S Congress (acc 118)

Baltimore, MD 21230: 2700 W Patapsco Ave (acc 115)

Birmingham, AL 35234: 1401 F. L. Shuttlesworth Dr (acc 107)

Charlotte, NC 28204: 1023 Central Ave (acc 118)

Dallas, TX 75235-7213: 5554 Harry Hines Blvd (acc 137)

Fort Lauderdale, FL 33312-1597: 1901 W Broward Blvd (acc 99)

Fort Worth, TX 76111-2996: 2901 NE 28th St (acc 109)

Houston, TX 77007-6113: 1015 Hemphill St (acc 167)

Hyattsville, MD 20781: (Washington, DC, and Suburban Maryland Center) 3304 Kenilworth Ave (acc 151)

Jacksonville, FL 32246: 10900 Beach Blvd 32216 (acc 121)

Memphis, TN 38103-1954: 130 N Danny Thomas Blvd (acc 86)

Miami, FL 33127-4981: 2236 NW Miami Court (acc 134)

Nashville, TN 37213-1102: 140 N 1st St (acc 86)

New Orleans, LA 70121-2596: 200 Jefferson Highway (acc 50)

Oklahoma City, OK 73106-2409: 2041 NW 7th St (acc 81)

Orlando, FL 32808-7927: 3955 W Colonial Dr (acc 105)

Richmond, VA 23220-1199: 2601 Hermitage Rd (acc 81)

San Antonio, TX 78204: 1324 S Flores St (acc 110)

St Petersburg, FL 33709-1597: Suncoast Area Center, 5885 66th St N (acc 119)

Tampa, FL 33682-2949: 13815 N Salvation Army Drive (acc 131)

Tulsa, OK 74106-5163: 601-611 N Main St (acc 86)

Virginia Beach, VA 23462: Hampton Roads Center, 5560 Virginia Beach Blvd (acc 123)

In addition, 16 fresh-air camps and 346 community centres, boys'/girls' clubs are attached to the divisions.

ENJOYING AN ARMY CUP OF TEA

United Kingdom Territory: Alongside a mobile canteen Commissioner John Matear (TC) meets some wartime veterans and chats over a cup of tea after the annual Remembrance Day parade in London's Whitehall

USA WESTERN TERRITORY

Territorial leaders:
**Commissioners Philip W. and
Patricia L. Swyers**

Territorial Commander:
Commissioner Philip W. Swyers
(1 Jan 2005)

Chief Secretary:
Lieut-Colonel Donald C. Bell (1 Jul 2002)

**Territorial Headquarters: 180 E Ocean Boulevard,
PO Box 22646 (90801-5646), Long Beach, California 90802-4709, USA**

Tel: [1] (562) 436-7000; web site: www.usw.salvationarmy.org

The Salvation Army was incorporated as a religious and charitable corporation in the State of California in 1914 as 'The Salvation Army' and is qualified, along with its several affiliated separate corporations, to conduct its affairs in all of the States of the territory.

Zone: Americas and Caribbean
USA states included in the territory: Alaska, Arizona, California, Colorado, Hawaii, Idaho, Montana, Nevada, New Mexico, Oregon, Utah, Washington, Wyoming, Texas (El Paso County), Guam (US Territory)
Other countries included in territory: Republic of the Marshall Islands, Federated States of Micronesia
'The Salvation Army' in Cantonese: Kau Shai Kwan; in Japanese: Kyu-sei-gun; in Mandarin (Kuoyo): Chiu Shi Chuen; in Spanish: Ejército de Salvación
Languages in which the gospel is preached: Cantonese, Chamarro, Chuukese, English, Haida, Hmong, Ilocano, Japanese, Kolrae, Korean, Laotian, Mandarin, Marshallese, Pohnpeian, Portuguese, Spanish, Tagalog, Tlingit, Tsimpshean, Visayan
Periodicals: *Caring, New Frontier, Nuevas Fronteras* (Spanish)

AN Army on the move, growing in numbers, expanding in territory and enlarging in scope of vision are the hallmarks of the USA Western Territory.

Saipan, the largest island in the Commonwealth of the Northern Marianas, became an authorised outpost of Guam Corps in February 2007. It is located 150 miles north of Guam.

Chief Secretary Lieut-Colonel Donald C. Bell presented the Army flag to Wayne and Annie Gillespie, the Salvationist couple responsible for initiating the outreach on Saipan. Six young people were enrolled as junior soldiers and 10 adults were welcomed as adherents.

Local government and community leaders, as well as the advisory council and local media, have demonstrated enthusiasm for The Salvation Army's work and provided practical support.

During the summer of 2006 five

Service Corps teams ministered at the FIFA World Cup in Germany; also in Italy, South Africa, Taiwan, the Pacific and Marshall Islands, and Las Vegas, Nevada.

For the first time cadets participated in mission trips to Alaska and Chitre and Colon, Panama, for their spring campaigns. Special guests from Australia for the commissioning of the Visionaries Session were Commissioners Earle and Wilma Maxwell (retired).

Representing nine divisions of the territory, 149 like-minded delegates met at the college for officer training campus for the Future Officers Fellowship (FOF) Retreat, with the theme 'Design for Life'.

Western Youth Institute delegates participated in the 120th anniversary celebrations of San Francisco Chinatown Corps.

The territory announced the institution of the Corps Cadet Graduate College Scholarship that is available to the territory's corps cadet graduates who are active Salvationists and attending college full-time.

The corps in Reno, Nevada, dedicated a 70-bed, $2.3 million adult rehabilitation programme at an 'open house' ceremony that drew various federal, state and city dignitaries, as well as donors, friends and staff.

The territory is focusing on disaster preparedness issues, asking the question 'Are we ready?' Ongoing disaster training is taking place throughout the territory.

A territorial business conference had as its theme 'Doing the Most Good – Managing God's Resources'.

In the area of music, September 2006 saw the debut of the Territorial Youth Band, comprised of musicians from each division, under the direction of Territorial Music Secretary Neil Smith.

SayTunes, an interactive website for Salvationist and other interested musicians, was launched (www.saytunes.com). The Western Music Institute celebrated 30 years of musical and spiritual transformation.

In January 2007 the Women's Ministries Department began a year-long observance of 100 years of the Home League.

The Spanish-language paper *Nuevas Fronteras* continued to address issues and feature stories that are particularly significant to the Hispanic population. The paper is read in all four USA territories, as well as in Mexico, South America, Latin America and Spain.

STATISTICS
Officers 993 (active 652 retired 341) **Cadets** 21 **Employees** 9,153
Corps 262 **Outposts** 16 **Institutions** 247
Senior Soldiers 16,702 **Adherents** 3,182 **Junior Soldiers** 5,574
Personnel serving outside territory Officers 45 Lay Personnel 5

STAFF
Personnel: Maj Ralph E. Hood
Business: Maj Ron Strickland
    Asst Sec for Business Admin: Maj Victor R. Doughty
    Asst Sec for Business Admin for Kroc Center Development: Maj Robert Rudd
Programme: Maj Eda Hokom
    Assoc Sec for Programme: Maj Pamela Strickland,
ARC Command: Maj Man-Hee Chang
Audit Dept: Maj Walter Fuge
Candidates and Recruitment: Maj Nancy Dihle

USA Western Territory

Community Care Ministries: Maj Ivy Hood
Community Relations/Development:
Capt Howard R. Bennett
Education: Maj Linda Manhardt
Finance: Maj Victor A. Leslie
Gift Services: Ms Kathleen Durazo
Human Resources: Ms Margaret (Miki) Webb
Information Technology: Mr Clarence White
Legal: Mr Michael Woodruff
Multicultural Ministries: Maj Elicio Marquez
Music: Mr Neil Smith
Officer Services: Capt Rhonda Lloyd
Officer Care and Development: Maj William
Nottle
Property: Capt Robert S. Lloyd
Risk Management: Mr John McCarthy
Senior Housing Management: Mrs Susan
Lawrence
Silvercrest Ministries: Maj Leslie Peacock
Social Services: Mr Gordon A. Bingham
Supplies and Purchasing: Mr Robert Jones
Training: Maj Donald Hostetler
Western Bible Conference Sec: Maj Kelly K.
Pontsler
Women's Ministries: Comr Patricia L. Swyers
(TPWM) Lt-Col Debora K. Bell (TSWM)
World Missions: Maj Mariam Rudd
Youth: Capt Kyle Smith

DIVISIONS

Alaska: 143 E 9th Ave, Anchorage,
AK 99501-3618 (Box 101459, 99510-1459);
tel: (907) 276-2515; Maj Douglas Tollerud
Cascade: 1785 NE Sandy Blvd, Portland,
OR 97232-2872 (Box 8798, 97208-8798);
tel: (503) 234-0825; Comr James Osborne
(pro-tem)
Del Oro: 3755 N Freeway Blvd, Sacramento,
CA 95834-1926 (Box 348000, 95834-8000);
tel: (916) 563-3700; Maj Linda Markiewicz
Golden State: 832 Folsom St, San Francisco,
CA 94107-1123 (Box 193465, 94119-3465);
tel: (415) 553-3500; Maj Joe E. Posillico
Hawaiian and Pacific Islands: 2950 Manoa Rd,
Honolulu, HI 96822-1798 (Box 620,
96809-0620); tel: (808) 988-2136; Maj David
E. Hudson
Intermountain: 1370 Pennsylvania St, Denver,
CO 80203-2475 (Box 2369, 80201-2369);
tel: (303) 861-4833; Lt-Col Raymond L.
Peacock
Northwest: 111 Queen Anne Ave N, Seattle,
WA 98109-4955 (Box 9219, 98109-0200);
tel: (206) 281-4600; Lt-Col Harold F.
Brodin
Sierra Del Mar: 2320 5th Ave, San Diego,

CA 92101-1679 (Box 122688, 92112-2688);
tel: (619) 231-6000; Lt-Col Douglas O'Brien
Southern California: 900 W James M Wood
Blvd, Los Angeles, CA 90015-1356 (Box
15899 Del Valle Station 90015-0899);
tel: (213) 896-9160; Lt-Col Paul E. Bollwahn
Southwest: 2707 E Van Buren St, Phoenix,
AZ 85008-6039 (Box 52177, 85072-2177);
tel: (602) 267-4100; Lt-Col Don R. Mowery

COLLEGE FOR OFFICER TRAINING

30840 Hawthorne Blvd, Rancho Palos Verdes,
CA 90275-5301; tel: (310) 377-0481;
fax: (310) 541-1697

SOCIAL SERVICES
Adult Rehabilitation Centres (Men)

Anaheim, CA 92805: 1300 S Lewis St;
tel: (714) 758-0414 (acc 147)
Bakersfield, CA 93301: 200 19th St;
tel: (661) 325-8626 (acc 58)
Canoga Park, CA 91304: 21375 Roscoe Blvd;
tel: (818) 883-6321 (acc 52)
Carpinteria, CA 93013: 6410 Cindy Lane, PO Box
780, 93014; tel: (805) 684-6999 (acc 85)
Colorado Springs, CO 80903: 505 S Weber St,
PO Box 1385, 80901; tel: (719) 473-6161
(acc 65)
Denver, CO 80216: 4751 Broadway;
tel: (303) 294-0827 (acc 96)
Fresno, CA 93721: 804 S Parallel Ave;
tel: (559) 490-7020 (acc 91)
Honolulu, HI 96817: 322 Sumner St;
tel: (808) 522-8400 (acc 75)
Long Beach, CA 90813: 1370 Alamitos Ave;
tel: (562) 218-2351 (acc 94)
Lytton, CA 95448: 200 Lytton Springs Rd,
Healdsburg, PO Box 668, Healdsburg, 95448;
tel: (707) 433-3334 (acc 95)
Oakland, CA 94607: 601 Webster St, PO Box
24054, 94623; tel: (510) 451-4514 (acc 130)
Pasadena, CA 91105: 56 W Del Mar Blvd;
tel: (626) 795-8075 (acc 107)
Phoenix, AZ 85004: 1625 S Central Ave;
tel: (602) 256-4500 (acc 92)
Portland, OR 97214: 139 SE Martin Luther King
Jr Blvd; tel: (503) 235-4192 (acc 72)
Riverside County, CA 92570: 24201 Orange
Ave, Perris, PO Box 278, Perris 92572;
tel: (951) 940-5790 (acc 125)
Sacramento, CA 95814: 1615 D St, PO Box 2948,
95812; tel: (916) 441-5267 (acc 85)
San Bernardino, CA 92408: 363 S Doolittle Rd;
tel: (909) 889-9605 (acc 77)
San Diego, CA 92101: 1335 Broadway;
tel: (619) 239-4037 (acc 131)

San Francisco, CA 94110: 1500 Valencia St;
tel: (415) 643-8000 (acc 112)

San Jose, CA 95126: 702 W Taylor St;
tel: (408) 298-7600 (acc 103)

Santa Monica, CA 90404: 1665 10th St;
tel: (310) 450-7235 (acc 60)

Seattle, WA 98134: 1000 4th Ave S;
tel: (206) 587-0503 (acc 100)

Stockton, CA 95205: 1247 S Wilson Way;
tel: (209) 466-3871 (acc 84)

Tucson, AZ 85713: 2717 S 6th Ave;
tel: (520) 624-1741 (acc 85)

Adult Rehabilitation Centres (Women)

Anaheim, CA 92805: 1300 S Lewis St;
tel: (714) 758-0414 (acc 28)

Arcadia, CA 91007: Pasadena Women's
Program, 180 W Huntington Dr;
tel: (626) 795-8075 (acc 14)

Arvada, CO 80002: Cottonwood, 13455 W 58th
Ave; tel: (303) 456-0520 (acc 24)

Fresno, CA 93704: Rosecrest, 745 E Andrews St;
tel: (559) 490-7020 (acc 14)

Pasadena, CA 91107: Oakcrest Women's
Program, 180 W Huntington Dr;
tel: (626) 795-8075 (acc 13)

Phoenix, AZ 85003: Lyncrest Manor, 344 W
Lynwood St (acc 12)

San Diego, CA 92123: Door of Hope, 2799 Health
Center Dr; tel: (858) 560-7398 (acc 14)

San Francisco, CA 94116: Pinehurst Lodge,
2685 30th Ave; tel: (415) 681-1262 (acc 26)

Seattle, WA 98102: The Marion-Farrell House,
422 11th Ave E; tel: (206) 587-0503 (acc 14)

UNDER DIVISIONS
Clinics

Fairbanks, AK 99701: Dental Care Access
Program, 723 27th Ave; tel: (907) 452-3103

Kalispell, MT 59901: 110 Bountiful Drive;
tel: (406) 257-4357

Lodi, CA 95240: 525 W Lockeford St;
tel: (209) 367-9560

Oxnard/Port Hueneme, CA: 622 W Wooley Rd;
tel: (805) 483-9235

Portland, OR 97204: Homeless Infirmary
Program (HIP), 30 SW 2nd Ave;
tel: (503) 239-1259

Reno, NV 89512: 1931 Sutro St;
tel: (775) 688-4555

San Diego, CA 92123: DOH, 2799 Health
Center Dr; tel: (858) 279-1100

Family Services

Anchorage, AK 99503: Family Services,
4611 Gambell St; tel: (907) 277-2593

Denver, CO 80205: Denver Family Services,
2201 Stout St; tel: (303) 295-3366

Honoka, HI 96727: Ke Kama Pono Outreach
Program, 45-511 Rickard Place;
tel: (808) 935-4111 ext 16

Honolulu, HI 96817: Honolulu Family Services
Offices, 420 Waiakamilo Rd, Unit 108;
tel: (808) 845-2544

Los Angeles, CA 90015-1352: Los Angeles
Family Service, 832 W James M. Wood Blvd;
tel: (213) 438-0933

Olympia, WA 98501: Social Services, 824 5th
Ave E; tel: (360) 754-2441

Phoenix, AZ 85034-2177: Family Service Center,
2702 E Washington; tel: (602) 267-4122

Richland, WA 99352: (Mid-Columbia) Social
Services, PO Box 1446; tel: (509) 547-2138

Sacramento, CA 95814: Family Service Center,
1200 North B St; tel: (916) 442-0303

San Diego, CA 92101: Family Development
Center, 726 F St; tel: (619) 231-6030

San Francisco, CA 94103: Family Service Center,
520 Jesse St; tel: (415) 575-4848

Seattle, WA 98101-1923: Emergency Family
Assistance, 1101 Pike St; tel: (206) 447-9944

Spokane, WA 99209: Family Services, 2020 N
Division; tel: (509) 325-6821

Tiyan, Guam: Family Services Center, 613-615
E Sunset Blvd; tel: (671) 477-3528

Vancouver, WA 98684: Family Services,
7509 NE 47th Ave; tel: (360) 694-9503

Yakima, WA 98907: Social Services, 9 S 6th Ave;
tel: (509) 453-3139

Yuba City, CA 95991: Family Services, 401 Del
Norte Ave; tel: (530) 216-4530

Adult Care Centres

Anchorage, AK 99508: 3350 E 20th Ave,
Serendipity Adult Day Services;
tel: (907) 279-0501 (acc 35)

Centralia, WA 98531: Evangeline Booth Adult
Care Program, PO Box 488;
tel: (360) 736-4339 (acc 40)

Henderson, NV 89015: 830 E Lake Mead Dr,
Box 91300, 89009; tel: (702) 565-9578 (acc 49)

Honolulu, HI 96817: 296 N Vineyard Blvd;
tel: (808) 521-6551 (acc 57)

San Pedro, CA 90731-2351: 138 S Bandini;
tel: (310) 832-7228 (acc 30)

Torrance, CA 90503: 4223 Emerald St;
tel: (310) 370-4515 (acc 40)

Alcoholic and Drug Rehabilitation Services

Anchorage, AK 99503-7317: Box 190567,
99519-0567, Clitheroe Center;

Captain Martin Cooper (Marshall Islands Coordinator) and Lieut-Colonel Donald C. Bell (Chief Secretary, USA Western) lead a march of witness on the Arno atoll in the South Pacific

tel: (907) 276-2898 (acc 58)

Bell, CA 90201-6418: Bell Shelter, 5600 Rickenbaker Rd 2a/b; tel: (323) 263-1206

Guam, GU 96910: Lighthouse Recovery Center, 440 E Marine Dr, PO Box 23038, GMF GU 96921, E Agana; tel: (671) 477-7671

Honolulu, HI 96816-4500: Women's Way/ Family Treatment Services, 845 22nd Ave; tel: (808) 732-2802 (acc 41)

Honolulu, HI 96817: Addiction Treatment Services, 3624 Waokanaka St; tel: (808) 595-6371 (acc 80)

Honolulu, HI 96822-1757: Therapeutic Living, 845 22nd Ave; tel: (808) 988-1786

Los Angeles, CA 90073: The Haven-Victory Place, 11301 Wilshire Blvd, Bldg 212; tel: (310) 478-3711 ext 48761 (acc 200)

Santa Rosa, CA 95401: Transitional Cooperative Living Program (After Recovering Housing), 93 Stony Circle; tel: (707) 535-4271 (acc 5)

Child Day Care Centres

Aiea (Leeward-Ohana Keiki), HI 96701: 98-612 Moanalua Loop; tel: (808) 487-1636 (acc 57)

Aurora, CO 80011: 802 Quari Ct, Box 31739, 80041-0739; tel: (303) 366-7585 (acc 123)

Boise, ID Booth, 83702: 1617 N 24th, Box 1216 83701; tel: (208) 343-3571 (acc 15)

Bozeman, MT 59715: 32 S Rouse, Box 1307, 59771-1307; tel: (406) 586-5813 (acc 14)

Colorado Springs, CO 80903-4023: Children's Development Center, 709 S Sierra Madre; tel: (719) 578-9190 (acc 30)

Denver, CO 80205-4547: Denver Red Shield Child Day Care (acc 163); Denver Red Shield Tutor Program, 2915 High St; tel: (303) 295-2108 (acc 250)

Denver, CO 80219-1859: Denver Citadel Tutor Program, PO Box 280750, 80228-0750, 4505 W Alameda Ave; tel: (303) 922-4540 (acc 15)

Globe, AZ 85501: Box 1743, 85502, 161 E Cedar St; tel: (928) 425-4011 (acc 20)

Greeley, CO 80632: Day Care Center, 1119 6th St, Box 87, 80632; tel: (970) 346-1661 (acc 45)

Honolulu, (FTS-Kula Kokua), HI 96816: 845 22nd Ave; tel: (808) 732-2802 (acc 24)

Honolulu, (Kauluwela-Ohana Keiki) HI 96817: 296 N Vineyard Blvd; tel: (808) 521-6551 (acc 75)

Kailua-Kona, (Ohana Keiki) HI 96740:

281

75-223 Kalani St, Box 1358 96745;
tel: (808) 325-7780 (acc 326)

Los Angeles, CA 90026: Alegria Day/After-School Care, 2737 Sunset Blvd;
tel: (323) 454-4200 (acc 90)

Los Angeles, CA 90021: 836 Stanford Ave;
tel: (213) 623-9022 (acc 250)

Los Angeles, CA 90025: Bessie Pregerson Childcare, Westwood Transitional Village, 1401 S Sepulveda Blvd; tel: (310) 477-9539 (acc 64)

Los Angeles, CA 90001: South Los Angeles, 7655 Central Ave; tel: (323) 277-0732 (acc 62)

Modesto, CA 95354, 625 'I' St, PO Box 1663 (mail), 95353; tel: (209) 342-5220 (acc 60)

Monterey, CA 93942: PO Box 1884 (mail), 1491 Contra Costa, Seaside, 93955;
tel: (831) 899-4915 (acc 105)

Oakland, CA 94607-4125: 601 Webster St;
tel: (510) 451-4514 (acc 132)

Phoenix, AZ 85008: 2707 E Van Buren St;
tel: (602) 267-4138 (acc 33)

Pomona, CA 91767: Box 2562, 91769, 490 E Laverne Ave; tel: (909) 623-1579 (acc 66)

Portland, OR 97296: 2640 NW Alexandra Ave;
tel: (503) 239-1248 (acc 18)

Riverside, CA 92501: 3695 1st St;
tel: (909) 784-4495 (acc 108)

Sacramento, CA 95814-1013: 1615 'D' St;
tel: (916) 441-5267 (acc 88)

San Diego, CA 92123: Door of Hope, 2799 Health Center Dr; tel: (858) 279-1100 (acc 108)

San Francisco, CA 94103: 407 9th St;
tel: (415) 503-3000 (acc 31)

Santa Barbara, CA 93111: Day Care and After-School Latchkey Program, Box 6190, 93160-6190, 4849 Hollister Ave; tel: (805) 683-3724 (acc 100)

Santa Fe Springs, CA 90606: Infant/Pre-School and After-School Care, 12000 E Washington Blvd; tel: (310) 696-7175 (acc 57)

Seattle, WA 98103: Little People Day Care, 9501 Greenwood Ave N Box 30638, 98103-0638; tel: (206) 782-3142 (acc 65)

Tacoma, WA 98405: Joyful Noise Child Care, 1100 S Puget Sound Ave; tel: (253) 752-1661 (acc 47)

Torrance, CA 90503: 4223 Emerald St;
tel: (310) 370-4514 (acc 60)

Tustin, CA 92680: 10200 Pioneer Rd;
tel: (714) 918-0659 (acc 90)

Correctional Services Offices

Los Angeles, CA 90015-1356: 900 W James M.

Wood Blvd, Box 15899, Del Valle Station 90015-0899; tel: (213) 896-9185

Portland, OR 97232: 1785 NE Sandy Blvd;
tel: (503) 239-1229

Tucson, AZ 85716: 1001 N Richey Blvd (no mail);
tel: (520) 795-9671

Emergency Shelters, Hospitality Houses

Anchorage, AK 99508: Booth Memorial, 3600 E 20th Ave; tel: (907) 279-0522 (acc 5)

Anchorage, AK 99501: Eagle Crest Transitional Housing, 438 E 9th Ave; tel: (907) 276-5913 (acc 76)

Anchorage, AK 99501: McKinnell House, 1701 'A' Street; tel: (907) 276-1609 (acc 110)

Anchorage, AK 99501: Cares for Kids (Crisis Nursery), 1701 'A' Street; tel: (907) 276-8511 (acc 20)

Bell, CA 90201: 5600 Rickenbacker;
tel: (323) 263-1206 (acc 484)

Boise, ID 83702: 1617 N 24th St;
tel: (208) 343-3571 (acc 24)

Cheyenne, WY 82001: Sally's House, 1920 Seymour St, PO Box 385, 82003 (mail);
tel: (307) 634-2769 (acc 6)

Colorado Springs, CO 80909: Bridge House, 2641 E Yampa St; tel: (719) 227-8773 (acc 7)

Colorado Springs, CO 80909-4037: 2649 E Yampa St, Freshstart Transitional Family Housing; tel: (719) 227-8773 (acc 61)

Colorado Springs, CO 80903-4023: R.J. Montgomery New Hope Center, 709 S Sierra Madre; tel: (719) 578-9190 (acc 200)

Denver, CO 80216: Crossroads Center, 1901 29th St; tel: (303) 298-1028 (acc 294)

Denver, CO 80221-4115: Denver New Hope (Lambuth) Family Center, 2741 N Federal Blvd; tel: (303) 477-3758 (acc 84)

El Paso, TX 79905: Box 10756-79997, 4300 E Paisano Dr; tel: (915) 544-9811 (acc 136)

Fresno, CA 93711-3705: Gablecrest Women's Transitional Home, 1107 West Shaw;
tel: (559) 226-6110 (acc 52)

Glendale, CA 91204-2053: Nancy Painter Home, 320 W Windsor Rd; tel: (213) 245-2424 (acc 19)

Grand Junction, CO 81502: Women's and Family Shelter, 915 Grand Ave, PO Box 578-0578 81501 (mail); tel: (907) 242-3343 (acc 10)

Hilo, HI 96720: Interim Home for Youth, Box 5085; tel: (808) 935-4411 (acc 18)

Honoka, HI 96727: Residential Group Home, 45-350 Ohelo St, PO Box 5085, Hilo, HI 96720; tel: (808) 935-4111 ext 14

Honolulu, HI 96816: FTS-Supportive Living, 845 22nd Ave; tel: (808) 732-2802 (acc 24)

World President of Women's Ministries Commissioner Helen Clifton celebrates the Home League centenary during her visit to India Northern Territory

Heavenly Father, thou hast brought us
Safely to the present day,
Gently leading on our footsteps,
Watching o'er us all the way.
Friend and guide through life's
  long journey,
Grateful hearts to thee we bring;
But for love so true and changeless
How shall we fit praises sing?

Song Book for The Salvation Army, 938

Top: Masai women sing their praises at an outpost in Tanzania

Below: The Home League centenary is celebrated with a lively dance during the women's camp in Latin America North Territory

In the USA Western Territory's 'WOW!' campaign (Win One Woman for Christ) Captain Melissa Viquez began a women's outreach group at Gilroy Corps, California, and saw her home league membership more than double within six months

Home League centenary souvenirs and clothing in Nigeria Territory

Junior Miss members in India Western Territory meet to celebrate the Home League centenary

Gender discrimination

Despite the adoption of the Convention on the Elimination of All Forms of Discrimination against Women in 1979, gender discrimination is pervasive in every region of the world

The consequences of gender discrimination...

At UN Headquarters in New York, World Secretary for Women's Ministries Commissioner Janet Street (far right) leads an international delegation of Salvationists attending the United Nations Commission on the Status of Women

Kahului, HI 96732-2256: 45 Kamehameha St;
tel: (808) 877-3042

Kailua-Kona, HI 96740: Interim Home-Youth
Shelter, 74-5045 Huaala St, PO Box 5085,
Hilo, HI 96720; tel: (808) 935-4411 (acc 8)

Kodiak, AK 99615-6511: Kodiak, Beachcombers
Transitional Housing, 1855 Mission Rd;
tel: (907) 486-8740

Las Vegas, NV 89030: Safehaven-Shelter,
31 W Owens Ave; tel: (702) 639-0277 (acc 22)

Las Vegas, NV 89030: Pathways, 37 W Owens
Ave; tel: (702) 639-0277 (acc 42)

Las Vegas, NV 89030: Lied Transitional Housing,
45 W Owens Ave; tel: (702) 642-7252 (acc 70)

Las Vegas, NV 89030: Emergency Lodge,
47 W Owens Ave; tel: (702) 639-0277 (acc 167)

Las Vegas, NV 89030: PATH, 47 W Owens
Ave; tel: (702) 639-0277 (acc 34)

Lodi, CA 95240-2128: Hope Harbor Family
Service Center, 622 N Sacramento St;
tel: (209) 367-9560 (acc 81)

Long Beach, CA 90810: The Village at Callebrio,
2260 Williams St; tel: (562) 388-7600 (acc 82)

Los Angeles, CA 90073: Naomi House (for
women veterans), Exodus Lodge (for mentally
ill), The Haven, 11301 Wilshire Blvd, Bldg 212,
Los Angeles; tel: (310) 478-3711 ext 48761
(acc 100)

Los Angeles, CA 90013: Safe Harbor, 721 E
5th St; tel: (213) 622-5253 (90013) (acc 56)

Los Angeles, CA 90015: Alegria (HIV/Aids
housing), 2737 Sunset Blvd; tel: (323) 263-1206
(acc 195)

Los Angeles, CA 90028: The Way In (teen
counselling), 5941 Hollywood Blvd,
Box 38668, 90038-0668; tel: (213) 468-8666
(acc 26)

Los Angeles, CA 90025-3477: Westwood
Transitional Housing, 1401 S Sepulveda Blvd;
tel: (310) 477-9539 (acc 60)

Marysville, CA 95901-5629: The Depot Family
Shelter, 408 'J' St; tel: (530) 216-4530 (acc 58)

Marysville, CA 95901, Transitional Living
Facility, 5906 B Riverside Dr;
tel: (530) 216-4530 (acc 40)

Medford, OR 97501-4630: 1065 Crews Rd;
tel: (541) 773-7005 (acc 43)

Modesto, CA 95354: Berberian Shelter,
320 9th Street; tel: (209) 525-9954 (acc 100)

Modesto, CA 95354: Emergency Shelter,
330 9th Street; tel: (209) 522-3200

Nampa, ID 83651: 1412 4th St South;
tel: (208) 461-3733 (acc 54)

Oakland, CA 94601: Family Emergency Shelter,
2794 Garden St, Box 510, 94604 (mail);
tel: (510) 437-9437 (acc 65)

Olympia, WA 98501: Hans K. Lemcke Lodge,
808 5th Ave SE, 98501; tel: (360) 352-8596
(acc 86)

Petaluma, CA 94975: PATH – Petaluma Area
Transitional Housing, PO Box 750684;
tel: (707) 769-0716 (acc 12)

Phoenix, AZ 85008: Kaiser Family Center,
2707 E Van Buren, Elim House, PO Box
52177, 85072; tel: (602) 267-4122 (acc 114)

Portland, OR 97296: Women's Shelter, 2640 NW
Alexandra Ave; tel: (503) 239-1248 (acc 10)

Portland, OR 97208: Women and Children's
Family Violence Center, PO Box 2398;
tel: (503) 239-1254 (acc 53)

Sacramento, CA 95814-0603: Emergency Shelter,
1200 N 'B' St; tel: (916) 442-0331 (acc 132)

Salem, OR 97303:
1901 Front St NE; tel: (503) 585-6688 (acc 83);
105 River St NE; tel: (503) 391-1523 (acc 6);
1960 Water St NE; tel: (503) 566-7267 (acc 10)

San Bernardino, CA 92410: Hospitality House,
845 W Kingman St; tel: (909) 864-3029
(acc 60)

Sand City, CA 93955: Good Samaritan Center,
800 Scott St; tel: (831) 899-4988 (acc 60)

San Diego, CA 92101: Family Development
Center, 730 'F' St, Box 122688, 92112;
tel: (619) 699-2223 (acc 60)

San Diego, CA 92101: STEPS, 825 7th Ave;
tel: (619) 446-0451 (acc 30)

San Francisco, CA 94103: SF Harbor House,
407 9th St; tel: (415) 503-3000 (acc 66)

San Jose, CA 95112: Santa Clara Hospitality
House, 405 N 4th St, Box 2-D, 95109-0004
(mail); tel: (408) 282-1175 (acc 79)

Santa Ana, CA 92701: 818 E 3rd St;
tel: (714) 542-9576 (acc 52)

Santa Barbara, CA 93101: 423 Chapala St;
tel: (805) 962-6281 (acc 40)

Santa Fe Springs, CA: Transitional Living
Center, 12000 E Washington Blvd, 90606,
Box 2009, 90610; tel: (562) 696-9562 (acc 116)

Seaside, CA 93955: Casa De Las Palmas
Transitional Housing, 535 Palm Ave;
tel: (831) 392-1762 (acc 12)

Seattle, WA 90101: Women's Shelter
(Emergency Financial Assistance), 1101 Pike
St, PO Box 20128; tel: (206) 447-9944 (acc 20)

Seattle, WA: Catherine Booth House (Shelter for
Abused Women), Box 20128, 98102;
tel: (206) 324-4943 (acc 17)

Seattle, WA 98134: William Booth Center –
Emergency Shelter and Transitional Shelter/
Living, 811 Maynard Ave S; tel: (206) 621-0145
(acc 183)

Seattle, WA 98136: Hickman House (Women),

5600 Fauntleroy Way SW, Box 20128, 98102;
tel: (206) 932-5341 (acc 35)

Spokane, WA 99201: Box 9108, 99209-9108,
Family Shelter, 1403 W Broadway;
tel: (509) 325-6814 (acc 48)

Spokane, WA 99201: Sally's House (Foster
Care Home), Box 9108, 99209-9108,
222 E Indiana; tel: (509) 325-6826 (acc 14)

Spokane, WA 99207-2335: Transitional Housing,
127 E Nora Ave; tel: (509) 326-7288
(acc 96)

Tacoma, WA 98405: Jarvie Family/Women's
Emergency Shelter, 1521 6th Ave, Box 1254,
98401-1254; tel: (253) 627-3962 (acc 72)

Tucson, AZ 85705: 1021 N 11th Ave;
tel: (520) 622-5411 (acc 91)

Tucson, AZ 85716: SAFE Housing,
3525 E 2nd St #1; tel: (520) 323-6080

Ventura, CA 93001-2703: 155 S Oak St;
tel: (805) 648-5032 (acc 51)

Watsonville, CA 95076-5048: Supportive
Housing Program for Women, 232 Union St;
tel: (831) 763-0131 (acc 60)

Whittier, CA 90602: 7926 Pickering Ave,
PO Box 954, 90608; tel: (562) 698-8348
(acc 17)

Harbour Light Centres

Denver, CO 80205: Denver Harbor Light, 2136
Champa St; tel: (303) 296-2456 (acc 80)

Los Angeles, CA 90013: Los Angeles Harbor
Light, Harmony Hall, Safe Harbor, PO Box 791,
90053-0791, 809 E 5th St; tel: (213) 626-4786
(acc 324)

Portland, OR 97204: Box 5635, 97228-5635,
30 SW 2nd St; tel: (503) 239-1259
(acc 143)

San Francisco, CA 94103-4405: 1275 Harrison St;
tel: (415) 503-3000 (acc 79)

Residential Youth Care and Family Service Centres

Anchorage, AK 99508: Booth Memorial Youth
and Family Services, 3600 E 20th Ave;
tel: (907) 279-0522 (acc 20)

Boise, ID 83702: Family Day Care Center,
Box 1216, 83701, 1617 N 24th St;
tel: (208) 343-3571 (acc 15)

Portland, OR 97210: Box 10027, 2640 NW
Alexandra Ave; tel: (503) 239-1248 (acc 33)

San Diego, CA 92123: DOH Haven, Transitional
Living Center, 2799 Health Center Dr;
tel: (858) 279-1100

Adult Rehabilitation Programs (Men)

Albuquerque, NM 87102: Box 27690, 87125-

7690, 400 John St SE; tel: (505) 242-3112
(acc 36)

Anchorage, AK 99503: 660 E 48th Ave;
tel: (907) 562-5408 (acc 61)

Chico, CA 95973: 13404 Browns Valley Dr;
tel: (530) 342-2087

Grand Junction, CO 81502: Box 578, 81502,
903 Grand Ave; tel: (970) 242-8632 (acc 32)

North Las Vegas, NV 89030: Box 30096,
211 Judson St; tel: (702) 649-2374 (acc 118)

Reno, NV 89502-1119: 835 E Second St;
tel: (775) 688-4570 (acc 66)

Reno, NV 89512-1605: 2300 Valley Rd;
tel: (775) 688-4559

Salt Lake City, UT 84102-2030: 252 South 500
East; tel: (801) 323-5817 (acc 51)

Adult Rehabilitation Programs (Women)

Chico, CA 95973: 13404 Browns Valley Dr;
tel: (530) 342-2087

Grand Junction, CO 81502: Adult Rehabilitation
Program – Women's Residence, 915 Grand
Ave, PO Box 578-0578 81501 (mail);
tel: (907) 242-8632 (acc 10)

Las Vegas, NV 89030: 39 W Owens;
tel: (702) 649-1469 (acc 42)

Ogden, UT 84401-3610: Women's Rehabilitation
Program, 2615 Grant Avenue;
tel: (801) 621-3580 (acc 29)

San Diego, CA 92123: Door of Hope, 2799 Health
Center Drive; tel: (619) 239-4037 ext 354

Senior Citizens' Housing

Albuquerque, NM: Silvercrest, 4400 Pan Am
Fwy NE, 87107; tel: (505) 883-1068 (acc 55)

Broomfield, CO 80020-1876: Silvercrest,
1110 E 10th Ave; tel: (303) 464-1994 (acc 85)

Capitola, CA 95010-2761: Silvercrest Senior
Citizens' Residence, 750 Bay Ave;
tel: (831) 464-6435 (acc 114)

Chula Vista, CA 91910: Silvercrest, 636 3rd Ave;
tel: (619) 427-4991 (acc 73)

Colorado Springs, CO 80909-7507: Silvercrest I,
904 Yuma St; tel: (719) 475-2045 (acc 50)

Colorado Springs, CO 80909-5097: Silvercrest II,
824 Yuma St; tel: (719) 389-0329 (acc 50)

Denver, CO 80219-1859: Silvercrest, 4595 W
Alameda; tel: (303) 922-2924 (acc 66)

Denver, CO 80221-2234: West Adams
Silvercrest, 2821 W 65th Pl, PO Box 211008
(mail); tel: (303) 657-1088 (acc 32)

El Cajon, CA 92020: Silvercrest, 175 S Anza St;
tel: (619) 593-1077 (acc 73)

El Sobrante, CA 94803-1859: Silvercrest,
4630 Appian Way; tel: (510) 758-1518
(acc 85)

Escondido, CA 92026: Silvercrest, 1301 Las
Villas Way; tel: (760) 741-4106 (acc 75)

Eureka, CA 95501-1264: Silvercrest, 2141
Tydd St; tel: (707) 445-3141 (acc 152)

Fresno, CA 93721-1041: Silvercrest,
1824 Fulton St; tel: (559) 237-9111 (acc 158)

Glendale, CA 92104: Silvercrest, 323 W Garfield;
tel: (818) 543-0211 (acc 150)

Hollywood, CA 90028: Silvercrest, 5940 Carlos
Ave; tel: (323) 460-4335 (acc 140)

Lake View Terrace, CA 91354: Silvercrest,
11850 Foothill Blvd; tel: (818) 896-7580
(acc 150)

Los Angeles, CA 90006: Silvercrest,
947 S Hoover St; tel: (213) 387-7278
(acc 120)

Mesa, AZ 85201: Silvercrest, 255 E 6th St;
tel: (480) 649-9117 (acc 81)

Missoula, MT 59802: Silvercrest, 1550 S 2nd St;
tel: (406) 541-0464 (acc 50)

N Las Vegas, NV 89030: Silvercrest,
2801 Equador Ct; tel: (702) 643-0293 (acc 60)

Oceanside, CA 92056: Silvercrest, 3839 Lake
Blvd; tel: (760) 940-0267 (acc 67)

Pasadena, CA 91106: Silvercrest, 975 E Union St;
tel: (626) 432-6678 (acc 150)

Phoenix, AZ 85003: Silvercrest, 613 N 4th Ave;
tel: (602) 251-2000 (acc 125)

Portland, OR 97232: Silvercrest, 1865 NE Davis;
tel: (503) 236-2320 (acc 78)

Puyallup, WA 98373: Silvercrest, 4103 9th St SW;
tel: (253) 841-0785 (acc 40)

Redondo Beach, CA 90277: Mindeman Senior
Residence, 125 W Beryl St;
tel: (310) 318-2827/0582 (acc 54)

Reno, NV 89512-2448: Silvercrest,
1690 Wedekind Rd; tel: (775) 322-2050
(acc 59)

Riverside, CA 92501: Silvercrest, 3003 Orange;
tel: (909) 276-0173 (acc 72)

San Diego, CA 92101: Silvercrest, 727 E St;
tel: (619) 699-7272 (acc 122)

San Francisco, CA 94133-3844: SF Chinatown
Senior Citizens' Residence, 1450 Powell St;
tel: (415) 781-8545 (acc 9)

San Francisco, CA 94107-1132: Silvercrest,
133 Shipley St; tel: (415) 543-5381 (acc 514)

Santa Fe Springs, CA 90670: Silvercrest,
12015 Lakeland Rd; tel: (562) 946-7717
(acc 25)

Santa Monica, CA 90401: Silvercrest, 1530 5th St;
tel: (310) 393-5336 (acc 122)

Santa Rosa, CA 95404-6601: Silvercrest,
1050 3rd St ; tel: (707) 544-6766 (acc 187)

Seattle, WA 98103, Silvercrest, 9543 Greenwood
Ave N; tel: (206) 706-0855 (acc 75)

Stockton, CA 95202-2645: Silvercrest, 123 N
Stanislaus St; tel: (209) 463-4960 (acc 82)

Tulare, CA 93274: 350 North 'L' St;
tel: (559) 688-0704 (acc 65)

Turlock, CA 95380: Silvercrest, 865 Lander Ave;
Box 116, 95380-5815 (mail);
tel: (209) 669-8863 (acc 82)

Ventura, CA 93004: Silvercrest, 750 Petit Ave;
tel: (805) 647-0110 (acc 130)

Wahiawa, HI 96786: Silvercrest Residence,
520 Pine St; tel: (808) 622-2785 (acc 159)

Senior Citizens' Nutrition Centres

Anchorage, AK 99501: Older Alaskans Program
(OAP), 1701 'A' Street; tel: (907) 349-0613

Denver, CO 80205-4547: Denver Red Shield,
2915 High St; (tel): (303) 295-2107

Denver, CO 80221-0395: West Adams,
2821 W 65th Pl; tel: (303) 428-6430

Fresno, CA 93712-1041: 1824 Fulton St;
tel: (559) 233-0139

Oakland, CA 94607: 379 12th St;
tel: (510) 834-1089

Phoenix, AZ: Laura Danieli Senior Activity
Center, 613 N 4th Ave; tel: (602) 251-2005

Portland, OR 97232-2822: Rose Centre – Senior
Citizens Program, 211 NE 18th Ave;
tel: (503) 239-1221

Salinas, CA 93906-1519: 2460 N Main St;
tel: (831) 443-9655

San Diego, CA 92101-1679: Senior Citizens
Program (9 Locations), 2320 5th Ave;
tel: (619) 843-9451

San Francisco, CA 94107-1125: Senior
Citizens Meal Program, 850 Harrison St;
tel: (415) 777-5350

San Jose, CA 95112: 359 N 4th St;
tel: (408) 282-1165

Tucson, AZ 85705; Nutrition and Home
Delivered Meals, 1021 N 11th Ave;
tel: (520) 792-1352

Tulare, CA 93274-4131: 314 E San Joaquin Ave;
tel: (559) 687-2520

Turlock, CA 95380-5815: 893 Lander Ave;
tel: (209) 667-6091

Watsonville, CA 95076-5203: 29-A Bishop St;
tel: (831) 724-0948

*In addition there are 14 fresh-air camps and
38 youth community centres attached to divisions,
as well as 470 service units in the territory*

ZAMBIA TERRITORY

Territorial Commander:
Commissioner Vinece Chigariro
(1 Aug 2004)

Chief Secretary:
Lieut-Colonel Grey Miyoba (1 May 2005)

Territorial Headquarters: 685A Cairo Road, Lusaka

Postal address: PO Box 34352, Lusaka 10101, Zambia

Tel: [260] 1 238291/228327; fax: [260] 1 226784; email: sathq@coppernet.zm

In 1922 emigrants from villages on the north bank of the Zambezi River working in a mica mine near Urungwe were converted. They carried home the message of salvation to their chief, and established meeting places in their villages. Two years later, Commandant Kunzwi Shava and Lieutenant Paul Shumba were appointed to command the new opening. The Zambia Division in the Rhodesia Territory became the Zambia Command in 1966. In 1988, the Malawi Division was transferred from the Zimbabwe Territory to form the new Zambia and Malawi Territory. The Zambia and Malawi Territory became the Zambia Territory on 1 October 2002 when Malawi became an independent region.

Zone: Africa
Country included in the territory: Zambia
Languages in which the gospel is preached: Chibemba, Chinyanja, Chitonga, English, Lozi

UNDER the theme 'Go and Make Disciples', the year was highlighted by extensive evangelistic ministry and numerous soul-saving events. As a result 1,949 soldiers were enrolled. Juniors soldiers were enrolled in every centre, leading to singing companies being formed in all corps.

Another area of children's ministry is the Scouting programme, funded by Sweden and Latvia Territory; it has become a successful means of winning young souls for Christ.

The five-day Territorial Home League Congress, held at Chipata, attracted 430 women. Some had to travel up to 585 kilometres, and on their way conducted six open-air meetings in five towns. The congress theme

was 'Bloom Wherever You Are' and 55 new souls were won for Christ.

The Men's Fellowship Congress was held with great success for the first time. Nearly 500 men camped at Mulikita Farm and were blessed by the visit of Commissioner Amos Makina (International Secretary for Africa).

The Territorial Youth Songsters attended the Malawi Command Congress, where the Chief of the Staff was guest of honour. The songsters were a source of blessing; their music moved many people and inspired them to seek and find Christ.

Even while travelling to and from Malawi the songsters shared their faith, such as organising an open-air meeting at the border post and preaching Jesus while someone attended to their passports.

The Territorial Youth Songsters also campaigned in Zimbabwe and returned encouraged.

The Projects Department assisted 11,776 orphans and vulnerable children with schooling requirements and personal needs. The territory's 914 trained care-givers and 248 peer educators brought hope into the lives of many HIV/Aids sufferers.

As a result, more than 2,500 people have benefited from home-based care through the Rapids project. Some 1,100 youths have been brought nearer God and themselves become channels of the gospel through programmes like sports ministry, skills training and drama.

As Chikankata Health Services continues to enhance its ministry to the community and the nation, a bio-medical college of sciences was opened for 30 young men and women.

Speaking as Territorial President of Women's Ministries, in an address to mark the Home League centenary, Commissioner Vinece Chigariro encouraged women to celebrate this special year under the leadership and Lordship of Jesus Christ. She called on women to allow the Holy Spirit to guide them as they wage war against human trafficking and child abuse.

She further said women should use most of their time to grow their home leagues as well as to mark this year with wonderful, adventurous and bright events to bring many to Christ.

STATISTICS

Officers 214 (active 196 retired 18) **Cadets** 23 (Zambia 19 Malawi 4) **Employees** 422
Corps 98 **Societies** 47 **Outposts** 174 **New Openings** 12 **Hospital** 1 **High School** 1 **Old People's Home** 1 **Farm** 1
Senior Soldiers 22,222 **Adherents** 1,437 **Junior Soldiers** 5,019
Personnel serving outside territory Officers 4

STAFF

Asst Chief Sec: Maj Bislon Hanunka
Sec for Personnel: Maj Metson Chilyabanyama
Sec for Programme:
Sec for Business Administration: Maj Davidson Varhgese
Audit:
Community Development and Social Services: Maj Alice Mankomba
Extension Training: Maj Ireen Hacamba
Finance: Capt Donald Hangoma
Property: Capt Emmanuel Manyepa
Micro-Credit: Maj Rosemary Chilyabanyama
Projects: Capt Kennedy Mizinga
Sponsorship: Capt Patricia Hangoma
Territorial Band: Brave Hanunka
Territorial Songsters: S/L Jericho Milambo
Trade: Medah Manyepa
Training: Maj Joster Chenda
Women's Ministries: Comr Vinece Chigariro (TPWM) Lt-Col Leniah Miyoba (Asst TPWM) Maj Saraphina Milambo (TSWM) Capt Rachel Kandama (TJHLS) Maj Melody Hannka (TLOMS, SAMF)
Youth and Candidates: Capt Ginger Kandama

TRAINING COLLEGE

PO Box 34352, Lusaka, 10101; tel: (01) 261755; email: saotc@zamnet.zm

DIVISIONS

Lusaka North West: PO Box 33934, Lusaka; Maj Frazer Chalwe
Lusaka South East: PO Box 34352, Lusaka; tel: (01) 221960; Maj Bernard Chisengele
Mapangazya: P Bag S2, Mazabuka; Maj Bexter Magaya
Mazabuka: PO Box 670017, Mazabuka; tel: (032) 30420; Maj Adeck Mwiinga

DISTRICTS

Copperbelt: PO Box 70075, Ndola; tel: (02) 680302; Capt Last Siamoya

Siavonga: PO Box 59, Siavonga;
  tel: (01) 511362; Capt Bryson Sitwala
Zambia Southern: PO Box 630537, Choma;
  Capt Cason Sichilomba

SECTION (reporting to THQ)
Eastern: PO Box 510199, Chipata;
  tel: (097) 881828; Capt James Gitangita

CHIKANKATA MISSION
P Bag S2, Mazabuka
Mission Director: Maj Christopher Mabuto

CHIKANKATA HEALTH SERVICES
P Bag S2, Mazabuka; tel: (01) 222060;
  email: administration@chikankata.com
Chief Medical Officer: Dr Trevor Kaile
Manager/Administration: Mr Richard
  Bradbury
**Manager/Aids Management Training
  Services:** (Acting) Mr Fred Nakanga
**Manager/Community Health and
  Development:** Mr Charles Mang'ombe
Manager/Nursing Education:
  Mrs Z. Ngalande
Hospital Chaplain: Maj Anna Mabuto
Nursing Officer: Mrs Mirriam Kalenga

Medical Clinics (under Chikankata)
Chaanga, Chikombola, Nadezwe, Nameembo,
  Syanyolo

Youth Project (under Chikankata)
Chikombola

CHIKANKATA HIGH SCHOOL
P Bag S1, Mazabuka; tel: (01) 220820;
  email: bhachitapika@chikankata.com
Headmaster: Mr Oscar Mwanza

OLD PEOPLE'S HOME AND VOCATIONAL TRAINING CENTRE
Mitanda Home for the Aged: PO Box 250096,
  Kansenshi, Ndola; tel: (02) 680460;
  email: mitanda@coppernet.zm

PRE-SCHOOL GROUPS
Chikankata; Chikanzaya; Chipapa; Chipata;
  Chitumbi; Choma; Dundu; George; Hapwaya;
  Ibbwe Munyama; John Laing; Kakole;
  Kalomo; Kanyama; Kawama; Kazungula;
  Lusaka Citadel; Maamba; Magoye; Mitchel;
  Mukwela; Mumbwa; Ngangula; Njomona;
  Nkonkola; Petauke; Peters; Siavonga;
  Sikoongo; Sinazongwe; Situmbeko

COMMUNITY SCHOOLS
Chipata (Lusaka); Choma; George; John Laing;
  Kanyama; Kasiwe; Kawama; Luanshya;
  Maamba; Mbala; Monze; Petauke.

COMMUNITY WORK
Agriculture Projects: Chikankata; Chitumbi;
  Dundu; Hamabuya; Malala; Ngamgula
Feeding Programme: Lusitu
Fish Farming Projects: George; Kanyama
Health Centres: George; John Laing; Kanyama
HIV/Aids Training, Counselling: Chikankata;
  John Lang; THQ
Micro-Credit Projects:
  Lusaka North West: George; Kabwe; Matero
  Lusaka South East: Chawama; Chelstone
  Mapangazya: Chikankata; Chitumbi
  Mazabuka: Kaleya; Njomona; Monze
  Copperbelt: Chimwemwe; Kabushi
  Siavonga: Chirundu; Lusitu; Mitchell; Sivonga

FARM (income-generating)
PO Box 250096, Kansenshi, Ndola; tel: (02) 680460

DISPLACED ARE FED

Sri Lanka Territory: Reaching out to needs in their community, Salvationists hand out bags of food to a group of internally displaced persons

ZIMBABWE TERRITORY

Territorial leaders:
**Commissioners Stanslous and
Jannet Mutewera**

Territorial Commander:
Commissioner Stanslous Mutewera
(1 Jul 2004)

Chief Secretary:
Lieut-Colonel Peter Dali (1 Feb 2007)

Territorial Headquarters: 45 Josiah Chinamano Avenue, Harare

Postal address: PO Box 14, Harare, Zimbabwe

Tel: [263] (4) 736666/7/8, 250107/8; fax: [263] (4) 726658; email: ZIMTHQ@zim.salvationarmy.org;
web site: www.salvationarmy.org/Zimbabwe

A pioneer party led by Major and Mrs Pascoe set out from Kimberley, South Africa, on 5 May 1891 in a
wagon drawn by 18 oxen, arriving in Fort Salisbury on 18 November. The then Rhodesia became a
separate territory on 1 May 1931. Work spread to Botswana where The Salvation Army was officially
recognised in 1997.

Zone: Africa
Countries included in the territory: Botswana, Zimbabwe
'The Salvation Army' in Ndebele: Impi yo Sindiso; in Shona: Hondo yo Ruponiso
Languages in which the gospel is preached: Chitonga, English, Ndebele, Shona, Tswana
Periodicals: *Zimbabwe Salvationist, ZEST* (women's magazine)

IN the midst of harsh economic
hardship, The Salvation Army has not
wavered in its mission to win
Zimbabwe for Christ. Establishing
'Set Apart for the Mission' as the
2007 territorial theme, Territorial
Commander Commissioner Stanslous
Mutewera challenged Salvationists to
passionately and wholeheartedly serve
God with joy and thanksgiving.

'We have not surrendered to the
economy, to despair or hopelessness,'
the commissioner declared. 'We have
not said: "Let us be content with the
size of our Army and wait until better
days." We will not surrender to the

devil. We will not retreat. We will
continue to carry out our mission.'

The territory experienced continued
growth, with thousands of new soldiers
enrolled and many corps and outposts
opened to the glory of God. Salvationists displayed their generosity as
they surpassed the financial targets set
for the international Partners in
Mission Appeal and the Territorial
Thanksgiving Appeal.

The territory embarked on a strategic
planning process, outlining its essential objectives for the next five years.
Officers and lay Salvationists participated, demonstrating the territory's

desire to see greater ownership and participation by soldiery. The territory also established new mission, vision and values statements.

Some 600 Salvationists experienced dynamic teaching, soulful worship and prayerful reflection at the Territorial Bible Convention. Led by Commissioner Linda Bond (Secretary for Spiritual Life Development and International External Relations, IHQ), the convention challenged delegates to fully embrace God's love and will for their lives.

The Territorial School of Music and Gospel Arts signalled a new direction for the territory. For the first time the school featured a fusion of drama, dance, mime and poetry with traditional brass banding, vocal and timbrels.

More than 3,200 men gathered for the Territorial Men's Fellowship Congress, where they were challenged to be strong in faith as they continued serving God through the ministry of The Salvation Army.

The Human Resources Development Department held a 'Training of Trainers' workshop. Delegates representing every region of the territory were equipped with skills necessary to establish training programmes in their corps and divisions.

Seventeen students from across the territory participated in the first-ever session of the Zimbabwe School for Youth Leadership (ZSYL). This is a school without walls, whose mission is to train and develop youth to be equipped with good leadership skills.

Over the course of the year, ZSYL students met together for six weeks of residential training, completed the necessary assignments and reading material, and participated in local mentoring and outreach opportunities.

Nearly 7,000 young Salvationists at the Territorial Youth Councils, hosted by the Midlands Division, were challenged to draw closer to God and follow his will for their lives. In addition to plenary sessions and workshops, delegates participated in four open-air meetings and a march of witness.

STATISTICS

Officers 529 (active 416 retired 113) **Cadets** 38 **Employees** 1,430
Corps 401 **Societies** 214 **Outposts** 179 **Institutions/Social Centres** 7 **Hospitals** 2 **Schools – Pre-Schools** 51 **Primary** 34 **Secondary** 18 **Vocational Training** 7
Senior Soldiers 116,988 **Adherents** 3,614 **Junior Soldiers** 27,391
Personnel serving outside territory Officers 9

STAFF

Sec for Business: Maj Clever Kamambo
Sec for Personnel: Maj Langton Zipingani
Sec for Programme: Maj Casman Chinyemba
Audit: Maj Moyo Marasha
Development Services: Capt Criswell Chizengaya
Extension Training: Mrs Rochelle McAlister
Finance: Capt Sheila Chitanda
Human Resources Development: Maj Beauty Zipingani
Literature Sec: Mr John McAlister
Property: Capt Edmore Zinyowera
Public Relations: Capt Anderson Chipiro
Social: Maj Nicholas Chigwaza
Sponsorship: Capt Lindani Nikisi
Statistics: Maj Daphne Kamambo
Territorial Bandmaster: B/M M. Mtombeni
Territorial Songster Leader: S/L K. E. Mushababiri
Trade: Capt Florence Pamacheche
Training: Maj Eleckson Rutanhira
Women's Ministries: Comr Jannet Mutewera (TPWM) Lt-Col Jessica Dali (TSWM) Maj Daphne Kamambo (TLOMS) Maj Martha Chinyemba (THLS)
Youth/Candidates: Capt Absolom Makanga

DIVISIONS

Bindura: PO Box 197, Bindura; tel: (071) 6689; Maj Frederick Masango

Chiweshe: PO Box 98, Glendale; tel: (077) 214524; Maj Dubayi Ncube

Greater Harare: PO Box 1496, Harare; tel: (04) 747359; Maj Funny Nyereyemhuka

Guruve: c/o Box 150, Guruve; tel: (058) 505; Maj Edwin Jeremiah

Harare Eastern: PO Box 26, Zengeza; tel: (070) 22639

Hurungwe: PO Box 269, Karoi; tel: (064) 629229; Maj Dominic Nkomo

Kadoma: PO Box 271, Kadoma; tel: (068) 23338; Maj Isaac Mhembere

Makonde: PO Box 33, Chinhoyi; tel: (067) 2107; Maj Joel Sundika

Masvingo: PO Box 314, Masvingo; tel: (039) 63308; Capt Onai Jera

Matebeleland: PO Box 227 FM, Famona, Bulawayo; tel: (09) 46934; Capt Sipho Mbangwa

Midlands: PO Box 624, Kwekwe; tel: (055) 3992; Maj Peter Innocent Kwenda

Mupfure: PO Box 39, Mt Darwin; tel: (076) 529; Maj Michael Bridge

Semukwe: PO Box Maphisa Township, Maphisa; tel: (082) 396; Maj Final Mubaiwa

DISTRICTS

Manicaland: PO Box DV8, Dangamvura, Mutare; tel: (020) 30014; Capt Manuel Nhelenhele

Murehwa: PO Box 268, Murehwa; tel: (078) 2455; Maj Lovemore Chidhakwa

AREAS

Harare Central: c/o Highfield Temple; Stand # 3300, Old Highfield; tel: 663 159; Area Coordinator: Maj Friday Ayanam

Harare West: c/o Dzivarasekwa Corps, PO Box 37, Dzivarasekwa; tel: (04) 216 293; Area Coordinator: Maj Tineyi Mambo

Hwange: PO Box 130, Dete; tel: 018 237; Area Coordinator: Capt Effort Paswera

TRAINING COLLEGE

PO Box CR95, Cranborne; tel: (04) 742298; fax: (04) 742575

MASIYE TRAINING CAMP

PO Box AC800 Bulawayo; tel: (09) 60727 Camp: tel: (0838) 222/261; tel/fax: (0838) 228; emails: info@masiye.com (camp), info@byo.masiye.com (town office)

EDUCATION: BOARDING SCHOOLS

Bradley Secondary School: P Bag 909 Bindura; tel: (071) 3421 (acc 516)

Howard High School: PO Box 230, Howard; tel: (0758) 45921 (acc 908)

Mazowe High School: P Bag 211A, Harare; tel: (075) 25603 (acc 670)

Usher Secondary School: P Bag P5271, Bulawayo; tel: (083) 2904 (acc 560)

MEDICAL

Athol Evans Hospital Home: Chiremba Rd, Queensdale, PO Box CR70, Cranborne; tel: (04) 572121; email: aec.sec@zol.co.zw (acc 164)

Bumhudzo Hospital Home: St Mary's Township, PO Box ZG 48, Zengeza, Harare; tel: (070) 24911; 'C' scheme hospital home (acc 55); 'B' scheme residential (acc 55)

Howard Hospital: PO Box 190, Glendale; tel: (0758) 2433; emails: howard.hospital@africaonline.co.zw, pthistle@healthnet.zw (acc 144)

Tshelanyemba Hospital: PO Tshelanyemba, Maphisa; tel: (082) 254; email: tshelanyemba.hosp@healthnet.zw (acc 103)

SOCIAL SERVICES
Bulawayo

Enterprise House: Josiah Tongogara St/12th Ave, PO Box 3208; tel: (09) 60012 (acc men 65)

Ralstein Home: Masotsha Ndhlovu Ave; tel: (09) 61972 (acc mixed 30)

Harare

Braeside Social Complex: General Booth Rd, Braeside, PO Box CR66, Cranborne; tel: (04) 742001 (acc women 20, men 64)

Arcadia Girls' Hostel: Jampies St, Arcadia; tel: (04) 770082 (acc 28)

Howard

Weaving and Dressmaking School: PO Howard; tel: (0758) 45921

❛ We will not surrender to the devil. We will not retreat. We will continue to carry out our mission. ❜

Biographical Information

Based on information received by 30 September 2007

1. The following list contains the names of all active officers with the rank of lieut-colonel and above, and other officers holding certain designated appointments.

2 (a) The place and date in parenthesis immediately following the name denote the place from which the officer entered Army service and the year of service commencement. Officers commissioned prior to 1 January 1973 have their active service dated from the conclusion of the first year of training. After 1 January 1973 active service begins at the date of commissioning following a two-year session of training.

(b) Details of married women officers' entry to active service are shown separately, including maiden name. If a wife was trained separately from her husband the word *and* joins the two entries, but if trained together the word *with* joins them.

(c) At the end of each entry of married officers a joint record of their service in other countries is given. Where applicable this includes countries each served in individually before marriage.

3. Where an officer is serving in a territory/command other than his/her own this is indicated by including the territory/command of origin after the corps from which he/she entered training. In all other instances the information given implies that the officer is serving in his/her home territory.

4. Details of appointments (where not given in this section) may be ascertained under the territorial or departmental headings.

5. A key to abbreviations is given on pages 340-341.

A

ABASTO, Franklin (Central Oruro, 1983); Maj, S Am W. b 25 Mar 47, and
ABASTO, Gladys (née Bustos) (Concepción, 1983) m 1984; Maj, S Am W. b 24 Apr 53.

ABAYOMI, Ebenezer (Ife Ife, 1988); Maj, Nig. b 4 Apr 60, and
ABAYOMI, Comfort (Ife Ife, 1990); Maj, Nig. b 12 Dec 63.

ABBULU, Sankurati Pedda (Achanta, 1978); Maj, Ind C. b 2 Jan 50, with
ABBULU, Vimala (née Kumari) m 1970; Maj, Ind C. b 10 Dec 53. Served in Tanz.

ÅBERG, Bert (Malmö 1, 1973); Maj, Swdn. b 14 Jan 51, and
ÅBERG, Inga (née Söderstedt) (Vasakåren, 1973) m 1974; Maj, Swdn. b 15 Jul 52.

ABRAHAM, Puthenparambil T. (Karimala, Ind SW, 1972); Lt-Col, CS, Ind C. b 17 Feb 48, and
ABRAHAM, Mariyamma (Central Adoor, Ind SW, 1975) m 1975; Lt-Col, TSWM, Ind C. b 30 Mar 52. Served in Ind SW

ADAMS, Clive (Claremont, S Afr, 1983); Lt-Col, CS, Nor. b 1 May 57. BTh, and
ADAMS, Marianne (née Jokobsen) (Oslo 3, 1985) m 1985; Lt-Col, TSWM, Nor. b 2 Oct 60. Served in S Afr, UK and at IHQ.

ADAMS, Shirley Ann (Houston, TX, USA S, 1973); Maj, Mex. b 1 May 51. AS (Business Admin). Served in USA S.

ADDISON, Edward (Swedru, 1981); Maj, Gha. b 24 Jan 54. Ww Lt Margaret, pG 1983, and
ADDISON, Mercy (née Simpson) (Swedru, 1985) m 1985; Maj, Gha. b 4 Nov 60.

ADU-MANU, Mike (Jamasi, 1987); Maj, Gha. b 10 Apr 48, with
ADU-MANU, Theresa (née Asante Pinamang) m 1970; Maj, Gha. b 1 Apr 48.

AGUILERA, Luis (Concepción, 1967); Lt-Col, S Am W. b 14 Aug 47, and
AGUILERA, Maria (née Caceres Morales) (Central Santiago, 1968) m 1969; Lt-Col, S Am W. b 31 Jan 45. Served in Sp and Mex.

AGUILERA, Miguel (Lo Valledor, S Am W, 1978); Maj, L Am N. b 9 Jul 55, and
AGUILERA, Angélica (née Cortes) (Lo Valledor, S Am W, 1978) m 1979; Maj, L Am N. b 11 Sep 58. Served in S Am W and Sp.

AGUIRRE, Bartolo (Salto, 1972); Maj, S Am E. b 4 May 45, with
AGUIRRE, Violeta (née Silveira) m 1969; Maj, S Am E. b 28 Oct 48.

AHN, Guhn-shik (Oh Ka, 1985); Maj, Kor. b 23 Dec 57, and
YANG, Shin-kyong (Sudaemun, 1984) m 1985; Maj, Kor. b 5 Jul 54.

AINSWORTH, Rodney (Mitchelton, 1973); Maj, Aus E. b 26 Nov 49, and
AINSWORTH, Leonie (née Matthews) (Woonona, 1976) m 1976; Maj, Aus E. b 6 Dec 53.

Biographical Information

AJUBIGA, Cornelius Kemakolam (Umudim, 1974); Maj, Nig. b 26 Jun 48, with
AJUBIGA, Caroline m 1971; Maj, Nig. b 29 Nov 53.

AKPAN, Joseph (Calabar, 1980); Maj, Nig. b 30 Sep 58, with
AKPAN, Patience m 1978; Maj, Nig. b 15 May 62.

AKPAN, Mfon Jaktor (Igbobi, Nig, 1969); Comr, TC, Con (Braz). b 21 Jul 49, and
AKPAN, Ime Johnnie (née Udo) (Ikot Udobia, Nig, 1974) m 1974; Comr, TPWM, Con (Braz). b 9 Nov 53. Served in Nig.

ALARCÓN, David (Punta Arenas, 1980); Maj, S Am W. b 24 Jun 56, and
ALARCÓN, María (née Arredondo) (Rancagua, 1980) m 1982; Maj. S Am W. b 3 Mar 55.

ALARCÓN, Juan Carlos (Punta Arenas, 1972); Maj, S Am W. b 25 Jan 51, and
ALARCÓN, Nancy (née Muñoz) (Punta Arenas, 1971) m 1973; Maj, S Am W. b 17 Sep 52. Served in USA E.

ALHBIN, Britt Gunborg (Höganäs, Swdn, 1966); Maj, Pak. b 1 May 41. Served in Swdn and Indon.

ALIP, Romeo (Manila Central, Phil, 1978); Maj, GS, Lib. b 2 Jan 49. BSc (Architecture), and
ALIP, Evelyn (née Kilong-Kilong) (Cebu Central, Phil, 1977) m 1979; Maj, Lib. b 1 Jul 55. Served in Phil and Indon.

ALLAN, Graham (Kokomo, IN, 1975); Maj, USA C. b 24 Feb 49. BA (Counselling/Bus Admin), and
ALLAN, Vickie (née Hardebeck) (Kokomo, IN, 1975); Maj, USA C. b 26 Jan 50.

ALLEMAND, Carolyn (née Olckers) (Cape Town Citadel, S Afr, 1980); Lt-Col, USA C. b 4 Oct 55. Served in S Afr, at IHQ and in S Am E. m 1989; Lt-Col Gustave, ret 2006.

ALLEN, Jennifer (née Cotterill) (Broken Hill, 1968) m 2006; Maj, Aus E. b 7 Nov 48, and
ALLEN, Raymond (Townsville, 1964); Maj, Aus E. b 20 Dec 41. Ww Maj Dorise, pG 2005

ALLEY, Kelvin (Belconnen, 1987); Maj, Aus E. b 3 Apr 54. BA (Pub Adm), BDiv, with
ALLEY, Julie (née Stewart) m 1975; Maj, Aus E. b 17 Jun 56.

ALM, Britt-Marie (née Johansson) (Hisingskåren, Göteborg, 1970); Maj, Swdn. b 28 Dec 45.

ALMENDRAS, Eduardo Lagos (Puento Alto, S Am W, 1975); Maj, L Am N. b 3 Aug 51, with
ALMENDRAS, Dalia Rosa Porras (née Diaz) m 1974; Maj, L Am N. b 23 Dec 48. Served in S Am W and Aus S.

AMBITAN, Harold (Manado 1, 1973); Lt-Col, CS, Indon. b 9 May 49, and

AMBITAN, Deetje (née Malawau) (Bandung, 1972) m 1975; Lt-Col, TSWM, Indon. b 8 Jun 49.

AMICK, Richard (Hutchinson, KS, 1978); Maj, USA C. b 24 Nov 54. BA (Bus Admin), and
AMICK, Vicki (née Anderson) (Grand Haven, MI, 1978) m 1979; Maj, USA C. b 29 Jun 55.

AMPOFO, Jonas (Asiakwa, 1981); Maj, Gha. b 6 Oct 1950, with
AMPOFO, Constance (née Nyamekye) m 2004; Capt, Gha. b 14 Apr 57.

AMPONSAH, Samuel (Wamfie 1987); Maj, Gha. b 30 Sep 59, with
AMPONSAH, Hagar (née Kissiwa) m 1985; Maj, Gha. b 9 Jul 62. Served at IHQ.

ANZEZE, Hezekiel (Naliava, 1980); Comr, TC, Ken. b 15 Mar 49. Ww Comr Clerah, pG 2005.

APPEATENG, Seth (Manso, 1989); Maj, Gha. b 9 Jun 62, with
APPEATENG, Janet (née Nkansah) m 1987; Maj, Gha. b 12 Dec 67.

ARGUEDAS, Antonio (Callao, 1974); Maj, S Am W. b 9 Sep 53, and
ARGUEDAS, Lilian (née Sánchez) (Lima Central, 1981) m 1981; Maj, S Am W. b 24 Nov 58.

ARNOLD, Wilfred D. (Hamilton, 1973); Lt-Col, NZ. b 22 May 45. BSoc Sc, MA (Soc Work), CQSW, with
ARNOLD, Margaret Dawn (née Fitness) m 1966; Lt-Col, NZ. b 6 Jul 45. BN, RGON, Grad Dip Soc Sc. Served in Aus S and Sing.

ASPERSCHLAGER, Gary C. (Orange, NJ, 1976); Lt-Col, USA E. b 20 Apr 46. BS (Biol), MA (Div), and
ASPERSCHLAGER, Pearl A. (née Samson) (White Plains, NY, 1973) m 1976; Lt-Col, USA E. b 20 Aug 46. BA (Ed).

B

BAAH, Samuel (Duakwa, 1987); Maj, Gha. b 13 Mar 63, with
BAAH, Theresa (née Kumi) m 1984; Maj, Gha. b 10 Sep 64.

BABU, P. V. Stanly (Chevalloor, 1983); Maj, Ind SW. b 28 Nov 55, and
BABU, Nirmala (Kanniyakuzhy, 1986) m 1986; Maj, Ind SW. b 14 Mar 63.

BAHAMONDE, Cecilia (Lo Vial, 1983); Maj, S Am W. b 23 Mar 63.

BAIGORRIA, Eduardo (Córdoba, 1989); Capt, S Am E. b 2 Mar 65, and
BAIGORRIA, Andrea (née Racelis) m 1989; Capt, S Am E. b 6 Sep 69.

Biographical Information

BAILEY, Christine (Barking, 1975); Maj, UK. b 15 Apr 49. BA (Hons) (Soc Sci – Pol), PGCE. Served in S Am E.

BAILEY, Fredrick Bradford (Kansas City (Westport Temple), MO, USA C, 1982); Maj, OC, Sp. b 4 May 58. BS (Soc Wrk), with **BAILEY, Heidi Juliette** (née Chandler) m 1978; Maj, CPWM, Sp. b 17 Jul 54. Served in USA C and S Am W.

BAILIS, Abel (Chenkody, 1980); Maj, Ind SE. b 20 Feb 53, and **BAILIS, J. Abaranam** (Chadayanvillai, 1972) m 1980; Maj, Ind SE. b 23 Aug 48.

BAILLIE, Kenneth (Warren, USA E, 1966); Comr, TC, USA C. b 3 Nov 42. BA (Soc), with **BAILLIE, Joy M.** (née Gabrielsen) m 1962; Comr, TPWM, USA C. b 30 May 41. BA (Biochem). Served in Can, USA E and E Eur (OC/CPWO).

BAKEMBA, Prosper (Mabenga, 1982); Maj, Con (Braz). b 21 Oct 49, with **BAKEMBA, Monique** (née Mafoua) m 1980; Maj, Con (Braz). b 28 Jun 52.

BAKER, Gary (Nundah, 1976); Maj, Aus E. b 23 Sep 48. ThA, with **BAKER, Judith** (née Wells) m 1969; Maj, Aus E. b 3 June 49.

BAKKEN, Solfrid (née Kristensen) (Tromsø, 1971); Maj, Nor. b 11 May 52.

BAMANABIO, Eugène (Mfilou, 1990); Maj, Con (Braz). b 10 Jul 62, with **BAMANABIO, Brigitte** (née Locko Oumba) m 1988; Maj, Con (Braz). b 13 Dec 63. Served in Rw.

BAMFORD, William A. III (Quincy, MA, 1989); Maj, USA E. b 11 Jun 57. BS (Pharm), MS (Org Ldrshp), with **BAMFORD, G. Lorraine** (née Brown) m 1980; Maj, USA E. b 25 Jul 53. BA (Mod Langs).

BANFIELD, Stephen (Quincy, MA, 1978); Maj, USA E. b 17 Mar 53. BA (Psych), with **BANFIELD, Janet Mae** (née Anderson) m 1976; Maj, USA E. b 27 Apr 55.

BANKS, Keith (Wokingham, 1963); Comr, UK. b 5 Nov 42, and **BANKS, Pauline** (née Jane) (Stowmarket, 1964) m 1965; Comr, UK. b 3 Feb 44. Served in PNG (OC/CPWO), Jpn (CS/TSWO) and at IHQ (IS Int Per/Int Statistician).

BANLASAN, Ronaldo (Davao, 1990); Maj, Phil. b 21 May 61, and **BANLASAN, Theresita** (née Mangalisan) (La Paz, 1983) m 1990; Maj, Phil. b 29 Jul 59.

BARKAT, Samuel (Thal, 1973); Maj, Pak. b 7 Aug 51, with

SAMUEL, Margaret m 1971; Maj, Pak. b 7 Aug 52.

BARNARD, Rodney (Norwood, 1982); Maj, Aus S. b 7 Apr 49, with **BARNARD, Jennifer** (née Rowe) Maj, Aus S. b 5 Nov 50. Served in UK.

BARR, John M. (Ian) (Saltcoats, 1972); Maj, UK. b 10 Aug 50. BD (Hons), MA Cert Ed, and **BARR, Christine** (née Hawkins) (Newport Maindee, 1972) m 1974; Maj, UK. b 23 May 49. BSc (Hons), MA. Served at IHQ.

BARTLETT, Royston R. (Croydon Citadel, 1971); Lt-Col, UK. b 28 May 44. Dip Mgt, MCI Mgt. Served at IHQ and in Swdn (CS).

BAUTISTA, Estelita (née Baquirin) (Asingan, 1994); Capt, Phil. b 12 Nov 62. BS (Comm), and **BAUTISTA, David** (Asingan, 1996) m 1996; Capt, Phil. b 12 May 61. BSc (Industrial Ed).

BECKMAN, Elisabeth (née Sundström) (Stockholm Temple, 2006); Capt, Swdn, b 18 Jan 65.

BELL, Donald C. (Spokane, WA, 1978); Lt-Col, CS, USA W. b 12 Oct 49. BA (Econ), JD (Law), and **BELL, Debora K.** (née Perry) (Hobbs, NM, 1977) m 1979; Lt-Col, TSWM, USA W. b 6 Feb 56. Served at USA Nat.

BELL, Mark (Hagerstown, MD, 1977); Maj, USA S. b 27 Mar 51, with **BELL, Alice** (née Armendariz) m 1975; Maj, USA S. b 26 Sep 54.

BEMBHY, Carlos A. (Caballito, 1972); Maj, S Am E. b 5 Sep 51, and **BEMBHY, Isabel Ines** (née Mamchur) (Tres Arroyos, 1968) m 1973; Maj, S Am E. b 10 Jun 48.

BERG, Gro (née Egeland) (Stavanger, 1985); Maj, Nor. b 11 Oct 62, and **BERG, Pål Thomas** (Nord Odal II, 1985) m 1985; Maj, Nor. b 12 Aug 1962.

BERG, Odd (Harstad, Nor, 1969); Lt-Col, CS, Ger. b 4 Mar 47. Cand Theol, and **BERG, Grethe Karin** (née Knetten) (Nor, 1969) m 1971; Lt-Col, TSWM, Ger. b 12 May 48. Served in Nor, UK and Den.

BERNAO, Raúl (Trelew, 1983); Maj, S Am E. b 11 Oct 61, and **BERNAO, Lidia** (née Lopez) (Santiago del Estero, 1981) m 1984; Maj, S Am E. b 20 Feb 59.

BERRY, Donald E. (Kearny, NJ, 1976); Maj, USA E. b 9 Jun 49, with **BERRY, Vicki** (née Van Nort) m 1970; Maj,

USA E. b 15 Jan 50. BA (Engl), MA (Strategic Comms & Ldrshp)

BIAKLIANA, S. (Hnahthial, 1981); Maj, Ind E. b 15 Feb 56, and
BIAKMAWII (Dolchera, 1982) m 1982; Maj, Ind E. b 10 Aug 62.

BIYENGA, Nzeza Simon (Kinshasa 4, 1968); Maj, Con (Kin). b 1 Jan 46, with
BIYENGA, Emilie (née Kinduelo) m 1966; Maj, Con (Kin). b 1 Jan 50.

BLACKMAN, William (St James, Winnipeg, MB, 1973); Maj, Can. b 12 Dec 44, with
BLACKMAN, Winifred (née Deacon) m 1969; Maj, Can. b 10 Dec 45. BA.

BLOOMFIELD, Glenn (Philadelphia NE, PA, 1972); Maj, USA E. b 25 Feb 50, and
BLOOMFIELD, Carol (née Thompson) (Cleveland Temple, OH, 1971) m 1972; Maj, USA E. b 1 Jun 48.

BODE, William H. (Alliance, OH, 1970); Maj, USA E. b 6 Sep 49, and
BODE, Joan I. (née Burke) (Brooklyn 8th Ave, NY, 1969) m 1971; Maj, USA E. b 30 Aug 48.

BOLLWAHN, Paul E. (Danville, IL, USA C, 1967); Lt-Col, USA W. b 20 Aug 42. BS, MSW (Admin), ACSW, CSW, CSWM, with
BOLLWAHN, Ronda G. (née Harvey) m 1965; Lt-Col, USA W. b 6 May 44. BS, MA (Admin). Served in USA C and at USA Nat.

BOMMELI, Walter Daniel (Freienstein ZH, 1974); Maj, Switz. b 25 May 50, and
BOMMELI, Hanny (née Eugster) (Heiden, 1974) m 1975; Maj, Switz. b 11 May 49. Served in Ger.

BOND, Eric (St Catharines, ON, 1987); Maj, Can. b 24 Dec 46. BA (Teachers Cert), with
BOND, Donna (née Williams) m 1968; Maj, Can. b 10 Mar 49.

BOND, Linda (St James, Winnipeg, Can, 1968); Comr, IHQ. b 22 Jun 46. BRelig Ed, BTS. Served in UK, Can (CS) and USA W (TC).

BONE, Cilla (South Croydon, UK, 1971); Maj, Aus S. b 24 Jul 49. Served in UK, at IHQ and in Aus E.

BOOTH, Patrick (Paris-Central, 1989); Maj, Asst CS, Frce. b 12 Jan 55, with
BOOTH, Margaret (née Miaglia) m 1983; Maj, TSWM, Frce. b 31 July 61. Served in UK

BORDE, Balu Ramji (Jalgoon, 1969); Maj, Ind W. b 6 May 48, with
BORDE, Kanchanmala m 1970; Maj, Ind W. b 1 Jun 48.

BOSCHUNG, Franz (Basle 2, 1977); Lt-Col, CS, Switz. b 21 Sep 49, with
BOSCHUNG, Hanny (née Abderhalden)

m 1971; Lt-Col, TSWM, Switz. b 7 Apr 50. Served in Con (Braz).

BOSH, Larry (Mansfield, OH, 1966); Lt-Col, CS, USA E. b 9 Jun 46. BS (Acct), MBA, and
BOSH, Gillian (née Reid) (Akron Citadel, OH, 1960) m 1967; Lt-Col, TSWM, USA E. b 4 Dec 40. Served at IHQ and USA Nat (Nat CS/NSWM, NRVAVS).

BOUZIGUES, Ricardo (Colegiales, 1976); Maj, S Am E. b 12 Sep 52. MA (Practical Theol), and
BOUZIGUES, Sonia (née Alvez) (Cordoba, 1979) m 1979; Maj, S Am E. b 12 Nov 54.

BOWLES, Marsha-Jean (née Wortley) (Woodstock, ON, Can, 1990); Maj, Ger. b 2 Mar 62, with
BOWLES, David m 1981; Maj, Ger. b 20 Jul 60. Served in Can.

BRADBURY, Clifford (Southsea, 1966); Maj, UK. b 17 Aug 45, and
BRADBURY, Jean (née Curtis) (Dorchester, 1965) m 1968; Maj, UK. b 2 Feb 45.

BREKKE, Birgitte (née Nielsen) (Copenhagen Temple, Den, 1980); Col, Nor. b 17 Sep 54. SRN. Served in Den, Nor, Sri Lan, Ban (CPWO), UK, E Eur and Pakistan (TPWM). Ww Col Bo, pG 2007.

BRIDGE, Michael (Umtali, 1974); Maj, Zimb. b 4 Sep 47, and
BRIDGE, Enlettah (née Madure) (Kwekwe, 1977); Maj, Zimb. b 2 Dec 55.

BRINGANS, David (Albion, Aus E, 1970); Col, TC, Sing. b 25 May 47, with
BRINGANS, Grace (née Palmer) m 1968; Col, TPWM, Sing. b 21 Sep 46. Served in NZ, HK, Sing (GS/CSWO), Vietnam and Tai (RC/RPWM).

BRODIN, Harold F. (Aberdeen, WA, 1964); Lt-Col, USA W. b 30 May 42, with
BRODIN, Joann (née Thompson) m 1962; Lt-Col, USA W. b 13 Aug 42.

BUCKINGHAM, Lyndon (Whangarei, 1988); Maj, NZ. b 13 Feb 62, with
BUCKINGHAM, Bronwyn (née Robertson) m 1986; Maj, NZ. b 21 Jun 65. Served in Can.

BUEYA, Nsoki Joseph (Kavwaya, 1981); Maj, Con (Kin). b 12 Jul 48, with
BUEYA, Germaine (née Nkenda Mbuku) m 1978; Maj, Con (Kin). b 10 Jun 52.

BULLOCK, Mary (Hucknall, 1980); Maj, UK. b 26 Oct 46. BA(Hons) French, Dip Applied Social Studies

BURGER, Kurt (Los Angeles Congress Hall, CA, USA W, 1972); Comr, TC, Switz. b 26 Aug 46. BS (Bus Admin), BA (Psych), MBA (Bus Admin), Cert CPA, and

BURGER, Alicia (née Pedersen) (San Bernardino, CA, USA W, 1976) m 1988; Comr, TPWM, Switz. b 6 Jul 46. Served in USA W.

BURN, Margaret (née Cain) (Lincoln Citadel, 1966); Lt-Col, UK. b 12 Nov 46.

BURNS, Alan (Harlow, 1976); Maj, UK. b 1 May 54. BSc, BSc (Hons), and
BURNS, Alison (née Hitchin) (Regent Hall, 1979) m 1981; Maj, UK. b 8 Oct 52. MA (Evan) Served at IHQ.

BURR, W. Howard (Lexington, KY, 1973); Lt-Col, USA E. b 8 Nov 47. BA (Psych), MS (Ed Admin), with
BURR, Patricia (née Stigleman) m 1970; Lt-Col, USA E. b 29 Jun 51.

BURRIDGE, Keith (Ealing, UK, 1967); Lt-Col, CS, Sing. b 21 Jun 44. MBE, with
BURRIDGE, Beryl (née Brown) m 1965; Lt-Col, TSWM, Sing. b 11 Nov 44. Served in UK.

BURROWS, David J. (Skipton, UK, 1970); Lt-Col, IHQ. b 30 Apr 47. SRN, and
BURROWS, Jean A. (née List) (Ware, UK, 1970) m 1972; Lt-Col, IHQ. b 19 Mar 48. SRN, SCM. Served in Pak, Tanz (OC/CPWM) and Mal (OC/CPWM).

BURTON, Joan (Goole, UK, 1978); Maj, Brz. b 5 Jul 55. Served in UK.

C

CACHELIN, Hervé (Biel, 1979); Maj, Switz. b 16 Feb 57, and
CACHELIN, Deborah (née Cullingworth) (Catford, UK, 1981) m 1983; Maj, Switz. b 2 Jul 57. Served in Aus E and UK.

CAFFULL, Wendy (née Hart) (Southend Citadel, UK, 1976); Maj, IHQ. b 24 Mar 57, and
CAFFULL, Michael (Worthing, UK, 1977) m 1978; Maj, IHQ. b 20 Dec 55. Served in UK.

CAIRNS, Philip (Campsie, 1982); Maj, Aus E. b 5 Feb 51. Dip Mus Ed, Dip Min, MTh, with
CAIRNS, Janice (née Manson) m 1972; Maj, Aus E. b 7 Oct 48. ATCL, LTCL.

CALDWELL, Anita Maye (née Howard) (Shreveport, LA, USA S, 1993); Capt, E Eur. b 1 Dec 64 with
CALDWELL, Bradley Joseph m 1989; Capt, E Eur. b 31 Aug 64. BA (Phil). Served in USA S.

CALVO, Esteban (Concepcion de Rios, 1987); Maj, L Am N. b 23 Jan 63, and
CALVO, Ileana (née Jimenez) (Concepcion de Rios, 1986) m 1989; Maj, L Am N. b 5 Jun 66.

CAMARGO, Iolanda (Niterói, Brz, 1969), Maj, TSWM, Brz. b 6 Aug 49.

CANNING, Donald William (Miami Citadel, FL,

1974); Lt-Col, USA S. b 28 Jan 43, with
CANNING, Constance Jean (née Osborne) m 1966; Lt-Col, USA S. b 20 Sep 46.

CANNING, Joan (Moncton, NB, Can, 1983); Maj, IHQ. b 27 Sep 62. BA (Bib and Theol Studies). Served in Can.

CAREY, Roderick (Dunedin Fortress, 1982); Maj, NZ. b 13 Mar 58, with
CAREY, Jennifer (née Cross) m 1980; Maj, NZ. b 5 Feb 61. Served Aust E.

CARLSON, William (Staten Island Port Richmond, NY, 1971); Lt-Col, USA E. b 9 Jan 48. BA (Soc Studies), and
CARLSON, Marcella (née Brewer) (Staten Island Port Richmond, NY, 1971) m 1971; Lt-Col, USA E. b 18 Sep 49.

CASTILLO, Luis (Antofagasta, S Am W, 1977); Lt-Col, CS, S Am E. b 7 Jan 48, and
CASTILLO, Aída (Quinta Normal, 1968) m 1972; Lt-Col, TSWM, S Am E. b 5 Nov 49. Served in S Am W (CS/TSWM) and Mex (CS/TSWM).

CASTOR, Onal (Aquin, Carib, 1979); Lt-Col, CS, Con (Kin). b 20 Jul 55, and
CASTOR, Edmane (née Montoban) (Duverger, Carib, 1980) m 1980; Lt-Col, TSWM, Con (Kin). b 1 Oct 57. Served in Carib and USA S.

CEREZO, Josué (Monterrey, 1985); Maj, CS, Mex. b 16 May 57. BS, with
CEREZO, Ruth (née Garcia) m 1983. Maj, TSWM, Mex. b 22 Oct 60. BA SocWk. Served in L Am N.

CHACKO, K. P. (Cherukole East, 1979); Maj, Ind SW. b 17 Apr 49. BA, with
CHACKO, Suseela (née Achamma) m 1974; Maj, Ind SW. b 22 Apr 47. BA.

CHAGAS, Edgar (São Paulo Central, 1988); Maj, Brz. b 24 Feb 58. BA (Phys) MA (Science), with
CHAGAS, Sara (née Parker) m 1982; Maj, Brz. b 26 Aug 60. BA (Psychol).

CHALWE, Frazer (Chikumbi, 1989); Maj, Zam. b 25 Jan 65, with
CHALWE, Rodinah (née Mukunkami) m 1986; Maj, Zam. b 8 May 68.

CHAMP, James (Chatham, ON, 1975); Maj, Can. b 29 Mar 52. BRE, and
CHAMP, Barbara (née Allington) (Earlscourt, ON, 1975) m 1976; Maj, Can. b 26 Jul 47. Served in UK.

CHANDRASIRI, Sarukkalige (Gonapinuwela, 1980); Maj, Sri Lan, b 9 Sep 53, and
CHANDRASIRI, Rohini (née Horathalge) (Siyambalangamuwa, 1968) m 1979; Maj, Sri Lan. b 7 Oct 50.

CHANG, Man-Hee (San Francisco Korean, CA,

Biographical Information

1993); Capt, USA W. b 31 Mar 58. BA (Bus Admin), MBA (Bus Admin), with
CHANG, Stephanie (née Shim) m 1983; Capt, USA W. b 1 Jun 59. BA (Math).

CHARAN, Samuel (Rampur, Ind N, 1978); Lt-Col, CS, Ind E. b 1 Apr 53, with
CHARAN, Bimla Wati (née Bimla Wati) m 1974; Lt-Col, TSWM, Ind E. Served in Ind N.

CHARLET, Horst (Berlin-Neukölln, 1969); Col, TC, Ger. b 1 May 46. Dip SW, Dip Soc Pedagogue, with
CHARLET, Helga (née Werner); Col, TPWM, Ger. b 18 Oct 48. Served in Ger (CS/TSWM)

CHAUHAN, Jashwant Soma (Tarapur, 1979); Maj, Ind W. b 20 Feb 52, with
CHAUHAN, Indiraben m 1976; Maj, Ind W. b 8 Jun 56.

CHAWNGHLUNA (Sawleng, 1983); Maj, Ind E. b 13 Apr 1959, and
K. LALCHHUANMAWII (Bethlehem, 1986) m 1986; Maj, Ind E. b 14 Jun 1965.

CHENDA, Joster (Matero, 1981); Maj, Zam. b 10 Jun 57, and
CHENDA, Christine (née Chingala) (Libala, 1983) m 1983; Maj, Zam. b 3 Mar 62.

CHEPKURUI, Stephen (Cheptais, Ken, 1982); Maj, RC, Rw. b 22 Feb 58, and
CHEPKURUI, Grace (née Madolio) (Vigeze, Ken, 1980) m 1985; Maj, CSWM, Tanz. b 15 May 55. Served in E Afr and Tanz (GS/CSWM, .

CHEYDLEUR, John Reeves (Philadelphia Northeast, PA, 1983); Maj, USA E. b 11 Mar 44. BA (Psych), MA (Counselling/ Psych), PhD (Org Psych), with
CHEYDLEUR, Judith Ann (née Kunkle) m 1965; Maj, USA E. b 27 Jul 39. BA (Psych/ Soc), MA (Writing).

CHIGARIRO, Vinece (Gunguwe, Zimb, 1975); Comr, TC, Zam. b 7 Mar 54. Served in Zimb and Tanz (GS).

CHIGWAZA, Nicholas (Harare Citadel, 1970); Maj, Zimb. b 9 Feb 48. DipSW, and
CHIGWAZA, Tendai (née M'loyie) (Tadzembwa, 1975) m 1975; Maj, Zimb. b 5 Sep 55.

CHILYABANYAMA, Metson (Chitumbi, 1987); Maj, Zam. b 30 Oct 55, with
CHILYABANYAMA, Rosemary (née Mboozi) m 1982; Maj, Zam. b 8 Aug 61.

CHINYEMBA, Casman (Chimbumu, 1989); Maj, Zimb. b 7 Jan 62, with
CHINYEMBA, Martha (née Gomo) m 1988; Maj, Zimb. b 16 Oct 63. Served in Tanz.

CHISENGELE, Bernard (Monze, 1983); Maj, Zam. b 1 Jan 51, and

CHISENGELE, Dorothy (née Mweemba) (Kaumba, 1985) m 1985; Maj, Zam. b 14 Nov 59.

CHISHOLM, Lindsay (Timaru, 1980); Maj, NZ. b 2 Jan 45, with
CHISHOLM, Raewyn (née Smith) m 1967; Maj, NZ. b 29 Sep 47.

CHITANDA, Sheila (née Mvere) (Kwekwe, 1992); Capt, Zimb. b 15 Oct 68, and
CHITANDA, Henry (Chinhoyi, 1991) m 1992; Maj, Zimb. b 6 Apr 66.

CHOO, Seung-chan (Yung Deung Po, 1980); Maj, Kor. b 15 Jun 50, with
LEE, Ok-hee m 1978; Maj, Kor. b 2 Aug 54.

CHOPDE, Surendra S. (Kodoli, 1992); Maj, Ind W. b 2 Sep 65, with
CHOPDE, Helen m 1989; Maj, Ind W. b 1 Jun 64.

CHRISTIAN, Gabriel Ibrahim (Muktipur, 1983); Maj, Ind W. b 24 Dec 59, and
CHRISTIAN, Indumati (née Samual Macwan) (Petlad Central, 1985) m 1986; Maj, Ind W. b 30 Aug 62.

CHRISTIAN, Paul Peter (Bhalej, Ind W, 1978); Lt-Col, CS, Ind N. b 22 Sep 48, and
CHRISTIAN, Anandiben (née Kalidas) (Ghoghawada, Ind W, 1980) m 1980; Lt-Col, TSWM, Ind N. b 12 Jul 57. Served at Ind Cent Off and in Ind W (CS/THLS).

CHRISTIAN, Prabhudas Jetha (Sinhuj, 1978); Maj, Ind W. b 23 Jan 52, and
CHRISTIAN, Persis (née Zumal) (Jhalod, 1978) m 1978; Maj, Ind W. b 5 Apr 48.

CHRISTURAJ, Rajamani (Elappara, 1983); Maj, Ind SW. b 27 Dec 61, with
MATHEW, Mary m 1983; Maj, Ind SW. b 11 May 59.

CHRISTIAN, Rasik Paul (Chunel, 1988); Maj, Ind W. b 7 Sep 65, and
CHRISTIAN Ramilaben (née Samuel) (Piplag, 1990) m 1990; Maj, Ind W. b 17 Apr 68.

CHUN, Joon-hung (Yong Dong, 1978); Maj, Kor. b 20 Jun 48, with
SHIN, Myung-ja m 1976; Maj, Kor. b 28 Sep 49.

CHUN, Kwang-Pyo (Duk Am, 1971); Comr, TC, Kor. b 15 Sep 41, with
YOO, Sung-Ja m 1969; Comr, TPWM, Kor. b 11 Jan 41.

CLIFTON, Shaw (Edmonton, UK, 1973); General (see page 26), with
CLIFTON, Helen (née Ashman) m 1967; Comr, World President of Women's Ministries, IHQ. b 4 May 48. BA (Eng Lang/Lit) (Hons), PGCE. Served at IHQ, in Zimb, USA E, Pak (TC/TPWO), NZ (TC/TPWM) and UK (TC/TPWM).

297

CLINCH, Ronald (Launceston, 1986); Maj, Aus S. b 6 Sep 54, with
CLINCH Robyn (née Mole) m 1982; Maj, Aus S. b 8 Nov 60.

COCHRANE, William (Barrhead, 1975); Lt-Col, CS, UK. b 7 Sep 54.

COCKER, James (Cleveland Temple, USA E, 1981); Maj, PNG. b 24 Jan 53, with
COCKER, Marcia (née Kelly) m 1978; Maj, PNG. b 21 Sep 58. Served in USA E.

COLE, Joan (Limón, 1995); Capt, L Am N. b 8 May 70.

CONDON, James (Shoalhaven, Aus E, 1971); Lt-Col, CS, PNG. b 29 Nov 49, and
CONDON, Jan (née Vickery) (Uralla, Aus E, 1971) m 1972; Lt-Col, TSWM, PNG. b 27 Jan 47. Served in Aus E and UK.

COPPLE, Donald (Flin Flon, MB, 1963); Lt-Col, Can. b 10 Apr 42, and
COPPLE, Ann (née Cairns) (Pt St Charles, QC, 1962) m 1965; Lt-Col, Can. b 15 Jul 42.

COTTERILL, Anthony (Regent Hall, 1984); Maj, UK. b 9 Dec 57. BA (Hons), with
COTTERILL, Gillian (née Rushforth) m 1979; Maj, UK. b 15 Sep 57. SRN.

COURT, Stephen (Etobicoke Temple, Can, 1994); Capt, Aus S. b 28 Feb 66, and
STRICKLAND, Danielle (Brampton, Can, 1995) m 1995; Capt, Aus S. b 14 Sep 72. Served in Can.

COWLING, Alison (Macleans, Aus E, 1978); Maj, IHQ. b 10 Feb 50. Served in Aus E.

COX, André (Geneva 1, Switz, 1979); Col, TC, Fin. b 12 Jul 54, with
COX, Silvia (née Volet) m 1976; Col, TPWM, Fin. b 18 Nov 55. Served in Switz and Zimb.

CRABSON, William L. (Baltimore Temple, MD, 1965); Lt-Col, USA S. b 27 Sep 42, with
CRABSON, LaVerne Jeanette (née Doyle) m 1962; Lt-Col, USA S. b 20 Apr 42.

D

DADDOW, Allan (Adelaide Congress Hall, 1978); Maj, Aus S. b 4 Jan 44, with
DADDOW, Lorraine (née Andrew) m 1965; Maj, Aus S. b 21 Sep 45.

DALBERG, Theodore J. (Omaha Citadel, NE, 1967); Lt-Col, USA C. b 9 Feb 42, with
DALBERG, Nancy (née Foubister) m 1963; Lt-Col, USA C. b 16 Jul 44.

DALI, Peter (Ebushibungo, Ken, 1978); Lt-Col, CS, Zim. b 2 Mar 52, and
DALI, Jessica (née Kavere) (Masigolo, Ken, 1978) m 1979; Lt-Col, TSWM, Zim.

b 25 Dec 55. Served in Ken, Tanz, at IHQ and in Gha (CS/TSWM).

DALY, Gordon (Wellington South, 1977); Maj, NZ. b 5 Mar 54, and
DALY, Susan (née Crump) (Te Aroha, 1976) m 1977; Maj, NZ. b 22 Oct 54. Served in Carib and S Am W.

DAMOR, Nicolas Maganlal (Jalpa, 1979); Maj, Ind W. b 1 Jun 55, and
DAMOR, Flora (née David) (Dilsar, 1980) m 1980; Maj, Ind W. b 26 Apr 58.

DANIEL, Edward (Meesalai, 1977); Lt-Col, CS, Sri Lan. b 18 Mar 56, and
DANIEL, Lalitha (née Ranchagodage) (Colombo Central, 1981) m 1981; Lt-Col, TSWM, Sri Lan. b 1 Oct 53.

DANIELS, Frank (Katanning, 1967); Maj, Aus S. b 10 Apr 47, and
DANIELS, Yvonne (née Knapp) (Melbourne City Temple, 1972) m 1972; Maj, Aus S. b 4 Oct 47.

DANIELSON, Douglas (El Paso, TX, USA W, 1987); Maj, Mex. b 19 Aug 58. BSc (Computer Sci), MA (Missiology), with
DANIELSON, Rhode (née Doria) m 1983; Maj, Mex. b 29 Jul 59. BSEd, MA (Maths). Served in USA W, S Am E, Carib and L Am N (CS/TSWM).

DANSO, Isaac (Asene, 1991); Maj, Gha. b 22 Feb 1960, with
DANSO, Eva (née Amoah) m 1988; Maj, Gha. b 1 Jul 61.

DAS, Sabita (Angul 1974); Maj, Ind N. b 1 Jan 53, with
DAS, Samuel m 1971; Maj, Ind N. b 22 Oct 51

DASARI, John Kumar (Pathamupparru, 1991); Maj, Ind C. b 7 Jan 61, with
DASARI, Mani Kumari m 1986; Maj, Ind C. b 3 May 66. BTh, MA.

DAVID, K. C. (Puthuchira, Ind SW, 1978); Maj, Ind Nat. b 5 Jan 53. BA, and
DAVID, Gracy (née Marykutty) (Thevalapuram, Ind SW, 1981) m 1981; Maj, Ind Nat. b 12 Nov 55. Served in Ind SW.

DAVIS, Trevor (Northampton Central, 1966); Lt-Col, UK. b 20 May 44. FTCL. Served in NZ and at IHQ. m 1968; Lt-Col Margaret, ret 2006.

DAWNGLIANA, C. (Chhilngchip, 1981); Maj, Ind E. b 1 Oct 55, and
MANTHANGI, H. (Champhai, 1982) m 1982; Maj, Ind E. b 20 Sep 61.

DEFIBAUGH, Sandra (Staunton, VA, USA S, 1978); Maj, USA Nat. b 19 Jan 51. Served in USA S.

Biographical Information

DEN HOLLANDER, Johannes A. (Treebeek, 1990); Capt, Neth. b 21 Nov 56, with
DEN HOLLANDER, Annetje C. (née Poppema) m 1978; Capt, Neth. b 4 May 57.

DE SÁ, Tomas (Suzano, 1972); Lt-Col, Brz. b 30 Nov 50, and
DE SÁ, Rute (née Almeida) (Alegrete, 1971) m 1975; Lt-Col, Brz. b 27 Nov 50. Served in USA C and Port (OC/CPWO).

DEVARAPALLI, Jayapaul (M. R. Nagaram, Ind C, 1974); Col, TC, Ind E. b 25 Dec 47. MA, BTS, Hon DD, with
DEVARAPALLI, Yesudayamma m 1971; Col, TPWM, Ind E. b 21 Nov 54. Served in Ind C.

DEVASUNDARAM, Samuel Raj (Vadasery, 1974); Maj, Ind SE. b 21 Sep 54, and
DEVASUNDARAM, Kanagamony (Brahmapuram, 1978) m 1978; Maj, Ind SE. b 5 Feb 52.

DIANDAGA, Frédéric (Nzoko, 1988); Maj, Con (Braz). b 26 May 55, and
DIANDAGA, Claudia (née Bayekoula) (Ouenze, 1990) m 1990; Capt, Con (Braz). b 29 Oct 66.

DIANTEZULWA, Makani Sébastien (Kingudi, 1977); Maj, Con (Kin). b 16 Apr 48, with
DIANTEZULWA, Martine (née Diatubaka Nyambudi) m 1975; Maj, Con (Kin). b 1 Nov 56.

DIKALEMBOLOVANGA, Eugène Nsona Lendo (Matadi, 1983); Maj, Con (Kin). b 30 Apr 52. BMgmt & Econ Sci, with
DIKALEMBOLOVANGA, Odile Nzuzi Simbi (née Simbi Luasa) m 1980; Maj, Con (Kin). b 2 Mar 58. Served at IHQ (SALT Afr).

DIXON, Robert (Philadelphia Germantown, USA E, 1981); Maj, OC, Lib. b 20 Mar 49, with
DIXON, Hester (née Burgess) m 1967; Maj, CPWM, Lib. b 20 Nov 49. Served in USA E.

DOLIBER, Robert (Champaign, IL, 1978); Maj, USA C. b 15 Jul 54, BS (Bus Adm), MBA, and
DOLIBER, Rae (née Briggs) (Champaign, IL, 1982); Maj, USA C. b 5 Jun 58.

DONALDSON, Robert (Dunedin South 1987); Maj, NZ. b 8 Jul 61. BSc, LTh, with
DONALDSON, Janine (née Hamilton) m 1983, Maj, NZ. b 23 Sep 62. Served in Zam.

DONZÉ, Jacques (St. Aubin, 1988); Maj, Switz. b 16 Feb 64, with
DONZÉ, Claude-Evelyne (née Roth) m 1983; Maj, Switz. b 5 Feb 63. Served in Belg.

DOWNER, Gillian (Great Yarmouth, UK, 1977); Lt-Col, IHQ. b 18 Mar 54. Served in UK, Phil, Vietnam, HK, Tai and Sing (GS and CS).

DREW, Marion (Boscombe, 1979); Maj, UK. b 12 Jan 49. BA (French & Law) Dip Inst Linguists. Served at ICO.

DUCHÊNE, Alain (Paris Montparnasse, 1971); Col, TC, Frce. b 1 Jan 45. Served at ESFOT and in Frce (CS). m 1972; Lt-Col Suzette, ret 2002.

DULA, Sangthang T. (Diakkawn 1986); Maj, Ind E. b 2 Jul 63. B Th, MA (Mission), MTh (Missiology), DMiss, with
MALSAWMI m 1984; Maj, Ind E. b 10 Jun 59.

DUNSTER, Robin (Dulwich Hill Temple, Aus E, 1970); Comr, CoS, IHQ. b 12 Jan 44. SRN, SCM, RPN, RMN, IPPF (Ed). Served in Aus E, Zimb (CS), Con (Kin) (TC, TPWO) and Phil (TC, TPWM).

DURSTON, Graham (Maryborough, Aus E, 1970); Lt-Col, CS, Phil. b 12 Nov 43. BDiv (Hons), MTh, Grad Cert Management (AGSM) with
DURSTON, Rhondda (née Rees) m 1966; Lt-Col, TSWM, Phil. b 11 Dec 45. L Th (MCD), B Admin Lead (UNE). Served in Aus E and Aus S.

DYALL, John (Regent Hall, UK, 1978); Lt-Col, IHQ. b 6 Jun 42. Served in UK, Thailand, Zam, HK, Hun and Pak (CS).

E

EDGAR, Samuel (Londonderry 1969); Maj, UK. b 26 Feb 49. Served in Ger.

EGGER, Paulette (Vallorbe, 1977); Maj, Switz. b 22 Nov 55.

ELIASEN, Anna Riitta (née Hamalainen) (Erie Central, PA, 1967); Lt-Col, USA E. b 11 Aug 45. BA (Org Mgmt). Ww Lt-Col Samuel E., pG 1997. Served in UK, Brz, S Am E, Sp and Fin (CS).

ELIASEN, Torben (Bosque, 1983); Lt-Col, CS, Brz. b 28 Nov 60, and
ELIASEN, Deise Calor (née de Souza) (Rio Comprido, 1985) m 1985; Lt-Col, Brz. b 22 Feb 66. BA (Journalism).

EMMANUEL, Muthu Yesudhason (Neduvaazhy, Ind SE, 1974); Col, TC, Ind C. b 8 May 51, and
REGINA, Chandra Bai (Valliyoor, Ind SE, 1978) m 1978; Col, TPWM, Ind C. b 3 Mar 55. Served in Ind SE, Ind N (CS/TSWM) and Ind E (TC/TPWM).

EMMANUEL, Walter (Green Town, 1983); Maj, Pak. b 7 Jul 57, with
EMMANUEL, Mussaraf (née Ullah) m 1981; Maj, Pak. b 1 Dec 65.

ESSIEN, Edet (Ikot Ebo, 1974); Maj, Nig. b 28 Apr 48, with

ESSIEN, Comfort Maj, Nig. b 25 Mar 53.

EXANTUS, Vilo (Arcahaie, Haiti, 1984) Maj, Carib. b 12 May 57, and
EXANTUS, Yvrose (née Benjamin) (Arcahaie, Haiti, 1985) m 1986; Maj, Carib. b 17 Jan 58. Served in LAN.

EXBRAYAT, Christian (Le Chambon s/Lignon, Frce, 1968); Maj, OC, Belg. b 11 Oct 46, and
EXBRAYAT, Joëlle (née Welleman) (Lille, Frce, 1972) m 1973; Maj, CPWM, Belg. b 27 Jul 48. Served in Frce.

EZEKWERE, Chika Boniface (Umuchu, 1978); Maj, Nig. b 1 Jan 49, with
EZEKWERE, Virginia Ete m 1976; Maj, Nig. b 1 Jan 54.

F

FALIN, John (Albany, GA, USA S, 1966); Lt-Col, USA Nat. b 9 Apr 42. AS (Bus Admin), BA, BS (Psych), and
FALIN, Judy (née Pegram) (Greensboro, NC, USA S, 1966) m 1967; Lt-Col, USA Nat. b 5 Jan 45. Served in USA S.

FARTHING, Peter (Dundas Outpost, 1978); Maj, Aus E. b 8 Mar 51. BSoc Studies (Hons), DMin, and
FARTHING, Kerrie (née Gale) (Wollongong, 1978) m 1978; Maj, Aus E. b 31 Aug 52. Served at IHQ.

FAULKNER, Donald S. (Norfolk, VA, 1977); Lt-Col, USA S. b 12 Jan 43. BSc, with
FAULKNER, Marian L. (née Horstemeyer) m 1965; Lt-Col, USA S. b 21 Feb 44.

FEENER, Maxwell (Port Leamington, NF, Can, 1966); Comr, TC, USA S. b 5 Jul 45, with
FEENER, Lenora (née Tippett) m 1967; Comr, TPWM, USA S. b 26 Dec 45. Served in Can, S Afr (CS/TSWM) and USA S (CS/TSWM).

FERGUSON, Lester (Nassau, Bahamas, 1988); Maj, Carib. b 1 Sep 65. BA (Bib and Theol), MA (Christian Ed), and
FERGUSON, Beverely (née Armstrong) (Bridgetown Central, Barbados, 1999) m 1999; Capt, Carib. b 12 Dec 64.

FERNANDEZ, Odilio (Diezmero, 1996); Capt, L Am N. b 8 Aug 63, with
FERNANDEZ, Ivis (née Diaz) m 1987; Capt, L Am N. b 7 May 70.

FERNANDEZ, Ricardo J. (Caparra Temple, PR, 1996); Capt, USA E. b 3 Jun 60, with
FERNANDEZ, Mirtha N. (née Benitez) m 1979; Capt, USA E. b 4 Jan 57.

FERNANDO, P. Anthony (Moratumulla, 1975); Maj, Sri Lan. b 5 Oct 47, with
FERNANDO, Freeda Esther (née Fernando)

m 1971; Maj, Sri Lan. b 7 Feb 53.

FERREIRA, Jorge (Cordoba, S Am E, 1972); Col, TC, S Am W. b 24 Jun 53, and
FERREIRA, Adelina (née Solorza) (Lauis, S Am E, 1974) m 1979; Col, TPWM, S Am W. b 19 Sep 55. Served in S Am E (CS/TSWM) and L Am N (TC/TPWM).

FINCHAM, Melvin (Croydon Citadel, 1981); Maj, UK. b 20 May 56, and
FINCHAM, Suzanne (née Kenny) (Stockport Citadel, 1981) m 1981; Maj, UK. b 19 Jan 59.

FINGER, Raymond (Hawthorn, 1974); Lt-Col, CS, Aus S. b 11 Jul 51, and
FINGER, Aylene (née Rinaldi) (Maylands, 1974) m 1976; Lt-Col, TSWM, Aus S. b 17 Apr 53.

FLINTOFF, Ethne (Dunedin North, NZ, 1971); Lt-Col, OC, Ban. b 11 Nov 46. RN, RM. Served in NZ, Ind W, Ind N and Pak.

FLORES, Eliseo (Cochabamba, 1977); Maj, S Am W. b 28 Jul 56, and
FLORES, Remedios (née Gutiérrez) (Oruro, 1977) m 1978; Maj, S Am W. b 6 Apr 55.

FLORES, Myline Joy (Lebe, 1988); Maj, Phil. b 2 May 63. BMin.

FOREMAN, Ronald (Concord, NH, USA E, 1978); Maj, USA Nat. b 17 Sep 1952. BA (Sociology), MSW Social Work, with
FOREMAN, Dorine (née Long); m 1972; Maj, USA Nat. b 6 Apr 1955. BSW Social Work, MSW Social Work. Served in USA E.

FORSTER, Malcolm (St Helier, UK, 1971); Lt-Col, S Afr. b 26 Mar 51, and
FORSTER, Valerie (née Jupp) (Croydon Citadel, UK, 1978) m 1979; Lt-Col, S Afr. b 5 Jun 55. Served in UK, at IHQ, in Zam & Mal, Gha & Lib, Mal (OC/CPWM) and Tanz (OC/CPWM).

FORSYTH, Robin W. (Edinburgh Gorgie, UK, 1968); Col, CS, NZ. b 30 Aug 46, with
FORSYTH, Shona (née Leslie) m 1966; Col, TSWM, NZ. b 25 Mar 48. Served in Aus S, Mex, UK and L Am N (TC/TPWM).

FOSEN, Jan Peder (Haugesund, 1976); Maj, Nor. b 18 Nov 55, and
FOSEN, Birgit (née Taarnesvik) (Trondheim, 1981) m 1979; Maj, Nor. b 27 Aug 1949.

FRANCIS, William (Paterson, NJ, USA E, 1973); Comr, TC, Can. b 5 Mar 44. BA (Mus/Hist), MDiv, Hon DD, with
FRANCIS, Marilyn (née Burroughs) m 1965; Comr, TPWM, Can. b 3 Feb 43. BA (Mus), MA. Served in USA E (CS/TSWM) and at IHQ (IS/SWM Am and Carib).

FRANS, Roy (Surabaya, Indon, 1977); Comr, TC, Neth. b 30 Oct 50, and

Biographical Information

FRANS, Arda (née Haurissa) (Jakarta 1, Indon, 1978) m 1978; Comr, TPWM, Neth. b 10 May 44. Served in Indon, Aus E, Sing, Ban, Sri Lan (TC/TPWM) and at IHQ (IS/SWM SPEA).

FREDERIKSEN, Miriam (née Larsson) (Paris Central, Frce, 1962); Lt-Col, IHQ. b 15 May 43. Served in Den and Nor (CS).

FRIEDL, Jörg (Munich, 1994); Capt, Ger. b 4 Jun 60. Dip SW, Dip Soc Pedagogue, with **FRIEDL, Susann** (née Harm) m 1982; Capt, Ger. b 25 Jul 62.

FRISK, Kristina M. (née Larsson) (Örebro 1, 1965); Lt-Col, CS, Swdn. b 22 May 45. m 1977; Lt-Col Anders, ret 2004.

G

GAIKWAD, Benjamin Yacob (Bodhegaon, 1974); Maj, Ind W. b 3 Oct 48, and **GAIKWAD, Sudina P.** (née Makasare) (Bodhegaon, 1975) m 1975; Maj, Ind W. b 23 Oct 57.

GAITHER, Israel L. (New Castle, PA, USA E, 1964); Comr, Nat Comm, USA Nat. b 27 Oct 44. Hon LHD, and **GAITHER, Eva D.** (née Shue) (Sydney, OH, USA E, 1964) m 1967; Comr, NPWM, USA Nat. b 9 Sep 43. Served in USA E (CS/TSWO), S Afr (TC/ TPWO), USA E (TC/TPWM) and at IHQ (CoS/WSWM).

GALVÁN, Guadalupe (Savo Loredo, 1975); Maj, Mex; b 28 Mar 51. Served in USA S and L Am N.

GARCÍA, Ángela (née Sanguinetti) (Lima, Perú, 1982); Maj, S Am W. b 15 Oct 1953, and **GARCÍA, Victor** (Trujillo, Perú, 1982) m 1983; Maj, S Am W. b 21 Jan 1955. Served in USA C and L Am N.

GARCÍA, Humberto (Monterrey, 1990); Maj, Mex. b 19 Jan 57. LLM, with **GARCÍA, Leticia** (née Castañeda) m 1981; Maj, Mex. b 9 Mar 59. BA (Primary Ed).

GENABE, Alexander (Cebu, 1981); Maj, Phil. b 27 Mar 1958, and **GENABE, Jocelyn** (née Willy) (Baguio 1993) m 1993; Maj, Phil. b 10 Feb 60. BSN, BSSW.

GEORGE, N. J. (Moncotta, 1978); Maj, Ind SW. b 24 Dec 51, with **GEORGE , Ruth M. C.** m 1979, Maj, Ind SW. b 23 Apr 48.

GEORGE, N. S. (Vayala-Adoor, 1980); Maj, Ind SW. b 19 Mar 50, and **GEORGE, A. Annamma** m 1983; Maj, Ind SW.

GHULAM, Yusaf (Shantinagar, 1975); Lt-Col, CS, Pak. b 4 Jan 55, and

GHULAM, Rebecca (née Charn Masih) (Shantinagar, 1975) m 1976; Lt-Col, TSWM, Pak. b 6 May 56.

GJERULDSEN, Frank (Brevik, 1981); Maj, Nor. b 21 Jan 58, and **GJERULDSEN, Tone** (née Olsen) (Templet, Oslo, 1984) m 1983; Maj, Nor. b 11 Feb 1959.

GONZALEZ, Henry (Orange, TX, 1967); Maj, USA S. b 18 Aug 46. BS (Sociol), and **GONZALEZ, Mary Dorris** (née McCollum) (Meridian, MS, 1967) m 1969; Maj, USA S. b 13 Sep 48.

GOODIER, William (Washington Southeast, DC, 1969); Lt-Col, USA S. b 27 Feb 42, with **GOODIER, Mary Lee** (née Cunningham) m 1963; Lt-Col, USA S. b 10 Jan 42. Served in Carib.

GOWER, Ross Richardson (Christchurch City, 1980); Maj, NZ. b 15 Dec 50, with **GOWER, Annette Veronica** (née Knight) m 1972; Maj, NZ. Served in UK.

GRAHAM, Keith Livingston (Bluefields, Jamaica, 1967); Maj, Carib. b 23 Dec 47, and **GRAHAM, Molvie** (née James) (St John's, Antigua, 1968) m 1970; Maj, Carib. b 13 Dec 46.

GREEN, Lynette (née Marion) (Bendigo, Aus S, 1965); Lt-Col, Aus E. b 30 Mar 44. Ww Maj Frederick, pG 1998. Served in Aus S, E Afr and Port (OC).

GRIFFIN, Stanley (St John's, Antigua, 1979); Maj, Carib. b 20 Feb 54, and **GRIFFIN, Hazel** (née Whyte) (St John's, Antigua, 1980) m 1981; Maj, Carib. b 23 Sep 57. Served in L Am N.

GRIFFIN, Terry W. (Seattle Temple, WA, USA W, 1970); Lt-Col, CS, USA S. b 2 Nov 46. BA (Bib Lit), MA (Relig), with **GRIFFIN, Linda** (née Bawden) m 1967; Lt-Col, TSWM, USA S. b 28 Aug 46. Served in USA W.

GRINDLE, David E. (Detroit Brightmoor, MI, 1966); Lt-Col, USA C. b 5 Mar 44, with **GRINDLE, Sherry** (née McNabb) m 1964; Lt-Col, USA C. b 25 Jul 45.

GYIMAH, William (Wiamoase, 1976); Lt-Col, CS, Gha. b 31 Dec 47, with **GYIMAH, Mary** (née Pokuaa) m 1974; Lt-Col, TSWM, Gha. b 14 Aug 48. Served in Gha & Lib.

H

HAMILTON, Ian E. (Clayton, 1971); Lt-Col, Aus E. b 8 Jun 47, with **HAMILTON, Marilyn** (née Rawiller) m 1968; Lt-Col, Aus E. b 6 Aug 48. Served in Aus S.

HANGOMA, Donald (Munali, 1995); Capt, Zam. b 15 Jan 70, and
HANGOMA, Patricia (née Michelo) (1993); Capt, Zam. b 19 Mar 70.

HANUNKA, Bislon (Chibbuku, 1985); Maj, Zam. b 10 Jun 58, with
HANUNKA, Melody m 1979; Maj, Zam. b 15 Dec 62.

HARFOOT, William (Detroit Brightmoor, MI, 1977); Lt-Col, USA C. b 6 Sep 48. BS, MA, with
HARFOOT, Susan (née Stange) m 1969; Lt-Col, USA C. b 21 Oct 48. Associate of Arts.

HARITA, Naoko (Shibuya, 1968); Maj, Jpn. b 19 Jul 43. BA (Sociol).

HARMS, Bennie (Johannesburg City, 1974); Maj, S Afr. b 15 Apr 52, with
HARMS, Jennifer (née Hall) m 1972; Maj, S Afr. b 21 Oct 48. Served in Zimb.

HARRIS, Ian W. (Penge, 1989); Maj, UK. b 1 Sep 56. MA, Dip Soc Work, with
HARRIS, Jean (née Foster) m 1979; Maj, UK. b 31 Jul 56.

HARTVEIT, Jørg Walter (Langesund, 1971); Lt-Col, Nor. b 22 Jun 47. m 1971; Lt-Col Rigmor, ret 2006.

HAUGHTON, Devon (Port Antonio, Jamaica, 1981); Maj, Carib. b 22 Jul 59, and
HAUGHTON, Verona Beverly (née Henry) (Havendale, Jamaica, 1976) m 1982; Maj, Carib. b 15 Apr 54. BA (Guidance and Counselling).

HEATWOLE, Merle D. (Milwaukee Citadel, WI, 1984); Maj, USA C. b 7 Jan 60. BS (Maths), with
HEATWOLE, Dawn Idell (née Lewis) m 1981; Maj, USA C. b 26 Nov 62.

HEDGREN, R. Steven (Chicago Mont Clare, IL, 1978); Maj, USA S. b 7 Mar 50. BS (Bus Admin), with
HEDGREN, Judith Ann (née White) m 1975; Maj, USA S. b 14 Feb 49. Served in USA C.

HEELEY, William (Rock Ferry, 1974); Maj, UK. b 6 May 48, and
HEELEY, Gillian (née Lacey) (Rock Ferry, 1975) m 1975; Maj, UK. b 18 Apr 52.

HEGGELUND, Brith-Mari (Harstad, 1972); Maj, Nor. b 22 Jul 49.

HENNE, Ingrid Elisabeth (Bergen 1, 1982); Maj, Nor. b 6 Sep 52.

HERRERA, Jaime (Hualpencillo, Chile, 1981); Maj, S Am W; b 27 Jul 59, and
HERRERA, Zaida (née Lopizic) (Santiago Central, Chile, 1983) m 1983; Maj, S Am W; b 12 Feb 58. Served in Braz.

HERRING, Alistair Chapman (Wellington City,

NZ, 1975); Lt-Col, CS, E Eur. b 4 Mar 51. DipSW, with
HERRING, Verna Astrid (née Weggery) m 1971; Lt-Col, E Eur. b 29 Oct 51. Served in NZ

HETTIARACHCHI, Nihal (Colombo, 1985); Maj, Sri Lan. b 20 Jun 64, and
HETTIARACHCHI, Rohini Swarnalatha (née Wettamuni) (Colombo Central, 1994) m 1994; Capt, Sri Lan. b 18 Oct 64.

HIGHTON, Michael (Hinckley, 1985); Maj, UK. b 27 May 53, with
HIGHTON, Lynn (née Edwards) m 1975; Maj, UK. b 10 Mar 53.

HIGUCHI, Kazumitsu (Nagoya, 1976); Maj, Jpn. b 9 Apr 51, and
HIGUCHI, Aiko (née Kutomi) (Shibuya, 1979) m 1982; Maj, Jpn. b 25 Sep 53.

HILL, Martin (Northampton Central, 1984); Maj, UK. b 3 Jul 55. BA (Hons) (Soc Sci), MTh (Ap Th).

HINTON, David (Blackheath, 1975); Maj, UK. b 28 Oct 53, and
HINTON, Sylvia (née Brooks) (Bedlington, 1975) m 1977; Maj, UK. b 2 Dec 53.

HIRAMOTO, Naoshi (Ueno, 1971); Lt-Col, CS, Jpn. b 24 Oct 46. BA (Law), and
HIRAMOTO, Seiko (née Kobayashi) (Kyobashi, 1968) m 1973; Lt-Col, TSWM, Jpn. b 7 Oct 43. BA (Eng Lit).

HIRAMOTO, Nobuhiro (Ueno, 1979); Maj, Jpn. b 28 Dec 51. BA (Chinese Lit), and
HIRAMOTO, Yasuko (née Kinoshita) (Ueno, 1979) m 1979; Maj, Jpn. b 7 Dec 51.

HISCOCK, David G. (Corner Brook Citadel, NF, 1965); Lt-Col, Can. b 11 May 45, and
HISCOCK, Margaret (née Brown) (Bay Roberts, NF, 1966) m 1967; Lt-Col, Can. b 27 Mar 45. BA.

HODDER, Kenneth G. (Pasadena Tabernacle, CA, USA W, 1988); Lt-Col, CS, Ken. b 16 Jun 58. BA (Hist), JD (Law), with
HODDER, Jolene (née Lloyd) m 1982; Lt-Col, TLWM, Ken. b 30 Jul 61. BA (Home Econ). Served in USA W and USA S.

HODGE, John (Wollongong, 1972); Lt-Col. Aus E. b 27 Aug 45. Dip Teach, MBA, BA (Relig Studies and Ed). Ww Lt Marie, pG 1974. Served in PNG, and
HODGE, Pamela (née Henry) (Bankstown, 1972) m 1975; Lt-Col. Aus E. b 29 Oct 49. Served in Carib (CS/TSWO), Phil (TC/TPWO) and NZ.

HOFER, Allan (Sissach, 1986); Maj, Switz. b 30 Mar 1961, and
HOFER, Fiona (née Pressland) (Barking, UK,

Biographical Information

1987) m 1987; Maj, Switz, b 15 Apr 1964. Served in Port, UK, Braz and USA S.

HOGAN, Olin O. (Aberdeen, WA, USA W, 1962); Col, TC, Mex. b 23 Sep 41. BA (Bus Admin), MA (Bible and Theol), and
HOGAN, Dianne C. (née Cagle) (Seattle Temple, WA, USA W, 1963) m 1964; Col, TPWM, Mex. b 10 Dec 43. Served in USA W.

HOKOM, Eda M. (Caldwell, ID, 1974); Maj, USA W. b 19 Mar 48. BA (Soc Sci), BS (Relig Ed). Served in PNG.

HOLLEY, Brian (Granville, 1966); Maj, Aus E. b 20 Nov 43. BAL, Th C, and
HOLLEY, Glenys (née Kingston) (Dulwich Hill Temple, 1967) m 1968; Maj, Aus E. b 30 Oct 42.

HOLLEY, Peter (Bankstown, 1969) Maj, Aus E. b 23 Mar 1946, and
HOLLEY, Eileen (née Lodge) (Narrabri, 1971) m 1971; Maj, Aus E. b 7 Nov 1947.

HOLNBECK, Brenda (Trenton, On, 1969); Maj, Can. b 24 Jun 46.

HONSBERG, Frank (Cologne, 1987); Maj, Ger. b 24 Jan 63. Grad Bus Mgmt, with
HONSBERG, Stefanie (née Gossens) m 1985; Maj, Ger. b 17 Dec 65.

HOOD, Brian (Bundaberg, 1974); Lt-Col, Aus S. b 23 Mar 44, with
HOOD, Elaine (née Toft) m 1970; Lt-Col, Aus S. b 19 Apr 51. Served in Aus E and PNG.

HOOD, George (Hamilton, OH, USA W, 1983); Maj, USA Nat. b 31 Jan 47. BS (Mgmt), MS (Mgmt), and
HOOD, Donna J. (née Morrison) (Newport, KY, USA W, 1984) m 1969; Maj, USA Nat. b 25 Oct 47. BS. Served in USA E and USA W.

HOOD, Sallyann (née Carpenter) (San Diego Citadel, CA, USA W, 1977); Maj, Mex. b 12 Nov 45. BA (Pre-med Zoology), MD Ob/Gyn, with
HOOD, James m 1971; Maj, Mex. b 27 Oct 46. BS (Agric Eng), MS (Civil Eng), Served in USA W and Ind SE.

HOOD, Ralph E. (Fresno, CA, 1966); Maj, USA W. b 13 Jul 42. BA (Bus Admin), BS (Relig Ed), and
HOOD, Ivy (née Hill) (Rockford West, IL, 1964) m 1967; Maj, USA W. b 20 Jun 41. Served in USA C.

HOSTETLER, Donald D. (Cincinnati Citadel, OH, 1971); Maj, USA W. b 2 Jan 49. BA (Soc), MA (Public Admin), with

HOSTETLER, Arvilla J. (née Marcum) m 1969; Maj, USA W. b 14 Aug 50.

HOUGHTON, Raymond (Woodhouse, UK, 1967); Comr, TC, Carib. b 12 Apr 44. MCMI, with
HOUGHTON, Judith (née Jones) m 1965; Comr, TPWM, Carib. b 15 Nov 45. Served in UK (CS/TSWO) and at IHQ (IS to CoS/ Mission Resources Sec).

HOWELL, Willis (Hyattsville, MD, 1985); Maj, USA S. b 3 Mar 56, with
HOWELL, Barbara (née Leidy) m 1978; Maj, USA S. b 3 Apr 57.

HRANGNGURA (Hnahthial, 1981); Maj, Ind E. b 16 Jan 52, with
BIAKSAILOVI (Hnahthial) m 1953; Maj, Ind E, b 9 Apr 53.

HUDSON, David E. (Portland Tabernacle, OR, 1975); Maj, USA W. b 28 Jun 54. BS (Bus Mgmt), and
HUDSON, Sharon (née Smith) (Santa Ana, CA, 1975) m 1976; Maj, USA W. b 14 Jun 52.

HULSMAN, Everdina (Nijverdal, 1975); Lt-Col, Neth. b 21 Dec 47.

HUNTER, Barbara (née Booth) (Tucson, AZ, USA W, 1967); Lt-Col, USA E. b 17 Mar 47. BS (Org Mgmt). Served in USA W and Rus (CSWO). Ww Lt-Col William, pG 2001.

HYNES, Junior (Happy Valley, NL, 1971); Maj, Can. b 6 Jan 51, and
HYNES, Verna (née Downton) (Windsor, NL, 1971) m 1973; Maj, Can. b 27 Aug 50. Served in UK.

I

IMMANUEL, Sam (Thulickal, 1984); Maj, Ind SW. b 27 May 59, with
IMMANUEL, Rachel P. C. m 1982; Maj, Ind SW. b 15 Jun 57.

INDURUWAGE, Malcolm (Colombo Central, Sri Lan, 1977); Col, TC, Phil. b 24 Sep 50, and
INDURUWAGE, Irene (née Horathalge) (Colombo Central, Sri Lan, 1977) m 1977; Col, TPWM, Phil. b 29 Nov 55. Served in Sri Lan and Phil (CS/TSWM).

IRVING, Ray (Shiremoor, 1989); Maj, UK. b 20 Apr 51. MVA, MCMI, and
IRVING, Angela (née Richards) (Torquay, 1972) m 1989; Maj, UK. b 12 Feb 51.

ISMAEL, Dina (Bandung 1, Indon, 1990); Maj, Phil. b 19 Jan 60. Served in Indon.

J

JACKSON, David (Romford, 1976); Maj, UK.

303

b 10 Nov 52. Served at IHQ.

JADHAV, Philip Baburao (Vishrantwadi, 1986);
Maj, Ind W. b 6 May 63, and
JADHAV, Rebecca (Byculla Marathi, 1992)
m 1988; Maj, Ind W. b 11 Nov 65.

JAMES, M. C. (Monkotta, Ind SW, 1979);
Comr, TC, Ind SE. b 20 Oct 54. MA Soc, and
JAMES, L. Susamma (Pothencode, Ind SW,
1983) m 1983; Comr, TPWM, Ind SE.
b 1 Mar 61. Served in Ind C (TC/TPWM).

JAYARATNASINGHAM, Packianathan
(Jaffna, 1973); Maj, Sri Lan. b 4 Nov 52, and
**JAYARATNASINGHAM, Delankage
Chandralatha** (née Delankage)
(Siyambalangamuwa, 1979) m 1980; Maj,
Sri Lan. b 28 Oct 59. Served at IHQ.

JAYASEELAN, Jebamony (Maharajaduram
1982); Maj, Ind SE. b 20 May 57, and
JAYASEELAN, Gnanaselvi (née Masih)
(1985); Maj, Ind SE. b 30 Dec 57.

JEBASINGH-RAJ, J. Daniel (Booth Tucker
Hall, Nagercoil, Ind SE, 1987); Maj, Ind Nat.
b 10 Jun 61. BA (Eng), MA (Social), BTh,
BD, MTh, with
JEBASINGH-RAJ, T. Rajam (Kuzhikalai,
Ind SE, 1992) m 1992; Maj, Ind Nat.
b 12 Mar 64; BA (Eng), MA (History), BTh
PM. Served in Ind SE.

JEFFREY, David (Morgantown, WV, USA S,
1973); Lt-Col, Nat CS, USA Nat. b 2 Aug 51,
and
JEFFREY, Barbara (née Garris) (Morgantown,
WV, USA S, 1966) m 1969; Lt-Col, NSWM,
USA Nat. b 1 Jan 46. Served in USA S
(CS/TSWM).

JERA, Onai (Marowa, 1992); Capt, Zimb.
b 10 Sep 67, and
JERA, Deliwe (née Gasa) (Gunguhwe, 1992)
m 1994; Capt, Zimb. b 18 Jun 68.

JEREMIAH, Edwin (Mupfure, 1990); Maj,
Zimb. b 30 Jun 60, with
JEREMIAH, Tambudzai (née Kabaya)
m 1979; Maj, Zimb. b 10 Feb 62.

JEWETT, Vernon Wayne (Atlanta Temple, GA,
1980); Maj, USA S. b 11 Dec 47. BA, MA,
with
JEWETT, Martha Gaye (née Brewer) m 1975;
Maj, USA S. b 22 Oct 52. BA.

JOHN, Morris (Rancho Lines, 1975); Lt-Col,
Pak. b 1 Jan 53, with
JOHN, Salma (née Feroz) m 1974; Lt-Col,
Pak. b 1 Jan 56.

JOHN, Rajan K. (Parayankerry, 1979); Maj,
Ind SW. b 26 Mar 52, with
JOHN, Susamma m 1977; Maj, Ind SW.
b 17 Oct 52.

JOHNSON, Kenneth (Charlotte Temple, NC,
1984); Maj, USA S. b 10 Aug 56. BS (Bus
Mgmt), with
JOHNSON, Paula (née Salmon) m 1981;
Maj, USA S. b 23 Nov 62.

JOHNSON, Paulose (Pallickal, 1969); Lt-Col,
Ind SW. b 24 Feb 46, and
JOHNSON, Thankamma (Mulakuzha, 1971)
m 1971; Lt-Col, Ind SW. b 3 May 49.

JOHNSON, Rex (Auckland Congress Hall, 1971);
Maj, NZ. b 24 May 48, and
JOHNSON, Geraldine (née Stratton)
(Dunedin Fortress, 1974) m. 1976; Maj, NZ.
b 6 Mar 54. Served in PNG.

JONAS, Dewhurst (St John's, Antigua, 1982);
Maj, Carib. b 20 May 56, and
JONAS, Vevene (née Gordon) (Rae Town,
Jamaica, 1980) m 1983; Maj, Carib. b 1 Jun 57.

JONES, John Roy, Jr (Gastonia, NC, 1971);
Maj, USA S. b 2 Feb 49, and
JONES, Arduth Eleanor (née Johnson)
(Charlotte Temple, NC, 1971), m 1973; Maj,
USA S. b 1 Jan 50.

JONES, Melvyn (Hoxton, 1976); Maj, UK.
b 21 Nov 51. MA (Nat Sci), with
JONES, Kathleen (née Hall) m 1974; Maj, UK.
b 15 Mar 51. SRN, SCM.

JOSHI, Devadasi (Musunuru, 1981); Maj,
Ind C. b 1 Oct 54, with
JOSHI, Leelamani m 1977; Maj, Ind C.
b 1 Jun 53.

JUNG, Verônica (Cachoeira Paulista, 1984);
Maj, Brz. b 15 Sep 59. BA (Trans and Interp).

K

KALA, Sere (Koki, 1990); Maj, PNG. b 1 Jul 58,
with
KALA, Hanua (née Malaga) m 1979; Maj,
PNG. b 10 Sep 59.

KALAI, Andrew (Koki, 1981); Col, TC, PNG.
b 18 Jan 56. BA (Psychology). Ww Capt Napa,
pG 1994, Ww Col Julie, pG 2006. Served
in UK.

KALE, Ratnakar Dinkar (Ahmednagar Central,
1977); Maj, Ind W. b 1 Jul 53, and
KALE, Leela (née Magar) (Byculla, 1981)
m 1981; Maj, Ind W. b 1 Mar 60.

KAMAMBO, Clever (Chrome Mine, 1979);
Maj, Zimb. b 28 Dec 57, and
KAMAMBO, Daphne (née Mhlanga)
(Mufakose, 1981) m 1984; Maj, Zimb. b 16
Dec 59.

KANG, Jik-koo (Pu Sang, 1978); Maj, Kor.
b 25 Aug 48; with
KIM, Chung-sook m 1976; Maj, Kor.
b 5 May 57.

304

Biographical Information

KANIS, Jacob (Kampen, 1968); Lt-Col, Neth. b 12 Oct 46, and
KANIS, Wijna (née Arends) (Kampen, 1968) m 1969; Lt-Col, Neth. b 21 Apr 47.

KARTODARSONO, Ribut (Surakarta, 1975); Col, TC, Indon. b 13 Dec 49. BA (Relig Ed), MA (Relig Ed & Public Societies), and
KARTODARSONO, Marie (née Ticoalu) (Bandung 3, 1975) m 1979; Col, TPWM, Indon. b 30 Nov 52. Served in Indon (CS/TSWM) and UK.

KARUNAKARA RAO, N. J. (Madras Central, Ind C, 1976) Lt-Col, Ind Nat. b 3 Apr 48. Dip Hosp Admin, MA (Soc Work), BSc (Bot), with
VIJAYALAKSHMI, N. J. m 1973; Lt-Col, Ind Nat. b 9 Jul 55. BA (Eng Lit), BD. Served in Ind SE, Ind C, Sri Lan (CS/TSWO) and Ind W (CS/TSWO).

KASAEDJA, Jones (Kulawi, 1982); Maj, Indon. b 22 Jun 68, and
KASAEDJA, Mariyam (née Barani) (Salupone, 1982) m 1989; Maj, Indon. b 10 Oct 1954.

KASBE, Devdan Laxman (Ahmednagar Central, 1970); Maj, Ind W. b 9 Feb 49, and
KASBE, Maria B. (née Devhe) (Dapodi, 1972) m 1972; Maj, Ind W. b 16 Oct 52.

KASUSO, Daniel (Pearson, Zimb, 1986); Maj, S Afr. b 15 Jul 65, and
KASUSO, Tracey (née Mashiri) (Torwood, Zimb, 1986); Maj, S Afr. b 19 Oct 64. Served in Zimb.

KATHENDU, Johnstone Njeru (Siakago, 1988); Maj, Ken. b 22 Jun 63, with
KATHENDU, Nancy (née Turi) m 1984; Maj, Ken. b 26 Feb 64.

KATHURI, Gabriel (Mombasa, 1982); Maj, Ken. b 13 Jan. 1951, with
KATHURI, Monica (née Minoo) m 1977; Maj, Ken. b 22 Feb 1954.

KATSUCHI, Jiro (Hamamatsu, 1984); Maj, Jpn. b 3 May 49, and
KATSUCHI, Keiko (née Munemori) (Nagoya, 1969) m 1986; Maj, Jpn. b 30 Jun 47.

KELLY, David E. (Cincinnati, OH, 1980); Maj, USA E. b 30 Nov 59. AS (Bus Adm), MA (Ldrshp & Min), and
KELLY, Naomi R. (née Foster) (Tonawanda, NY, 1977) m 1981; Maj, USA E. b 14 Sep 56. BA (Org Mgmt).

KHAIZADINGA (Bukpui, 1974); Maj, Ind E. b 20 Jan 1950, with

RAMTHANMAWII m 1970; Maj, Ind E. b 23 Nov 1953.

KHARKOV, Alexander (Moscow Central, 1993); Maj, E Eur. b 31 Jan 58, with
KHARKOV, Maria (née Seleverstova) m 1979; Maj, E Eur. b 30 Nov 49.

KHOZA, Jabulani (Mbabane, 1985); Maj, S Afr. b 8 Jun 62, and
KHOZA, Fikile (née Mkhize) (Ezakheni, 1986) m 1986; Maj, S Afr. b 28 Aug 66.

KIHI, Mais (Kainantu, 1988); Maj, PNG. b 9 Sep 1956, with
KIHI, Paula (née Anton) m 1980; Maj, PNG. b 18 Mar 63.

KIM, Nam-sun (Ah Hyun, 1983); Maj, Kor. b 11 Sep 54.

KIM, Oon-ho (Eum Am, 1979); Maj, Kor. b 31 Jan 52, with
LEE, Ok-kyung m 1977; Maj, Kor. b 9 Jun 53.

KIM, Young-tae (Chin Chook, 1986); Maj, Kor. b 23 Mar 56. BAdmin, MBA, with
PYO, Choon-yun m 1977; Maj, Kor. b 29 Jul 53.

KING, Charles (New Barnet, UK, 1975); Maj, IHQ. b 29 Nov 48. Served in UK.

KJELLGREN, Hasse (Östra Kåren, Swdn, 1971); Comr, IS Eur, IHQ. b 1 Nov 45. BSc, and
KJELLGREN, Christina (née Forssell) (Hisingskaren, Swdn, 1971) m 1971; Comr, SWM Eur, IHQ. b 21 May 47. Served in S Am E (TC/TPWO), Switz (TC/TPWM) and Swdn (TC/TPWM).

KLARENBEEK, Elsje (Amsterdam Zuid, 1979); Maj, Neth. b 2 Jun 52.

KLEMAN, Johnny (Boras, Swdn, 1982); Maj, Fin. b 29 Jul 59, and
KLEMAN, Eva (née Hedberg) (Motala, Swdn, 1981) m 1982; Maj, Fin. b 6 Sep 60. Served in Swdn.

KLEMANSKI, Guy (Lewiston-Auburn, ME, 1970); Maj, USA E. b 21 Nov 50, and
KLEMANSKI, Henrietta (née Wallace) (Cleveland, West Side, OH, 1970) m 1972; Maj, USA E. b 27 Jul 47.

KNAGGS, James (Philadelphia Roxborough, PA, USA E, 1976); Comr, TC, Aus S. b 5 Dec 50. MPS (Urban Min), and
KNAGGS, Carolyn (née Lance) m 1972; Comr, TPWM, Aus S. b 19 Sep 51. Served in USA E (CS/TSWM).

KNAPP, Jocelyn (Camberwell, 1969); Lt-Col, Aus S. b 7 Apr 44. Served in Aus E.

KNECHT, Hans (Wetzikon, 1967); Maj, Switz. b 17 Jan 43. m 1969; Maj Heidi, ret 2007.

KNEDAL, Jan Øystein (Templet, Oslo, 1974); Maj, Nor. b 25 Aug 52, and
KNEDAL, Brit (née Kolloen) (Templet, Oslo, 1976) m 1978; Maj, Nor. b 27 Apr 58

KORNILOW, Petter (Parkano, 1981); Maj, Fin. b 21 Aug 53, and
KORNILOW, Eija Hellevi (née Astikainen) (Tampere Kaleva, 1981) m a1981; Maj, Fin. b 28 Jun 56.

KROMMENHOEK, Dick (Amsterdam Congress Hall, Neth, 1983); Col, IHQ. b 18 Jun 52. MA (Music), with
KROMMENHOEK, Vibeke (née Schou Larsen) m 1978; Col, IHQ. b 27 Nov 56. MA (Th). Served in Neth, Den (TC/TPWM) and Frce (TC/TPWM).

KUMAR, K. Y. Dhana (Khajipalem, Bapatla, 1980); Maj, Ind C. b 21 Sep 1957. BCom, with
KUMAR, Yesamma (née Dasari) m 1978; Maj, Ind C. b 18 May 1961.

KWENDA, Innocent Peter (Mutondo, 1976); Maj, Zimb. b 10 Apr 57, and
KWENDA, Norma (née Nyawo) (Dombwe-Makonde, 1977) m 1977; Maj, Zimb. b 10 Jul 55.

KWON, Sung-dal (Son Chi, 1977); Maj, Kor. b 17 Apr 47, with
KIM, Moon-ok (Son Chi, 1977) m 1973; Maj, Kor. b 29 Oct 53.

L

LAHASE, Kashinath V. (Chapadgaon, Ind W, 1972); Col, TC, Ind N. b 1 Nov 49, with
LAHASE, Kusum K. m 1970; Col, TPWM, Ind N. b 7 Jun 49. Served in Ind W, Ind SW and Ind N (CS/TSWM).

LAL, Rounki (Amritsar, 1972); Maj, Ind N. b 15 May 48, with
LAL, Agnes m 1968; Maj, Ind N. b 3 Feb 50.

LALBULLIANA (Darlawn, Ind E, 1987); Maj, Ken. b 20 Sep 64, and
LALBULLIANA, Lalnunhlui (Thingsulthliah, Ind E, 1990) m 1990; Maj, Ken. b 12 Dec 65. Served in Ind E.

LALHMINGLIANA (Chaltlang, 1994); Capt, Ind E. b 29 Sep 71. BA (Hons) (Hist), and
LALHLIMPUII (Bethel, 1994) m 1994; Capt, Ind E. b 28 Oct 71. Served at IHQ.

LALHRIATPUIA (Republic 1982); Maj, Ind E. b 1 Jun 62, and
LALCHHUANMAWII (Temple, 1985) m 1986; Maj, Ind E. b 18 Sep 64.

LALKIAMLOVA (Kahrawt, 1971); Comr, IS S Asia, IHQ. b 7 Mar 49. BA, and

LALHLIMPUII (Saitual, 1973) m 1973; Comr, SWM S Asia, IHQ. b 25 Sep 53. Served in Ind E, Ind SW (CS/TSWO) and Ind C (TC/TPWM).

LALNGAIHAWMI, Naomi (Aizawl Central, 1978); Lt-Col, CS, Ind E. b 1 Jan 54. MA. Served at Ind Nat

LALRAMHLUNA (Chaltlang, Ind E, 1981) Lt-Col, CS, Ind W. b 9 May 51, and
KAWLRAMTHANGI (Chaltlang, Ind E, 1981) m 1972, Lt-Col, TSWM, IndW. b 14 Nov 52. Served in Ind E.

LALZAMLOVA (Tuinu, Ind E, 1986); Col, TC, Sri Lan. b 20 May 62. BA, with
NEMKHANCHING (Nu-i) m 1984; Col, TPWM, Sri Lan. b 23 Feb 63. Served in Ind E and Ind N.

LAMARR, Armida Joy (Old Orchard Beach, ME, USA E, 2002); Capt, Ken. b 10 Jul 75. Served in USA E.

LAMARR, William (Yonkers Citadel, NY, 1967); Lt-Col, USA E. b 8 Apr 45, and
LAMARR, Judy (née Lowers) (East Liverpool, OH, 1962) m 1968; Lt-Col, USA E. b 14 Sep 41. LPN (Nursing)

LAMARTINIERE, Lucien (Petit Goave, Haiti 1992); Maj, Carib. b 13 Jun 57, with
LAMARTINIERE, Marie (née Bonhomme) m 1980; Maj, Carib. b 26 May 57. Served in Can.

LANCE, Donald W. (Philadelphia Roxborough, PA, 1980); Maj, USA E. b 7 Feb 53. BA (Business), and
LANCE, Renee (née Hewlett) (Scranton, PA, 2002) m 2003; Capt, USA E. b Jun 53. RN (Nursing).

LANGA, William (Witbank, 1977); Maj, S Afr. b 15 Jul 49, with
LANGA, Thalitha (née Themba); Maj, S Afr. b 1 Sep 50.

LAPEÑA, Marilou (née Hercer) (Quezon City 1, Phil) m 1987; Maj, Sri Lan. b 26 Sep 61. Served in Phil.

LARSSON, Per-Olof (Orebro 1, 1978); Maj, Swdn. b 7 Dec 51, and
LARSSON, Karin (née Blomberg) (Dala-Jarna, 1977) m 1978; Maj, Swdn. b 5 Jun 50.

LAUA, Abner (Palu, 1968); Lt-Col, Indon. b 8 Mar 45, and
LAUA, Mina (née Hohoy) (Surabaya Kulawi, 1972) m 1972; Lt-Col, Indon. b 14 Dec 46.

LAUKKANEN, Arja (Turku 2, 1975); Lt-Col, CS, Fin. b 29 Apr 46.

LAWS, Peter (Wauchope, 1973); Maj, Aus E. b 23 Oct 1950. BAL, MBA, with

Biographical Information

LAWS, Jan (née Cook) m 1970; Maj. Aus E. b 18 Jun 50.

LEAVEY, Wendy (Street, UK, 1980); Maj, Gha. b 17 Feb 53. SRN, SCM. Served in UK.

LECOCQ, Noélie (Quaregnon, 1973); Maj, GS, Belg. b 29 Feb 48.

LEE, Kong Chew (Bob) (Balestier, 1983); Maj, Sing. b 8 Oct 57. BDiv, and
LEE, Teoh Gim Leng (Wendy) (Penang, 1983) m 1982; Maj, Sing. b 24 Aug 57.

LESLIE, Victor A. (Port-of-Spain, Carib, 1980); Maj, USA W. b 5 Nov 56. BA (Mgmt), MA (Relig Studies), Cert (Chem Dependence), JD (Law), MBA (Mgmt), and
LESLIE, Rose-Marie (née Campbell) (Lucea, Carib, 1977) m 1980; Maj, USA W. b 15 Aug 57. BS (Soc Work), AS (Nursing), RN (Nursing), BS (Nursing), Cert (Public Health Nurse). Served in Carib.

LEWIS, Douglas (Toronto Temple, 1972); Maj, Can. b 14 Jan 47, with
LEWIS, Elizabeth (née Legge) m 1966; Maj, Can. b 30 Jul 46. Served in Ger.

LIANHLIRA (Ratu, 1979); Maj, Ind E. b 28 Apr 51, with
THANZUALI m 1975; Maj, Ind E. b 20 Jan 57.

LIANTHANGA (Darlawn, 1974); Maj, Ind E. b 1 Mar 50, and
RINGLIANI (Darlawn, 1974) m 1975; Maj, Ind E. b 10 Jan 52.

LIM, Hun-taek (Kunsan, 1979); Maj, Kor. b 28 Feb 50; with
CHUN, Soon-ja m 1977; Maj, Kor. b 15 Aug 50. Served in Aus S.

LIM, Young-shik (Shin An, 1975); Maj, Kor. b 26 Jun 49, with
YEO, Keum-soo m 1972; Maj, Kor. b 6 Dec 50.

LINARES, Orestes (Camaguey, 1997); Capt, L Am N. b 13 Aug 60, with
LINARES, Sandra (née Fernández) m 1986; Capt, L Am N. b 26 Jun 63.

LINCOLN, Abraham Maddu (Guduru, 1991); Capt, Ind C. b 12 Sep 64, with
MERCY, Manjula m 1988; Capt, Ind C. b 22 May 66.

LING, Fona (née Chan) (Lok Man, HK, 1973); Maj, RC/RPWM, Tai. b 29 Jun 53. Ww Maj James, pG 2001. Served in HK and Aus E.

LÖFGREN, Kehs David (Norrköping, 1968); Col, Swdn. b 8 Nov 45, and
LÖFGREN, Edith (née Sjöström) (Borlänge, 1974) m 1977; Col, Swdn. b 2 Mar 51. Served in UK and Nor (CS/TSWO).

LOSSO, Mesak (Jakarta 2, 1968); Lt-Col, Indon. b 12 Nov 45, and

LOSSO, Mona (née Warani) (Turen, 1971) m 1972; Lt-Col, Indon. b 13 Jun 44.

LOUBAKI, Urbain (Bakongo, 1992); Capt, Con (Braz). b 20 Dec 64, with
LOUBAKI, Judith (née Bikouta) m 1989; Maj, Con (Braz). b 16 Apr 68.

LOUKOULA, Cécile (Ouenzé, 1990); Maj, Con (Braz). b 30 Aug 56.

LUDIAZO, Jean Bakidi (Salle Centrale, Kinshasa, Con (Kin), 1971); Comr, TC, Nig. b 19 Nov 45, with
LUDIAZO, Véronique (née Lusieboko Lutatabio) m 1970; Comr, TPWM, Nig. b 26 Sep 53. Served in Con, Can and Con (Kin) (TC/TPWM).

LUFUMBU, Enock (Londiani, Nakuru, 1982); Maj, Ken. b 10 Feb 52, with
LUFUMBU, Beatrice (née Kageha) m 1978; Maj, Ken. b 22 Feb 57.

LUKAU, Mangiengie Joseph (Kimbanseke 1, Con (Kin), 1977); Lt-Col, CS, Frce. b 18 Sep 53, with
LUKAU, Angélique (née Makiese) m 1975; Lt-Col, TPWM, Frce. b 1 Sep 54. Served in Con (Kin).

LUTHER, Lise (Harstad, 1992); Maj, Nor. b 20 May 65.

LYDHOLM, Carl A. S. (Gartnergade, Den, 1966); Comr, TC, Nor. b 14 Nov 45, and
LYDHOLM, Gudrun (née Arskog) (Odense, Den, 1967) m 1967; Comr, TPWM, Nor. b 5 Aug 47. MTh. Served in Den, UK, Rus/CIS (GS/CSWM) and Fin (TC/TPWM).

M

MA, Tony Yeung-mo (Tai Hang Tung, 1985); Maj, HK. b 20 Oct 55, and
MA, Elen Yi-lung (née Lu) (Tainang, 1981) m 1985; Maj, HK. b 4 Nov 52.

MABANZA, Alexandre (Makaka, 1975); Maj, Con (Braz). b 15 Dec 50, with
MABANZA, Madeleine (née Mantseka) m 1972; Maj, Con (Braz). b 24 Jan 54.

MABASO, Timothy John (Witbank, 1988); Maj, S Afr. b 10 Jun 57. BA (Bus Admin), with
MABASO, Flemah Ntombizakithi (née Zulu) m 1983; Maj, S Afr. b 16 Dec 57.

MACMILLAN, M. Christine (North York, Can, 1975); Comr, IHQ. b 9 Oct 47. Served in UK, Aus E, PNG (TC, TPWM) and Can (TC, TPWM).

MACWAN, John Purshottam (Alindra, Ind W, 1969); Maj, Ind Nat. b 1 Feb 48, and
MACWAN, Miriam (née Peter) (Bhalej, Ind W, 1974) m 1974; Maj, Ind W. b 13 Oct 55. Served in Ind W.

307

MACWAN, Natwarlal M. (Ghoghawada, 1969); Maj, Ind W. b 23 Jan 46, and
MACWAN, Savitaben (Sundha-Vansol, 1983) m 1976; Maj, Ind W. b 1 Jun 56.

MACWAN, Phulen W. (Poona, 1981); Maj, Ind W. b 21 Apr 51.

MACWAN, Punjalal Ukabhai (Lingda, 1980); Maj, Ind W. b 8 Jul 55, with:
MACWAN, Margaret m 1975; Maj, Ind W. b 17 May 55.

McINTYRE, Robert George (New City Road, 1967); Maj, UK. b 15 Oct 44, and
McINTYRE, Isobel (née Laird) (Partick Temple, 1969) m 1969; Maj, UK. b 23 Sep 48.

McKENZIE, Garth (Wellington City, 1975); Comr, TC, NZ. b 19 Feb 44, with
McKENZIE, Merilyn (née Probert) m 1968; Comr, TPWM, NZ. b 20 Jul 46. Served in Aus S.

McKENZIE, Sydney (Havendale, Jamaica, 1970); Lt-Col, Carib. b 24 Dec 47, and
McKENZIE, Trypheme (née Forrest) (Bluefields, Jamaica, 1971) m 1973; Lt-Col, Carib. b 14 Jan 50.

McLAREN, Mickey L. (Midland, MI, 1970); Lt-Col, USA C. b 13 Oct 44. BA (Bus Admin), with
McLAREN, June C. (née Monroe) m 1964; Lt-Col, USA C. b 11 Jun 42. Served in Gha.

McLEOD, Margaret (Medicine Hat, Can, 1994); Capt, PNG. b 29 Apr 63. BEd, MTS. Served in Can.

McMILLAN, Susan (Montreal Citadel, Can, 1979); Lt-Col, CS, S Am W. b 20 Oct 54. BAS, MBA, CGA. Served in Can, Mex & Central Am and S Am E.

MAELAND, Erling Dag (Bryne, Nor, 1964); Col, TC, Den. b 9 Oct 43, and
MAELAND, Signe Helene (née Paulsen) (Bryne, Nor, 1964) m 1965; Col, TPWM, Den. b 12 Jun 45. Served in UK, at IHQ and in Nor (CS/TSWM).

MAGANLAL, Paul (Vaso, 1979); Maj, Ind W. b 7 Jan 54, with
MAGANLAL, Febiben m 1973; Maj, Ind W. b 11 Jun 52.

MAGAR, Bhausaheb J. (Dahiphal, 1977); Maj, Ind W. b 2 Jun 53, and
MAGAR, Pushpa (née Gajbhiv) (Dahiphal, 1978) m 1979; Maj, Ind W. b 2 Jun 54.

MAGAYA, Bexter (Chitumbi, 1981); Maj, Zam. b 29 Jan 56, with
MAGAYA, Jessie (née Milambo) m 1979; Maj, Zam. b 20 Sep 63.

MAHIDA, Jashwant D. (Vishrampura, 1984); Maj, Ind W. b 12 Jun 60, and

MAHIDA, Ruth (née Maganlal) (Anand Central, 1990) m 1990; Maj, Ind W. b 12 Nov 67.

MAKINA, Amos (Gwelo, Zimb, 1971); Comr, IS Afr, IHQ. b 28 Jun 47, and
MAKINA, Rosemary (née Chinjiri) (Mutonda, Zimb, 1973) m 1973; Comr, SWM Afr, IHQ. b 8 Aug 52. Served in Gha and Zimb (TC/TPWM).

MALABI, Joash (Mulatiwa, Ken, 1984); Lt-Col, CS, S Afr. b 17 May 55, and
MALABI, Florence (née Mutindi) (Webuye, Ken, 1988) m 1988; Lt-Col, TSWM, S Afr. b 26 Jun 64. Served in E Afr and Rw (RC/RPWM).

MARKIEWICZ, Linda V. (Rome, NY, USA E, 1981); Maj, USA W. b 15 Oct 50. BA (Arts/English). Served in USA E and at IHQ and ICO.

MARQUEZ, Paulina (née Condori) (Viacha, Bolivia, 1987); Capt, S Am W. b 2 Mar 1964, and
MARQUEZ, Manuel (La Esperanza, Perú, 1995) m 1997; Capt, S Am W. b 12 Feb 1971.

MARSEILLE, Gerrit Willem Jan (Ribe, Den, 1978); Maj, S Afr. b 8 Jun 51. MSc and MEd, with
MARSEILLE, Eva Elisabeth (Ribe, Den, 1978) m 1976; Maj, S Afr. b 18 Jun 52. MD (RSD). Served in Neth, Zai and Den.

MARSHALL, Norman Stephen (Chicago Mont Clare, IL, 1978); Maj, USA C. b 17 Jun 45. BA (Sociol), MS (Human Services Admin), MA (Org Devpt), with
MARSHALL, Diane Bernice (née Hedgren) m 1974; Maj, USA C. b 30 Sep 47. BS (Ed).

MARTI, Paul-William (Templet, Oslo, 1980), Maj, Nor. b 24 Jan 61, and
MARTI, Margaret Saue (née Saue) (Voss, 1980) m 1983, Maj, Nor. b 29 Aug 58. Served in Switz.

MARTIN, Larry R. (Edmonton Northside, AB, 1980); Maj, Can. b 31 Jul 1950, BA, MA, MTS, with
MARTIN, Velma (née Ginn) m 1972; Maj, Can. b 4 Oct 50. Served in UK.

MASANGO, Frederick (Mangula, 1971); Maj, Zimb. b 24 Jul 49, and
MASANGO, Rosemary (née Handiria) (Karambazungu, 1981) m 1981; Maj, Zimb. b 13 Feb 56.

MASIH, Bashir (Talwandi, Ind N, 1969); Lt-Col, CS, Ind SE. b 10 Apr 48, and
MASIH, Bachini (Gurdaspur, Ind N, 1972) m 1972; Lt-Col, TSWM, Ind SE. b 24 Nov 50. Served in Ind N and Ind C (CS/TSWM).

Biographical Information

MASIH, Edwin (Bareilly, 1979); Maj, Ind N.
b 6 Oct 57, and
MASIH, Sumita (Gurdaspur, 1983) m 1983;
Maj, Ind N. b 9 Oct 63.

MASIH, Gian (Jalalabad, 1972); Maj, Ind N.
b 1 Oct 50, and
MASIH, Salima (Barnala, 1972) m 1978;
Maj, Ind N. b 1 Dec 54.

MASIH, Joginder (Bhoper, Ind N, 1982); Maj,
GS, Ban. b 13 Jul 58, with
MASIH, Shanti m 1980; Maj, CSWM, Ban.
b 15 May 59. Served in Ind N.

MASIH, Kashmir (Khushadpur, 1990); Capt,
Ind N. b 1 Mar 63, with
MASIH, Veena m 1987; Capt, Ind N. b 1 Sep 66.

MASIH, Lazar (Rampur, 1974); Maj, Ind N.
b 20 May 52, with
MASIH, Sharbati (née Sharbati) m 1969;
Maj, Ind N. b 15 Jun 53.

MASIH, Makhan (Shahpur Guraya, 1990); Maj,
Ind N. b 30 Mar 68, and
MASIH, Sunila Makhan (City Corps, Amritsar,
1992) m 1988; Maj, Ind N. b 5 May 66.

MASIH, Manuel (Amritsar, 1994); Capt, Ind N.
b 1 Apr 64, with
MASIH, Anita m 1991; Capt, Ind N.
b 22 Apr 62.

MASIH, Peter (Daburjie, Amritsar, 1968); Maj,
Ind N. b 23 Oct 48, and
MASIH, Darmi (Bakhatpur, 1966) m 1968;
Maj, Ind N. b 15 Nov 46.

MASIH, Prakash (Khunda, 1984); Maj, Ind N.
b 10 Mar 58, with
MASIH, Mariam m 1981; Maj, Ind N.
b 2 Apr 62.

MASIH, Salamat (Shantinagar, 1989); Maj,
Pak. b 12 Aug 64, with
SALAMAT, Grace (née Sardar) m 1987;
Capt, Pak. b 18 Apr 64.

MASIH, Shafqat (Rehimabad, Sheikhupu,
1981); Maj, Pak. b 30 Oct 48, with
SHAFQAT, Parveen (née Sardar) m 1979;
Maj, Pak. b 26 Jun 51.

MASIH, Sulakhan (Dina Nagar, 1988); Maj,
Ind N. b 15 Apr 64, and
MASIH, Sheela (Hayat Nagar, 1984) m 1988;
Maj, Ind N. b 5 Apr 64.

MASIH, Yaqoob (Chamroua, 1986); Maj, Ind N.
b 6 Jun 62, with
MASIH, Sumitra m 1980; Maj, Ind N.
b 6 Jan 63.

MASON, Raphael (Mandeville, Jamaica, 1967);
Lt-Col, CS, Carib. b 7 Jul 47, and
MASON, Winsome (née De Lisser) (Montego
Bay, Jamaica, 1967) m 1969; Lt-Col, TSWM,
Carib. b 19 Feb 49. Served in USA E.

MASSIÉLÉ, Antoine (Yaya, 1982); Maj,
Con (Braz). b 20 Feb 53, with
MASSIÉLÉ, Marianne (née Ngoli) m 1978;
Maj, Con (Braz). b 2 Jan 50.

MATA, Mayisilwa Jean-Baptiste (Kisenso,
1983); Maj, Con (Kin). b 21 Oct 51, with
MATA, Marie (née Mundele Kisokama)
m 1981; Maj, Con (Kin). b 22 Mar 58.

MATEAR, John (Whifflet, 1978); Comr, TC,
UK. b 26 Apr 47, and
MATEAR, Elizabeth (née Kowbus) (Greenock
Citadel, 1977) m 1978; Comr, TPWM, UK.
b 16 Aug 52. Dip Youth, Commun and Soc
Work, Emp Law. Served in UK and Carib
(TC/TPWM).

MATTHEWS, Ward (Atlanta Temple, USA S,
1984); Maj, Carib. b 27 Jul 60. BS, and
MATTHEWS, Michele (née Matthews)
(Tampa, FL, USA S) m 1999; Capt, Carib.
b 1 Feb 67, BA Soc Services/Psychology,
BS Nursing. Served in USA S.

MATONDO, Isidore Mayunga (Boma, 1989);
Maj, Con (Kin). b 6 Jul 56, with
MATONDO, Lily Nlandu (née Luzoladio)
m 1987; Maj, Con (Kin). b 7 Dec 62.

MAVOUNA, Nkouka François (Nzoko, 1988);
Maj, Con (Braz). b 15 Mar 60, with
MAVOUNA, Louise (née Matondo) m 1986;
Maj, Con (Braz). b 11 Dec 62.

MAVUNDLA, Ntandane Hezekiel (Barberton,
S Afr, 1970); Lt-Col, OC, Tanz. b 19 Jan 47,
and
MAVUNDLA, Busisiwe Mirriam (née
Maphanga) (Barberton, S Afr, 1970) m 1970;
Lt-Col, TSWM, Tanz. b 2 Aug 52. Served in
S Afr (CS/TSWM).

MAXWELL, Wayne (Canberra City Temple,
1984); Maj, Aus E. b 31 May 58. BMin,
with
MAXWELL, Robyn (née Alley) m 1980;
Maj, Aus E. b 14 Feb 60.

MAYNOR, Kenneth (Cleveland South, OH,
1980); Maj, USA E. b 1 Feb 59. BS (Org
Mgmt), with
MAYNOR, Cheryl Ann (née Staaf)
m 1977; Maj, USA E. b 27 Sep 58.
BS (Church Mgmt).

MBAJA, Tiras Atulo (Kibera, 1986); Maj, Ken.
b 13 Jul 54, with
MBAJA, Mebo (née Mukiza) m 1983; Maj,
Ken. b 25 Mar 60.

MBALA, Lubaki Sébastien (Kifuma, 1987);
Maj, Con (Kin). b 23 Jun 58, and
MBALA, Godette Mboyo (née Moseka)
(Kintambo, 1987) m 1988; Maj, Con (Kin).
b 26 Sep 62.

MBANGWA, Sipho (Bulawayo, 1995); Capt, Zimb. b 5 Jun 67, and
MBANGWA, Nyarai (née Matambanadzo) (Tshabalala, 1997) m 1997; Capt, Zimb. b 1 Nov 74.

MBOTO, Martin Mathias (Chambai, Tanz, 1972); Maj, Ken. b 1950, with
MBOTO, Grace (née Mulengeka) m 1970; Maj, Ken. b 1952.

MENDES, Marcio (Belo Horizonte, 1980); Maj, Brz. b 24 Feb 57, and
MENDES, Jurema (née Mazzini) (Quarai, 1979) m 1981; Maj, Brz. b 4 Aug 57. BA (Ed).

MENDEZ, Jorge (El Faro, 1988); Maj, L Am N. b 5 Oct 51, with
MENDEZ, Idali (née Jiminez) m 1973; Maj, L Am N. b 24 Aug 52.

MENIA, Virgilio (Asingan, 1990); Maj, Phil. b 2 Jun 1961. BSCE (Civil Engr), and
MENIA, Ma Luisa (née Araneta) (Negros Occ, 1984) m 1990; Maj, Phil. b 7 Jan 1962.

MERAS, Marja (Turku 2, 1977); Maj, Fin. b 6 May 49.

MEYNER, Marianne (née Stettler) (Basle 2, 1983); Maj, Switz. b 14 Apr 57, with
MEYNER, Urs m 1978; Maj, Switz. b 30 Jan 51.

MHASVI, Evan (née Mhizha) (Shirichena, 1977); Lt-Col, Zimb. b 1 Feb 55. Served in Zam. Ww Lt-Col Henry, pG 2006.

MHEMBERE, Isaac (Mukwenya 1989); Maj, Zimb. b 5 May 69, and
MHEMBERE, Charity (née Muchapondwa) (Muchapondwa, 1990) m 1991; Maj, Zimb. b 2 Jan 67.

MILAMBO, Saraphina (née Shikawala) (Kafue, 1989); Maj, TSWM, Zam. b 1 Feb 55. Ww Maj Vincent, pG 2007.

MILLER, Gary (Youngstown Citadel, OH, USA E, 1962); Maj, USA Nat. b 24 May 42. BGS (General Studies), and
MILLER, Cheryl (née Harvey) (Wilmington, DE, USA E, 1966) m 1966; Maj, USA Nat. b 31 Jan 45. Served in USA E.

MIYOBA, Grey (Chitumbi, 1975); Lt-Col, CS, Zam. b 14 Mar 54, and
MIYOBA, Leniah (née Mweemba) (Chitumbi, 1977) m 1977; Lt-Col, Asst TPWM, Zam. b 5 Jan 56. Served in USA W.

M'MEMI, Naphas (Sabatia, 1984); Maj, Ken. b 10 Aug 56, with
M'MEMI, Grace (née Kasaya); Maj, Ken. b 28 Aug 58.

MNTAMBO, Sibongile Ivy (née Ngwenya) (Soweto Central, 1988); Maj, S Afr. b 13 Sep 57.

MNYAMPI, Benjamin Amosi (Dar-es-salaam, 1985); Maj, GS, Tan. b 1 Mar 54, with
MNYAMPI, Grace (née Sage) m 1984; Maj, CSWM, Tan. b 3 Jun 63. Served in Zimb.

MOCHARLA, Elisha Rao (Anganna Gudem, 1970); Maj, Ind C. b 29 Sep 49. BTS, with
MOCHARLA, Prema Mani (née Ganta) m 1969; Maj, Ind C. b 8 Aug 51.

MOCKABEE, William (Anniston, AL, 1975); Maj, USA S. b 1 Nov 54, and
MOCKABEE, Debra (née Salmon) (Oklahoma City, OK, 1976) m 1976; Maj, USA S. b 9 Sep 54.

MONI, Chelliah (Oyaravillai, 1976); Maj, Ind SE. b 18 May 55. MA, and
MONI, Mallika (Alady, 1978) m 1978; Maj, Ind SE. b 6 Mar 57.

MORAN, Peter (Bradford West Bowling, 1979); Maj, UK. b 11 Feb 51, with
MORAN, Sandra (née Clapham) m 1971; Maj, UK. b 16 Jul 49.

MORETZ, Lawrence R. (Sunbury, PA, 1964); Comr, TC, USA E. b 22 Jul 43, and
MORETZ, Nancy A. (née Burke) (Kingston, NY, 1964) m 1965; Comr, TPWM, USA E. b 29 Nov 44. Served in S Am W (TC/TPWO) and USA C (TC/TPWM).

MORIASI, Stephen (Keng'uso, Ken, 1984); Maj, GS, Uga. b 7 Jun 60, and
MORIASI, Rose Mmbaga (née Onchari) (Embago, Ken, 1988) m 1990; Maj, CSWM, Uga. Served in E Afr and at IHQ.

MORRIS, Richard (Glenfield 1994); Capt, NZ. b 18 Mar 61. BCom, with
MORRIS, Jennifer (née Walker); m 1989; Capt, NZ. b 20 Feb 67.

MOTCHAKAN, Sundaram (Aramboly, 1974); Maj, Ind SE. b 17 Mar 50, and
MOTCHAKAN, Selvabai (Kaliyancaud, 1974) m 1975; Maj, Ind SE. b 2 May 50.

MOTHERSHED, David (Tampa, FL, 1977); Lt-Col, USA S. b 17 Oct 41, with
MOTHERSHED, Martha (née Suarez) m 1961; Lt-Col, USA S. b 5 Mar 41.

MOULTON, Jean (née Pittman) (Kitchener, ON, 1970); Maj, Can. b 30 Mar 46. BA.

MOULTON, Raymond E. (Wychwood, ON, 1967); Lt-Col, Can. b 26 Oct 42. BA, with
MOULTON, Marilyn K. (née Petley) m 1963; Lt-Col, Can. b 5 Dec 41. Served in USA W.

MOWERS, John D. (Kansas City (Westport Temple), MO, USA C, 1976); Maj, S Am E. b 25 Sep 52. BA (Sociology), with
MOWERS, Nancy J. (née Hultin) m 1970;

Maj, S Am E. b 26 Apr 49. BA (Psychology). Served in USA C and L Am N.

MOWERY, Don R. (Salt Lake City, UT, 1969); Lt-Col, USA W. b 29 Aug 44. Cert Alcohol and Drugs, with
MOWERY, Jan (née Dempsey) m 1961; Lt-Col, USA W. b 7 Oct 42.

MUASA, Jackson (Kivaku, 1980); Maj, Ken. b 9 Jan 56, and
MUASA, Ciennah (née Mwandi) (Kee, 1980) m 1982; Maj, Ken. b 10 Oct 57.

MUBAIWA, Final (Nyarukunda, 1990); Maj, Zimb. b 29 June 60, with
MUBAIWA, Pfumisai (née Ngwenya) m 1988; Maj, Zimb. b 12 May 69.

MUKONGA, Julius (Kwa Kyambu, 1978); Lt-Col, Ken. b 10 Mar 53, with
MUKONGA, Phyllis (née Mumbua) m 1976; Lt-Col, Ken. b 28 Mar 57.

MUNGATE, Stuart (Mabvuku, Zimb, 1970); Comr, TC, Con (Kin). b 15 Nov 46. BA, Grad Cert Ed, Dip Bus Admin, and
MUNGATE, Hope (née Musvosvi) (Mucherengi, Zimb, 1974) m 1974; Comr, TPWM, Con (Kin). b 23 Mar 53. Dip Journ. Served in Zimb, Con (Kin) (CS/TSWM) and Nig (TC/TPWM).

MUNN, Richard (Lexington, KY, 1987); Maj, USA E. b 16 Jan 56. BA (Ed), MDiv (Theol), DM (Chrstn Ldrshp), with
MUNN, Janet (née White) m 1980; Maj, USA E. b 22 Oct 60. BA (Psych/Spanish), MA (Ldrshp &Min).

MUÑOZ, Manuel (Limón, 1989); Maj, L Am N. b 25 Mar 57, and
MUÑOZ, Nancy (née Letóna) (Central Corps, Guatemala, 1984) m 1985; Maj, L Am N. b 29 Dec 62.

MUTEWERA, Stanslous (Sinoia, 1970); Comr, TC, Zimb. b 25 Dec 47, and
MUTEWERA, Jannet (née Zinyemba) (Tsatse, 1973) m 1973; Comr, TPWM, Zimb. b 11 Nov 52. Served in UK.

MUTHURAJ, Solomon (Perumpazhanchy, 1967); Maj, Ind SE. b 7 May 48, and
MUTHURAJ, Gracemony (Chemparuthivillai, 1971) m 1972; Maj, Ind SE. b 23 Jul 43.

MUZORORI, Trustmore (Alaska Mine, Zimb, 1987); Maj, Asst CS, Ken. b 4 Mar 66. BA (Eng and Comm Studies), and
MUZORORI, Wendy (née Kunze) (Mutukwa, Zimb, 1989) m 1989; Maj, Ken. b 16 Feb 68.

MWIINGA, Adeck (Hakantu 1985); Maj, Zam. b 2 Aug 58, and
MWIINGA, Harriat (née Mukwesha)

(Chakanyemba, 1995) m 1995; Capt, Zam. b. 3 Mar 60.

N

NAMAI, Kiyoshi (Wakamatsu, 1984); Maj, Jpn. b 20 Apr 42, with
NAMAI, Fumiko (née Isago) m 1971; Maj, Jpn. b 1 Jan 48.

NANGI, Masamba Henri (Kinzadi, 1979); Maj, Con (Kin). b 21 May 53, with
NANGI, Josephine (née Nsimba Babinga); Maj, Con (Kin). b 30 Dec 53.

NANLABI, Priscilla (San Jose, Phil, 1980); Maj, GS, HK. b 15 Nov 58. Served in Phil.

NATHANIEL, Alladi (Bhogapuram, 1980); Maj, Ind C. b 9 Dec 52. BA, with
NATHANIEL, Rajeswari (née Yesu) m 1971; Maj, Ind C. b 6 Jul 55.

NAUD, Daniel (Paris-Montparnasse, 1979); Maj, Frce. b 8 Mar 54, and
NAUD, Eliane (née Volet) (Strasbourg, 1980) m 1980; Maj, Frce. b 3 Apr 60. Served in Belg.

NAUD, Francis (Paris Villette, Fra, 1987); Maj, Ger. b 15 Mar 58, and
NAUD, Anne-Dore (née Kaiser) (Hamburg, 1987) m 1987; Maj, Ger. b 26 Nov 59. Served in Fra and Belg.

NAUTA, James (Grand Rapids Heritage Hill, MI, 1989); Maj, USA C. b 18 Apr 44. BA (Psych), MSW, with
NAUTA, Janice B. (née Rager) m 1964; Maj, USA C. b 28 Jul 42.

NCUBE, Dubayi (Ndola, 1972); Maj, Zimb. b 8 Jun 52, and
NCUBE, Orlipha (née Ndlovu) (Mpopoma, 1976) m 1976; Maj, Zimb. b 25 Dec 54.

NEEDHAM, John (Atlanta, GA, 1977); Maj, USA S. b 11 Aug 51. MTS, with
NEEDHAM, Marthalynn (née Ling) m 1973; Maj, USA S. b 5 Jun 52. Served in UK.

NESTERENKO, Alex (Vitarte, 1986); Maj, S Am W. b 13 Dec 63, and
NESTERENKO, Luz (née Henríquez) (Santiago Central, 1990) m 1991; Capt, S Am W. b 10 May 67. Served in Rus/CIS.

NGANDA, Francis (Kanzalu, 1978); Maj, Ken. b 11 Jan 52, with
NGANDA, Lucy (née Njioka) m 1976; Maj, Ken. b 8 Apr 59.

NGKALE, Pilemon (Palu, 1978); Maj, Indon. b 10 Jul 54, and
NGKALE, Christien (née Kapoh) (Jakarta 2, 1979) m 1982; Maj, Indon. b 25 Dec 52.

NICOLASA, Pablo (Buenos Aires Central, 1989); Maj, S Am E. b 20 Feb 61, with
NICOLASA, Estela (née Ocampo) m 1984; Maj, S Am E. b 4 Jul 60.

NIELSEN, Jostein (Stavanger, Nor, 1980); Maj, E Eur. b 2 Jul 56, and
NIELSEN, Magna (née Våje) (Arendal, Nor, 1987) m 1978; Maj, E Eur. b 23 Sep 57. Served in Nor.

NJIRU, Nahashon Kidhakwa (Mombasa, 1984); Maj, Ken. b 30 Apr 53, with
NJIRU, Zipporah (née Ndeleve) m 1976; Maj, Ken. b 22 Feb 56.

NKANU, Bintoma Norbert (Kavwaya, 1981); Maj, Con (Kin). b 29 Jun 54, with
NKANU, Hélène (née Makuiza Lutonadio) m 1978; Maj, Con (Kin). b 18 Nov 61.

NKOMO, Dominic (Hwange, 1986); Maj, Zimb. b 24 Oct 59. Ww Maj Sitabile, pG 2005.

NLABU, Nzolameso Ferdinand (Kingudi, 1971); Lt-Col, Con (Kin); b 10 Aug 48, with
NLABU, Hélène (née Kingondi) m 1968; Lt-Col, Con (Kin). b 1 Mar 49.

NORE, Henoch (Kalawara, 1977); Maj, Indon. b 17 Aug 50, and
NORE, Agustina (née Warani) (Malang, 1974); Maj, Indon. b 25 Jan 51.

NSUMBU, Mambueni Emmanuel (Kingudi, 1981); Maj, Con (Kin). b 14 Aug 52, with
NSUMBU, Clémentine (née Mbimbu Bamba) m 1978; Maj, Con (Kin). b 10 Jun 59.

NUESCH, Nestor (New York Temple, NY, USA E, 1977); Col, TC, S Am E. b 1 Dec 49. BA (Bus Admin), MBA, and
NUESCH, Rebecca (née Brewer) (Ithaca, NY, USA E, 1977) m 1977; Col, TPWM, S Am E. b 17 Jan 55. Served in USA E.

NYAGA, Henry Njagi (Kagaari, 1986); Maj, Ken. b 21 Feb 54, with
NYAGA, Catherine (née Njoki) m 1984; Maj, Ken. b 3 Sep 59.

NYAMBALO, Francis (Migowi, Mal, 1982); Maj, GS, Zam. b 15 Mar 50, with
NYAMBALO, Jamiya (née Khumani) m 1980; Maj, CSWM, Zam. b 14 Aug 56. Served in Mal.

NYEREYEMHUKA, Funny (Dombwe, 1973); Maj, Zimb. b 15 Dec 50, and
NYEREYEMHUKA, Ellen (née Mpofu) (Gandiwa Society, 1978) m 1978; Maj, Zimb. b 9 Jul 55.

NZITA, Jerôme (Bakongo, 1977); Maj, Con (Braz). b 15 Oct 48, with
NZITA, Jeanne (née Nsongala Jeanne) m 1976; b 26 Jun 52.

O

OALANG, David (Sta Barbara, 1995); Capt, Phil. b 20 Feb 66, and
OALANG, Elsa (Quezon City 1, 1988); Maj, Phil. b 25 May 62. BSc (Mass Comm)

OBANDO, Maria Eugenia (née Venegas) (Central, Costa Rica, 1991); Capt, L Am N. b 21 Apr 65, with
OBANDO, Javier m 1988; Capt, L Am N. b 2 Mar 66.

OBENG-APPAU, Richmond (Suame, 1989); Maj, Gha. b 1 Nov 61, with
OBENG-APPAU, Dora (née Kwane) m 1986; Maj, Gha. b 26 Jun 60.

O'BRIEN, Douglas G. (San Francisco Citadel, 1976); Lt-Col, USA W. b 1 Aug 49. BA (Speech), MA (Relig), and
O'BRIEN, Diane (née Lillicrap) (Staines, UK, 1975) m 1988; Lt-Col, USA W. b 8 Nov 50. FTCL, GTCL. Served in UK.

ØDEGAARD, B. Donald (Oslo 3, Nor, 1966); Comr, IS Prog Res, IHQ. b 18 Dec 40. Cand Mag, and
ØDEGAARD, Berit (née Gjersøe) (Tønsberg, Nor, 1964) m 1967; Comr, IHQ. b 27 Sep 44. SRN. Served in Zimb, S Afr, Nig (TC/TPWO), E Afr (TC/TPWO) and Nor (TC/TPWM).

ODURO, Elizabeth (née Nimfa) (Achiase, Gha, 1983); Maj, TSWM, Lib. b 13 Jul 70, with
ODURO, James m 1981; Maj, Lib. b 21 Jun 59. Served in Gha.

ODURO, Godfried (Kyekyewere, 1981); Maj, Gha. b 17 Jul 54, with
ODURO, Felicia (née Obeng) m 1978; Maj, Gha. b 25 Jun 60.

ODURO-AMOAH, Peter (Achiase, 1989); Maj, Gha. b 26 Aug 58, with
ODURO-AMOAH, Grace (née Fosua) m 1984; Maj, Gha. b 11 Feb 64.

OKLAH, Samuel (Accra Newtown, Gha, 1983); Maj, Ken. b 5 Mar 58, with
OKLAH, Philomina (née Addo) (Tema, Gha, 1985) m 1985; Maj, Ken. b 21 Dec 65. Served in Gha.

OKOROUGO, Edwin Rapurnchukwu (Amesi, 1982); Maj, Nig. b 2 Aug 49. BA (Relig Studies), MA (Eth and Phil), with
OKOROUGO, Agnes (née Nwokekwe) m 1978; Maj, Nig. b 5 Apr 52.

OLAUSSON, Kjell Edor (Hisingskår, 1978); Maj, Swdn. n 12 Nov 56, and
OLAUSSON, Gunilla (née Lind) (Helsingborg, 1986) m 1986; Maj, Swdn. b 23 Aug 60.

OLEWA, John (Mukhombe, 1986); Maj, Ken. b 12 Nov 54, with

312

OLEWA, Mary (née Kadzo) m 1982; Maj, Ken. b 19 Sep 1960.

OLORUNTOBA, Festus (Supare, 1976); Lt-Col, CS, Nig. b 7 Jul 55, and
OLORUNTOBA, Gloria (Egbe, 1986) m 1986; Lt-Col, TSWM, Nig. b 8 Mar 61.

ONYEKWERE, Paul I. (Umuogo, 1984); Maj, Nig. b 27 Jul 58, with
ONYEKWERE, Edinah P.; Maj, Nig. b 29 Oct 61.

ORASIBE, Patrick (Akokwa, 1988); Maj, Nig. b 9 Oct 58, with
ORASIBE, Blessing (née Chituru) Maj, Nig. b 5 Dec 58.

ORD, Norman (Peterborough Citadel, 1992); Capt, UK. b 28 Sep 55. MA (Hons) (French & Music), PGCE, CDRS, with
ORD, Christine (née Ross) m 1980; Capt, UK. b 8 Dec 54. MBChB (Hons), Dip CH (Child Health), CDRS, DipTh (App Theol).

OTA, Haruhisa (Hamamatsu, 1973); Maj, Jpn. b 30 Jan 50, and
OTA, Hiromi (née Nakatsugawa) (Hamamatsu, 1973) m 1976; Maj, Jpn. b 21 Jun 48.

OWEN, Graham (Nuneaton, UK, 1977); Maj, CS, Den. b 8 Jul 53, and
OWEN, Kirsten (née Jacobsen) (Copenhagen Temple, 1977) m 1978; Maj, Den. b 2 May 56. Served in UK.

OYESANYA, Michael (Iperu, 1984); Maj, Nig. b 17 May 61, and
OYESANYA, Roseline (Iperu, 1988) m 1988; Maj, Nig. b 21 Jun 65.

P

PAEZ, Jorge O. (Bahía Blanca, 1961); Lt-Col, S Am E. b 19 May 41, and
PAEZ, Azucena (née Berenguer) (La Unión, 1968) m 1973; Lt-Col, S Am E. b 1 Dec 45.

PANG, Kie-chang (Yung Chun, 1975); Maj, Kor. b 7 Oct 44, and
PARK, Keum-ja (Ah Hyun, 1973) m 1975; Maj, Kor. b 16 Mar 44.

PAONE, Massimo (Naples, 1977); Lt-Col, OC, It. b 8 Jun 52, and
PAONE, Elizabeth Jane (née Moir) (Nunhead, UK, 1982) m 1982; Lt-Col, CPWM, It. b 17 Dec 58. BA (Hons). Served in UK and Frce.

PARAMADHAS, Arulappan (Elanthiady, 1972); Maj, Ind SE. b 11 May 54, and
PARAMADHAS, S. Retnam (Changaneri, 1974) m 1976; Maj, Ind SE. b 30 May 51.

PARDO, Zoilo B. (Santa Ana, CA, USA W, 1989); Maj, CS, L Am N. b 9 Dec 53. BA (Acct), with

PARDO, Magali (née Pacheco) m 1980; Maj, TSWM, L Am N. b 20 Apr 56. BA (Gen Ed), BA (Acct). Served in USA W and Mex.

PAREDES, Tito E. (La Paz, S Am W, 1976); Lt-Col, USA E. b 14 Aug 54, and
PAREDES, Martha (née Nery) (Cochabamba, S Am W, 1976) m 1977; Lt-Col, USA E. b 3 Jun 54. Served in S Am W and L Am N (CS/TSWM).

PARK, Chong-duk (Pupyung, 1977); Maj, Kor. b 22 May 50, with
YOON, Eun-sook m 1975; Maj, Kor. b 23 Oct 50.

PARK, Man-hee (Chung Ju, 1975); Lt-Col, CS, Kor. b 11 Aug 47, with
KIM, Keum-nyeo m 1973; Lt-Col, TSWM, Kor. b 5 Feb 51.

PARK, Nai-hoon (Syn Heung, 1978); Maj, Kor. b 23 Oct 46, with
KIL, Soon-boon m 1971; Maj, Kor. b 26 Nov 49.

PARKER, Michael (Hucknall, 1977); Maj, UK. b 28 Jul 50, with
PARKER, Joan (née Brailsford) m 1971; Maj, UK. b 16 Jan 52. Served at IHQ.

PARMAR, Kantilal K. (Ode, 1983); Maj, Ind W. b 1 Jun 53. BA, BEd, and
PARMAR, Eunice K. (née Gaikwad) (Mohmedwadi, 1977) m 1983; Maj, Ind W. b 30 Oct 52.

PATRA, Samir (Calcutta Central, 1985); Maj, Ind N. b 6 Aug 57, with
PATRA, Sita m 1983; Maj, Ind N. b 5 Apr 65.

PAULSSON, Christian (Centrumkåren, Stockholm, 1984); Maj, Swdn. b 28 Jun 64, and
PAULSSON, Anna-Lena (née Wiklund) (Arvidsjaur/Malmberget, 1984); m 1986; Maj, Swdn. b 18 Aug 63.

PAWAR, Suresh S. (Ahmednagar EBH, 1981); Maj, Ind W. b 10 Feb 60, and
PAWAR, Martha (née Shirsath) (Ahmednagar Central, 1981) m 1981; Maj, Ind W. b 17 Nov 63.

PAYNE, Goff (Godfrey) (Tunbridge Wells, UK, 1980); Maj, OC, Mal. b 15 Oct 51, with
PAYNE, Diane (née Harris) m 1975; Maj, CPWM, Mal. b 28 Dec 52. Served in UK, E Afr, Zam & Mal and Uga (OC/CPWM).

PEACOCK, Raymond L. (Denver Citadel, CO, 1963); Lt-Col, USA W. b 9 Mar 42. BA (Soc), MSW (Soc Prog Admin), and
PEACOCK, Carolyn Bea (née Irby) (Portland Harbour Light, 1968) m 1969; Lt-Col, USA W. b 7 Aug 47. Served at USA Nat.

PEARCE, Lynette J. (Parkes, Aus E, 1972); Comr, IS Int Per, IHQ. b 13 Jan 45. BA. Served in Aus E and at ICO.

Biographical Information

PEDDLE, Brian (Dildo/New Harbour, NF, Can, 1977); Maj, NZ. b 8 Aug 57, and
PEDDLE, Rosalie (née Rowe) (Carbonear, NF, Can, 1976) m 1978; Maj, NZ. b 17 Jan 56. Served in Can.

PETER, K. C. (Amarakunnu, 1980); Maj, Ind SW. b 15 Apr 48. BSc, with
PETER, K. J. Annamma; Maj, Ind SW. b 4 Feb 51.

PETTERSEN, Per Arne (Sarpsborg, 1969); Maj, Nor. b 20 Mar 47, and
PETTERSEN, Lillian (née Madsø) (Namsos, 1969) m 1971; Maj, Nor. b 5 Jun 45.

PHILIP, Alister (Colombo Central, 1988); Maj, Sri Lan. b 11 Oct 61, and
PHILIP, Nilanthi (née Fernando) (Moratumulla, 1987) m 1989; Maj, Sri Lan. b 24 May 67.

PHILIP, P. K. (Thottamon, 1975); Maj, Ind SW. b 12 Dec 48, and
PHILIP, Rachel (Kottarakara Central, 1980) m 1979; Maj, Ind SW. b 10 Nov 54.

PIGFORD, Raymond E. (Wellsville, NY, 1970); Lt-Col, USA E. b 26 Jun 44. BA (Sci), MA (Ed Admin), with
PIGFORD, Edith Helen (née Waldron) m 1966; Lt-Col, USA E. b 12 May 45. BA (Chr Ed and Fr). Served in Can.

PILKINGTON, George A. (Lamberhead Green, 1971); Maj, UK. b 11 Apr 50. SRN. m 1974; Maj Vera, ret 2007.

POA, Selly Barak (Jakarta, 1979); Maj, Indon. b 25 Sep 55, and
POA, Anastasia (née Djoko Slamet) (Surakarta 2, 1984) m 1985; Maj, Indon. b 29 Jun 1962.

POBJIE, Barry R. (Paddington, Aus E, 1965); Comr, IS SPEA, IHQ. b.25 Jan 45 Ww Capt Ruth, pG 1978. Served in PNG and E Eur (TC), and
POBJIE, Raemor (née Wilson) (Port Kembla, Aus E, 1971) m 1980; Comr, SWM SPEA, IHQ. b 22 Sep 48. Served in NZ, Aus E and E Eur (TPWM).

POKE, Victor (Burnie, Aus S, 1968); Comr, TC, Swdn. b 8 Jan 46, and
POKE, Roslyn (née Pengilly) (Maylands, Aus S, 1968) m 1970; Comr, TPWM, Swdn. b 20 Jun 45. Served in Aus S and UK (CS/TSWM).

PONNIAH, Masilamony (Periavilai, 1969); Lt-Col, Ind SE. b 2 Jun 49, and
PONNIAH, Sathiyabama (Layam, 1974) m 1974; Lt-Col, Ind W. b 14 Apr 56. Served in Ind W and Nor.

POSADAS, Leopoldo (Dagupan City, 1981); Maj, Phil. b 18 Aug 58, and
POSADAS, Evelyn (née Felix) (Hermoza, 1982) m 1982; Maj, Phil. b 2 Aug 57. Served in Ban.

POSILLICO, Joseph E. (Los Angeles Lincoln Heights, CA, 1972); Maj, USA W. b 29 Dec 50, and
POSILLICO, Shawn L. (née Patrick) (San Francisco, CA, 1984) m 1988; Maj, USA W. b 3 Aug 57. BS (Bus Econ).

PRASAD, P. C. (Annavaram, 1981); Maj, Ind C. b 9 Sep 58, with
PRASAD, Krupamma m 1979; Maj, Ind C. b 4 Jun 59.

PRITCHETT, Wayne (Deer Lake, NF, Can, 1970); Lt-Col, IHQ. b 13 Aug 46. BA, BEd, MTS, and
PRITCHETT, Myra (née Rice) (Roberts Arm, NF, Can, 1969) m 1972; Lt-Col, IHQ. b 19 Jun 50. BA, MTS. Served in Can.

PUOTINIEMI, Tella (née Juntunen) (Helsinki IV, 1983); Maj, Fin. b 17 Oct 52, and
PUOTINIEMI, Antero (Oulu, 1981) m 1983; Maj, Fin. b 15 Oct 48.

R

RAINES, Timothy (Mt Vernon, NY, 1971); Lt-Col, USA E. b 30 Dec 47. BS (Org Mgmt), and
RAINES, Lynda Lou (née Swingle) (Zanesville, OH, 1969) m 1969; Lt-Col, USA E. b 23 Aug 48. BS (Org Mgmt).

RAJAKUMARI, P. Mary (née Desari) (New Colony, Bapatla, Ind C, 1978); Comr, TC, TPWM, Ind W. MA (Engl), MA (Hist). Served in Ind M & A, at IHQ, at Ind Cent Off, in Ind W (THLS), Ind N (TPWM) and Ind SE (TPWM). Ww Comr P. D. Krupa Das, pG 2007

RAJU, M. Daniel (M. R. Nagaram, 1984); Maj, Ind C. b 20 Jun 54. MA (Econ), with
RAJU, Rachel (née Kondamudi) m 1982; Maj, Ind C. b 15 Jun 62.

RAJU, K. Samuel (Kakulapadu, 1980); Maj, Ind C. b 5 May 58, and
RAJU, K. Raja (née Kumari) (Pedaparapudi, 1980); m 1981; Maj, Ind C. b 3 May 64.

RANDIVE, Benjamin B. (Shevgaon, 1981); Maj, Ind W. b 11 Jan 60, and
RANDIVE, Ratan S. (née Teldune) (Shenegaon Central, 1981) m 1981; Maj, Ind W. b 17 Aug 62.

RANGI, Gidion (Kulawi, 1990), Maj, Indon. b 7 Aug 60, with
RANGI, Lidia (née Norlan) m 1985; Maj, Indon. b 25 Nov 1965.

Biographical Information

RAO, S. Jayananda (Madras Central, 1981); Maj, Ind C. b 29 Oct 52, with
RAO, S. Christiansen m 1976; Maj, Ind C. b 22 Dec 60.

RASELALOME, Johannes (Seshego, 1982); Maj, S Afr. b 3 May 60, and
RASELALOME, Veliswa Atalanta (née Mehu) (Tshoxa, 1982) m 1985; Maj, S Afr. b 16 Jul 62.

RATNAM, Guddam Venkata (Guraza, 1973); Maj, Ind C. b 5 Apr 49, with
RATNAM, Gaddam Rajakumari m 1969; Maj, Ind C. b 15 Mar 52.

RAWALI, Lapu (Koki, 1983); Maj, PNG. b 27 Jul 54. BA, with
RAWALI, Araga (née Heroha) m 1974; Maj, PNG. b 19 Apr 55.

REDDISH, Graeme John (Thames, NZ, 1974); Lt-Col, IHQ. b 28 Aug 49. Ww Maj Nola, pG 2002, and
REDDISH, Wynne (née Jellyman) (Miramar, NZ, 1982) m 2005; Lt-Col, IHQ. b 22 Apr 57. Served in NZ.

REEL, Robert J. (Wilkes-Barre, PA, 1970); Maj, USA E. b 28 Dec 44. BA (Org Mgmt), with
REEL, Lynette M. (née Hufford) m 1964; Maj, USA E. b 2 Sep 45. BA (Org Mgmt).

REES, John (Ipswich, 1974); Maj, Aus E. b 29 Jun 47, with
REES, Narelle (née Lehmann) m 1969; Maj, Aus E. b 27 Jun 48. Served in PNG and Rus.

REFSTIE, Peder R. (Mandal, Nor, 1965); Comr, TC, Brz. b 13 Jul 43, and
REFSTIE, Janet M. (née Dex) (Bedford, UK, 1966) m 1969; Comr, TPWM, Brz. b 7 Jul 43. Served in UK, S Am W, Port, Nor, Sp (OC/ CPWM), at IHQ and in S Am E (TC/ TPWM).

REYNOLDS, James (Canton Citadel, OH, 1976); Maj, USA E. b 2 Jun 48. BS (HRM), with
REYNOLDS, Blanche Louise (née Labus) m 1972; Maj, USA E. b 16 Dec 49.

RICE, Sandra (Roberts Arm, NF, 1980); Maj, Can. b 16 Feb 58. BEd, BA, MTS.

RICHARDSON, Alfred (Mount Dennis, ON, 1967); Maj, Can. b 5 Dec 44, with
RICHARDSON, Ethel (née Howell) m 1964; Maj, Can. b 2 Apr 43.

RICHARDSON, Lonneal (Bloomington, IN, 1983) Maj, USA C. b 3 Mar 59. BA (Bus Admin), and
RICHARDSON, Patty (née Barton) (Omaha South, NE, 1979) m 1983; Maj, USA C. b 30 Jan 57. BA (Bus Admin).

RIEDER, Beat (Basle 1, Switz, 1989); Maj, Ger. b 8 Oct 58, and

RIEDER, Annette (née Pell) (Cologne, 1986) m 1989; Maj, Ger. b 9 May 64. Served in Switz and Can.

RISAN, Jan (Stavanger, 1990); Maj, Nor. b 28 Mar 63, with
RISAN, Kjersti Håland m 1982; Maj, Nor. b 30 May 63.

ROBERTS, Campbell (New Brighton, 1969); Maj, NZ. b 15 Feb 47. BTh, and
ROBERTS, Marlyn (née Robertson) (Naenae, 1969) m 1971; Maj, NZ. b 26 Oct 46.

ROBERTS, Jonathan (Leicester Central, 1986); Maj, UK. b 20 Feb 62. BA (Hons) (Econ), BA (Hons) (Theol), and
ROBERTS, Jayne (née Melling) (Southend Citadel, 1985) m 1986; Maj, UK. b 23 Apr 58. BA (Hons) (Eng).

ROBERTS, William A. (Detroit Citadel, MI, USA C, 1971); Comr, IS Bus Admin, IHQ. b 26 Feb 46. BS, MA, with
ROBERTS, Nancy Louise (née Overly) m 1968; Comr, IHQ. b 27 Oct 43. BS, MA. Served in USA C and S Am E (TC/TPWM).

ROBINSON, Ian (Santa Ana, CA, USA W); Capt, Sing. b 15 Oct 48. BA (Pastoral Ministries), with
ROBINSON, Isobel (née Lawrie) m 1976; Capt, Sing. b 15 Mar 56. Served in USA W.

ROTONA, Kabona (Boregaina, 1983); Maj, PNG. b 10 Jan 59, with
ROTONA, Margaret (née Michael) m 1978; Maj, PNG. b 14 Jan 62.

ROWE, Dennis (Norwood, 1982); Maj, Aus S. b 25 Jun 48, and
ROWE, Patricia (née Muir) (Woodville Gardens, 1950) m 1972; Maj, Aus S. b 18 Mar 48. Served in HK and Tai.

ROWE, Lindsay (Chance Cove, NF, Can, 1972); Maj, S Afr. b 21 Sep 51. BA (Hon), M Div, and
ROWE, Lynette (née Hutt) (Winterton, NF, Can, 1971) m 1974; Maj, S Afr. b 13 Feb 52. Served in Can and Carib.

ROWE, Raymond (Chance Cove, NF, 1968); Maj, Can. b 3 Nov 47, and
ROWE, Audrey (née Knee) (Corner Brook, NF, 1968) m 1970; Maj, Can. b 30 Jul 44.

ROWLAND, Mervyn (Granville, Aus E, 1967); Lt-Col, OC, HK. b 11 Jul 43. BAL, Grad Dip (Conflict Resolution), and
ROWLAND, Elaine (née Holley) (Granville, Aus E, 1968) m 1968; Lt-Col, CPWM, HK. b 11 Oct 46. BAL. Served in Aus E and HK (GS/CPWM).

RUTANHIRA, Elackson (Dubugwani, 1988); Maj, Zimb. b 27 Jul 62. Dip (Gen Mgmt), with

Biographical Information

RUTANHIRA, Shiellah (née Jakaza) m 1986; Maj, Zimb. b 6 Oct 68.

S

SAAVEDRA, Lidia (Tucumán, 1979), Maj, S Am E. b 9 May 49.

SAKAMESSO, Jean-Aléxis (Ouenze, 1979); Maj, Con (Braz). b 25 May 50, with
SAKAMESSO, Pauline (née Louya) m 1976; Maj, Con (Braz). b 19 Jan 56.

SALOGI, Sakius (Kulawi, 1973), Maj, Indon. b 10 Aug 51, and
SALOGI, Femmy (née Rawung) (Manado, 1980) m 2001; Maj, Indon. b 16 Jun 56.

SAM DEVARAJ, Appavoo (Palayamcottai, 1976); Maj, Ind SE. b 23 Jun 51. BA, MA (Public Admin), and
DEVARAJ, Kanagaretnam (Anducodu, 1975) m 1977; Maj, Ind SE. b 19 Oct 51.

SAMRAJ, Jeyaraj (Booth Tucker Hall, Nagercoil, 1982); Maj, Ind SE. b 14 Aug 58. MA (Sociol), and
SAMRAJ, Jessi Thayammal (Gnaniahpuram, 1986) m 1986; Maj, Ind SE. b 21 Oct 63. MusB. Served at Ind Nat.

SAMUEL, Chadalavada (Achanta, 1970); Maj, Ind C. b 15 Aug 48, with
SAMUEL, Mary Rani Maj, Ind C. b 5 Jul 52.

SAMUEL, Johns (Central Corps, Trivandrum, 1984); Maj, Ind SW. b 22 May 53. BSc. Ww Maj Annamma, pG 2007.

SAMUEL, M. (Central, Kottarakara, 1974); Maj, Ind SW. b 15 Dec 51, and
SAMUEL, K. Thankamma (Ommanoor, 1977) m 1976; Maj, Ind SW. b 15 Oct 53.

SAMUELKUTTY, Simson (Kanacode, 1979); Maj, Ind SW. b 27 May 57, with
SAMUELKUTTY, Lilly Bai m 1982; Maj, Ind SW. b 10 Jul 55.

SANCHEZ, Oscar (Lima Central, S Am W, 1982); Col, TC, L Am N. b 21 Nov 56, and
SANCHEZ, Ana Rosa (née Limache) (Huayra K'assa, S Am W, 1985) m 1987; Col, TPWM, L Am N. b 12 Jun 60. Served in Sp, S Am W, USA W and Brz.

SANGCHHUNGA (Ratu, 1974); Maj, Ind E. b 15 Mar 52, and
VANLALAUVI (Ngopa, 1975) m 1975; Maj, Ind E. b 10 Jun 52.

SATHYADHAS, N. Edwin (Kolvey, 1981); Maj, Ind SE. b 10 Aug 55, with
SATHYADHAS, Gnana Jessibell m 1980; Maj, Ind SE b 15 Jun 57

SAVAGE, Peter J. (Linwood, 1969); Lt-Col, NZ. b 21 Oct 42. CFRE, with
SAVAGE, Raeline J. (née Allan) m 1966;

Lt-Col, NZ. b 29 Dec 46. BMus.

SCHMID, Fritz (Adelboden/Thun, 1980); Maj, Switz. b 20 Nov 53, and
SCHMID, Margrit (née Dössegger) (Seon, 1981) m 1981; Maj, Switz. b 4 Dec 52.

SCHOLLMEIER, Rudolf (Mannheim, 1968); Maj, Ger. b 9 Nov 43, and
SCHOLLMEIER, Christine (née Harvey) (Cologne, 1968) m 1970; Maj, Ger. b 31 Jul 48.

SCHOLTENS, Teunis (Zwolle, 1980); Maj, Neth. b 28 Aug 52, with
SCHOLTENS, Hendrika (née Stuurop) m 1977; Maj, Neth. b 28 May 56.

SCHWARTZ, Barry Richard (Goodwood, 1973); Maj, S Afr. b 17 Apr 48, with
SCHWARTZ, Anja Jacoba (née Kamminga) m 1967; Maj, S Afr. b 28 Jul 48.

SEILER, Paul R. (Hollywood Tabernacle, CA, USA W, 1981); Lt-Col, CS, USA C. b 23 May 51. MBA, BS (Bus Admin), with
SEILER, Carol (née Sturgess) m 1978; Lt-Col, TSWM, USA C. b 6 Apr 52. RN, BS (Nursing), MPH. Served in USA W.

SERÈM, Alberto (Lisbon Central, 1985); Maj, OC, Port. b 27 Nov 56, and
SERÈM, Maria José (née Leitão) (Picheleira, 1977) m 1980; Maj, CPWM, Port. b 13 Dec 52. Served in UK and It.

SEVAK, David Keshav (Sokhada, 1981); Maj, Ind W. b 15 Nov 50, and
SEVAK, Vimalaben (Bharoda, 1983) m 1983; Maj, Ind W. b 5 Jun 63.

SEWELL, Roland (Buckingham, 1976); Lt-Col, UK. b 26 Dec 44. MBE, BSc (Hons) (Eng), CEng, MICE, with
SEWELL, Dawn (née Towle) m 1967; Lt-Col, UK. b 25 Dec 46. RN. Served in Zam, Nig (CS/TSWM) and at IHQ.

SEYMOUR, Geanette (Belmore, 1973); Lt-Col, CS, Aus E. b 20 Feb 50. BA (Soc Work).

SHAKESPEARE, David (Catford, UK, 1981); Maj, IHQ. b 8 Oct 59. Served in UK, and
SHAKESPEARE, Karen (née Grainger) (Catford, UK, 1980) m 1981; Maj, UK. b 2 Aug 54. BEd (Hons), MA (Pastoral Theol), MA (Adult Ed with Theol Reflection).

SHAROV, Svetlana (née Blagodirova) (Chisinau Botannica, 1999); Capt, E Eur. b 18 Jun 65, with
SHAROV, Alexander m 1986; Capt, E Eur. b 6 Jul 57.

SHAVANGA, Edward Alumasa (Matunda, 1982); Maj, Ken. b 9 Mar 58, with
SHAVANGA, Florence (née Vulehi) m 1979; Maj, Ken. b 11 Oct 60.

Biographical Information

SHAVANGA, Moses (Musudzuu, 1984); Maj, Ken. b 10 Jun 57, with
SHAVANGA, Gladys (née Sharia) m 1982; Maj, Ken. b 18 Mar 61. Served in Tanz.

SHEKWA, Albert Zondiwe (Emangweni, 1974); Maj, S Afr. b 12 Mar 51, and
SHEKWA, Peggy (née Maimela) (Louis Trichardt, 1974) m 1974; Maj, S Afr. b 3 Jun 54.

SHEPHERD, Glen (Winnipeg Citadel, 1981); Col, CS, Can. b 7 Feb 48. BA, MA (Econ-Sociol), with
SHEPHERD, Eleanor (née Pitcher) m 1969; Col, TSWM, Can. b 4 Mar 47. BA (Econ-Sociol). Served in Frce (TC/TPWM) and at IHQ.

SHIN, Moon-ho (Yang Chung, 1973); Maj, Kor. b 1 May 44, with
CHO, In-sook m 1970; Maj, Kor. b 12 Aug 47.

SIAGIAN, Pieter (Solo, 1973); Lt-Col, Indon. b 5 May 45, and
SIAGIAN, Sukarsih (née Sosromihardjo) (Turen, 1972) m 1975; Lt-Col, Indon. b 2 Aug 49.

SIJUADE, Michael A. (Ife Ife, 1992); Capt, Nig. b 13 Jun 64, with
SIJUADE, Comfort m 1990; Capt, Nig. b 11 Nov 67.

SIMATUPANG, Lidia (Semarang, 1981); Maj, Indon. b 7 Jun 50.

SIMON, T. J. (Perumpetty, 1977); Maj, Ind SW. b 15 Nov 52, with
SIMON, Ammini, m 1979; Maj, Ind SW. b 1 Feb 60.

SINGH, Dilip (Simultala, 1990); Maj, Ind N. b 4 Nov 68, and
SINGH, Nivedita (née Christian) (Fatapukur, 1992) m 1992; Capt, Ind N. b 14 Sep 71.

SJOGREN, Daniel (St Paul (Temple), MN, 1972); Maj, USA C. b 12 Nov 51, and
SJOGREN, Rebecca (née Nefzger) (Hibbing, MN, 1973) m 1973; Maj, USA C. b 11 Jun 53.

SMITH, Charles (Kansas City (Blue Valley), MN, 1978); Maj, USA C. b 22 Aug 57, with
SMITH, Sharon (née Cockrill) m 1975; Maj, USA C. b 7 Mar 54.

SMITH, Jeffrey (Flint Citadel, MI, 1986); Maj, USA C. b 19 Jan 54. BA (Bible), MRE, with
SMITH, Dorothy R. (née Kumpula) m 1974; Maj, USA C. b 22 Oct 54. BA (Psychol/Sociol), MA (Pastoral Counselling).

SMITH, Peter (Malvern, UK, 1980); Maj, IHQ. b 6 Sep 43. Solicitor of the Supreme Court. Served in UK.

SOLOMON, K. M. (Oramana, 1978); Maj, Ind SW. b 3 Jun 55, and

SOLOMON, P. K. Elizabeth (1982) m 1982; Maj, Ind SW. b 5 Nov 56.

SONDA, Jean-Pierre (Mahita, 1990); Maj, Con (Braz). b 28 Nov 56, with
SONDA, Jeannette (née Ndoudi) m 1988; Maj, Con (Braz). b 25 Jan 67.

SOUZA, Maruilson (Petrolina, 1987); Maj, Brz. b 6 May 64. BA(Acct), MBA, BA (Theol), MA (Theol), with
SOUZA, Francisca m 1982; Maj, Brz. b 15 Oct 66.

SPILLER, Lyndon S. (Springvale, 1970); Lt-Col, Aus S. b 26 May 45, with
SPILLER, Julie (née King) m 1968; Lt-Col, Aus S. b 7 Aug 47. Served in Aus S, Pak, Zam, Gha (CS/TSWO) and E Afr (CS/TSWM).

STARRETT, Daniel L. (Roswell, NM, USA W, 1973); Lt-Col, USA Nat. b 1 Jun 52. BS (Appl Bus & Mgmt), MBA, and
STARRETT, Helen (née Laverty) (San José, CA, USA W, 1973) m 1974; Lt-Col, USA Nat. b 20 Jul 48. Served in USA W and at IHQ.

STERLING, David (Tottenham Citadel, UK, 1975); Maj, IHQ (SALT Afr). b 11 Mar 49. BA (Eng) (Hons), and
STERLING, Brenda (née Turner) (Tottenham Citadel, UK, 1975) m 1976; Maj, IHQ (SALT Afr). b 17 Jun 44. MA. Served in UK.

STOCKMAN, Mona Valborg (née Ericson) (Uppsala, 1978); Maj, Swdn. b 24 Nov 46. BA (Sociology), and
STOCKMAN, Björn (Kalmar, 1981) m 1984; Maj, Swdn. b 12 Nov 51.

STRASSE, Wilson S. (Rio Grande, 1988); Maj, Brz. b 20 Jul 63, with
STRASSE, Nara m 1985, Mjr; Brz. b 12 Feb 68.

STREET, Robert (Stotfold, UK, 1968); Comr, IS to CoS, IHQ. b 24 Feb 47, with
STREET, Janet (née Adams) m 1967; Comr, WSWM, IHQ. b 19 Aug 45. Served in UK and Aus E (CS/TSWM).

STRICKLAND, Ron (Santa Barbara, CA, 1978); Maj, USA W. b 7 Aug 45. BS (Bus Mgmt), and
STRICKLAND, Pamela (née Fuss) (Minot, ND, 1969) m 1970; Maj, USA W. b 1 Dec 48.

STRISSEL, Dennis L. R. (St Louis Northside, MO, USA C, 1974); Col, TC, Gha. b 4 Mar 52, and
STRISSEL, Sharon (née Olson) (Sioux City, IA, USA C, 1974) m 1975; Col, TPWM, Gha. b 7 Oct 51. Served in USA C and S Afr.

STRONG, Leslie J. (Kalbar, 1965); Comr, TC, Aus E. b 5 Apr 43. BAL, and
STRONG, Coral (née Scholz) (Kalbar, 1966)

Biographical Information

m 1967; Comr, TPWM, Aus E. b 30 Mar 44.
Served in Aus S (CS/TSWM).

SUNDIKA, Joel (Karambazungu, 1988); Maj,
Zimb. b 1 Sep 56, with
SUNDIKA, Auxillia (née Makanda) m 1985;
Maj, Zimb. b 4 Apr 57.

SUSEELKUMAR, John (Pallickal, 1978); Maj,
Ind SW. b 11 Oct 51. Ww Maj Aleyamma,
pG 2007.

SUTHANANTHA DHAS, Perinbanayagam
(Booth Tucker Hall, Nagercoil, 1986); Maj,
Ind SE. b 14 Oct 56. MA, HACDP, and
SUTHANANTHADHAS, Esther Evangelin
(Attoor, 1986) m 1986; Maj, Ind SE.
b 18 Apr 63. BSc.

SUTHERLAND, Margaret (Sleaford, UK,
1968); Comr, Principal, ICO. b 22 Jul 43. MA,
ARCO. Served in Zam, UK, Zimb (CS) and
at IHQ (ISAfr).

SWAMIDHAS, Chelliah (Kannankulam, 1977);
Maj, Ind SE. b 21 Apr 55, and
SWAMIDHAS Joice Bai (Kaliancaud, 1973)
m 1977; Maj, Ind SE. b 16 Feb 53.

SWANSON, Barry C. (Chicago Mt Greenwood,
IL, USA C, 1978); Comr, IS Am and Carib,
IHQ. b 22 Apr 50. BS (Marketing), with
SWANSON, E. Sue (née Miller) m 1975; Comr,
SWM Am and Carib, IHQ. b 13 Aug 50. BA
(Soc Work). Served in USA C (CS/TSWM)
and at USA Nat CS/NSWM).

SWYERS, Philip W. (Dallas Temple, TX,
USA S, 1968); Comr, TC, USA W.
b 22 Apr 44. BBA, and
SWYERS, Patricia Lyvonne (née Lowery)
(Charlotte, NC, USA S, 1962) m 1968; Comr,
TPWM, USA W. b 26 Aug 41. Served in USA
C (CS/TSWM) and USA S (CS/TSWM)

T

TADI, Patrick (Bimbouloulou, 1984); Maj,
Con (Braz). b 17 Apr 59, with
TADI, Clémentine (née Bassinguinina)
m 1982; Maj, Con (Braz). b 4 Apr 58.

TAMPAI, Yusak (Turen, 1993); Capt, Indon.
b 25 Feb 66, and
TAMPAI, Widiawati (Anca, 1995) m 1997;
Capt, Indon. b 19 Apr 73. Served at ICO.

TAN, Thean Seng (Penang, 1966); Lt-Col, Sing.
b 24 Jul 45, and
LOO, Lay Saik (Penang, 1966) m 1969;
Lt-Col, Sing. b 12 Jul 47. Served at IHQ, in
Sing (OC/CPWM) and HK (OC/CPWM).

TANAKA, Teiichi (Omori, 1983); Maj, Jpn.
b 19 Feb 52, and
TANAKA, Chieko (née Hirose) (Nishinari,
1977) m 1984; Maj, Jpn. b 22 Apr 48.

TARI, Samuel (Shantinagar, 1970); Maj, Pak.
b 7 Sep 49, and
SAMUEL, Victoria (née Khurshid) (Khanewal,
1971) m 1973; Maj, Pak. b 15 Oct 52.

TATY, Daniel (Pointe-Noire, 1982), Maj,
Con (Braz). b 14 Feb 54, with
TATY, Angèle (née Louya) m 1980; Maj,
Con (Braz). b 6 Dec 56.

TELFER, Ivor (Clydebank, 1982); Maj, UK.
b 26 May 54. MSc (Strategic Management), with
TELFER, Carol (née Anderson) m 1980; Maj,
UK. b 26 Aug 59. Dip Post Traumatic Stress,
Stress Consultant, CIPP.

TEMINE, David (Lembina, 1992); Capt, PNG.
b 12 May 70, and
TEMINE, Doreen (née A'o) (Kamila, 1999)
m 2002; Capt, PNG. b 24 Feb 73.

THANHLIRA (Ratu, 1971); Maj, Ind E.
b 15 Feb 49, and
THANTLUANGI (Central, 1975) m 1975;
Maj, Ind E. b 5 Jan 50.

THEODORE, Sinous (Luly, Haiti, 1981); Maj,
Carib. b 20 Oct 52, and
THEODORE, Marie Lourdes (née Doralus)
(Port-au-Prince, Haiti, 1981) m 1982; Maj,
Carib. b 22 Sep 57.

THOMAS, Gera (EBLH, Bapatla, Ind C. 1988);
Maj, Ind N. b 12 Jul 65, with
THOMAS, Gera Sion Kumari m 1984; Maj,
Ind N. b 9 Oct 67. Served in Ind C.

THOMSON, Robert E. (Evansville Asplan
Citadel, IN, 1971); Maj, USA C. b 20 Nov 50.
BS (Soc Work), MSW, with
THOMSON, Nancy (née Philpot) m 1972;
Maj, USA C. b 4 May 50.

TILLSLEY, Mark W. (East Northport, NY,
1987); Maj, USA E. b 20 Nov 57. BA
(Psychol/Sociol), MSW, with
TILLSLEY, Sharon (née Lowman) m 1979;
Maj, USA E. b 21 Jun 57. BS (Nursing).

TOLLERUD, Douglas (Santa Ana, CA, 1983);
Maj, USA W. b 16 Mar 57, with
TOLLERUD, Sheryl (née Smith) m 1978; Maj,
USA W. b 12 Jan 59. BS (Organztnl Mngmnt).

TRAINOR, Iain (Orillia, Can, 1974); Maj,
Aus S. b 18 Jan 45, with
TRAINOR, Dawn (née McCormack) m 1965;
Maj, Aus S. b 19 Jun 44. Served in Can.

TRIM, Kester (Scarborough Citadel, ON, 1983);
Maj, Can. b 16 Jun 53, with
TRIM, Kathryn (née Webster) m 1976; Maj,
Can. b 2 Jun 54. Served in Zai and at IHQ
(SALT College).

TSILULU, Dieudonné Nzuzi (Bandalungwa,
1997); Capt, Con (Kin). b 16 Dec 66, and
TSILULU, Philippine Kiasala (née

Ngudiankanga) (Kimbanseke 1, 1995)
m 1998; Capt, Con (Kin). b 18 Nov 67.
TUCK, Trevor M. (Kensington Citadel, 1969);
Comr, TC, S Afr. b 11 Sep 43, and
TUCK, Memory (née Fortune) (Benoni,
1965) m 1968; Cmr, TPWM, S Afr.
b 28 Apr 45. Served in S Afr (CS/TSWM) and
PNG (TC/TPWM).
TURSI, Massimo (Naples, 1983); Maj, GS, It.
b 14 Nov 57, and
TURSI, Anne-Florence (née Cachelin) (Bern 1,
Switz, 1983) m 1983; Maj, CSWM, It.
b 25 Mar 59. Served in Switz and Ger.
TVEDT, Hannelise (née Nielsen) (Copenhagen
Temple, 1976); Maj, Den. b 13 Dec 55.
Served in Nor.

U

UDOH, Etim (Oboyo Ikot Ita, 1984); Maj, Nig.
b 9 May 56, with
UDOH, Ekerebong; Maj, Nig. b 1 Apr 61.
UMOH, Smart (Ikot Akpan, 1974); Maj, Nig.
b 18 Nov 50, with
UMOH, Dorothy m 1971; Maj, Nig.
b 12 Dec 56.
UNDERSRUD, Arne (Drammen, 1969); Maj,
Nor. b 15 Mar 44, and
UNDERSRUD, Anne Lise (née Bendiksen)
(Finnsnes, 1969) m 1974; Maj, Nor.
b 12 Feb 48. Served in UK.
UWAK, Udoh (Ikot Obio Inyang, 1992); Capt,
Nig. b 2 Oct 66, with
UWAK, Esther m 1990; Capt, Nig.
b 12 Dec 73.
UZOHO, Stephen (Umuobom, 1974); Maj, Nig.
b 22 Sep 49, with
UZOHO, Edith; Maj, Nig. b 2 Jul 53.

V

VALE, John (Bairnsdale, 1981); Maj, Aus S.
b 8 Jan 44. m 1965; Maj Adele, ret 2006.
VAN DER HARST, Willem (Scheveningen,
Neth, 1966); Comr, TC, E Eur. b 13 Mar 44.
Ww Capt Suzanne, pG 1985, and
VAN DER HARST, Netty (née Kruisinga)
(Amsterdam Congress Hall, Neth, 1984)
m 1985; Comr, TPWM, E Eur. b 15 Feb 58.
Served in Cze R and Neth (TC/TPWM).
VAN DUINEN, Susan (née Jewers)
(Mississauga, ON, 1978); Maj, Can.
b 11 Mar 50. BA, MDiv, with
VAN DUINEN, Dirk m 1970; Maj. b 13 Jun 49.
Served Ger and Cze Rep.
VAN HAL, Jeanne E. (Rotterdam Congress
Hall, 1965); Maj, Neth. b 6 May 42.
Served in UK and at IHQ.

VAN VLIET, Johan C. J. (Baarn, 1975); Maj,
Neth. b 17 Jul 52. D (Soc Serv Admin), with
VAN VLIET, Maria E. (née de Ruiter)
m 1971; Maj, Neth. b 9 May 51.
VANDER WEELE, Richard E. (Kalamazoo, MI,
1976); Maj, USA C. b 19 May 48. BS (Soc),
MSW.
VANLALTHANGA (Ruallung, 1979); Maj,
Ind E. b 4 Jul 57, with
HMUNROPUII m 1977; Maj, Ind E.
b 25 Oct 59.
VARGHESE, Davidson (Trivandrum Central,
Ind SW, 1986); Maj, Zam. b 13 Dec 58. BA,
and
DAVIDSON, Mariamma (née Chacko)
(Adoor Central, Ind SW, 1985) m 1988;
Maj, Zam. b 1 May 65. Served in Ind SW.
VARUGHESE, Wilfred (Trivandrum Central,
Ind SW, 1985); Maj, Ind Nat. b 25 Mar 58.
BSc (Botany), and
VARUGHESE, Prema Wilfred (Anayara,
Ind SW, 1987) m 1987; Maj, Ind Nat.
b 25 May 60. BA, BD. Served in Ind SW.
VENTER, Alistair (Cape Town Citadel, 1981);
Maj, S Afr. b 19 Aug 58. ThA, BTh, and
VENTER, Marieke (née van Leeuwen)
(Benoni, 1988) m 1987; Maj, S Afr. b 31 Dec 62,
BCur (Hons), MTh.
VIJAYAKUMAR, Thumati (Denduluru, Ind C,
1970); Lt-Col, Ind Nat. b 10 Jun 49, and
VIJAYAKUMAR, Keraham Manikyam (née
Karuhu) (Denduluru, Ind C, 1970) m 1971;
Lt-Col, Ind Nat. b 17 Apr 53. Served in Ind C,
Ind SE and Ban (GS/CSWM).
VIRU, Zarena (Bhogiwal, 1973); Lt-Col, Pak.
b 1 Jan 52.
VOORHAM, Christina (The Hague South,
1970); Lt-Col, Neth. b 2 Sep 46.
VYLE, Bruce (Hamilton City, 1995); Capt, NZ.
b 5 Jun 46. MA, BA, DipT, with
VYLE, Elaine (née French) m 1968; Capt,
NZ. b 9 Jul 48.

W

WAGHELA, Chimanbhai Somabhai (Ratanpura,
1968); Comr, TC, Ind SW. b 1 Jun 47, with
RAHELBAI, Chimanbhai Waghela m 1972;
Comr, TPWM, Ind SW. b 1 May 52. Served in
Ind SE (CS/TSWO) and Ind E (CS/TSWO).
WAINWRIGHT, John (Reading Central,
1979); Maj, UK. b 13 Mar 51, with
WAINWRIGHT, Dorita (née Willetts)
m 1976; Maj, UK. b 19 Oct 51. Served in
E Afr and Zimb.
WALKER, Peter (Morley, 1982); Maj, Aus S.
b 2 Mar 54, with

WALKER, Jennifer (née Friend) m 1975; Maj, Aus S. b 26 Feb 56. Served in Mlys.

WANDULU, Moses (Bumbo, 1986); Maj, OC, Uga. b 5 Aug 60, with
WANDULU, Sarah (née Rwolekya) m 1982; Maj, CPWM, Uga. b 30 Aug 1964. Served in E Afr

WANJARE, Sanjay (Vithalwadi, 1994); Capt, Ind W. b 10 Oct 67, with
WANJARE Sunita m 1992; Capt, Ind W. b 1 Jun 70.

WARD, H. Alfred (Atlanta Temple, GA, 1971); Lt-Col, USA S. b 2 Aug 46. BA, MBA, with
WARD, Mary M. (née Busby); Lt-Col, USA S. b 13 Nov 47. BVA. Served in Aus E.

WARD, Robert (Brock Avenue, TO, Can, 1970); Col, TC, Pak. b 22 Apr 48. MHSc (Health Mgmt), BA (Admin), and
WARD, Marguerite (née Simon) (Swift Current, Can, 1970) m 1971; Col, TPWM, Pak. b 13 May 48. Served in Can, S Afr, Zimb (CS/TSWM) and USA C.

WATT, Neil (Montreal Citadel, 1977); Maj, Can. b 4 Nov 48, with
WATT, Lynda (née Westover) m 1968; Maj, Can. Served in UK.

WEBB, Geoff Robert (Ulverstone, Aus S, 1984); Maj, Pak. b 18 Jan 59. BEd, BD, Phd Theol, and
WEBB, Kalie Maree (née Down) (Box Hill, Aus S, 1997) m 1993; Maj, Pak. b 18 Jan 59. BTheol. Served in Aus S.

WEBB, Neil (Nottingham New Basford, 1983); Maj, UK. b 6 Sep 58, and
WEBB, Christine (née Holdstock) (Bromley, 1983) m 1983, Maj, UK. b 1 Mar 55. BA, CQSW, Dip RS.

WHITE, Charles (Owensboro, KY, 1967); Lt-Col, USA S. b 7 May 46, with
WHITE, Shirley (née Sanders) m 1962; Lt-Col, USA S. b 24 Apr 43.

WHITE, Larry Wayne (Orlando, FL, 1972); Maj, USA S. b 27 Aug 45, and
WHITE, Shirley Anne (née Knight) (Lake Charles, LA, 1967) m 1969; Maj, USA S. b 7 Mar 42.

WICKINGS, Margaret (Welling, UK, 1976); Maj, Gha. b 15 Apr 51. Served in UK, Zam and E Afr.

WILLERMARK, Marie (Göteborg 1, Swdn, 1980); Maj, E Eur. b 18 Jun 54. Served in Swdn and Den.

WILLIAM, Appavoo (N Karayankuzhy, 1969); Lt-Col, Ind SE. b 2 Jun 48, and
WILLIAM Thavamony (Booth Tucker Hall,

1971) m 1972; Lt-Col, Ind SE. b 18 Mar 47.

WILLIAMS, John (Murukondapadu, 1991); Maj, Ind C. b 7 May 65. Ww Capt K. Mary Rani, and
WILLIAMS, Ratna Sundari (Murukondapadu, 2000) m ; Maj, Ind C. b 22 Nov 67.

WILLIAMS, Michael (Bristol Easton Road, UK, 1967); Lt-Col, IHQ. b 16 Dec 46. Served in UK. m 1969; Lt-Col Ruth, ret 2004.

WOLTERINK, Theo (Hengelo, 1974); Lt-Col, CS, Neth. b 16 Jun 47, with
WOLTERINK, Albertina (née Riezebos) m 1970; Lt-Col, TSWM, Neth. b 17 Feb 46. Served at IHQ.

WOODALL, Ann (Croydon Citadel, UK, 1969); Lt-Col, IHQ. b 3 Feb 50. MA, MSc, FCCA, PhD. Served in Con, Zam, Zaï and UK.

WOODWARD, Cecil (Coorparoo, 1969); Maj, Aus E. b 3 Jun 46. BSW (Hons), MSWAP, MBA, and
WOODWARD, Catherine (née Lucas) (Miranda, 1970) m 1970; Maj, Aus E. b 20 Jan 48

Y

YAMANAKA, Masaru (Fukuoka, 1970); Maj, Jpn. b 10 Jul 44, and
YAMANAKA, Machiko (née Matsui) (Tenma, 1963) m 1973; Maj, Jpn. b 21 Jan 39.

YANG, Tae-soo (Chun Yun, 1978); Maj, Kor. b 14 Feb 47, with
CHUN, Ok-kyung m 1968; Maj, Kor. b 14 Jul 47. Served in Sing.

YOHANNAN, C. S. (Kaithaparambu, 1975); Maj, Ind SW. b 8 Jan 54, and
YOHANNAN, L. Rachel (Pathanapuram, 1979) m 1978; Maj, Ind SW. b 31 Jul 55.

YOHANNAN, P. J. (Oollayam Kangazha, 1978); Maj, Ind SW. b 17 May 49, and
YOHANNAN, Annamma (Oollayam Kangazha, 1981) m 1981; Maj, Ind SW. b 31 Aug 55.

YOSHIDA, Makoto (Shibuya, 1969); Comr, TC, Jap. b 7 Dec 45. BS (Engin), and
YOSHIDA, Kaoru (née Imamura) (Omori, 1971) m 1974; Comr, TPWM, Jap. b 13 Jan 45. Served in Jpn (CS/TSWM) and at IHQ (IS/SWM, SPEA).

YOSHIDA, Tsukasa (Shibuya, 1982); Maj, Jpn. b 26 Nov 54, and
YOSHIDA, Kyoko (née Tsuchiya) (Kiyose, 1980) m 1982; Maj, Jpn. b 13 Oct 53.

YOUNIS, Joseph (Kamalia, 1979); Maj, Pak. b 12 Dec 54, with
YOUNIS, Margaret (née Gabrial) m 1978; Maj, Pak. b 5 Dec 57.

Z

ZACHARIAH, Jupalli (Hutti, Ind C, 1983);
Maj, Sri Lan. b 6 May 54. BA, with
ZACHARIAH, Usha Rani (née Perumalla)
m 1980; Maj, Sri Lan. b 15 Jun 65.

ZIPINGANI, Langton (Pearson, 1987); Maj,
Zimb. b 22 Nov 61, and
ZIPINGANI, Beauty (née Chimunda)
(Mutonda, 1987) m 1989; Maj, Zimb.
b 2 Aug 66.

ZOLA, Ambroise (Kingudi, Con (Kin), 1979);
Lt-Col, CS, Con (Braz). b 6 Sep 52, with
ZOLA, Alphonsine Kuzoma (née Nsiesi)
m 1976; Lt-Col, TSWM, Con (Braz).
b 2 Jan 57. Served in Con (Kin).

ZUÑIGA, Francisco Javier (Nuevo Laredo,
1972); Maj, Mex; b 3 Aug 52, and
ZUÑIGA, Carolyn (née Jones) (Gastonia, NC,
USA S, 1969) m 1975; Maj, Mex; b 18 Jun 46.
BA Music. Served in USA S and Sp.

Retired Generals and Commissioners

The following list contains the names of retired Generals,
commissioners and lieut-commissioners, and widows of
lieut-commissioners and above, as at 30 September 2007

A

ADIWINOTO, Lilian E. (Malang, 1954);
Comr. b 31 Jul 27. Served in UK, Indon (TC)
and at IHQ.

ASANO, Hiroshi (Shizuoka, 1950); Comr.
b 5 May 27. m Lt Tomoko Ohara (Kyoto,
1953) 1955. Served in Jpn (TC).

B

BASSETT, W. Todd (Syracuse Citadel, NY,
USA E, 1965); Comr. b 25 Aug 39. BEd, with
BASSETT, Carol A. (née Easterday) m 1960;
Comr. BEd. b 10 Dec 40. Served in USA E, at
IHQ (IS to CoS/ Mission Resources Sec) and
at USA Nat (Nat Comm/NPWM).

BATH, Vida (née McNeill) (Moree, 1945);
m 1951; Mrs Comr. Served in Sri Lan, Ind W,
Ind NE, Ind SW, at IHQ and in Aus E.
Ww Comr Robert, pG 2006.

BAXENDALE, David A. (Pittsburgh, PA, USA,
1954; Comr. b 23 Apr 30. MA (Col), BSc
(Sprd), with Alice (née Chamberlain); BMus
Ed (Syra). Served in USA E, USA W (CS),
Carib (TC), S Am W (TC), ICO (Principla)
and IHQ (IS Am and Carib).

BIMWALA, Zunga Mbanza Etienne (Central
Hall, Kinshasa 1, 1959); Comr. b 29 Sep 32.
Served in Zaï (TC/TPWO) and Switz.
Ww Comr Alice, pG 2004.

BIRD, Patricia (Fulham, UK, 1958); Comr.
b 7 Aug 35. Served in Nig, UK, Zam (TC)
and at IHQ (IS Fin, IS Afr).

BOVEN van, Johannes (The Hague, 1955);
Comr. b 9 Jan 35, and

BOVEN van, Klazina (née Grauwmeijer)
(Rotterdam, 1959) m 1960; Comr. b 22 Sep 35.
Served in Neth (TC/TPWO).

BRAUN, Edouard (Vevey, Frce, 1968); Comr.
b 16 Aug 42, with
BRAUN, Françoise (née Volet) m 1966; Comr.
b 8 Dec 43. Served in Frce (TC/TPWM) and
Switz (TC/TPWM).

BROWN, Jean (née Barclay) (Montreal
Citadel, Can, 1938); Mrs General. Served at
IHQ and in Can. Ww General Arnold Brown,
pG 2002.

BUCKINGHAM, Hillmon (Waimate, NZ,
1960); Comr. b 20 Jan 36, with
BUCKINGHAM, Lorraine (née Smith)
m 1958; Comr. Served in Aus S, NZ
(CS/TSWO) and Aus E (TC/TPWO).

BURROWS, Eva Evelyn General (1986-93)
(see page 25).

BUSBY, John A. (Atlanta Temple, GA, USA S,
1963); Comr. b 14 Oct 37. BA (Asbury), with
BUSBY, Elsie Louise (née Henderson)
m 1958; Comr. b 11 Jun 36. Served in
Can (CS/TSWO), USA S (TC/TPWO) and
USA Nat (NC/NPWM).

C

CACHELIN, Genevieve (née Booth) (Paris
Central, Frce, 1947); Mrs Comr. MA. Served
in Switz, Belg, Frce, Ger, BT and at IHQ.
Ww Comr Francy, pG 2007

CAIRNS, Alistair Grant (West End, Aus E,
1942); Comr. b 12 Dec 16. AM, Order of
Australia (1996). Served in Kor, Aus E (CS),

at ITC and in S Afr (TC). Ww Mrs Comr Margery, pG 2006.

CAIRNS, William Ramsay (West End, Aus E, 1947); Comr. b 25 May 23. Served in Aus E (CS) and at IHQ (IS SPEA). AM, Order of Australia (1981). Ww Bernice, pG 1983. m Major Beulah Rae Ann Harris (Parramatta, NSW, Aus E, 1959) 1984.

CALVERT, Ruth (Port Hope, ON, 1955); Mrs Comr. b 8 Feb 35. Served in Aus E. Ww Comr Roy, pG 1994.

CAMPBELL, Donald (Highgate, WA, 1945); Comr. b 31 Oct 23. Served in NZ (TC) and Aus S (TC). m Capt Crystal Cross (Highgate, WA, 1944) 1947.

CHANG, Peter Hei-dong (Seoul Central, Kor, 1960); Comr. b 12 May 32. BD, STm (Union, NY), BTh MEd (Columbia, NY), and **CHANG, Grace Eun-Shik** (née Chung) (Seoul, Kor, 1963) m 1963; Comr. BA, BMus (Seoul Nat). Served in USA W (TC/TPWO), UK, Sing, HK, USA E, Kor (CS and TC/TPWO) and at IHQ.

CHEVALLY, Simone (née Gindraux) (Lausanne 1, 1947); Mrs Comr. Ww Comr Robert, pG 1989.

CHIANGHNUNA (Ngupa, 1951); Comr. b 10 Jun 29. Served in Ind N (CS), E (CS) and W (TC). m Maj Barbara Powell (Ware, UK, 1948) 1968.

CLAUSEN, Siegfried (Catford, UK, 1958); Comr. b 4 Mar 38, and **CLAUSEN, Inger-Lise** (née Lydholm) (Valby, 1958) m 1961; Comr. b 1 Oct 39. Served in UK, S Am W, Sp (OC/CPWO), L Am N (TC/TPWO), Ger (TC/TPWO) and at IHQ (IS/SWM Am and Carib).

CLINCH, John H. (Fairfield, Vic, 1956); Comr. b 30 Nov 30, with **CLINCH, Beth** (née Barker); Comr. Served in Aus S, Aus E (CS), at IHQ (IS SPEA) and Aus S (TC/TPWO).

COLES, Alan C. (Harrow, UK, 1953); Comr. b 2 Feb 25. ACIB. Ww Heather, pG 1978. m Maj Brenda Deeming (Tipton, UK, 1959) 1980. Served in Zimb (TC) and at IHQ.

COLES, Dudley (North Toronto, ON, Can, 1954); Comr. b 22 Mar 26. m 2/Lt Evangeline Oxbury (Powell River, BC, Can, 1954) 1956. Served in Can, Ind Audit, Ind W, Sri Lan (TC) and at IHQ (IS S Asia).

COOPER, Raymond A. (Washington Georgetown, DC, 1956); Comr. b 24 May 37, and **COOPER, Merlyn S.** (née Wishon) (Winston Salem Southside, NC, 1957) m 1959; Comr.

b 2 Sep 36. Served in USA C and USA S (TC/TPWO).

COX, Hilda (née Chevalley) (Geneva, 1949); Mrs Comr. Served in UK, Zam, Zimb, Frce, Neth and at IHQ. Ww Comr Ron, pG 1995.

CUTMORE, Ian (Tamworth, Aus E, 1954); Comr. b 27 Sep 33, and **CUTMORE, Nancy** (née Richardson) (Atherton, Aus E, 1957); Comr. Served in Aus E, PNG, UK (CS), ICO (Prin) and NZ.

D

DAHLSTRØM, Eili (née Holme) (Molde, 1937); Mrs Comr. Served in UK, Nor, Gha, Nig, Fin and Nor. Ww Comr Haakon, pG 2006

DAVIS, Douglas E. (Moreland, 1960); Comr. b 12 Feb 37, with **DAVIS, Beverley J.** (née Roberts) m 1958; Comr. b 23 Feb 38. Served in NZ, UK (CS/TSWO) and Aus S (TC/TPWO).

DELCOURT, Raymond Andre (Montpellier, 1935); Comr. b 25 Oct 14. Served in BT and Frce (TC). Croix de Guerre (1939-40), Medaille Penitentiaire (1973), Medaille d'Honneur de la Ville de Paris (1976), Chevalier de la Legion d'Honneur (1978). m Lt France Bardiaux (Lyon 1, 1943) 1943.

DEVAVARAM, Prathipati (New Colony, Ind C, 1964); Comr. b 15 Nov 46. MBBS, BSc, and **DEVAVARAM, P. Victoria** (Bapatla Central, Ind C, 1970) m 1974; Comr. b 25 Nov 49. BSc, BEd, BLSc. Served in Ind C, at Ind Nat, in Ind E and Ind SE (TC/TPWM).

DIAKANWA, Mbakanu (Poste Francais, Kinshasa, 1949); Comr. b 1923. Officier de l'Ordre du Leopard, 1981. Served in Zaï (TC). Ww Mrs Comr Situwa, pG 1998.

DITMER, Anne (née Sharp) (Dayton Central, OH, 1957) m 1992. Mrs Comr. Ww Comr Stanley, pG 2003.

DU PLESSIS, Paul (Salt River, S Afr, 1968); Comr. b 3 Jul 41. MB, ChB, MRCP, DTM&H, with **DU PLESSIS, Margaret** (née Siebrits); Comr. b 17 Jul 42. BSoc Sc. Served in Zam, Ind C (TC/TPWO), S Afr (TC/TPWO) and at IHQ.

DURMAN, David C. (Bromley, UK, 1940); Comr. b 21 Aug 20. Served in UK, Ind W (TC) and at IHQ (Chancellor of the Exchequer and IS S Asia). m Capt Vera Livick (South Croydon, UK, 1942) 1949.

DWYER, June M. (Windsor, NS, Can, 1952); Comr. b 28 Aug 32. Served in USA Nat, S Afr (CS) and at IHQ (IS Admin).

Retired Generals and Commissioners

E

EDWARDS, David (New Market Street, Georgetown, Guyana, 1962); Comr. b 15 May 41, and
EDWARDS, Doreen (née Bartlett) (Wellington St, Barbados, 1957) m 1966. b 4 Mar 35. Served in USA E, Carib (TC/TPWO), at IHQ (IS/SWO Am and Carib) and in USA W (TC/TPWO).

EGGER, Verena (née Halbenleib) (Solothurn, 1945); Mrs Comr. Served in Carib and C Am, Zaï, Mex and C Am, S Am E and Switz. Ww Comr Jacques E., pG 2001.

ELIASEN, Carl S. (Gartnergade, Den, 1951); Comr. b 28 Mar 32. Served in Port (OC), Brz (TC), S Am W (TC) and at IHQ (IS Americas). Ww Comr Maria, pG 2003.

EVANS, Willard S. (Greenville, SC, 1949, w wife, née Marie Fitton); Comr. b 2 Sep 24. Served in USA S, USA E (CS) and USA W (TC). BA (Bob Jones Univ).

F

FEWSTER, Lilian (Lt Hunt, Hanwell, 1931); Mrs Comr. Served in UK, Can and Zimb. Ww Comr Ernest F., pG 1973.

FREI, Werner (Rorbas, Switz, 1965); Comr. b 6 Mar 40, and
FREI, Paula (née Berweger) (Heiden, Switz, 1965) m 1967; Comr. b 19 Mar 36. Served in Switz (CS/TSWO) and Ger (TC/TPWM).

FULLARTON, Frank (Bromley, UK, 1955); Comr. b 3 Mar 31. BSc, DipSoc, and
FULLARTON, Rosemarie (née Steck) (Croydon Citadel, UK, 1958) m 1959; Comr. BEd (Hons), MITD. Served at IHQ (CS to CoS and IS Eur), Soc S (GBI) (Leader) and in Switz (TC/TPWO).

G

GAUNTLETT, Caughey (Wood Green, UK, 1952, w wife, née Marjorie Markham); Comr. b 10 Aug 20. Served at ITC, in Zimb, Frce (CS), Ger (TC) and at IHQ (CoS).

GOODIER, William Robert Henry (Atlanta Temple, GA, 1941, w wife, née Renee L. Tilley); Comr. b 23 May 16. Served in USA S (CS), at USA Nat (CS), in Aus S (TC) and USA E (TC).

GOWANS, John General (1999-2002) (see page 26), and
GOWANS, Gisèle (née Bonhotal) (Paris Central, France, 1955) m 1957; Comr. Served in USA W, France (TPWO), Aus E (TPWO), UK (TPWO) and at IHQ (WPWM).

GRIFFIN

GRIFFIN, Joy (Maj Button, Tottenham Citadel, UK, 1957); Mrs Lt-Comr. Ww Lt-Comr Frederick, pG 1990.

GRINSTED, Dora (Lt Bottle, Sittingbourne, UK, 1950); Mrs Comr. Served in UK, Zam, Zimb, Jpn and at IHQ. Ww Comr David Ramsay, pG 1992.

GULLIKSEN, Thorleif R. (Haugesund, Nor, 1967); Comr. b 26 Apr 40, with
GULLIKSEN, Olaug (née Henriksen) m 1962; Comr. b 25 Jan 38. Served in Nor, Neth (TC/TPWO) and at IHQ (IS/SWM Eur).

H

HANNEVIK, Anna (Bergen 2, Nor, 1947); Comr. b 9 Aug 25. Served in Nor, UK, Swdn (TC) and at IHQ (IS Eur). Paul Harris Medal (1987), Commander of the Royal Order of the Northern Star (Sweden).

HANNEVIK, Edward (Oslo 3, Nor, 1954); Comr. b 6 Dec 32, and
HANNEVIK, Margaret (née Moody) (Newfield, UK, 1956) m 1958; Comr. Served in UK, Den (TC/TPWO), Nor (TC/TPWO) and at IHQ (IS/SWO Eur).

HARITA, Nozomi (Shibuya, Jap, 1966); Comr. b 10 May 39. BA (Mus), and
HARITA, Kazuko (née Hasegawa) (Shibuya, Jap, 1966) m 1969; Comr. b 19 Dec 37. BA (Ed). Served in Aus E and Jap (TC/TPWM).

HARRIS, Bramwell Wesley (Cardiff Stuart Hall, UK, 1948); Comr. b 25 Nov 28. m Capt Margaret Sansom (Barking, UK, 1949), 1955. Served in UK, Aus S (CS), at IHQ, in Scot (TC), NZ (TC) and Can (TC).

HAWKINS, Peter (Croydon Citadel, UK, 1948); Comr. b 16 Oct 29. FCIS. m Lt Mary McElroy (Partick, UK, 1949) 1952. Served in UK and at IHQ (IS Finance).

HEDBERG, Lennart (Nykoping, Swdn, 1954); Comr. b 12 Oct 32, and
HEDBERG, Ingvor (née Fagerstedt) (Nykoping, 1955) m 1956; Comr. Served in Den, Swdn (TC/TPWO) and at IHQ (IS/SWO Eur).

HINSON, Harold D. (High Point, USA S, 1955); Comr. b 7 Sep 35, and
HINSON, Betty M. (née Morris) (New Orleans, LA, 1955); Comr. b 1 Jun 35. Served in USA C (TC/TPWO) and USA S (CS/THLS).

HODDER, Kenneth L. (San Francisco Citadel, CA, 1958); Comr. b 30 Oct 30. BA (Richmond), DSS (Hons) (Richmond) JD (California) and

HODDER, Marjorie J. (née Fitton) (San Francisco Citadel, CA, 1958). Served in USA W, USA C, Aus S (CS), USA S (TC/TPWO) and at USA Nat (NC).

HOLLAND, Louise (née Cruickshank) (Invercairn, UK, 1958); Mrs Comr. Served in UK, E Afr, Nig, Gha, Pak and at IHQ. Ww Comr Arthur, pG 1998.

HOOD, H. Kenneth (Denver Citadel, CO, 1954); Comr. b 27 Jan 33, and
HOOD, Barbara (née Johnson) (Pasadena, CA, 1952) m 1957; Comr. Served in USA W (CS), at USA Nat (CS/THLS) and in USA S (TC/TPWO).

HOWE, Norman (Dartford, UK, 1957); Comr. b 13 Aug 36, and
HOWE, Marian (née Butler) (Boscombe, UK, 1953) m 1959; Comr. b 9 Feb 30. Cert Ed. Served in UK, at ITC (Principal), in Aus S (TC/TPWO), Can (TC/TPWO) and at IHQ (IS Prog Res/SWO Eur, General's Travelling Representative).

HUGHES, Alex (Paisley West, UK, 1960); Comr. b 29 Jan 42, and
HUGHES, Ingeborg (née Clausen) (Catford, UK, 1964) m 1971; Comr. b 2 Jan 42. Served in L Am N, S Am E (CS/THLS and TC/TPWO), S Am W (TC/TPWO), at IHQ (IS/SWO Am and Carib) and in UK (TC/TPWM).

HUGUENIN, Willy (Le Locle, Switz, 1954); Comr. b 22 Sep 31, and
HUGUENIN, Miriam (née Luthi) (La Chaux-de-Fonds, 1953) m 1955. Served in Zaï (GS), Con (TC/TPWO), Switz (TC/TPWO) and at IHQ (IS/SWO Afr).

HUNTER, Denis (Poplar, UK, 1938); Comr. b 22 May 19. Served in Zimb (GS), NZ (CS), Scot (TC), at IHQ (IS S Pacific and Far East, IS Afr) and in BT (Brit Comr). MA (Cantab), O St J. Ww Mrs Comr Pauline, pG 2002.

I

IRWIN, Ronald G. (Philadelphia, PA, 1957); Comr. b 4 Aug 33. BS (Rutgers), MA (Columbia), and
IRWIN, Pauline (née Laipply) (Cincinnati, OH, 1953) m 1967; Comr. Served in USA W (CS/THLS) and USA E (TC/TPWO).

ISRAEL, Jillapegu (Peralipadu, 1957, w wife, Rachel née Amarthaluri); Comr. b 31 May 32. BA, BEd. Served in Ind M & A (CS/THLS), Ind N (TC/TPWO) and Ind SW (TC/TPWO).

K

KANG, Sung-hwan (Noh Mai Sil, Kyung Buk, Kor, 1973); Comr. b 15 Dec 39, with
LEE, Jung-ok m 1970; Comr. b 10 Nov 49. Served in Aus S and Kor (TC/TPWM).

KELLNER, Paul S. (Miami Citadel, FL, USA S, 1963); Comr. b 1 Sep 35. B Mus, with
KELLNER, Jajuan (née Pemberton); Comr. b 23 Feb 39. Served in USA S, Carib, Con (Braz) and Zimb (TC/TPWO).

KENDREW, K. Ross (Sydenham, NZ, 1962); Comr. b 7 Dec 38, and
KENDREW, Marion June (née Robb) (Wanganui, NZ, 1961) m 1964; Comr. b 8 Oct 39. Served in NZ (TC/TPWO) and Aus S (TC/TPWM).

KERR, Donald (Vancouver Temple, BC, Can, 1955); Comr. b 25 Oct 33, and
KERR, Joyce (née Knaap) (Mt Dennis, ON, 1955) m 1957; Comr. b 12 Jan 35. Served in UK (CS).

KIM, Suk-tai (Choon Chun, 1957); Comr. b 23 Jan 26. ThB, BA, MSoc. m Capt Lim, Jung-sun (Sudaemun, 1969) 1975. BMus. Served in Korea (TC).

KING, Margaret (Lt Coull, Fairview, 1936); Mrs Comr. Ww Comr Hesketh K., pG 1990.

L

LALTHANNGURA (Ratu, 1963); Comr. b 15 Sep 38. BA, with
KAPHLIRI; Comr. b 9 Sep 43. Served in Ind C (CS/THLS) and Ind E (TC/TPWM).

LANG, Ivan B. (Auburn, Aus S, 1967); Comr. b 18 Jul 40, with
LANG, Heather C. (née Luhrs) m 1961; Comr. b 8 Dec 42. Served in Sing (OC/CPWO), Aus E (CS/TSWO), at IHQ (IS/SWM SPEA) and in Aus S (TC/TPWM).

LARSSON, John General (2002-06) (see page 26), and
LARSSON, Freda (née Turner) (Kingston-upon-Thames, UK, 1964) m 1969; Comr. Served in S Am W (THLS), at ITC, in UK (TPWO), NZ (TPWO), Swdn (TPWO) and at IHQ (WSWM, WPWM).

LEE, Sung-duk (Cho Kang, 1963); Comr. b 10 Jun 35, with
CHO, In-sun (Taejon Central, 1963) m 1961; Comr. b 8 May 40. Served in Kor (TC/TPWO).

LIM, Ah Ang (Balestier Rd, Sing, 1954); Comr. b 30 May 32, and
LIM, Fong Pui Chan (Singapore Central, 1954) m 1958; Comr. Served in Sing, HK (OC/CPWO), Phil (TC/TPWO) and at IHQ (IS/SWO SPEA).

Retired Generals and Commissioners

LINDBERG, Ingrid E. (Norrköping, Swdn, 1951); Comr. b 12 Dec 25. Served in Swdn, Zimb, Phil (OC), Den (TC) and Fin (TC).

LINNETT, Merle (Capt Clinch, Hindmarsh, 1947); Mrs Comr. Served in NZ, at IHQ, ITC, ICO and in Aus S. Ww Comr Arthur, pG 1986.

LOVATT, Olive (née Chapman) (Doncaster, UK, 1949); Mrs Comr. Served in UK, Aus S, Aus E & PNG and at IHQ. Ww Comr Roy, pG 2000.

LUTTRELL, Bill (Greeley, CO, USA W, 1958); Comr. b 4 Jul 38. BA Soc, and
  LUTTRELL, Gwendolyn (née Shinn) (Long Beach, CA, USA W, 1961) m 1962; Comr. b 3 Sep 38. Served at IHQ (IS/SWO Am and Carib), in Can (TC/TPWM) and USA W (CS/TSWO and TC/TPWM).

LYSTER, Ingrid (Valerenga, Nor, 1947); Comr. b 7 Apr 22. Served in Nig, Zimb, Nor (CS) and at ICO (Principal). BA (S Afr).

M

MABENA, William (Bloemfontein, 1959); Comr, b 23 May 40, and
  MABENA, Lydia (née Lebusho) (Bloemfontein, 1959) m 1960; Comr, b 25 Jun 39. Served in UK, S Afr (CS, TC/THLS, TPWM), Gha (TC/TPWO) and at IHQ (IS/SWO Afr).

MAILLER, Georges (Neuchatel, 1961); Comr. b 9 Nov 36. BTh, and
  MAILLER, Muriel (née Aeberli) m 1959; Comr. b 15 Apr 35. Served at ESFOT (Principal), in Frce and Switz (TC/TPWO).

MAKOUMBOU, Antoine (Bacongo, Con (Braz), 1968); Comr. b 2 Mar 40, with
  MAKOUMBOU, Véronique (née Niangui) m 1967; Comr. b 30 Aug 46. Served in Con (Braz) (TC/TPWM).

MANNAM, Samuel (Duggirala, 1946); Comr. b 3 Jun 21. Served in Ind M & A (TC), Ind W (TC), Ind SW (TC), Ind E (TC) and Ind N (TC). Ww Mrs M., pG 1974. m Maj Ruby Manuel (Leyton Citadel, UK, 1953) 1975.

MARSHALL, Marjorie (P/Lt Kimball) (New York Temple, 1944); Mrs Comr. Served in USA C, USA E, at USA Nat and at IHQ. Ww Comr Norman S., pG 1995.

MARTI-JÖRGENSEN, Aase (née Jörgensen) (Oslo, Nor, 1959); Comr. Served in Nor, Den, Ger (TPWO) and Switz (TPWO). Ww Comr Paul Marti, pG 1999.

MASIH, Mohan (Khundi, 1961); Comr. b 29 Sep 39, with
  MASIH, Swarni m 1958; Comr. b 14 Mar 42. Served in Ind N (CS/THLS), Ind C (TC/ TPWO), Ind SW (TC/TPWO) and Ind W (TC/TPWM).

MAXWELL, Earle Alexander (Orange, NSW, Aus E, 1954); Comr. b 8 Jul 34. FCIS, ASA, CPA, and
  MAXWELL, Wilma (née Cugley) (Camberwell, Vic, Aus S, 1956) m 1957; Comr. Served in Sing (OC/CPWO), Aus E, Phil (TC/TPWO), NZ (TC/TPWO) and at IHQ (CoS/WSWO).

MILLER, Andrew S. (Newark, NJ, 1943); Comr. b 14 Oct 23. Served in USA E, USA C (CS), USA S (TC) and at USA Nat (NC). BSc (Akron Univ, OH), Hon LLD (Asbury), Hon LHD (Akron Univ, OH). m Lt Joan Hackworth (Hamilton, OH, 1945) 1946. Hon LHD (Wesley Biblical Seminary, MS).

MORGAN, K. Brian (Bairnsdale, Aus S, 1958); Comr. b 5 Oct 37, and
  MORGAN, Carolyn (née Bath) (Melville Park, Aus S, 1958) m 1961; Comr. b 5 Mar 38. Served in Rus/CIS (OC/CPWO), Aus S (CS/ TSWO) and Aus E (TC/TPWM).

MORRIS, Louise (née Holmes) (Charleston, W VA, USA S, 1953) m 1957; Comr. Served in USA S and Jpn (TPWO). Ww Comr Ted, pG 2004.

MOYO, Gideon (Chikankata, 1963); Comr. b 3 May 33. Served in Zam (GS) and Zimb (TC). Ww Comr Lista, pG 2001.

MOYO, Selina (née Ndhlovu) (Bulayao Central, 1951); Mrs Comr. Served in Zimb (TPWO). Ww Comr David, pG 2005.

N

NEEDHAM, Florence (née Jolly) (Baltimore 4, MD, 1939); Mrs Comr. Served in USA S, USA C, Carib and C Am, UK and at USA Nat. Ww Comr John D., pG 1983.

NEEDHAM, Philip D. (Miami Citadel, USA S, 1969); Comr. b 5 Dec 40. BA (Rel), MDiv ThM, DMin, with
  NEEDHAM, Keitha (née Holz) m 1963; Comr. b 9 Oct 41. BA (Ed). Served at ICO (Principal), in USA W and USA S (TC/ TPWM).

NELSON, John (Victoria Citadel, BC, Can, 1952); Comr. b 19 Aug 32, and
  NELSON, Elizabeth (née McLean) (Chatham, Ont, 1953) m 1956; Comr. Served at IHQ (IS/SWO S Asia), in Can, Carib and Pak (TC/TPWO).

NELTING, George L. (Brooklyn, Bushwick, NY, 1942, w wife née Kathleen McKeag); Comr. b 20 Jun 18. Served in USA E, at USA Nat (CS), Neth (TC), at IHQ (IS Afr and

IS Far East) and in USA C (TC). Ww Mrs N.,
pG 1976. m Capt Juanita Prine (Cincinnati
Cent, OH, 1962) 1977.

NEWBERRY, Inez Margaret (Monroe, LA,
USA S, 1944); Comr. b 19 Mar 24. Served
in USA S, Sri Lan, Ind S, Ind NE,
Ind M & A (CS), Ind SE (TC) and
Ind SW (TC).

NGUGI, Joshua (Nakuru, 1945); Comr.
b 29 Jan 16. Served in E Afr (TC). Ww Mrs
Comr Bathisheba, pG 2005.

NILSON, Birgitta K. (Boone, IA, USA C,
1964); Comr. b 2 Oct 37. AB (Chicago), MSW
(Loyola). Served in USA C, Swdn (TC) and at
IHQ (IS Eur).

NILSSON, Sven (Vansbro, 1940); Comr.
b 27 Jul 19. Served in Nor (CS), Den (TC)
and Swdn (TC). King's Medal (12th size),
Sweden (1983). m Capt Lisbeth Maria
Ohlqvist (Trelleborg, 1937) 1946.

NOLAND, Joseph J. (Santa Ana, CA, USA W,
1965); Comr. b 17 Jul 37. BA, MS, and
NOLAND, Doris (née Tobin) (Los Angeles
Congress Hall, CA, USA W, 1965) m 1966;
Comr. RN. Served in USA W, Aus E and USA
E (TC/TPWO).

NTUK, Patience (née Ekpe) (Ibadan, Nig, 1969);
Comr. Served in Nig (TPWM). Ww Comr
Joshua, pG 2007.

NUESCH, Ruben D. (Rosario Cent, 1946);
Comr. b 28 Feb 21. Served in Brz (TC),
S Am W (TC) and S Am E (TC).
m 2/Lt Rosario Legarda (Bahia Blanca,
1946) 1948.

O

OLCKERS, Roy (Uitenhage, 1952); Comr.
b 16 Jul 29. Served in S Afr (TC). m Lt
Yvonne Holdstock (Fairview, 1952) 1955.

ORD, John (Easington Colliery, UK, 1948);
Comr. b 7 Sep 29. m Lt Lydie Deboeck
(Brussels, 1951) 1953. Served in Frce,
Belg (OC), at ITC, at ICO, in UK and
Nor (TC).

ORSBORN, Howard (Rutherglen, UK, 1940);
Comr. b 1 May 17. Served at ITC, in Can,
Aus S, NZ (CS), UK (CS), Swdn (TC) and
Aus E (TC). Ww Olive, pG 1967.
m Maj Amy Webb (Adelaide North, Aus S,
1951) 1968.

OSBORNE, James (Washington 3, DC, w wife
née Ruth Campbell, 1947); Comr. b 3 Jul 27.
Served in USA W (CS), USA S (TC) and at
USA Nat (NC).

ØSTERGAARD, Rigmor (née Hansen)
(Helsingør, 1944); m 1949; Mrs Comr. Served

in Fin, Den and at IHQ. Ww Comr Egon,
pG 2006.

P

PARKINS, May (Maj Epplett) (Seattle Citadel,
WA, 1951); Mrs Lt-Comr. Served in USA E,
USA S and USA W. Ww Lt-Comr William,
pG 1990.

PATTIPEILOHY, Blanche (née Sahanaja)
(Djakarta 1, 1955) m 1955; Mrs Comr. Served
in Indon. Ww Comr Herman G., pG 2000.

PATRAS, Gulzar (Punjgarian, Pak, 1973);
Comr. b 19 Aug 47, and
GULZAR, Sheila (née John) (Amritnagar, Pak,
1973) m 1973; Comr. b 22 Sep 46. Served in
Pak (TC/TPWM).

PENDER, Winifred (née Dale) (Godmanchester,
UK, 1954); Comr. Served in NZ (THLS),
S Afr (THLS and TPWO), Scot (TPWO), at
IHQ, in Aus S (TPWO) and UK (TPWO). Ww
Comr Dinsdale, pG 2006.

PINDRED, Gladys (Brig Dods, Kitsilano, BC,
1941); Mrs Comr. Served in Can and Carib.
Ww Comr Leslie, pG 1990.

PITCHER, Arthur Ralph (St John's, NF,
1939); Comr. b 30 Oct 17. Served in S Afr
(CS), Carib (TC), USA S (TC) and Can (TC).
m Capt Elizabeth Evans (Bishop's Falls, NF,
1935) (b 1 Feb 14) 1942.

PRATT, William (Ilford, UK, 1947); Comr.
b 8 May 25. Served at IHQ, in BT (CS),
USA W (TC) and Can (TC). m Lt Kathleen
Lyons (Harlesden, UK, 1948) 1949.

R

RADER, Paul A. General (1994-1999) (see
page 25), with
RADER, Kay F. (née Fuller) m 1956; Comr.
BA (Asbury), Hon DD (Asbury Theol
Seminary), LHD (Hon) (Greenville) 1997,
Hon DD (Roberts Wesleyan) 1998. Served in
Kor (THLS), USA E (THLS), USA W (TPWO)
and at IHQ (WPWO).

RANGEL, Paulo (Rio Comprido, Brz, 1968);
Comr. b 19 Nov 41, Hon DD, and
RANGEL, Yoshiko (née Namba) (São Paulo,
Brz, 1967) m 1969; Comr. b 1 Sep 44. Served
in Brz (TC/TPWM).

READ, Harry (Edinburgh Gorgie, UK, 1948);
Comr. b 17 May 24. Served in UK, at IHQ,
ITC (Principal), Can (CS), Aus E (TC) and
BT (Brit Comr). Ww Mrs Comr Winifred,
pG 2007

RIGHTMIRE, Robert S. (Cincinnati, USA E,
1946); Comr. b 23 Jun 24. Served in USA E,
S Afr (CS), Jpn (TC), Kor (TC) and USA C

(TC). m Capt Katherine Stillwell (Newark Citadel, USA E, 1942) 1947.

RIVERS, William (Hadleigh Temple, UK, 1952); Comr. b 22 Dec 27. m 2/Lt Rose Ross (Aberdeen Torry, UK, 1956) 1957. Served in UK and at IHQ (IS Admin).

ROBERTS, William H. (Detroit Brightmoor, MI, USA C, 1943); Comr. b 27 May 22. Served in USA C, Aus S (CS) and at IHQ (IS Americas and Carib and for Dev). BA (Wayne State). m Lt Ivy Anderson (Marshalltown, IA, USA C, 1943) 1945.

ROOS, Rolf (Uppsala, Swdn, 1962); Comr. b 13 Nov 40, and
ROOS, Majvor (née Ljunggren) (Uppsala, Swdn, 1964) m 1965; Comr. b 15 Sep 38. Served in Fin (TC/TPWO) and Swdn (TC/TPWM).

RUTH, Fred L. (Shawnee, OK, 1955); Comr. b 21 Aug 35. BA (Georgia State), Dip Ed, MA (Counselling and Psychological Studies) (Trinity). Served in Kor, USA W, USA S , at USA Nat and IHQ (IS SPEA). Ww Sylvia (née Collins), pG 1990.

S

SAUNDERS, Robert F. (Philadelphia Pioneer, 1962); Comr. b 16 Jan 37. C Th (Fuller), and
SAUNDERS, Carol J. (née Rudd) (Seattle Temple, 1966) m 1967. b 10 Sep 43. Served in Carib, USA E, USA W, Kor (CS/TSWO), Phil (TC/TPWO) and at IHQ (IS/SWO SPEA).

SCHURINK, Reinder J. (Zutphen, Neth, 1947); Comr. b 2 Dec 27. Officer Order of Orange Nassau (1987). m 2/Lt Henderika Hazeveld (Utrecht 1, 1950) 1951; pG 1961. Served in Ger (CS), Neth (TC) and Rus (Commander). Ww Mrs Comr Wietske, pG 1997. m Lt-Col Dora Verhagen, 1998.

SCOTT, Albert P. (Lawrence, MA, USA E, 1941); Comr. b 15 Oct 18. Served in USA E (CS) and at IHQ (IS Am and Carib, and IS Dev). Ww Mrs Dorothy, pG 1970. m Maj Frances O. Clark (Concord, NH, USA E, 1953) 1971.

SHIPE, Tadeous (Mukakatanwa, Zimb, 1969); Comr. b 13 Jul 43, and
SHIPE, Nikiwe (née Jani) (Zimbara Zowa, Zimb, 1972) m 1972; Comr. b 24 Dec 49. Served in Zimb, Zam & Mal (TC/TPWM) and Zam (TC/TPWM).

SHOULTS, Harold (St Louis Tower Grove, MO, 1949); Comr. b 6 Mar 29. m Lt Pauline Cox (St Louis Tower Grove, MO, 1951) 1952. Served in USA E (CS), USA N (CS) and USA C (TC).

SKINNER, Verna E. (West End, Qld, Aus E, 1957); Comr. b 5 May 36. Served in Aus E, HK, Sri Lan (TC), Aus S (CS), at IHQ (IS Resources) and in E Afr (TC).

SMITH, Lawrence Robert (Portland Citadel, OR, 1936); Comr. b 28 May 15. Served in NZ (TC), at IHQ and in USA W (TC). m Lt Wilma Cherry (Portland Citadel, OR, 1937) 1939.

SOLHAUG, Karsten Anker (Sandvika, Nor, 1936); Comr. b 9 Nov 14. Kt, St Olav. Served in UK, Den (CS) and Nor (TC). Ww Else (née Brathen), pG 2006.

SUNDARAM, T. G. (Denduluru, 1963); Comr. b 1 Oct 35, with
SUNDARAM, Suseela (née Thota) m 1955; Comr. b 16 Apr 36. Served in Ind C, Ind SE (TC/TPWO) and Ind W (TC/TPWO).

SWINFEN, John M. (Penge, UK, 1955); Comr. b 24 Jan 31. BA, Cert Ed, Chevalier de l'Ordre du Merite Exceptionnel (Congo), with
SWINFEN, Norma (née Salmon); Comr. Served in Zimb, ITC, UK, E Afr (CS/ THLS), Con (TC/TPWO) and at IHQ (IS/SWO Afr).

SWYERS, B. Gordon (Atlanta Temple, GA, 1959); Comr. b 25 Jul 36. BBA (Georgia State), and
SWYERS, Jacqueline (née Alexander); Comr. b 25 Dec 29. Served in USA S and at IHQ (IS Admin/SWO SPEA).

T

TAYLOR, Margaret (née Overton) (Aylsham, UK, 1962); Comr. Served in UK, E Afr, Pak and at IHQ (IS Prog Res). Ww Comr Brian, pG 2004.

TAYLOR, Orval A. (Seattle Citadel, USA W, 1940); Comr. b 21 May 19. Served in USA W, USA S, USA N (CS), Carib (TC), at IHQ (IS Planning and Dev) and USA E (TC). m Capt Muriel Upton (Long Beach, USA W, 1937) 1943.

THOMPSON, Arthur T. (Croydon Citadel, UK, 1961); Comr. b 23 Dec 32. BSc, PhD, PGCE, Freeman of the City of London, and
THOMPSON, Karen (née Westergaard) (Camberwell, 1961) m 1962; Comr. BA, PGCE. Served in Zimb, Zam, UK, NZ (CS/THLS) and at IHQ (IS Admin/IS Res, SWO Eur).

THOMSON, Robert E. (Racine, WI, w wife née Carol Nielsen, 1951); Comr. b 21 Feb 28. BM (St Olaf); Mrs T. BA (St Olaf). Served at USA Nat, in USA C (CS), at IHQ (IS Am and Carib) and in USA E (TC).

TILLSLEY, Bramwell Howard General (1993-94) (see page 25), with
TILLSLEY, Maud (née Pitcher). Mrs General. Served in Can, at ITC, in USA S, Aus S (TPWO) and at IHQ (WSWO, WPWO).
TONDI, Roos (née Mundung) (Sonder, Indon, 1958) m 1967; Comr. Served in Aus S and Indon (TPWO). Ww Comr Victor, pG 2002.

V

VERWAAL, Sjoerdje (née Zoethout) (Zaandam, 1947); Mrs Comr. Ww Comr Cornelis, pG 2002.

W

WAHLSTROM, Astrid (Lt Gronlund, Helsinki, 1936); Mrs Comr. Served in UK, Fin, S Am E and at IHQ. Ww Comr Per-Erik, pG 1995.
WAHLSTRÖM, Maire (née Nyberg) (Helsinki 1, Fin, 1944); Mrs General. Served in Fin, Swe, Can and at IHQ. Ww General Jarl Wahlström, pG 1999.
WALTER, Alison (née Harewood) (Calgary Citadel, AB, 1955); Mrs Comr. Served in Zimb, E Afr, Can, S Afr and at IHQ. Ww Comr Stanley, pG 2004.
WATERS, Margaret (née Eastland) (Niagara Falls, 1953); Comr. b 1 Mar 34. Served in Can and at IHQ. Ww Comr Arthur W., pG 2002.
WATILETE, Johannes G. (Bandung 3, Indon, 1963); Comr. b 9 Sep 41. BA, MTh, DTh, DMin (HC) and

WATILETE, Augustina (née Sarman) (Bandung 3, Indon, 1962) m 1966; Comr. b 16 Aug 39. Served in Sing (GS/CHLS), Phil (CS/THLS and TC/TPWO) and Indon (TC/TPWM).
WATSON, Robert A. (Philadelphia Pioneer, PA, USA E, 1955); Comr. b 11 Aug 34, and
WATSON, Alice (née Irwin) (Philadelphia Pioneer, PA, USA E, 1956) m 1957; Comr. Served in USA E (CS/THLS) and at USA Nat (NC/NPWO).
WICKBERG, Eivor (Maj Lindberg, Norrköping 1, Swdn, 1946); Mrs General. Ww General Erik Wickberg, pG 1996.
WILLIAMS, Harry William George (Wood Green, UK, 1934); Comr. b 13 Jul 13. Served in Ind W, Ind NE, Ind S (TC), NZ (TC), Aus E (TC) and at IHQ (IS Am and Australasia, IS Planning and Dev). OBE (1970), FRCS (Edin), FICS. Ww Eileen M., pG 2002.

Y

YOHANNAN, Paulose (Kalayapuram, Ind SW, 1974); Comr, b 1 Dec 45. MA (Sociol), DD, PhD, with
YOHANNAN, Kunjamma (née Jesaiah) m 1966; Comr. b 15 Jun 47. Served in Ind SW, Ind E, Ind SE (TC/TPWM) and Ind N (TC/TPWM).
YOSHIDA, Ai (née Yamamoto) (Kyoto, Jap, 1934) m 1939; Mrs Comr. Ww Comr Shinichi, pG 2004.

Retirements from Active Service

AUSTRALIA EASTERN

Maj Elizabeth Gittins from Faith Cottage on
1 Jun 2006

Comrs Ivan and Heather Lang (née Luhrs)
from THQ (TC/TPWM) on 1 Jul 2006

Maj Ian Hutchinson from Gungahlin on
1 Oct 2006

Maj Margaret Sanz from on 1 Oct 2006

Majs Russell and Betty Adams (née Pennall)
from Fairhaven Recovery Services Centre on
1 Jan 2007

Maj Alan Harley from College of Further
Education on 1 Jan 2007

Capt Dudley Mortimer from Palm Beach/
Elanora on 1 Jan 2007

Maj Eva Hill from Rural Ministries on
1 Feb 2007

Maj Robyn Proud from Calamvale on
1 Feb 2007

Capt Robert Stephens from Red Shield Defence
Services on 1 Feb 2007

AUSTRALIA SOUTHERN

Maj David Brunt from Melbourne Central
Division on 1 Aug 2006

Majs Paul and Edna Winter (née Exon) from
Melbourne Central Division and THQ on
1 Aug 2006

Capts Graham and Christine Isaac (née White)
from Tasmania Division on 1 Sep 2006

Maj Margaret Newdick from THQ on 1 Sep 2006

Lt-Col Pam Trigg from Eastern Victoria Division
on 1 Sep 2006

Maj Adele Vale from THQ on 1 Nov 2006

Maj Howard Smith from South Australia
Division on 1 Dec 2006

Maj Barry Shearer from South Australia
Division on 1 Jan 2007

Majs Dudley and Valma Mortimer (née Ray)
from South Queensland Division on 1 Jan 2007

Majs David and Laraine Philp (née Klein) from
THQ and Melbourne Central Division on
1 Feb 2007

Maj Barbara Munro from THQ on 1 Mar 2007

Lt-Cols John and Helen Staite (née Hewitson)
from National Secretariat on 1 May 2007

Major Jean Dale from THQ on 1 July 2007

Majs Robert and Valis McDonald from South
Australia Division on 1 Jul 2007

Major Ian and Heather Dawson from Red
Shield Defence Services on 1 Jul 2007

Major Heather Dawson from Red Shield
Defence Services on 1 July 2007

Major Colin Littlechild from Tasmania Division
on 1 Jul 2007

Lt-Col Ian Southwell from IHQ on 1 Jul 2007

Maj Athol Jackson from THQ on 1 Aug 2007

BRAZIL TERRITORY

Maj Benoni Campos from Campos do Jordão
Old People's Home on 10 Oct 2006

Majs Adonias and M. José Souza (née Calôr)
from Pirai do Sul on 30 Dec 2006

Majs Antonio and Edei Moitinho (née Silva)
from Uruguaiana Children's Home on
14 Jan 2007

Maj Ismael Rodrigues from Boqueirão on
31 Jan 2007

CANADA AND BERMUDA

Cols Roy and Joy Bungay (née Sturge) from
Newfoundland and Labrador West DHQ on
1 Sep 2006

Maj Lois Dueck from Manitoba and NW Ontario
Division on 1 Sep 2006

Majs James and Sheila Ellis (née McClure)
from The Scarborough Hospital on 1 Oct 2006

Maj Fronie Samson (née Sansome) from THQ
on 1 Oct 2006

Maj Laureen Twyne (née Worden) from
Midland CRC on 1 Dec 2006

Maj Barbara Hustler from THQ on 1 Mar 2007

Capts William and Barbara Gower (née Arnold)
from Gravenhurst Community Church on
1 Apr 2007

Maj Robin Cuff from Hamilton Grace Haven
on 1 Jul 2007

Majs Martin and Vera Youden (née Squires)
from Bayview on 1 Jul 2007

Majs Clyde and Gladys Osmond (née Brace)
from THQ on 1 Jul 2007

Majs Fredrick and Winnie Randell (née Freake)
from Comfort Cove/Newstead on 1 Jul 2007

Majs Ernest and Sandra Reid (née Ratcliff)
from Kitchener on 1 Jul 2007

Majs Robert and Shirley Ratcliff (née
Hutchinson) from Alberta and Northern
Territories DHQ on 1 Aug 2007

Majs Donald and Greta Oakley (née Banfield)
from Brantford Booth Centre on 1 Aug 2007

Majs Kenneth and Glennice Bonnar (née Gray)
from Ontario East DHQ on 1 Aug 2007

Retirements from Active Service

CARIBBEAN
Maj Alice Buckley from Belize Region on 24 Apr 2007

CONGO (BRAZZAVILLE)
Maj Pascal Kongo on 30 Nov 2006
Maj Badila on 31 Dec 2006
Maj Nkoua on 31 Dec 2006

CONGO (KINSHASA) & ANGOLA
Maj Julienne Ndilu from Sapu (Angola) on 27 Jan 2007
Lt-Cols Ferdinand and Hélène Nlabu from Kinshasa 2 DHQ on 25 Mar 2007

DENMARK
Maj Fanny Worm from THQ on 31 Dec 2006

FINLAND AND ESTONIA
Maj Reijo Pitkonen from THQ on 31 Mar 2006
Maj Leena Savolainen from Helsinki on 30 Sep 2006
Maj Marja-Liisa Toivonen from Kotka on 31 Oct 2006
Maj Pirkko Santala from Mikkeli on 31 Mar 2007
Maj Pirkko Vauhkonen from Rovaniemi on 31 Jul 2007
Maj Leila Nygrén from Oulu on 31 Aug 2007
Maj Kalevi Kortelainen from Tampere on 31 Aug 2007
Maj Seija Kortelainen (née Tuupainen) from Tampere on 31 Aug 2007

FRANCE
Maj Mado Allegre-Gros from Monnetier-Mornex on 1 May 2007
Maj Denise Munch from Toulon on 1 May 2007

GERMANY AND LITHUANIA
Majs Rolf and Ursula Metzger (née Wiessell) from THQ on 31 Aug 2007

INDIA EASTERN
Majs Kapluaia and Zodingliani from Thiangfal on 14 Jan 2007
Majs Rotluanga and Rothangpuii from Thingsultliah on 18 Feb 2007
Lt-Cols Rohmingthanga and Lalkungi from Kawrthah on 25 Feb 2007

INDIA NORTHERN
Majs Rafiq and Sheela Masih from MacRobert Hospital, Dhariwal, on 30 Oct 2006
Majs Nazar and Gladys Masih from Beas on 1 Mar 2007

Majs Bua and Miriam Masih from Dera Baba Nanak on 1 Jul 2007

INDIA SOUTH EASTERN
Majs M. John Rose and Jebamoni on 30 Oct 2006
Majs P. David and Regibai on 30 Oct 2006
Lt-Cols C. Rajamonickam and Marthal on 31 Jan 2007
Majs M. Isac and Salam on 6 Feb 2007

INDIA SOUTH WESTERN
Majs M. Samuel and Rachel Samuel on 31 Sep 2006
Maj M. D. Annamma Joseph on 31 Jan 2007
Majs V. Subhanantharaj and Hebsibai Subhanantharaj on 28 Feb 2007
Majs V. C. John and Aleyamma John on 31 Mar 2007
Majs D. Samuel and Swornamma Samuel on 30 Apr 2007
Majs T. J. Joseph and Gracy Joseph on 31 May 2007
Majs P. Joseph and Sosamma Joseph on 30 Jun 2007

INDIA WESTERN
Cols Sumant and Nalani Parkhe from THQ (CS/TSWM) on 30 Apr 2007
Lt-Cols Gideon and Ushaben Chhaganlal from Petlad Division on 30 Apr 2007
Majs Natwarlal and Savitaben from South Gujarat Division on 30 Apr 2007
Majs Shiva and Shardabai Mangal from Petlad Central on 30 Apr 2007
Majs Dashrath and Pramila Gajbhiv from Aurangabad Extension on 30 Apr 2007
Capts Joel Solomon and Jashwantiben Joel from Chune on 30 Apr 2007
Majs David and Roshanben Padale from HRD Centre, Ahmednagar, on 1 May 2007

INDONESIA
Majs Jacob and Julie Habel from East Palu Division on 1 May 2006
Majs Fanolo and Henny Sarumaha from Waturalele on 1 May 2006
Maj Adriana Ngale from Ampera on 1 July 2006
Majs Aming and Mina Noerman from Batujajar on 1 Jul 2006
Majs Tukimin and Rostani Tjondrosiswojo from Jepon on 1 Aug 2006
Comrs Johannes and Augustina Watilete from THQ (TC/TPWM) on 1 Oct 2006
Majs Muchsen and Esthefien Kaswadie from Kulawi on 1 Feb 2007

JAPAN
Majs Koji and Akiko Nishimiya (née Onodera) from Fujinryo Women's Home and Booth Hospital and THQ on 30 Sep 2006

Maj Kunio Nakagawa from Kyoto on 31 Jan 2007

Maj Masumi Takahashi (née Imamura) from Shinseiryo Women's Home on 31 Jan 2007

Maj Noriko Konishi from Shizuoka on 31 Mar 2007

KENYA
Majs Wilson and Tafroza Adego (née Kadenyi) from Matunda on 7 Dec 2006

Majs Joseph and Mary Ndeda (née Livanga) from Madegwa on 7 Dec 2006

Majs Joseph and Margaret Juma (née Akuku) from Viyalo on 7 Dec 2006

Majs Joel and Monicah Kuria (née Mwelu) from Makadara on 7 Dec 2006

Majs Ephraim and Mary Migeke (née Lovega) from Ikengero on 7 Dec 2006

Majs Abisai and Jesca Bulimu (née Lovembe) from Dandora on 7 Dec 2006

Majs Thadayo and Mical Ogonji (née Kusa) from Muusini on 7 Dec 2006

Majs Zebedayo and Janet Evelya (née Kahivugutsa) from Masigolo on 7 Dec 2006

Capt Beatrice Kidai (née Anzilimu) from Thika on 7 Dec 2006

KOREA
Lt-Col Son, Myong-shik and Lt-Col Chung, Yang-soon from Seoul DHQ on 28 Feb 2007

Lt-Col Lee, Sang-hyung and Lt-Col Kim, Kyung-soon from THQ on 28 Feb 2007

Maj Lee, Oong-ho and Maj Hong, Shin-ja from Hapjeong Community Centre, Pyongtaek, on 28 Feb 2007

Maj Oo, Soo-il and Maj Lee, Hwa-soon from Yung Duk Corps on 28 Feb 2007

Maj Kim, Chong-tae and Maj Choi, Jeong-ja from Sang Kei Corps on 31 Mar 2007

Maj Kim, Kie-duk and Maj Park, Chung-ja from Seoul South DHQ on 30 Jun 2007

MALAWI
Majs George and Nelesi Nkhululu from CHQ and Chirimba on 1 Apr 2007

THE NETHERLANDS AND CZECH REPUBLIC
Majs Bert and Elly Sprokkereef (née van den Berg) from THQ on 1 Feb 2007

Maj Aad Plaisier from Goes/Zierikzee on 1 May 2007

Majs Peter and Cathy Slingerland (née Rozema) from THQ on 1 May 2007

NEW ZEALAND, FIJI AND TONGA
Maj Graeme McMurdo from Auckland Congress Hall on 30 Jun 2006

Maj Robert Millar from Canterbury Northwest DHQ on 1 Jul 2006

Maj Roger Horton from Southern DHQ on 31 Aug 2006

Maj Harold Robertson from Epsom Lodge on 31 Aug 2006

Maj Ian Spargo from THQ on 31 Aug 2006

Majs Eroni and Makereta Serukalou (née Timi) from Community Ministries Eastern (Suva) on 31 Aug 2006

Maj Christopher Brunskill from Thames on 31 Oct 2006

Maj Rex Cross from Timaru on 31 Oct 2006

Maj Evelyn Millar (née Jarvis) from Canterbury Northwest DHQ on 31 Oct 2006

Maj Lorna McMurdo (née Johnson) from Auckland Congress Hall on 10 Jan 2007

Maj June Robertson (née Reilly) from Epsom Lodge on 10 Jan 2007

Majs John and Christine Kendall (née Smith) from Wanganui on 18 Jan 2007

Maj Ian Knight from Motueka on 22 Jan 2007

Maj Carol Horton (née Cosgrove) from Southern DHQ on 31 Jan 2007

Maj (Dr) Patricia Hill (née Cruickshank) from Special Services (Medical) on 31 Jan 2007

Majs Seth and Pamela Le Leu (née Duffell) from THQ on 31 Jan 2007

Maj Kevin Goldsack from THQ on 28 Feb 2007

Majs Sainivalati and Ledua Toganivalu (née Wasa) from Fiji DHQ on 30 Apr 2007

Maj Judith Bennett (née Muirhead) from Tawa on 30 Jun 2007

Maj Harold Hill from THQ on 30 Jun 2007

Maj David Bennett from THQ on 31 Aug 2007

Maj Thomas Kopu from Thames on 31 Aug 2007

Majs David and Christine Stone (née Henrickson) from Court and Prisons on 31 Aug 2007

NORWAY, ICELAND AND THE FÆROES
Maj Frank Nymoen from Mo i Rana on 28 Feb 2007

Maj Clara Inger Georgsen from THQ on 28 Feb 2007

Maj Anna Skogly from Social Services on 31 Mar 2007

Comrs Thorleif and Olaug Gulliksen from THQ on 31 May 2007

Retirements from Active Service

Maj Liv Astrid Iversen from THQ on
31 May 2007

PAKISTAN
Majs Allah Lok and Surriya Allah Lok from
Paddri on 6 Apr 2007

PAPUA NEW GUINEA
Capts Avee and Sandra Keire (née Beraro)
from Community and Social Services and
HIV/Aids, Goroka, on 12 Dec 2006
Majs Rabona and Gabi Rotona (née Kanau)
from South Eastern DHQ on 1 Feb 2007
Majs Keroro and Molly Eric from Uaripi on
7 May 2007

THE PHILIPPINES
Lt-Col Anita Orane from THQ on 28 May 2006

SOUTHERN AFRICA
Majs George and Irene Pavey (née Wright) from
Firlands Children's Home on 28 Feb 2007

SRI LANKA
Majs Ananda and Nanda Subasinghe from
Maradana on 17 Feb 2007
Maj Bisomanie Kumarage from
Siyambalangamuwa on 22 Apr 2007

SWEDEN AND LATVIA
Maj Berith Ståhl from THQ on 30 Sep 2006
Maj Jean Kjellgren from THQ on 31 Oct 2006
Maj Milton Tourn from Stockholm 6/Sundbyberg
on 31 Dec 2006
Envoy Jerry Widman from Offerdal on
22 Dec 2006
Maj Ulla Gallardo from Stockholm on
10 Jan 2007
Envoy Gun Bohman from Helsingborg on
27 Feb 2007

SWITZERLAND, AUSTRIA AND HUNGARY
Lt-Col François Thöni from Romandie DHQ
on 31 Oct 2006
Maj Hans Bösch from Basel 1 on 30 Nov 2006
Maj Bernard Hanselmann from Geneva on
30 Nov 2006
Maj Käthi Mosimann from Waldkirch on
30 Nov 2006
Maj Thérèse Villars from Budapest (Hungary)
Social Services on 31 Dec 2006
Maj Erwin Saugy from Ost DHQ on
31 Jan 2007
Maj Paul Balmer from Zofingen on 31 Mar 2007
Maj Yvonne Geiser from Vevey on 31 Mar 2007

Maj Marie-Madeleine Rossel from Les Ponts-
de-Martel and Fleurier on 31 Mar 2007
Maj Heinz Weidmann from Social Programme,
Liestal Corps, and Thrift Stores Pastoral Care
on 31 Mar 2007
Maj Martha Schwendener from Arbon on
31 May 2007
Maj Sonja Balmer from Zofingen on 30 Jun 2007
Lt-Col Ursula Dollé from Berne on 30 Jun 2007
Maj Paul Burch from Frutigen on 31 Jul 2007
Maj Heidi Knecht from Nordwestschweiz DHQ
on 31 Jul 2007

UNITED KINGDOM WITH THE REPUBLIC OF IRELAND
Capt Isobel Carson (née McCarthy) from
Portadown on 1 Sep 2006
Maj Barbara Howe from Ottery St Mary on
1 Sep 2006
Maj Vera Pilkington (née Bailey) from London
Central DHQ on 1 Sep 2006
Maj Miriam Scutt (née McGilchrist) from THQ
on 1 Sep 2006
Maj Patricia Charlesworth from Whitby
Outreach Centre on 1 Oct 2006
Maj Alistair Dawson from THQ on 1 Oct 2006
Maj Alan Hickman from Millom on 1 Oct 2006
Majs Colin and Maureen Hunt (née Sheehan)
from Southampton Sholing on 1 Oct 2006
Maj Olivia Milner (née Greenwood) from
Davis House Soc S, Swindon, on 1 Oct 2006
Maj Leslie Cook from Whitehaven on 1 Nov 2006
Maj Jean Kjellgren (née Mitton) from Sweden
and Latvia THQ on 1 Nov 2006
Capt Ruth Lewington (née Davies) from
Midsomer Norton on 1 Nov 2006
Maj Keith Lloyd from THQ on 1 Nov 2006
Majs Mervyn and June Marshall (née Kirk)
from Shotton Colliery on 1 Nov 2006
Majs Frank and Mavis Pascoe (née Jolley) from
Sutton in Ashfield on 1 Nov 2006
Majs Derek and Gillian Smith (née Mullins)
from Prison Chaplains, Southern Division, on
1 Nov 2006
Lt-Col David Jones from Nelson on 1 Dec 2006
Maj Pauline King (née Smith) from Ashbrook
Soc S, Edinburgh, and Eagle Lodge Eventide
Home on 1 Dec 2006
Maj Madeliene Lloyd (née Moon) from
Bradbury Eventide Home, Southend-on-Sea,
on 1 Dec 2006
Maj Marlene Bishop (née Simpson) from
Wellingborough on 1 Jan 2007
Lt-Col Joan Dunwoodie from IHQ on 1 Jan 2007
Maj Janet Gilson from Leigh-on-Sea on
1 Jan 2007

Retirements from Active Service

Cols Graeme and Anne Harding (née Lewis)
from Ghana Territory (TC/TPWM) on
1 Feb 2007

Comrs Alex and Ingeborg Hughes (née Clausen)
from Maidenhead on 1 Feb 2007

Majs Robert and Helena Boyd (née Hall) from
Airdrie on 1 Feb 2007

Majs Terence and Yvonne Jones (née Price)
from Bristol Easton on 1 Feb 2007

Maj Margaret Yuill (née Jackson) from Central
North DHQ on 1 Feb 2007

Majs David and Sandra Dalziel (née Snape)
from THQ on 1 Mar 2007

Maj Alan Austin from Bovington Red Shield
Club on 1 Apr 2007

Maj Steven Booth from London Central DHQ
on 1 Apr 2007

Capt Wilma Perfect (née Laird) from Port
Talbot on 1 Apr 2007

Lt-Col Ronald Smith from THQ and North
Shields on 1 Apr 2007

Maj Christine Kilpatrick (née Finch) from
London Central DHQ on 1 May 2007

Majs John and Jean Howarth (née White)
from Dudley on 1 Jun 2007

Maj James Cunningham from Belfast Citadel
on 1 Jul 2007

Majs Peter and Olive Dickson (née Fisher)
from Clacton on 1 Jul 2007

Maj Margaret Hardy (née Finlay) from South
and Mid Wales DHQ on 1 Jul 2007

Majs John and Shirley Knight (née Hallam)
from Lye on 1 Jul 2007

Cols Michael and Ina Marvell (née Nissen)
from Denmark Territory (TC/TPWM) on
1 Jul 2007

Majs Raymond and Dawn Bates (née Tout)
from THQ on 1 Aug 2007

Lt-Cols Peter and Sylvia Dalziel (née Gair)
from The Netherlands and Czech Republic
Territory (CS/TSWM) on 1 Aug 2007

Maj David Gill from Sunderland Millfield on
1 Aug 2007

Majs John and Janette Howie (née Young)
from Barrhead on 1 Aug 2007

USA CENTRAL

Majs Dallas and Phyllis Raby (née Gilmour)
from Rockford, IL, on 31 Jan 2007

Majs James and Linda Porterfield (née
Sorensen) from Waukegan, IL, ARC on
31 Mar 2007

Lt-Cols Harry and Barbara Brocksieck (née
Cooke) from THQ on 30 Jun 2007

Majs Leroy and Margarett (née Simpson) from
Albert Lea, MN, on 30 Jun 2007

Majs Gerald and Sharon Smelser (née Larson)
from Richmond, IN, on 30 Jun 2007

USA EASTERN

Majs Washington and Catherine Navarro (née
Crispell) from Perth Amboy, NJ, on 1 Oct 2006

Majs Frank and Evelyn Psaute (née Foulke)
from New Haven, CT, ARC on 1 Oct 2006

Maj D. Sue Smith from THQ on 1 Nov 2006

Majs William and Kathleen Bentley (née
Rexicker) from Cleveland, OH, DHQ on
1 Jan 2007

Maj Mary Fitch (née Johnson) from Oneonta,
NY, on 1 Jan 2007

Majs Warren and Diana Smith (née Small)
from THQ on 1 Jan 2007

Lt-Cols Fred and Barbara Van Brunt (née
Huntsman) from Boston, MA, DHQ on
1 Jan 2007

Maj Dorothy Hitzka (née Drown) from NHQ
on 1 Mar 2007

Majs Raymond and Sheila Patrick (née Patno)
from Alliance, OH, on 1 Mar 2007

Majs Donald and Priscilla Klemanski (née
Hardy) from Ten-Eyck, NY, on 1 Apr 2007

Maj Sylvia Rebeck from THQ on 1 Jun 2007

Majs Bruce and Lorraine Fleming (née Carroll)
from New Kensington, PA, on 1 Jul 2007

Majs Robert and Camilla Pfeiffer (née Bigelow)
from Providence, RI, on 1 Jul 2007

Majs Joseph and Judith Robinson (née Kearns)
from Tonawanda, NY, on 1 Jul 2007

Majs John and Catherine Wettlaufer (née
Fullmer) from Glen Falls, NY, on 1 Jul 2007

USA SOUTHERN

Lt-Cols Danny and Esther Morrow (née
Pritchard) from Louisville, KY, DHQ on
1 Sep 2006

Majs James and Elma Brogden (née Blackwell)
from Atlanta, GA, ARC on 1 Sep 2006

Majs James and Bertha Worthy (née Dacres)
from Charlotte, NC, DHQ on 1 Feb 2007

Maj Sue Ann Jervis (née Wade) from Eden,
NC, on 1 Apr 2007

Maj Patricia Ann Wixson (née Breedlove) from
Greensboro, NC, on 31 May 2007

Majs David and Patricia Johnston (née Miles)
from Gaffney, NC, on 1 Jun 2007

Majs Joseph and Judith Knobel (née
Bridgeman) from Sanford, FL on 1 Jul 2007

Majs Robert and Beatrice Hopper (née
Tidman) from Charlotte, NC DHQ on
1 Jul 2007

Majs Charles and Sylvia Nowell (née Smith)
from St Petersburg, FL, ARC on 1 Jul 2007

Majs Charles and Sharon Smith (née Lynn) from West Palm Beach, FL on 1 Jul 2007

Majs John and Jacquelyn Tolan (née Henderson) from Memphis, TN, on 1 Jul 2007

Majs John and Mary Tracey (née Shockley) from Washington, DC, DHQ on 1 Jul 2007

Majs Jack and Janice Repass (née Mills) from Bradenton, FL, on 1 Jul 2007

Majs John and Bonnie Jordan (née Bergren) from THQ/Atlanta, GA, ARC on 1 Aug 2007

Majs Larry and Evelyn Repass (née Tyrell) from THQ on 1 Aug 2007

USA WESTERN

Majs Theodore and Rosalyn Mahr (née Bricknell) from Long Beach, CA, on 1 Jan 2007

Lt-Cols Jerry and Jeanine Gaines (née Wheeler) from New York, NY, on 1 Feb 2007

Majs William and Bernadita Begonia (née Cabanes) from Ontario, CA, on 1 Apr 2007

Majs Ronald and Shirley McKay (née Dillman) from Alamogordo, NM, on 1 Apr 2007

Maj Mark Sparks from Sacramento, CA, DHQ on 22 Jun 2007

Majs Ronald and Marilyn Bawden (née Andreasen) from Glendale, AZ, 1 Jul 2007

Majs Russell and Jacqueline Fritz (née Blake) from San Bernardino, CA, on 1 Jul 2007

Majs William and Judith Nottle (née Dart) from THQ on 1 Jul 2007

Majs Marvin and Carol Samuelson (née Robertson) from Medford, OR, on 1 Jul 2007

Majs James and Judy Goodwin (née Garner) from Idaho Falls, ID, on 1 Aug 2007

Maj Janet Summerfield (née Smith) from Great Falls, MT, on 1 Aug 2007

ZIMBABWE

Majs Sydney and Gladys Mabhiza from Greater Harare on 1 Nov 2006

Majs Jonathan and Thandiwe Yafele from Mupfure on 1 Dec 2006

WORDS OF LIFE

THE Salvation Army's international Bible reading plan, *Words of Life* offers an invaluable aid to daily devotional study. The readings cover a wide selection of Scripture over a period of time and the comments offered give opportunity to build a lasting library for further study and reflection. Points for prayer and praise are a further enrichment to personal devotion. Retired General John Gowans begins a term as writer of *Words of Life* with the May-June 2007 edition.

WE BELIEVE IN SALVATION

'We are a salvation people. This is our speciality – getting saved and keeping saved, and then getting somebody else saved. . . . We believe in salvation! We believe in old-fashioned salvation. Ours is the same salvation taught in the Bible, proclaimed by prophets and apostles, preached by Luther, Wesley and Whitfield, sealed by the blood of the martyrs – the very same salvation which was purchased by the sufferings and agony and blood of the Son of God.' – *William Booth*

Promotions to Glory

AUSTRALIA EASTERN
Mrs Comr Margery Cairns on 7 Aug 2006
Mrs Maj Rita Limpus on 21 Aug 2006
Maj Cyril Bugler on 28 Aug 2006
Capt Ernie Hill on 15 Sep 2006
Maj Ray Wilson on 18 Sep 2006
Mrs Lt-Col Doreen Brooks on 19 Sep 2006
Capt Coral Warren on 20 Sep 2006
Mrs Brig Edith Johnson on 27 Oct 2006
Maj Ray Cugley on 14 Nov 2006
Brig Clyde Wilkie on 15 Nov 2006
Col Charles Sheppard on 21 Nov 2006
Mrs Maj Ann Terracini on 4 Dec 2006
Brig Lionel Bray on 14 Dec 2006
Mrs Maj Cherie Wise on 4 Feb 2007
Maj Noel Kay (A) on 13 Feb 2007
Mrs Maj Catherine Creamer on 22 Mar 2007
Mrs Brig Lucy Reddie on 24 Mar 2007
Mrs Maj Myrtle Smith on 5 May 2007

AUSTRALIA SOUTHERN
Aux-Capt Dorothy Oakley on 4 Jul 2006
Brig Ruby Berry on 16 Jul 2006
Aux-Capt William Edmonds on 13 Aug 2006
Brig Victor Pedersen OF on 13 Aug 2006
Brig Merle Hewitt on 4 Sep 2006
Brig George Jones on 18 Sep 2006
Col Jean Linsellon 2 Oct 2006
Capt Frank Swift on 3 Oct 2006
Maj David Henderson on 8 Oct 2006
Brig Eileen Johnston on 28 Oct 2006
Lt-Col Anne Bautovich on 4 Nov 2006
Maj Lorna Cooper on 16 Nov 2006
Col Ronald Sketcher on 20 Nov 2006
Maj William Cooper on 8 Dec 2006
Lt-Col Hedley Preston on 20 Jan 2007
Brig Isabel McCormack on 12 Feb 2007
Brig Thelma Miller on 15 Feb 2007
Maj Dorothy Collins on 4 May 2007
Aux-Capt Agnes Craddock on 8 May 2007
Envoy June Rundle on 16 May 2007
Lt-Col Dulcie Magill on 29 May 2007
Maj Doreen Whan on 25 Jun 20
Maj Marjorie Nelson on 3 Jul 2007

BANGLADESH
Capt Niskalanka Halder (A) from Dhaka on
3 Sep 2006

BRAZIL
Capt M. Lúcia Silva on 10 Aug 2006
Maj Darcy Santos on 15 Oct 2006

CANADA AND BERMUDA
Brig Dora Taylor on 20 Sep 2006
Brig Dorothy Wells on 30 Sep 2006
Aux-Capt Donald Miller on 28 Oct 2006
Brig Etta Pike on 11 Nov 2006
Mrs Maj Lili Jedlicka on 15 Nov 2006
Mrs Aux-Capt C. Nellie Nichol on 26 Nov 2006
Brig Florence Hill on 29 Nov 2006
Brig Dorothy Thompson on 29 Dec 2006
Mrs Brig J. (Doris) Monk on 2 Jan 2007
Aux-Capt Emma Thompson on 5 Feb 2007
Aux-Capt Dorothy Gosling on 26 Feb 2007
Maj Edith Taylor on 7 Mar 2007
Mrs Brig Mae Ellsworth on 25 Apr 2007
Lt-Col Margaret Rea on 4 May 2007

CARIBBEAN
Maj Kenneth Gibbons on 7 Aug 2006
Brig Alma Rollock on 19 Oct 2006

CONGO BRAZZAVILLE
Capt Pulchérie Mavoungou (A) from Moungali
on 5 May 2006
Maj Bernard Mavoungou on 27 Mar 2006
Maj Pascal Kongo on 20 Dec 2006

CONGO (KINSHASA) AND ANGOLA
Maj Antoinette Ntumba Kinioko on
13 Aug 2006
Maj Germaine Boma Nseke on 2 Jan 2007
Maj Sylvie Kisaka Nkuakala on 13 Feb 2007

DENMARK
Brig Agda Jensen on 13 Mar 2007

FINLAND AND ESTONIA
Brig Hilkka Hämäläinen (née Viman) on
11 Apr 2007
Brig Niilo Kortelainen on 18 May 2007
Lt-Col Irma Salmi (née Määttä) (A) from THQ
on 19 Jun 2007

FRANCE
Maj Henriette Benaben on 16 Aug 2006
Maj Paule Lautard on 1 Feb 2007
Commandant Elie Bordas on 9 Feb 2007

HONG KONG AND MACAU
Maj Andrew Lo Wai-hing on 6 Nov 2006

INDIA EASTERN
Maj Darrinpui on 22 Jan 2007

Maj Ngunthanga (A) from Bualpui on
14 May 2007

INDIA NORTHERN

Maj B. N. Sahu on 22 Nov 2006
Maj (Mrs) Manasini Sahu on 11 Feb 2007
Maj (Mrs) Mukhtara Karnail Masih on
27 Feb 2007
Maj Masih Dayal on 21 Apr 2007
Brig (Mrs) Elizabeth Rahmat Masih on
23 May 2007

INDIA SOUTH EASTERN

Maj Peter Yesudian (A) from Tuticorin District
Office on 22 Nov 2006
Maj Gnanammal Abel on 27 Jan 2007
Maj Retnaraj (A) on 3 Feb 2007
Maj Abraham on 8 Feb 2007
Maj Nesam Sebagnanam on 5 Apr 2007

INDIA SOUTH WESTERN

Maj N. Rajamma Paulose on 12 Jun 2006
Capt Mathew Joseph (A) on 4 Aug 2006
Maj Lysamma Alexander on 19 Aug 2006
Maj Mariamma George on 26 Aug 2006
Maj S. Gnanam Swamidhas on 26 Sep 2006
Maj P. J. Sosamma Thomas on 12 Nov 2006
Maj T. J. Gnanamma Daniel on 06 Dec 2006
Lt-Col John Benjamin on 7 Dec 2006
Maj P. M. Wilson on 20 Mar 2007
Maj Aleyamma John Suseelkumar (A) from
THQ on 17 Apr 2007

INDIA WESTERN

Maj Saubai Prabhakar Jadhav on 7 Aug 2006
Maj Sumatibai Waman Mhaske on 16 Aug 2006
Maj Kmlabai Petrus Balid on 26 Aug 2006
Maj Waman Mhaske on 28 Aug 2006
Maj Tulsabai S. Bodhak on 1 Sep 2006
Maj Manilal Lalu from on 3 Sep 2006
Brig Marthabai Howard on 10 November 2006
Maj Yamunabai Bhambal from on 11 Dec 2006
Maj Mamtabai Makasre on 23 Dec 2006
Maj Godhaji Magar on 12 Jan 2007
Maj Miriam Samuel Jetha on 21 Jan 2007
Brig Howard Bavji on 23 Feb 2007

INDONESIA

Maj Sally Higgi on 24 Apr 2006
Maj Ertji Deitje Panggaudju (A) on 17 Dec 2006
Maj Alfina Sango (A) on 14 Jan 2007
Maj Nicolas Sumu (A) on 1 Feb 2007
Maj Sri Rahayuni Salmon (A) on 15 Feb 2007

JAPAN

Mrs Lt-Col Kimie Usui on 9 Jan 2007

Maj Toshio Izumo on 11 Feb 2007

KENYA

Maj Grace Mbugua on 1 Aug 2006
Maj Damaris Mwugusi on 17 Oct 2006
Maj Joel Kuria (A) from Makadara on
18 Oct 2006
Maj Marita Kirui on 10 Nov 2006
Maj Elizabeth Bwasio on 19 Nov 2006
Maj Bramwel Ogada (A) from Wabukhonyi on
25 Jan 2007
Maj Dickson Juma on 11 Feb 2007
Maj Esther Machayo on 2 Mar 2007
Maj Salome Akombo on 11 Mar 2007
Maj Rosalia Ajuang on 12 Mar 2007
Col Wyciffee Angoya on 21 Mar 2007

KOREA

Maj Kang, Bong-nam on 19 Jul 2006
Lt-Col Kwon, Tai-hoon on 13 Sep 2006
Maj Shin, Young-hee on 24 Jan 2007
Lt-Col Song, Young-sook on 19 May 2007
Maj Kim, Chung-sook (widow of Maj Choi,
Dong-geun) on 1 Jul 2007

MEXICO

Lt-Col Isidoro Cerezo on 7 Dec 2005
Maj Eligio Martínez on 10 Nov 2006
Lt-Col Mireya Sánchez on 12 Jul 2007
Maj Irene Martínez on 29 Sep 2007

NEW ZEALAND, FIJI AND TONGA

Maj Isabella Ramsey on 10 Mar 2006
Maj Violet Medland on 15 Apr 2006
Lt-Col Lawrence Weggery on 11 May 2006
Maj Raymond Knight on 16 Jun 2006
Maj Daphne Irwin (née Simpson) on 21 Jun 2006
Lt-Col Lancelot Rive on 24 Jun 2006
Capt Fauoro Kaurasi (née Semantafa) on
3 Jul 2006
Brig Margaret Hill (née Cunningham) on
24 Jul 2006
Maj Ngaire White (née Mayfield) on 20 Aug 2006
Maj Neville Stark on 27 Jul 2006
Col Lorna Kendall (née Pedersen) on
28 Aug 2006
Brig Maisie Harris on 9 Feb 2007
Brig Joshua Taylor on 21 Apr 2007
Maj Peter Thorp on 30 Apr 2007

NORWAY, ICELAND AND FÆROES

Mrs Brig Edith Heimark on 1 Aug 2006
Mrs Maj Klara Enstad on 16 Sep 2006
Maj Solveig Nilsen on 17 Oct 2006
Maj Christine Frøshaug on 19 Oct 2006
Comr Haakon Dahlstrøm on 31 Oct 2006

Promotions to Glory

Lt-Col Henny Driveklepp on 24 Nov 2006
Maj Ella Nesset on 7 Dec 2006
Maj Steinar Austevik (A) from THQ on
3 Jan 2007
Mrs Lt-Col Sigrid Moen on 10 Jan 2007
Mrs Lt-Col Norunn Rasmussen on 17 Jan 2007
Maj Svanhild Kjeilen on 10 Mar 2007
Mrs Maj Britta Brodtkorb on 10 Mar 2007
Mrs Lt-Col Valborg Raubakken on 14 Mar 2007
Mrs Col Metta Kristiansen on 14 Mar 2007
Mrs Maj Signe Vavik on 29 Mar 2007
Mrs Maj Lilly Lund on 6 May 2007
Maj Edith Olsen on 12 May 2007
Maj Hanna Winther Gundersen on 2 Jun 2007
Maj Ruth Pettersen on 22 Jun 2007
Mrs Brig Liv Eikeland on 30 Jun 2007

PAKISTAN

Maj Mable Hanzal (A) from Greetn Town on
22 Jan 2007
Maj Alice Gulzar on 10 Jan 2007
Maj Barkat Masih on 26 Mar 2007

PAPUA NEW GUINEA

Capt Joseph Tomaliso (A) from Lealea on
18 Jul 2006
Col Julie Kalai (née Kiofi) (A) from THQ
(TPWM) on 2 Oct 2006
Maj Aero Tauaru (née Kou) on 9 Feb 2007

THE PHILIPPINES

Maj Erene Gascon (née Osorio) on 12 Apr 2007

SINGAPORE, MALAYSIA AND MYANMAR

Capt Rothianga (A) from Myanmar Regional
HQ on 8 Aug 2006

SOUTH AMERICA EAST

Brig Orlando Franchetti on 4 Aug 2006

SRI LANKA

Capt Violet Silva on 11 Jul 2006

SWEDEN AND LATVIA

Envoy Karl Aringstam on 10 Aug 2006
Maj Betty Ölmeklint on 5 Oct 2006
Mrs Brig Lisen Sundberg (née Granberg) on
16 Oct 2006
Envoy Greta Karlsson Pallone (née Karlsson)
on 23 Oct 2006
Mrs Brig Margit Öhneskog-Lendin (née
Jansson) on 5 Dec 2006
Brig Helny Sandberg on 13 Dec 2006
Lt-Col Arne Henning on 19 Dec 2006
Lt-Col Kurt Larson on 19 Dec 2006

Mrs Comr Lisbeth Nilsson (née Ohlqvist) on
30 Jan 2007
Brig Rune Karlsson on 13 Feb 2007
Maj Florence Ringqvist on 22 Feb 2007
Envoy Göta Sahlman (née Arestav) on
18 Mar 2007
Maj Ester Klaar on 26 Mar 2007
Aux-Capt Ulla Jespersen (née Bengtsson) on
10 Apr 2007
Mrs Lt-Col Stina Wallin (née Wikström) on
4 May 2007
Lt-Col Stina Malmström on 28 June 2007
Maj Viola Lundkvist (née Berglund) on
17 Jul 2007

SWITZERLAND, AUSTRIA AND HUNGARY

Maj Vreni Raas-Müller on 12 Sep 2006
Maj Fleur Booth on 19 Oct 2006
Maj Steinmann Ruth on 26 Nov 2006
Maj Johanna Schmid-Anderegg on 4 Feb 2007
Brig Marie Jäggi on 14 Apr 2007
Brig Martha Reist on 4 May 2007

UNITED KINGDOM WITH THE REPUBLIC OF IRELAND

Brig Ivor Howells on 16 Sep 2006
Maj Winifred Scott on 21 Sep 2006
Maj Donald Heness on 11 Oct 2006
Maj George Saltwell on 13 Oct 2006
Lt-Col John Archibald on 16 Oct 2006
Mrs Brig Mary Parker on 26 Oct2006
Col Colin Durman on 30 Oct 2006
Mrs Brig Edith Johnson on 27 Oct 2006
Capt David Clift on 1 Nov 2006
Maj Joan Middlehurst on 8 Nov 2006
Aux-Capt Joan Mends on 16 Nov 2006
Maj Lindsay Anderson (A) from Clacton-on-
Sea on 22 Nov 2006
Maj Margaret Constable on 29 Nov 2006
Mrs Maj Ivy White on 3 Dec 2006
Comr Dinsdale Pender on 3 Dec 2006
Brig Kathleen Middleton on 8 Dec 2006
Brig Gwenyth Anderson on 10 Dec 2006
Brig Jessie Broom on 14 Dec 2006
Maj William Cook on 14 Dec 2006
Maj Clive Bishop (A) from Wellingborough on
25 Dec 2006
Maj Wallace Holliday on 4 Jan 2007
Maj Mrs Margaret Shaw on 13 Jan 2007
Comr Geoffrey Dalziel on 31 Jan 2007
Mrs Aux-Capt Betty Ford on 8 Feb 2007
Brig Olive Buttress on 13 Feb 2007
Maj Maureen McKenzie on 17 Feb 2007
Lt-Col James Chandler on 15 Mar 2007
Maj Janet Cooper on 27 Mar 2007

Mrs Lt-Col **Violet Smith** on 3 Apr 2007
Maj **Keith Lloyd** on 20 Apr 2007
Maj **Ron Doust** on 28 Apr 2007
Mrs Lt-Col **Ada Graver** on 29 Apr 2007
Maj **Glenna Hughes (A)** from Buckingham on
  1 May 2007
Mrs Aux-Capt **June Gibbs** on 10 May 2007
Mrs Maj **Stella Ward** 11 May 2007
Mrs Lt-Col **Mabel Bowes** on 27 May 2007
Mrs Comr **Winifred Read** on 5 Jun 2007
Brig **Douglas Burgess** on 6 Jun 2007
Maj **Valerie Blake** on 7 Jun 2007
Mrs Maj **Margaret Cox** on 12 Jun 2007
Maj **Eric Blake** on 21 Jun 2007
Maj **Mary Deacon** on 22 Jun 2007
Maj **Jessie (Netty) Hendry** on 16 Jul 2007
Maj **Ronald Mariner** on 20 Jul 2007
Mrs Lt-Col **Margaret Smith** on 21 Jul 2007
Maj **Mary Templeton** on 29 Jul 2007
Mrs Maj **Jean Pearce** on 5 Aug 2007

USA CENTRAL

Col **Stig W. Franzen** on 31 Aug 2006
Maj **Alvin A. Parker** on 14 Sep 2006
Mrs Brig **Ernest (Kathryn) Hammer** (née
  Ripley) on 20 Sep 2006
Mrs Maj **David (Flossie) Amick** (née Matthews)
  on 18 Oct 2006
Maj **George Scofield** on 26 Oct 2006
Mrs Maj **Robert (Violette) Hallquist** (née
  Gustafson) on 26 Oct 2006
Brig **Arlene Finley** on 2 Dec 2007
Maj **Orville Butts** on 3 Dec 2007
Col **Gordon Foubister** on 7 Feb 2007
Mrs Maj **Oliver (Betty) Poling** (née Hills) on
  24 Feb 2007
Lt-Col **Raymond Carroll** on 15 Mar 2007
Lt-Col **Kathleen Zehm** on 15 Mar 2007
Mrs Maj **Roy (Janet) Rowland** (née Gilchrist)
  on 22 Mar 2007
Maj **Thomas Line** on 12 Apr 2007
Aux-Capt **Kenneth (Marilyn) Sharp** (née
  Watson) on 23 Apr 2007
Maj **Ruth Lohr** on 27 May 2007
Maj **James Barker** on 16 Jun 2007
Col **John Paton** on 17 Jun 2007
Mrs Brig **Erma Rush** on 17 Jul 2007
Maj **Helen L. Prosser** on 22 Jul 2007

USA EASTERN

Mrs Brig **Ella V. Lowman** on 21 Sep 2006
Maj **Leann J. Klemoswki** on 23 Sep 2006
Mrs Brig **Mary H. Moody** on 30 Sep 2006
Maj **Edsel D. Wheatley** on 5 Oct 2006
Mrs Brig **Lisen T. Sundberg** on 16 Oct 2006
Maj **Robert E. Manning** on 20 Oct 2006

Brig **E. Walter Lamie** on 10 Oct 2006
Lt-Col **Wm Arthur Bamford** on 28 Nov 2006
Maj **John Ryans** on 12 Dec 2006
Maj **Martha J. Coleman** on 27 Dec 2006
Brig **Everett Henry** on 14 Jan 2007
Mrs Col **Dorisceil L. Hooper** on 26 Jan 2007
Brig **Alice V. Thileen** on 1 Feb 2007
Maj **Betty Margaret Myers** on 2 Feb 2007
Maj **Mary Ellen MacKay** on 4 Feb 2007
Maj **Graham Barnes Mills** on 4 Feb 2007
Mrs Lt-Col **Gertrude Charron** on 17 Feb 2007
Maj **James Francis (A)** from Buffalo, NY on
  21 Feb 2007
Maj **Edith I. Bassett** on 23 Feb 2007
Maj **Ann M. MacMurdo** on 13 Mar 2007
Maj Mrs **Hilda E. Wickens** on 25 Mar 2007
Lt-Col **Raymond J. Wilson** on 4 Apr 2007
Brig **Clyde P. Green** on 8 Apr 2007
Mrs Lt-Col **Betty Wilson** on 10 Apr 2007
Brig **Constance Tanner** on 1 May 2007
Brig **H. Wilbur Smith** on 30 May 2007
Brig **Lambert Bittinger** on 5 Jun 2007
Mrs Maj **Lorna Shaffstall** on 31 Jul 2007

USA SOUTHERN

Maj **Earl Short** on 13 Aug 2006
Mrs Maj **James (Jeannette) Tritton** on
  27 Aug 2006
Mrs Maj **Christine Wixon** on 30 Aug 2006
Mrs Maj **Otis (Hazel) Street** on 31 Oct 2006
Mrs Maj **Doris McQuay** on 18 Nov 2006
Mrs Brig **Robert (Flora) Moore** on 19 Nov 2006
Mrs Brig **Louis (Grace) Amberger** on
  2 Jan 2007
Mrs Lt-Col **John (Irene) Mikles** on 5 Feb 2007
Lt-Col **James Jay** on 5 Feb 2007
Maj **Alta Belle (Billie) Walker** on 5 Apr 2007
Maj **James Walker** on 19 Apr 2007
Maj **Samuel Crowder** on 19 Apr 2007
Mrs Brig **Katherine (Payne) Millsap** on
  30 Apr 2007
Maj **Herbert R. Bergen** on 5 Jun 2007
Mrs Maj **Mildred (Kirby) Foden** on
  20 Jun 2007
Maj **Everett Howard Lynch** on 13 Jul 2007
Mrs Maj **Hymon (Erna) Davis** on
  16 Aug 2007

USA WESTERN

Snr-Maj Mrs **Georgina Panter** on 6 Aug 2006
Mrs Lt-Col **Bennetta Rody** on 26 Jan 2007
Maj **Wilfrid Hunter** on 20 Apr 2007
Aux-Capt W. **Gene Lantz** on 20 Jun 2007
Mrs Col **Eleanor Murray** on 10 Jul 2007
Mrs Maj **Dianne Bassett** on 10 Aug 2007
Mrs Maj **Donna Miller** on 23 Aug 2007

ZIMBABWE

Envoy J. Kurwakumire (A) from Hurungwe on
   15 Jul 2006
Maj Stanley Gorejena (A) from Seke Materera
   on 12 Aug 2006
Maj E. Mukau Bindura on 12 Sep 2006
Maj W. Gore on 24 Sep 2006
Lt-Col Henry Mhasvi (A) from THQ on
   28 Sep 2006

Capt Mpiliso Magugu (A) from Harare Central
   on 4 Nov 2006
Maj K. Mpofu in Nov 2006
Maj Shadrack Muchenje on 22 Dec 2006
Brig Mpakaira Nyamunetsa on 21 Apr 2007
Maj Mashayamombe on 16 May 2007
Capt Christopher Pamacheche (A) from THQ
   on 12 Jul 2007

PROMOTED TO GLORY

THERE are many descriptions to soften the harshness of the word
'death' but one of the most radical is the Army's descriptive phrase,
'promoted to Glory'. It sounds a triumphant, positive note in support
of the Army's belief in eternal life, Heaven and an unending period
in Glory with the Father. It declares incontrovertibly that death is not
the end, but the beginning of a new and glorious experience for those
redeemed by the blood of Jesus Christ.

The term was first used in *The War Cry* of 14 December 1882, at a
time when so many other military phrases were being introduced
following the advent of the name 'The Salvation Army' four years
earlier. It seems to have found ready acceptance and soon entered
common usage.

It was also consistent with the Founder's dislike of sombre black
clothing as a sign of mourning. He believed that, while Christ
sympathises with sorrow, he desires to make personal tragedy a
stepping stone to greater faith by seeing death as a victory.

LEGACIES

Abbreviations used in *The Year Book*

A

(A) (active officer pG); Acc (Accommodation); Afr (Africa); Am (America); AO (Area Officer); Apt (Apartment); Appt (Appointment); ARC (Adult Rehabilitation Centre); Asst (Assistant); Aus (Australia); A/Capt (Auxiliary-Captain).

B

b (born); Ban (Bangladesh); Belg (Belgium); B/M (Bandmaster); Braz (Brazzaville); Brig (Brigadier); Brz (Brazil); BT (British Territory).

C

Can (Canada and Bermuda); Capt (Captain); Carib (Caribbean); CIDA (Canadian International Development Agency); CO (Commanding Officer); Col (Colonel); Comr (Commissioner); Con (Congo); CoS (Chief of the Staff); CS (Chief Secretary); CWMO (Command Women's Ministries Officer); Cze R (Czech Republic).

D

DC (Divisional Commander); Den (Denmark); Dis O (District Officer); DO (Divisional Officer).

E

E Afr (East Africa); E Eur (Eastern Europe); ESFOT (European School for Officers' Training).

F

Fin (Finland and Estonia); Frce (France); FS (Field Secretary).

G

Ger (Germany and Lithuania); Gha (Ghana); GS (General Secretary).

H

HK (Hong Kong and Macau); HL (Home League); Hun (Hungary).

I

ICO (International College for Officers); IES (International Emergency Services); IHQ (International Headquarters); IHS (International Health Services); Ind C, E, etc (India Central, Eastern, etc); Ind M & A (India Madras and Andhra); Indon (Indonesia); Internl (International); IPDS (International Projects and Development Services); IS (International Secretary); It (Italy); ITC (International Training College).

J

JHLS (Junior Home League Secretary); Jpn (Japan).

K

Ken (Kenya); Kin (Kinshasa); Kor (Korea).

L

L Am N (Latin America North); Lat (Latvia); Lib (Liberia); Lt or Lieut (Lieutenant); Lt-Col or Lieut-Colonel (Lieutenant-Colonel); LOM (League of Mercy).

M

m (married); Maj (Major); Mal (Malawi); Mlys (Malaysia); Mol (Moldova); My (Myanmar).

N

Nat (National); Nat Comm (National Commander); Neth (The Netherlands and Czech Republic); NHQ (National Headquarters); Nor (Norway, Iceland and The Færoes); NZ (New Zealand, Fiji and Tonga).

O

OC (Officer Commanding); ODAS (Order of Distinguished Auxiliary Service); OF (Order of the Founder); O&R (Orders and Regulations).

P

Pak (Pakistan); pG (promoted to Glory); Phil (The Philippines); PINS (Persons in need of supervision); PNG (Papua New Guinea); Port (Portugal); PO (Provincial Officer); Pres (President); PRD (Public Relations Department); PS (Private Secretary).

R

RC (Regional Commander); ret (retired); RO (Regional Officer); Rus (Russia).

S

S/ (Senior); SAAS (Salvation Army Assurance Society); SABAC (Salvation Army Boys' Adventure Corps); S Afr (Southern Africa); SALT (Salvation Army Leadership Training); S Am E (South America East); SAMF (Salvation Army Medical Fellowship); S Am W (South America West); SAWSO (Salvation Army World Service Office); Scot (Scotland); SFOT (School for Officers' Training); Sgt (Sergeant);

Abbreviations

Sing (Singapore, Malaysia and Myanmar); S/L (Songster Leader); Soc S (Social Services); Sp (Spain); SP&S (Salvationist Publishing and Supplies Ltd); Sri Lan (Sri Lanka); Supt (Superintendent); Swdn (Sweden and Latvia); Switz (Switzerland, Austria and Hungary).

T

Tai (Taiwan); Tanz (Tanzania); TC (Territorial Commander); tel (telephone); TCCMS (Territorial Community Care Ministries Secretary); THQ (Territorial Headquarters); TLWM (Territorial Leader of Women's Ministries); TPWM (Territorial President of Women's Ministries); TPWO (Territorial President of Women's Organisations); TSWM (Territorial Secretary for Women's Ministries); TSWO (Territorial Secretary for Women's Organisations); TWMS (Territorial Women's Ministries Secretary).

U

Uga (Uganda); UK (United Kingdom); Uk (Ukraine); USA (United States of America); USA Nat, USA C, etc (USA National, Central, etc).

W

WI (West Indies); WSWM (World Secretary for Women's Ministries); Ww (Widow).

Z

Zai (Zaïre); Zam (Zambia); Zimb (Zimbabwe).

International Direct Dialling

Telephone country codes to territorial and command headquarters are listed below

In *The Year Book* the international prefix, which varies from country to country, is indicated by [square brackets]. Local codes are indicated by (round brackets)

Argentina	[54]	India	[91]	Portugal	[351]
Australia	[61]	Indonesia	[62]		
		Italy	[39]	Russia	[7]
Bangladesh	[880]			Rwanda	[250]
Belgium	[32]	Jamaica	[1876]	Singapore	[65]
Brazil	[55]	Japan	[81]	South Africa	[27]
				Spain	[34]
Canada	[1]	Kenya	[254]	Sri Lanka	[94]
Chile	[56]	Korea	[82]	Sweden	[46]
Congo (Democratic				Switzerland	[41]
Republic)	[243]	Liberia	[231]		
Congo (Republic)	[242]			Taiwan	[886]
Costa Rica	[506]	Mexico	[525]	Tanzania	[255]
		Malawi	[265]		
Denmark	[45]			United Kingdom	[44]
		Netherlands (The)	[31]	USA	[1]
Finland	[358]	New Zealand	[64]		
France	[33]	Nigeria	[234]	Zambia	[260]
		Norway	[47]	Zimbabwe	[263]
Germany	[49]				
Ghana	[233]	Pakistan	[92]		
		Papua New Guinea	[675]		
Hong Kong	[852]	Philippines (The)	[63]		

INDEX

Index

Index

Index

Haiti, 19, 28, 36, 87, 264,
  see also Caribbean 88-92
Harding, Col Anne, 117
Harding, Col Graeme, 116, 117
Hawaiian Islands, 17, 201
Herring, Lt-Col Alistair, 103
Herring, Lt-Col Astrid, 104
Herter, Dr Walter, 41
Higgins, General Edward J., 18, 22, 23
High Council, 3, 18, 19, 20, 22, 23, 43
Hills, Maj Cedric, 38, 44
Hiramoto, Lt-Col Naoshi, 153
Hiramoto, Lt-Col Seiko, 154
Hodder, Lt-Col Jolene, 77, 157
Hodder, Lt-Col, Kenneth, 156
Hogan, Col Dianne, 172, 173
Hogan, Col Olin, 172
Holy Land, 17
Home League, 13, 17, 21, 34, 73, 127,
  131, 134, 137, 138, 141, 164, 188, 195,
  207, 215, 248, 278, 286, 287
Honduras, 20, 28, *see also* Latin America
  North 163-167
Hong Kong, 18, 20, 28, 39, 50, 51, 229,
  241, 242
Hong Kong and Macau, 31, 119-124
Hope HIV, 40
Houghton, Comr Judith, 37, 88, 89
Houghton, Comr Raymond, 37, 88
Howard, Comr Henry, 36, 48
Hughes, Comrs Alex/Ingeborg, 72
Hungary, 18, 19, 28, 51, *see also*
  Switzerland, Austria and Hungary
  237-240
Hurricane Katrina, 255

I

Iceland, 17, 28, *see also* Norway, Iceland
  and The Faeroes, 191-194
In Darkest England and the Way Out,
  13, 17
India, 9, 16, 17, 21, 28, 38, 39, 71, 87,
  210, 257
  National Secretariat, 33, 51, 125-126
  Central, 31, 33, 40, 50, 51, 127-130
  Eastern, 31, 33, 36, 50, 51, 126,
  131-133

  Northern, 31, 33, 50, 51, 112, 130,
  134-136
  South Eastern, 31, 50, 51, 126, 137-139
  South Western, 31, 33, 50, 51, 140-142
  Western, 31, 33, 50, 51, 132, 143-146
Indian Ocean tsunami, 20
Indonesia, 17, 18, 28, 39, 50, 51, 147-150,
  169, 210
Induruwage, Col Irene, 201, 203
Induruwage, Col Malcolm, 201
International Centenary, 19
International College for Officers, 17, 19,
  48, 50
International Commission on Officership, 20
International Conference of Leaders, 19, 20
International Conference for Personnel
  Secretaries, 20, 21, 45
International Conference for Training
  Principals, 20
International Congress, 16, 17, 18, 19,
  20, 46
International Corps Cadet Congress, 19
International Doctrine Council, 3, 5, 43
International Education Symposium, 20
International Emergency Services, 38-39, 44,
  208, 246
International Headquarters, 14, 18, 19, 20,
  23, 24, 26, 32, 36, 42-51, 247
  Administration Department, 43
  Business Administration Department, 44
  International Administrative Structure, 46
  International Management Council, 43
  International Personnel Department, 44
  Programme Resources Department, 44
  Zonal Departments, 44-45
International Health Services, 44
International Heritage Centre, 250
International Projects and Development
  Services, 40-41, 44
International Literary and Publications
  Conference, 20
International Literature Programme,
International Music and Other Creative
  Ministries Forum (MOSAIC), 20
International Poverty Summit, 20
International Self-Denial Fund, 50
International Staff Band, 17, 249

Index

Index

Panama, 17, 28, 278 *see also* Latin America

North 163-167

Paone, Lt-Col E. Jane, 151, 152

Paone, Lt-Col Massimo, 21, 151, 152

Papua New Guinea, 19, 21, 28, 32, 33, 37, 50, 51, 153, 198-200

Paraguay, 18, 28, *see also* South America

East 214-216

Pardo, Maj Magali, 164

Pardo, Maj Zoilo, 163

Park, Lt-Col Man-hee, 159

Payne, Maj Diane, 170, 171

Payne, Maj Godfrey, 170

Pearce, Comr Lyn, 44, 47

Peru, 18, 28, 39, 95, 192, *see also* South America West 217-222

Philippines, The, 18, 28, 32, 34, 39, 50, 51, 52, 201-205

Pobjie, Comr Barry, 45, 47, 103

Pobjie, Comr Raemor, 45

Poke, Comr Roslyn, 232, 233

Poke, Comr Victor, 232

Poland, 20, 28, 43, 51

Portugal, 19, 28, 50, 51, 164, 206-207

Portuguese East Africa, 18

Project Warsaw, 20, 43

Promoted to Glory, 15, 339

Puerto Rico, 19, 28, 255

R

Rader, Lt-Col Lyell, 218

Rader, Comr Kay, 223

Rader, General Paul A., 20, 22, 25, 223

Radio Help (Sweden), 41

Railton, Comr George Scott, 6, 255

Rajakumari, Comr P. Mary, 143, 144

Redhead, Col Robert, 72, 189

Refstie, Comr Janet, 74, 75, 214

Refstie, Comr Peder, 74, 214

Regina, Col Chandra Bai, 127, 128

Reliance Bank Ltd, 17, 47

Roberts, Comr Nancy, 43

Roberts, Com William, 44, 47

Roger Carllson Foundation (UK), 41

Romania, 20, 28, *see also* Eastern Europe 103-105

Rowland, Lt-Col Elaine, 119, 120

Rowland, Lt-Col Mervyn, 119

Russia (Russian Federation), 18, 19, 20, 28,

see also Eastern Europe 103-105

Rwanda, 20, 21, 28, 39, 50, 51, 208-209

S

Sabah (East Malaysia), 20

St Helena, 16, 28, *see also* Southern Africa 223-226

St Kitts, 18, 28, *see also* Caribbean 88-92

St Lucia, 17, 28, *see also* Caribbean 88-92

St Maarten, 28, *see also* Caribbean 88-92

St Vincent, 17, 28, *see also* Caribbean 88-92

Saga Shipping (UK), 41

Saipan, 277

Salvation Army

Blue Shield Fellowship, 35

Honours, 36-37

International Trustee Company, 47

Leaders Training College (SALT) of Africa, 49, 51

Medical Fellowship, 18, 35

Scouts and Guides Jamboree, 20, 192

Students' Fellowship, 19, 35

Salvation Army Act 1931, 18, 22

Salvation Army Act 1980, 11, 19, 22

Salvation Army Australia Development Office (SAADO), 41

Salvation Army World Services, 9

Salvation Army World Service Office (SAWSO), 41, 50, 229

Salvation Story, 3, 20

Sanchez, Col Ana Rosa, 163, 164

Sanchez, Col Oscar, 163

Sawichhunga, Col, OF, 36

Scotland, 16, 23, 24, 25, 26, *see also* United Kingdom, 247-254

Seiler, Lt-Col Carol, 259

Seiler, Lt-Col Paul, 257

Self-Denial Appeal, 15

(*see also* International Self-Denial Fund)

Self-Denial World Mission Fund, 258

Serém, Maj Alberto, 206

Serém, Maj Maria, 206, 207

Index

Index

Six New Books from International Headquarters

All these books are available direct from International Headquarters on payment by sterling cheque and from territorial and command trade departments in national currencies (check prices locally)

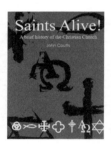

Saints Alive!
by John Coutts
price £4.95
A brief history of the Christian Church showing where The Salvation Army fits in

Unsung Heroes
by Derek Elvin
price £4.95
Biographies of 11 courageous 20th-century Salvationists

For Such A Time
by Jenty Fairbank
price £4.95
The story of the young Florence Booth

Purity of Heart
by William Booth
price £3.95
The first of a new series of
Classic Salvationist Texts

Seasons
by JoAnn Shade
price £4.95
A woman's calling to ministry

Saying Yes to Life
by John Larsson
price £8.95
The autobiography of
The Salvation Army's 17th General

TERRITORIES (T), COMMANDS (C) AND REGIONS (R) BY ZONES

AFRICA
Congo (Brazzaville) (T)
Congo (Kinshasa) and Angola (T)
Ghana (T)
Kenya (T)
Liberia (C)
Malawi (C)
Nigeria (T)
Rwanda (R)
Southern Africa (T)
Tanzania (C)
Uganda (C)
Zambia (T)
Zimbabwe (T)

AMERICAS AND CARIBBEAN
Brazil (T)
Canada and Bermuda (T)
Caribbean (T)
Latin America North (T)
Mexico (T)
South America East (T)
South America West (T)
USA Central (T)
USA Eastern (T)
USA Southern (T)
USA Western (T)

EUROPE
Belgium (C)
Denmark (T)
Eastern Europe (T)
Finland and Estonia (T)
France (T)
Germany and Lithuania (T)
Italy (C)

The Netherlands and Czech
  Republic (T)
Norway, Iceland and
  The Færoes (T)
Portugal (C)
Spain (C)
Sweden and Latvia (T)
Switzerland, Austria and
  Hungary (T)
United Kingdom with the
  Republic of Ireland (T)

SOUTH ASIA
Bangladesh (C)
India Central (T)
India Eastern (T)
India Northern (T)
India South Eastern (T)
India South Western (T)
India Western (T)
Pakistan (T)
Sri Lanka (T)

SOUTH PACIFIC AND EAST ASIA
Australia Eastern (T)
Australia Southern (T)
Hong Kong and Macau (C)
Indonesia (T)
Japan (T)
Korea (T)
New Zealand, Fiji and Tonga (T)
Papua New Guinea (T)
The Philippines (T)
Singapore, Malaysia and
  Myanmar (T)
Taiwan (R)